WHILE AMERICA SLEEPS

Contents

Preface   vii

Introduction   1

PART I   Britain Between the Wars   11

1 The Brave New World   13

2 Britain's Defense Dilemma   44

3 The First Challenge to Peace   67

4 The Paper Lion Roars   78

5 Retreat from Responsibility   98

6 The Search for Security   118

7 The Unraveling of Versailles   140

8 The Locarno Treaty   160

9 The Spirit of Locarno   176

10 The Bill Comes Due   194

11 The Price of Self-Deception   217

PART II   The United States After the Cold War   235

12 The New World Order   237

13 The Peace Dividend   267

14 Increased Commitments, Reduced Forces 300

15 Kicking the Can Down the Road 321

16 Proliferation and Blackmail 341

17 Another Versailles 367

18 A Legacy of Half Measures 400

Conclusion 424

Notes 437

Bibliography 465

Index 469

Donald Kagan
Frederick W. Kagan

WHILE
AMERICA
SLEEPS

Self-Delusion, Military Weakness,
and the Threat to Peace Today

St. Martin's Griffin ⚞ New York

For Myrna and Kim

www.stmartins.com

Library of Congress Cataloging-in-Publication Data

Kagan, Donald.
    While America sleeps / Donald Kagan and Frederick W. Kagan
        p. cm.
    Includes bibliographical references (p. 465) and index.
    ISBN 0-312-20624-0 (hc)
    ISBN 0-312-28374-1 (pbk)
    1. United States—Foreign relations—1989– 2. United States—Military Policy. 3. National security—United States—Forecasting. 4. Great Britain—Foreign relations—20th century. 5. Great Britain—History, Military—20th century. I. Kagan, Frederick W., 1970– II. Title.

E840.K3 2000
355'.033573—dc21   00-031818

10 9 8 7 6 5 4 3 2

Preface

In 1940 a young man published what had been his college senior thesis, entitled *Why England Slept*. In that year, German armies destroyed those of France and England, conquered France, and subjected England to the most terrible and destructive bombing campaign the world had ever seen. *Why England Slept* aimed to explain to an America just beginning to wake up to the danger it faced why England had failed to protect the peace of the world, or to ensure its own security. It was too late—one year later as Japanese bombs shattered the American battle fleet at Pearl Harbor, the United States was drawn willy-nilly into yet another war it had failed to deter and for which it was woefully unprepared. The book was reprinted in 1961 when its young author, John F. Kennedy, was President of the United States.

Two years before Kennedy had written his thesis, Winston Churchill, long out of favor and out of control of British politics, published a collection of his speeches given from 1932 to 1938 under the title *While England Slept*. Those speeches pointed to the rapid rise of Germany as a major threat to England and to the peace of the world. In them he called for a foreign policy to deter German *revanchisme* and for military preparedness to support that policy. His advice, and those of others similarly minded, was ignored consistently by a British government preoccupied with domestic concerns and both afraid and unwilling to face the new realities. As a result, it was clear not only to Churchill that by 1938 England had let slip by her best chance either to deter or to prepare for war. Thenceforth it would be Hitler who would call the tune, and for a time it looked very much as though England would have to pay the piper.

The present work harkens back to these earlier efforts to warn unwilling democracies to prepare for the dangers of war, fully aware that the situation America faces today is by no means so dire as the one she faced in 1940, or the one England faced in 1938. Few today would agree that America's current situation is in any way dire. On the contrary, it is almost an article of faith in the few public discussions on foreign policy that one can find today that America is in the most secure of all possible positions. Since the United States desires nothing but peace and stability in the world, it is most difficult to imagine that any other state might threaten us. Since our armed forces are so powerful, it is hard to believe that any enemy could defeat them or be so foolish as to try. Above all, since the world is now so peaceful and prosperous, and our military preponderance apparently so great, we can hardly conceive of any major state desiring or daring to upset the world order.

It is our aim in this work to challenge such complacent and comfortable opinions, and to do it before it is too late to repair the deficiencies in our foreign and defense policies and address the dangers that we see ahead. In our view the peace that concluded World War I was lost not in the 1930s, when the British allowed their leading position in the world to deteriorate through inaction and so set the stage for disaster in the following decade. The neglect, wishful thinking, and self-delusion of the 1920s, "the years of the locust," so undermined Britain's position as to make the task of its leaders in the 1930s too great for them to manage. For the history of the 1930s shows that democracies almost inevitably act too slowly, even when the danger is upon them. The warnings Churchill and Kennedy issued in 1938 and 1940 came far too late, even if they had been heeded.

Our hope is to provide warning early enough to bring about a necessary change of course, even in a democratic state concerned, as democratic states usually are, with domestic preoccupations. Major war need not be just around the corner, as it was then. If the United States assumes the true burdens of world leadership on which peace depends and that it alone has the resources to bear, major war may be put off for longer than it has ever been. But the military preparations on which such an undertaking must rest are inadequate today, and will be less adequate in the future, if the current insufficient and confused direction of our policies continues. Unless we change them soon our efforts to deter aggression and to maintain world stability will fail. As a vital first step Americans must stop thinking and acting as though there can never be another war. We must understand that the world and the United States, as they have always been up to now, are simply in an interwar period. It is up to us to determine how long it will last and how well it will end.

We could not have completed this project without the support and encouragement of many people. First and foremost, we must thank Robert Kagan. His work, his thinking, and his constructive criticism have been an essential part of the development of our own thoughts. The excellent faculty, past and present, at the Department of History of the U.S. Military Academy have played an invaluable role in educating us and helping us to see the strengths and weaknesses in our arguments. In particular, the support and encouragement of Colonels Robert S. Doughty and Cole C. Kingseed, as well as the intellectual support of Lieutenant Colonel Conrad Crane, have been extremely important. We are also indebted to Lieutenant Colonels David T. Fautua and H. R. McMaster for a series of conversations long ago that helped to spark this project in the first place.

In the course of our work, we have had several opportunities to present our findings to audiences whose questions helped us to sharpen our thinking. For this we are grateful to Professors Paul Kennedy and Charles Hill of Yale University and Aaron Friedberg of Princeton University for inviting us to speak to their organizations.

This project could not have been completed without the support provided to Fred Kagan by the John M. Olin Foundation. The authors are grateful to the foundation and to its executive director Jim Piereson for the vital support they give to scholarship in the fields treated in this book, fields largely neglected by others.

This work was the product of a team that consisted not only of the two authors, but of their wives, Myrna and Kim, as well. Their patience in the face of many, no doubt wearisome, historical conversations and arguments, their insightful contributions to those discussions, and their support and encouragement throughout, have made the completion of this book not merely possible, but enjoyable.

Any flaws, errors, or omissions in this work are, of course, the responsibility of the authors.

Introduction

America is in danger. Unless its leaders change their national security policy, the peace and safety its power and influence have ensured since the end of the Cold War will disappear. Already, increasing military weakness and confusion about foreign and defense policy have encouraged the development of powerful hostile states and coalitions that challenge the interests and security of the United States, its allies and friends, and all those with an interest in preserving the general peace. Without American support, the friends of democracy and human rights will cry in vain for protection against the forces of repression, which persist and will intensify in areas from which American power will have to be withdrawn for lack of strength and will. Despite that withdrawal, those forces will continue to identify the United States as the source of a modernization that threatens them, as the propagator of values they find evil and abhorrent, as their principal enemy. Over time the technologies of which the United States and its allies are the chief possessors will fall into these unfriendly hands and may be used against them directly.

In the past, the collapse of an international system that suited the United States deprived Americans of access to markets or caused American casualties on faraway battlefields. In the future, it will bring attacks on the American homeland, not merely by terrorists, but as part of deliberately planned and carefully executed military strikes against critical targets in the United States of America. The happy international situation that emerged in 1991, characterized by the spread of democracy, free trade, and peace, so congenial to America, has begun to decay at an alarming rate and will vanish unless there is a change of course. The costs of failure now are far higher than ever before.

These statements must seem alarmist. Even now, with NATO still committed in Yugoslavia, with Saddam Hussein free of inspections and real trammels on his development of weapons of mass destruction, with a hostile and reckless North Korea relentlessly developing nuclear weapons and long-range ballistic missiles on which to put them, with China more openly hostile, antagonistic, and threatening, with Russia stuck on its presumed road to democracy and free markets and openly opposed to American policies in the Balkans and Iraq, most Americans believe that we are in a peaceful interlude that will last a long time, and that any danger is comfortably far into the future. Most policy makers assert or assume that America faces no significant threat today, and that it is not likely to take the form of a "peer competitor," an enemy like the old Soviet Union that could challenge the United States globally and threaten America's very survival. The worst prospect they see would be another Saddam—some regional power whose bid for hegemony in its area would challenge our interests and compel us to intervene.

But the Gulf War showed that American arms will easily prevail, did it not? How could any future enemy of that kind stand up to the much more technologically advanced forces America will have in a decade or two? By the time a serious threat could arise, the United States will have developed the weapons to defeat it. On that assumption the National Defense Panel argued that the United States should take advantage of the current "strategic pause," cutting forces now to fund modernization programs for the future.

Another argument is that future threats will arise not from nation-states, none of which can hope to compete with the United States, but only from "non-state actors." International terrorist organizations will gain possession of the new technology and will exploit the increasing vulnerability of technologically advanced societies to the disruption of critical pieces of equipment. International criminal organizations may also use technology to infiltrate national governments, causing all sorts of disasters. The collapse of nation-states around the world, moreover, will create chaos in the international system, and the United States may be drawn into an endless series of Bosnias and Somalias to try to shore up the failing international structure. Those sharing this view point to the enormous difficulty of tracking individual terrorists with suitcase nuclear weapons or vials of sarin nerve gas and urge every effort to coordinate the activities of the armed forces with the FBI and local police departments. These scenarios lead some to the conclusion that the defense of the homeland against such threats is the most challenging task, so that preparations made for fighting even against a major regional adversary in any conventional sense are unnecessary or, at any event, less important.

Still others see in the advent of the "information age" a complete change in the nature of war as well as of society. Wars in the future will no longer be concerned with territory or natural resources, but with the struggle for "information." Pessimists worry about terrorists and other enemies infiltrating our computer systems, corrupting information, and planting "logic bombs." Optimists believe that America's predominance in information technology will continue indefinitely, allowing the United States to have forces so deadly to its enemies and so safe to its own soldiers that no one will dare challenge it. The Pax Americana will reign so thoroughly that there will never be need to use the systems that maintain it. All of these arguments conclude that there is no serious threat to America now, and that none is likely to arise in the near future. In the unspecified long term, new dangers may require more attention to America's defenses, but there will be ample time for that.

Deeper thinkers point out that no political development serious enough to revolutionize the international situation takes place in a vacuum. There will be warnings years before the threat emerges, and America's leaders need only be alert and ready to respond to those warnings. In the meantime, the "strategic pause" provides the opportunity not only to modernize American forces but also to turn to domestic needs. The "peace dividend" and the surpluses generated by the booming economy can be used to improve the lot of American citizens and to strengthen the industrial-information base. The United States can reduce its defenses, for this is an era without threats.

That way of thinking is the normal one for liberal, democratic, prosperous nations after victory in a great conflict. In his biography of his ancestor John Churchill, Duke of Marlborough, Winston Churchill describes similar thoughts and policies among the English after the Peace of Ryswick ending one of the wars against Louis XIV in 1697:

> The wars were over; their repressions were at an end. They rejoiced in peace and clamoured for freedom. The dangers were past; why should they ever return? Groaning under taxation, impatient of every restraint, the Commons plunged into a career of economy, disarmament, and constitutional assertiveness which was speedily followed by the greatest of the wars England had ever waged and the heaviest expenditure she had ever borne. This phase has often recurred in our history. In fact it has been an invariable rule that England, so steadfast in war, so indomitable in peril, should at the moment when the dire pressures are relaxed and victory has been won cast away its fruits. Having made every sacrifice, having performed prodigies of strength and valour, our countrymen under every franchise or party have always fallen upon the ground in weakness and futility when a very little more perseverance would have made them supreme, or at least secure.[1]

Churchill wrote in the years between the world wars of the twentieth century, when his countrymen were once again demonstrating these same habits. Americans were doing the same at the same time and, after fifty years of unprecedented effort and responsibility crowned by unprecedented success, they are slipping back to their old ways, so terribly dangerous to the safety of America and the world. For all the novelty of the "information age" and the "transformation" of war, society, the economy, and politics, the current epoch is not unusual in the history of countries like the United States and Great Britain. In the past such assumptions have repeatedly left them profoundly unready to meet a new danger. The United States' forces were inadequate before the War of 1812, the Mexican War, the Spanish-American War, World War I, World War II, and the Korean War. Losing the first battle has been a regular part of the American "way of war," yet in each of those wars the United States ultimately triumphed. Britain also suffered defeats at the beginning of the wars against Napoleon, the Crimean War, the Boer War, World War I, and World War II, but in every case was able to achieve victory before the end. Each time, the almost complete demobilization of the victorious armed forces resulted from a feeling that the end of war had brought the return of "normal" peacetime conditions when large armed forces are not needed. In each war the unprepared nation paid a much higher price for victory than necessary, and sometimes it barely escaped defeat. In many of them war came when the aggressor knew of its enemy's unpreparedness.

The day is long past when the separation from other nations by bodies of water, even oceans, provides a degree of security that permits isolation from the rest of the world. Apart from the threat posed by intercontinental missiles, no nation dependent upon international peace and free trade for its well-being can avoid playing an important role in the international arena. Historical experience reveals that when the states most interested in preserving the peace are weaker than dissatisfied states willing to advance their cause through war, the result is war. Still another teaching of the experience of the past is that a foreign policy not backed by sufficient military force is doomed to failure. But these are unwelcome lessons that, if properly learned, impose unwelcome responsibilities. The record of liberal, democratic, commercial nations, no matter how great their strength, in keeping the peace over the long run is abysmal. The absence of an immediate threat permits democracies to focus on domestic comfort. Maintaining a secure international climate through adequate military power seems an unnecessary luxury to people and policy makers who do not reflect on the danger the deterioration of that climate would pose.

Like any insurance policy, the maintenance of sufficient armed forces and an active, engaged foreign policy in an era with no immediate serious threats seems wasteful. Americans, and the British before them, have always felt that there would be time to create the force necessary to win the war. So there was, up to now, although the price both nations have paid for buying that time has been great, and has increased on each occasion. Much more seriously, military unpreparedness has prevented deterrence, thereby repeatedly costing the liberal democracies the chance to avoid horrific wars altogether. Time after time their military weakness has persuaded potential adversaries that the democracies would tolerate changes they opposed rather than fight or that they would be too weak to win. The one great exception was the performance of the United States and its allies in the Cold War, when the challenge presented by the Soviet Union was so inescapable that they created and maintained a formidable military power in peacetime for almost half a century. The cost in effort, wealth, and lives was considerable but infinitesimal compared to the costs of a great modern war. The results were the avoidance of such a war, which many thought inevitable, and a peaceful resolution to a serious confrontation. Unless the same nations take their bearings for future policy from this last and most successful course rather than relapsing into the previous comfortable irresponsibility, the future will be grim.

Predicting the future is a difficult and uncertain business, but for those who make international and military policy there is no escape from it. Any future course of action rests on assumptions about how events are likely to develop and how political and military leaders will try to shape and react to them. Simply to project the behavior of the past in a straight line into the future is a mistake, for history does not repeat itself with precision. A far worse mistake, however, is to project a future that is entirely different from the past, to assume that all previous human behavior has been made irrelevant by some current developments or discoveries. It is so tempting to construct a vision of the future that, however pleasing, is entirely unprecedented and most unlikely. Men have been making such optimistic projections since the eighteenth century, at least, predicting the end of war because of new conditions and always turning out to be devastatingly wrong.

For all its shortcomings, past behavior remains the most reliable predictor of future behavior. History can enlighten critical elements of the debate over our national security policy by examining what once was as a way of conceiving what might be. The center of any argument against the need to maintain large armed forces and an active foreign policy as a way of preventing war is the refusal to admit that we could face a serious threat in a very short time. A corollary to that refusal is the assumption that warning signs will be seen well before the threat materializes, and that effective action will be taken in good time.

At its heart is the belief that the sky, which was so blue in 1991, will remain so indefinitely, and that if a storm should come, it will come as a gradual clouding-over and we will have the time, the means, and the will to prepare for it. Already, recent events should have undermined such optimism. Experience shows that terrible storms can appear with little or no warning and that when they do they cause the greatest harm.

After World War I, Great Britain found itself in a situation very similar to the one in which we live today. Military experts proclaimed that a "revolution" in war was under way. Politicians and professors proclaimed that a new international order had dawned. A nation exhausted by the "war to end war" happily turned its attention from the politics of the external world to its own internal economic and social concerns, starving its armed forces of the resources they needed and, thereby, taking from its diplomacy the tools without which no foreign policy can be effective. The British believed then, as we do now, that no storm was on the horizon and none could appear before they were able to respond. They were wrong.

Less than a decade after the collapse of the Soviet Union, it is well to recall that in 1926, only eight years after the collapse of the German Empire, the international scene seemed as tranquil and promising to Britain as it does now to us. The notion that within seven years Germany's Weimar Republic would reject its democracy for a military dictatorship and then rearm so rapidly as to threaten the very survival of Britain was laughable. The idea that only five years would see the beginning of the Japanese drive that would result, even after a victorious war, in the virtual elimination of Great Britain as a power in the Far East seemed no less unlikely. Similarly absurd was the thought that Germany, not Britain, would perfect the revolution in military affairs that had started in England, and would use it to destroy the French army, the strongest ground force in the world in 1926, within six weeks. There seemed to be no credible threat in 1926, and the English felt free to focus their time, energy, and resources on domestic concerns. They assumed that the world would continue to pursue the peaceful course they desired even without their active and constant intervention. They were wrong. Are we?

The purpose of this work is to challenge the widely held beliefs that the United States and its allies face no serious threat now or in the foreseeable future, that our current policies and power are adequate to ward off serious dangers, that the greater threat is too much involvement, too much alertness, too much attention to military capacity. The most effective argument against those opinions can come only from the study of a past whose relevance is clear and becomes more persuasive the more closely it is examined. Such a study reveals that for all the significant differences between them, the United States has been pursuing a path remarkably similar to the one taken by Great Britain, both in foreign and in military policy, so that the history of the collapse of peace and the destruction of the international order in the 1930s may have more significance for the future than we would like to think.

In the years following the Treaty of Versailles in 1919, Britain slashed its armed forces, allowed its military modernization programs to stagnate, and pinned its hopes for peace on the economic wonders to be performed by international trade and on international organizations and treaties that it did not have the military power to support and enforce. Its leaders assured themselves and the populace that the smaller armed forces would be sufficient both because of the peaceful state of the world and because technological advances would make up for their smaller size. But their military and civilian planners produced little new technology and failed to make the organizational changes needed to convert new technology into effective weapons of war. As late as 1939, the British army was unprepared to fight modern war. In the meantime, Britain's military weakness and, especially, its inability even to contemplate fighting major regional competitors in two different theaters paralyzed its foreign policy throughout the 1930s. The British allowed Mussolini's aggression in Ethiopia in 1935 to go unopposed for fear of weakening Britain's position in East Asia, where Japan had suddenly become a serious threat. Britain's inability or unwillingness to resist this aggression encouraged Hitler to march into the Rhineland in 1936. The policies Britain had pursued in the 1920s of military decline and an unwillingness to use force in defense of peace and the established international order and the weakness it produced robbed its statesmen and its allies in the 1930s of the determination to resist aggression and defend their own security. The same weakness made possible the unhampered rise to international power of military dictatorships in Italy, Germany, and Japan, ultimately producing a coalition of these unlikely allies, World War II, and the near conquest of Britain itself.

How does this compare with the record of the United States today? The United States has reduced its armed forces by more than one-third across the board. Its leaders acclaim the advantages new technologies will bring to its forces to offset those reductions, but not one new major weapons system has been put into service since 1991, and most new weapons are still only in the planning phase. For the first time in its history, NATO has been expanded to include countries that the alliance has no real intention of defending, for it has not strengthened NATO forces to meet the additional burden. Just as Britain signed the Treaty of Locarno in 1925 knowing that it could not support it militarily, so the United States and its allies have expanded the NATO alliance without making any plans to meet the military commitments thereby involved. The United States has already reached the point where its armed forces are not capable of fighting two major regional competitors at once, although its proclaimed strategy and the experience of history make it clear that such a capacity is necessary. Today in America, as in Britain in the 1920s, air power enthusiasts make extravagant and undemonstrated claims that air power and modern technology can close the gap.

No historical analogy is perfect, and there are significant differences between Britain's situation in the interwar years and the situation the United States faces in what may well be today's interwar years, but most of the differences give no cause for comfort. Britain's unwillingness to spend what was needed for defense was intensified by serious economic difficulties. An adequate defense program would have caused a degree of hardship. America today is the richest nation in the world, its economy growing at record levels, its people better off materially than any in the world's history. The additional cost of an adequate defense would be trivial as a proportion of the great national wealth.

Another difference arises from a crucial disparity in the international situation faced by each nation. In their darkest hours, British statesmen and soldiers knew that there was in the wings a potential ally of enormous power whose assistance could shift the balance of force in their favor, the United States. Americans today can hope for no similar genie to emerge from a bottle, for none exists. There is no nation to come to its rescue if its leaders choose to endanger its security and the peace of the world by pursuing a policy of military weakness and international indifference or timidity.

No one can predict that a nationalistic autocrat will soon seize power in Russia and begin rearming at a pace that will threaten its neighbors and the security of Europe. It is not inevitable that the Chinese military will take control of their country and launch a policy of expansion and hegemony in East Asia. Nor is it certain that Iraq will recover, rearm, and strike again, having learned the lessons of the Gulf War, or that Iran will take advantage of its neighbor's weakness to seek a hegemony of its own. Precisely following any historical analogy is not wise. But it is no less foolish to be certain that such things will not happen, as the study of Britain in the two decades between the wars makes clear.

The understanding of British policy in the interwar years has been seriously distorted by the knowledge of what happened in 1939. We now can see in Germany even as early as 1935 the Germany that invaded Russia in 1941 and wonder how anyone in England could have failed to see the threat. It seems inconceivable that we could be as blind as they were, for we see the mistakes of men like Stanley Baldwin and Neville Chamberlain as part of the failed policy of appeasement, and we believe we have learned that lesson. But the story of the 1930s is not merely the story of appeasement. It is also the tale of how hard it is for a liberal democracy to react to a change in the international scene. It is the tale of lost opportunities to avert a horrible war because a democracy would not pay the premiums on its life insurance in the form of the will to maintain and use adequate armed forces large and strong enough to deter a war by being obviously capable of winning it. It demonstrates how, even with the best intentions after understanding its errors, it may be impossible to rearm fast enough even to win a war that its disarmed forces had failed to deter.

British statesmen in the interwar years made serious mistakes. They were the kinds of mistakes that the statesman of a nation so similar as the United States are most likely to make again. Therein is one of the great values in making the comparison. Even as late as 1939, Germany and Japan were each simply "major regional competitors"—neither was a peer competitor to Britain around the world. The collapse of Britain's position in the world resulted in considerable part from its failure to maintain a true "two major regional competitor" strategy and the capability to support it, as the United States is now failing to do. We will tell the story of Britain's security policy from 1919 to 1929, and trace how similar has been the development of America's military and foreign policy since 1991. We will tell the story of the collapse of the peace in the 1930s that resulted, and ask: can this happen to us? The answer is that such a development is as foreseeable and as hard to foresee today as it was in 1929, and if we take no better precautions to prevent it from occurring than the British did, our fate may be the same, or worse.

Today's readers may be skeptical about the warning we derive from the historical comparison. If we have done our work well, they will see that the circumstances, ideas, and actions of the earlier period are sufficiently similar to those of the later one as to be alarming. We hope they will understand the high price of failing to preserve the peace through an actively engaged foreign policy backed by dominant military force, understand that the cost of deterring war is infinitesimal compared to the cost of fighting it. We hope they will see that the work of keeping the peace does not cease and requires permanent commitment and attention, that we cannot wait until the danger is upon us, when it is too late to avert the war, maybe even too late to win it. Given the military technology of the twenty-first century, the danger we and the world face is not just a setback in a foreign war, but the bombing of our own cities and the killing of our own civilians, if not by nuclear weapons, then by devastating conventional "smart" weapons, whose use in future wars is certain. Perhaps if the British had an example before them like the one they present to us, more of them might have made better decisions. If we get it wrong we will have no such excuse.

PART I

Britain Between
the Wars

1

The Brave New World

At five in the morning of November 11, 1918, German and Allied representatives formally signed the Armistice, which came into effect at eleven o'clock that day. The Armistice ended the fighting, but it did not end the war. For almost a year after its signing, the wartime Allies, England, France, the United States, Italy, and others, wrangled among themselves and with the Germans over the terms of the peace treaty that concluded the bloodiest war the world had ever seen. The Treaty of Versailles was not signed until June 1919, and was not ratified by all the powers (except the United States, which never ratified it) until January 1920. Even then the war was not "over," for Versailles established peace only between the Allies and Germany—peace with Turkey and Austria was still further delayed.

World War I destroyed the international order from which it had originated in Europe, Africa, the Middle East, and Asia. The writing and signing of peace treaties did not restore that order, nor did it establish a new order. The peace merely ratified the abolition of the old way of doing things and the destruction of four great empires, the Ottoman, Russian, Austro-Hungarian, and German, upon which the old order had been based. If the victorious powers wanted a new order and a new stability, they would need to create it and see to its preservation.

Before the war a precarious balance among five great powers—Britain, France, Germany, Austria-Hungary, and Russia—had been the basis for European peace and stability. In November 1918, there could be no "balance." Only Britain and France retained their former strength, and the war had destroyed both their rivals, Germany and Austria-Hungary, and their former ally, Russia. The United States had appeared as a major player on the international scene, and the British and the French placed great hopes on an Anglo-Franco-American alliance to guide the world toward a new stability. Those hopes proved to be misplaced, however, for America rapidly withdrew from the international scene, refusing to ratify the Treaty of Versailles or to remain involved in Europe in any meaningful way.

November 1918 saw the dawn of a new epoch in Europe of a nature unparalleled in European experience. The "balance of power" is so deeply rooted a concept in European history that it continues to pervade our thinking even today, when no balance has emerged in the world. It dominated the thinking of British politicians throughout the interwar period, even when, as in the early 1920s, it did not exist and the form it might take was unclear. There was no rival power to balance Great Britain and France, and, despite foolish talk of Anglo-French antagonisms, those two states were so closely bound in their mutual interests that they could not in any way "balance" each other. For the first time in centuries, a European order (which included Asia, the Middle East, and Africa) had to come into existence based not on the "balance of power" but on some other principle. November 1918 was a unique and fleeting moment in history when a great power with global vision could take the lead, guiding the international community in the direction it saw fit. Was there any power that could take that lead in 1918?

Germany, Austria-Hungary, and Russia were devastated. The United States would soon choose isolation. France could not play the role of international leader after the war. It continued to be fixated on the German problem, the fact that with its greater rate of population growth and greater industrial capacity, Germany must inevitably eclipse France's military power, given time. France saw the solution to this problem only in the creation of an international order that would prevent Germany from ever again rising to threaten France. French politicians and the French people had some interest in the world outside of Europe, and they were satisfied to make gains that could be secured easily and cheaply, but they were not willing to invest significant resources in the maintenance of general peace and order. France's worldview was too Eurocentric and too circumscribed even in Europe to allow it to take the leading role in creating a new international order.

Britain was the only power with the inescapable need and the ability to do so. The war brought a vast mobilization of the power of the British Empire. With a strength, including all reserves, of 733,000 soldiers in August 1914, the British army had received more than 8.5 million recruits in the four years of war. On the day the Armistice was signed, more than 1,794,000 British soldiers were serving in France alone.[1] The power of the British Empire had never been tapped to such a degree.

In contrast to the French effort, which was concentrated on the eastern frontiers of France (although numerous French forces served elsewhere as well), the British army had fought the Entente's foes on three continents and many fronts. British troops were in France, Belgium, Italy, the Balkans, Greece, European Turkey, Palestine, Egypt, Syria, Iraq, Persia, the Caucasus, and Russia. During the war, Britain had promised independence or various forms of protection to many small states and peoples. Because of its worldwide interests and its capabilities, Britain alone of the victorious powers could take the lead in creating a new global order.

Britain's war aims developed during the course of the war, moreover, seemed to point the way to such a role. In 1916, Prime Minister Asquith declared that Britain's chief object in the war was "to ensure that all the States of Europe, great and small, shall in the future be in a position to achieve their national development in freedom and security." To this end, he declared that Britain would insist that the peace be based upon a redefinition of European boundaries to accord with national identities.[2] David Lloyd George, who succeeded Asquith as Prime Minister in 1916, added that the principle of nationalism should be extended to the territories of the Ottoman Empire. Subsequently the British added the provision that an international agency should be established to help preserve order after the peace treaties had been signed. The famous Fourteen Points that President Woodrow Wilson presented to the Allies and the Germans as the basis for the Armistice were little more than the war aims of Great Britain laid out in greater specificity. By the time the fighting had ended on the Western Front, Great Britain, in conjunction with America and France, had declared that it had fought this bloodiest of all wars in order to create a wholly new international order based on the principle of nationalism, guaranteeing the freedom and security of all states to develop in peace and secured by an international organization of states, the League of Nations. It was no accident that these goals and this arrangement would best serve Britain's chief postwar needs: to preserve the new international arrangements without another resort to major war. On November 11, 1918, Britain had the need, the ability, and the stated aim to organize the world in such a way as to ensure its continued peacefulness and its own continued security and prosperity. It remained to be seen if it had the vision and the will.

The immediate priority for Britain's leaders in the months following the Armistice, however, was not the restoration of the world order, but the restoration of order and normality at home. In the electoral campaign after the armistice, Prime Minister Lloyd George, in effect, promised to end conscription entirely and to speed up the demobilization process as much as possible. The army of 3.5 million in being on Armistice Day shrank to 800,000 by November 1919, and to 370,000 by the following November.[3]

The war was over, and it was necessary and appropriate to reduce those forces considerably, but that did not provide any guide to how fast the armed forces should be demobilized or what their final peacetime strength should be.

It is easy to sympathize with the feeling that it was time to "bring the boys home," but Britain demobilized at a dangerous pace, too rapidly and too fully. The peacetime armed forces that it ultimately decided to maintain were too small to accomplish its declared aims and to meet its real needs. As we shall see, British leaders never fairly took up the challenge of seeking to shape a favorable international order, but by failing to maintain adequate military forces, they forfeited their fleeting chance to do so. Britain lost the opportunity to guide the world in a direction that could have preserved the peace on which its own security depended. Instead, it helped create the conditions in which disorder, conflict, and, ultimately, fascism and war could incubate. Why did Britain evade its responsibilities? Why did it miss its chance?

Britain's leaders lacked a vision of Britain's future place in the world, and, therefore, of any strategy to attain and keep it. The Prime Minister might assert that Britain sought a world with boundaries based on nationality, with the security and freedom of states great and small guaranteed and supported by the League of Nations, but what did that mean for the British army, the Royal Navy, and the recently created Royal Air Force? How large were the forces needed to defend those boundaries, to protect that security, and support the League? Where should they be deployed? As the Chief of the Imperial General Staff (CIGS), Sir Henry Wilson frequently noted that it was impossible to determine the appropriate speed and scale of the demobilization until it was known what the demobilized army would have to do. The government had to begin by establishing a strategy for national security and a military policy before serious thought could be given to the permanent size and deployment of the armed forces.

Lloyd George failed to produce such a policy because he was preoccupied with other matters. For him, demobilization was the critical issue. After the election of 1918, Lloyd George turned to the Peace Conference, which ended on June 28, 1919, with the signing of the Treaty of Versailles. In the seven months following the Armistice, therefore, the Prime Minister was so thoroughly preoccupied that there was no time to formulate any coherent national security strategy.

But how could Lloyd George negotiate the peace treaty without a clear security strategy? It is likely that he did not wish to have any clear strategy, because any version that might have emerged would surely conflict with his domestic political objectives. He wanted to reduce the armed forces as much as possible and to ensure that conscription was ended. He also wanted to pursue negotiations for international arms limitation accords and to establish the League of Nations. He hoped that the League might replace Britain in its traditional role of keeper of the balance of power, and he did not see, or, perhaps, refused to recognize, that Britain must take the lead if League actions were to be effective, which required that its armed forces be ready and able to enforce League decisions. He believed "that there would have to be, of course, an efficient army to police the Empire, but [he] looked forward to a condition of things with the existence of a League of Nations 'under which conscription will not be necessary in any country.' "[4] In this nearest thing to a statement of national security strategy, Lloyd George showed that he saw the League, not Britain and its allies, as the maintainer of international order; the British armed forces would serve only as the police force of the British Empire. He wished to turn away from international responsibilities and to concentrate on the home front. Instead of serving as an important instrument in preserving the peace, the League would serve as a screen meant to conceal Britain's unwillingness to do what it must.

In his memoirs, the Prime Minister asserted that "the policy of reconstruction which I sketched out . . . is the most comprehensive, thorough, and far-reaching ever set before the country by any political leaders." He continued:

> The formation of a League of Nations, reduction of armaments (including the abolition of conscription), self-government for India and Ireland, the housing of the people as a national and not a local undertaking, larger opportunities for education, improved material conditions, the prevention of degrading standards of employment, the control of drinking facilities, the development of the resources of the country in such a way as to avoid the waste which had dissipated and depressed them, improved agricultural and transport conditions, measures for securing employment for the workers of the country—these were some of the reforms I indicated. . . . Our policy was summed up in a phrase which in a perverted form became historic: "What is our task? To make Britain a fit country for heroes to live in."[5]

In sum, Lloyd George thought that the end of the war and the establishment of the League of Nations would allow him and the nation to turn their attention inward, to correct the failures and flaws in the British body politic, to mend the holes in Britain's social fabric. The only real threats to Britain had been destroyed; the signing of peace treaties would put an end to an ugly chapter of the world's history. It was time to "make victory the motive power to link the old land up in such measure that it will be nearer the sunshine than ever before," and in doing that, "There is no time to lose."

It was true that there was no time to lose, but not in the way that Lloyd George thought. Britain's moment in history was fast slipping away. In the aftermath of the World War, with America retiring and Britain predominant, Lloyd George had the chance to make the world a safer and more secure place, his repeatedly stated goal. But with every day that went by, the situation slipped more and more out of his control, and by mid-1919 Britain's role in the world became almost completely reactive. The chance to create a stable new order came quickly and passed unheeded.

The failure to develop a coherent national security strategy led to a dangerous divergence between foreign and military policy. New and old responsibilities and old, sometimes ancient, assumptions about Britain's interests drove a confused foreign policy. Military policy, on the other hand, was driven by the Cabinet's determination to reduce military expenditure to as low a level as possible. The development of the force structure of the armed services, their size and organization, did not result from an evaluation of the military forces required by the nonexistent national security strategy. It became, instead, a game in which the Treasury and the Cabinet sought to press the Chiefs of Staff to accept lower force strengths and budgets than they thought appropriate, while the Chiefs fought to convince the Cabinet and the Parliament that they needed more. The pressure of a daily changing international scene drove foreign policy while the pressure of budget-cutting drove military policy. There was nothing to ensure that the two policies were mutually supporting, and so they were not.

The formation of Britain's military policy in 1918 was decentralized and occasionally chaotic. Since there was no central ministry of defense, the individual services set their own agendas and made their own plans independently of one another. Their policies were placed before the Cabinet and the Parliament by the Secretary of State for War and Air, Winston Churchill,[6] and the First Lord of the Admiralty, Sir Eric Geddes. In the end, the Prime Minister had the predominant role, always constrained by the fact that he had to be able to get his budget through a Parliament that was not eager to spend a lot of money on defense.

In the first few years after the war, the services made several independent attempts to define a national military strategy to serve as a context for their force structure and budget proposals. Not all of these attempts were narrowly self-serving. In a December 1918 discussion strikingly reminiscent of the current defense debate in the United States, the Chief of the Air Staff, Sir Frederick Sykes, noted, "In writing this paper I am faced with the fundamental question as to whether armaments more or less on pre-war lines will continue or whether the future forces of sea, land and air will have a semi-police semi-commercial basis." The Prime Minister had already decided that the primary purpose of the armed forces would be to police the empire, but Sykes gently questioned the wisdom of that decision:

It seems improbable that for some years there will be a great war between first-class powers. It seems equally unlikely that there will be a satisfactory league of nations other than that which perhaps may be possible between the British Empire, America and France. In any case there will be a period of deep-seated disturbance throughout the world. The Commonwealth, which has carried the greater share of the responsibilities of civilisation during the war, must continue to bear them into more stable times.[7]

Sykes argued that Britain should continue to play an active role in the world in restoring and maintaining order, and that it should not confine itself simply to policing the empire, which assumed either that no threats existed or that the League of Nations would handle any that did. But he also made the case for his own service, asserting that the RAF would be not only effective but economical in policing the empire: "In air power we possess a rapid and economical instrument by which to ensure peace and good government in our outer Empire, and more particularly upon its Asian and African frontiers. . . ." He sought to ensure that whether or not Lloyd George accepted a broader view of the purpose of the armed forces, the RAF would be able to argue that it was the cheapest and most efficient of the services.

The RAF was the most forward-thinking service and was the most aggressive in laying out both a national military strategy and a view of future war, because the RAF had been created during the war as an adjunct of the army, and its leaders felt that they had to advance their case clearly and convincingly to assure the institution's survival. They wanted to become an independent service, a status that the RAF achieved in 1921, and to increase the resources available to the new service to allow it to grow and develop.

The RAF represented the cutting edge of military technology and practice in 1918. Its leaders knew that they had seen only the beginning of a major change in the nature of war, what we would now call a revolution in military affairs. Far from fearing such a change, as the conservative natures in the army and the navy did, afraid that their "backward" services would suffer, the Royal Air Force enthusiastically embraced the notion that the nature of war was changing. They may be accused of excessive optimism and of using self-serving arguments, ostensibly based on the changing nature of war but really aimed at increasing the RAF budget; nonetheless, they were on to something. Warfare truly was changing, and those who simply fought to stop the change handicapped themselves and their country.

In the December 1918 discussion, Sykes sketched out a vision of future warfare that would be repeated and developed by a succession of airpower theorists between the wars:

Future wars between civilised nations will be struggles for life in which entire populations, together with their industrial resources, will be thrown into the scale. Evolution has brought about the creation of air fleets to meet the demands of such warfare. These will consist of home defence units and striking forces. The objectives of striking forces will be nerve centres, the armies and navies of the opponent, the population as a whole, his national moral[e] and the industries without which he cannot wage war.

The RAF, therefore, began to argue in 1918 for the creation of an offensive striking force with which to carry out what would later be called strategic bombing, aimed at critical command and communications nodes, industry, and even the civilian population, in order to bring an enemy rapidly to its knees. Sykes pointed out that future wars might well begin as surprise air attacks, without preliminary declarations of war or detectable mobilizations, and, moreover, that Britain was more vulnerable than any other state to such a strike because of the concentration of population and industry in and around London, so close to the French coast. He argued, therefore, for the maintenance of a large home defense force, in addition to the forces needed to protect Britain's sea lines of communication, a function he proposed that the RAF take over from the navy, and to police the empire, a function he proposed to take over from the army.

Sykes painted a picture of future airpower in which strategic bombing, and defense against it, was predominant, in which an independent air force could take over certain functions from the navy, and in which any ground-attack role in support of the army was a secondary or even tertiary concern. This focus on what would come to be called "strategic bombing" has been much praised by airpower advocates then and since who saw its proponents as visionaries, and much reviled by airpower adversaries who saw it as a distraction from the "real" revolution in military affairs—"blitzkrieg."[8] Sykes and his successor as Chief of the Air Staff, Sir Hugh Trenchard, and other airpower enthusiasts of the 1920s were neither fools nor knaves. The "strategic bombing" view of future airpower was a linear extrapolation of the events of the Great War into the geopolitical environment that those thinkers could perceive in the postwar world.

Throughout 1917 and 1918, German bombers, first Zeppelins and then Gotha fixed-wing bombers, struck London and southeastern England repeatedly with what would now be considered minor bomb attacks. These attacks were not seen to be minor during the war, however, when England had little effective defense against them, and a feeling of helplessness spread throughout the cities and the countryside. At the same time, aircraft performing aerial reconnaissance and tactical interdiction over the battlefield were truly helping to transform war in Europe. Why did the RAF adopt only one of these attributes of airpower rather than the other, or both?

The RAF leaders knew that they had a fight on their hands if they wanted to preserve the RAF as an independent service, and this led them to advocate the mission that conferred and required service independence—strategic bombing—at the expense of the mission that seemed to require subservience to the army—the ground attack role. But the strategic bombing arguments also made sense in the context of the postwar world in a way that ground attack missions did not. Britain faced no "peer competitor" (as we would now say) and could look forward to years without the prospect of a major war. The international environment was uncertain and disorderly, however, and conflict could be expected to continue for a long time to come. Sykes did not explicitly lay out the next part of the argument, but implicit in his conclusion was the assertion that although no great power was likely to arise in the foreseeable future to draw Britain into a major ground war, a power that sought to thwart Britain would follow the cheaper course of simply building a large air force capable of striking Britain's industrial heartland.

In other words, Sykes implicitly described what we would now call the "asymmetrical response" to Britain's global power. Realizing that no state foreseeable in 1918 could hope to fight the mobilized strength of the British Empire, Sykes argued that an aggressive state could hope to cripple or even destroy Britain using new technologies that would allow it to avoid Britain's great, but latent, strength. The old style of war and of reckoning military power was gone, Sykes was saying, and a new era of technological and asymmetrical threats was approaching. The RAF had to continue to perform the ground attack role, particularly in supporting the army in policing the empire, but its primary assignment must be to counter this dangerous new threat. Sykes and the other airpower enthusiasts of the time were quite wrong about the new nature of war, as we shall see, but their mistakes are much more understandable considering the geopolitical environment in which they were made.

The flexible and foresighted approach adopted by the RAF was not equaled by the army. The CIGS, Sir Henry Wilson, did not believe that Britain should police the world and violently opposed any new responsibilities that Lloyd George's foreign policy seemed likely to impose upon the army. His constant refrain that Britain should get out of those areas that do not concern it and "hang on like hell" to those that do resembles that of modern "realist" political theorists who warn against American involvement in "peripheral" conflicts. It reflects his concern that the military requirements of Britain's foreign policy were rapidly outstripping the army's resources. Wilson made several attempts to get Lloyd George to adopt a clear policy about the postwar army immediately after the Armistice, but with no success.[9] Thereafter, demobilization and the Peace Conference largely prevented any more serious attempts to do so. By April, Wilson had become extremely concerned that the de facto commitments the British army faced were exceeding its capabilities and had concluded that he could not get Lloyd George to lay down a broad military policy. In response to a request from the navy, Wilson wrote:

> You want me to send a general to help in the Baltic Border States. Yes, on one condition. That is that the Big Four lay down a broad policy. Other-

wise—No. Since November 22 of last year I have been trying to get a policy—trying, trying, trying, and not a shadow of success.

That being so, my whole energies are now bent to getting our troops out of Europe and Russia, and concentrating all our strength in our coming storm centres, viz. England, Ireland, Egypt, and India. . . . Since the statesmen can't and won't lay down a policy, I am going to look after and safeguard our own immediate interests. . . .[10]

On April 23, Wilson wrote, "I really have not enough troops to cope with our possible difficulties."[11]

By the end of April, a mere five months after the signing of the Armistice, Wilson submitted to the Cabinet a memorandum entitled "The Military Situation Throughout the British Empire, with Special Reference to the Inadequacy of the Numbers of Troops Available," bringing to the Cabinet's attention his concerns.[12] The note began with the ominous statement "In view of recent events, both in the United Kingdom and in the more distant parts of the British Empire, I feel compelled to bring to the notice of the War Cabinet the grave possibilities which confront us, and to draw attention to the serious shortage of troops with which we are threatened." He noted that the army was well below its authorized complement of 900,000, especially in vital specialties, and that recruiting had become extremely difficult in view of the fact that the recently instituted unemployment "donation" made military service relatively unattractive to out-of-work youth.

But Wilson noted,

apart from the numberless requests for British troops which are constantly being received from every quarter of Europe, our liabilities in vital portions of the British Empire have increased rather than diminished. Industrial unrest in Great Britain, incipient rebellion in Ireland, insurrection in Egypt and revolt in India, added to the latent hostility on the part of the Turks throughout the Middle East, all result in urgent demands for reinforcements which are too well-founded and too insistent to ignore.[13]

Wilson was not exaggerating Britain's troubles. In Ireland the revolutionary movement Sinn Fein established an independent legislative assembly, the Dail Eireann, in January 1919. On January 21 the Dail proclaimed Ireland's independence from Great Britain and announced that a state of war existed between Britain and Ireland. A sporadic guerrilla campaign began that showed every sign of danger.[14] Britain's General Officer Commanding-in-Chief (GOC) of Ireland urgently requested eight infantry battalions and two machine gun battalions; Wilson sent five infantry battalions and one machine gun battalion. Even those reinforcements were sent over the objections of the GOC of the forces in Great Britain, who feared that industrial unrest brought on by too-hasty demobilization resulting in unemployment could spread and turn into revolutionary activity.

Crisis in Egypt had been brewing from the first months of the Great War when it became clear that Turkey would intervene on the side of the Central Powers. Since the 1880s, Britain had held a protectorate over Egypt and the Suez Canal, but the Ottoman Sultan held nominal suzerainty over the area through the Khedive, whom he (theoretically) appointed to run the country. With the outbreak of war between Britain and Turkey, this situation was, of course, unacceptable, and Britain dismissed the Turkish Khedive and established one of its own choosing, thereby, in effect, making Egypt an "independent" state subject to British control. The war had suppressed the development of the consequences of this action—Egypt remained quiet. The peace soon brought rising Egyptian nationalism and disarray. The arrest in March of a prominent Egyptian nationalist led to rioting in Cairo, which rapidly spread to engulf much of the Nile Delta region. By the end of the month, British officials in Egypt reported that "we have no means of regaining control in Upper Egypt, from whence there is practically no news. . . ."[15]

The original Army of Occupation planned for Egypt consisted of two Indian divisions and one British infantry brigade.[16] This force was to be obtained by selectively demobilizing the much larger British, Indian, and dominion forces then in Egypt. Since that force was obviously inadequate to handle the rebellion, however, the demobilization was reversed and a division dispatched from the Balkans to Egypt. By the end of April, General Allenby, the GOC in Egypt, had succeeded in putting down the rebellion, but he wrote ominously that "this quiet can only be considered temporary and that an outbreak on a far more serious scale is in preparation." He requested, accordingly, still another British and another Indian division as reinforcements, as well as replacements to fill out his remaining depleted units.[17] Wilson found it difficult to meet this request.

Iraq was quiet for the moment, although British units were understrength, but India was not. Nationalist stirrings began appearing in India immediately on the signing of the Armistice, and local officials took a hard line in dealing with any unrest. On April 10, 1919, a mob got out of hand in the city of Amritsar, killing four Europeans; three days later, General Dyer killed 379 Indian protesters who had gathered for a prohibited meeting. At the same time, India's neighbor Afghanistan had been unsettled by the convulsions of war, and the government of India feared lest it become entangled in an Afghan conflict.

The Viceroy was not overly concerned about these developments, noting that "we can deal with even the worst contingency (internal disorder plus tribal-cum-Afghanistan complications) so long as the loyalty of Indian troops remains undoubted."[18] The Indian army was less sanguine about the situation, however, and on April 19 a telegram arrived at the War Office asking Wilson to hold "four divisions and four cavalry brigades in readiness to be sent out as reinforcements."[19] Wilson duly reported this request to the Cabinet in his May 19 memorandum, but added, "It is the duty of the General Staff to point out that at the present moment we are not in a position to provide these units." To prove this assertion, he continued by pointing out that British forces were inadequate even in the most critical theaters:

> It has already been shown that neither from Great Britain nor Ireland can we spare any troops. On the contrary we have not sufficient for Ireland as it is. . . .
>
> Of the ten divisions and one cavalry division which nominally compose General Robertson's force [on the Rhine], only six divisions are in a position to move forward in case of necessity and then for a limited distance only and with a reduced establishment of artillery, engineers, signalers and mechanical transport. These six divisions are the minimum required by Marshal Foch for operations in the event of the German Government refusing to sign the Treaty of Peace. But, even if it were decided to draw on these units for India, it is estimated that owing to the large majority of the battalions composing this Army being young soldiers' battalions, not more than one division could be organized for service in India, and to do this would break up every division in the Army, which would be thereby reduced to impotence.[20]

The inadequacy of the forces on the Rhine was particularly dangerous. The British had originally promised to maintain a force of ten infantry and two cavalry divisions to support the allied Army of the Rhine, which was essential to compelling Germany to accept the Allies' peace terms. In January 1919, Wilson said, "Foch is quite satisfied with our 10 infantry and 2 cavalry divisions, provided we keep them up."[21] By May, according to Wilson, although ten infantry divisions and one cavalry division were nominally present, only six were ready to fight—the British had not "kept up" the forces they sent there. Moreover, those forces were clearly not adequate for anything more than a demonstration should the Germans prove recalcitrant—their youth and relative immobility would render them useless for the task of imposing a treaty by force on a resisting Germany. Not only could these forces not supply reinforcements for India, they were evidence that Britain was already breaking faith with its allies and endangering its policies in Europe.

Wilson also pointed out that British forces in Turkey had been dramatically reduced, concluding that the commander in the region, General Milne, "will have none too many troops to enforce the terms of peace on Turkey, and that (assuming that this task will fall to us) all he has will be wanted in the neighbourhood of Constantinople for this purpose." Since no treaty for Turkey had even been drawn up, and Lloyd George contemplated a truly Carthaginian peace for Constantinople, this weakness posed serious dangers.

Wilson concluded, "The above survey will suffice to show that there is no available source from which the 4 Divisions and 4 Cavalry Brigades can at present be provided if the worst should happen in India."[22] He went on to say that the likelihood of disturbances in every theater had been increased by the "unfortunate incidents which have lately occurred at the Peace Conference, following on a long period of uncertainty and delay." In April a crisis had arisen over the Italian claims to the port of Fiume, which President Wilson absolutely rejected. The crisis came to a head—and to the world's attention—when the Italian delegates walked out of the peace conference at the end of the month. The CIGS was extremely concerned that this public display of disagreement among the victorious Allies would undermine their ability to guide the world scene peacefully: "The sharp divergence of view between the various Allied and Associated Powers which has now been advertised to the world at large is more likely to re-act on every centre of disturbance from Ireland to the Far East, and it would be foolish to ignore the possibility of aggravated trouble occurring at all danger points more or less simultaneously."

Having shown that, in a variety of possible circumstances, Britain might find itself without the military force to defend its interests and commitments, Wilson drew three conclusions. First, he insisted that "all military commitments not vital to the British Empire should be cut down with a view to concentrating all available troops at the essential points." Second, he called for British policy toward Turkey to be framed so as to avoid upsetting Muslim sentiments. He believed that such a policy was necessary to avoid inflaming revolutionaries in India by "the threatened extinction of Turkey as a Sovereign State . . . [as] occurred before the Indian Mutiny." Finally, noting that "we must face the fact (and prepare public opinion to face the fact) that we may be called on in the near future to furnish a military effort in defence of vital British interests that is beyond the strength of the forces now available," he concluded that "it may therefore be necessary to have recourse to some form of remobilization, that is to say compulsion."[23]

This memorandum had no material effect on British policy. It was a classic example of the army's reaction to the lack of a national security strategy and the absence of a coherent military policy. Unlike Sykes, Wilson did not lay out a vision of the future international scene, but described the present one. He did not look toward a future view of warfare, but assumed that the present style would continue. Above all, he did not seek to adapt the army to the new geopolitical circumstances, as Sykes sought to do for the RAF. Instead, he sought to adapt the geopolitical circumstances to suit the army.

Wilson's arguments that Britain should withdraw from its international commitments were not based on any view of the international situation, any assumption of a national security strategy, or any careful analysis of Britain's security needs. They were based, instead, on the knowledge that Britain's army was overstrained in meeting present commitments, and on a desire to relieve that strain. Wilson knew that getting the Cabinet to provide a larger standing army was virtually impossible, and he rarely tried to fight for such an outcome. He hoped that conscription could be retained in some form so as to provide the nucleus for a national mobilization plan that would make sense. But Lloyd George and almost every other politician of any stature had long ago abandoned any serious thought of maintaining conscription in peacetime.

Wilson's eloquence in laying before the Cabinet the real crisis that did face the British army in April 1919, as well as the possible and much more serious crisis that might face it shortly after that, was wasted. In April 1919 the British army was overstretched; only good fortune saved Britain from conflicts for which it had not the necessary resources. The point that Wilson needed to make was that Lloyd George and the Cabinet supported an army too small to carry out the roles which their foreign policy required of it. In the event, he made no impact at all.

Sir Henry Wilson was widely seen as one of the best Chiefs of the Imperial General Staff there has ever been. He was extremely current in the makings and doings of foreign policy, traveling between Paris and London with Lloyd George and communicating freely with his opposite number in France, Marshal Foch. Why was Wilson's memorandum so futilely ineffective, while Sykes's memorandum proved to be the statement of the military policy Britain would pursue for two decades? Why could Sykes look ahead and write cogently and coherently about policy and about the future, while Wilson could only write darkly about today and apocalyptically about tomorrow? The best explanation lies in the relative opportunities and difficulties that face armies and air forces in such periods.

The British army was committed, with boots on the ground, in at least seven theaters in April 1919. Air units were present in some but by no means all of those theaters, and only in very small numbers, and they, unlike the army, could fly away at the first sign of danger. If things went badly, as Wilson feared they would, the first result would be the killing of a good number of British soldiers for whom he was responsible. Next would come the receipt in London of frantic requests for reinforcements—that did not exist. Wilson feared that the sequel to that telegram would be the news that British officers had died with their commands. Besides, Wilson's army had responsibility for maintaining peace and order in Egypt, India, Ireland, and Great Britain herself, to say nothing of the secondary theaters. Any CIGS would be driven to focus on the details of current threats, looking for short-term solutions to short-term problems. The danger and responsibility of his position was almost certain to overwhelm the long view in any CIGS.

Sykes neither faced the danger nor bore the responsibility. He had to defend England from the air, but there was no hostile power with an air force. He had to support British military operations around the globe with airpower, but he did not have the responsibility for any theater. It is almost certain that RAF forces in a collapsing theater would have died trying to help their army comrades rather than "bugging out," but because they could leave at a moment's notice, Sykes or any other Chief of the Air Staff (CAS) need not be overwhelmed by that danger. As a result, the CAS was in a much better position to think in the long term, develop meaningful plans and strategies for the distant future, and work on the policies to realize them. Since the RAF, unlike the army, was convinced from the outset that it represented a fundamental change in the nature of war and, therefore, a change in the nature of British military policy, it was natural for its leaders to focus their attention on developing new policies and new concepts of war.

For the next two months it appeared that Britain and the allies had lost control of the situation entirely. As they continued to wrangle with each other over the terms of the treaty to be presented to the Germans, British forces fought with White Russian forces against the Bolsheviks, German irregulars fought Bolshevik sympathizers in the Baltic States, and Bela Kun, who had momentarily seized power for the Communist Party in Hungary, threatened war with Czechoslovakia.

Trouble also arose in regard to Turkey. During the war, parts of Turkey, even in Anatolia, had been promised to the Greeks and the Italians. In May, with British knowledge and Lloyd George's support, the Greek Prime Minister, Venizelos, sent a large force to seize and hold the Turkish city of Smyrna. Wilson strenuously disapproved, going so far as to ask Lloyd George "if he realized that this was starting another war, but [Lloyd George] brushed that aside."[24] Another war looked as if it was well under way in Afghanistan when Wilson learned that the Afghans had declared a jihad against the empire and that the Viceroy of India was moving forces to seize Jalalabad in Afghanistan itself. At the end of the month, the German delegates replied to the draft of the treaty they had received by refusing several of its terms and pointing out its various problems. Wilson constantly complained to Lloyd George about the dangers, but could not suggest alternate solutions.

On June 21, the German sailors in what remained of the High Seas Fleet, interned at Scapa Flow, scuttled their ships—a crime, as those ships were prizes of war taken by the Royal Navy, and a problem, since various plans for solving naval tensions among the Allies revolved around the ships now on the bottom. It seemed likely, moreover, that the Germans would refuse to sign the treaty altogether. In a prophetic comment, Wilson wrote in his diary:

I don't think that the Boche signature, in the present discredited position of [the Peace Conference at] Paris, is worth having. I am sure that, if he signs, he does so with no intention of carrying out his engagements, and I am equally sure that, after signature, the Allies will never agree to employ force again—so the whole thing would be a farce.[25]

On June 22, the day after the scuttling of the German fleet at Scapa Flow, the German delegates requested an additional forty-eight hours to consider the peace terms and their reply. The request was refused, and Wilson again conferred with his subordinates on the subject of how British forces could advance into Germany to enforce the peace treaty. General Robertson, the GOC of the detachment on the Rhine, had already reported that his troops could not advance farther than the Weser—Berlin was out of the question—and could get that far only if the Germans assisted by running the railways, telegraphs, and telephones![26] Fortunately, the Germans "saw reason." They agreed to sign the treaty.

The war against Germany had been won by a threat based on strength. The peace against Germany had been won by a bluff based on weakness. This is not to say that the Allies could not have enforced their terms on the Germans. Germany was weak, divided, and starving from the blockade still being enforced upon it, pending its signature of the treaty, while the Allies could mobilize millions, if necessary, to suppress it. But that mobilization would have taken time and been difficult, painful, and costly. It would have been much cheaper to have maintained the forces in being adequate for the task, as Britain had promised its allies it would do—and as it had not done.

Lloyd George and England escaped; they did not have to pay any price for their weakness in Germany. The treaty was signed, the bells were rung, and the war was over officially. But damage had already been done to the new order. The wartime coalition had shattered—Italy withdrawing itself, America about to do the same. A schism had developed even between France and England over the harshness of the treaty to be imposed on the Germans—a split that events and the Germans themselves would widen over time. The precedent, moreover, had been set that the small nations, and even the larger ones, in Eastern and Central Europe could flout the orders of the Peace Conference at Versailles at will, and that neither the force nor the will existed to impose its decrees. Small wars raged unchecked across Central and Eastern Europe, to say nothing of Russia, despite the best "shuttle diplomacy" of Entente diplomats.

Little seemed to come of these dangers. Béla Kun's communist government was short-lived, and peace soon reigned between Czechoslovakia and Hungary. German irregular forces in the Baltic states withdrew after a time. The treaty with Austria was signed. Italy did not set herself against the other Allies—yet. The war between India and Afghanistan also fizzled out, as did the disorders within India itself, and in Egypt. Many of the dangers against which Wilson had warned came to naught. But others would not.

THE BRAVE NEW WORLD   29

The Ten-Year Rule

The peace with Germany seemed to set the stage for a return to peacetime conditions, which led to intensified debate over the budget. In early July 1919 the
Admiralty presented its first postwar memorandum addressing naval strategy
in the context of unexpectedly high expenditures. Noting "that the question
will be asked: Against what possible enemy are you preparing?" the Admiralty
responded that "owing to the peculiar geographical constitution of the British
Empire, we run constant risks of unexpected and unforeseen troubles." Reaching desperately for the only plausible "enemy" in sight, the Admiralty continued, "Is it not at least prudent to bear in mind that if trouble arises in
Ireland—and this seems almost inevitable—it is at least within the bounds of
possibility that the United States of America may be forced by political exigen-
cies of their own to assume hostile action towards ourselves; I do not mean, to
make war—but to attempt to dictate." The memorandum concluded that only
by remaining absolutely in command of the sea and, among other things, superior to the U.S. Navy could Great Britain be assured of a free hand in Ireland.

Attempting to steal a march on the RAF, the memorandum also argued
that "in peace time the British Navy is the cheapest and most efficient police
force that the Empire can possess. . . . It is a fact that when trouble is threatened in almost any of our oversea possessions, the first thing asked for is the
appearance of the White Ensign."[27] In contrast to the army, then, both the
navy and the RAF felt that imperial commitments were in their parochial interest. Each argued that it was the premier force for policing the empire cheaply
and efficiently. In the meantime, imperial policing remained almost purely an
army job.

In response, the Chancellor of the Exchequer, Sir Austen Chamberlain,
clearly laid down the Treasury's fundamental assumptions:

> It will be a profound shock to Parliament and the public to learn that de-
> spite the fact that in the years before the war Great Britain was straining
> every nerve to keep an adequate margin of superiority over the German
> Fleet Programme . . . despite the surrender of the German Fleet (and its
> sinking at Scapa Flow), despite the surrender of the Austrian and Turk-
> ish Fleets, it will be necessary to maintain in the view of the Admiralty,
> not in the remainder of 1919/20 but in the period of reduced Fleets
> 1920/21 a Fleet almost if not quite as large as that which with the Ger-
> man menace still looming was only maintained with extreme difficulty.[28]

This argument was to be the Treasury's rallying cry for years to come: if we
fought and won this war to accomplish anything, surely it should have been to

increase our security. If our security has been increased, why, then, can we not reduce our armed forces dramatically from what we maintained in an era of danger and tension before the war? This argument was echoed by the Minister of Housing and Health a few weeks later in a note on the financial situation referring to the army estimates: "The War will certainly prove to be very disappointing in its results, if in the near future we cannot look for a substantial reduction in these enormous charges."[29]

Chamberlain also gave a classic example of how interservice rivalry provides a parsimonious treasury (or legislature) with solid arguments for cutting all the services. The navy proposed its vast expenditures, he wrote, "in spite of the fact that the Navy is no longer our only weapon of defence: that we have an Air Force capable of operating on Sea and Overseas, and millions of trained soldiers and sailors available in case of need." Chamberlain then addressed directly the question that the services, for the most part, had avoided: against what enemies should Britain prepare?

> The British Navy is intended for Defence not aggression. It is therefore worth considering the possible Powers or possible combinations of Powers from whom attack might come. To begin with, the Enemy Fleets are destroyed: and Germany, Austria and Turkey need surely be no longer considered. Russia? For operations in the Baltic perhaps, but not for defence of Great Britain against invasion. France? Is it seriously supposed by anyone, even those who are most struck by the chauvinistic attitudes of France in Victory, that a war with Great Britain, especially an attempt at invasion or a naval struggle has the faintest degree of probability? Or Italy? Is Italy with her difficult internal situation, her high prices, her coal difficulties, likely to try conclusions at sea? I venture to suggest that all the continental powers whether singly or in combination may be ruled out.[30]

Chamberlain noted that America and Japan might conceivably pose greater threats, quite generously omitting to attack the assertion that Britain and America might come to blows. He waved the American danger aside, however, asserting that "it must surely be years before the United States of America can be our equal in Fleet material." Simultaneously, however, he assumed that America would support Britain in the Far East against Japan: "the improbability that [Japan] could go to war with Great Britain without also bringing in the United States of America" was shown by the fact that "the Admiralty disposition of their capital ships places none nearer to Japan than the Mediterranean." He asserted that "a coup de main by Japan, if such were contemplated, could not be anticipated by any Fleet action even under the intended Admiralty disposition of the Fleet," and that, therefore, it was appropriate to reduce the active strength of the navy still further. He suggested a reduction of one-third of the active strength of the navy, both in men and in capital ships.[31]

Chamberlain's critiques of the Admiralty's position seemed sound. No enemy threatened Britain's survival, no state anywhere in the world could sensibly contemplate an attempted invasion of the British Isles, and none would be able to for years to come. The apparent validity of this argument was buttressed by the bureaucratic incompetence of the Admiralty, arguing for a larger force size based on the American threat. Virtually every member of the Cabinet of the time would have agreed with Chamberlain's assertion "I cannot believe that War between the United States of America and Great Britain is anything but unthinkable, above all in the course of the next few years, and the idea of an invasion of these islands from the United States is even more incredible."

The weakness of Chamberlain's line of reasoning was the assumption that the navy existed solely for the purpose of defending Great Britain, and primarily for the purpose of preventing an invasion of the British Isles. The navy had made some attempt to argue for an imperial policing mission, but Chamberlain brushed that argument aside.

Neither the Admiralty nor Chamberlain, apparently, gave any thought to the navy's role in helping Britain to create an international situation that would guarantee its security in the long run. Since Britain is an island, the navy's role in such a mission had to be crucial.

The existence of a powerful Treasury Department that took a very active role in the formulation of policy made the British security-policy-making process very different from that of America today. In America, the services formulate their polices and their force structures and submit the results through the Secretary of Defense and the President to Congress. Congress may accept those proposals or modify them, but it is not likely to enunciate general principles of policy in doing so. The Treasury Department, on the other hand, regarded itself as having the right not merely to comment on the services' proposals but to suggest alternative bases for the formulation of security policy in Britain. Throughout the interwar years the Treasury Department took the most simplistic and backward view of Britain's security policy. Reasoning that the armed forces existed to defend the nation first and to police the empire second, the Treasury remained steadfastly unwilling to sanction any forces beyond those it felt were needed to accomplish those aims. The debate rages over how powerful the Treasury was at various times in this period, but there can be no doubt that its influence on the formulation of security policy, at least in the 1920s, was uniformly baneful.

The services, to be sure, did not help themselves in their arguments with the Treasury. Chamberlain's memorandum stung the Admiralty to demand a statement of the "general policy of the Government, especially in regard to foreign relations." They insisted upon answers to two questions: "What is to be the policy of the Government as regards the supremacy of the seas—(a) over the United States of America? (b) over any probable combination?"[32] Noting that "there has never been any dispute as to the fact that no one Power could be permitted to surpass us in Naval Strength" (which was not entirely true, as the prewar standard specifically omitted the United States from that calculation), the Admiralty admitted the justice of Chamberlain's remarks regarding Austria, Germany, France, and Italy, but disputed Chamberlain's claim that Britain would not have to worry about America for some years to come. By 1923, they estimated, the Americans would have almost achieved equality "and some of their ships will outclass ours in fighting power." Even a small reduction in what the Admiralty was asking for, they continued, "would place this Country in a position of manifest inferiority." Having raised the specter of naval inferiority before a neutral power, rapidly withdrawing itself from the world and hardly likely, in any event, to contemplate aggressive war with any European nation, the Admiralty tried to clinch the debate with an appeal to emotion and politics: "It is unnecessary for me to remind the Cabinet of the strength of feeling in this country and throughout the Empire in favour of the maintenance of our sea supremacy. . . . The Government must now definitely decide whether they are prepared to maintain the supremacy which we have held for so long."[33] The Admiralty did note, almost in passing, that "while the demands for reductions and economies are made with growing insistence, the demands upon the Navy show no signs of decrease—quite the contrary. . . . If we have to admit that we cannot meet these and other calls, will not the effect upon the Empire and, indeed, the world, be disastrous?"

It is easy to ridicule the Admiralty's attempts to scare the Cabinet with the bogey of potential American naval superiority. It is true that war between America and Great Britain was virtually as unthinkable then as it is now. The British army, indeed, had sworn off America as a threat before World War I, deciding that it would not have to defend Canada against a renewal of the attack of 1812, and that in any event it would not prepare for such an eventuality. The fact remains, however, that since the defeat of the Spanish Armada in 1588, naval supremacy had been the lynchpin of Britain's security policy. As long as Britannia ruled the waves, the safety of the English people and their empire was assured. The admission that Britain would not hold naval supremacy meant that for the first time in almost three and a half centuries, it would live at the sufferance of another power. That the other power would almost certainly suffer it to live forever and without interference did not change the fact that a fundamental shift in the basis of Britain's security policy was at hand.

The argument, however, was beside the point. Politically it was absurd: the Cabinet would never sanction a naval race with America just to be the biggest fish in the ocean. Strategically it was mindless: America was not and would not be a real threat. But it was also a distraction. Arguing about the need to match America not only ensured that the Admiralty would lose the debate but also meant that the debate would not focus on the true needs of the time—the calculation and political defense of the forces needed to support a foreign policy aimed at creating a safe and secure world, Lloyd George's stated aims.

In the context of its American nightmare, however, the Admiralty also posed a fundamental question, the answer to which would shape Britain's security policy throughout the 1920s: "What should be the period of time during which we may reckon on immunity from war with a great Power or combination of small Powers giving an equivalent enemy force. . . ." Noting, "It has been suggested that it should be for a period of either five or ten years," the Admiralty pointed out that a period of five years gave greater security: Britain knew the building plans of America and Japan throughout that period. A period of ten years, however, "would undoubtedly enable us to make more effective reductions at present."

The five- or ten-year period mentioned in the memorandum was fully in accord with the direction the government was already taking. In a Cabinet meeting a week before the memorandum was written, Lloyd George had identified a series of domestic social and political issues as the top priorities of his government. Saying that "we were faced today with diminished resources" and that "it was necessary for us to realise that we could not have the best of everything," he continued:

> The Government must be prepared to take risks, just as the soldier had to take risks; and they must decide what risks they could best afford to take. As regards our Naval and Military position, our Armies had destroyed the only enemy we had in Europe; his military force was now reduced to 100,000 men; and his Navy was at the bottom of Scapa Flow. If, therefore, in such circumstances, we maintained a larger Army and Navy and Air Force than we had before we entered on the War, people would say, either that the War had been a failure, or that we were making provision to fight an imaginary foe. The War Cabinet had to decide . . . not a matter of Naval or Military policy, but rather a question of foreign policy, or statecraft. That is, what provision in respect to our armed forces we must make for say, the next five to ten years. It was for the Government to say to their Military Advisors: "These are the risks which you have to provide against" and "This is the basis on which you must act" . . . In five or ten years it would be necessary to review the situation, but so far as external forces were concerned, he felt that risks could be taken. No risks, however, could be taken with respect of the health and the labour of the people.[34]

Lloyd George mentioned risks, but he did not believe that he was really risking anything. Britain's enemies were destroyed and not likely soon to arise. He had no intention of fighting France or America. Where was the risk?

Believing that there really was no risk, Lloyd George was appealing to the services through their political chiefs to support his short-term "risk-taking" in order to help him put the nation's house in order. And the Secretary of State for War and Air, Winston Churchill, supported him wholeheartedly. He asserted:

> It was for the War Cabinet clearly to define the various responsibilities of the fighting services; in other words, they must state that there would be no great European war for the next five or ten years. They must also define what arrangements should be made for the maintenance of a sufficient force to support the civil power in a case of emergency; further, the Government must determine the size of the garrisons to be maintained in Ireland, Mesopotamia, India, Egypt, etc. It would then be for the fighting departments to consider how the obligations imposed upon them by the Government could best and most economically be discharged. He would venture . . . that the expenditure on the Army and Air Force in 1919/20 would not exceed £100,000,000.[35]

In the conversation that ensued, the Prime Minister continually pressed Churchill to justify the army size he advocated, as well as the sizes of particular garrisons throughout the world. He went so far as to point out that "the War had shown how immense was the superiority of equipment, such as tanks, guns, and aeroplanes. In the old days the use of armour had saved the employment of men; and so to-day a possible extension of the use of equipment should be taken into account in considering the size of the post-war Army." Churchill, who agreed with that principle, as events would show, made no comment, but granted that "the expenditure on the Army in 1914 should be taken as a datum line, and that definite justification should be shown for every extension of expenditure beyond that line."[36]

Between them at this meeting, Churchill and Lloyd George laid out the principles that would guide British security policy in the 1920s and served as the basis of the Cabinet conclusions ten days later outlining that policy.[37] They both proceeded from the same erroneous assumptions: they assumed that the prewar army had been designed to fight Germany; yet they also assumed that, having been designed to fight Germany, an army of the size of 1914 should be large enough to serve Britain's very different interests in 1919. There was no basis for either assumption.

The prewar army was not designed specifically to fight Germany. On the contrary, its basic structure came into being in the late nineteenth century when England was friendly to Germany, a balance of power existed on the continent, and the army's mission was simply to defend the empire. The rise of a German threat should have led to a realization that Britain might have to fight on the continent to maintain or restore the balance of power and should have led to an increase in the standing army. It did not—the army remained the same through the first fourteen years of the twentieth century. It was so weak, in fact, that the German General Staff virtually disregarded the British Expeditionary Force in its plans for the invasion of France. It was so weak that it could not deter Germany from attacking, and so small that a year of war elapsed before Britain could put a new, mass-mobilized army into the field. Reckoning from the starting point of the prewar army, the disappearance of the German threat had no significance—that army had never been designed to fight Germany.

The other assumption was more insidious—that the prewar army, ready, it was wrongly thought, to fight Germany, should surely be large enough and more than large enough to handle the international situation in which Britain found herself in 1919. Churchill knew better. He repeatedly reminded Lloyd George and the Cabinet that the empire had many new responsibilities that had not existed before the war, but in his zeal for supporting the Prime Minister's budget-cutting efforts, he conveniently forgot that fact. He seemed not even to notice that the entire nature of the international scene had changed. The continued references to the size and cost of the prewar army showed that the postwar leadership had not come to terms with the changed world—their thought patterns were simply out of date.

This debate finally led Lloyd George to try to wrench the formation of security policy away from the services, laying down his own policy line. He did that in a Cabinet meeting of August 15, 1919, at which it was concluded:

The Admiralty, and the War Office and Air Ministry, should work out their Estimates on the following bases:
(1) It should be assumed, for framing revised Estimates, that the British Empire will not be engaged in any great war during the next ten years, and that no Expeditionary Force is required for this purpose.
(2) No alteration should be made, without Cabinet authority, in the pre-war standard governing the size of the Navy.
(3) No new Naval construction should be undertaken, and the Admiralty should make every effort to stop constructional work on vessels that have no value for mercantile purposes. . . .
(4) The principal function of the Military and Air Forces is to provide garrisons for India, Egypt, the new mandated territory (other than self-governing) under British control, as well as to provide the necessary support to the civil power at home.
(5) As regards Ireland, the present conditions may necessitate a garrison in excess of the normal, but within twelve months there is a reasonable probability that a normal garrison will suffice.
(6) In order to save man-power, the utmost possible use is to be made of mechanical contrivances, which should be regarded as a means of reducing Estimates.

(7) In framing the Estimates, the following maximum figures should be
     aimed at:-
     Royal Navy   £60,000,000
     Army and Royal Air Force   £75,000,000.[38]

This much-cited passage from the Cabinet Minutes is the government's official
adoption of the "ten-year rule," about which much of the debate concerning
interwar British military policy has revolved.[39] It has frequently been asserted
that the ten-year rule kept the armed forces excessively weak and prevented
Britain from rearming in time. Some have argued that although its adoption in
1919 made sense, its continuation on a rolling basis after 1928 did not. Still
others have pointed out that the rule was formally abandoned in 1932, seven
years before the outbreak of the war in Europe, and was not a bad estimate for
a rule like that.[40] All of these arguments miss the significance of the adoption
of this principle for the Britain of 1919, and also miss the significance of the
other principles established in this Cabinet Minute.

What did the Cabinet really decide? It concluded that Britain would not be
involved in a great war for at least ten years. Since there was no longer any
great power that Britain was likely to confront in 1919, and since Britain's traditional enemies had been utterly devastated by the war, this conclusion was
sound.

The Cabinet decided that no expeditionary force would be needed during
that period to fight a great war. The concept of an "expeditionary force" was
tied up with the idea of a continental commitment—that Britain might participate in a war on the continent of Europe against a great power. The idea that it
might do so in 1919 generated such revulsion that the notion of maintaining
an expeditionary force was specifically excluded. The argument was specious,
however, for Britain had not maintained a designated expeditionary force before 1914 either. The nature of the British method of deployment, the Cardwell
System,[41] ensured that forces that could compose an expeditionary force
would always be available, although that was not its purpose. The army had
never maintained special units or requested particular funding for the maintenance of such a force before.

Regarding the navy, the Cabinet did not change the "prewar standard" requiring the Royal Navy to be 60 percent larger than that of any other power
excluding the United States. Historically, this rule had always also ensured that
the Royal Navy would be larger than the American—although not necessarily
160 percent larger. On the other hand, the Cabinet imposed what amounted to
a unilateral naval building holiday, which, the Admiralty had assured it, would
definitely allow the American navy to surpass the Royal Navy within a few
years.

Perhaps the most significant part of this minute was the definition of the
"principal function" of the armed forces, which was to provide garrisons for

all territory under British control. This provision was absolutely inappropriate in August 1919. If the world had been peaceful and stable, and if some other agency had existed to ensure its continued peace and stability, and if Britain had had no national interests that conflicted with those of other states, then this provision might have made sense. None of those conditions held. Civil war still raged in Russia, Germany edged ever closer to revolution, and border conflicts kept the newborn states of Eastern Europe at more or less constant, if low-level, war. Worse still, there was no treaty of peace with Turkey yet, and that was a problem, since Lloyd George proposed to dismember the Turkish state and remove the Turkish Sultan from his role as titular secular head of Islam.[42] A powerful nationalist movement was already arising in Turkey under the leadership of Mustapha Kemal Pasha, later known as Ataturk, and it seemed clear that he would not accept such terms without a fight. Meanwhile, the Cabinet estimates concerning Ireland were wildly optimistic, and unrest continued to simmer in Egypt and India. The world was not a peaceful, stable place in which the British armed forces could be content simply to guard Britain's frontiers. This Cabinet conclusion is the most straightforward evidence that Lloyd George never faced up to the military requirements of the foreign policy he advocated, inadequate though even that policy was to the task at hand.

The Cabinet also concluded that manpower (meaning money) could be saved by the use of "mechanical contrivances." The British Cabinet of 1919 was as blinded by the promise of technology, especially military technology, as American administrations have been since the Gulf War. Within the British government it was a widely held belief that tanks and airplanes had won the World War, and that those "mechanical contrivances" would transform war itself. We will explore below the details of the conversion of the British Cabinet to the religion of the machine in war, but here it is enough to note that as early as August 1919 the increased use of machines to replace men (and thereby save money) became a fixed part of British security policy.

The last principle the Cabinet established was the creation of a "ceiling" for service estimates. The conclusion referred simply to "maximum figures [which] should be aimed at," but the meaning was clear. The armed forces resisted the imposition of this cap,[43] but to no effect. Wilson objected to the principle, noting in his diary that he was calculating "what troops we require to keep our four storm-centres quiet—Ireland, Egypt, Mesopotamia, India. From these requirements we can build, and not from the allotment of an arbitrary sum."[44] Wilson was correct, although the alternate principle he suggested for calculating the army's requirements would not have been sufficient in the world as it was, since it would only have guaranteed the defense of the empire.

But no one challenged the assumption that underlay Lloyd George's conclusion. Defining a cap for spending and adhering to it implies a willingness to accept weakness and defeat. No armed force can guarantee that, for a fixed amount of money not determined by strategic requirements, it can ensure that all strategic requirements can be met. The corollary is that some requirements may not be met, and the adoption of the ceiling is the acceptance of that corollary. For the next several years the Cabinet would neither impose the ceiling uniformly—emergency requests from the army had constantly to be met—nor provide adequate resources to support its foreign policy. After 1922 it applied the ceiling, and Britain's ability to influence international events with military force thereafter declined rapidly.

Is it fair to charge Lloyd George or the Cabinet as a whole with failing to respond to a danger that no one seems to have noticed? In fact, the danger had been noticed, and not three weeks before the adoption of the ten-year rule. On July 27, A. J. Balfour, the Lord President of the Council, submitted a memorandum to the Cabinet called "Armies and Economics, Being Reflexions on Some Aspects of the Allied Situation on July 27th, 1919."[45] It laid out the dangers of Britain's military weakness:

> It must be obvious to everyone who has followed contemporary developments that Allied diplomacy is being seriously embarrassed by Allied military weakness. Ever since Peace with Germany seemed in a fair way to be established, it has been a race between the Great Powers which should demobilise the fastest. . . .
>
> I am not concerned here to justify this procedure. It has the best of all justifications—it is inevitable. But I must say a word about its consequences, for these have to be faced.
>
> We have at present two kinds of Military obligations; the one imposed by Treaty, the other by policy. Neither of these should seem very formidable to the States which only a few months ago had, I suppose, some fifteen million men under arms. But so rapidly have our Armies melted away that both are burdensome, and both lead to unedifying recrimination in the Conference Room about the share which the different Allies are taking the common burden. Upper Silesia, for example, has by Treaty to be occupied till a plebiscite be held. The soldiers say, or did say, that a division was required for the purpose. Where is it to come from and how is it to be composed? It is to come, say the soldiers, from the Army of Occupation on the Rhine. It is to be composed, says M. Clemenceau, of Allied troops in equal proportion. The discussion is not yet concluded, but I conjecture that in the end this arrangement will prove inconvenient or impracticable; that if a division be really required, it will have in the main to be French. . . .

Balfour then described the complaints the French would make about that procedure and about the way, in general, they felt that they alone of the Allies were being constantly required to send troops hither and yon in defense of the interests of all. He drew no real conclusions from this problem, although the conclusions should have been obvious: Britain's military weakness imposed a burden on its allies that they did not appreciate. That in itself might start a split in the alliance that other irritants could exacerbate, but it also meant that Britain did not control the application of force on behalf of the Allies, for it did not supply the force. That factor would soon become very significant.

Balfour continued in another vein:

These little controversies [with France] are harmful, but doubtless they can be arranged. Indeed, if I could only find out exactly what are our own Military commitments and our own Military resources, I should not despair of coming to some clear understanding, at least between France and ourselves.

The fact that Balfour, a member of the Cabinet and a close confidant of Lloyd George, should profess himself ignorant of Britain's military commitments and military resources reflects Lloyd George's presidential, almost imperial, style of governing—Lloyd George would never have made such a complaint. But it also reflects the fact that Lloyd George and the military authorities were at odds over what Britain should be doing—he wanted to play a greater role in shaping the world, but he did not wish to maintain the forces necessary to do that. Seeing that he would not have enough forces to play a large role in the world, the CIGS, Wilson, wanted to play a smaller role. Balfour's confusion reflected a disagreement between the CIGS and the Prime Minister both over ends and over means.

Balfour was not confused about the consequences of that disagreement, however. He continued:

But there is another aspect of the problem not so easily dealt with, the aspect which relates to our small Allies and our small enemies. The former, one would suppose, would obey us through gratitude; the latter through fear. But the gratitude is being rapidly worn away by our persistent efforts to prevent the nations we have saved or created from cutting each other's throats and seizing each other's territory; while the fear cannot easily survive the continued spectacle of our obvious Military weakness. Greeks, Roumanians, Poles, Czechs, Jugo-Slavs, (I may say nothing of the Italians), have all at different times disobeyed our explicit instructions. The Hungarians at the present moment are breaking the Armistice with impunity. The cases are many in which a Division or Brigade or even a Battalion would have made a situation easy which is now difficult, and have effectually smoothed the diplomatic path to Peace. But asking the War Department of a Great Power for soldiers is like asking a mendicant for a thousand pounds, and you get much the same reply. The Conference is therefore compelled to talk when action is required. Even the threat of action is denied us; for so notorious is our impotence that we cannot afford to bluff.[46]

Bluffing, as we shall see, was not impossible, at least for a time, but action was. The history of Central and Eastern Europe in this time need not be recapitulated in detail here, but the outcome is simply put. After the war, a host of new states including Poland, Czechoslovakia, Hungary, Yugoslavia, and the Baltic States were created from the detritus of the German, Russian, and Austro-Hungarian empires. Those states quarreled among themselves and with their neighbors about their frontiers: Poland with Germany, Lithuania, Russia, and Czechoslovakia, Hungary with Rumania, Yugoslavia with Italy, and so on. The Conference of Ambassadors at Versailles, which continued to meet after the signing of the Versailles Treaty because peace remained to be established with the other former Central Powers, attempted to mediate the various disputes, but to no avail. In the end, after a very small war, Hungary and Rumania worked out their differences, and after skirmishing, Poland and Czechoslovakia did the same. Poland's problems with Germany generated further violence and were never fully resolved, and Poland would shortly be at war with Lithuania and then with Russia over its differences with those states. By 1922, Eastern Europe was largely peaceful, although antagonism remained high, particularly among the Poles and their neighbors.

But Britain (and the other Allies) had missed an opportunity. Eastern Europe should have been a powerful stabilizing factor in European politics after the war. It should have served as a buffer state keeping Germany and Russia apart and preventing them from either making common cause on the basis of their pariah status, as Churchill always feared, or from making war on one another. Eastern Europe should also have served as a restraining factor on German ambitions, but it could do so only if it was united by the leadership of some great power. Looking forward, for a moment, to the crisis of 1938, imagine the situation if when Germany threatened Czechoslovakia, not merely Britain and France but Poland and Hungary came to its defense. Then direct and limited military action to defend Czechoslovakia would have been not merely possible but easy. It lay within the power of the Allies, specifically Britain, to bring about a situation in which such action would have been possible by acting forcefully in 1919. As Balfour noted, very few troops would have been needed to cause the minor states to desist from their minor attacks. The result would have been a composition of differences in that critical region with minimum inflammation of national hatreds, rather than the maximum inflammation that ensued. Although the minor states would not accept the leadership of any of their own number, they would almost certainly have accepted the leadership of a great power. Britain's military and diplomatic weakness was to have a higher price even than Balfour imagined, although his warning was clear enough at the time.

Balfour did not suggest increasing Britain's military strength. On the contrary, he noted, "I assume that this disease is incurable," but he asked, "[I]f we have no soldiers wherewith to help and shepherd our friends or control and perhaps coerce our foes, have we any substitute?" The substitute, he suggested, was the "economic weapon," and he pleaded for a "closer study of its capabilities." After argument on behalf of economic levers, however, Balfour concluded that they were not likely to suffice in a passage that should resonate strongly in our own day:

> Where the results of such an examination [of the efficacy of economic measures] are satisfactory we may be well content to lack Military force; though even at the best we cannot hope that the remote threats of economic ills will always give pause to greedy Governments or peoples intoxicated with a perverted patriotism. There are many nations at this moment who understand no argument but force; and on them the sight of a British Battalion would have a more immediate effect than the remoter prospects of poverty and want.[47]

But there were no battalions to be had, as Balfour well knew.

No mention of this dramatic statement of the problems Britain's military weakness was causing appears in the Cabinet discussions leading to the adoption of the ten-year rule. Part of the reason for that omission surely lay in Lloyd George's desire that it should not, but part lay also in the response that Churchill put before the Cabinet in a memorandum of August 4. He wrote:

> Mr. Balfour's complaint . . . of the absence of any military force to support the decisions of the Peace Conference and the consequent impotence of that body is not justified so far as Great Britain is concerned.
>
> Ten British divisions in good order stand upon the Rhine and will obey orders to go to any place which the Cabinet may wish. Whether it will be wise to involve them in Central European disputes is another question. But there they are and there they have been kept with no enemy in front of them for the last six months at a great expense.
>
> There is no validity in the plea that force is not available. There is plenty of force; it is the decision to employ it which has been lacking.[48]

Why did Churchill, the Secretary of State for War and Air, so emphatically destroy an argument he could well have used to strengthen the position of the services for which he was responsible? He had taken control of the War Office ready and willing to cut the army, for he believed that with the Great War over, Britain needed little or no army and that merely to police the empire. He was eager to move the Army of the Rhine somewhere else because he vigorously opposed the harsh treaty the Allies had imposed upon Germany and the harsh treatment in the future that was threatened by the maintenance of a strong army on the Rhine. He sought to bring Germany back into the community of nations by generous treatment and bridled at the notion that Britain should spend a great deal of money preserving a force on the Rhine whose only purpose, as he saw it, was to pursue misguided French policies. His retort to Balfour, therefore, was largely aimed at supporting his own foreign policy objectives rather than at taking care of the services that were his responsibility. The result was that Balfour's warnings were not addressed in the discussions leading to the adoption of the ten-year rule. The Cabinet had been warned of the danger both present and future of the policy it was pursuing, but had chosen to disregard the warning completely.

The decision to adopt the ten-year rule arose from the determination of Lloyd George and the Treasury to cut the military budget in order to save money, and the ten-year rule provided a principle to support their intention. Despite warnings, Lloyd George was unwilling to face the military and financial costs of his foreign policy, unwilling to recognize the limitations even of that seemingly aggressive foreign policy to create a stable and secure world, and unwilling to contemplate the consequences of pursuing such a foreign policy without adequate military backing. He was aided in making this bad decision by the confusion among those who would have warned him away from it. Balfour's warning was that Britain's foreign policy was too weak, because of military inadequacy. Wilson warned that the foreign policy was too aggressive, noting that it was overstraining limited military resources. Neither called for an increase in the military resources: halfheartedly, Balfour sought other tools for pursuing an aggressive policy; Wilson advocated pursuing a meeker policy. Churchill, pursuing a policy all his own, gutted Balfour's arguments as only the civilian head of a military service department can, but also presented Wilson's arguments for cutting commitments although he himself favored an entirely different set of commitments (he favored supporting the White forces in the Russian Civil War by deploying British ground forces there)—for which he knew the army did not have the resources. If Lloyd George did not find the warnings sent him very clear, it is not surprising.

Still, the Prime Minister must bear the chief responsibility. He had reason to know that the armed forces were dangerously weak, he had reason to see that Britain was losing control of the situation in Eastern Europe, and he had reason to fear that regarding German policy Britain would soon lose the initiative to France. He may be excused, perhaps, for not seeing the dangers that were soon to come, but he cannot be excused for imagining that there would be no such dangers.

Britain had the opportunity to shape the international scene in the months immediately following the Armistice. It alone among nations could have played the role of global leader, seeing to it that the international order that came into being in the aftermath of war was stable and secure, establishing the

League of Nations as a powerful tool for peace by taking a leading diplomatic and military role in it, and sending a message to European powers great and small that resort to military force was not an acceptable tool of diplomacy. To do all this, it would have had to retain its armed forces at a much higher level of strength and readiness, and that would have cost money. It might even have been difficult to find enough voluntary recruits for such a force, although Wilson's constantly expressed fears in that regard should be taken with a grain of salt, as he so obviously sought to defend the need for peacetime conscription.

It would have been very hard for a political leader in November 1918, or even November 1919, to follow such a course. Britain's populace was exhausted by war and weary of the world and had focused its attention inwardly on its own pains and problems. Britain had become, for the first time in centuries, a debtor rather than a creditor nation, and the politicians of the time may be excused for overstating the consequences of that transformation.

It is not enough, however, to say of a democracy that it could not follow a particular policy because the people did not wish to do so. For the necessary and proper role of leaders is to lead, and we must remember clearly that Lloyd George himself led the people to look inwardly, led them to believe that Britain had no foreign policy concerns, led them to believe that Britain's security was assured. He never undertook to combat the argument that the end of the war should produce an enormous "peace dividend" as we would now call it, for he took the lead in saying it was time to make Britain "a land fit for heroes to live in"—implying that the time for heroism had passed. Could he not have pursued a different policy? Could he not have warned the people of the dangers that lay ahead? Could he not have created a national consensus on the need to win the peace for real, since they had given up so much to win the war? Perhaps not, but we shall never know, because no attempt was made.

Lloyd George himself, and most of the Cabinet, did not see the need. Although the Prime Minister spoke and wrote about the need to shape the world in a good way, he did not think through what that meant. He did not consider how serious and hard a thing it is, even for the leading global power, to shape a chaotic world into one dominated by peace, order, and stability. In his heart, Lloyd George believed that with England's enemies defeated, the world would go its way more or less peacefully, more or less pleasantly for Britain. He led the people also to that view, and he trampled on any in the Cabinet who opposed it. By August 1919, he laid down as Britain's security policy that Britain would not undertake to maintain the forces needed to shape the international arena but would concentrate only on defending the British Empire and the British Isles. Britain chose to ignore its responsibilities and withdraw from the world at the very moment when its decisive engagement was so desperately needed. For the part that he played in that decision, it was, perhaps, only poetic justice that Winston Churchill would live to reap the whirlwind he had helped to sow.

2

Britain's Defense Dilemma

During World War I, British leaders had enunciated as one of their war aims to create conditions of peace and stability in the world that would render war a rare and controllable event. They looked to the Versailles Treaty, the League of Nations, and the expansion of the British Empire by means of League mandates to secure a new era of peace: Versailles would keep the German menace down, Britain's new mandates gave it control over strategically vital and congenitally unstable regions, and the League of Nations would maintain order in the rest of the world. There was much justice in the view that if Versailles was properly enforced (and the entente with France required by that enforcement sustained), the mandates were secured and pacified, and the League of Nations was properly led and supported by Britain, peace would largely reign. The years immediately following the armistice tested Britain's resolve to meet these three principal policy goals, and largely found it wanting, a failure that led gradually but inexorably to Britain's loss of control over the international scene.

The first test was the easiest—a large-scale revolt broke out in Iraq, a new mandate carved out of the Ottoman Empire, and Britain was required to defend its control over an area in which it already had considerable armed forces and a commitment of honor and interest. In the end, it passed the test, but even in this success the warning signs were ominous. The debate over the right policy to pursue with regard to Iraq before, during, and after the uprising was confused, frequently missing the main points, and focused almost exclusively

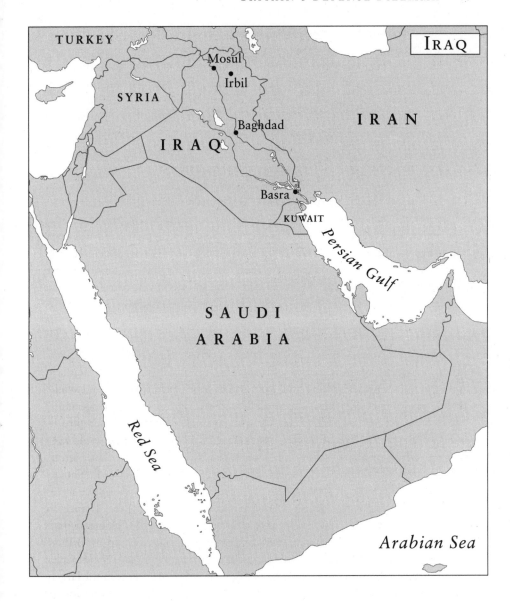

on the financial aspects of the problem. It revealed that many of Britain's senior leaders did not understand the true needs and obligations of the leading
global power and mistook an era of peace shaped by force and active involvement for an inherently peaceful era.

The debate over Iraq was complicated by the politicians' primitive grasp of
and enthusiasm for the dawning revolution in military affairs. The policy implications of the developments in military technology and theory were evident
during the war itself. The Smuts Report stated the linkage very clearly:

The progressive exhaustion of the man-power of the combatant nations will more and more determine the character of this war as one of arms and machinery rather than of men. And the side that commands industrial superiority and exploits its advantages in that regard to the utmost ought in the long run to win. Man-power in its war use will more and more tend to become subsidiary and auxiliary to the full development and use of mechanical power. The submarine has already shown what startling developments are possible in naval warfare. Aircraft is destined to work an even more far-reaching change in land warfare.[1]

The notion of "mechanization" in the 1920s was similar to the concept of "digitization" that reigns supreme in the armed forces today. In both cases, the idea is that with the addition of "mechanism" or computers, enormous combat power will be added as well, and that it will therefore be possible greatly to reduce the size of the armed forces without losing, and perhaps gaining, combat power. During the war this issue was not too important, as resources for the war effort were not stinted. After the war it became critically important.

We have seen how Britain's imperial commitments in 1919 and 1920 complicated the efforts of Lloyd George and others to attain fiscal savings simply by cutting the armed forces. For all their wishing, the rebellion in Ireland would not go away, India remained unstable, Egypt still simmered, domestic unrest in the form of strikes and riots increased. There was no treaty with Turkey yet, and British forces spread throughout that country watched with trepidation as a war raged between Turkish nationalist forces under the leadership of Mustapha Kemal Pasha—Ataturk—and Greek divisions based at Smyrna. Worst of all, a serious rebellion raged throughout Iraq that periodically isolated British garrisons in their forts, threatening to overrun them completely.

At the same time, the British economy had taken a turn for the worse. The immediate postwar boom rapidly gave way to a period of recession. Unemployment was high, prices fluctuated dangerously, businesses and individuals suffered. Lloyd George had adopted the policy, then thought to be fiscally most sound, of withdrawing the government from the economy as rapidly as possible. Orders for military goods were summarily canceled, and factories and mines nationalized during the war were turned over to the private sector as rapidly as possible. The government's aim was to restore the normal economy of the country as rapidly as possible while reducing both government spending, which was seen as nonproductive, and the taxes to pay for that spending, which were harmful. The result of these policies was immediate economic dislocation, and the government soon heard the voice of the people raised against it. The people called for an end to "government waste"—the budget had to be cut.

The armed services inevitably bore the brunt of that cut. According to the fiscal and political orthodoxies of the time, spending on the military was entirely nonproductive. Lloyd George defended spending on social programs both as part of his program to make England "a land fit for heroes," and as part of a more urgent plan to placate a restless and increasingly unhappy populace. He was, therefore, much less likely to accept cuts in government programs in housing, for instance, than to cut the military. The government knew that military industries were a source of employment and repeatedly pressed the armed forces to retain factories and programs they did not need, solely in order to avoid increased unemployment. The fiscal orthodoxy of the time, however, argued that "priming the pump" of the economy by increasing government expenditures was harmful in the long run, because it required either raising taxes or increasing the debt burden, both of which were unacceptable.

But the troubled international conditions of 1920 and 1921 made cuts in the armed forces highly problematic. Rebellion in Ireland continued throughout that period, requiring the commitment of a large number of British ground forces and ending in a truce on July 11, 1921. The Anglo-Irish Treaty signed in December 1921 effectively granted southern Ireland independence, and all British regular forces were withdrawn from southern Ireland, now the Irish Free State, by the spring of 1922. British policy in Ireland had been totally defeated.

Whether Lloyd George should have sought to retain British control over southern Ireland or not, that policy required a large commitment of ground forces to Ireland that, in the end, proved inadequate. The inadequacy of those forces was probably due largely to errors in their use and to a series of important political blunders on the part of the London and Dublin governments, but there is no escaping the fact that counterinsurgency is a manpower-intensive activity. Given the tools the government was determined to use to suppress the Irish uprising, Lloyd George's military policies did not provide enough forces to meet the need. His determination to hold Ireland regardless of cost, however, combined with the military weakness his policies imposed stripped the rest of the empire of adequate force to meet contingencies. That problem was illustrated clearly first in Iraq in June 1920.

Great Britain had been holding Iraq under a military administration since its armies had taken the area from the Turks during the World War. Because Iraq was nominally a collection of Turkish provinces, and because the formal treaty of peace with Turkey had been delayed by the prolonged Versailles negotiations, the military administration set up during the war continued to rule the country through mid-1920. But that administration began to lose its legitimacy in the eyes of more radical Arab nationalists who saw in the prolonged interregnum the opportunity to move for an independent Arab state in Iraq. British military weakness and Bolshevik gains encouraged them in this venture. A British attempt to arrest the ringleaders of this movement in June 1920 backfired, setting off a widespread revolt that soon engulfed most of the country. The local commanders screamed for reinforcements—not fewer than two divisions, they said, would be needed to suppress the revolt. Otherwise, Britain would have to abandon Iraq.

The two divisions were found, but with great difficulty, most being drawn from the Indian army over the protests of the Indian government that its forces were stretched to the limit. More ominous than those protests was the fact that the constant deployment and redeployment of British forces was having a serious impact on their readiness to do anything at all. One of the local commanders wrote, " 'One of our great difficulties . . . is the fighting capacity of troops here.' Many soldiers had 'never fired a musketry course, much less seen a shot fired.' "[2] Those soldiers, he felt, were only useful for garrison duty.

The British army was small, and the political leadership knew it but implicitly believed that the force would make up in quality what it lacked in quantity. That had been the hallmark of the small but extremely proficient British Expeditionary Force that had helped fight the Germans to a standstill in 1914. This problem was not an isolated one, for in June 1920 the thirty infantry battalions in Ireland had "a total effective strength of about 23,000 of which, however, 3,000 have not fired a musketry course."[3] The system was clearly suffering from overstrain. These inadequacies should have been an important warning to the government to bring Britain's military strength into line with its commitments before disaster struck.

For the moment, disaster did not strike, and Lloyd George's government was once more able to avoid making hard decisions. The government of India complained loudly, but supplied the necessary troops that, used skillfully in conjunction with the few airplanes in Iraq and powerfully aided by the concessions Britain made in July 1920 toward autonomy for Iraq, suppressed the uprising by the fall. The policy objective was achieved, and the warnings went unheeded. Similar problems in Egypt, which remained restless after the abortive revolt of 1919, were put off with political declarations, but tensions there would resurface throughout the 1920s. Palestine, likewise, although relatively quiet, remained a potential powder keg the fire from which, if once ignited, was beyond the capacity of the forces stationed there to put out.

British security policy in 1920 and 1921 faced a fundamental paradox. All had seen a revolution in military affairs beginning during the war that appeared to hold out hope of a great reduction in the size, and therefore expense, of the armed forces without any cost to their combat power. Britain's imperial commitments, however, were so great that the already reduced armed forces were not able to meet them adequately without suffering training breakdowns and incurring substantial risks. But both financial and political pressures seriously constrained the budgets the armed forces could have, which were inadequate for current needs, let alone for developing the armed forces appropriate during a revolution in military affairs (RMA). Even if one believed the RMA enthusiasts who argued that "mechanized" forces would save money, there was still the financial hump of "mechanizing" the armed forces to get over in the short term, when there was not enough money even for normal operating expenses. The only reasonable solutions were to reduce international commitments dramatically, as Wilson repeatedly suggested, or to spend more money on the armed services, as the service chiefs periodically demanded. In the event, Lloyd George did neither.

The process of determining the budget for the armed forces for fiscal year 1920–1921 began with the presentation of the Army Estimates to the Cabinet in early February 1920. The estimates rested on the assumption that policy aimed at the re-creation of the army of 1914, and they separated the normal operating cost of the army—calculated by figuring the cost of the prewar army in 1920 pounds—from the "extra charges due to temporary obligations," such as the maintenance of control in Iraq. Figured that way, the ordinary expenses were £55.5 million, which would rise to £62 million when war-surplus stocks had finally been consumed. The budget agreement arrived at when the ten-year rule was adopted had allocated £75 million to the army and the Royal Air Force together, of which Churchill, the Secretary of State for War and Air, chose to allocate £62 million to the army and £13 million to the RAF. The Army Estimates for 1920–1921, then, seemed to have brought the army in line with Cabinet policy. But the "extra charges" for that year were estimated at £48 million, of which £21.5 million were to go to the forces in Iraq.[4]

In an accompanying memorandum, Churchill explained the various problems that beset the army. He noted that the army of 1920 was a wholly new creature—almost all of the conscripted soldiers of World War I had been released, and almost all of the soldiers then in arms were new volunteers. He warned that "the battalions and batteries of the new Army have certainly not yet reached the standard at which they could be safely committed to any serious military enterprise or have any great responsibility thrown upon them, either at home or abroad." He predicted that two years would see the proper reestablishment of the professional British army, but cautioned, "This is, in fact, the year when the expenses of the peace time British Army will be at its highest and the results at their very lowest."[5]

This honesty aimed to disarm criticism and deflect the budget cuts he clearly foresaw away from the meat of the army. Churchill hoped, instead, to convince the Cabinet to bring foreign policy into line with the army's capabilities, since it seemed to him so obviously impossible to bring the capabilities into line with the policy. He went carefully through the "extra charges" section of the estimates to argue for foreign policy withdrawals across the board. The £5 million required to support the army in Germany, he noted, should be recovered from Germany in reparations (and not, therefore, charged to the army). The forces around Constantinople, he continued, cost some £6.5 million per year, an expense which "can be terminated and the total reduced by a decision of policy." He cautioned that the commander in chief of the forces in Egypt and Palestine would strongly protest against any reduction in his forces, costing some £15 million a year, but recommended that he be approached again with reductions in mind.

But he really took aim at the garrison in Iraq: "The cost of the military establishment in Iraq appears to me to be out of all proportion to any advantage we can ever expect to reap from that country." Its garrison would cost more than £18 million annually, and even more in the erection of permanent housing for the troops, essential for the maintenance of their health in that climate. He practically begged the Cabinet simply to withdraw from Iraq but, failing that, suggested they pull all forces back to Baghdad and Basra and "let our influence gradually radiate out from there in the next 10 or 15 years as was done from Khartoum in the Soudan." Such a scheme would cut the expenditure necessary from £18.5 to £5.5 million a year, and "if there is no other method of holding the country, I am of opinion that our commitments should be reduced."

But Lloyd George did not wish to pull out of Egypt, Constantinople, Palestine, Persia, and Iraq, nor was the Cabinet solidly behind such a policy. The Foreign Secretary, Lord Curzon, cherished the hope of establishing a powerful British empire in the Middle East, finally securing the critical link between Britain itself and its possessions in the Far East. He maintained emphatically the need for a strong British presence in Egypt, Palestine, Persia, and Iraq. Others argued strongly for the maintenance of Iraq on the grounds of its oil. Then as now a considerable portion of the world's oil came from the area of Basra, and vast oil reserves around Mosul were guessed at, although mostly not yet proven. Since it was clear that oil had become a vital strategic resource, many were unwilling to give up the richest oil-bearing region yet found.

But the most important reason Lloyd George did not happily contemplate withdrawing from all of those regions was simply that England's presence there had already committed its prestige and its honor—factors that Churchill and Wilson studiously ignored when it suited them. Britain had made promises and commitments to many local individuals and groups in the course of the war and in 1919, and these would be abandoned if Britain withdrew; any withdrawal would seem a major defeat in the eyes of Britain's enemies. The Soviets would have been much heartened by Britain's withdrawal from the Middle East and might well have pushed farther into Persia, a traditional Russian objective, traditionally thwarted by Britain. Considering the strategic importance of the Suez Canal, any withdrawal in Egypt seemed a dangerous move. Although Britain had little strategic interest in Palestine, its presence there was part of a complicated political game with France—simply withdrawing would have affected Britain's relationship with its most important ally in unpredictable ways. Lloyd George, finally, was determined to impose a particularly harsh peace on Turkey, and no prospect of such a peace was in sight if Britain withdrew from all of the territories it held around and in Turkey. Foreign policy interests are what they are, not always what we would like them to be, and it is not easy to decide that a state has no interests in a region to which it has already committed itself, simply because it would be convenient to do so. That is why Churchill's proposals and Wilson's constant carping were largely irrelevant in shaping British foreign policy, and it is all the more reason why Lloyd George, who understood that his policies and desires committed Britain to active roles in the regions of the Middle East, must be held to account for failing to provide the military forces necessary to support those commitments.

The Cabinet Finance Committee, meeting to discuss the Army Estimates on February 9, was equally unrealistic. Hearing that the basis for establishing the postwar army was the re-creation, as nearly as possible, of the prewar Army (at 1920's prices), the committee commented:

> Some question was raised as to whether this was the correct basis to adopt having regard to the alteration in circumstances. No reduction, however, appeared practicable owing to the disappearance of Germany as a military Power, in view of the fact that the pre-war Army, though organised to meet an emergency on the Continent, had been designed, so far as its strength was concerned, solely with a view to the defence of the Empire, and our liabilities in this respect, so far from being diminished, had been increased by the acceptance of the mandates over Palestine and Iraq.[6]

The British took it for granted that victory in the war should yield what we would now call a "peace dividend," that with so powerful a foe as Germany finally vanquished, it should be possible to cut expenditures on the armed forces. The leaders of the armed forces had the constant and painful duty to point out that the prewar army had not been designed to fight Germany at all and that the mission for which it had been designed had grown, not shrunk, since 1914. When they pointed out that the postwar army should be larger than the prewar army, few were willing to accept their simple logic. The prewar army was accepted as the standard against which the postwar force would be measured.

The need to reduce expenditures on Iraq, therefore, was obvious and urgent: "It was recognized that the cost of such a garrison for Iraq was prohibitive and that it must be curtailed."[7] But how to curtail it without withdrawing from Iraq entirely? Churchill offered a nonanswer that was eagerly accepted: "the sum £21,500,000 proposed for the maintenance of the garrison in Iraq should be halved, discretion being left to the War Office to determine the method by which this reduction should be secured."[8] A similar decision arbitrarily cut the allotted garrison of Palestine in half as well, since "provision on this scale, especially for the maintenance of order in Palestine, where no serious trouble could be anticipated, was indefensible."[9] It is difficult to understand how anyone in 1920 could assert that no serious trouble could be anticipated in Palestine, but that assumption became one of the bases for determining the size and posture of the British army.

But Churchill, the Secretary of State for War and Air, had saddled himself with a problem, for he had promised to cut the cost of the Iraq garrison in half without withdrawing from substantial portions of the country, and the CIGS, Wilson, proved obstinately unhelpful to him. He argued that "any withdrawal at present would have a serious effect on the internal condition of Iraq, and might well involve us in grave internal disorders." Attempting to sway the Cabinet with appeals to finance, he noted in addition that "the possibility of Iraq paying its way within a reasonable time depends greatly on whether the vilayet of Mosul is included or not," and that "it would be an act of extremely short-sighted policy to throw away the best chance we have of recouping ourselves for the outlay already incurred" by abandoning it.[10] So much for limiting Britain's commitment in Iraq.

As for the possibility of holding all of Iraq, including Basra, Baghdad, and Mosul, with the force Churchill proposed, Wilson warned that "any attempt to hold Baghdad and the Line of Communication to Basra with the force suggested is to invite disaster." He thought reductions in the force would be possible only by reestablishing order and security in the region, and his proposed method for accomplishing that was to abandon Lloyd George's plans for imposing a harsh peace on Turkey. He reminded the Cabinet that "the General Staff have, for many months, repeatedly pointed out that the policy of antagonizing the Turks, and thereby embittering the whole Mussulman world, was involving us in unnecessary expense at the present time and laying up for us untold liabilities in the future." The key for Wilson, of course, was forcing Lloyd George to moderate his views on Turkey, and to this end he offered him two unpalatable alternatives: public and international humiliation in the form of a withdrawal from Iraq or abandonment of his harsh policy with respect to Turkey.

Wilson's attempt backfired. On May 20, 1920, Churchill sent the Cabinet a proposal by Sir Hugh Trenchard, the Chief of the Air Staff, for policing Iraq using only airplanes and a few armored car squadrons.[11] Churchill's proposal took direct aim at British policy in Iraq and offered the Cabinet a forceful alternative: get out of Iraq or adopt Trenchard's proposal.

Churchill's notion of how foreign policy and military policy should be coordinated is the most interesting part of the document:

> The sole line of argument on which it is safe to proceed is, first, to fix the amount that may be spent. Secondly, to give the administering department the power of choosing the policy within those limits. And thirdly, having chosen its policy, to indent upon the War Office or the

Air Ministry for the military force required. Of this force the War Office or the Air Ministry must be the judge. We must be entitled to say, "To hold this district will require these troops and will cost you so much." We must also be entitled to say, "These forces must be so disposed as to be militarily safe and not liable to be overwhelmed or surrounded." As a result of such a consultation between the two departments concerned, it will often happen that political officers will be forbidden to go into large districts for several years to come because the troops are not available within the limits of the grant-in-aid, instead of as at present these officers pushing out wherever they will and drawing a blank cheque upon our resources in money and men.

In operations of this sort, which we might call peacekeeping or peacemaking operations, the tension between the military authorities and the political authorities is almost inevitably high. It is true, as Churchill noted, that the department setting the policy, in this case the Foreign Office, is not the department that has to pay for it, in this case the War Office. The best solution to that problem is not, however, to determine in advance the amount of money to be spent and then offer the Foreign Office, in effect, a menu of military options, with prices attached, from which they might choose, for the option that can accomplish the policy might not be on the menu.

When the money to be spent on a policy is fixed in advance, the government must accept the possibility that the policy will not be achieved at the price. When the money has been spent and the policy is not achieved, what then? Is it better to spend more money to accomplish the mission or throw away all that had been done and spent already? The first course is by far the more likely, particularly since abandoning a partially completed policy is usually wasteful and embarrassing. Churchill's cost-limitation proposal, therefore, was not only unwise but impracticable.

This episode shows that it does not take a "Vietnam syndrome" to create a fixation on departmental responsibility, "mission creep," and "exit strategies." It is enough for a military department to fear that it must execute a policy it does not control, and that it will be blamed both for the cost and for the failure of that policy. That is often the way with "political" missions such as peacekeeping operations, because those operations, unlike major wars, are dominated by the interests of the "political" departments, while the relatively low level of military threat seems not to justify real military control of the operation. The response of the military is often, as in this case, to grasp for a clear separation of power and responsibility so that it can at least control the allocation and use of its own resources. Such solutions, however, rarely work well.

Churchill's attempt to constrain policy in Iraq gained support from the need for economy and from Trenchard's novel proposal for maintaining order on the cheap. The policy of "air policing" in Iraq marked a change in Trenchard's attitude toward airpower. During the war, he had been an unwavering opponent of the idea of an independent role for the air force. In the "air policing" policy, he identified for the first time in peacetime an independent role and mission for the RAF.

Although most of the development of the RAF during the war had taken place on the Western Front in operations dominated by the army and the Royal Navy, Trenchard claimed that "in more distant theaters . . . such as Palestine, Mesopotamia, and East Africa, the war has proved that the air has capabilities of its own which can be usefully employed in operations against the enemy's ground forces. . . ."[12] There, to be sure, ground forces predominated in determining the outcomes of the campaigns, but aircraft played a much more independent role in those relatively free-flowing and changeable theaters than they did on the static Western Front. Trenchard acknowledged that the RAF might not be able to defend a country against external attack on its own, as yet, but claimed that "the Air Force may yet impose considerable delay on an enemy whose lines of advance are limited and lengthy, and has proved itself a powerful agent for the attack and dispersal of considerable bodies of ground troops."

He asserted, however, "If the air power be applied for the purpose of keeping order in a partially pacified area, the requirements of the garrison of such a country may be considered from an entirely novel point of view." He described the expense and inefficiency he saw in stationing ground troops all around the country in small groups which were too small to be secure but amounted to quite a large number of troops overall. In his own plan, most of the ground troops would be withdrawn except for garrisons in Baghdad and around a few centrally located airfields. Aircraft would patrol the country, for "the speed and range of aircraft makes it practicable to keep a whole country under more or less constant surveillance." He referred frequently to the almost primordial fear that the local population had of aircraft: "It must be remembered that from the ground every inhabitant of a village is under the impression that the occupant of an aeroplane is actually looking at him, and the frequent, perhaps daily, appearance of aircraft apparently overhead will do much towards establishing the impression that all their movements are being watched and reported."

If unrest, nevertheless, broke out, the RAF would receive "early information of hostile concentrations of marauding tribes" and send out aircraft to attack and disperse them much faster than the army could put together a punitive expedition. "The capacity of the Air Force to deal a swift and unexpected blow," he said, "affords the chance of stifling the outbreak in its early stages, before unrest has time to spread." Even if the RAF failed to nip the uprising in the bud, however, airpower would still carry the day, for "it is within the power of the air to continue its offensive action day after day and week after week, without intermission, until success is assured."

The key to his plan was that ground troops were to be excluded from all aspects of the operation. Citing conjectures as though they were physical laws, he noted:

The Air Staff are convinced that strong and continuous action of this nature must in time inevitably compel the submission of the most recalcitrant tribes without the use of punitive measures by ground troops, and they hold this opinion even in the light of recent events on the North-Western Frontier of India. With certain stubborn races time is essential to prove to them the futility of resistance to aerial attack by a people who possess no aircraft, but it is held that the dislocation of living conditions and the material destruction caused by heavy and persistent aerial action must infallibly achieve the desired result.

The following up of air attacks by ground troops is only playing into the hands of the tribesman by substituting for a foe against whom their efforts can effect little, an enemy whom they can meet on comparatively favourable terms.

The principle Trenchard cited as the basis for his plan has turned out not to be valid. Even people who cannot fight back against aerial bombardment will not necessarily surrender, no matter how long or how intense the bombing—think of Britain in 1940, Germany in 1944–1945, Japan in 1945, Vietnam, and Iraq in 1991. The inevitability of the surrender of a people attacked from the air is a key tenet of airpower doctrine, and has never yet been proved. Trenchard, advancing the argument for the first time, however, may be forgiven for not understanding a point that has continued to elude more modern students of airpower with much less excuse.

Trenchard, however, did not abjure the use of ground troops entirely. He insisted that the RAF be provided with armored car detachments "to enable military forces to complete the work of aeroplanes and reap the fruits of their success." In the subsequent campaigns in Iraq, in fact, armored car detachments would prove critical to the RAF's success in keeping Iraq quiescent.

The plan was adopted, but its implementation had to be postponed because of the outbreak of rebellion in Iraq in July. This revolt clearly revealed the dangers of Britain's military weakness. Caught by surprise, London soon began studies of the rebellion's origins. The Civil Commissioner of Iraq, A. T. Wilson, "pointed out how our apparent military weakness emboldened the disaffected to make a trial of strength, and how, having been unexpectedly successful in their initial attempts, they have succeeded in spreading rebellion."[13] The commander in chief of the British forces in Iraq reported:

I am afraid that one cannot escape the facts that this country can't be kept quiet without a strong garrison. [Sir Percy] Cox [the incoming

High Commissioner of Iraq] will not be able to alter that fact "charm he never so wisely." The Arabs say so themselves and the townsmen dread a weakening. The Arab, according to one his proverbs, "has his brains in his eyes"—or seeing is believing. It was the speedy demobilization and the fact that we had never shown force north of Samawah that encouraged him to try a throw with us.[14]

Britain's obvious military weakness contributed to the outbreak of the rebellion, for Arab nationalist propaganda claimed it was possible to throw the British out of the country "because the British did not have enough soldiers."[15] Of a later spate of anti-British propaganda the Civil Commissioner, Wilson, wrote, "So long as our military weakness was not apparent, this propaganda . . . had little success. . . . It was not, however, until our enemies in Syria demonstrated to people of Iraq that we could be dislodged . . . that movement became dangerous."[16] In his list of the causes of the uprising in an August 12 telegram, Wilson said that "perhaps first in order of importance comes perception of our military weakness. To kick a man when he is down is the most popular pastime in the East. . . ." Britain's military weakness alone did not cause the outbreak—the factors that led to the rebellion were much more systemic and fundamental—but these causes, by themselves, did not cause the discontented to risk war. The Arab nationalist leaders knew of Britain's weakness, felt that that weakness offered an opportunity, and took it. They provided the clearest evidence yet that England's weakness was a real danger to it and to the peace of the world, and once again spurred the military leadership to call attention to the problem.

Wilson had already tried to warn the Cabinet of the dangers England faced before the uprising in Iraq. Aware that much hope was being placed on "mechanization," Wilson warned that reality lagged behind the Cabinet's desires in this regard:

It is true that if we had plenty of aeroplanes and air personnel; if our Administrative Services were fully manned by a competent personnel; if we had large numbers of armoured cars, tanks, mobile machine-gun units, all complete with trained personnel; if we had wireless stations, railways and roads; if we had well organized gas units; we could now and at once commence a progressive, even a rapid, reduction of our garrisons. But what is the story of all these mechanical services? We have struggled, and struggled hard, ever since the Armistice to fit out these services, and you know as well as I do with what poor results.

The aeroplane programme is moving forward, but moving slowly; but the armoured cars, the tanks, the wireless, the gas and the Administrative Services have gone steadily back, with a deplorable result on the efficiency of the fighting units.

> These are some of the reasons why, in our opinion, we cannot at pres-
> ent reduce our garrisons in these theatres [Palestine and Iraq].[17]

The overextension of the British army was also leading to serious shortfalls in training, vitally needed in the newly reformed volunteer army and in support services:

> Under normal conditions we might have hoped that the newly consti-
> tuted Regular Army would have acquired increased efficiency during the
> last 6 months. Unfortunately the abnormal strain which has been placed
> upon it in every theatre outside Great Britain has not unnaturally pro-
> duced an exactly opposite effect. Combatant units have been depleted to
> make up for shortage in ancillary services; troops have been ill-housed
> and constantly on the move; guards have been excessive, with the result
> that training and musketry in the true sense of the word have been im-
> possible.[18]

The importance of support services is not commonly appreciated except by careful students of militaries. Support services include transportation, supply, communications, etc.—all the elements of glue that hold the combat forces of an army together, feed it, allow its various parts to communicate with each other, and move it. The collapse of the support services under an excessive bur-den of activity results in the immobilization of the army and renders it unable to conduct any operations, including training. This urgency led the British army to take soldiers out of combat units and put them in supply units—de-pleting the combat units and filling the supply units with untrained and inexpe-rienced personnel.

The appeals in May fell on deaf ears, but Wilson and Churchill tried again in mid-June, just weeks before the outbreak of the Iraqi revolt. Churchill said, "I am sure we are trying to do too much with our present forces and certainly it is impossible, within the present financial limits for me to continue to meet the varied and numerous obligations of our policy."[19] Wilson insisted on the need of "our policy being brought into some relation with the military forces available to support it. At present this is far from being the case."[20] He went on to paint a worrying picture of the British Army in June 1920:

2. Is it realized that at the present moment we have absolutely no reserves whatever (in formations) with which to reinforce our garrisons in any part of the world where an emergency may at any
   moment develop without warning?
3. The present garrison in Ireland is 1,500 rifles below the minimum of
   25,000, and a considerable number even of these are both immature
   and only partially trained.

4. The garrison of Great Britain . . . is even now below the strength of 30,000 rifles which has been laid down as the minimum required to preserve internal order in case of industrial trouble, and from this attenuated force six more infantry battalions are being held in readiness to move to Ireland at short notice, in addition to the two recently dispatched.

5. The Army Reserve is practically non-existent . . . and we have no means of mobilising even one complete division for service abroad, except by breaking up other formations in this country and thereby still further depleting the minimum garrisons. At the same time the situation in India and the Middle East is such that we may at any moment be called on to send a force of from 3 to 5 divisions to succour the British garrisons in those territories. . . .[21]

He concluded, "I cannot too strongly press on the Government the danger, the extreme danger, of His Majesty's Army being spread all over the world, strong nowhere, weak everywhere, and with no reserve to save a dangerous situation or to avert a coming danger."

Still, Wilson refrained from a serious challenge to government, contenting himself with the request to withdraw a few battalions from duty supervising plebiscites in Poland, from the Caucasus, and from Persia. He asked for so little because he was certain that Lloyd George would not give him any more, but he and Churchill kept making the case that British foreign policy vastly outstripped its military resources and yet failed to request more resources chiefly because they did not like the policy. Again and again, the CIGS and the Secretary of State for War and Air used Britain's military weakness as a weapon in a political argument over what the right policy should be. Churchill was disappointed in Lloyd George's failure to confront Bolshevism and his determination to crush Turkey and Germany both under harsh peaces, and he chose, since he could not persuade the Prime Minister, to favor withdrawal. Wilson was determined to ignore the change in the world situation from before the war and to set his course for a resurrection of the prewar army, with its mission and force structure intact. Neither of them had responsibility for considering the needs of Britain's foreign policy on the grand scale, which Lloyd George and the Foreign Minister, Lord Curzon, could not avoid. The separation of the military from the formation of policy in England was all too complete, and its harmful influences spread throughout the government.

The Royal Air Force, by contrast, suffered from no such aversion to the foreign policy of the government, and no such disinclination to ask for more resources. On the contrary, Trenchard's parallel memorandum called not for withdrawal from any theater, but instead for the formation of additional RAF units. He painted an equally grim picture of the RAF's ability to carry out its various missions in mid-June 1920. The strength of the RAF, he wrote, "is already well below our requirements to meet existing liabilities, and still more so to deal with a further unfavourable development in even one theatre of operations."[22] In Turkey, "applications for aerial assistance to our military forces . . . have had to be refused, not because we do not agree that air units are very necessary, but because we cannot provide them." In Ireland, the War Office had warned him that more aircraft might be needed, but "[s]hould extra squadrons be required none are available." In Germany, queries about the possibility of increasing Britain's aerial presence met with the answer "No possibility of increasing our strength in that area presents itself." Iraq was "a storm center"; "If our national policy is to continue to maintain forces in Persia, Iraq requires immediate reinforcements." One request from the Persian government for aerial support had already had to be refused. In sum, "the possible calls on the services of the Air Force are numerous, while no reserve whatever exists to meet the demands. . . . Thus it has come about that both internally in each area and also considered as a whole the Air Force is working at breaking strain. The Air Staff is convinced that this strain can be no longer sustained. . . ." Trenchard called for the immediate establishment of five more squadrons as a central reserve.

The differences between Trenchard's and Wilson's memoranda help to explain why the RAF emerged from the Lloyd George administration as the favored force while the army was relegated to political irrelevance. From the outset, Trenchard aimed to support the government's foreign policy, while Wilson tried to force it to change to suit him. Both openly and honestly pointed out the serious deficiencies their services faced, but while Wilson called for a reduction in foreign policy commitments that was unrealistic and that Lloyd George resented, Trenchard simply asked for more resources to accomplish his mission. Nor did the request for resources flatter the army: since Churchill had volunteered to cut the funding for the Iraq garrison in half at the beginning of the year, the army was forced to submit a request for £11 million in supplementary estimates in order to accomplish the same mission with the same forces; Trenchard's request for £960,000 bought five new squadrons![23] In the mood of the time neither policy had much immediate benefit for either service, but in the long run Trenchard's approach was much more effective and Wilson's was doomed to failure.

Wilson's constant repetitions of the warning that there were no reserves anywhere in the empire and no forces with which to meet contingencies raise a question: how did the army survive all those months under intolerable strain, constantly having to find manpower where there was none? Was Wilson lying? Were there reserves somewhere that he was concealing? In a sense, there were. Under pressure, Wilson drew down the forces available in England more than he would have liked, for he still feared that industrial unrest would lead to disorders that the army would be called upon to quell. There was a small reserve, therefore, in England in the form of Wilson's "irreducible minimum" of forces that, as it turned out, proved to be reducible, at least when the alternative was the destruction of British forces elsewhere in the empire. But the other "hidden" reserve of manpower was India—and the Iraqi revolt contributed powerfully to eliminating that reserve as well.

When the commander in chief in Iraq called for two divisions as urgent re-inforcements, Wilson urgently requested them from India. He got them—and more than he bargained for as well. Traditionally the Indian government, run by the Viceroy in Delhi, supported an Indian army from Indian taxes. When the London government needed troops, it was in the habit of "renting" them from India—India would deploy forces abroad for a fixed fee at the behest of London. But the situation in India was changing. The reforms of 1919 intro-duced an elective Legislative Assembly in India that had to approve budgets, taxes, and so forth, and the viceregal government was very much concerned that it might have to ask it for increases in taxes to pay for maintaining an army for the benefit of England. The Viceregal Army Department wired a warning to London:

> Recent demands received by us for reinforcements for Iraq on a large scale have forced us to consider whole question regarding supply of overseas garrisons from Indian Army.
>
> It would appear that His Majesty's Government is counting on India to provide a quota of the permanent garrisons of the mandatory territo-ries in addition to certain colonial garrisons. . . .
>
> We have evidence to show that the great bulk of educated opinion in India is opposed to our undertaking extensive obligations in regard to overseas garrisons, and the subject has already attracted considerable at-tention in the Press and on the platform. . . . Further, moderate opinion, including many Europeans, considers India is being exploited in being asked to provide for service outside India an unreasonably large propor-tion of troops now employed for Imperial purposes, since it is clear that no similar demand has been made on the Dominions, and that all British troops were demobilised as quickly as possible, with the inevitable result that, in case of trouble, the increased demands must be met from India and not from home.[24]

The Indian government hit the nail on the head—London was using the Indian army to make up for Britain's excessive demobilization. India was paying the part of the bill for Britain's foreign policy that Lloyd George chose not to pay. With the rise of a semiautonomous legislature with budgetary powers, that state of affairs could not be expected to continue.

The Indian Government put its case bluntly and even more ominously:

Attention is drawn to the fact that India is an original member of the League of Nations, but it is Great Britain and not India which has received a mandate for the new territories, and the troops employed are largely Indian.

This was a serious warning. England's relationship with its empire was changing, and the old style of imperial command-as-leadership was not going to work anymore. The time was coming when Britain would have to exercise dynamic leadership within the empire if it was to receive the support it desired. And its military weakness compromised the exercise of that leadership.

As the Indian government noted, it seemed unreasonable to India that it should be required to send forces hither and yon simply because Britain had chosen to demobilize its army. When a country that has disarmed too rapidly and publicly has to ask others to make up for the armed forces it lacks, the resulting embarrassing situation makes it difficult to exercise leadership, as the British quickly discovered. The British General Staff became seriously concerned that the well of Indian reserves might dry up. Wilson reminded the Cabinet that "our many commitments in the United Kingdom, Europe, Egypt, &c., already exhaust our available resources in British troops and there is no prospect under our present voluntary system of providing troops to meet the possible requirements of both Iraq and India."[25] He suggested asking the other dominions, Canada, Australia, and New Zealand, to provide assistance by replacing British garrisons in their regions of the world with their own forces, thus freeing British reserves.

This request was met with derision in Canada and Australia—New Zealand offered to find volunteers for a new battalion.[26] The dominions had turned to peace as forcefully as Britain or more so, and were unlikely to increase their military commitments under any circumstances, but even had they been willing to increase their commitments, Britain had done nothing to deserve their assistance. The dominions had long constituted more of a coalition than an empire, and a coalition needs both leadership and cooperation. Britain had not exercised leadership either globally or within the empire since the end of the war, yet Lloyd George and the Cabinet obstinately refused to take the dominions into their confidences. The Cabinet refused to consult about policy in advance, for they were not willing to allow the dominions to affect British policy at all. It should have been no surprise, therefore, that the dominions withheld support. The revolt in Iraq brought Britain near the end of its ready resources with no help in sight.

This crisis, however, like the previous manpower crises, passed and the lesson was lost. By December, with over 100,000 men and three squadrons of airplanes at his disposal, Haldane, the commander in chief of British forces in Iraq, succeeded in quelling the revolt. The British, moreover, established an Arab administration of the whole territory with limited autonomy. This change went a long way toward assuaging the feelings of the Arab nationalists—it has been hailed as the beginning of an independent Iraqi state—and, combined with the demonstration of British power and determination during the revolt itself, kept Iraq relatively peaceful for years to come.

When order had been established, Haldane was asked to draft a report on the operations of the RAF during the Iraqi revolt.[27] The report and the RAF commentary bring into sharp relief the sort of arguments used by RMA enthusiasts to get around problems encountered by their favored technologies in actual practice, arguments that persist to this day, as we shall see.

Haldane reported that RAF reconnaissance flights were very important in a land where few maps existed and where the terrain changed so rapidly that such maps as the British had became almost instantly out of date, but he also pointed out that reconnaissance flights over mountainous parts of Iraq exposed the aircraft to attack. The inhabitants, moreover, were learning how to take countermeasures against British airpower. The rebels "and more especially those who have experienced the visits of aeroplanes, have realised the possibilities and advantages of concealing themselves and their flocks before the arrival of the machines within bombing range." This, in addition to the fact that "the buildings have flat roofs, overgrown with vegetation, which render them on many occasions invisible from above" and the absence of known landmarks by which to navigate, hindered the operations of the RAF. As a result, "It has even occurred that observers in aeroplanes have passed over the camps of a large section of Arabs, comprising hundreds of black tents and thousands of cattle and other animals, without seeing anything unusual, although they were especially looking for this section." Thus the value of airplane reconnaissance was limited by the fact that negative reports could never be relied upon.

Haldane also reported that technological limitations seriously hindered operations. The aircraft had no radios; troops on the ground could not communicate with them, so the troops could not call in air support at need. On the Western Front in the Great War, operations were carefully planned weeks and sometimes months in advance, allowing the RAF to consider where and how best to deploy its aircraft in anticipation of heavy fighting in which they would be able to see the need to help ground forces. The situation was quite different in Iraq. Columns marched not knowing where the enemy was; sometimes they were attacked by an enemy they had not known was nearby. In those cases, aircraft could have intervened with most decisive assistance, if it had been possible to communicate with them.

Haldane also pointed out that the planes available at the time simply could not bring in enough weight of supplies to make much of a difference, but aircraft were highly useful in pursuing rebel groups that had been defeated in ground combat—better than cavalry in its traditional role. In a section with the modern-sounding heading "Distant Attack," Haldane explained how aircraft could be used to strike at rebel concentrations deep in the rear and in inaccessible terrain, which the army could have attacked only when the rebels were ready: "Large concentrations which offer good targets can in this way sometimes be dispersed, with the result of completely upsetting the plans of the insurgent leaders."

Haldane's conclusion was mixed:

> I wish to point out that aeroplanes as an auxiliary to troops on the ground are of great value, but I do not consider that as a primary force they have the qualities which will enable them without the assistance of land forces to bring into subjection tribes who have committed themselves to insurrection. In this view I am aware that the Royal Air Force do not concur.

Indeed it did not! For the Air Staff saw the report as an attack on the RAF and undertook to refute it point by point:

> The great value of the Air Force in the pursuit of a beaten enemy has been once more proved in Iraq: with a greater strength of Air Forces available, aircraft should of themselves effect the enemy's defeat. It is admitted that the Air Force has at times failed to dislodge the enemy from his chosen position. Such attacks have often been carried out in insufficient force, but in any case it is unreasonable to expect an enemy to leave his trenches while he is actually being bombed and exchange his position for one still less safe. The assumption of the Air Force is that if he is attacked by numbers of aircraft and subjected to a long bombardment he will take advantage of the night to disappear from the danger point. If he does not, the attack must be renewed the following day in still greater strength, and it will be impossible for any enemy to offer continuous resistance.

This minute does not respond to any charge made in Haldane's report—the Air Staff felt the need to preempt such a complaint. It also contained a key underlying assumption of RMA enthusiasts—if some new technology does not solve the problem, more will definitely do so: "it will be impossible for any enemy to offer continuous resistance."

This theme reappears in other minutes:

> [Haldane] is more doubtful about supply by air, but it must be remembered that he had very few aircraft available and that these were not of a weight-carrying type. There are in existence in the Air Force aeroplanes of such capacity that a mountain gun complete with crew and ammunition can be carried by two of them to reinforce a post, while a single ma-

chine can transport 2,000 lb. of food or ammunition to a distance of 200 miles and return without landing. Practice in dropping these supplies will lead to increased accuracy being attained.

These arguments are valid. Haldane had fighters and bombers, not transport aircraft, and very few planes of any type. Nor had the aircrews practiced airdropping supplies, which is always a tricky business. Nevertheless, subsequent history would show that air supply is not always possible. As armies became more mechanized, moreover, the weight of supplies they needed increased dramatically. One ton of fuel will not take a tank company very far. Although the Air Staff correctly pointed out particular problems that led to failure in this case, their confident assumption that all problems would disappear in time turned out not to be correct.

The argument that more aircraft would overcome any problems surfaced again in the section headed "Distant Attack":

> Even with the limited strength in the country, aircraft have succeeded in creating considerable effect by attacking concentrations out of range from or inpenetrable [sic] to troops. The Air Staff is informed that the towns of Umm-el-Barur, Abu Sukhair and Saarah (all noted insurgent centres) surrendered as a result of bombing alone. It is certain that villages liable to this attack are evacuated by day: with more aircraft available and by the use of large delay action bombs they can be made unapproachable by night. Improved "man-killing" bombs will increase the effectiveness of air attack on tribesmen in the field as opposed to disaffected villages.

It turns out that although improvements in ordnance and aiming now make it possible to obliterate villages and massacre their inhabitants, they do not make villages unapproachable by night (as the Soviets learned to their chagrin in Afghanistan). Even if our equipment today could accomplish such a feat, no equipment available in 1920 or for half a century thereafter could do so. Once again, the assumption that new technology would solve the problems simply was not valid.

The chief claim of the RMA enthusiasts, then as now, was not simply a "quantity equals victory" argument. Instead, it was an argument that an enemy's knowledge that we can destroy it from the air will lead it to surrender. Concerning Haldane's section on "Demonstrations," the Air Staff minuted:

> This is the most significant paragraph of the G.O.C.-in-C. Iraq's report by reason of the statement that delicate situations which could not be dealt with by troops have been at least temporarily stabilised by aircraft demonstrations: in the case quoted an outbreak was constantly antici-

pated but never materialised owing to the visits of aircraft. This is a striking confirmation of the Air Staff view, and as the power of aircraft is more frequently demonstrated and respect for that power becomes more securely rooted in the minds of the people, the efficacy of these demonstrations will be increased. With greater strength in air squadrons in the country it should be possible to stabilise in this manner a situation in any district: the delay which the use of ground troops involves merely permits the outbreak to go unchecked until unrest develops into insurrection.

Subsequent history has called this statement into question. A weak foe, weakly committed to its cause, may be dissuaded from action by air attacks alone, but the general statement that any enemy grows less determined to fight the longer an air attack goes on has been shown decisively to be false. The failed record of strategic bombing is enough to show that prolonged bombing frequently loses its effectiveness over time when the target is the morale or will of the people to fight.

But the Air Staff had to cling to the generality wherever Haldane called it into question, because the Air Staff needed to "point to what has actually been achieved under great difficulties by exiguous Air Forces" as direct confirmation of belief in the power of the air to control a country of this kind economically "without the use of large military columns."

But there were large military columns in Iraq throughout the rebellion—by December some 102,000 British and Indian soldiers roved the countryside. The Iraqis knew that ground forces were nearby and that if the air attacks failed, ground columns would surely follow. Even as British aircraft attacked their villages, British ground columns occupied the critical centers and severely punished attempts at rebellion elsewhere. The Air Staff ignored the obvious fact that the presence or absence of ground troops elsewhere in the theater has an important effect on the behavior of the enemy being attacked solely from the air. British experience and other subsequent history, however, show clearly that independent air operations can achieve great and economical successes, but only when ground forces are available as a further threat.

The outcome of this debate did not matter for the future of Iraq. The massive show of British force and determination in crushing the rebellion, combined with the grant to Iraq of a semiautonomous position under an Arab ruler, dampened the fires of rebellion throughout the interwar period. Air policing, supplemented by British armored car units and an ever-growing indigenous Iraqi army, worked. The real importance of this dispute arises from the impressions it left in the minds of the policy makers.

Although its role in the pacification of Iraq had been essential, the army did not come out well. Questions were asked almost at once as to why the army had not foreseen and prepared for the possibility of the revolt in the first place. The RAF arguments made the army leadership seem like dinosaurs—here was a promising new way of maintaining peace and order cheaply and effectively, and the army, which hated being in Iraq, seemed to hate even more the prospect of losing Iraq to the RAF. But the most important outcome of this crisis was that it seemed to many to prove the argument that "mechanization," in the form of aircraft here, could revolutionize war, making it cheap and decisive. The RAF's future, which had still been in question before the Iraqi revolt, was solid and promising after it. The perceived success of "mechanical devices" in policing the empire, by promising cheap solutions to Britain's security problems, encouraged a neglect of more traditional military forces that was welcome to its political leaders and baneful for its future security.

3

The First Challenge
to Peace

The repeated crises between 1918 and 1922 came to nothing. Wilson had warned that England's army was overstretched, Churchill had called for reductions in Britain's foreign commitments, and Lloyd George had repeatedly been told that his foreign policy was outstripping the resources he chose to devote to the military. But the crises in Ireland, Egypt, Palestine, Iraq, and elsewhere all subsided before exacting any serious price from England for its unpreparedness. The year 1922 saw the first crisis that did not pass without cost.

Like the Iraqi revolt, the Chanak crisis tested England's willingness to defend its own interests. Lloyd George and others felt that a certain type of settlement with the Ottoman Empire was essential to the security and well-being of the British Empire, and they were determined to impose it on Turkey, even against its opposition. That task should have been easy, for in January 1919 the Allies were all-powerful, at least with regard to Turkey. "The Ottoman Empire was regarded by the statesmen of Europe as a matter of secondary importance—as a mere cloud no larger than a man's hand." In the next few years, however, "the cloud had swollen into a typhoon."[1] The decline of Britain's military power and her failure to exercise international leadership led to serious bloodshed, helped bring about a split in the victorious coalition, and almost produced a humiliating military defeat and the destruction of British prestige and influence.

The war had put an end to Turkey's claims to Egypt, Libya, Cyprus, the

Adrianople
Maritza R.
Constantinople
Bosphorus
Ismid Peninsula
Black Sea
Caucasus Mts.
THRACE
Gallipoli
Imbros
Tenedos
Mudros
Zone of the Straits
ARMENIA
Sea of Marmara
Dardanelles
Mudania
Chanak
Ankara
T U R K E Y
Aegean Sea
A N A T O L I A
GREECE
CILICIA
Dodecanese Islands
IRAQ
Aleppo
SYRIA
Mediterranean Sea

TROUBLE IN TURKEY

Dodecanese Islands, and the islands of the Aegean, all lost before the war. In addition, the armistice signed between Britain and Turkey at Mudros on October 30, 1918, which followed the sudden collapse of Turkish military resistance, deprived the Turks of all their Arab provinces: Syria, Lebanon, Palestine, Iraq, and the lands now called Yemen, Jordan, and Saudi Arabia. They also lost Cilicia in southern Anatolia and the area they had controlled in Persia and the Caucasus.

The Armistice merely reflected the location of Allied, largely British, forces. The process of establishing a lasting peace in the area of the former Ottoman Empire based on realistic and acceptable or enforceable new boundaries was difficult and complicated; it was not achieved until five eventful and dangerous years had passed. Secret treaties during the war had envisaged the decomposition of the Turkish Empire. Apart from the Arab lands, which would be divided between Britain and France, parts of Anatolia had been promised to Greece, Italy, Russia, and a newly created Armenia. The Russian claims could be ignored, since they were denounced by the new Bolshevik government, but the others were very much alive and, to some degree, in conflict with one another. They also conflicted with a statement made in January of 1918 by Prime Minister Lloyd George, who said: "Nor are we fighting to deprive Turkey of its capital, or of the rich and renowned lands of Asia Minor and Thrace, which are predominantly Turkish in race. . . ."[2] The decisions resolving such conflicts would be made by the statesmen at the Peace Conference in Paris, where British opinion on the Turkish settlement was bound to play a powerful role.

The dominant view in the British Cabinet was that Turkey should be driven from everywhere except Anatolia, that the Turks should be expelled from Europe "bag and baggage," but more moderate voices argued for leaving them Constantinople and some part of eastern Thrace. At the San Remo Conference in April 1920 the victorious Allies carved up the Ottoman Empire in a draft treaty that was presented to the Turks at Sèvres the next month.

According to the Treaty of Sèvres, Greece received all of Thrace, almost to the defense lines that protected Constantinople itself, and the islands of Imbros and Tenedos. Smyrna and a large region in Anatolia that extended to its east were made an autonomous region under Greek control; after five years a plebiscite would be held that could give it permanently to Greece. The Greeks gained full sovereignty over the Dodecanese Islands. The territory most important to Britain bordered the sea lane from the Aegean to the Black Sea. The treaty created a Zone of the Straits that included both shores of the Dardanelles, the Sea of Marmora, and the Bosphorus. This was to be controlled by a commission appointed by the League of Nations from which Turkey was excluded. Allied forces would remain "in permanent occupation" of the zone, from which Turkish troops would be barred. Armenia was established as an independent state. Turkey was formally deprived of its Arab provinces: the future Saudi Arabia was turned over to the Arabs, while France received Syria and Britain Iraq and Palestine as mandates under the League of Nations. The Turkish navy and air force were abolished and the army limited to 50,000 men. When the Turks objected, the Allies made the trivial concession of permitting a Turkish representative to join the Straits commission.[3]

Britain's Foreign Minister, Lord Curzon, would have liked to limit the new Turkey to Anatolia and to exclude any foreign occupation of that Turkish homeland. He would thus have liked to deprive the Turks of Constantinople and of all their European territory, chiefly for reasons of grand strategy and the security of the British Empire. "For nearly five centuries," he said,

> the presence of the Turk in Europe has been a source of distraction, intrigue and corruption in European politics: of oppression and misrule to the subject nationalities; and an incentive to undue and overweening ambitions in the Moslem world. It has encouraged the Turk to regard himself as a Great Power, and has enabled him to impose upon others the same illusion. It has placed him in the position to play off one Power against another, and in their jealousies and his own machinations to find pretexts for his continued immunity.[4]

Although the treaty left the Turks Constantinople and some small part of Europe, it still promised to accomplish Curzon's goals: it would remove Turkey as a "deadly threat to Britain's imperial security in the Middle East and India" and it would reduce her "in the eyes of the Islamic world" to the status of a nation, "at best, of the second rank."[5]

The treaty represented Britain's hope to make its empire secure by establishing hegemony over the Middle East. Its crafters' ambitious plan was to control Egypt, Palestine, and Iraq and to gain a dominant influence in the Caucasus region, Persia, and a curtailed Turkey. The success of this arrangement depended on two conditions: (1) that the British would continue to have the overwhelming military dominance that obtained at the end of the war, and (2) that Turkey would continue to be governed by the weak and ineffective regime of the Ottoman Sultan Mehmed IV.

Government policy swiftly undid the first condition, as we have seen. Even before the treaty was presented to the Turks, moreover, events began to undermine the second condition as well. On May 15, 1919, with the approval of the Supreme Council of the Allied Powers as part of its policy of breaking up the Ottoman Empire and dividing it among the victorious states, 20,000 Greek troops landed in Anatolia and occupied the port city of Smyrna.[6] The landing stirred great hostility among the Turks; they soon rallied around the banner of Mustapha Kemal, a hero of the recent war who quickly established himself as leader of the nationalist forces that opposed the dismemberment of the Turkish homeland. Only a week after the Greek landing, Kemal set up headquarters in eastern Turkey and insisted on the removal of all foreign forces from Anatolia and Turkey's European lands, even as the Greeks expanded inland from Smyrna, the Italians occupied Cilicia in southwestern Anatolia, and the British, French, and Italians occupied Constantinople and the Straits.[7]

This early success masked darker realities that threatened. Churchill, keenly aware of the decline of British military power, urged the Prime Minister to use the moment to make a more generous peace with Turkey, pointing out, "We have maintained a force of some 40,000 men in Constantinople and on the Black Sea shores ever since the 11th November. The strain of this upon our melting military resources is becoming insupportable . . . the length of time which we can hold a sufficient force at your disposal to overawe Turkey is limited. . . ."[8] These circumstances did not escape Kemal and his nationalist forces.

> The British Government were demobilising: from every area of the Middle East they were rapidly withdrawing their troops: only a few unhappy Majors remained scattered throughout Anatolia, relying solely upon their red tabs, their excellent manners, and their confidence in the clean-fighting Turk. Kemal quickly realized that these amiable officers could be ignored and even insulted. He was much encouraged by this realisation.[9]

In February 1920, even as the Supreme Council was discussing what harsh terms it would impose on Turkey, a Turkish army of regular troops took up the nationalist cause, routing the French forces in Cilicia and challenging the delusion that the nationalist forces were a disorganized rabble that posed no threat.[10] A newly elected Turkish Parliament met in January 1920, dominated by Kemal's supporters. When they adopted Kemal's National Pact, the Allied armies occupied Constantinople and arrested several officials. The Kemalist deputies fled to Ankara to join their leader in forming a new National Assembly. The removal of the Kemalist faction to the interior of the country, where the center of government of modern Turkey has remained ever since, also eliminated a traditional Turkish vulnerability. In the past, governments that desired to overawe the Turks could hope to achieve their purpose by bombarding the capital in Constantinople. As it was impossible to bombard Ankara from the sea, this lever disappeared and the Turks became much harder to influence other than by direct force. Events in Constantinople, Greek atrocities and expansion in Anatolia, and the revelation of the harsh terms the Allies meant to impose all turned Turkish sentiment toward the nationalists and brought thousands of recruits to Kemal's army. By June he had gained enough confidence to lead his army against the British force holding the Ismid Peninsula across the Bosphorus from Constantinople.[11] (See map on page 68.)

On June 17–18 a conference of the relevant ministers met to consider the several military crises facing Britain in Persia, northern Iraq, and Turkey, as well as troubles that might arise in Palestine and Egypt. Of these "the most immediately menacing was in the Ismid Peninsula," where the mere six British battalions stationed there "were very weak in numbers."[12] As they had many times before, Churchill and Wilson warned of Britain's military inadequacies:

> The Secretary of State for War and the Chief of the Imperial General Staff placed on record their view that the military forces at the disposal of Great Britain were insufficient to meet the requirements of the policies now being pursued in the various theatres. An immediate curtailment of British responsibilities was indispensable if grave risk of disaster was not to be incurred. Should the Cabinet decide to continue the attempt to maintain simultaneously our existing commitments at Constantinople, Palestine, Mesopotamia and Persia, the possibility of disaster occurring in any or all of these theatres must be faced, and the likelihood of this will increase every day.[13]

The Cabinet was told that reinforcements were needed in several places immediately and would soon be required in others, but "[i]n the present stage of our military development . . . when the War Army has been completely demobilised and the post-war Army is in its infancy, no general reserve exists, and reinforcements for one theatre could only be obtained by withdrawing troops from another."[14] The ministers, nevertheless, agreed that "to retire from Constantinople before a bandit like Mustapha Kemal would deal a shattering blow to our prestige in the East, and . . . this could not possibly be contemplated."

Field Marshal Wilson, however, painted an alarming picture of the British situation. The Turks controlled the southern shore of the Sea of Marmora; against them on the southern side of the Dardanelles there were only two British battalions, "and there was really no reason why these should not be driven into the sea if the forces under Mustapha Kemal chose to attack them." General Milne, commander in chief of the Army of the Black Sea, in charge of British forces in Constantinople, warned that if the Turks took Ismid,

> [i]t was hard to say what the position of Constantinople might be as it would be possible . . . to shell the town night and day. Moreover, the Bosphorus would be closed and it would be more than likely that the populace would get out of hand. If the Turkish Nationalist Army are by any chance to seize the Chanak side of the Dardanelles the situation would be even more difficult. He saw no reason why Mustapha Kemal should not in about six weeks' time have some 40,000 troops at his disposal. If he (the C.I.G.S.) were in the position of Mustapha Kemal he would advance against Chanak at once.[15]

The placement of Turkish guns at Chanak would drive the British fleet out of the Dardanelles and the Allies out of the Straits entirely.

To deal with the emergency Wilson asked for reinforcement by one division at once and others later on. In the midst of the conversation a telegram came from General Milne that perfectly coincided with Wilson's estimate of the situation. A division was needed at once and more later, but no British forces were available and none could be expected from France or Italy. "It was clear," the minutes of the meeting record, "that the menacing situation could only be adequately and immediately met by the employment of Greek troops." Greek Prime Minister Elevtherios Venizelos was at hand and quickly offered to send the needed division to General Milne at once "to do what he liked with."[16]

In accepting this offer Lloyd George placed Britain's policy and the security of its position in Turkey into the uncertain and incapable hands of the Greek government and its army. Events would soon demonstrate the inadequacies of both, and the leading British military and civilian authorities warned against backing the Greeks. Why did the Prime Minister take this questionable and dangerous action? Suggested answers are that he suffered from a romantic and emotional philhellenism, that he was taken in by the wiles of the clever and persuasive Venizelos, or that he had a visceral hatred of the Turks.[17] A less irrational suggestion is that he made an erroneous estimate of the future capacity of the heated rivals and planned to adopt a new grand Middle Eastern strategy based upon a new predominance by the Greeks. Although his hopes for an Anglo-Greek partnership were shared by some of his senior colleagues,[18] they were quickly belied by events, so such a plan would be no less irrational.

There is, however, no need for recourse to irrationality. The hard fact is that in the face of a resurgent Turkish army under Kemal, Lloyd George had little or no choice. Unless he was prepared to face the disgrace of withdrawal, which would have forfeited the fruits of the victory over Turkey, or to accept a military disaster that would have the same result, British military weakness, produced by his own policy of ruthless reduction in the armed forces, especially the army, tied his hands.

Lloyd George's ambitious foreign policy, assuming continued British military predominance and Turkish weakness, and his military policy, which was shaped by domestic economic and political considerations, were incompatible. As usual, the hard truth of military necessity had its way. Churchill, among others, argued for a milder, negotiated peace that would meet the new realities. In the House of Commons on February 23, 1920, he said, "I trust that, having dispersed our armies, we shall not now take steps which will drive the Turkish people to despair, or undertake any new obligation, because our resources are not equal to the discharge."[19] It was good advice, but it required abandoning Greek goals and aspirations; so long as British policy and security depended on the Greek army it could not be taken. The Turks insisted on driving the Greeks out of Anatolia and eastern Thrace. The Greeks would not go, so Britain's fate depended on the prospects of their military success. Lord Curzon expressed surprise that Lloyd George should have approved Greek rule even over Smyrna. On April 9 he wrote to the Prime Minister: "I am the last man to wish to do a good turn to the Turks . . . but I do want to get something like peace in Asia Minor, and with the Greeks in Smyrna, and Greek divisions carrying out Venizelos' orders and marching about Asia Minor, I know this to be impossible."[20]

On June 22 the Greek army set out from Smyrna to relieve the British at the Straits. Confounding most expectations, they quickly drove the Turks back and joined the British on the Ismid Peninsula. In July a second Greek army forced the surrender of a Turkish army in eastern Thrace and captured Adrianople. "The Turks," Lloyd George told the House of Commons, "are broken beyond repair."[21] His confidence in the Greek army seemed confirmed, and the harsh treaty devised at San Remo was imposed upon the Turks, who signed it as the Treaty of Sèvres in August 1920.

Even before the agreement, however, many of its terms were obsolete and its prospects in doubt. The Greek army had defeated Kemal's forces without destroying them. The Sultan's government, which had signed the peace, controlled only the territory occupied by the British. Kemal himself became more popular than ever with the angry Turks. He withdrew to Ankara, calling for a Grand National Assembly, denouncing the treaty as an act of aggression against Turkey. "Henceforth, he declared, the Angora [Ankara] Government was at war with the Allies, and would drive them from Turkish soil."[22]

This might seem a vainglorious declaration by a recently defeated general, but the weaknesses in the position of his enemies gave it weight. The power of the Supreme Council of the Allies was crumbling. Much had been expected from the Americans. President Wilson had led his allies to believe that the United States might accept a mandate over Armenia and perhaps over Constantinople and the Straits, but the failure of the Senate to ratify the Treaty of Versailles put an end to any hope of American support. The Greek victories may have buoyed British spirits, but they did not delight the other allies. Italian ambitions had been forced to give way to those of Greeks in the Smyrna area, and their hopes for any gains in Anatolia were severely dampened by the Turkish victory that drove the Allies out of Cilicia. As early as April 1920 the Italians secretly made a separate arrangement with the Turks in which they agreed not to give further support to the Greeks, in exchange for promises of future economic opportunities in Turkey. "It was the first open crack in the Western Alliance."[23]

Much more serious for Britain's plans was the beginning of French defection. The defeat of their forces in Cilicia, of course, had been discouraging, but even earlier, in September 1919, the French had begun talks with the Kemalists, and further conversations brought them still closer in 1920. "They realized that, if Kemal was to be crushed, it could not be with French force, and hence that Britain and Greece would be the beneficiaries."[24] They greeted the Greek victory not with pleasure but with alarm and irritation.

> The triumphant justification of M. Venizelos and Mr. Lloyd George was too much for the nerves of the French and Italians. They insisted that the Greeks, in freeing the zone of the Straits, had already accomplished the task demanded of them and must now be restrained. A telegram was despatched in the name of the Supreme Council ordering the Greeks to advance no further. At the eleventh hour Kemal and his recruits were thus rescued from destruction.[25]

None of this, it is safe to say, could have happened if the bulk of the victorious army had been British. The British were discovering that it is not possible to maintain the leadership of an effective alliance without making a leader's sacrifice and commitment. Britain's military weakness and its consequent reliance on Greece thus assisted the collapse of the more important alliance with France and Italy, which further undermined British policy.

By relying on the Greeks the British had, in fact, given a major hostage to fortune, and fortune soon undid their apparent success. In October 1920 the young King Alexander of Greece was bitten by a pet monkey and died of blood poisoning. He was succeeded by the former king, Constantine, brother-in-law

to the Kaiser and notoriously pro-German during the late war. Then, in November, Venizelos was defeated at the polls and forced to leave office. This
combination of events seriously undermined support for or tolerance of Greek
ambitions and Lloyd George's policies. It was hard to maintain support even in
England, where, according to Churchill, "the feeling was not resentment, but a
total extinction of interest."[26] His own views were those of many who now
questioned Lloyd George's policy: "In our present state of military weakness
and financial stringency we cannot afford to go on estranging the Mohammedan world in order to hand over a greater Greece to Constantine."[27] King
Constantine, however, was determined to continue the war, and Lloyd George
had little choice but to support the Greeks.

The Allies leaped on the new situation to justify their estrangement from
Britain's policy and rejection of its leadership. Behind the backs of the British,
the French carried on conversations with the nationalists in which they sought
to trade recognition and concessions for economic opportunities.[28] As rumors
and knowledge of the Italian and the French maneuvers reached the British it
became increasingly evident that they could not confidently rely upon them
even for diplomatic, much less for military, support. Any change in the military
situation would clearly reveal the gap between the goals of the British and
those of their allies.[29]

Pressure from the allies and from some within his own cabinet compelled
Lloyd George grudgingly to consider revisions of the Treaty of Sèvres to
achieve a more moderate negotiated peace. In February 1921 a conference met
at London to consider revisions of the treaty. Although ready to make concessions at the expense of the Armenians and Kurds and to restore a cosmetic
suzerainty, but not control, over the Greek-held province of Smyrna, Lloyd
George and Curzon were not prepared to yield on the main issues: Thrace,
Constantinople, the Straits, and the Greek occupation of Smyrna.[30] The conference, therefore achieved nothing. Soon after its failure, Churchill warned of
the consequences of the renewal of the war and urged peace talks with the
Turks on terms that would include Greek evacuation of Smyrna, a sine qua
non for peace. Britain continued, however, to depend upon Greek forces for
success and safety, so such a solution "was ruled out by the extent of the Greek
military success of the summer."[31]

On July 10, 1921, the Greek army launched an offensive that produced astonishing success. The Turkish army was compelled to withdraw to within fifty
miles of Ankara. King Constantine, in personal command of the army, expected to take Ankara and thereby humiliate and defeat Kemal and his nationalist government. He hoped that a new government would then be forced to
accept the Greek occupation of Smyrna and, perhaps, even yield Constantinople.[32] These heady dreams came crashing to earth with the battle at the
Sakarya River in late August and early September. The battle itself was a
standstill, but it produced a major strategic defeat for the Greeks, "in retro-

spect the decisive watershed of the war in Asia Minor."[33] From then on the Greek army was on the defensive.

Greece had suffered serious casualties, and its economy was hard pressed by the cost of the war. The British could no longer count on a Greek victory to achieve their goals, and the many demands on their inadequate military forces as well as the defection of their allies precluded the possibility of achieving them by their own efforts. There was no choice but to rely on diplomacy, to try to persuade Kemal to make peace by softening the terms of the Treaty of Sèvres. In March 1922, Curzon met with the French and Italians and hammered out a proposal that included the Greek evacuation of all of Asia Minor. The Turks insisted that the evacuation take place before any armistice could go into effect. This was unacceptable, as Lloyd George told the House of Commons: "The Greeks could not retire and leave 500,000 of their nationals to the mercy of the Turks without guarantees against . . . massacres."[34]

The deadlock continued until July 29, when King Constantine decided to break it with the bold gamble of seizing Constantinople. He secretly moved two divisions from Smyrna to the vicinity of the city and slipped his fleet into the Sea of Marmora to assist them. He was gambling not only that his forces could overcome the Turks but that the Allies would allow him to take the city they occupied. Instead, the Allies, which in May declared their neutrality in the Greco-Turkish conflict, inevitably announced their intention to prevent the seizure of Constantinople. The British government has been blamed for not acting more decisively, for neither supporting the Greeks more firmly and helping them to win, nor taking them in hand and compelling them to accept terms that would include the evacuation of Smyrna.[35] This is completely to misunderstand the situation. The Greeks could not defeat the Turks without military forces the British were unable and financial resources they were unwilling to commit. Without such a commitment, moreover, the British could not hope to regain the support of the Allies, which, in fact, were already maneuvering for favorable relations with the Turks. To use compulsion against the Greeks, on the other hand, would have been a betrayal beyond what was possible. As Harold Nicolson put it, how could the British "oblige Greece by force to evacuate a territory which we were pledged by treaty to assign to her and which she had occupied at our own express invitation?"[36]

As the ancient Greeks might have seen it, Constantine's adventure was the result of a foolish blindness brought on by arrogance, which swiftly brought terrible retribution. Kemal took advantage of the weakening of the Greek forces before Smyrna to launch a long-prepared assault on August 18. A week later the Greeks were fleeing for their lives. "Within a fortnight nothing but the corpses of Greek soldiers remained in Anatolia."[37]

British policy had allowed the Greeks to launch their offensive in 1921 as a way to prevent the Turkish nationalists from reaching the Straits without the use of British troops. So long as the Greeks had been successful, Lloyd George and Curzon could defend their policy against domestic criticism and open Allied defection. At the same time, Greek success had allowed the government to avoid the question of Britain's real interests in regard to Turkey and what Britain was prepared to do in their defense. The destruction of the Greek army for the first time compelled the British government "to consider how the supposed requirements of imperial strategy in the Near East could be guaranteed by British power and British diplomacy without benefit of the Greek shield."[38]

The British were right to seek a peace that reflected their decisive victory in the war and secure control of the strategic Straits. They refused to recognize, however, that these appropriate political and strategic goals required the maintenance of armed forces to guarantee their achievement. The result was a deadly menace to their forces, their policy, and their prestige.

4

The Paper Lion Roars

The period following the Greek debacle, from early September 1921 to the signing of a truce at Mudania on October 11, historians have called "the Chanak crisis," a time when it appeared that Great Britain might find itself alone, deserted by its allies, at war against a reinvigorated Turkey. The crisis began when a triumphant Kemalist army marched north from Smyrna toward the Straits amid reports that its goal was not merely to drive out any remaining Greek forces, "but to liberate all former Turkish territory, Thrace, Gallipoli and the old capital itself, from Allied control."[1] The Cabinet wasted little time in deciding Great Britain must resist the attempt, by force if necessary,[2] for the stakes were high. Unchecked, Kemal would certainly tear up the Treaty of Sèvres, undoing by force the Allied victory only a few years after the end of the war. As Churchill said: "If the Turks take the Gallipoli Peninsula and Constantinople, we shall have lost the whole fruits of our victory. . . ."[3] Such an outcome would undermine the prestige of the victors, and with it their capacity to uphold any of the peace treaties concluded at Paris. Churchill thought that yielding to Turkish power would have dire practical consequences: "another Balkan War would be inevitable."[4] Lloyd George agreed that Gallipoli was of vital importance:

> It was the most important strategic position in the world and the closing of the Straits had prolonged the war by two years. It was inconceivable that we should allow the Turks to gain possession of the Gallipoli Peninsula and we should fight to prevent their doing so.[5]

His remarks in the midst of a Cabinet debate may have been exaggerated, but the central idea, the vital strategic importance of the Straits, was widely shared. Two months later, in the calm of his study, Harold Nicolson wrote a memorandum on the subject with which few British leaders would have quarreled.[6] He remembered that at the beginning of the war the Turks, while ostensibly neutral, had allowed two German warships through the Straits and then closed the waterway to the British fleet. This permitted the *Goeben* and the *Breslau* to use Sea of Marmora as a safe haven from which they emerged when ready and did great harm to British shipping. Victors in the late war, the British were determined that never again should the Turks "be able to bar passage of the British fleet into the Black Sea."[7]

Consideration of both the past and the future persuaded almost all British ministers of the need to resist Kemal. In Curzon's view, which most shared, one of the great values of the victory over Turkey that must not be surrendered was its denial to Turkey of "the opportunity of repeating the tactics of 1914, and manipulating European conflict for its own purposes."[8] For the future, Churchill warned, "Grave consequences in India and among other Mohammedan populations for which we are responsible might result from a defeat or from a humiliating exodus of the Allies from Constantinople. . . ."[9]

Britain's expanded interests and responsibilities, moreover, made Turkey more important than merely its control of the Straits. In the postwar era the old policy of supporting the decrepit Ottoman Empire in Asia was no longer feasible. Turkey, along with Persia and Iraq, had become crucial places "where the whole drive of British policy was to construct political settlements which would strengthen and enhance the safety of the British world-system."[10] The British saw the rise of Kemal's nationalist regime, however, as a first step in the restoration the Ottoman Empire.

> Coexistence with Turkish nationalism seemed impossible. As a result its containment and suppression became the centre-piece of imperial policy in the Middle East; and the possibility of Turkey re-establishing herself as a Eurasian power—coupling the intrigues of Europe to her designs in Asia—the greatest threat to the hard-won victory on the strategic frontiers of the British Empires. . . .[11]

There was consensus, therefore, to resist Kemal, but questions remained as to where and with what forces. The British would have liked to keep the Turks out of the entire Zone of the Straits, but they knew they lacked the forces needed. In case of a war they planned to evacuate Constantinople and the Ismid Peninsula across from it, but they meant to be able to threaten the city and to use the Dardanelles. For that purpose they decided to defend and hold Gallipoli and Chanak, on the Asian shore opposite.[12] (See map on page 68.) The French and Italians were eager to make an agreement with Kemal on his terms and determined not to fight him. Without consultation, they withdrew their troops entirely from the Asian side of the Straits, leaving the small British force alone at Chanak. General Sir Charles Harington, commander of the Allied forces at the Straits, was instructed that it was Chanak that was his most important responsibility, "since it was the key to the control of the Gallipoli channel and hence of the Straits as a whole."[13]

On September 15, when the Cabinet met to consider the problem, the British at Chanak numbered only 1,000 men and three battleships anchored offshore,[14] and there were grounds for apprehension. Sir Laming Worthington-Evans, Secretary of State for War, painted a grim picture of the forces on the ground. There were 7,600 Allied troops in the entire zone, including Constantinople. Against them were arrayed 6,000 Turks near Ismid, 5,000 near Chanak, and 40,000 more marching north from Smyrna. Curzon opposed military resistance to Kemal, citing Sir Horace Rumbold, British High Commissioner in Constantinople, who had telegraphed a warning that the publication by the press of the government's intentions not to give way "may inspire Kemal to act with great rapidity in seeking to threaten allied forces in Chanak district and Ismid peninsula. I do not think," said Rumbold, "that in his present temper it would be safe to try to bluff Kemal."[15] At a Cabinet meeting three days later, Lord Cavan, Chief of the Imperial General Staff, was even gloomier. He reckoned that the 1,000 British soldiers at Chanak faced as many as 52,000 of the enemy, and he warned that "the Kemalists could push that small force into the sea within a fortnight." To regain it would require a large war and the use of at least 300,000 men.[16]

The most potent members of the cabinet, however, were not dismayed. Churchill, previously the most caustic and determined critic of the policy of imposing a harsh settlement upon the Turks by the use of the Greek army, was one of the group, whose membership and purposes he later described:

> I found myself in this business with a small group of resolute men: the Prime Minister, Lord Balfour, Mr. Austen Chamberlain, Lord Birkenhead, Sir Laming Worthington Evans. . . . We made common cause. The Government might break up and we might be relieved of our burden. The nation might not support us: they would find others to advise them. The Press might howl, the Allies might bolt. We intended to force the Turk to a negotiated peace before he should set foot in Europe. The aim was modest, but the forces were small.[17]

With the benefit of hindsight, Churchill knew that all these possibilities would be realized.

Where would the forces come from to achieve this "modest" goal? Both Churchill and Lloyd George indulged in wishful thinking to provide an answer. The French would do their part. The Greek army would recover from its smashing defeat. The Serbs and Rumanians would also contribute to the fight against the Turks. "Mustapha Kemal ought to know," said the Prime Minister, "that if he crossed the Straits with 60,000 rifles he would be met by 60,000— to say nothing of the British fleet. The time had come to do something concrete."[18]

Orders for the transfer of two British battalions from Malta and Gibraltar were the first "concrete" steps taken to defend Chanak. In the next three weeks these forces were increased by troops from Egypt and elsewhere; by October 7 the original 1,000 soldiers at Chanak had risen to 9,900.[19] Hopes for help from the Balkans were illusory, but the Cabinet counted on considerable help from the dominions, despite their previous refusal to assist England during the Iraq crisis. Churchill, with the approval of Lloyd George, drafted a telegram to the dominions' Prime Ministers, telling them of the decision to defend the Neutral Zone with force and asking them to send military reinforcements. The two men also released a statement to the press on September 17, explaining the dangers presented by Kemal's advance to the Straits, including the following language:

> The British Government regard the effective and permanent freedom of the Straits as a vital necessity. . . . It would be futile and dangerous in view of the excited mood and extravagant claims of the Kemalists, to trust simply to diplomatic action. Adequate force must be available to guard the freedom of the Straits and defend the deep water line between Europe and Asia against a violent and hostile Turkish aggression. . . . [The British Government has appealed to the Dominion Governments and to Foreign Powers], inviting them to be represented by contingents in the defence of interests for which they have already made enormous sacrifices. . . . It is the intention of His Majesty's Government to reinforce immediately . . . the troops at the disposal of Sir Charles Harington and orders have been given to the British fleet in the Mediterranean to oppose by any means an infraction of the neutral zones by the Turks or any attempt by them to cross to the European shore.[20]

The statement "defied, not the whole world, merely, but the full hysterical force of British public opinion."[21] Instead of rallying national support, it was denounced in the hostile press as "deliberately designed to promote a most disastrous and costly war." The headline in the *Daily Mail* the next day read STOP THIS NEW WAR! On September 19 its readers were told that dominion soldiers should not be made to die "in order that Mr. Winston Churchill may make a new Gallipoli."[22] Curzon, who read the statement in the newspaper "with consternation," called it bellicose and a "flamboyant manifesto."[23] He hurried off to Paris, where he found his fears justified: the French had recalled the contingent they had sent to Chanak to present a united front against the Turks, and the Italians did the same. Both were engaged in secret negotiations with the Turks behind the backs of their British allies. Response from the dominions was tepid at best, with only New Zealand and Newfoundland expressing support, while Australia and Canada responded with cold negativity. The call for help from the Balkans never accorded with reality.

Britain—that is, the small group in the Cabinet who held fast to their policy—stood alone, the group's isolation made clear by the reactions to their seemingly misguided public statement. "Yet," as Harold Nicolson pointed out, "Kemal had also read the Churchill communiqué. He sheered away from Chanak and marched onwards to the Ismid peninsula. Great Britain thereby was granted a respite of ten incalculably valuable days."[24]

On September 13, Kemal had told an American reporter that he would be in Constantinople in eight days. When asked what he would do if the British opposed him, he asked "why should they oppose him? He had no quarrel with Britain, but only with the Greeks. But, anyhow, he would be in Constantinople in eight days' time."[25] To carry out that promise Kemal would have to drive out the tiny British force at Chanak, challenge the British navy preventing his crossing to the European side of the Straits, or both. Instead, confronted by British determination, he avoided the confrontation. No one has offered a better explanation for his restraint than Nicolson's.

Events would reveal that Kemal's strategy was to try to achieve his maximum goals, full command of Anatolia, the Straits, Constantinople, and Thrace up to the line of the Maritza River, without concessions but by the threat of overwhelming military force. He knew that the French and Italians would present no difficulty; they were scrambling to win his favor and to gain any economic concessions they could negotiate and would happily undermine the British position in the process. There was reason, too, to doubt that the British truly had the resolve to fight a war in Turkey. Their national military forces had melted away like snow in a spring thaw; their forces on the ground were pitifully few. Public opinion in Britain opposed any fighting. Before the Cabinet's communiqué, Kemal had good reason to believe that the British would give way. Face could be saved merely by holding a conference in which all Kemal's wishes were granted in advance, as the French advocated.[26]

The British navy, on the other hand, was formidable. So soon after the war, moreover, the hard-earned reputation of the British army for toughness was very much alive. A real war against a committed British nation was not a happy prospect. When the British appeared to commit themselves to serious military resistance, Kemal drew back from the conflict. Thereafter his game would be to try to undermine British resolve by working on the Allies, by menacing the British with overwhelming military force on the scene and probing for weakness with provocative actions that always fell short of real combat.

The British leadership, on the other hand, in spite of the warning from Rumbold, their man in Constantinople, had always thought that Kemal could be made to agree to an acceptable peace if the Allies stood fast. Their goal, instead, was to deter a war and bring Kemal to the bargaining table for a diplomatic solution by a show of grit and determination.

As early as September 5, Rumbold advised that the Turks could not be cajoled but could be deterred: "We should do everything to (keep?) alive their fear that even if they dispose of the Greeks they will still have to reckon with us."[27] At the same time he urged the opening of negotiations as quickly as possible.[28] The Cabinet's position was that "if we are to maintain our position in a Conference, it must be supported by adequate force."[29] This double-track, firm resistance as a prerequisite to negotiation was at the heart of the government's policy. Retreat or expulsion from Chanak, however, would destroy Britain's credibility and its ability to compel an acceptable peace. This understanding was behind Churchill's insistence that "there could be no greater blow to British prestige than the hurried evacuation of Chanak in face of Turkish threats." It also explains Lloyd George's statement that the British should evacuate Ismid and even Constantinople rather than Chanak, because "the threat to Chanak was a blow to Great Britain alone. . . ."[30] General Harington was instructed accordingly: Chanak was more important than Ismid or Constantinople, and he should dispose his forces on that assumption. He should warn Kemal "against any violation of the neutral zones." If there was any serious collision at Chanak, "we shall take that as a definite challenge to the power of the British Empire, mobilize our two divisions and call for volunteers to reinforce and supplement them. . . . If we are forced to fight we will take all help we can get from any quarter."[31]

A memorandum from the General Staff of September 17 spoke of the British stand as a "gigantic bluff,"[32] but the words and actions of the Cabinet throughout the crisis prove this judgment wrong. The British sent all the reinforcements they could find as swiftly as they could and gave the generals at Chanak orders to fight if the Turks forced their hand. At one point, as we shall see, they instructed Harington to deliver an ultimatum to the Turks whose rejection would have meant war. In retrospect, Lloyd George wrote, "It was not a bluff, I certainly meant to fight and I was certain we would win."[33]

British policy, however, was not to provoke a war but to force a conference that might produce an acceptable peace. On September 23, Curzon was able to hammer out an agreement with the French and Italians on the text of an invitation to a conference to be sent to Kemal. On the one hand, it indicated a willingness "to restore the greater part of Thrace to Turkish sovereignty" and promised the withdrawal of Allied forces from Constantinople after a peace was signed. On the other, this was to depend on the Turks' giving guarantees "for the permanent maintenance of the freedom of the waters between the Black Sea and the Mediterranean" and of "the protection of racial and religious minorities" under the League of Nations.[34]

This "Paris Note" of September 23 became the focus of the rest of the crisis, its acceptance being the goal of Britain's determined resistance. Lloyd George might not have negotiated such terms, but once the note had been issued it became the basis of policy. Kemal did not leap at the opportunity. For days he made no response. All the while Turkish troops moved into the neutral zone near Chanak, provokingly showing themselves to the British soldiers but taking no hostile action. A private letter by Churchill gives a vivid sense of the moment:

> Thank God that awful pro-Greek policy against which we have so long inveighed has come to an end. We have paid an enormously heavy price for nothing. However, at the very end I have had to throw in my lot with L. G. in order to try to make some sort of front against what would otherwise have been a complete Turkish walk-over and the total loss of all the fruits of the Great War in this quarter. They make a great deal of fuss about the communique which I drafted for the P.M. at his request and which he issued. All the same, I am convinced, that if we had not got a move on there would be no question of the Turks accepting the terms we have now offered, and even now it is possible that they will prove uncontrollable.[35]

And so it seemed when, on September 27, news arrived that Kemal had not only not replied to the Paris Note but had rejected the British demand to withdraw his soldiers from the neutral zone. The next day Churchill telegraphed to the dominion Prime Ministers that the situation at Chanak was "extremely critical and unsatisfactory." Turkish forces were getting into position to command the heights overlooking Chanak, and Harington was told to fire on them if they did not turn back. Kemal was not expected to answer the Paris Note for a week. The Turks were concentrating both at Ismid and Chanak. "At any moment fresh violations may take place."[36]

The Conference of Ministers met on September 29. They were told of intelligence reports that the Turks were planning to attack Chanak the next day, pressed forward by the Russians, with whom they had made an agreement.[37] Following the advice of their service chiefs, the Ministers decided that an ultimatum was needed, and they sent a telegram with fateful orders to Harington:

> Kemalists are obviously continuing to move up troops and are making efforts to net you in. General Staff advises that the defensive position will be seriously endangered if this is allowed to continue and that the time has come to avert this disaster. . . . Immediate notification is to be sent to the local commander of the Turkish troops around Chanak, that unless his troops are withdrawn by a time set by you . . . all the forces at our disposal, naval, military and air will open fire on the Turks. . . . Time limit given should be short. It should not be forgotten that we have

been warned by intelligence reports of September 30th as the date of a possible attack.[38]

Even at this critical moment the British hoped that their firmness would bring peace, not war. When Curzon the next day urged the Cabinet to cancel the ultimatum, Churchill joined those who firmly refused. He "had by no means lost hope that there might still be a peaceful settlement. He did not think the action to be taken would exclude conversations being reopened in a few days' time." A show of strength and determination would carry the day, he thought. "What Mustapha Kemal thought . . . was that the British could be trampled on and ignored. He might get over that if a lesson were given him locally at Chanak."[39]

Kemal had shown no sign of softening. On the 28th, Rumbold reported in a telegram marked "Very Urgent" that Turkish forces at Chanak were acting under direct orders from Kemal. He told of Kemal's interview with a French official in which he refused to withdraw his troops and had the effrontery to suggest the removal of British forces from Chanak. Rumbold's estimate was that the situation "evidently contemplated by Kemal is that British and Turks should watch each other whilst Turkish forces are piling up until Mustapha Kemal thinks he is strong enough to attack."[40] Since Lord Cavan, the CIGS, reported 23,000 Turks at Chanak to 3,500 British, that moment could not be far off. Kemal was fully aware of the heavy attacks being launched against the British government from the press and various public groups, and he knew through direct contact that the French and Italians were working against their British allies. He must have thought that they were bound to give way if he maintained the pressure. War against great odds seemed imminent and unavoidable.

Alarming news, however, was not traveling in only one direction. Since the telegram to the dominions and the publication of its content in Churchill's communiqué, the message coming out of London had been consistently tough and defiant. Kemal would have known from the French how fiercely the British resisted their efforts to give the Turks what they wanted even before a conference, and the words had been backed by deeds. The Turks could see with their own eyes that the British were reinforcing Chanak, and they knew that more help was on the way. Lloyd George deliberately was as open as possible in sending reinforcements, declaring that "it was desirable that it should be made clear that we were serious, and it would be a good thing if it became generally known in Constantinople of the action we were taking to send troops, aeroplanes and ships. . . ." He told his colleagues that "by a show of force and firmness it was possible that fighting might be prevented."[41]

As the days passed and the British Cabinet remained firm, as the British forces grew at Chanak and boldly confronted the immensely more numerous Turks, Kemal must have come to realize that his plan was not working. If he persisted in it the result would be a difficult war he did not want. Perhaps it would be better not to insist on an outcome that would humiliate the British and force them to fight, to accept an armistice and do the best he could at a peace conference. Although General Harington never delivered the ultimatum, the French press reported it at once, and it is inconceivable that Kemal was unaware of it.[42] It appears that the British ultimatum, backed by the commitment of significant military forces obviously ready to fight, caused him to accept negotiations.

That is certainly the likeliest explanation for Kemal's sudden change of tack. Harington and Rumbold were on the scene and in a position to detect the change. The navy received a telegram from Kemal to Harington that took an entirely new tone, saying that Kemal had given orders to his troops to avoid any incidents. "This was the first intimation that Kemal was willing to avoid a clash with Britain, and to negotiate a truce."[43] In the language of a later crisis, Kemal had "blinked first." Harington had received this news at the same time as the Cabinet's ultimatum. It was one of several signs of a change in the Turkish demeanor. He had taken a tough line with Hamid Hasancan Bey, Kemal's representative in Constantinople: "I have been very careful to warn Hamid that I have the [power] of England behind me and that I shall not hesitate to use it if the time comes. General Marden has full powers from me to strike when he thinks fit. . . ."[44] There were other signs that fighting would be unnecessary and that Britain's firm stand had been effective:

> Confidence has re-appeared in last few days since reinforcements marched in and I was every day feeling more hopeful that I might see the end with principle of the neutral zones preserved without firing a shot and with British flag flying high here. . . . I have received from General Marden a report says things are now much easier at Chanak and there is no more movement and in cases where Turks have been told to go back they have done so. . . . There are now no Turkish troops at ERENKEUI.[45]

Erenkeui was a village west of Chanak where a week earlier the Turks had challenged British troops and refused to withdraw when asked. "Here they remained," Churchill later wrote, "contumaciously and encroachingly . . . in undoubted violation of the neutral zone,"[46] but on September 30 they were gone. It was another hopeful sign. Finally Hamid told Harington that a meeting between Kemal and the Allies would take place within two or three days.[47] In these circumstances, and with Rumbold's concurrence, Harington did not deliver the ultimatum and asked the Cabinet "that matters be left to my judgment for moment."[48] That judgment was vindicated: at noon on October 1, Rumbold's telegram arrived at the Foreign Office announcing that Kemal had agreed to meet General Harington at Mudania (see map on page 68) to discuss the disposition of the Neutral Zone, the Straits, and Thrace. The Cabinet sent a telegram to Harington drafted by Churchill granting permission not to deliver the ultimatum, but even then they were concerned to stiffen his spine and avoid any appearance of softness or yielding to threats:

> You are indeed right in supposing that H.M.G. earnestly desire peace. We do not however, desire to purchase a few days peace at the price of actively assisting a successful Turkish invasion of Europe. Such a course wd deprive us of every vestige of sympathy & respect & particularly in the United States. Nor do we believe that repeated concessions & submissions to victorious orientals is the best way to avoid war.[49]

The conference at Mudania opened hopefully on October 3. Ismet Pasha, the Turkish negotiator, accepted the Paris Note of September 23, and the Turkish army at Chanak withdrew a thousand yards from the British forces. For three days, discussions went agreeably; the British, French, and Italians agreed on a protocol emerging from the three days of talks with Ismet Pasha, which they all believed gave "very great and important concessions" to the Turks and which they hoped could be signed on the 5th. But any idea that the crisis was over was premature. On that day the Turks suddenly raised difficulties, introducing new demands that went against the Paris Note and were unacceptable to the British: they wanted unlimited Turkish gendarmes in Thrace that amounted, in fact, to an army and menaced the safety of the resident Greeks; they wanted Karagatch, a suburb of Adrianople on the west side of the Maritza, and a right to continue military operations after the armistice was signed and until it was ratified, and insisted that Allied missions and forces be withdrawn immediately after the withdrawal of the Greeks. They demanded the right to occupy eastern Thrace and refused to leave the Neutral Zone.[50]

General Harington reported, "The Nationalists will not give one single point and came near breaking down the whole conference last night."[51] His fuller account said:

> At the last moment Ismet Pasha demanded that Eastern Thrace should be handed over to the Turks before peace treaty and that all the allied contingents and missions should be withdrawn. This demand is entirely at variance with allied proposal of September 23rd.
>
> Ismet Pasha intimated that he would set his troops in motion if allied generals did not agree to this proposal, which annuls the whole basis of the conference.[52]

The Turks had returned to the policy of intransigence, confrontation, and the threat of military force. What had changed their attitude? The British were convinced it was the machinations of the Italians and, especially, the French. As early as October 4, Rumbold had passed on his suspicion about Henri Franklin Bouillon, in charge of France's secret negotiations with Kemal. His

> personal influence and intervention with Mustapha Kemal have been prejudicial to British interests. . . . [H]e has probably offered Turks more than Great Britain . . . is prepared to give. . . . I heard that he informed Mustapha Kemal that England was not unwilling but incapable of going to war owing to hostility of labour and England's fear of complications in her Moslem possessions. Interventions of this nature by conveying a totally false impression would have effect of increasing chances of war rather than of . . . peace.[53]

Coming from Britain's most powerful ally, a reminder of the government's political troubles must have been comforting, and the Turks could only be further encouraged by what appeared in the London newspapers on the morning of October 7. There was the report of a speech attacking the government's policy toward Turkey by the former Liberal Prime Minister H. H. Asquith. Far more serious, there was also a letter from Bonar Law, former Leader of the Conservative Party, that Britain, as the ruler of millions of Muslims, should not "show any hostility of [or?] unfairness to the Turk" and should not undertake any military action without, at least, the support of the French. He said, "We cannot act alone as the policeman of the world."[54]

Rumbold confirmed that the French were prepared to give the Turks what they wanted and that the Italians "argued strongly in favor of yielding to the Turks."[55] Harington was recalled from Mudania to Constantinople.[56] For the moment the talks had broken down.

On the same day the Foreign Secretary was in Paris, trying to get the Allies to hold fast. The French Prime Minister would give no satisfaction. Curzon made it clear that the British would make no further concession. What, he asked, would Poincaré do if Kemal attacked? "M. Poincaré retorted that if the Turks advanced he would do nothing. Let there be no doubt about that. He would do nothing in any circumstances. French troops should never fire a shot in the East, and would not."[57] Kemal, of course, was well informed of this deep split that divided Britain from her allies, and conversation with Franklin Bouillon must have encouraged him to try to exploit it to make the British back down.

The argument continued, Poincaré embarrassed and beleaguered, Curzon pressing and accusing the French, by implication, of cowardice and breach of faith. Perhaps he was also influenced by attacks on him by the French press accusing him of abandoning the British at Chanak.[58] The key moment came when Curzon asked if the French general at Mudania "had instructions to give way on anything to avoid war." If so, he went on, "those instructions meant the breakdown of the Mudania Conference and of common action."[59] This was the critical moment. Poincaré realized that the British were serious. Their words were backed by armed forces in position to fight. Curzon's aggressive firmness convinced him of Britain's determination to fight, alone if necessary. The recurrence of war had incalculable possibilities, all bad for France. What, for instance, would happen to Franco-British relations if the British believed that the French had deserted and betrayed them? Poincaré's tone changed at once. "Perhaps," he said, he had "explained himself badly." Before the session was over the Prime Minister had accepted the British formulation of an agreed Allied position. Harington was sent back to Mudania, and the talks could resume, "on the clear understanding that the reservations and conditions insisted upon by the Cabinet and by Lord Curzon in Paris are accepted by the generals and embodied in the convention to be signed by the generals."[60]

With a common position for the Allies established, talks could go forward, but the Turks remained difficult. Although Ismet made some concessions at Mudania, Rumbold reported during the negotiations on the 9th, "Turks are very difficult and obstinate. . . . We have done all in our power to get agreement, but I am not very hopeful."[61] At the same time Harington reported penetration of the Neutral Zone near Ismid in violation of Turkish assurances. Once again, collapse of negotiations and the outbreak of war threatened.[62]

Suddenly, on October 11, after an all-night negotiating session, the word came from Rumbold to Curzon: "Military convention between allies and Turks was signed early this morning and takes effect as from midnight October 14th/15th." The crisis was over. What had caused the Turks to back down and make an armistice? In his letter to Rumbold of the 8th, Harington said:

> I am issuing an ultimatum to Izmet tomorrow (i.e. this, October 8th) morning to say that latter has broken faith regarding frontier and cessation of movements, and that unless he withdraws I will oppose him with all available forces.[63]

This time the ultimatum was delivered, for, as Rumbold explained to the French and Italians two days later,

> that ultimatum and consequent measures were necessary to ensure as far as possible safety of British troops whose position was being endangered by gradual infiltration of Kemalist forces not only in neutral zones but into Constantinople, and that General Harington could not accept responsibility for further delay.[64]

Once again, the French had made it clear that not in any case would they go to war against Turkey, but on the previous night they and the Italians, together with the British, had given the Turks the military convention that their ministers had worked out in Paris, and the "French and Italian Generals agreed that convention was their last word."[65] On the same day, therefore, the Turks had received a military ultimatum from the British and a diplomatic one from the united Allies. The Turkish negotiators requested an adjournment to consult Kemal in Ankara, after which they launched the lengthy negotiating session that produced an armistice.

The military agreement gave the Turks most of what they wanted, but it, and the way it had been achieved, preserved British dignity and prestige and prevented the Turkish "walkover" that might have threatened British interests in the Straits and the safety of the Greeks in European Turkey, and possibly brought on a war in the Balkans. Allied forces would occupy eastern Thrace for a month, allowing the orderly withdrawal of the Greeks. The Turks would withdraw from the Neutral Zone along the Straits and not increase their forces in the neighborhood or in eastern Thrace. The Allies would retain control of Constantinople, Ismid, Chanak, and Gallipoli until a final peace was signed.[66]

In his message conveying the good news, Rumbold said, "Factors which probably determined Turks to sign were knowledge of arrival of British reinforcements, presence of British warships, and fact that these would be used in last resort." In a telegram sent the next day he passed on the view of General Harington "that it was only due to action of His Majesty's Government in sending reinforcements—naval, military and air—so promptly, and to the wonderful restraint of troops that he was able to score some measure of success at Mudania."[67] On this point there is no reason to question their judgment.

The prospect of peace did not save the government that achieved it. Domestic considerations and the weariness of many Conservatives of a coalition government under Lloyd George were chiefly responsible for its overthrow, but foreign policy and the recent crisis played a part. The impression outside the Cabinet was that men like Lloyd George and Churchill had wanted war, and the enemies of the governing coalition used such suspicions on a party and a nation that wanted to turn inward and ignore the world. Bonar Law and Stanley Baldwin led a rebellion of the Conservatives, and Lloyd George resigned on October 19. Bonar Law became Prime Minister of a new Conservative government that was confirmed in office by a general election on November 15. The "small group of resolute men" who preferred to pay a political price for pursuing an unpopular but necessary policy were now required to pay it.

Curzon, who was not among them, continued as Foreign Secretary in the new government, and it was left to him to conclude a treaty with Turkey at the conference that opened at Lausanne in November 1922. Harold Nicolson, who served under him there, believed that "[t]he odds against him were tremendous," because the Turks were confident of their military superiority on the scene and "could claim a conqueror's peace . . . that not Russia only, but

also France and Italy, were Turkey's allies," and that "the British people, in re-
pudiating Lloyd George and Churchill, had demonstrated that they would in
no circumstances oppose Turkish desires."[68] Increasing Curzon's difficulties
was a lack of strong support within the new Cabinet. Lord Derby, the new
Minister for War, was convinced, probably rightly, that Britain could send no
more reinforcements to Harington without partial mobilization of the nation,
which the new government would never contemplate. Bonar Law, the new
Prime Minister, in the midst of the hardest negotiations in January 1923, told
Neville Chamberlain that he

> was afraid that Curzon might get committed to a position in which we
> must either fight or lose prestige by apparently running away. He then
> repeated what he had said to me just before the election. What special
> British interest have we got in the Dardanelles? What interest have we
> got in the freedom of the Straits that is not equally the interest of other
> nations? If no one else is willing to fight then why should we take all the
> burden?[69]

So narrow and unrealistic a view of the nation's interests would be used often
in the future to justify inaction and retreat. The Foreign Secretary knew better,
but while such opinions reigned in London his task was formidable.

His chief tangible goals were, first and foremost, to gain a satisfactory situation in the Straits, to give as much protection as possible to minorities under
Turkish rule, and to settle in Britain's favor the disagreement with Turkey over
ownership of the Mosul region in northern Mesopotamia. Beyond these, he
wanted "to cool the new friendship between Turkey and the Soviets and,
above all to restore British prestige."[70] Because of his unmatched knowledge of
the relevant regions, his great skill and experience, and his personal force and
toughness he was able to achieve remarkable results, in spite of his handicaps.

Throughout the conference Curzon continued to contend with his allies
and with British opinion, governmental and public. He met with Bonar Law
on December 31, in the midst of one of the tensest episodes of the conference.
On his return he reported, "The feet of the Prime Minister were glacial. Positively glacial." To his wife he wrote, "I found Bonar Law longing to clear out
of Mosul, the Straits, Constantinople; willing to give up everything and anything rather than have a row; astonished at the responsibility I have assumed
at Lausanne and prepared for me to back down everywhere."[71] Curzon tried
to stiffen the Prime Minister's spine: "Staggered at his flabbiness and want of
grip, [I] endeavoured to give him some spirit and courage," but to no avail.[72]

This attitude was especially important when the talks turned to Mosul.
Curzon fought especially hard over Mosul, not only because of its important
oil resources but because of "the strategic disadvantage to Britain's position in

Iraq if Mosul remained in Turkish hands, and the possible loss of face if the district were ceded."[73] The Prime Minister was afraid that if Curzon stood firm in the British interest the Turks might break off the talks and renew the war. Nicolson reports Bonar Law's anguished communications to Curzon:

> This would be the most unfortunate thing which could happen in every way, since half of our people, and the whole of the world would say that we had refused peace for the sake of oil. . . . If I made up my mind that we were free to leave, I would certainly not be responsible for continuing to hold the mandate [over Iraq]. . . . It is perhaps well . . . that I should again repeat that there are two things that seem to me vital. The first is that we should not go to war for the sake of Mosul; and second, that if the French, as we know to be the case, will not join us, we shall not by ourselves fight the Turks to enforce what is left of the Treaty of Sèvres. I feel so strongly on these two points that, unless something quite unforeseen should change my view, I would not accept responsibility for any other policy.[74]

In London the *Daily Express* took the same line: "Mosul is not worth the bones of a single British soldier. Our interests in Mosul are non-existent." Several days later a headline screamed: "No war to defend Mosul! Out of Mesopotamia! Bag and baggage the only policy!"[75]

By force of personality and tough determination, Curzon gained the leading and dominant position at the conference. With bold cleverness he forced a split between the Soviets and the Turks on the question of the Straits. In the end, the Turks accepted what was essentially the British position over Soviet objections.[76] They also agreed to join the League of Nations, further separating them from the Soviets, who were outside that organization.

By January 1923 the Mosul question came to the fore. The Turks were adamant. Curzon asked them to submit the matter to the League. The Turks refused, and Nicolson describes his response:

> In solemn tones, and to the astonishment of those present, he read out the terms of Article II of the [League] Covenant. "Any war," he read, "or threat of war, whether immediately affecting any of the members of the League or not, is hereby declared a matter of concern to the whole League, and the League shall take any action that may be deemed wise and effectual to safeguard the peace of nations." Having read through the whole article he paused in silence. "If," he continued, "the Turkish Delegation refuse my proposal I shall act upon the article. I have stated on behalf of my Government the action which I shall be compelled to take, and I shall take it without delay."[77]

The article used the deadly word "war," and Curzon had delivered still an-other ultimatum. Nicolson's judgment was: "This, for the purpose of the Lausanne Conference, was the end of the Mosul dispute. The Turkish position had been pierced, shattered, and turned."[78]

In the event, Curzon postponed his appeal to the League in favor of direct negotiations with Turkey. Although the matter had later to be referred to the League and then to the World Court, a treaty was finally signed between the two countries and Mosul and its oilfields became part of the British mandate in Iraq.[79]

By the end of January, Curzon had achieved all that Britain could hope to get. All that remained was some financial and administrative issues that were important to the French and Italians, but of no concern to the British.

One last time Curzon delivered an ultimatum: he would leave Lausanne on February 4; the Turks had until then to agree to the proposed treaty. The Turks asked for an extension of eight days and were supported by the French and Italians. Curzon refused. The Turks produced a counterproposal that gave to the British all they wanted but not to the Allies. It was an attempt to split the British from the French and Italians, but Curzon refused. On the day set for departure, Ismet Pasha came to see Curzon. Nicolson recorded the meeting in his diary. Curzon said to the Turkish representative:

> "I wish you," he says, "Ismet Pasha, to realise that I have given up more than I thought possible." (This is a lie: he has gained more than he thought possible and the old blighter knows it.) "I have done this for the sake of peace. Peace . . . is in your hands. If, within the next two hours, we do not conclude peace—then there will be no peace. There may be war, Ismet Pasha; there may be war. We cannot wait. I do implore you to accept . . . the concessions we have made and to realise that we have come"—here the Marquis paused and hissed the last words in a dramatic Tennysonian whisper—"to an end. . . ." [After an interruption] I find Curzon looking at his watch. "You have," he says, "only half an hour to save your country. . . ."
>
> Ismet dabs his handkerchief against his lips. He bounces on the chair. He puts the tips of his fingers against his forehead which is beaded with sweat. "Je ne peux pas," he mumbles wretchedly. "Je ne peux pas."[80]

Curzon's train left without an agreement, but he had achieved his goal. The Turks were eager to arrive at a peace, and the conference resumed at Lausanne from April to July 1923. The time was spent arguing about the economic issues that concerned France and Italy. "Curzon's own work at the conference remained untouched."[81] The peace was signed in July and ratified in August.

The response to Curzon's work was mixed. A French newspaper greeted his arrival in Paris from Lausanne in February with the words *"Le triomphe de Lord Curzon."* The British ambassador in Berlin reported that the Germans held the same view. He himself enthused that "Curzon has rendered an immense service, not only to England, but to the world." In London, however, the *Daily Mail*'s headline was "Failure of Lord Curzon." "The British negotiators," the *Mail* said, "are returning under the cloud of a humiliating blunder."[82]

The final settlement was also the target of criticism. Lloyd George, out of office and bitter, called it a rout.[83] In spite of all the efforts by him and his colleagues, the British had been compelled to back down a long way from the victorious Treaty of Sèvres and to abandon many of the goals with which they had begun. Turkey remained in Europe; Constantinople and Gallipoli remained Turkish; there was no partition of Anatolia; although the Straits were demilitarized, they remained under Turkish sovereignty. Protections for minorities under Turkish rule were inadequate and the plan to restore an independent Armenia was abortive. Curzon himself regarded the treaty as disappointing. In a private letter to a member of Parliament he defended it, but conceded and explained its shortcomings: "Admittedly the treaty which finally resulted was not what we could have wished. But we had to restore peace in the Near East and to withdraw our troops, and we were not prepared to exact our conditions by force of arms."[84] In a debate in the House of Commons on August 2, 1923, Ronald McNeil, Under-Secretary of State at the Foreign Office made a similar point while defending the treaty: "We were no longer in a position at Lausanne to dictate peace. We had to negotiate a peace with the Turks on an equal footing, discussing every clause and line in the same way as we discuss Bills in this House."[85]

These were reasonable defenses. The gross inadequacy of Britain's military forces had encouraged the Turks, weakened the alliance, and undermined support at home. In the face of these handicaps the praise awarded by the consensus of modern scholarship is well deserved. The main achievements of the conference concerned the Straits and Mosul, and "against the background of September [1922], they were remarkable. . . . These were solid achievements, and the British delegation ran risks to secure them."[86] "The Treaty of Lausanne secured the freedom of the Straits. . . . It was the most successful and the most lasting of all the post-war treaties."[87] "Britain gained her main desiderata in the peace treaty. . . ." Curzon's "achievement at Lausanne has stood the test of time and still ranks as an example of British diplomacy at its best."[88]

The judgment of Curzon's younger colleague was that Curzon had "by the sole force of his own personality, demonstrated that Great Britain still retained the major voice in any settlement on international affairs." To his wife he wrote at the time, "Britannia has won . . . against the Turks, against treacherous allies, against a week-kneed cabinet, against a rotten public opinion."[89]

Nicolson, perhaps, was somewhat hyperbolic, but there can be no doubt that Lausanne put an end at least to the imminent threat of a great military and diplomatic defeat, the disgrace of Great Britain, and the swift decline in influence that would have followed with incalculable but surely dangerous results.

What is even clearer is that success at Lausanne was entirely dependent on Britain's bold stand at Chanak. Had the British yielded there, they would have been driven out ignominiously and any peace treaty would have been dictated by Turkey. Nicolson, a thoroughly well-informed diplomat who was on the inside of the situation but was not involved in the Cabinet's decision to resist at Chanak, had no doubt about its centrality and importance. The communiqué announcing the stand and calling for help from the dominions "had been a stroke of reckless genius and had been justified by the result. . . ." Among the "meagre" assets Curzon brought to Lausanne were his personality.

> Secondly, and perhaps predominantly, there was Chanak. The impression created abroad by that superb gesture of unwisdom cannot be overstated. In spite of its repudiation by the British electorate, in spite of the repeated assurances of the *Daily Mail*, the Turks and the Russians never, after that fierce spasm of vitality, felt absolutely certain that the British lion was absolutely dead.[90]

Once again, Nicolson may have been somewhat enthusiastic, but even Bonar Law recognized the importance of the stand at Chanak. His letter to the newspapers on October 7, 1922, said, "When the Greek forces were annihilated in Asia Minor and driven into the sea at Smyrna, it seems to me certain that, unless a decisive warning had been issued, the Turks, flushed with victory, would have attempted to enter Constantinople and cross into Thrace."[91] A modern strategic study points out, "Had Chanak fallen Britain would have lost men, prestige and the ability to use the Dardanelles," and endorses the stand: "Britain was prepared to fight but its real aim was to show resolution so as to deter war and to force the Turkish nationalists to the negotiating table. This was the best possible policy. . . ."[92] When the government took its stand, Kemal's victorious army was about to sweep the pitifully small military units of the Allies from Turkey by force of arms, destroying their prestige and their ability to influence the course of events.

The success of the stand at Chanak was not inevitable. The British General Staff, keenly aware of Britain's military weakness, regarded the Cabinet's policy as a bluff. What if Kemal had chosen to fight? One view is that the British at Chanak could have held their own, at least for a time. That was the view of Lloyd George and of General Harington. The small British force, a modern scholar points out, was only a shield that could soon have been strengthened, since the Royal Navy controlled the sea. "Opinion in Britain would probably have soon rallied round the government had war broken out," but even he is doubtful about the outcome of such a war and of the real commitment of British opinion.[93]

A more thorough strategic analysis paints a darker picture. The British had 4,700 men at Chanak against a potential Turkish force of 36,000 men and 112 guns. Any Turkish penetration of the British line would probably have brought collapse. Lloyd George's plan was to substitute firepower for manpower in the form of artillery, naval guns, and airplanes, but "it is doubtful whether this was more than a mirage." The artillery and naval weapons seem to have been inadequate for the purpose. The Royal Air Force was crucial to the Prime Minister's idea of "mechanical superiority," and its commander, General Sir Hugh Trenchard, confidently promised to disrupt the Turks' ground attacks and nullify their artillery. In fact, he exerted much effort in preparing to bomb Ankara, which would have done no good whatever for the forces at Chanak. "Unfortunately the RAF could not have honoured Trenchard's promise," for its planes were too few and in poor condition and many of their crews lacked adequate training. If the Turks held off until after October 30 the prospects for the British at Chanak would have been grim. "Had war occurred, Britain's forces could not have maintained Britain's political aims and might even have failed to defend themselves."[94]

The idea of withdrawing peacefully, however, contained dangers of its own. Though guilty of some exaggeration, Lloyd George was right to point out the terrible consequences of abandoning Chanak to the Turks without a fight: "the evacuation of Chanak . . . would be the greatest loss of prestige which could possibly be inflicted upon the British Empire. . . . [If] we had to scuttle from Chanak, our credit would entirely disappear." Churchill agreed in general, but made the valid additional point that "there could be only one more disastrous event, namely a British defeat at Chanak involving compulsory abandonment of that position."[95]

That Britain should find itself in so dangerous a predicament was the direct result of its recklessly divided foreign and defense policies since 1918. Even as they increased their global responsibilities and expected to exercise a dominant role in world affairs, the British government slashed their military forces to a point that made them vulnerable everywhere. That weakness, in the face of rising Turkish nationalism, left them little choice but to associate their fate with that of the Greek army, "the only large force in Anatolia at the disposal of the Supreme Council. Britain did not have the troops at her disposal to be able to dispense with the services of the Greek army. . . ."[96]

When the Greeks were routed, British forces and British policy were greatly at risk, yet men like Lloyd George, Churchill, and their associates were right to see that even in these dangerous circumstances there was no escape in retreat. At a most threatening moment in the crisis, Churchill wrote to a distinguished London financier in response to Bonar Law's famous letter. He agreed that it was unfair for Britain to be asked to carry the burden alone, but warned against underestimating the consequences of a "violent Turkish inroad into Europe." It would surely bring "war and massacre in Thrace, and no one can tell how far the conflagration may spread." With terrible prescience he pointed out:

> Even after this conflict is finished the evil consequences will endure and Europe in another generation will reap a harvest of blood and tears which might all have been prevented without great expense or effort by common action and loyalty between the signatories of the Treaty of Sèvres.[97]

The British chose to stand at Chanak, and the immediate danger was overcome, but the effect was not lasting. The significance of Chanak was not absorbed by a British public that wanted the fruits of world leadership without the costs. The crisis had shown once again that British military forces were overstretched even to meet their current commitments. It also made a mockery of the ten-year rule, "by showing that a great emergency could arise suddenly rather than waiting until 1929, and that in the interim other powers might threaten British interests."[98] But the lesson was not to be learned either by the British people or by their new government. "Middle-class resentment against high taxation for whatever purpose, coupled with mushroom growth of new financial commitments in debt servicing and social services, ensured that the rapid reduction of military and imperial expenditure to its pre-war standard would be rapid and ruthless."[99]

Chanak temporarily gave an exaggerated sense of British military power and determination. Curzon's remarkable performance reinforced that impression. Without Chanak, Britain would have been ignominiously driven from Turkey, losing its power to shape international events. Without Curzon, Bonar Law would have given everything away at Lausanne. But Chanak was quickly forgotten, and memories of Britain's apparent military might faded with the reality of its decline. Curzon was a relic of a previous age of British strength and confidence. No one like him would guide British foreign policy again until after the outbreak of World War II.

The Chanak crisis has been called "the last occasion on which Great Britain stood up to a potential aggressor before the outbreak of the second World War."[100] A. J. P. Taylor dismissed this as "a melodromatic verdict," but there is no other instance of the use by Britain of the credible threat of military force in a diplomatic crisis in Europe or its vicinity before the war. Even as it signaled the dangerous consequences flowing from Britain's excessive disarmament and despite the fact that Britain failed in this crisis to achieve anything like its original aims, Chanak marked the end of the approach that won the war and the beginning of a new one that would lose the peace.

5

Retreat from
Responsibility

In the same month that Turkey ratified the Treaty of Lausanne another challenge arose to test the policy of Britain's new Conservative government.[1] The affair in Turkey represented an effort to foster and defend British interests in the Near East by means of the wartime alliance with France and Italy, the Entente. Divisions among the Allies and a reluctance on the part of British politicians and the British public to supply and use adequate military power for such a purpose hampered that effort. The Corfu affair of August and September 1923 would provide the first test of the new doctrine of "collective security," whereby the League of Nations was meant to serve as the focus for resistance to aggression and the preservation of a decent and secure international order.

One of the issues remaining unsettled from the Peace Conference in Paris was the establishment of the border between Greece and Albania. That was the task of an Allied Commission under the supervision of the Ambassadors' Conference. On August 27, General Enrico Tellini and other Italian members of the commission were murdered on Greek territory in Epirus.[2] On the 28th and 29th, the Italians demanded that the Greek government arrest and punish the killers, and on the 30th the Greek Foreign Minister promised to do his best to comply. Without waiting for the reply, however, on the 29th the Italians presented a list of seven demands as an ultimatum with a time limit of twenty-four hours. The demands were for a formal apology, a funeral service for the victims in *Athens,* a salute to Italian ships in Phaleron Bay by Greek battleships, a

very strict inquiry into the murders to be carried out by Greece "with the assistance of the Italian Military Attaché," a death penalty for the guilty parties, a payment of 50 million lire as a penalty to be delivered within five days, and military honors to be paid to the victims as they embarked.[3] No evidence then or since has ever shown Greek complicity in the murder, and the commission that ultimately investigated the matter for the Allied Commission of Ambassadors did not blame the Greeks even for culpable negligence. The questions of who committed the murders and why were never of true importance.[4]

Lord Curzon, among others, was struck by the similarity between this situation and the assassination of the Archduke Franz Ferdinand at Sarajevo in June of 1914, which sparked World War I: "The terms demanded by Mussolini seem to me extravagant—much worse than the ultimatum after Sarajevo, and I can hardly conceive any self-respecting Gov[ernmen]t acceding to them."[5] The Greeks met the time limit and accepted four of the demands but rejected those for Italian participation in the investigation, for the death penalty, and for the financial penalty as "outraging the honour and violating the sovereignty of the State." The answer, too, resembled the Serbian response to the Austrian ultimatum in 1914. In 1923, however, the smaller nation had recourse to a newly established protector, and the Greek note included the statement that if the Italians were not satisfied, the Greeks would "appeal to the League of Nations in accordance with the Covenant and undertake to accept its decisions."[6]

Ever since his arrival in power in 1922, Benito Mussolini had sought a triumph in foreign policy to raise Italian international prestige and to start the restoration of the ancient Roman Empire in the Mediterranean. Disappointed in their disputes with Yugoslavia and Albania, the Italians considered action against the Greeks, with whom they were in dispute over control of the Dodecanese Islands in the Aegean. A month before the Corfu incident, discussions in the Foreign Office in Rome considered naval actions to be taken against Greece in case any "offense" by the Greeks called for them. In that event Corfu was to be occupied and held hostage for the fulfillment of Italian demands. At the same time, Italian naval units would operate from the island of Leros to threaten Athens. On August 29, the day they presented their demands to Greece, the Italians sent a fleet to Leros; twenty-four hours later another fleet sailed for Corfu.[7] Corfu is strategically placed at the entrance to the Adriatic Sea, "which the Fascists liked to regard as 'mare nostrum.'"[8] Once the island was occupied, whatever the pretext, it could be difficult to expel the Italians. That is how they had acquired the Dodecanese Islands from Turkey, an acquisition recently ratified by the Treaty of Lausanne. "Given this precedent and the contrived search for a Greek slight to Italy, there is little doubt," according to one scholar, "that Mussolini's object was to seize and hold Corfu permanently."[9] It is not hard to see why the suggestion has been made that the assassins were in the pay of the Italians.[10]

The next day, August 31, the Italian naval squadron sailed into the harbor of Corfu and demanded the island's surrender. They bombarded an old fortress whose only use was for housing Greek and Armenian refugees from Turkey, killing fifteen and wounding many others. Italian troops then landed on the island and occupied it.[11] "Mussolini's first act of aggression had been consummated."[12]

The Greeks appealed to the League under Articles 12 and 15 of the Covenant. "Here," wrote Harold Nicolson,

> if ever, was the very type of international incident for which the League had been created. A Great Power had, in circumstances of sensational brutality, violated the articles of the Covenant by taking direct action against a Small Power. The latter had appealed to Geneva for protection. The League, at that very moment, happened to be in full session of the Fourth Assembly. Should the Assembly fail, in such flagrant circum-

stances, to enforce obedience to the Covenant, it was realised that the authority of the League would be forever impaired.[13]

The first British reactions were sharp and clear. On August 31 the ambassador to Italy, by no means unfriendly to the government at Rome, reported that the Italian press "seized on the opportunity to give vent to their deep-seated hatred of Greece. . . . [T]he extreme nationalist elements are well pleased to make the most of the opportunity to show the world that Italy is a strong Mediterranean power who will tolerate no offence at the hands of her neighbors and hope that . . . it may be possible to satisfy nationalist aspirations by definitely taking over the Dodecanese or even other islands."[14] The next day, Lord Robert Cecil, Britain's representative to the League, telegraphed to Curzon his opinion that Italy's action at Corfu was a violation of Article 15 of the Covenant and exposed it to the actions in Article 16, which included sanctions, both economic and military. An ardent supporter of the League and collective security, he made his feelings clear: "In absence of instructions, presume His Majesty's Government will desire me to do everything possible to uphold Covenant."[15] Only hours later, Harold Nicolson, in the Foreign Office in London, reported to the British Embassy in Paris, "His Majesty's Government, faithful to the letter and spirit of the Covenant of the League of Nations, will observe the procedure established by the articles of the Covenant and have instructed their representatives accordingly." Nicolson accurately foresaw that the Italians would try to keep the League out of the affair and that the French would assist them in deflecting it to the Ambassadors' Conference, where Italy and France were represented but Greece was not. "We assume," he said, "that you will wish to leave the matter in the hands of the League."[16]

Curzon was no less positive. He saw two reasons for concern. The strategic one was that Italian retention of Corfu "would constitute intolerable disturbance of naval balance in Medterranean." The other was political and moral, that "our attitude finds an even stronger justification in desire to support League on first occasion on which a small power has appealed to it against high-handed action of a great power." He told Prime Minister Baldwin: "Italian ultimatum seemed to me precipitate, while their action in seizing Corfu placed them definitely in the wrong. . . . I do not know what attitude of other members of Council will be, if faced with defiance of Council by one of its powerful members [Italy]. But you may rely upon support of His Majesty's Government in upholding the Covenant."[17] "Italy's conduct is violent and inexcusable. And if we don't back up the appeal to the League, that institution may as well shut its doors."[18]

Curzon swiftly acted in accordance with these views. He returned from France to London on September 2. After a briefing from his staff in his train compartment he said, "Yes, there can be no doubt about it. The machinery of the League must be put in motion. Telegraph to Bob Cecil instructing him to go full steam ahead."[19] The telegraph was duly sent. The next day Curzon called the Italian ambassador in and expressed his opinions with firmness, to say the least:

> The Italian government had launched an ultimatum of almost unprecedented severity without waiting for any . . . process and had followed it by bombardment of undefended town and killing of innocent people. Public opinion might be pardoned for being somewhat disturbed at these proceedings, and puzzled at the assurance that they were acts of peace and not war. Would the Italian government . . . have acted in precisely the same way had the presumed culprits belonged to a great power instead of a petty, impoverished, enfeebled people? Public opinion would . . . be even more disturbed at refusal of Italian government to consent to reference of matter to League of Nations. I know of no article in the covenant which provides for such a refusal on the plea of honour. . . . Would the humiliation of Greece even before her complicity had been ascertained either set a desirable precedent or produce the expected result? . . . Our representative at the League had already received instructions to uphold the Covenant, and upon these I felt sure he would act. . . .
>
> [M]y impression was that small states represented on council would regard matter as vital to their own security as well as to future existence of League. . . . [P]olicy of ultimatums and bombardment before enquiry would find no place in accepted canons of international practice. . . .

He instructed the British ambassador in Rome to persuade the Italians that "repudiation of the League is an unwise procedure" and that they should seek an inquiry by the League.[20] On reading Curzon's telegrams, Prime Minister Baldwin responded with full support: "I approve entirely language held by you to Italian Ambassador. I regard attitude of Italian government towards League of Nations as test case of their sincerity to respect the rights of small countries."[21]

In Geneva the British delegation to the League was firm and confident in the rightness of their cause and the support they were receiving. On September 2 they told Curzon that they were certain that the League Council had jurisdiction, under Article 15, since the bombardment and occupation of Corfu were "clearly an act of war and Council could not abstain from intervention without forfeiting confidence of the whole world in League of Nations." He reported the view of Karl H. Branting, the Swedish representative, that the smaller powers believed that "in this question existence of League was at stake; action of Italy was menace to all small nations." The Italian plan was to persuade the French and British to remove the matter from the competence of the League and turn it over to the Conference of Ambassadors. He felt sure, however, that there was "no danger of such a deplorable decision so far as His Majesty's Government are concerned, as any failure of League in this grave crisis would do irreparable harm and perhaps lead to disintegration of the League itself."[22]

Popular opinion in Britain was overwhelmingly outraged at Italy's behavior. Throughout the crisis the Italians repeatedly complained of the hostility of the British press, claiming it was "unanimous in condemning Italian action."[23] In fact, there was one exception, The *Daily Mail,* which conducted "a hysterical campaign against our support of the League of Nations, accusing Lord Robert Cecil, Lord Curzon and the Foreign Office of 'war-mongering.'"[24] With that single exception, the Italians were right, and the rest of the press reaction to Italy's actions was characterized as "severe."[25] To the Italian ambassador Curzon explained that the English press, "across the political spectrum," wanted the League to intervene. To have told Cecil to support the Italian position, he said, "would have provoked the fall of the Ministry."[26] In addition, unlike in their plight in the Chanak affair, the British government would also have had the support of the dominions. Writing to Mussolini, the Italian ambassador in London said that they demanded that the League deal with the matter. Led by South Africa's Jan Smuts, they made the League their "essential stronghold."[27] Public reaction reflected the broad and deep support for the League and for collective security through the League that existed during the first decade after the war. A government prepared to act vigorously against the obvious Italian aggression would, likewise, have had strong public support in Britain and the empire.

In the words of Harold Nicolson, "It was at this stage that Curzon unaccountably collapsed."[28] On September 5, Curzon sharply reversed direction, sending to Cecil instructions "not in any case [to] commit H[is] M[ajesty's] G[overnment] to any course of action without first consulting us fully."[29] Pressed by France, the Ambassadors' Conference in Paris produced a scheme meant to let the Italians have their way. Mussolini insisted that the complaints should not be dealt with by the League, indicating that he would leave Corfu if he was satisfied with the decision of the conference. On September 10, Lord Crewe, in Paris, was instructed to accept the proposal. "The Council of the League," said Nicolson, "were also obliged, in view of our surrender, to renounce their own authority. A settlement was imposed upon Greece which was demonstrably unfair. Corfu was evacuated, but the League of Nations had suffered a defeat from which it has never recovered."[30]

What had happened to produce this remarkable reversal? Most answers have been uncertain and unpersuasive. One scholar attributes it to press criticism,[31] but we have seen that attacks came from only one newspaper and there was strong support for strong action from all the rest. Nicolson, close to Curzon and a participant in the events, found his action merely "unaccountable." Another scholar attributes it to "an attack of weariness on Lord Curzon's part."[32] But there were deeper and more specific reasons than that. Although Curzon had proved himself a tough and courageous negotiator, he now belonged to a government that was much less ready to fight than its predecessor. Prime Minister Stanley Baldwin, the successor to Bonar Law, had, like Law, opposed Britain's bold stand at Chanak and helped bring the Lloyd George government down, in part, on that issue. The new regime, as we have seen, had pressed Curzon to yield rather than risk a renewal of the fight during the Lausanne negotiations. Such a regime can be more readily intimidated than others. The Italian diplomat Guariglia may have been right in suggesting, "Perhaps the sensation of finding themselves confronting an abnormal political man whose reactions were very difficult to foresee was one of the reasons that induced England and France to seek a transaction that would safeguard the prestige of Mussolini and not push Mussolini towards a new adventure."[33]

France, however, did not need to be intimidated into supporting Italy. During the Corfu crisis the French were engaged in the occupation of Germany's Ruhr district in an effort to force the payment of war reparations. That action had increased the rift with Britain and brought considerable criticism from many sides. The French were keenly aware of the parallel that might be drawn between their occupation of the Ruhr to compel the payment of war reparations and the Italian seizure of Corfu, allegedly to obtain reparations for the murder of the Italians. The French "would not dare countenance the League's arbitration of the Corfu affair lest a precedent be set for intervention in the analogous Ruhr crisis."[34] The French, moreover, wanted the friendship of Italy, one of the victorious Entente powers, both to support their current policies and to stand with France against a resurgent Germany in the future. They would certainly not risk that friendship over the question of justice for Greece, and they would insist on salving the Italians' pride when they were compelled to leave Corfu.

Part of the explanation for the reversal of British policy is the difficulty presented by the policy of France, but it also lies in a fundamental difference of opinion within the British Foreign Office. Scholars have distinguished between "collectivists," like Sir Robert Cecil, who was said to want to make the League the center of world affairs, and "traditionalists," like Sir William Tyrrell in the Foreign Office, who saw the League of Nations as supplementary and subordinate to the ordinary and conventional instruments of national policy. He had little belief in the League and wanted to avoid a confrontation. "Sir William's motto was 'avoid trouble.'"[35] Curzon certainly belonged with the traditionalists, but his first response to the crisis placed him with the collectivists. In the immediate shock and horror of the response to Mussolini's bullying there was no objection to a hard line against Italy, but soon more traditional voices began to be heard. As early as September 3, the British ambassador in Rome warned against any action that might anger Mussolini and the Italians. He

urged the solution preferred by the Italians: avoidance of the League, no intervention by either of the Allied Powers (given France's support for Italy, this
had to mean Britain), but a settlement by the Conference of Ambassadors.
Otherwise, he advised, Italy would withdraw from the League. Even more serious, a direct intervention by Britain "might induce a premier of Mussolini's
temperament to take some rash and impulsive step which might greatly react
on the people of Europe."[36]

A few days later, perhaps detecting a change of mood in Whitehall, his
message was more plain. If the League "insist on strongest measures I think
that Mussolini is capable of any ill-considered and reckless action which might
even plunge Europe into war." He therefore recommended "some formula
which would extricate Mussolini from his present predicament. he must be regarded as a mad dog who may do infinite harm before he is despatched."[37]
This striking metaphor emerged again and was used frequently in the crisis
over Abyssinia that Mussolini provoked in 1935. It was used to advocate a
policy of concession and appeasement in the face of rage and intimidation, regardless of justice or security. Accepting the metaphor, it would seem wise, at
least, to consider the policy of trying to capture him and lock him up or to
shoot him on the spot to eliminate the threat once and for all. It might be more
reckless and dangerous to throw him a bone in the hope he will calm down.
Kennard, the ambassador in Rome, rejected such an approach: "it might be
thought preferable to despatch the mad dog without delay," but then "a period
of anarchy might ensue which would be followed by either military dictatorship or even some worse form of government."[38] Mussolini's own government,
of course, would soon be generally recognized as a military dictatorship. The
threat of anarchy or something worse would become a common excuse for
those who would accommodate aggressive regimes in Italy and elsewhere.

Kennard had spoken of war, but the League had other sanctions available,
if its members chose to use them against aggressors. In his message to Cecil of
September 5, Curzon included the Treasury's answer to his inquiry concerning
possible actions the League might take against Italy. The Treasury poured a
large pitcher of cold water on the idea of economic sanctions, asserting that
their imposition would require a return to wartime control over most economic activities. "The result would be a complete stoppage of all foreign business and all imports and exports until such time as declarations [under the
war-time system] could be obtained." Even if all that were done, economic
sanctions would not work. "Unless every state, in particular the U.S.A., joined
in these measures, they would be completely ineffective." Italy could evade the
sanctions with the complicity of other states to the detriment of British business.

Without war-time machinery including censorship, high class bankers
and trading houses will lose business to less scrupulous competitors and

no such machinery will work unless generally and willingly accepted. We do not believe banking or trading community will accept bureaucratic control and dislocation of trade unless essential to prosecuting a war in which national feelings are intensely aroused.[39]

There would be difficulties, no doubt, in imposing effective economic sanctions. There always are, and such sanctions rarely achieve their purpose against a determined opponent, but it is hard to believe that the Treasury officials would have painted so dark a picture in a cause in which they believed. The last sentence gives the game away: the Corfu affair, in their opinion, was not important enough to justify sanctions of any kind.[40]

If economic sanctions, however, would not avail, why not use military sanctions, which were also permitted by the Covenant for use against aggressors? Only the British delegation at Geneva seems to have contemplated military action.[41] Cecil approached the French with a proposal to make a joint naval demonstration to force the Italians from Corfu, but the French responded negatively.[42] No one appears to have considered using or even threatening purely British armed force. The closest thing to that appears to have been a suggestion from Cecil at Geneva on September 6 that the aircraft carrier *Ark Royal* and other elements of the Royal Navy should concentrate at Malta. "I believe," he wrote, "that if some such steps . . . could be taken they would certainly become known to Italian government . . . and would produce excellent effect in Rome." Curzon was not persuaded. "I think that at the present stage your proposal might give rise to serious misinterpretation, and therefore had better not be pursued. But I will bear it in mind should circumstances render such a step desirable."[43] Before the crisis was over, Mussolini's behavior, especially his reluctance to evacuate Corfu, caused Curzon considerable anxiety, but such circumstances did not seem to him to arise.

Cecil approached the French, no doubt, because "the British fleet was thought to be in no position to challenge the Italians, therefore, incapable of participating at Corfu in a unilateral naval demonstration."[44] In a letter dated September 7, Vice Admiral Sir Roger Keyes, Deputy Chief of Naval Operations, wrote, "From a Naval point of view [the situation] was even more serious than the economic." Ships could neither rush to the Adriatic nor concentrate at Malta because the Mediterranean fleet was "almost to a keel, still holding a watching brief in the Near East." Help from the Atlantic fleet would be "difficult" since, after concentrating in the Mediterranean, it "had already been dispersed."[45] One naval officer has concluded that Italy's freedom to act as it did at Corfu shows that "the British Fleet normally in the Mediterranean was not of sufficient strength to deal with two simultaneous and separate crises."[46] When Cecil suggested the minatory concentration of the British fleet at Malta, Admiral Keyes scoffed, saying the *Ark Royal* would be of no help. He thought the whole scheme of Cecil's was "intolerable." There might be "something in all these threats if we really meant to fight, but it can only end in climbing down and trying to save face in the humiliating way we did at Lausanne." Nicolson tried to soothe him by informing him that Curzon had already "scotched" any idea of naval action.[47]

The Deputy Chief of Naval Operations was surely too pessimistic about the capacity of the Royal Navy. The ratification of the Treaty of Lausanne before the Corfu crisis made it possible to move at least a significant part of the fleet from Turkish waters without danger. Whatever the capabilities of the Royal Navy, moreover, they were plainly much greater than those of the Italians. Minister of Marine Grand Admiral Thaon di Revel had constructed a plan of action against Britain that called for a crucial air base at Trapani in Sicily, needed to defend the southern coast of Italy and to attack the key British base at Malta. A report he delivered on September 13, however, "made sad reading. After an eighteen-point description of Italy's naval weakness and unpreparedness, the minister recommended that there would have to be an evacuation of the ports of Genoa, Livorno, Civitavecchia, Cagliari, *Trapani* [emphasis added], and perhaps Palermo." Because of "insufficient means" the Italian fleet would not be able to defend its merchant ships at sea.[48]

Against such an enemy Admiral Keyes's opinions seem excessively negative. His arguments are those dredged up by someone looking for excuses not to do what he does not wish to do. He was influenced, no doubt, by the opposition of the Treasury and the knowledge that the government really did not want to take action. His sneer at the presumably pusillanimous civilians is unjustified, for the navy in the Dardanelles before Lausanne was not eager for a fight. Underlying the navy's reluctance, however, was something more important. Its officers were keenly aware of the swift and tremendous reductions suffered by the navy in the previous five years. Expenditures for the fleet had shrunk below prewar levels, even as the new mandates had increased responsibilities. Even more serious, Japan, which had been Britain's ally in 1914, had become a potentially dangerous enemy, since the British had allowed the alliance to lapse in 1922. In general terms, the Royal Navy truly was inadequate to meet all its commitments, a situation that makes military and naval leaders nervous and extremely, often excessively, conservative. This would not be the last time between the wars that such considerations would help limit the options available for the conduct of policy. In this way it is true that "Britain's military weakness, the feeling that coercive action through the League was impossible . . . provide[s] the key" to British policy.[49]

Because of the deeper reasons that underlay British policy, Curzon found it easy to accept that any form of sanctions was impractical and to turn away from his earlier indignation and support for a policy in support of the League's resistance to Italian demands and aggression. Without saying so openly, he pursued a policy of separating the issue of what reparation the Greeks must pay for the murdered Italians, from Italy's evacuation of Corfu, the former being a problem for Greece and the League, the latter for Britain and France. In so doing he would tacitly accept Greek responsibility for the murders, though none had been proved, and the removal of the matter from the purview of the League of Nations, though it plainly came under the terms of the Covenant.

From September 3 the French worked with the Italians to delay proceedings in the League long enough to permit the Conference of Ambassadors to take the question of the assassinations out of the hands of the League.[50] The conference was all but certain to produce an outcome to Italy's liking. It included both France and Italy but not Greece. It met in secret and rarely failed to attend to the national interests of the Entente powers. "Paris and Rome could therefore confidently expect the conference to give a judgment based on political expedience rather than on some principle of abstract justice. . . ."[51]

Together France and Italy convinced the League Council to delay action. At the crucial meeting of September 5, Lord Cecil, not yet restrained by Curzon, took a strong stand. He requested the reading of Articles 10, 12, and 15 of the Treaty of Versailles (the Covenant of the League of Nations was part of that Treaty) in French and English. He reminded the Council "that the same stipulations appeared in the Treaty of St. Germain, Treaty of Neuilly, Treaty of Trianon: if they are disregarded the whole foundation of new Europe would be shaken"[52] and demanded a vote on the question of the League's jurisdiction within twenty-four hours. His remarks were plainly directed toward the French, who were currently using a strict interpretation of those clauses to justify their occupation of the Ruhr even as they were conspiring with the Italians to undermine their application to Italy. Their reading aloud did not have the intended effect, for the French continued to help the Italians stall and prevented the vote, which was most likely to go against them. September 5 "was the League's last real opportunity to act," for on the same day the Conference of Ambassadors informed the League that it would deal with the Italo-Greek dispute.[53]

The next day, the League Council acquiesced, de facto, in its surrender of the League's authority. To save face it approved a "tentative solution" to be suggested for the consideration of the Ambassadors' Conference whereby Greece would accept responsibility for the assassinations and deposit 50 million lire as a guarantee for whatever indemnity would be imposed by a judgment of the World Court in the Hague. The French were able to persuade the Italians to accept this, since the "solution" was only a recommendation. "In reality, on September 6, the League gave up all hope of exerting any authority and influence. As an interested bystander, the League "'would be glad to receive information as to the deliberations of the Conference of Ambassadors . . .' so ran the meek words of the League Council's communication. The Allied ambassadors in Paris were given carte blanche; the League's abdication was complete."[54]

On September 7, the Conference produced its own plan. It proposed an international commission to supervise the inquiry into the assassinations. Its members would be British, French, and Italian serving under a Japanese president. There would be no representation from the League. As in the League Council's recommendation, Greek responsibility was assumed and the 50 million lire were to be deposited subject to a ruling by the World Court, based on the findings of the Ambassadors' Conference's commission of inquiry. In return for these concessions the Italian member promised to evacuate Corfu when the Greeks paid the assessed indemnity. On September 9 the Greeks accepted these terms.

The next day Curzon instructed his representative at the Ambassadors' Conference to accept the proposal. In a very different vein from his earlier communications, he presented this decision to Cecil not as the disaster to the League that it was, but as its vindication:

> I trust that League while reaffirming, if this indeed be thought necessary, their own competence will be satisfied with substantial triumph that had won in almost unqualified acceptance of their proposals by the Ambassadors' Conference. I am so far from regarding the issue as a rebuff to the League that I should be prepared to contend that main principles for which they fought have been vindicated.[55]

It is hard to believe that Curzon, for all his self-assurance and sang-froid, could have written that message with a straight face.

Still, with Greek and British acquiescence, a solution appeared to be imminent. It turned out, however, that his representative's promise did not speak for Mussolini, who informed him that "the prompt acceptance on the part of Greece of the demands formulated by the Conference of Ambassadors cannot import a simultaneous evacuation of Corfu." The deposit of the 50 million lire was not enough, The Duce also required "the search and punishment of the assassins" before the evacuation of Corfu. "The capture of the assassins was highly improbable—and Mussolini knew it. He merely wanted an excuse to remain at Corfu."[56]

On September 10, Mussolini's demands were put before the Ambassadors' Conference. Shocked by this development, it adjourned for two days. In that period the character of the crisis changed. The new Italian conditions for leaving Corfu were accompanied by detailed information that "the Italian authorities in Corfu acted as if they wished to remain there permanently."[57] From the British point of view, this was something different. Injustice and humiliation for the Greeks was one thing, but the possession by Mussolini of an island of Corfu's strategic importance was quite another. On this point, the French agreed with Great Britain. What mattered to them was preventing action by the League; they were willing, gently and up to a point, to join the British in pressing Mussolini to leave Corfu. At the conference meeting of September 10, Lord Crewe, the British ambassador, had complained that under Mussolini's conditions "the occupation might last indefinitely." Sensing the new mood, Mussolini's ambassador wrote to the Duce, "The question is changing its character, and the Italo-Greek conflict may give way to an Anglo-Italian contest."

Mussolini was impressed enough to send another proposal to the conference that suggested with some vagueness that if the assassins could not be identified or captured he might accept the 50 million lire as an acceptable form of reparation.[58] Lord Crewe insisted on Italy's setting a specific date for evacuation of Corfu, precisely and formally, no later than September 27. Otherwise Britain would "tomorrow resume complete liberty of action in the whole question."[59]

The Italian ambassador, Romano Avezzana, bitterly complained that he had received "an ultimatum on the question of Corfu."[60] He wrote in alarm to Mussolini that he could no longer count on France's unconditional support and pointed out the danger of a confrontation with Britain that could result in the loss of Italy's gains. The Italian naval attaché in Paris reported a rumor that Curzon might offer the use of the Royal Navy to the League of Nations. He also told the Duce that sources close to Crewe said that Italian refusal would lead to a "grave" situation. That is the diplomatic language used to hint at the possible use of force. The Italian ambassador in London reported a conversation with Sir William Tyrrell in which he warned that Britain might be willing to take "special action" in regard to the evacuation. The ambassador noted that "British public opinion was unanimous in insisting on an immediate evacuation of Corfu."[61] In the midst of all this alarming news, on September 13, Mussolini received two reports from the Ministry of Marine on Italy's prospects in a war against Britain. They painted the darkest of pictures leading to the conclusion that it would be "madness to think of fighting Britain for Corfu."[62] In the face of the new British firmness and the momentary defection of the French, Mussolini gave way and agreed to evacuation of Corfu no later than September 27.

There is no reason for belief in the truth of the rumors that so alarmed the Italians. No evidence has appeared to show that the British ever contemplated naval or military action against Italy during the Corfu crisis, either on behalf of the League or on their own. On the contrary, in a message to Curzon on September 27, Lord Crewe defended his ultimate retreat by pointing to the unlikelihood of action by the League, the collapse of French support, and the impossibility of imposing economic sanctions. "The only effective weapon in my hands," he said, "was the threat of referring the matter back to the League."[63] Nothing is said about the use of force, because none was ever considered. Stiffer British language, no more than a bluff, had panicked the Italians and made them yield. Had the British stuck to their guns throughout the rest of the crisis, with or without a naval demonstration, there can be little doubt that Mussolini would have been compelled to back down and accept a humiliating defeat, his reputation badly damaged and his ability to intimidate greatly diminished. Resolute British action might also have compelled the French to go along, however reluctantly, as they had at Chanak and Lausanne. Had the British chosen to take action in the name of the League of Nations, that might have helped that infant organization toward a useful role in preserving the peace and the security of Europe and the world. With our knowledge of Italian capacities and intentions, we can be sure that there would have been no risk, but even at the time it should have been clear that the risk was small. In September 1923, however, Britain chose not to accept the opportunity.

Embarrassed and angered by his retreat, Mussolini tried to save as much face as possible. He agreed to evacuate Corfu on the specified date but insisted that "if, on that date, the guilty parties have not been discovered and if it is not established that the Greek government has not been negligent in pursuing and seeking them . . . the conference will impose on Greece, in virtue of penalty, the payment to Italy of the sum of 50 million Italian lire, waiving from that moment any appeal to the Permanent Court of Justice at The Hague [the World Court]."[64] The multiple negatives had the effect of requiring the Greeks to prove themselves innocent in order to escape or modify the maximum financial penalty. Crewe was torn between the need to resist unreasonable Italian demands and the need to get Mussolini out of Corfu, but the latter was clearly the overwhelming priority. A letter from Curzon made that clear, even as it tried to put the two concerns together. "Unless," he said, "we get the Italians out of Corfu pretty quickly a great blow will have been struck at the public law of Europe."[65] The treatment of Greece was not mentioned.

In his letter to Curzon of September 27 in which he defended his performance, Crewe described the course of events:

> I should be loath to have to defend it from an ethical standpoint, but . . .
> I cannot see what other solution could have been reached, if effect was
> to be given to the universal desire to see the Italians evacuate Corfu. . . .
> The critical point of the discussion was reached on September 13th
> when the Italian ambassador made a declaration in the name of his
> Government. . . . Monsieur Laroche [the French ambassador], accepting
> the Italian thesis . . . used the formula "if it is not established that the
> Greek Government has committed no negligence in their pursuit and
> their investigation," which threw on the Greek Government the onus of
> proving its innocence. I immediately objected to this wording and urged
> that instead of being put in the negative the phrase should be drafted in
> the positive, so as to lay on the Commission of Enquiry the onus of establishing the negligence of the Greek Government. . . . [A]fter consider-

able discussion in which I received no support from Monsieur Cambon [the French minister], I was compelled to yield.

Crewe tried to embarrass the Italians by pointing out that the world would think they had been bribed with the 50 million lire to evacuate Corfu, but Avazzini insisted it was not a matter of money but of Italian honor. Cambon did not deny that the money was a bribe but pointed out that if the bribe was not paid, "Signor Mussolini might refuse to evacuate Corfu on the 27th, or, if he did, would seize some other Greek territory." No one mentioned the possible use of force to resist such eventualities.

Far from being troubled by the injustice to the Greeks, Crewe was irked with them. They had not made his task easier by the usual devices of dismissing or reprimanding some of their officials. "They had not even gone through the farce . . . of producing some shepherds, at most accessories after the fact, as the actual perpetrators of the crime." In a minute on Crewe's complaint about the Greeks, Alexander Cadogan in the Foreign Office wrote: "The last paragraph . . . —on the subject of Greek 'negligence'—seems hardly fair. The Greek Gov[ernment] would have been prejudging the whole case if they had taken the actions there indicated."[66] but there is nothing so annoying in international relations as complaints on behalf of an innocent victim whose interest you are in the process of betraying.

Without even the assistance of false accusations and arrests by the Greeks, Crewe had no choice. The preliminary report, as Avezzana pointed out, said that "Commission did not regard the Greek Government as necessarily implicated, they had failed to establish that the Government had been guilty of no negligence in the search for the murderers." In that situation, Crewe asserted, it would have been futile to refuse the full penalty and given the Italians an excuse not to evacuate Corfu. He concluded that once it had been decided to make the Italians leave Corfu "before complete satisfaction had been given to their original demands it was inevitable that with the inadequate means of pressure at our disposal we should be compelled in effect to pay the price demanded by Signor Mussolini."[67]

In fact, Crewe had not immediately given way. Abandoned by all the delegates, and most emphatically by the French, who vigorously insisted on the immediate full payment of the penalty by the Greeks, he insisted on referring the question to London for instructions. Later on, Curzon, in a letter to Crewe, tried to elude responsibility by claiming that on reading Avezzani's argument "I found (I wish I hadn't) that your colleagues [the ambassadors] had apparently given the case away. . . ."[68] As a result, in light of the French defection and the danger that continued Italian occupation of Corfu "might lead to disaster," he wrote, I think you have no alternative but to defer to Italian contention."[69] The fact is that Curzon could have instructed Crewe to reject the

Italian version, threatened to refer the matter to the League of Nations if the Italians' did not evacuate Corfu by the stated date, and called Mussolini's bluff. As an American diplomat observed, "it was apparent at every moment that fear of something occurring in Geneva was the driving power" behind Italian diplomacy.[70] Curzon would have had British public opinion solidly behind him had he done so, but ultimately such an action implied the use of force, and Baldwin's Foreign Minister was not willing to do that. On September 14, after Crewe had been instructed to accept the Italian version, Baldwin wrote to Curzon that if he could get Mussolini out of Corfu by the end of the month he would have done "a great thing. I am delighted with your general direction of affairs in a most difficult situation, and I hope the country will realize what an awkward corner you have got them round."[71]

The Conference of Ambassadors rushed to judgment, accepting the Italian position that Greece must pay a penalty of 50 million lire, although even the preliminary report of the Commission of Inquiry had not found them guilty of anything. Major Harenc, the British member of the commission, later reported in detail that only the intransigence of the Italian member had prevented the commission from sending to the ambassadors a final report that "would practically have exculpated the Greek Government, . . . and that subsequent inquiry had not revealed any evidence to condemn that Government. . . ."[72] The Greeks, nevertheless, quickly paid the penalty, and the Corfu affair was over.

Though he put up a bold front, Curzon understood that things had not gone perfectly well. In a burst of realism he wrote to Crewe on the 26th, "It is rather a humiliating finale (if indeed it is that) of the episode. But I daresay even the Greeks would sooner pay than see the Italians remain in Corfu."[73] He did not address the question of what the effect was on larger questions, but Leopold Amery, First Lord of the Admiralty, did. On September 26, when Curzon gave the reasons why he had instructed Crew to accept the Italian proposal, Amery observed that it "was a really bad blow to the League of Nations . . . [and] was bound to shake the faith of all the small powers."[74]

Two weeks later, Curzon explained his decision to the Imperial Conference. Once again, he blamed the Council of Ambassadors for giving "away the case by the language they had accepted," as though he himself had not instructed his ambassador to accept that language. He spoke of the great responsibility Britain felt not to take any action that might bring on "a great European conflagration which really was on the verge of breaking out." Britain had made this "sacrifice" to preserve "the great cardinal principle of European policy at this moment, namely, the entente between ourselves and our allies." The conference's decision, to be sure, "was unjustified by the evidence. . . ." Its only "justification . . . was that it saved . . . Europe from the chances of a great complication."[75]

Lord Crewe was not entirely comfortable with his own role in the affair.

He wrote to Curzon on the question of publishing an account of the Ambassadors' Conference. He blamed the behavior of the French and Italians for "having wished to condone a quite indefensible act," but he did not think that publication was a good idea. "I do not think," he said, "that a serious moral defence can be advanced for having accepted Italy's action at all, and I am greatly afraid that any attempted explanations at this stage will only make things worse. . . ."[76] The government decided not to publish.

Among themselves, then, the British acknowledged that their treatment of the affair was a moral failure. But what of their defense on the basis of *realpolitik*? The Corfu affair was about much more than assigning guilt for assassinations and even getting Mussolini out of Corfu. It was, as Curzon claimed, about larger questions of war and peace and the future condition of Europe, but his understanding of these matters was narrowly limited. Britain's greatest interest was to establish and maintain a stable and secure order, where resort to violence to achieve national ends would not be permitted. The Italian ultimatum to Greece, which reminded everyone of Austria's ultimatum to Serbia, was another case where a great power sought to impose its will on a small state by the threat and use of force. Less than a decade before, such an action had led to the World War. If so dangerous an action was allowed to stand, the situation would soon revert to the one that produced that war. If the victorious powers meant to preserve what they had won they needed to perform their function as guardians of the peace. If aggression was neither deterred nor punished, nothing was safe. The French ought to have understood this, but their obsession with the danger from Germany prevented them from looking beyond the moment.

Britain's deepest interests required a stand against aggression. The best course would have been to rally the League of Nations as the center of resistance to international bullying and begin to turn it into a useful weapon for preserving the peace. Failing that, the British should have tried to act, in concert with France, if possible, but finally they should have acted alone, if necessary. They undoubtedly had the naval power needed to compel Mussolini to back down, but the severe cuts in their forces made it a more difficult procedure than it should have been and provided an excuse for inaction. Deterring or defeating Mussolini in 1923 would have been easy. Each passing year, as British power declined and as memories of British strength and determination gave way to the perception of British weakness, inaction and lack of will would make it more difficult to act against him and other disturbers of the peace.

For Mussolini the outcome of the affair was more than satisfactory. If he wanted to take permanent control of Corfu the brief collaboration of France and Britain had thwarted him. That bothered him, and privately he said "he would not forgive the British for making him back down."[77] Over time, however, he came to see the affair as a great victory. He "remained convinced, as he declared every year afterwards, that the Corfu incident had been the most beautiful page in his foreign policy activity in these first years of his government."[78] With his control of the press and his great skills as a propagandist he soon convinced the rest of Italy. "The impression of Corfu remained in Fascist historiography as a great international triumph for Mussolini." In November 1923 he told the Roman Senate, "You should not believe that the occupation of Corfu took place only as a means of compelling Greece to accept our conditions. It also took place to increase the prestige of Italy."[79] Internally, the Corfu affair did him enormous good: "among Italians, liberals as well as conservatives, the first example of violence on an international scale won him a useful reputation for courage and patriotic zeal." The Fascist press spoke of it as "a magnificent display of strength . . . and a first step in conquering for Italy a place in the sun."[80] It helped solidify his popularity in the country and, thereby, helped free this low-born interloper from the constraints Italy's upper-class professional diplomats tried to impose upon him.

The affair at Corfu, moreover, at once emboldened him externally. "He believed he had achieved a great success, which encouraged him to begin one of his personal actions in the conduct of our relations with Yugoslavia."[81] For some time Italy and Yugoslavia had disputed possession of the city of Fiume. In 1922 the Treaty of Rapallo established it as an autonomous state. On September 16, when it had become clear that Britain would not use force in his conflict with Greece, Mussolini appointed an Italian general as military governor of Fiume "and simply took over the city."[82] No one raised a whisper of objection. The lesson he learned from the events of September 1923 was that "the other states of Europe would not stand together against a treaty-breaker, and that by control of the newspapers he could at any time rally opinion in Italy in favour of bullying a smaller and weaker state."[83]

For the League of Nations the Corfu affair was a terrible blow. In the midst of the crisis, when its outcome was clear, its Secretary-General, Sir Eric Drummond, spelled out the significance of what was taking place. Its lofty goals required practical implementation. If it was to keep the peace it needed not only to help resolve disputes peacefully "but also to . . . build up a tradition and a practice that will prevent dangerous disputes from developing in the future." To that end the League must preserve its moral authority and create "a general confidence that the clear and precise obligations of the covenant will be loyally fulfilled and carried out." The crisis had weakened and undermined both of these elements:

> A powerful member of the League has refused to carry out its treaty obligations under the Covenant, and has succeeded in doing so with impunity, some might even say, with an increase in its prestige . . . the authority of the League has been challenged in a sphere which is precisely that for which it was created, and . . . this challenge has brought into question the fundamental principles which lie at the root of

public law of the new world order established by the League. . . . Until they are re-established in the minds of Governments and peoples, there will be a sense of uncertainty which will rapidly disintegrate the power of the League.[84]

There can be no doubt that his assessment was correct. "Only three years after its establishment as the body to avert and deter war, and punish aggression, the League had abdicated its responsibilities following a threat by one of its members."[85]

For Britain in 1923 the Corfu affair was a minor affair, its true character publicly denied, its significance ignored, the incident itself brushed aside and quickly forgotten. Its weakness at Corfu undid what little had been achieved by its stand at Chanak. In letting the League down both Britain and France undermined an instrument whose success would have served chiefly their own interests. International order, public law, deterrence of violent actions, all served the victors in the war and the status quo they had established, and a proper understanding of that long-term benefit ought to have led both Britain and France to smack down Mussolini and defend the League in their own behalf. Britain's leaders, moreover, were embarrassed by what had taken place. In a letter to Crewe, without conceding his own culpability, Curzon admitted that the penalty imposed on Greece was "unjust and in reality indefensible." The Italians had been bribed to go away. "To such a pitch of immorality," he said, "have we sunk."[86] What Curzon said in private was apparent to all interested observers. In the Corfu incident Britain had behaved dishonorably. In the judgment of an admiring subordinate, Curzon's "hesitation over the Corfu incident damaged our prestige in Europe and the world."[87] Everyone, including Mussolini, believed the British had the military power to humiliate him and compel him to back down. They had failed to do so, either because their power was inadequate, after all, or because they lacked the will to use it. In international relations dishonorable behavior by a great power carries a practical price.

Part of that price is the strengthening of dissatisfied powers who are prepared to overthrow the order of the world in their own interests by violence or its threat. So it was with Mussolini after Corfu.

The tragedy of the Corfu crisis . . . was that it in no way denied Mussolini the fruits of his aggression. The Duce retired from this perilous adventure unscathed and with his prestige enhanced. The incident . . . gave Mussolini the reputation of a dangerous international firebrand and strengthened his position in subsequent Balkan negotiations. In a dramatic way it was an announcement that a vigorous Italy under a new and dynamic leadership had begun to play a more important role in world affairs. . . . In Rome, the Corfu settlement produced the greatest contempt for the League and all that the League system personified, an attitude seen again a decade later in Hitler's Germany.[88]

Scholars, with the benefit of after-knowledge, have pointed out the consequences of the affair at Corfu. Because of what it revealed about the League of Nations and the Western Powers, some have compared it with the Japanese occupation of Manchuria. "In 1931 the Japanese government repeated in Manchuria on a much vaster scale what Mussolini had done at Corfu in 1923."[89] Others connect Corfu with Italy's adventure in Abyssinia in 1935:

> Corfu was not merely the harbinger of a policy and methods which became apparent in the 1930s in a general way; it constituted a veritable dress rehearsal of Mussolini's quarrel with the League over Ethiopia in 1935. Both times Italy aspired to annex territory. Both times when the League was called on to defend the integrity of one of its smaller members, first France and then Britain sought a solution by undercutting and bypassing the League. . . . But in both cases the loser was the League of Nations and its status as an agent of collective security. More than any other individual Mussolini was responsible for the collapse of the League; Ethiopia was the climax of the erosion begun at Corfu.[90]

The author of the fullest study of the Corfu affair draws even more sinister conclusions. France's determination to deal with current items of national interest and to ignore larger considerations helped persuade Britain to reverse its championship of collective security. "But Britain's defeat and France's pyrrhic victory undermined the very settlement they were committed to uphold; this was the beginning of that long road that fifteen years later ended at Munich."[91]

6

The Search for Security

A much larger problem lay behind Britain's troubled relations with its erstwhile ally France, which had so greatly hampered British policy in the Near East and in the Corfu affair. The British had never come to grips with the need to guarantee France's security against a future attack by Germany. In the absence of such a guarantee the French were fearful and resentful, displaying attitudes and pursuing policies that annoyed and hampered the British. The challenge of establishing a peaceful and confident Europe, paving the way for prosperity and stability, was made immensely more difficult by the complicated and uncomfortable relationship between the two powers on which the responsibility most fully rested.

The division between Britain and France began to emerge immediately, during negotiations over the peace treaty after the Great War. The most critical problem facing postwar Europe remained the future of Germany. Even with the losses imposed by the Treaty of Versailles it remained Europe's largest and most populous nation west of Russia, with a well-educated, disciplined, highly skilled people and a higher birth rate than victorious France. Relatively, it was potentially even more powerful than before the war, since Russia, in the form of the Soviet Union, devastated by military defeat and social revolution, had been driven out of Europe, and both the Habsburg and Ottoman empires were gone.

These facts threatened the future security of the victorious powers and the settlement they were making. Something needed to be done to contain the power that Germany was otherwise certain to recover. One obvious possibility would have been to dismantle Germany and rearrange it in such a way as might

NORWAY
SWEDEN
FINLAND
ESTONIA
GREAT BRITAIN
DENMARK
POLISH CORRIDOR
LATVIA
LITHUANIA
SOVIET UNION
NETH.
GERMANY
EAST PRUSSIA
Cologne
BEL.
RHINELAND
POLAND
Eupen
LUX.
SAAR
Pilsen
CZECHOSLOVAKIA
Rhine R.
BOHEMIA
ALSACE-LORRAINE
FRANCE
AUSTRIA
HUNGARY
ROMANIA
ITALY
YUGOSLAVIA
BULGARIA
TURKEY

THE SEARCH FOR SECURITY

Mediterranean Sea

prevent its resurgence. Such division of territory in disregard of ethnic considerations was commonplace in Europe from the seventeenth to early in the nineteenth century. Even after the cult of nationalism had been born in the French
Revolution, similar segmentations had taken place. Germany had separated the
Danes of northern Schleswig from Denmark in 1864 and then incorporated the
people of Alsace-Lorraine, Frenchmen at least since the seventeenth century,
without a qualm. Germany had been only a geographical expression until less
than a half century before. Why should it not be dismembered?[1] The French
plan for establishing a separate Rhenish republic as a buffer state made consid-

erable sense from the traditional point of view of establishing a durable balance of power and was no more outrageous than the annexation of Alsace-Lorraine had been in 1871.

At the peace conference the French stubbornly argued for making the Rhine Germany's western frontier on thoroughly strategic grounds: "what happened in 1914 was possible only for one reason; Germany, because of her mastery over offensive preparations made by her on the left bank of the river, thought herself capable of crushing the democracies, France and Belgium, before the latter could receive the aid of the overseas democracies, Britain, the Dominions and the United States." Peace in the future, therefore, required a common guarantee against an attack from Germany, but "[t]his guarantee cannot be completely assured, either by the limitation or the suppression of Germany's military power or by the proposed clauses of the Covenant of the League of Nations . . . [it can be found] only in the fixation at the Rhine of the western frontier of Germany and in the occupation of the bridges by an international force." They suggested a plan for an "independent Rhineland" and included a study of its economic consequences.[2] The British member of the committee receiving the French memorandum rejected the idea firmly. "England," he said, "is opposed both to a permanent Army and to the use of British troops outside of English territory." He predicted conflicts resulting from an independent Rhenish state and warned, "If war results from these conflicts, neither England nor her Dominions will have that deep feeling of solidarity with France which animated them in the last war."[3] The fundamental and stubborn difference between British and French attitudes thus revealed itself at once in 1919 and continued even after the outbreak of World War II.

In spite of British and American resistance the French refused to yield. The only way they could be made to agree to the Peace of Versailles was by a compromise that pleased neither side. France received Alsace-Lorraine and the right to work the coal mines of the Saar for fifteen years. To compensate for the rejected buffer state, Germany west of the Rhine and fifty kilometers east of it was permanently to be a demilitarized zone, and Allied troops on the west bank could stay there for fifteen years. Most important of all, the stipulation without which French agreement would not have been given, the treaty provided that Britain and the United States would guarantee to aid France if it was attacked by Germany. The bill containing the guarantee swept through the House of Commons with no more than one dissenting vote.[4]

Britain's promise, however, was contingent on America's ratification of the guarantee. That assured the British that they would not need to carry out its duties alone. They did not, moreover, imagine that they would ever need to meet that responsibility, thinking that the other peace terms would be enough to keep the Germans quiet. "The original British conception was that of a stopgap insurance policy, which could be surrendered when the world returned to 'normality' after the postwar upheavals."[5] The French, on the other hand, grasped at the guarantee as a permanent substitute for the territorial security an independent Rhenish state would have given them. The compromise achieved, therefore, was worse than inadequate. "[T]he frictions between Britain and France engendered by the left bank question, British mistrust of French imperialism and French lack of confidence in British understanding of strategic realities, acted as the solvents of the Franco-British accord, an accord which, with the eventual defection from the peace settlement of the United States, alone stood against the military revival of Germany."[6] When the American Senate refused to ratify the Versailles Treaty, which contained the guarantee, the British allowed their promise to lapse as well.

British advocates of the guarantee would later demand a new one by Britain alone on the grounds of honor. As a French ambassador sent to London in 1922 said, "Our English friends keep in their hearts or consciences, like an intolerable weight, this breach of promise, as they say, a saying that means, across the Channel, the breaking of a promise of marriage. Often, people from every milieu, including members of the Cabinet, Lloyd George told me, say 'We must do something for France.'"[7] One of the reasons given to the House of Commons by Lloyd George in 1922 for considering a new guarantee to France made a similar point:

> This undertaking was given by us in the course of the negotiations at Versailles in order to counter what is known as the advanced Rhine policy, a policy which proposed that there shall be something in the nature of annexation of territory on the left bank of the Rhine in order to avoid what we regarded as a permanent disaster to the whole of Europe. I myself and President Wilson gave the guarantee, and upon it that policy was abandoned. I think the consideration having been paid by France, we are in honour bound.[8]

In the course of the debate one member dealt with the excuse that America's defection had ended Britain's obligation:

> It never occurred to me as possible that because the President of the United States, having himself signed it, found it impossible to get a ratification in the Senate, we should draw back and say to France, "It is quite true we promised to protect you against a gross outrage, it is quite true we said our reason was you are a gallant people, who had suffered so severely, that we could not bear to think that so great a wrong should be inflicted upon you again. After all those are fine words and when we see a loophole of escape we are going to leave you in the lurch."[9]

There is much to be said for these arguments, but they had no effect on British policy until more practical considerations moved the British Government in 1921 to think again about the problem of French security. The British believed that the restoration of their trade and prosperity depended on the economic recovery of Germany, which, they thought, required the reduction or elimination of reparations payments and the withdrawal of allied troops from the Ruhr and the Rhineland. To an imperial conference in 1921 Lord Curzon said: ". . . our policy is frankly the re-establishment of Germany as a stable state in Europe. She is necessary with her great population, her natural resources, with her prodigious strengths of character. . . . : and any idea of obliterating Germany from the comity of nations or treating her as an outcast is not only ridiculous but insane."[10]

France, devastated, alone, and fearful, stood in the way. The French, as we have seen, also presented problems in the Near East, making it difficult for the British to achieve many of their goals in foreign policy. To some British leaders it seemed that French fear of Germany and resentment at Britain's defections stood behind these difficulties. They thought that if Britain were to provide France with the guarantee promised at Versailles or even a full alliance, these difficulties might dissolve.

By late 1921 these views began to have some effect. In anticipation of a conference between the Allies in London in February, Sir Eyre Crowe, Permanent Under-Secretary of State in the Foreign Office, suggested a course of action to his chief, Lord Curzon. He feared that without some general settlement of the German question to suit France, Britain might face "a definite breach, with France," which "cannot be contemplated without grave anxiety." Britain did not have good relations with any of the European powers or the United States at a time when the empire was threatened with dangers around the world. All these troubles would be alleviated "[i]f we could at this juncture reconstitute, or if possible fortify, the solidarity of the entente with France." Although the forthcoming conference would deal with disarmament and reparations, these were only symptoms of the basic trouble.

What is ultimately in the French mind is . . . the apprehension that within a measurable time there will arise on the other side of the French frontier a new Germany rapidly returning to a position approaching her former strength, while France, exhausted by the war and with a stationary population, will be powerless to meet the rivalry of a neighbour thirsting for revenge. It was this feeling which inspired all the French attempts to extend the French frontiers to the Rhine. It will be remembered that these attempts were only definitely given up at the Peace Conference when Great Britain and the United States offered France a military and naval guarantee against a new German attack. . . . It is for consideration whether we should not look for the key of the situation, so far as our relations with France are concerned, in the definite conclusion of that so far abortive agreement. If we came forward with an offer to give definite security to France against a fresh German attack . . . the French would be disposed to prove far more conciliatory, not only in matters where she can make concessions to British interests in the East, and perhaps elsewhere, but also in regard to her attitude towards Germany herself.[11]

Crowe's suggestion did not come before the Cabinet, and relations with France grew worse. There were disagreements about the disposition of Silesia, about Tangier, about policy in Turkey and the French treatment of Germany. Considerable friction also arose at the Washington Conference on disarmament, where the British complained of the great size of the French army and were especially troubled by French plans for a large fleet of submarines. This led some to intensify the quarrel with strong anti-French statements, but it led others to take another tack. Viscount Arthur Lee, First Lord of the Admiralty, for instance, suggested a renewal of the prewar guarantee by the British navy to protect the French coast as a better way of gaining French cooperation.[12]

At an imperial conference in July 1921, Winston Churchill pursued a similar line. The goal was "to get an appeasement of the fearful hatreds and antagonisms which exist in Europe and to enable the world to settle down," and "a greater assurance to France" was the way to achieve those goals. The failure to ratify the guarantee promised in the peace negotiations had produced a natural fear "which this poor mutilated, impoverished France has of this mighty Germany which is growing up on the other side of the Rhine." He presented the picture as the French saw it.

> The French say, well we are left alone; we are left to shift for ourselves. We have not a friend in the world except Belgium, Little Belgium is with us. England has not come in; America has not; and we have not got the line of the Rhine; therefore we must have Poland. We must have Poland on our side, and make of Poland a counterpoise to the enormous millions growing up against us in Germany. They look at it in a feverish and anxious state of mind, and in this mood they approach the seizure of the Ruhr Valley. The seizure of military positions is more and more in the minds of the French military party, and these military men have matters very much in their own hands because France is alone. They can say "we (France) have the only army worth anything; now we can march where we will and take any securities we like, but if we wait, where shall we be?"

He favored good and close relations between Britain and Germany but pointed out that these would produce fear and suspicion among the French. The best answer, he thought, was a British alliance with France, even without the United States, which "bound the British Empire to protect France against unprovoked aggression." That would give Britain greater freedom to work with Germany in the reconstruction of Europe,

> and it might well be that being at once the Ally of France and the friend of Germany, we might be in a position to mitigate the frightful rancor and fear and hatred which exist between France and Germany at the present time and which, if left unchecked, will most certainly in a generation or so bring about a renewal of the struggle of which we have just witnessed the conclusion.[13]

This suggestion bore no fruit, but toward the end of the year the French raised the subject of an alliance themselves. Their plans for security contained several elements, all of which were at odds with British desires. On both economic and ideological grounds the British wanted general disarmament, but the French meant to retain military dominance on the continent while preventing German rearmament. To balance German numerical and eventual industrial superiority France wanted to be sure of the security of her allies on Germany's eastern borders, Poland and the Little Entente states of Czechoslovakia, Yugoslavia, and Rumania. The French would also have liked a British military guarantee against German aggression, not only against France in the west but also against her eastern allies, but the British shrank from any commitment in Central Europe.

In a conversation with Curzon on December 5, 1921, the French ambassador, St-Aulaire, on his own initiative, introduced the subject of a general alliance between their countries that would provide mutual guarantees against attacks direct or indirect. Aristide Briand, the French Prime Minister, pursued the matter in a talk with Lloyd George. What he had in mind was "a very broad Alliance in which the two Powers would guarantee each other's interests in all parts of the world, act closely together in all things and go to each other's assistance whenever these things were threatened." Lloyd George replied that a British guarantee of France against a direct attack by Germany was possible, but "Great Britain was hardly prepared for so broad an undertaking as that." The British would not be willing to take part in quarrels involving such places as Silesia, Danzig, or Poland. "There was a general reluctance to get mixed up in these questions in any way. The British people felt that the populations in that quarter of Europe were unstable and excitable; they might start fighting at any time and the rights and wrongs of the dispute might be very hard to disentangle."[14] Briand suggested that a general pact could, in time, include other nations, Germany among them, and could serve as a general organization that could preserve the peace of Europe.

> If other nations felt that France and Great Britain were firmly united to maintain peace and order, peace will not be threatened soon again, and

Germany would find it to her advantage to join them. That very fact would block the way to reactionary forces in Germany by making unassailable the order of things they wished to challenge. Some such understanding between Great Britain and France would prevent the Germans from formulating designs against the people on their frontiers. With such a guarantee, the Germans would probably give up militarist designs, for example on Poland and Russia. It would help German democracy to provide facilities for the return of Germany to the community of nations and generally tend to stabilise Europe for a long period.[15]

Lloyd George agreed to discuss the matter further with Briand at Cannes before the next conference, scheduled to be held there in January 1922. In preparation for that meeting, Curzon wrote a memorandum expressing his views on the proposed alliance that reveals much about the attitude of many British leaders. Although he came down firmly against an alliance, he carefully listed its potential advantages as well as its disadvantages. There was no doubt about its advantages, which would be "immediate, continuing and almost immeasurable in value." It would free Great Britain "from the ever-present and formidable menace of a German war of revenge—a revenge which it requires small knowledge of the German character to be sure that the country will systematically and relentlessly pursue so long as she has a chance of success." That would allow a reduction in armaments and their expense and permit a swifter return to economic prosperity for France and Europe. That, of course, would be good for Britain, but the benefit to the British would be far greater than that. All the disturbances roiling Europe sprang from "the fear of a resuscitated and revengeful Germany," which "is so ruinous to trade, so fatal to exchanges and such an irritant poison in the relations between France and this country. What nation and what Government would not be willing to pay a heavy price to exorcise such a spectre and to return to the only condition under which Europe can rebuild its shattered existence?" Germany, "though assuredly destined to recover," could not threaten the peace if France and Britain stood together. "A definite and publicly announced agreement between the two countries to stand by one another in case either were attacked would offer a guarantee of peace of the strongest kind."

No French leader could have stated the case from a mutual defensive alliance more strongly, yet Curzon came down against it. Why? The French, he argued, had far more to gain from such an alliance than the British. The threat to them was great and would surely require British military assistance, while it was hard to imagine where in the world French forces might be needed and able to defend British territory. France, in fact, was Britain's likeliest enemy in imperial matters. An alliance would eliminate that problem, "but for such a result the price of a defensive alliance would be exorbitant." Besides, Curzon questioned France's suitability as an ally. Even though British opinion, as expressed in the press and elsewhere, had never been so friendly to France, "there has rarely been a period when British policy and British statesmen were more coarsely or vindictively assailed in the French press." Such a time "seems to be hardly propitious for the creation of a much closer union."

French ministries, moreover, were notoriously unstable. Sometimes they conducted foreign policy in such a way as to shore up their domestic situation rather than with sincerity. French statesmen, even those as friendly as Briand, could not be trusted. Even as they offered friendship to Britain they took such actions as the recent treaty with Turkey behind the British back. Could "the man or the men who cannot be true to an entente . . . be faithful to an alliance?" In fact, at that moment all over the world the French were conducting policies in their own selfish interests inconsistent or even hostile to British interests. "You cannot pledge yourself to go to the assistance of a man with all your resources, in the event of his being attacked, if in the interval he is always delivering stealthy and surreptitious attacks upon you."

These were not satisfactory reasons against an alliance that, presumably, would eliminate precisely such complaints, and they were not the real ones. Curzon conceded as much in turning to difficulties he described as "of a more profound or formidable character." The first was that an alliance with France would be seen as a return to the old system of alliances that was widely believed to be the cause of great wars in general and the recent war in particular. This would occur just when "such arrangements were believed to have been superseded by the newer conceptions embodied in the League of Nations, in international courts and conferences, and in the theory of corporate action as opposed to the rival groupings of Powers." This would alienate other European states, especially Italy, and also the United States.

Besides, such a commitment would not be accepted either by Parliament or the British people.

> A proposal . . . to commit this country to go to war again—not for a narrowly defined and easily intelligible object, such as the defense of the eastern frontier of France, *which is also the external frontier of Britain* [emphasis added]—but for objects which it will be difficult to define in words, and in contingencies which, though unlikely to arise, cannot be described as impossible, will, I think, excite in many quarters the gravest disappointment and alarm.

Victory in the Great War had brought a feeling "widely preached and passionately believed, that an era of general peace had set in, and that wars in the future would be banished by the operation of the League of Nations." The possibility and reality of British troops being involved in various trouble spots since 1920 had led to their withdrawal from the Caucuses, Persia, and

Mesopotamia, "where their presence was regarded as implying a continuance of hostilities rather than the maintenance of peace." A French alliance, therefore, would bring "a feeling of profound mistrust, if not worse, at the acceptance of fresh warlike commitments; and this will be enhanced by the fear that a treaty of alliance with France may drag us into a war in which direct British interests are not involved, and which might have been avoided had not our ally been encouraged to take up an unbending attitude [by the alliance]."

A final argument against an alliance rested on the fundamentally different spirit in which the two nations conducted diplomacy. It was the British way to try "to deal with the current problems of diplomacy, as they arise, on the merits of the particular case," while the French subordinated "even the most trivial issues to general considerations of expediency, based on far-reaching plans for the relentless promotion of French prestige and the gratification of private, generally monetary and often sordid interests or ambitions, only too frequently pursued with a disregard of ordinary rules of straightforward and loyal dealings which is repugnant and offensive to normal British instincts." If the self-satisfied, anti-French rhetoric is ignored, Curzon was distinguishing the French attempt to pursue a consistent policy based on an estimate of lasting national needs and strategic realities with the British liking for "splendid isolation" without entangling obligations, for a return to the prewar policy of the "free hand" pursued by Lord Grey down to the war. Two nations, said Curzon, with such divergent approaches could not be satisfactory allies.

In light of the French request, however, and the Prime Minister's willingness to discuss it, Curzon was prepared to go part of the way. He would consider returning to the guarantee of France against an unprovoked attack by Germany promised by Britain at Versailles in 1919. But even that offer should be contingent on the French clearing up all British complaints against them around the world. "I earnestly hope," said Curzon, "it will not be proposed to give the guarantee for nothing."[16]

The Cannes conference met chiefly to deal with the question of economic recovery that was at the center of Lloyd George's approach to Britain's foreign policy. In his conversations with Briand about security issues and the proposed alliance he repeatedly brought the discussion around to them, expressing great determination. He made it a condition of any such agreement that "Great Britain and France should march together for the economic and financial reconstruction of Europe. They would be able to carry this much further if the United States came in, but failing the United States he was convinced that France and Great Britain must take the initiative."[17] He did not show the same initiative and determination in seeking a diplomatic and military accord. He was not prepared to offer an alliance of mutual defense, but only a reaffirmation of the guarantee against an unprovoked attack on France by Germany. He firmly opposed the French desire for the protection of Poland as part of the preservation of the Versailles settlement. The British people, he declared, would consider no commitment except to France. "They would not undertake responsibilities in Eastern and Central Europe, in which their interest is necessarily small."[18] The British "did not understand the necessity of fighting for Poland and Czechoslovakia and they would never allow themselves to be concerned in an alliance with liabilities of that kind."[19]

Several days later the French presented a memorandum containing their views. They did not want a unilateral guarantee but a reciprocal agreement of mutual defense. Beyond that, they wanted the British guarantee to cover not only French soil but also the demilitarized zone of the Rhineland. They also wanted the two countries to take action together in case Germany should violate the military clauses of the Versailles Treaty. Since these actions would involve joint military actions, the French wanted an agreement regulating the strength of their respective military forces. Finally, they wanted an agreement to act in concert when any question threatened the general peace.[20]

Lloyd George told Briand clearly that the British wanted only a guarantee, not a mutual alliance. The draft treaty the Prime Minister sent to London for the Cabinet's approval provided for British assistance to France only "in the event of direct and unprovoked aggression *against the soil of France*" (emphasis added). The guarantee would jointly be extended to Belgium. Should the Germans threaten the demilitarization of the Rhineland or violate the military clauses of the Versailles Treaty, Britain would agree only to consult with the French. The French would have liked a treaty for thirty years; Lloyd George's draft specified ten.[21]

For a variety of reasons, one of them being criticism by the President of the French Republic of his Prime Minister's negotiations at Cannes, Briand resigned on January 12, 1922, bringing the conference to an end. He was replaced by Raymond Poincaré, former President of the Republic, a man from the restored province of Lorraine, a hard bargainer, deeply distrustful of the Germans and suspicious of the British, who pursued French interests with ferocity and an insistence on clarity and precision. Yet, except for this insistence, his position was not different from Briand's. Lloyd George met him in Paris on his way home on January 14, and the differences between the two sides were quickly apparent. Poincaré emphasized the importance of a reciprocal guarantee supported by a military convention, without which, he pointed out, a guarantee would have little value. Lloyd George replied that the guarantee would be backed by whatever forces Britain had in being, as well as the reserves trained in the late war. The dominions, he asserted, would never agree in advance to provide armed forces. Poincaré said that joint plans regularly reviewed by the General Staffs, backed by a reference in the treaty, would suffice. What, after all, would be the value of a British guarantee if Britain decided to disarm entirely? Lloyd George ignored that question; he would not pledge Britain to any stated military strength. The conversation seems to have become heated, and the British Prime Minister stood on his wounded dignity: "If the word of the British people was not sufficient for France, he feared the draft treaty must be withdrawn. The British people would honour their pledge, if France were attacked, with the whole of their strength, but they would never bind themselves by military conventions as to the forces which they would maintain in present conditions during a time of peace." Unperturbed, Poincaré said he did not doubt Britain's word but asked how France could decide on what forces she needed without knowing the resources of her ally. Lloyd George blustered that it was absurd to talk about such things when Germany was disarmed. If the Germans revived there would be plenty of time to make military conventions then.[22]

The French then prepared a new draft of their own, which Ambassador St-Aulaire took to Curzon. It differed very little from their previous positions, providing for a reciprocal guarantee against unprovoked aggression in which not merely "the soil of France" but also the Rhineland was to be protected. In case of:

> threat of violation, or breach of the military, naval, or air clauses of the Treaty of Versailles; there would be constant staff contacts; and the two governments would consult on all questions of a nature to endanger peace or jeopardise the order established by the peace treaties, and would examine together measures to ensure a quick, peaceful and equitable solution. The two countries were to concert together in case of any solution. The treaty was to last for thirty years and be renewable.

St-Aulaire explained some of the provisions in accompanying notes. He conceded that at the moment Germany was in no condition to attack France or Britain. "There was little doubt," however, "that she would invade Poland or Czechoslovakia, or absorb Austria, if she thought she could do so with impunity, and success would give her new strength which would be turned against the west later." Another note considered in detail different scenarios that might or might not be violations of the clauses in the Versailles Treaty dealing with the Rhineland. The main conclusion was that "if German forces actually went in, either without asking permission or after it had been refused, it would be a violation and the *casus foederis* would arise. Such a provision was essential if the protection afforded by the demilitarization of the Rhineland was to be real."[23]

These arguments had little force with the British leaders. Curzon was willing to grant the French reciprocity of guarantees and to consider a duration of a treaty for more than ten years, but he recommended rejection of any guarantee that covered the Rhineland and of any mention of staff conversations in any form lest it suggest a military commitment. Further discussions within the Foreign Office did not change the direction of British policy. Neither Curzon nor Lloyd George was eager to move quickly, both thinking it best to hold the pact out as a lure to get the French to make concessions on other matters. The Prime

Minister wanted French cooperation in a forthcoming conference at Genoa meant to bring Soviet Russia into the European economic sphere; the Foreign Secretary wanted French cooperation in Turkey. They did not coordinate their strategy, and time passed without further discussion of the proposed treaty.

The conference at Genoa failed in its purpose, and, worse than that, the Russians and Germans went off in mid-conference to sign a treaty at nearby Rapallo. The French were angry and more fearful than ever, even as a new crisis over German failure to pay reparations loomed. Poincaré responded with threats and strong language that angered the British. Enthusiasm for any pact waned. When the French raised the question again at the end of May, they were told that outstanding disagreements between the two countries, including the Turkish question and the character of European reconstruction, must be settled before a treaty could be concluded. Poincaré said the French were prepared to settle the other issues but that including the reconstruction of Europe on the list amounted to an indefinite postponement. He also revealed the weakness of the British effort to use the prospect of a limited guarantee as a bargaining chip to achieve other purposes. Without the provisions required by France a pact with Britain was of little value: "the pact in the limited form preferred by Britain was of no importance to him since Britain, in her own interest, would always come to the assistance of France and Belgium if German aggression took place whether there was a pact of not. Britain was giving nothing and expected obedience in all things from France in return."[24] That exchange effectively ended negotiations for an Anglo-French treaty. Disagreements over reparations at a London conference in August and the French invasion of the Ruhr on January 23, 1923 left the entente shattered and made further talks inconceivable.

For France the failure was yet another blow to her efforts to preserve her security against the future rise of a vengeful Germany, but it was a fateful defeat for British interests, as well. To be sure, the chief British purpose seems to have been to gain French concessions on other matters in return for very little of substance. Britain was not prepared to defend France in the ways that really mattered: to guarantee the demilitarization of the Rhineland, to protect Poland and Czechoslovakia, to maintain a military force adequate to deter even a German attack against French soil, to engage in military cooperation with the French without which serious deterrence was impossible. As a keen student of the negotiations puts it, "the British Government never intended the guarantee to be militarily meaningful. It was conceived as a political gesture, partly to pay an obligation outstanding since 1919 but chiefly to induce France to fall in with British policy elsewhere."[25] British policy need not have failed even in that short-sighted goal had the government been more serious about achieving success. No one can say what might have been the positive effect if Britain had held to its guarantee in 1919, even after the Americans reneged. Certainly, relations between France and Britain could hardly have been much worse in the years down to 1923. Even so late as 1922 a British alliance or guarantee might have produced greater French cooperation, in spite of the real differences between the two countries. "The number of occasions, in 1919, in 1924, and in 1925, when French Governments of different complexions, faced with the choice between gaining British support and pursuing French interests single-handed, chose Britain, suggests that the same might have been the case in 1922."[26]

The collapse of negotiations was far more damaging in Britain's long-range interests. Except when exercised or when they used the French bogey as a calculated weapon in argument, Britain's leaders knew that France neither would nor could pose any threat to their islands' security. The only plausible threat could come from a rejuvenated Germany that defeated France, gained control of the channel ports in France and the Low Countries, and could then launch aerial attacks on Britain which could make a successful invasion possible. Even an armchair strategist could understand that in the new circumstances Britain's frontier was no longer on the channel but on the Rhine, as Curzon conceded. The German menace was the only one that could directly threaten British safety. Should that threat recur, Britain's security rested on a powerful France with an army strong enough to keep the Germans away from the Channel. Demography demonstrated that France could not do that job for long without considerable help. What Britain ought to have required was not merely a marginal advantage for the French but one so clearly invincible as to deter any attempt by Germany to achieve its goals by force or its threat. German disarmament could not be maintained forever, any more than its temporary economic and financial weakness. A recovered and rearmed Germany could be restrained only with difficulty. The most important element of such restraint was to deprive the Germans of a launching platform in the Rhineland for an invasion of France and the Low Countries. British security, therefore, rested on the permanent demilitarization of the Rhineland. Another important element was the threat that if the Germans attacked in the west they would face a second front in the east by Poland and Czechoslovakia. A third element was a clear and irrevocable commitment by Britain, backed by adequate military forces, to send a sufficient British army to the continent in case of a German military move into the Rhineland, or a German attack on the Low Countries, France, or its eastern allies.

If anything could have deterred a German war of revenge, it would have been a policy pursuing that strategy. Even one that omitted France's Central European allies but guaranteed the west and backed up the guarantee with adequate military forces and cooperation with France could well have been enough. This latter policy was the one supported by the British advocates of a French alliance. There is good reason to think that they were right in believing that a France reassured by solid British support might take a more reasonable attitude in their areas of conflict with Britain and in their dealings with Germany. Their harsh demands and strong measures in regard to reparations and other questions made perfect sense in a situation in which they were alone against an inevitably stronger enemy which their erstwhile allies were helping to recover its strength with frightening speed. In that situation they must depend for survival on maintaining their own power and depriving the Germans of theirs. Had the British followed a different course, the French would surely have acted differently, and the course of European history must have taken a very different direction.

It might be thought that the dangers of a future war begun by Germany could not be visible in the 1920s or at least until the rise of Hitler in 1933 but are the product of hindsight, yet there is striking evidence that these developments could readily be foreseen. As we have seen, Eyre Crowe foresaw that if Britain did not act to allay French fears the result would be increased estrangement between the Allies and increased hostility between France and Germany. Churchill was even more clear, foreseeing another great war with Germany. St-Aulaire predicted the steps on the road to World War II with almost perfect precision.

British military leaders and statesmen repeatedly warned of the danger over the next decade. In 1924, Herriot, the new French Prime Minister, again raised the question of a guarantee and an alliance with the new British Labour government. The British General Staff provided a long commentary, observing that "under conditions as they are now and are likely to be for many years to come German aggression is the greatest danger that faces us, and French security is our security."[27] Earlier in that same year the General Staff had favorably considered the question of an alliance with France. That would only acknowledge the fact that Britain could not avoid fighting alongside France if Germany attacked again, but it would also have significant advantages. It would bolster French resolve, permit closer staff contacts and the exchange of military information, and "would give Britain the great advantage of having definitely enlisted the most powerful army and air force in Europe as a screen between herself and Germany."[28] The General Staff was well aware that for the moment Germany was too weak to defend itself against the Allies, much less to undertake aggression, but it had no trouble seeing ahead. The Germans greatly outnumbered the French already, and the advantage would grow in the next decade. They had plenty of industrial capacity to rearm. They must not be allowed to do so in peacetime. "In no circumstances," the General Staff said, "must the Allies be so supine as to sacrifice the initiative in a future war." The Allies, therefore, must keep control of Lorraine, of the Saar, too, for some time, and they must keep the Rhineland demilitarized. For all this France needed the moral and material support of Britain. The plain implication was that without such an alliance and such a policy there was grave danger of a future German war of aggression.

In January 1925 the new Foreign Secretary, Sir Austen Chamberlain, asked his subordinates to suggest a course of action providing for European security. "I see no prospect," he said,

> of the continuation of cordial relations with France in Europe or else-
> where unless we somehow give her a sense of security. Looking at Ger-
> many, I see no chance of her settling down to make the best of new
> conditions unless she is convinced that she cannot hope to divide the Al-
> lies or to challenge them with any success for as long a time as any man
> can look ahead. As long as Security is absent, Germany is tempted to pre-
> pare for the Revanche. "The Day" will still be the national toast and
> with far more reason, whilst French fears, goading France to every kind
> of irritating folly, will keep alive German hatred and lead us inevitably,
> sooner or later, to a new catastrophe.[29]

The most precise and fully argued prediction came from the pen of Sir James Headlam-Morley, Historical Adviser in the Foreign Office. In January 1922 he wrote a comparison between the situation in 1919 and that after the Napoleonic Wars a century earlier in regard to the question of guarantee treaties.[30] The comparison seemed to him apt. Concern for France's "revolutionary doctrines" in 1815 existed, as did concern about "German militarism" in 1919. Europe needed a guarantee against a new aggression by France just as it needed protection from "a fresh outburst of German militarism." Germany and Belgium needed guarantees of security in the earlier period as France did in the later. After 1814 the British made treaties with continental powers guaranteeing Europe against renewed French aggression, and they worked: "it was the policy—the continuance of the alliance as a potential weapon which, at any moment might become operative—by which, in fact, the peace of Europe was maintained, and the key to the whole system was the participation of Great Britain." By analogy, a treaty guaranteeing France against German aggression in 1922 could have the same result. The Foreign Office's Historical Adviser, however, pointed out an important difference:

> We can . . . give a guarantee against German aggression on the Rhine or
> through Belgium. But in the future the real danger may lie, not here, but
> rather on the eastern frontiers of Germany—Danzig, Poland, Czechoslo-
> vakia—for it is in these districts that the settlement of Paris would be,
> when the time came, most easily overthrown. But in these districts no
> military help would be available from this country, and this is one reason
> why it is impossible now to satisfy the demands of our French allies in
> the way in which a hundred years ago it was possible to satisfy the Prus-
> sians and the Austrians.[31]

In March 1925 he again addressed the problem of what Britain meant to do to defend France against a German aggression. "This," he said, "is a narrow and misleading point of view. It is an English as much as a French problem. We are concerned with it not merely as friends or allies of France, but because of our own interests. It is not only France, but England that we have to defend, and if we are concerned with the security of France and Belgium, it is because in this matter our interests are identical. The entente and alliance with France was not a cause of our concern in this problem but the result of it."[32] He traced Britain's involvement with the continent from the time of the Plantagenet kings, describing formal military commitments of guarantee and alliance with such states as Holland, Austria, and Prussia, among others. The danger to Britain of a single power dominating all Europe was always serious but was even more deadly in his own time when "the invention of the aeroplane and the airship go far to destroy the security of the island."[33] The future danger would come from a restored Germany. "If Germany were to recover her full military power, then, as in the past, the German army, occupying the country between Cologne, Aachen and Trèves, would be a spearhead directed at France and Belgium. It is the obvious dictate of wisdom and foresight to avoid this danger in the future." The best means for this purpose was indicated by a study of past success which pointed to "these old alliances [which] are in all essentials similar to the pact for the defence of France and Belgium, which has been under consideration during the last five years."

Headlam-Morley saw an opportunity to escape from the cycle of wars in history based not on the general principles on which the League of Nations rested but on strategic realities built into treaties that guaranteed frontiers backed by adequate forces. He hoped these could ultimately be spread to include all of Europe, but he was confident that a western alliance would work, "for it would be a general treaty for the preservation of peace and not a partial treaty in preparation for war." It might also be "a model and example towards which we could work when dealing with the other danger points of Europe." To be sure, Central and Eastern Europe were not yet ready for a similar pact, but there was hope that the Little Entente might be the base for such a development in the future. Paper agreements, however, were of no value: "a treaty of this kind is of no use, unless there is real force and power behind it." The key to success lay in British hands. "It is," he wrote, "on Great Britain and if necessary on the British Empire, that in the time of emergency the world must depend for the necessary force," and he explained why:

In this matter we have a very peculiar position. The whole arrangement is . . . of vital necessity to ourselves; on the other hand, we alone of all the nations concerned, have, and can have in the future, no direct territorial interests. It is therefore essential that the world should be made to understand that our accession to any such agreement will be the symbol of a firm resolution at all costs to enforce its observance. There must be no hedging, no justification for the suspicion that we might on some finesse of interpretation attempt to avoid our engagements. If, in signing a treaty of this kind, the Government have behind them the nation and the Empire, that will be the one sure means of avoiding war. No nation in the future will be willing to put itself in the position of Germany in 1914. . . . The world must understand that in the future, as in 1914, those in this country who are in principle most opposed to war, will actively and vigorously support a war undertaken in defence of law and justice against aggressive violence.[34]

The Foreign Office's Historical Adviser had written yet another memorandum the month before in which he confronted, without naming it, the "blue water" or "maritime" school of British strategists who had great vogue between the wars, "a party among us . . . who had advocated a complete separation from continental affairs, and have declared that it was not our duty to interfere in what did not concern us. Experience shows that if we are misled by advice of this kind the ultimate result is that we do not take steps in time to avert an impending danger, and are just for that reason forced into war." Their kind of thinking is what brought on the Great War of 1914. Britain had allowed its guarantee of Belgium, first made in 1839, to grow vague and uncertain. After 1897, Germany had adopted the Schlieffen Plan, entailing an attack on Belgium and probably Holland, made inescapably clear by the building of strategic railroads to mass troops on the Belgian frontier. This was "well known—it was in fact the common talk of Europe," yet not once before the war did any British authority warn the Germans off. "If we are equally remiss in the future, similar consequences will almost inevitably follow." Headlam-Morley asserted that "the paramount interest of this country requires that we should not allow Belgium or the North of France in any circumstances to fall under German control . . . , and in order to prevent this, the whole resources of the Empire must be used without stint." A guarantee of France and Belgium must include the demilitarized Rhineland, and the whole would be "analogous to the older system of barrier fortresses" that protected the Netherlands against the France of Louis XIV.[35]

All this could be done and depended only on the British adopting the right policy and backing it to the full. Once again, however, he faced the problem of the east. Geographical problems made it difficult if not impossible to intervene effectively there, yet "[i]t is in the real interest of this country to prevent a new alliance between Germany and Russia, *an alliance which would no doubt be cemented by an attack on Poland* [emphasis added]. We cannot now be indifferent if Germany breaks through upon the east and there begins to acquire a new accession of territory and strength which would inevitably in the future be brought to bear upon the Rhine." France's system of alliance with the small states of Central Europe was a good thing for that reason. To those who regarded Eastern Europe as not involving British interests and none of Britain's business, Headlam-Morley asked this question: "what would happen if there were to be a new partition of Poland, or if the Czechoslovak State were to be so curtailed and dismembered that in fact it disappeared from the map of Europe? The whole of Europe would be in chaos." He spelled out the nightmare in greater detail:

> Imagine, for instance, that under some improbable condition, Austria rejoined Germany; that Germany using the discontented minority in Bohemia, demanded a new frontier far from the mountains, including Carlsbad and Pilsen, and that at the same time, in alliance with Germany, the Hungarians recovered the southern slope of the Carpathians. This would be catastrophic, and even if we neglected to interfere in time to prevent it, we should afterwards be driven to interfere, probably too late.[36]

Though not prepared to make an alliance with these states, Headlam-Morley sought a more reliable device for protecting them than the League of Nations provided because "we cannot dissociate ourselves from responsibility in regard to what happened in Eastern and Central Europe. . . . What is wanted is some arrangement by which, in close connexion with the League of Nations, special responsibility for dealing with European questions should be thrown immediately upon the States of Europe themselves. We want a European protocol."[37]

Headlam-Morley, it should be remembered, writing between 1922 and 1925, could not even imagine anything like the Germany that would be, the demonic Germany of Adolf Hitler and the Nazi Party. He imagined that the threat was posed by something like the Weimar Germany of his day, without a militarist Kaiser and Junker ruling class, whose people would be no less eager for peace than the French and British. He knew, however, that this Germany was dissatisfied with the peace settlement and its place in the world, and that was enough to require precautions, but "German ambitions need not alarm us so long as we see to it that Germany is confined within her present limits; that we shall be able to do with the help of our former allies."[38]

Germany was not the only state that was dissatisfied with its place in the world. Russia had been a great power before the war but, for the time being, was no longer of that rank. The loss of the Baltic states, Finland, Poland, and Bessarabia had removed her from Europe, but "at any moment she may once again become a great danger in Europe. The fall of Trotsky has presumably checked tendencies toward military aggression, but no one can foresee how soon they will be resumed. . . ." Russia would continue to be a threat to its border states, and that must be a concern for Britain. Not every local quarrel need cause alarm, but "a concerted and determined attack, whether on Roumania or Poland or on the Baltic States, could not leave us indifferent."[39]

Headlam-Morley did not look at the world with general alarm. He observed that in many ways the outcome of the war had reduced the danger of war. The end of the Ottoman and Austrian empires and the retreat of the Russians had made it most unlikely that a Balkan quarrel could again lead to general war. Only a resurgent Germany or Russia could lead to such a war, and those threats could be deterred or contained if Britain would play her part. Beyond these, the main threats were internal. "We want, for instance, the Poles to realize how much harm may be done to their own cause by injustice in the treatment of their minorities at home or by foolish and wanton affronts to any of their neighbors." Britain could help here by helping the new states build sound institutions, through advice, diplomacy, and commerce. But the effectiveness of all these depended on "the belief that they can look to us for help in grave danger."[40]

Headlam-Morley foresaw the return of Germany and Russia to power and their possible union against Poland. He saw that the future of peace in Europe rested first on a firm alliance between the Western Allies that guaranteed the safety of France and the Low Countries and, therefore, of Great Britain. He saw the strategic importance of the Rhineland and insisted on its inclusion in any guarantee. He understood that stability in the west was connected to stability in the east. He predicted in remarkable detail the way in which World War II would come. His idea of the means to a lasting peace foreshadowed NATO after the Cold War. Seeing that peace in Europe was the most vital of Britain's interests, he thought clearly and strategically about how to preserve it, concluding that because of its central importance to Britain, its preservation called for its continuing responsibility and commitment, since Britain, on account of its resources, its relative objectivity, and its lack of territorial grievances or ambitions, was essential to it.

Headlam-Morley was unusually well grounded in the relevant historical experience, remarkably wise and far-sighted, yet the essence of his thinking was neither recondite nor beyond the understanding of anyone willing to think carefully along strategic lines. As we have seen, a number of his contemporaries shared similar perceptions and opinions. Lloyd George and the supporters of the alliance with or guarantee to France, and even opponents like Lord Curzon, could clearly see the danger of a German revanche against France and the threat it would pose to Britain. In parliament Lloyd George said:

One of the real dangers in Europe, not in five, ten, or twenty years, but maybe the next generation . . . is that the young people of Germany may be brought up with thoughts of vengeance—a vengeance of recovering old possessions and old prestige, old ascendancy, and punishing old de-

feats and generally ministering to the national pride. That is one of the
great dangers to France and Europe in the future, and when you are
making peace you must not think only of the moment but think of years
to come. . . . I say you must make Germany feel that that is a policy
which will not pay, that a war of revenge is a war that will bring not
merely France but will bring other lands in as well. By that means you
will discourage that sentiment at the very outset and you will convince
every German that that is a policy which is fatal to his own country.[41]

A supporter, Sir C. Townshend, spoke in favor of a firm alliance and the military preparations needed to make it effective: "France is under the knife; the
Rhine is our frontier, not the Channel. . . . I hope I have made it clear about the
necessity of an alliance, which is what I want rather than this entente. I am tired
of these mild platitudes about friendship and then not preparing to help them.
How long would it take us at this moment to put 150,000 men on the Rhine
alongside the French? . . . A strong agreement with the French is absolutely
necessary."[42]

But whatever a backbencher might say, Lloyd George and his colleagues in
the government were never serious about undertaking the obligations such an
agreement would impose, much less the broader burden of playing a central
role in keeping the peace of Europe. In Parliament they defended the idea of deterrence through a French alliance, so long as that idea was in play, but they
were more than a little sympathetic to the criticisms of its opponents about the
dangers of alliances and commitments such as the following spoken in the same
debate:

We are convinced that French security and French prosperity can be
found more certainly by gaining the good opinion of the world, by gaining through a world-wide League of Nations or association of peoples
that strength and that guarantee against further aggression which cannot
be found to the same degree by any arrangement merely between France
and one or two other countries. I think that history and the lessons of all
wars have taught us that groupings between small rings of nations tends
only to a recurrence of war and to counter-grouping. It is certain that if
a few countries in any part of the world are linked together on the
ground that such linking is essential because of risks of aggression outside, then those who are suspected of such acts of aggression will begin
to group, and in a generation or two . . . there will be a recurrence of
war.[43]

That was the sort of historical judgment, unlike the informed detailed investigation of Mr. Headlam-Morley, that was tossed about by most in Britain.
At bottom, the reigning ideas were that strategic thinking, active involvement,

armaments for any purpose, and alliances were the real causes of war, and that disengagement, disarmament, sympathetic understanding of discontented nations, and economic prosperity achieved through increased commerce were the true road to peace. These ideas were all the more welcome because they permitted sharp reductions in military costs, greater expenditure for welfare programs, and lower taxes.

7

The Unraveling
of Versailles

B ritain's policy of rapid and deep disarmament was especially dangerous in light of the problems presented by the Treaty of Versailles. That peace that ended the war between the Western Powers and Germany was called a "Carthaginian Peace" in England for the harshness of the terms the Allies imposed upon their defeated German foes. In France, on the other hand, the treaty was widely regarded as too lenient, for it left intact a German state that would inevitably reacquire the strength to threaten France and the European order. In truth, the peace was both too hard and too soft, for it imposed harsh and humiliating conditions on Germany guaranteed to generate hatred, resentments, and the determination to readjust the "new world order" of that time without taking effective measures to deter, prevent, or defeat the reappearance of that German menace.

By far the most serious flaw of the Versailles Treaty, however, was that the harsh terms it imposed on Germany to prevent that resurgence required the constant and seemingly perpetual willingness of the Allies to use force to compel German adherence to the treaty. This flaw was fatal, because the detailed complexity of the treaty's terms ensured that each crisis would arise from a German violation of one of the innumerable minor clauses of the treaty, and the victors would need to decide if they really wanted to fight again to impose such a piece of legalism, trifling in itself. Inevitably, many German violations, too small in themselves to merit armed conflict, would be allowed to pass. Yet the totality of those violations over many years would seriously undermine the validity of the treaty and the Allies' determination to enforce it, while strengthen-ing the Germans' determination and ability to unravel it.

The Treaty

The Treaty of Versailles deprived Germany of territory, imposed limitations on its armed forces, and subjected it to economic penalties. Alsace-Lorraine, which Germany had seized from France in the war of 1870–1871, was returned to France. In addition, areas of Poland that Prussia had received during the parti-tions at the end of the eighteenth century were recombined with the Austrian and Russian sections of that country to resurrect the old Polish state. The an-cient Prussian territory of East Prussia remained in German hands, but a "Pol-ish Corridor" was created separating East Prussia from the rest of Germany. The port city of Danzig (Gdansk today) was made a "free city" so that Poland might not be completely landlocked. The German frontiers with Belgium and Czechoslovakia were also drawn to Germany's disadvantage. All the territory to the west of the Rhine and for fifty kilometers to the east of the Rhine was to be demilitarized and occupied by Western forces for a period of ten years.

The treaty legislated the disarmament of Germany in minute detail. By March 31, 1920, the German army must consist of no more than seven infantry and three cavalry divisions. Including all rear services and depots, the army must not exceed 100,000 soldiers, of whom not more than 4,000 could be offi-cers. Germany could not retain more than two corps headquarters and staffs, and the German General Staff was to be disbanded and prohibited. The num-ber and caliber of artillery pieces, machine guns, and small arms were strictly limited in minute detail, as was the number of rounds of ammunition that could be maintained for them. All excess munitions were to be destroyed or handed over to the Allies within two months after the treaty came into force. Germany was forbidden to manufacture, import, or use poison gas, armored vehicles of any variety, or military aircraft of any type. The size of the German navy was sharply constricted, the number and types of permitted vessels delineated. Ger-many could not possess any submarines at all. Universal military service was abolished in Germany. Soldiers were required to serve for twelve consecutive years, officers for twenty-five. Not more than 5 percent of the army was to be discharged per year. An Inner-Allied Control Commission would oversee the implementation of all these clauses.

The economic terms of the treaty are notorious. The treaty established Ger-many's "responsibility for the war" and compelled Germany to pay reparations to the Allies of an unspecified amount to be determined by an Allied commis-sion. The terms of the treaty made clear that the Allies expected reparations to be in the hundreds of billions of gold marks. In addition, Germany was obliged to turn over to France the rights to mine the coal fields of the Saar River Basin for a period of fifteen years in order to recompense France for the destruction of the mines in northeastern France. Germany was also required to surrender a large portion of its merchant and fishing fleet to make good the Allies' losses to German U-boats. The treaty also specified the number of stallions, mares, rams, sheep, goats, and sows Germany must turn over to France and to Belgium in "average health and condition."

The purposes of these three categories of terms were (1) to create a European order based more nearly on national demarcations than it had been under the German, Austrian, Ottoman, and Russian empires, (2) to compensate France and Belgium economically and territorially, and other powers financially, for the losses they suffered during the war, and (3) to prevent Germany from maintaining a military force capable of planning, preparing for, or executing another war of aggression. The Allies did not find it enough simply to reduce Germany's army virtually to nothing, for the fear remained that if Germany could acquire the most modern and deadly instruments of war, particularly aircraft, tanks, and chemical weapons, then even the small but highly professional army allowed to the defeated power could be turned to aggression. The goal of the victors was to assure that if Germany ever started down the road toward aggression again, it would be easy militarily to check that advance.

The Failures of the 1920s

The alliance that won the Great War fractured almost immediately upon its conclusion, the United States withdrawing from European affairs almost altogether (except for its demands that its erstwhile allies repay their war loans), while Britain and France drifted steadily apart. Whereas Lloyd George and subsequent British ministers were determined to avoid crushing and antagonizing Germany so as to cause its internal collapse and eternal enmity, the French were equally determined to destroy the German menace to France forever. Prevented from accomplishing that aim through the dismemberment of Germany and then, failing that, through a series of mutual alliances with Britain and America, the French were determined to enforce the disarmament clauses of the Versailles Treaty to cripple the German armed forces, while using the reparations clauses to strangle the German economy. They were zealous in their willingness to use military force to compel the Germans to bend to the terms of the treaty, while the British, who sought accommodation rather than confrontation, became increasingly unwilling even to contemplate the use of force.

Occasions that might call for the use of force, however, were frequent, as Germany repeatedly failed to implement the disarmament clauses and aggressively fought the successive reparations agreements offered by the British and the French. The collapse of order in Germany that occurred at the end of 1918 aggravated the problem. As millions of disgruntled German soldiers returned home, bringing their weapons with them, the unstable infant Weimar Republic proved unable to maintain order throughout the countryside. Hundreds of thousands joined the *Freikorps,* local paramilitary groups engaged in a running fight with socialist and radical right-wing military groups in many of Germany's major cities. Whole regions fell outside the control of the central government for various periods, and the prospect of restoring order seemed daunting enough to Weimar officials without the added problem of disarmament.

For that reason, as well as because of a determination to sabotage the terms of the dictated peace, the German government set out to obstruct the implementation of those terms. The Germans greeted the arrival of the advance elements of the Inter-Allied Control Commission (IACC) with hostility and with efforts, from the most trivial to the serious, both to intimidate them and to obstruct their work.[1]

The German government met with a delegation from the advance element of the IAAC in its Foreign Office building. After waiting a considerable time in an antechamber, the members of the Allied team found that the head of the German delegation proposed to chair the meeting. The head of the IACC asserted that "it was for the Allied delegation to state their requirements." The Germans countered by insisting that as the building was part of the German Foreign Office, "it is for us to receive you." The IACC delegation walked out of the conference room. Other trivial irritants followed. The naval delegation was housed in poor quarters without baths. Its complaints went unanswered for a week until the head of that delegation sent a note to the German government announcing that the delegation would leave Berlin the following day unless adequate quarters were found. The delegation was moved to a luxurious hotel—where they found that the locked drawers in their writing desks were broken open as soon as they had gone out.[2] Five days after the unpleasant scene in the Foreign Office, an article appeared in *Die Deutsche Zeitung* headed "Kill the Lot! The Last Great Judgment Will Hold You Blameless!" and exhorting Germans to kill the British and French soldiers "strolling carelessly, cigarette in mouth, and staring ironically at the statues of the Hohenzollerns."

At the request of the IACC, the German army established an Army Peace Commission to be the liaison organ between the IACC and Germany. At its first meeting the Germans put forth a plan to render the IACC useless as an agency for enforcing the terms of the treaty. Arguing that the text of the Versailles Treaty did not permit "the exercise of local control by the medium of the District Committees of Allied officers," which the IACC proposed to create, the Germans insisted that the IACC be strictly limited in its numbers and that its officials confine their activities to Berlin. They further asserted that in light of Germany's shortage, the government would be hard pressed to find housing for so many as the four hundred officials the IACC proposed. Because of the hostility of the German population to the IACC, moreover, the German government declared that it "could not be responsible for 'the grave incidents' which the presence of so many officers might excite among the civil population." To avoid such incidents, the Germans requested that the members of the IACC, conduct their inspections and move about in mufti rather than in uniform—a request that would have placed the members of the IACC in great personal danger, for they would have been unidentifiable as foreign officials and liable to attacks that could be discounted as local banditry.[3] The IACC rejected these demands.

The Army Peace Commission, nonetheless, rapidly emerged as a major obstacle to the IACC's inspections. The IACC had divided itself into three sub-commissions, "Effectives," "Armaments," and "Fortifications," to verify Germany's compliance with the provisions of the treaty concerning demobilization, military industry, and weaponry respectively. Germany's Army Peace Commission created a parallel structure of some 140 liaison officers organized along exactly the same lines. These "liaison officers" worked hard to disrupt the IACC's inspections:

> Two of our Control officers presented themselves at the barracks at Potsdam accompanied by the inevitable liaison officer, only to be met by a tough-looking N.C.O. who informed them that the C.O. and all the officers of the unit were absent. Even the adjutant could not be found. The liaison officer professed, with an artless expression, complete ignorance of where they were. The inspection, of which due notice had been given by us in accordance with the agreement, had to be abandoned. At Duisburg the exact reverse happened. The C.O. of the unit to be inspected and its officers were all present, but the liaison officer was unaccountably absent and the C.O. professed to know nothing of his existence. No doubt in this case, as in the former, the comedy had all been carefully rehearsed on the telephone before the Control officers arrived. The result was the same in the one case as in the other—the inspection had to be abandoned. Occasionally the comedy was varied by the introduction of a new "gag." In one district the liaison officer professed, on his arrival at the barracks, to be new to his duties and suggested an adjournment of the inspection in order that he might obtain information from the liaison office . . . as to how to proceed. After compliance with his request, the Control officers came again on the appointed day, only to find a new liaison officer who requested another adjournment on the same ground as his predecessor.

Not all of the obstructions were so humorous, however:

> As if at a given signal, the liaison officer accompanying the Control officers on an inspection would suddenly disappear. The next moment the

soldiers of the unit to be inspected would pour out of the barrack room, hoot the Control officers and assail them with clods of earth and a shower of stones. This happened, with a singular unanimity, at Prenzlau, at Bremen, at Doberitz, and a score of other places. At Bremen two French officers were struck, thrown to the ground and threatened with bayonets. The troops were quite impartial in their unpleasant attentions—a British Army officer, Colonel Irvine, was their target at Prenzlau, while at Bremen—so we heard from the Naval Commission, a British naval officer was thrown into the water.[4]

These tactics succeeded in delaying or stopping particular inspections of particular installations, but they neither intimidated the IACC nor prevented the inspectors from learning what they sought.

The minor skirmishes between the IACC and the Army Peace Commission took place against an even more ominous background. On March 15–16, Marshal Foch and Field Marshal Wilson took part in a war game that revealed, according to Wilson,

> that with the Allies at their present strength and distribution it is a perfectly feasible operation of war for the Germans to force the line of the Rhine and to engage the Allies in a series of operations on the left bank of the river which would probably entail their having to bring up considerable reinforcements from the mother countries.

The Germans, moreover, knew what was happening and what it meant:

> The German to-day is a very different man from what he was when I was here last August. He is no longer taking the overwhelming strength of the Allies for granted, and he is measuring, with a military eye, the military values of the very indifferent and inefficient Belgian troops, the small and wholly untrained British force, the Americans who may at any moment be withdrawn and the French forces, composed, as they are, in large part (60 per cent) of black troops.
>
> To a military nation like Germany there is no longer much to fear from the Allied garrisons of the Rhine, which possess no offensive power whatever. In short, the German of to-day realizes that the Allied troops on the Rhine are no longer an instrument capable of being used to coerce him should he do something which incurred the displeasure of the Supreme Council. From such a frame of mind it is a short step for a German to pass to open contempt and flagrant disobedience of Allied commands.[5]

Wilson, seeking to force the Cabinet to withdraw from Germany altogether, overstated the Allies' weakness and the Germans' strength, as subsequent events were to show. His warnings that the Germans no longer feared the Allies and were determined to undermine the treaty, however, were accurate and prescient.

The Treaty of Versailles came into effect on January 10, 1920. It stipulated that the disarmament provisions, including the reduction of the German army to 100,000 soldier and officers, were to be completed within a few months. By March it was clear that the Germans were violating the terms of the treaty. Field Marshal Wilson relayed to the Cabinet Marshal Foch's reports of the Germans' violations. As of March 10, the Germans had not surrendered any of their war material to the Allies. They claimed to have destroyed some, but such destruction was carried out without prior inspection and without Allied supervision. The German government had not permitted the IACC to inspect its fortifications, as required. Regarding the size of the German army, Wilson reported, "As reduction of the strength of the German Army to 200,000 men has not to be carried out until 10th April, no definite violation of the Treaty yet exists; no progressive demobilization of effectives has, however, been attempted. On the contrary, the introduction of unauthorized formations, Einwohnerwehr, Sicherheitspolizei, &c., have provided fresh cadres for the reception of trained classes released after the war." Wilson also reported the Germans' obstructions of the IACC: "The German Government have failed to make good the facilities guaranteed to the Commission of Control by the Peace Treaty. On the contrary, there have been numerous cases of ill-will and insult to Allied officers whilst fulfilling their duties on the Commission." Exports of war material to Holland, prohibited by the treaty, "have been reported almost daily." The air and naval clauses were being violated. Wilson summed up, ". . . Marshal Foch's indictment is a very, serious matter. Germany has disregarded the authority of the Supreme Council and is encouraged to do so by the indecision of the Allies as to whether or how they intend to enforce the Peace Treaty."[6]

On the night of March 12–13, the right-wing Kapp putsch appeared to succeed in Berlin, which prompted local socialist organizations in the Ruhr valley to set up quasi-Soviet governments in order to oppose the newly installed right-wing regime. The putsch collapsed quickly in Berlin, but the Ruhr region was not equally quick to disband its soviets, and the reinstalled Weimar government asked the Allies for permission to suspend its disarmament and to send troops into the Ruhr, which had been neutralized by the treaty.[7] A British response to this request was slow to evolve, but a French response was not. On April 2, 1920, German forces began the reconquest of the Ruhr; on April 6 the French seized Frankfurt, Darmstadt, and their immediate surroundings in retaliation. The Ruhr was reconquered, and French forces withdrew in May.[8]

A British member of the IACC, Brigadier General Morgan, later claimed that the Ruhr uprising was largely orchestrated by the German government both to justify its requests that the permanent army allowed to Germany be increased from 100,000 to 200,000 men and to dramatize the extent of the resentment on the part of the German people against the Allied occupation of German territory. He claims that one of the members of the IACC traveled to the Ruhr during the disturbances and discovered that the leaders of the "soviets" were Reichwehr agents provocateurs and the whole thing was staged. According to Morgan, this report was instrumental in stiffening Lloyd George's spine temporarily in subsequent dealings with the Germans.[9]

However that may be, the Germans certainly took advantage of the uprising to demand a revision of the Versailles Treaty. The government presented the Allies with a note containing a host of unrelated arguments to support the demand to increase the size of the army to 200,000.[10] It claimed that "the events of the last few days have clearly shown how shaky is the political foundation on which Germany rests. These events have once more and in the gravest way shaken the political and economic situation." Germany's army was "scarcely sufficient to re-establish the power of the Government." At the same time, "it will be only by remaining indisputable masters of the situation that the Government will be able to compel the rebels to give up the arms which are illegally in their possession." The "Bolsheviks" (the revolutionaries in the Ruhr had been socialists, not communists, and certainly not "Bolsheviks," but the German government relied on the emotional appeal of this appellation) had been unprepared for this uprising, but the strength of their response was "surprising": "If these elements on their part assume the initiative of a revolution, it is to be feared that this move would break out still more vigorously and simultaneously throughout Germany." The Germans' failure to destroy their war matériel, as they had pledged to do in the treaty, was coupled with the disorder in the countryside, which, in turn, was joined to the threat of Bolshevism. Because of these factors, "it is inconceivable that one hundred thousand men can be enough to maintain the Government of a nation of sixty millions." The note continued, "Besides, the lack of adequate military forces would turn out to the disadvantage of the Allied Governments, because the German Government would find it impossible to conform to stipulations of an economic nature," that is to say, would refuse to pay reparations.

The German note also attributed the cause of the Kapp putsch to the over-hasty forced demobilization of the German army:

> The Government saw themselves forced by the conditions of peace to turn into the street men and officers to whom they had appealed in the distressing moments of the Spring of 1919. It was easy for the conspirators to put a false complexion on the fact that the Government could take no other course. This event showed that the German Government have been confronted with an almost insoluble task in the demand being addressed to them in present circumstances to dissolve further bodies of troops. The soldier who has engaged expects to be for a certain time free from the economic battle of life. If he is compelled to enter civilian life

again before his existence can be guaranteed to him, he feels that he has been duped and falls an easy prey to seducers.

All these arguments were calculated to appeal to the British. Many in London feared the resurgence of Bolshevism, against which British forces had only recently been in direct combat in support of the White Armies in Russia. For many months after the end of the war, the Cabinet received reports of the "revolutionary" situations in England and abroad. The threat that the German army would be too weak to resist a future communist uprising played on this fear. The warning that "prematurely" demobilized soldiers would be an easy prey for revolutionaries likewise played to the economic and social problems caused in England by a too-rapid demobilization.

The note did not, however, achieve its aim. The French had no sympathy for the argument that disorders in Germany were the cause of the Germans' failure to honor the terms of the treaty. Marshal Foch declared that "if the Treaty had been executed there would have been no arms in the Ruhr during the recent troubles in this area."[11] The German request, accordingly, met a very hostile reception, yet the Allies' answer showed hints of weakening.

The Allied note of response began with the stern admonition "The Allies wish to state at once that a proposal of this nature cannot even be examined so long as Germany fails in the most important obligations of the Treaty of Peace and does not proceed with a disarmament upon which depends the peace of the world."[12] The Allies declared that "Germany is not living up to its engagements either in the destruction of the material of war, or in the reduction of its effectives. . . . She has given neither satisfaction nor apologies for the assaults to which on several occasions the members of the Allied Missions have been subjected." The Germans also had failed to take any steps toward coming to an agreement about the reparations terms as required under the treaty. The Allies were "unanimous in declaring that they cannot permit a continuation of these infractions of the Treaty of Versailles . . . and that they are determined to take all measures, even to the extent, if necessary, of the occupation of further German territory, which will have the effect of ensuring the execution of the Treaty.

The repeated declarations that "the unity of the Allies for the execution of the Treaty is as solid as it was for the war," however, began to ring a bit hollow, for the note also spoke of a relaxation of the treaty's terms: "The Allies do not ignore the difficulties with which the German Government is faced, and do not intend to insist upon a too literal interpretation of the Treaty." If "a satisfactory settlement" could be arrived at concerning the German violations of the treaty, "the Allied Governments will be willing to discuss with the German representatives any question which affects the internal order and economic well-being of Germany." The medium for that discussion was to be a face-to-face exchange by the respective heads of state.

The German role represented a direct attempt to revise the treaty. It was written at the very moment that the Germans were violating the treaty, occupying the Ruhr by military force without the advance permission of the Allies. The Allies responded with some harsh words, even as they assured the Germans that the Allies did not intend to enforce the treaty "too literally," meaning that they might be willing, in effect, to revise it. The Germans' obstruction of the inspections and violations of the treaty were not to be punished but rewarded.

Lloyd George tried to achieve through harsh language what he was unwilling to use force to gain. In June he "complained about the 15,000 guns said to be lying about in Germany. 'It was very important,' he said . . . , 'to create the necessary atmosphere of alarm on the part of Germany in order to induce it to put forward reasonable proposals in regard to reparation and not such proposals as would not even form a basis of negotiations.'"[13] He said that "the time had come when the Germans 'must be made to hear the crack of the whip.'" The Allies rejected the Germans' request to maintain a 200,000-man army, demanded that the Reichswehr be reduced to 100,000 immediately, insisted upon the disbanding of the Sicherheitspolizei, a paramilitary organization raised to combat the disorders, and also complained about German foreign economic policy.[14]

The direct meeting of heads of state, however, showed more weakness than toughness. At the Spa Conference in July the Germans announced that "owing to the political unrest in Germany and the presence in that country of 2 million rifles which the authorities were unable to trace, no date could be set for the reduction of the Reichswehr to the treaty figure of 100,000 men." They admitted to other obstructions of the treaty but undertook no definite commitments to make good their defaults. By now Lloyd George abandoned even his harsh language, saying that "the German Government could not be expected to do the impossible; he favoured requiring them to issue a proclamation ordering the surrender of arms by the civil population and fixing appropriate penalties."[15] The French had something more practical in mind. Agreeing to allow the Germans until January 1, 1921, to reduce the Reichswehr to the stipulated size, they, in turn, compelled Lloyd George's reluctant agreement to their occupation of the Ruhr if the Germans failed to live up to their pledges. Armed with this compromise, Lloyd George announced to the House of Commons on July 21 that "the time of troubles with Germany was largely over."[16]

Yet in early June, Lloyd George had received a document revealing a large-scale failure of the Germans to meet the terms of the treaty, as well as intentional efforts on the part of German officials to obstruct the Inter-Allied Control Commission charged with conducting on-site inspections in Germany to verify its compliance with the treaty.[17] The Germans had not yet promulgated a law banning universal military service and maintained paramilitary forces in the form of *Sicherheitspolizei* (security police) specifically banned by the treaty. Of the numbers of guns, machine guns, and hand weapons the Germans claimed they were obliged to destroy by the beginning of 1920, fewer than one-third had been destroyed by June, notwithstanding the fact that "the total number of hand weapons which the Germans have to hand over to us in accordance with their lists is patently inadequate . . ." The Germans also provided lists of other weapons, and of munitions factories, that were "obviously too small." During an inspection of one of the Krupps factories, moreover, the commission discovered the illicit production of guns and ammunition wagons.

The IACC also reported that *Freikorps* continued to exist, and that groups of short-term soldiers, *Zeitfreiwilligen,* ordered to be dissolved, still existed, and "it may be said that the German military authorities are not using any haste to bring [their dissolution] about." Other paramilitary groups were ordered to dissolve by the Weimar Republic, "but this order . . . was issued in such terms as to render its execution improbable. It was more a suggestion to camouflage the Citizen Guards still further, by altering their armament and abstaining from military exercises, rather than an order for their abolition."

The IACC also encountered systematic efforts on the part of the German government to obstruct their inspections. It said that this resistance

> is due to an order issued by the Central German Bureau to its various representatives, and tending to make any unexpected exercise of control by the Commissions impossible.
>
> At Breslau, Colonel von Luck, head of the German liaison service, informed the officers belonging to the Commission of Control that he had received instructions from Berlin that such officers were not to ask any direct questions of the units or services which they might visit, but were only to ask for a programme communicated beforehand to be carried out and to check the replies given in writing by the German representative.

One of the inspectors was actually attacked while conducting an investigation: "Missiles were hurled at his car, the windows of which were smashed." The IACC also reported German violations of the reparations and economic provisions of the treaty in wearying detail.

Even so, Lloyd George insisted on conceding the German request for a delay in the final reduction of the Reichswehr to 100,000 for one year and declared in the House of Commons that all was well. The British government desperately sought to finesse Germany's violations of the treaty rather than to confront them, and it worked to keep the public in the dark about those violations by issuing misleading accounts of events in Germany. Lloyd George's reluctance to use force had already overcome his waning determination to enforce the treaty.

General Hans von Seeckt, the new head of the Reichswehr,[18] publicly described the Spa Conference as a defeat for Germany. His proclamation to the army declared, "The negotiations at Spa have not brought the desired result.

The struggle for the preservation of a stronger Wehrmacht has been in vain."[19] But this first Ruhr crisis and the Spa Conference had positive results for the German policy of resistance. They showed clearly that for all the Allied declarations of unity, France and Britain disagreed. France consistently sought to enforce the treaty strictly, while England continued to show signs of a willingness to relax its terms. This first crisis also revealed that since France was unwilling to act alone, the Allied position was closer to England's—the allies would not insist on "too literal" an interpretation of the treaty. The Germans were free to continue to undermine the treaty and obstruct the Allied inspections with redoubled efforts.

After the Spa Conference the British Imperial General Staff prepared a thoughtful and ominous memorandum.[20] "Germany is faced with two alternatives:—(a.) To continue in its present state of subjection to the Entente, under the iron heel of French militarism. . . . (b.) To ally herself with Bolshevik Russia, or nationalist Russia, as the case may be, and to break the Versailles Treaty by force of arms." Although both alternatives were likely to appear unpleasant to most Germans, the second offered them "real possibilities and . . . far brighter prospects."

> [I]f the German people ponder these two alternatives, and have no others to consider, they may perforce be led to some agreement with Soviet Russia; their hatred of France may strengthen them in this decision. The only way to prevent such a disastrous alliance, which would destroy the Treaty of Versailles and all other treaties, and possibly Bolshevise the whole of Europe, is to give Germany more hope for the future and more strength for the present.

The German warnings of the threat of Bolshevism had not fallen on deaf ears. Yet the General Staff's suggestion amounted to a call to destroy the Treaty of Versailles in order to save it, for how else could Germany be given a large enough force to fight the Russians, the Czechs, the Poles, and the others identified by the General Staff as the most dangerous enemies except by allowing Germany to maintain a large and powerful army?

The General Staff distorted reality to support its point: "We should treat Germany, as long as she has a moderate Government like the present one, which moreover appears to be making an honest effort to carry out the Peace Treaty, as a Sovereign Great Power, though as a debtor to the Entente."[21] The General Staff knew of the German cheating on the Treaty, which gravely undermined the claim to "honest efforts" by the German government. Why did the General Staff close its eyes to German perfidy? The first part of the answer came at once—it blanched at the thought of compelling the Germans to adhere to the treaty by the continual use of force: "[W]e must give up the plan of grinding Germany down by a constant display of military strength. Had Germany remained helpless and without any chance of escape, such a course of action might have been possible, though it would not have been desirable or sound; in the present circumstances it might well end in disaster." The present circumstances appeared to reflect not only the weakness and disorganization of the British army, but the threat of international revolution, particularly of the Bolshevik kind, that so held the attention of Wilson and the General Staff. At any event, the memorandum declared, "a German military danger may still exist, [but] it is a future, and not a present danger. The Bolshevik peril is a present one and far greater, and we must deal with it first, or we shall go under."

This dismissal of the German danger into the distant, and therefore irrelevant, future was an escape from reality. The General Staff's memorandum itself showed that the Versailles Treaty and the actions of the Entente after its signing were provoking hatred and the determination to undo the treaty in the hearts of the Germans—otherwise, there was no need for Germany to seek an accord with the Bolsheviks, whom the German government, and especially the military, cordially disliked. But the minor palliatives raising the numerical restrictions on the Reichswehr while keeping the reparations obligations in place would not erase that hatred and determination. Only a complete overturning of the Versailles settlement could have appeased the Germans, as the General Staff had every reason to know. In the absence of the complete destruction of the Versailles Treaty, which would leave the peace settlement and European and British security in a shambles, the future German danger was assured. To dismiss it was dangerously irresponsible.

The General Staff, however, was moved by what seemed to be a more immediate fear. Unless the Allies "give the German people reasonable hope for the future and allow Germany to retain sufficient armed strength for the present, a German-Bolshevik . . . combination seems inevitable. . . . The result cannot fail to be diastrous to the Entente, and would mean a fresh war." Yet,

> Great Britain cannot afford to be involved in a renewal of hostilities on the Continent of Europe; our commitments are too great. Nor can the nations of Europe stand another great war. They want peace, and unless they get it, there is a serious danger of such chaos and anarchy as would mean the end of civilization, as we know it. The Spa Conference was the first step towards the restoration of peace and reasonably good relations with Germany. It is absolutely essential for us to continue on these lines of conciliation and discussion, tempered with firmness.

As early as 1920, then, the British Imperial General Staff had come to the conclusion that England's military weakness and unwillingness even to contemplate another European war imposed upon it the obligation to appease Germany and to support its efforts to destroy the Versailles settlement.

This view was unduly apocalyptic. Armed intervention, even occupation of territory in reprisal for Germany's refusal to abide by the treaty, would not destroy civilization as it was then known. Such a policy was not impossible, but it would have been extremely difficult for Britain, considering the unstable situations it faced in Ireland, Egypt, Palestine, India, and even at home. Military leaders, moreover, often confuse the difficult with the impossible when faced with a mission they do not want to perform. And Britain's excessive demobilization and its decision not to provide itself with the armed forces required by the international situation made the suppression of German violations of the treaty a dubious and difficult project that daunted its generals. Their reluctance, in turn, strengthened Lloyd George's inclination to avoid conflict with Germany, however much evidence emerged that Germany was subverting the treaty. Instead of providing their civilian masters with the professional opinion that Britain's forces were inadequate to compel German adherence to the treaty, they chose to recommend a different policy toward Germany.

Taking the view that Britain's chief objective should be the modification of the Versailles Treaty, the General Staff pointed out, "The greatest obstacle to any policy of conciliation is the attitude of France and Belgium." The solution they proposed was to form a defensive alliance with France and Belgium which would "strengthen our position against the menace of Bolshevism . . . by the spirit of conciliation which could be called into being and developed in our relations with Germany." The ideas that would produce the Treaty of Locarno in 1925 flourished within the General Staff five years earlier, as did the willingness to ignore the military requirements of such a treaty: "A defensive alliance with France and Belgium would not increase our military commitments. In the event of German aggression, with or without the aid of Russia, we should in any case be forced to come to the assistance of France and Belgium, as in 1914, in the interests of self-defense." But the General Staff had just said that England had no ability to intervene in a continental war! As early as 1920, the General Staff had dismissed the German threat far into the future, determined that the Versailles Treaty must be modified to suit the Germans, and concluded that France and Belgium must be "bought off" to accomplish that with a "defensive alliance" that England had no intention of maintaining the military forces to support. British policy was to depend upon a declared adherence to a treaty Britain was determined to ignore, support by promises it could not redeem and a military force adequate for none of the tasks required either to uphold the treaty or to revise it.

The next few years saw continued conflict between the Allies and the Germans over reparations and other violations of the treaty, which came to a head with the French occupation of the Ruhr in 1923.[22] By that time, British policy had drifted so far away from the French determination to enforce the treaty that open breaches in the alliance became visible. The French withdrew, as a compromise, ultimately unsatisfactory to France, was reached. The Ruhr Crisis of 1923 convinced the British that a more permanent solution must be found, leading to the Locarno Treaty of 1925 that largely implemented the policy recommended by the General Staff in 1920.

In 1925 the IACC was still reporting that Germany was not in compliance with the terms of the Versailles Treaty. A general inspection in Germany produced a damning final report.[23] The IACC noted that the police put up little resistance to the inspectors, but "[s]trong resistance was on the other hand put up by the military authorities. This was largely overcome after some time in regard to the inspection of armaments, but continued to the end in the case of the effectives. The inspecting officers met with both obstruction and dissimulation, and this was so general that the inference is that it was part of an organised plan."[24] The report identified significant breaches of the treaty throughout German industry, in German legislation, in the paramilitary organizations, and in the organization of the army:

> [T]he Reichswehr, instead of being organised for internal purposes as laid down in the treaty, is being built up under the direction of the High Command to prepare the nation for war. The High Command is itself contrary to the treaty, as is also the Great General Staff which is still in existence. The various arms are instructed and organised in ways forbidden by the treaty, e.g., no essential modification has been made in the pre-war military railway organisation. In regard to numbers, supplementary cadres of officers and non-commissioned officers and short-term recruits have been observed. The treaty is infringed by the system of short-term recruiting, and other infringements have been noted, such as an undue percentage of discharges per annum. . . .
>
> All these infractions taken together are, in the opinion of the commission, sufficiently important to require putting right, and the commission will not on its own initiative to be able to declare the military clauses fulfilled until these points are sufficiently advanced to have attained the degree of disarmament required by the treaty, which is now far from being the case.[25]

This report, like the others before it, made it perfectly clear that the Germans were not in compliance with the treaty and had no intention of coming into compliance. All along the inspectors had documented the Germans' deception but the Allies' unwillingness to use significant force prevented the enforcement of compliance. By 1925, the disarmament clauses of the Versailles Treaty were largely a dead letter.

The Locarno Treaty was signed in October 1925, less than five months after the commission sent its final report to the German government demanding compliance with the Versailles Treaty. No such compliance took place before the Locarno Treaty was signed. On the contrary, the army leadership had come to believe by then that the Locarno Treaty was the only way to encourage the Germans to comply with the Versailles Treaty.[26] Yet the inevitable result of the Locarno Treaty was to shelve the question of German compliance and ensure the withdrawal by 1927 of the IACC. The world was encouraged to believe that the Germans had complied with the treaty's terms and that there was no longer any reason to be concerned, particularly in the wake of Germany's new membership in the League of Nations. More than ever, it was essential to the British government to conceal the extent of Germany's treaty violations.

General Morgan had already been recalled from the IACC in 1922 because of "a continuing difference of opinion between a certain higher authority and myself, he insisting that Germany was 'totally disarmed' and I insisting that she was not."[27] Morgan, accordingly, began to write his book in 1924 to expose Germany's fraud to the world. Then, as Morgan later explained,

> in 1925, came the fateful overtures by Herr Stresemann for a "Pact of Security" known, and now notorious, as the Pact of Locarno. The price exacted by Stresemann for that Pact was not only the withdrawal of the Control Commission, but silence. He got it. It became "bad form" for any one to question whether Germany was, or was not, in a state of grace in the matter of disarmament. To have proceeded, under such circumstances, with the publication of a history of the attempt to disarm her under the Treaty of Versailles would have involved such a revelation of the bad faith of Germany, in her all too successful obstruction to the work of the Control Commission, as to amount, in the language of diplomacy to "an unfriendly act," particularly in view of her spectacular entry into the comity of the League of Nations. The only course open to the Author was therefore to abandon his unfinished task.[28]

He completed the work for publication only in 1946, hoping to warn the leaders of that later time to avoid making a mistake similar to the one made in 1919—which they did.

The lesson to be learned from Morgan's message is important. The IACC seemed to many to be nit-picking; Germanophobic members were simply determined to find cheating where there was no intent to cheat—only the poor circumstances of a war-ravaged and revolution-torn country. German violations identified in the IACC's reports all seemed rather small and insignificant. Excess machines or equipment in this or that factory, a surplus of 30,000 policemen in a force of 180,000, delays in reducing to the 100,000 effectives mandated by the treaty—none seemed to pose any immediate threat. The threat they posed, however, was long-term and deadly.

A recent student of Germany's covert rearmament divides Germany's activities into three periods: disarmament (1918–1920), covert arms evasion

(1920–1926), and clandestine rearmament (1927–1935), followed by overt rearmament and bluff.[29] In the first period, the IACC carefully inventoried German stockpiles, examined factories, and inspected barracks as the Germans more or less complied with the disarmament terms of the treaty. In the second period, as the IACC worked to settle the remaining questions about German disarmament, the Allies' focus shifted to what we would now call monitoring—ensuring that the Germans stayed disarmed. After the debacle of the Ruhr occupation in 1923 and the Locarno Treaty, the inspectors withdrew, so that the third period saw German activities unfettered by intrusive Allied inspections.

Even in the first period, which saw the most aggressive operations of the IACC, the Germans worked hard to cheat the inspectors. The massive arms firm of Krupp acquired control of the Swedish firm of Bofors and the Dutch firm of Blessing. Its most skilled and important personnel went to Sweden and Holland, where they continued to design and build artillery, antiaircraft guns, and light tanks. Blessing, in fact, took a stockpile of 1,500 of Krupp's artillery pieces and continued to explore ways to improve them.[30] Holland's arms industries also received prototypes of Fokker aircraft, some of them smuggled out under the eyes of IACC inspectors. In all, Fokker managed to get 220 airplanes and 400 aircraft engines, all proscribed by the Versailles Treaty, to Holland, where they became part of a new Fokker empire, now renamed Nederlandische Vliegtuigenfabriek NV. The new company was brazen enough to persuade the Dutch government to cancel a contract for aircraft and engines placed with the British firm of Vickers and transfer it to Fokker![31]

These violations were minor in themselves: "Throughout the 1920s, Germany looked and indeed was substantially disarmed. The small army was a strictly light infantry force suitable only for internal security, the minuscule navy was a ragtag coastal defense force only, the air corps had been abolished entirely, and Krupp was busy making the implements of peace. Or so it all seemed, equally to the casual observer and to those intelligence services that bothered to keep watch." Yet the truth was much more ominous: "[I]f the letter of Versailles was being more or less observed, the intent was not. The potential for rapid rearmament was present and growing and so was the desire for it."[32]

During the period of covert arms evasion, 1920 to 1926, the Germans worked to stabilize their military industry, maintain such military manpower as they could in official and paramilitary organizations, and develop surreptitiously the best tools of modern warfare.[33] Because the IACC continued to pursue aggressive inspections, the Germans had to continue to be clever in foiling it. The aircraft firm of Heinkel was given a secret order in 1923 to develop a reconnaissance plane, the first military aircraft it had been asked to design. The hangar in which the prototype was built was inspected several times by the IACC, but the tricks of the Army Peace Commission succeeded admirably:

"The Allied control commission inspectors only saw the hangar empty, because hours before each inspection all aircraft and components were loaded onto trucks and driven to hidden spots in the heath or among nearby sand dunes."[34] The softening of the provisions of the Versailles Treaty following Locarno eased the Germans' task considerably, even before the inspectors were withdrawn. Thus in 1926 the Pact of Paris allowed the Germans to build a limited number of "nonmilitary" aircraft to participate in international flying competitions. The aircraft produced under this eased restriction were the prototypes of the Bf-109 fighter, the Ju-52 bomber, which became the basic Luftwaffe transport aircraft, and the He-111 bomber, which almost bombed London into submission. The eased restrictions also made it easier for the Reichswehr to train a large number of "civilian" pilots.[35]

With the easing of tensions in 1925, Krupp grew even bolder, setting up an ordnance-design team in the heart of Berlin, a short walk from the central Reichswehr offices under the name of Koch and Kienzle (E)—the (E) standing for Entwicklung or development. Koch and Kienzle developed a series of "agricultural tractors" of "light," "medium," and "heavy" types. On one occasion, careless designers included sketches of the "heavy tractor" equipped with a 75-mm gun. Another slip emerged from the Nuremberg trials: one set of plans noted that "specifications for power tractors . . . must meet the requirements for transportation on open railroad cars in Belgium and France."[36] The peaceful firm of Koch and Kienzle also developed artillery pieces and mobile 210-mm mortars.

The development of the tank force was also assisted by German expatriates. Thus Joseph Vollmer, Germany's tank designer during World War I, emigrated first to Sweden and then to Czechoslovakia, where by 1925 he was producing tanks at Skoda. As a result of this violation and Chamberlain's agreement at Munich, the German army was able to absorb peacefully some 469 Czech tanks in 1939.[37] The result of Germany's covert rearmament in this second period, according to a Krupp memorandum, was that "with the exception of the hydraulic safety switch, the basic principles of armament and turret design for tanks had already been worked out in 1926." As a result of these efforts, Hans Guderian, then a major, "drove his first tank as a guest of the Swedish army's lone tank company. Appropriately, his machine was one of Vollmer's smuggled ex-German alias M-21s."[38]

The British General Staff had been right in one belief, that the Germans would turn to Russia for help in undoing the results of the war both had lost. Well before the Locarno Treaty, a Russo-German cooperative effort was underway, based in Russia, to develop modern tools of war and methods for using them. German-designed tanks were run on Russian exercise fields by German crews. German engineers designed poison gases and tested their effects and the means to deliver them. Aircraft parts smuggled out of Germany in the early 1920s were assembled and then the designs perfected in Holland by enterprising German military industrialists—and the aircraft were sent to Russia for testing and training. Finland proved a suitable base for developing submarines and training crews. The 1920s probably saw more experimentation, research, and development of the tools and methods of modern war by German officers in other countries than by English officers in England.

The paramilitary groups, supposedly banned by the Treaty of Versailles, flourished even during the inspection regime. Hundreds of thousands of German citizens kept handguns and underwent regular military training in the service of these various organizations. In the end, this surplus of militarily trained manpower, the right-wing portions of which were actively supported by the Reichswehr, helped undo the Weimar Republic—paramilitaries supported the Papen coup of 1932, and then supported Hitler's rapid rise to power. One such group, the Stahlhelm or "steel helmets," numbered 800,000 in the mid-1920s and was absorbed completely into the SA, Hitler's first army. These groups led to the death of the Weimar Republic and the rise of Nazi Germany, and they then provided Nazi Germany with an immediately available source of partly trained draftees.

When Hitler came to power, therefore, he inherited a state that had little military power, but enormous military potential. It had a large base of semi-trained military manpower, an industrial base configured to move rapidly to war production, and a highly sophisticated research and development system that had already designed the equipment that military industry would produce. The British, who had come to believe that Germany was disarmed by the time of Hitler's rise to power, were taken by surprise by the speed with which Germany rearmed. They should not have been. The reports of the IACC had made it clear all along that the capacity for so rapid a rearmament was being carefully and deliberately conserved by the German government. It was not the knowledge of German violations of the treaty that had been lacking, but the will to do anything about it. In the end, the British paid a very high price for their willful blindness.

Germany was disarmed in 1920, disarmed in 1925, and disarmed in 1930. The German military predicted in 1932, when the rearmament began in earnest, that Germany would not be ready for war for a decade. Hitler's ascent to power changed that calculus somewhat, but even in 1939, Germany was woefully ill prepared in critical areas for the world war it was about to set off. In a sense, the disarmament provisions of the Versailles Treaty achieved their purpose—they rendered Germany no threat at all for more than a decade, and delayed the resurrection of German military power even after that. In the end, however, it would have been better had the provisions failed utterly and obviously.

The fact that Germany was disarmed in 1925 meant that the German threat could be comfortably put off into the irrelevant future. It was a powerful psychological factor underlying the "ten-year rule," which continued to be valid as far as Germany was concerned until 1929. As far as the Germans' own esti-mates of when their preparations would be complete goes, that ten-year rule was abandoned at just the right moment—1932 was ten years before the Ger-man military leadership thought it would be ready to go to war.

But the Germans did not reckon with how successfully they had positioned their country to rearm, and the British had given the matter no thought at all. When the German rearmament began, therefore, the speed of its progress was itself an important factor in undermining England's willingness to respond—for a time in the mid-1930s, Baldwin and Chamberlain, stunned at that speed, were willing to believe almost any claim Hitler might make regarding the size of the Luftwaffe. In fact, the claims were exaggerated; the Luftwaffe was much smaller than Hitler proclaimed, its aircraft not as dangerous, its trained pilots few and far between. If the British had maintained their own air force, tank force, and navy at adequate levels throughout the 1920s, the new German threat could have been regarded with equanimity. But they did not. The appar-ent disarmament of Germany, combined with the placidity induced by the Lo-carno era, undermined the feeble efforts made by the armed forces to maintain adequate strength. The fact that it had become "bad form" by 1925 to speak of Germany's violations of the disarmament provisions of the treaty, each so mi-nor in itself, meant that there was no popular backing for maintaining adequate armed forces. Worst of all, the two-small British army, air force, and navy placed too few orders with England's own munitions factories. As the Germans carefully nurtured a deceitful program to maintain their arms industries, there-fore, the British carelessly destroyed their own. When the time came to race to rearmament in the 1930s, the Germans were ready and the British were not.

None of these events were inevitable. At any point the Allies could have at-tempted by force to compel the Germans actually to adhere to the treaty they had signed. The British could have kept up their armed forces, or at least the ability to reconstitute them. They could have proclaimed Germany's violations to the world and thereby prepared their people for the struggle that was loom-ing. All of those things could have been done. But it was extremely unlikely that they would be done, because of the nature of the Versailles Treaty and the mood that at once created and was created by that pact. The Versailles Treaty was designed to achieve by *diktat* what the Allies had not achieved by force; it was no stronger than the willingness of the Allies to use force to impose it, and that willingness had to be perpetual. It had to span Prime Ministers, govern-ments, and parties. It could never end. Every day that went by hardened in the minds of successive German governments the desire to overthrow the treaty and strengthened their vast and complex arrangements to subvert it in time. It was a waiting game the Allies were almost certain to lose.

8

The Locarno Treaty

The lapse of negotiations for an Anglo-French alliance brought no relief for the problem of French security. France's search for security did not end, nor did Britain's tortuous efforts to achieve its own ends without making any firm commitments that might have military consequences. One historian has described Great Britain's policy as follows: "It never abandoned France entirely, encouraging false hopes here, and it never supported Germany completely, causing bitterness there. But in general, it supported concessions to Germany at the expense of France."[1] The British believed that only the revival of the European economy and especially the restoration of prewar levels of trade with Germany would restore strength to its own industries and prosperity for England. As Stanley Baldwin said soon after he became Prime Minister in 1924: "We have got to settle Europe. . . . We live by our export trade. We can't afford to let Europe go to pieces with all the serious economic consequences."[2]

The British believed that significant reparations payments would hamper German recovery and unduly stimulate Germans exports in competition with British goods.[3] Lloyd George "proposed a new mystique: the economic reconstruction of Europe through German recovery."[4] This led to the subordination of security and strategic considerations to economic ones, sometimes even to their rejection.

For England to take a generous attitude toward a defeated Germany accorded with long-standing habit. Lloyd George and the British leaders who followed him sought to pursue a policy that allowed Britain to maintain a "free hand," to hold the decisive balance between contending powers without being truly committed to any of them. More than ever they wanted to be free of a "continental commitment" such as might compel them to fight a war in Europe.

In January 1923 the Germans defaulted for the thirty-fourth time in thirty-six months on their monthly reparations obligation to deliver a quota of coal, and the Reparations Commission declared the Germans formally in default. The Belgians and French chose to occupy the Ruhr, the great industrial area critically important to the German economy. The British denounced the action as illegal and immoral.

The German government ordered a campaign of passive resistance. The French reacted by crushing strikes and sending in their own workers, miners, and officials, protected by soldiers. The Germans were deprived of the vast majority of the coal that ran their industry, causing unemployment all over Germany, as well as in the Ruhr. The government was forced to support the great numbers placed in distress from an already overstrained budget. The result was a staggering inflation.

As the occupation became longer, nastier, and more costly, the French conceived greater goals: control of mines in the Ruhr, permanent Allied control of railroads in the Rhineland, even the creation of an independent Rhenish state, the buffer state they had always sought as a guarantee of their security.[5] Poincaré knew this was France's last chance to use the single advantage it had to prevent the collapse of the Versailles settlement, the resurgence of German preponderance, and the menace to French security it represented.

At last, the Germans gave way. In August 1923, Gustav Stresemann became German Chancellor, committed to compliance with the treaty. Poincaré tried to get support for a plan that would give France control of important German assets in the Ruhr and the Rhineland, depriving the Germans of sovereignty in the area. This was unacceptable to the British and Americans, who increasingly turned away from France and toward support of Germany. Isolated, threatened by collapse of the franc, pressed by political opponents, Poincaré was forced to yield. Settlement of the problems of reparations, financial stability, and the future of the Ruhr and the Rhineland—i.e., the de facto revision of the Versailles Treaty—would be determined not by the French in possession of the Ruhr but by international groups in which the French would stand alone.

Such a group produced the Dawes Plan in April 1924. It reorganized Germany's finances, supported them by a large international loan, and effectively reduced Germany's reparations debt and payment schedule. Payments, in any case, were made easier by considerable American investment in Germany. The Germans enjoyed the opportunity to make almost no payments in the first two years and rightly expected to achieve further reductions when heavier payments became due. Arrangements for the implementation of the new reparations plan and the withdrawal of France from the Ruhr were left to the London Conference in the summer of 1924. By that time Poincaré had been forced out of office and replaced by the pliable and inexperienced Édouard Herriot. France was required to end economic occupation of the Ruhr almost immediately and to withdraw its troops within a year. The Reparations Commission was revised in such a way as to make future punishment of default all but impossible. It was a major defeat for the French, who were deprived of all means to enforce the provisions of the treaty meant to afford them security. The treaty had been revised against their wishes and interests, and the process of revision was far from over.

The British welcomed the outcome of the Ruhr crisis, but it revealed that Britain and France no longer stood together as a check against German ambitions. The French were too weak to withstand the opposition of their former allies again. "The result was a decisive French moral defeat; never again was France to hold the upper hand which she had enjoyed from 1918 to 1923. . . . Henceforth that military strength with which France could alone offset the potentially overwhelming superiority of German national power, relapsed into a posture of defensiveness and passivity . . ."[6]

After their Ruhr debacle the French sought other ways to defend their security. They explored the policy of collective security through the League of Nations. Together with Britain's Socialist Prime Minister Ramsay MacDonald, Herriot promoted the Geneva Protocol for the Pacific Settlement of Disputes. It provided that all members of the League agree to submit unsolved disputes to binding arbitration rather than resort to war and to give military aid to the victims of aggression. The French government hoped this would provide the protection France needed, but such hopes were excessive. MacDonald was interested chiefly in conciliating Germany, pressing forward with disarmament, especially of France, and avoiding the use of force. In the conditions of 1924 he did not imagine that fighting would be needed. Less even than most British statesmen did he believe that Germany was a menace, even potentially. The promises of military aid to defend France against a German attack looked "[b]lack . . . and big on paper," said MacDonald, but were really "a harmless drug to soothe nerves." Problems could be solved by "the strenuous action of good-will." One historian has described MacDonald's thinking in this way:

> The important thing was to launch negotiations. If the French could be lured into negotiating only by promises of security, then the promises should be given, much as a small child is lured into the sea by assurances that the water is warm. The child discovers that the assurances are false; but he gets used to the cold, and soon learns to swim. So it would be in international affairs. Once the French began to conciliate Germany, they would find the process less alarming than they imagined. British policy should urge the French to concede much, and the Germans to ask little. As MacDonald put it some years later: "Let them especially put their demands in such a way that Great Britain could say that she supported both sides."[7]

Negotiations produced a document full of loopholes; even so, the British dominions opposed anything that committed Great Britain to military action, and the Conservative government that succeeded MacDonald had no intention of accepting the Geneva Protocol.[8]

The new British Foreign Minister was Austen Chamberlain, half brother of the future Prime Minister Neville Chamberlain. He described himself as "the most pro-French member of the government."[9] Unusual in his time in understanding that the security question could not be brushed aside, he was determined to take action. He was scheduled to go to France to inform Prime Minister Herriot that Britain would not approve the Geneva Protocol. He did not want to go to him empty-handed but to bring him something to replace that scheme for security. The urgency was more intense because of the danger presented by the recent report of the international committee monitoring German disarmament. The Versailles Treaty provided that the Allies should withdraw from their occupation of the Rhineland in three stages. The first was to be the evacuation of Cologne and the surrounding district on January 1, 1925, provided that the Germans had fulfilled their treaty obligations. As we have seen, however, the Germans resisted. Although Germany was still effectively disarmed, the committee's preliminary report issued in December 1924 revealed major German failures to meet significant disarmament requirements. On that basis the Allies informed Germany that the withdrawal would not take place until Germany had given clear evidence of compliance.

In light of the report it seemed likely that France would refuse to evacuate the Cologne zone. The British were far less concerned about Germany's failure to disarm than about the possibility that France would remain in the Rhineland. The Belgian Foreign Minister had warned Chamberlain that "many people in France and Belgium genuinely believed that it would be unwise to give up the existing guarantees on the Rhine unless an equally weighty substitute were forthcoming."[10] Chamberlain was convinced that in the absence of some guarantee, France would act in such a way as to bring on new trouble with Germany, which would surely embroil Britain. If the British would not agree to a guarantee or an Anglo-French alliance, there must be a substitute. To his colleagues in the Foreign Office, after his Cabinet had made clear their opposition to the Geneva Protocol, he wrote: "Rejection, pure and simple, makes matters much worse, as every unsuccessful attempt to settle a great political problem always does." He had "failed to convey . . . the urgency, the difficulty, the complexity and the absolutely vital character of the problem which remains for solution."[11] He saw no prospect for lasting peace without a sound guarantee of French security and called the Central European Department of the Foreign Office to recommend the best way to achieve that goal.

An early opinion came from Lord D'Abernon, ambassador to Germany, so friendly to Germany and its leaders that he was known as their "Lord Protector" and *"praeceptor Germaniae."*[12] He believed that Germany must be restored and trusted and saw no chance that Germany could rearm swiftly without being attacked and defeated by France or that it would rearm gradually without being detected; he rejected the likelihood of Germany's return to military predominance. He dismissed the danger of a Russo-German alliance, declaring that "any military combination between the aristocratic imperialist military leaders in Germany and the Communist forces in Soviet Russia is unthinkable."[13]

The diplomats in London had a different view. The response of Sir Maurice Hankey, Secretary to the Cabinet and Secretary of the Committee of Imperial Defense, was especially interesting since, as he pointed out, in the past his "general sentiment towards the idea of a Guarantee Pact to France and Belgium has been decidedly adverse."[14] He had feared that an alliance might needlessly involve Britain in a war, make France even less accommodating to Germany and no more so to Britain, and involve Britain in great and unnecessary military commitments and armaments. Finally, he was concerned that it would be very hard to overcome "the average Britisher's instinctive dislike of any Continental commitment (which I share), and in persuading public opinion in this country" and in the dominions.

Most reluctantly, Hankey allowed these considerations to be overcome by his realization that a war against the French would cause Britain "grave inconvenience and grievous loss." It would be even more dangerous if Germany conquered France and gained control of the Channel ports. Britain, therefore, needed good relations with France, but the Geneva Protocol was far worse than a simple alliance, which could limit British commitments clearly, while the protocol's commitments would be "vague, unlimited geographically, and not within our own control." An alliance "appears by far the less objectionable as a choice of evils." Even so, any alliance should leave the decision as to whether aggression has taken place entirely to "the discretion of the British Government," should involve "no increased expenditure in armaments," and should contain a provision for periodic consideration."[15]

There was no such hesitation in the clearly expressed opinion of Ronald McNeill:

> The real and only source of fear is Germany. France and Belgium fear Germany's vengeance. Great Britain has more reason to fear the same thing than she admits, and it is only her habitual blind complacency that saves her from being as "jumpy" as her neighbor. The latter have learned their history lesson more thoroughly than we have or ever will. . . . Security against German aggression can be obtained by no treaty or protocol, but only by making aggression too dangerous to herself.[16]

Since Germany could not for long be kept disarmed, "maintaining superior military forces ready to resist her . . . is the only possible means of security." Without an alliance with Britain, France must depend on its own resources, but what if they proved inadequate? The Germans would invade again. How would Britain respond? "Is it conceivable that we should look on while France is invaded through Belgium, the Channel ports seized, Paris occupied, and a dictated and vengeful peace imposed on France? . . . Has not the introduction of submarine and aerial warfare made this policy more, and not less, necessary to us than ever?"

Since such an attack would surely bring Britain into a war on the side of France and Belgium, what are the pros and cons of "proclaiming that intention in advance"? The advantages would include the allaying of French fear, better relations with France, the reduction of the danger of a German invasion of France and, therefore, of another war. What are the disadvantages?

> Against these solid advantages the only objection to proclaiming our policy seems to be our traditional dislike of putting our signature to any document that may commit us to engage in a future war, and the opposition to which the dislike would give rise in the press and in Parliament. . . . But this objection . . . resolves itself into a disinclination to face the facts. To say in one and the same breath that under given circumstances we should undoubtedly take such-and-such action, but that we must not commit ourselves to do so, is absurd self-contradiction.[17]

A definite defensive alliance with France and Belgium, since they preferred it, would provide greater security than a unilateral declaration of guarantee by Britain. "Such a pact with France and Belgium seems the only policy really calculated to give the rest and security which Europe needs today. . . . A defensive pact for twenty-five years should at all events prevent German aggression and give us peace and relief from fear of war, for that period."[18]

The fullest analysis came from the pen of Harold Nicolson, who painted a picture of a dangerously unstable situation where "[o]ne-half of Europe is dangerously angry; the other half is dangerously afraid."[19] Although Germany, for the moment, was too weak to undertake aggression,

> it is certain that with her great military and chemical potentialities she will sooner or later again become a powerful military factor. . . . So soon as Germany recovers, there will be a steady movement towards the righting of what are, for a German, the two most objectionable provisions of the Peace Settlement, namely, the Polish corridor and the partition of Silesia. . . . There is obviously a danger that a nation of over 60 millions will not permanently acquiesce in being thus sundered from the province [East Prussia] which was the cradle of the Prussian State, or in being deprived of those mineral resources [in Silesia] on which the national prosperity was largely based.

Demographics were also ominous. The French population was already less than two-thirds of the German and declining while the number of Germans was increasing. These facts have "inevitably and justifiably led the French to place their own security above all other considerations."

They had tried to obtain an independent Rhineland to obtain security, but were prevented by the British and Americans, who substituted a guarantee against German invasion in its place and then withdrew it. "The French were thus left with the impression that not only had they been refused the Rhine barrier, but they had also been deprived of the only serious compensations offered to them. . . ." They naturally turned to secure their own safety. The creation of the Little Entente, which seemed to encircle Germany and help with the disparity in manpower, "was nonetheless a policy of desperation." The alliance itself stood on shaky ground, and the vulnerability of Poland and Rumania to threats from Germany and Russia made them "an element not of security but of added apprehension."

Perhaps it was an understanding of that reality that led the French to press for the Geneva Protocol. Now that Britain's refusal would destroy that project, France could be expected to return to the original position of Marshal Foch, and it would "be increasingly difficult for any French Government to evacuate the Rhineland unless and until they receive some compensating guarantee for the future security of France." From all this Nicolson concluded:

> Germany will sooner or later recover. She will certainly desire to revise the Polish clauses of the Treaty of Versailles. If France were isolated, and British neutrality to be assured, she might also endeavour to attack France.
>
> Unless France can be secured against the menace, she will be driven to expedients which in the end will only provoke the German revenge of which she stands in terror.

What did this mean for Britain? The old policy of "splendid isolation" was not possible. "History and economics show that isolation in present conditions spells danger, vulnerability and impotence. Geography and aeronautics show that isolation is not in our case a scientific fact." The defense of Great Britain itself required that Europe's instability be cured, that all threats to the Channel and North Sea ports be prevented. The upshot was that "it is consequently a necessity of British and therefore of Imperial defence to reach some understanding with France and Belgium which may entail a guarantee on our part that these territories shall not fall into other hands." If that was done the French would know that Britain regarded their security as essential to its own. A center of security and stability would be established that could in time be enlarged, eventually, perhaps, to include Germany. "But until we can quieten France, no concert of Europe is possible, and we can only quieten France if we are in a position to speak to her with the authority if an Ally."[20]

Nicolson's memorandum, dated February 20, 1925, was the most important, for Chamberlain circulated it to the Cabinet with a covering letter stating that it had been written by instruction of the Foreign Secretary under the supervision of Crowe, the Permanent Under-Secretary, and resulted from a conference of the senior officers in the department. Lest it be taken lightly, Chamberlain wrote that "it represents not only the personal opinion of the Secretary of State, but the considered opinion of the Foreign Office as a whole. . . ." It presented "the basis and outline of the policy which I urgently recommend."[21]

In spite of the power of its arguments and the credentials of their proponents, the memorandum ran into serious trouble in the Cabinet at meetings on March 2 and 4. A majority was strongly opposed either to a guarantee or to an alliance with France. There was no carefully considered refutation of the Nicolson-Crowe presentation, but different individuals expressed different reasons for their opposition.

> The opponents of commitment were the larger party, but their views were inconsistent. They argued that a war in Europe was not imminent but that an alliance with France might lead to "Armageddon No. 2." They knew that Britain must defend France against German aggression but doubted that they could defeat Germany. They believed that German aggression was possible but favoured an agreement in which unenforceable arbitration alone could check that possibility.[22]

The reaction was more emotional than rational, reflecting the majority's panic at the thought of seriously committing Britain to a firm promise to deter potential aggression backed by military power.

It appears, however, that Chamberlain knew of the strength of the opposition even before the meeting and that from the first he proposed not a pact with France and Belgium but a quadruple pact that included Germany.[23] The idea came from the Germans. Rumors of a British alliance with France and Belgium had reached them and alarmed Gustav Stresemann, now their Foreign Minister. Stresemann was a German nationalist who sought to undermine and revise the Versailles Treaty in order to restore Germany to the position of Great Power, the greatest in Europe. The war had convinced him that this required intelligence and patience as well as military power. An Anglo-French alliance would be a fearful barrier to his plans. Germany's "reasons for taking the initiative, were fear of an Anglo-French alliance, the need to find some way forward from the setback over the Cologne zone, and fear of League of Nations supervision over German disarmament,"[24] but the chief "unstated reason" for approaching

Britain before France, "no doubt, was at the earliest possible moment to try to head Chamberlain off from a renewal of the Cannes guarantee to France."[25]

In January 1925, therefore, Stresemann proposed to the British a plan for the preservation of European peace through international agreement in which France, Germany, and Great Britain, among others, would all take part, the basis for what would become the Locarno agreements. That was the core of the plan Chamberlain took to his Cabinet on March 2 and 4. Chamberlain rightly suspected that the German proposal for a four-way pact was intended to prevent a Franco-British alliance and to drive a wedge between France and Britain. But he was the only important British official who had favored a commitment to France. Members of the Committee of Imperial Defence wanted to give the French no commitment of any kind, and the Cabinet was overwhelmingly of the same opinion. On March 2, to balance the rejection of the Geneva Protocol and a British alliance with France and Belgium, he managed to get a carefully hedged statement for Herriot from the Cabinet that an agreement including Germany "stands on a different footing" from an Anglo-French alliance.[26] Two days later, however, the Cabinet took some steps back, "severely limiting" what Chamberlain could tell the French Premier. All he could say was that Britain would do its best to work out some "quadrilateral agreement of mutual security." The Cabinet did not say what, if any, pact it might prefer, and the discussion was terribly confused. "Curzon and Amory at least hoped that the approach would wreck Chamberlain's policy and avoid any commitment." Determined to take some action, Chamberlain interpreted the instructions as support for a quadrilateral pact.[27]

The next day he told the House of Commons, "No nation can live, was we live, within 20 miles of the Continent of Europe and remain indifferent to the peace and security of the Continent." With approval he cited Lord Grey, who had spoken the night before: "It was for British public opinion to recognise that the one thing it could do to help the European situation was to make some firm offer to promote European security in which the British Empire can join."[28]

Then Chamberlain came to Paris and reported to Herriot that the British would neither adopt the Geneva Protocol nor make an alliance with France. This came as a blow to the French Premier, who said: "From my heart I tell you I look forward with terror to [Germany] making war on us again in ten years." Chamberlain asked him to consider the new idea for achieving security that the British might support, but he feared that the French would not cooperate. He was "oppressed by the danger," he wrote to Crowe, that they would stay in Cologne, "for reasons which are within the terms of the Treaty" but would be rejected by British opinion. The British would then want to withdraw their own troops from the Cologne area, as promised by the treaty, but if they did so they ran the risk of alienating the French totally, which was even worse than continuing the occupation. Chamberlain, still in Paris, asked Crowe to find out from the Cabinet what they thought about these matters and about his conversation with Herriot.

At a meeting on March 11 the Cabinet tried to take back even its tepid agreement to let Chamberlain discuss the German proposal with the French. Conservative imperialists like Balfour, Lord Curzon, Leo Amery, and Winston Churchill, now returned to the Conservative fold, were entirely opposed to an Anglo-French alliance and against any commitment in Europe "that might restrict Britain's freedom to mediate between the powers."[29] There was considerable reservation about any involvement at all. Churchill argued that there was no danger of a breach with the French, who would soon calm down, so there was no need to take any action.[30] It was only with the greatest difficulty, including a threat of resignation, that Chamberlain got Prime Minister Stanley Baldwin's help in persuading the government to propose to the French serious consideration of the plan proposed by Stresemann. The French, rather than stand alone against the British, agreed to join the negotiations.

In its final form the Locarno agreement consisted of two main elements: (1) the Treaty of Mutual Guarantee, or the Rhineland Pact, and (2) a treaty of nonaggression by the states bordering on the Rhine, Germany, France, and Belgium. In the first, Britain, France, Germany, Belgium, and Italy agreed to maintain the demilitarization of the Rhineland, "to defend the existing borders between Germany and France and Germany and Belgium and to render military assistance to any signatory who was the victim of a violation of these two promises."[31] The arbitration agreements (2) were between Germany and her neighbors, France, Belgium, Poland, and Czechoslovakia.

These agreements were not what Chamberlain had originally wanted, but they were the best he could get, and he soon began speaking of them as the best imaginable. The Locarno agreements were greeted with rapture by ordinary people, the press, the diplomats, and, for a long time, the historians. Headlines in the *New York Times* announced, "France and Germany Bar War Forever," and the London *Times* proclaimed, "Peace at Last."[32] Stresemann made much of the voluntary nature of the agreements. Unlike the Versailles Treaty, Locarno had been negotiated and accepted by Germany; thus, it was legitimate in the eyes of the Germans and would therefore be effective and lasting. Germany tacitly accepted the loss of Alsace-Lorraine and the permanent demilitarization of the Rhineland, and the Rhineland Pact seemed to bind Britain to give France the assurance it wanted against a German attack. The east, to be sure, was not so protected, but at least Germany had agreed to arbitration treaties with the new states.[33] Beyond all that there was "the spirit of Locarno," a spirit of accommodation and cooperation more important, many said, than the particular provisions. Germany would be conciliated and France reassured, and a true peace would emerge. Chamberlain told the House of Commons that the Locarno agreements were "yet more valuable for the spirit that produced them. . . . We regard Locarno, not as the end of the work of appeasement and reconciliation, but as its beginning. . . .[34]

The realities were very different from these pleasant imaginings. Germany emerged from Locarno with a great victory and the certainty that its position would improve still further. The Locarno agreements left the Germans free to pursue revision of their frontiers in the east. Pressed to negotiate an "eastern Locarno," Stresemann flatly refused. After much discussion, he agreed not to try to change the eastern settlement by force, but even that he refused to put in writing. Territorial revision in the east was supported by just about every German, and Stresemann called it "the most important task of our policy."[35] The Locarno agreements, in fact, prevented the French from providing effective military help to their eastern allies. If a war should break out over the Polish Corridor, for instance, France could not attack Germany without violating the Rhineland Pact. The alliances with Poland and Czechoslovakia lost much of their value to France and, of course, to its eastern allies, because of Locarno. As one perceptive German diplomat put it: "I am a poor German but would not wish to be Polish for there would not pass a night when I would sleep tranquilly."[36] Abandonment of the Poles and Czechs would save the Germans from the threat of another two-front war.

In the west, France was out of the Ruhr and in five years would be out of the Rhineland.[37] If the French ever tried to reenter German territory, even to seize customs houses, they would be chastised by the League Council, and Britain and Italy would be bound to come to the aid of Germany. If the Germans refused to meet reparations or disarmament requirements the French had abandoned all means of enforcement. The main point of the Rhineland Pact was to fix the German frontiers with France and Belgium permanently by consent and so to remove a major danger of war, but not even that was secure. Days after the conclusion of the Locarno agreements, Stresemann asked Belgium to return Eupen and Malmédy, "claiming that he had only promised not to alter the frontier by military means."[38] The French accepted these disadvantages because they seemed to have no choice. Desperate for some kind of protection and unwilling to be isolated, they accepted what they could get: Germany's promise of nonaggression and Britain's conditional promise of military assistance.

The promise of British military assistance was a weak reed on which to support French security, for military considerations had never been a serious part of Chamberlain's thinking. During the negotiations, Sir Maurice Hankey, secretary to the Committee of Imperial Defence, had warned the Foreign Secretary that an agreement would commit England to take action, that "some day the cheque would be presented and we should have to honour it." But Chamberlain would not allow the committee to assess the strategic aspects of the proposed agreements; he "did not wish to wreck his policy on the technicalities of military consideration."[39] Nor was the British promise a firm guarantee against

German attack. In case of war between Germany and France the British and Italians would need to decide who was the aggressor and then support the victim. The French and British could not make concerted plans against a German attack, as they had before 1914, because Britain could not prejudge which of the two might be the aggressor. Locarno was not "a guarantee against invasion," only a guarantee to come to the aid of the attacked party after the fact. "Once the Rhineland was evacuated, Locarno guaranteed [only] that British troops would return to the Continent to liberate France from the German Army."[40] Britain's capacity to deter future German aggression was thereby sharply reduced.

In 1925, moreover, the British had no thought of going to war to defend France.

> Britain retained wide latitude for deciding when and how to act and accepted this commitment in the expectation that it would never have to be honoured. Furthermore, it could do so only through strong military forces and plans for their use with its potential allies. Yet the treaty led Britain to believe that Europe would remain peaceful during the foreseeable future and encouraged it to reduce its forces, while Britain's position as the guarantor between the signatories hampered the making of such plans. As Amery noted, Britain could scarcely send "its officers simultaneously to Paris and Berlin to work up arrangements for fighting with the French and against the French." Britain soon rejected a Belgian request for staff talks about Belgium's defences because this would contravene Britain's "special position."[41]

For the moment a German attack was impossible. For the future, the British government hoped and expected that all would be well. Austen Chamberlain believed that Britain's guarantee of its border would calm the French and remove their fears. Britain's own safety would also be assured by Germany's conciliation and its return to the Concert of Europe. British friendship and support of France would remove tensions and allow peaceful resolution of outstanding issues.

Winston Churchill, among others, insisted that Britain must not make a commitment that tied its hands, that prevented it from standing between France and Germany as an arbiter. Chamberlain, to be sure, said in 1926 that "the true defence of our country . . . is now no longer the Channel . . . but upon the Rhine,"[42] but he never expected to fight in defense of that line. Still less did the British contemplate defending Germany's eastern neighbors, who were deliberately excluded from Locarno. Of the Polish corridor, which had now become "the danger-spot in Europe,"[43] Chamberlain considered it a place "for which no British Government ever will or ever can risk the bones of a British grenadier."[44] Even at the center of the agreement, the Rhineland Pact, Britain sharply limited its commitment. Britain was bound to defend the current situation there and to guarantee the arbitration treaty between Germany, France, and Belgium only if a violation involved a military movement into the demilitarized zone or amounted to unprovoked aggression. Any violation, moreover, had to be "flagrant," Britain herself "being in every case the judge, and it had to constitute 'unprovoked aggression,' the definition of which was again left to Britain."[45] In the ratification debate, Chamberlain rightly told Parliament that Britain's obligations could not "be more narrowly circumscribed as [sic] they are in the Treaty of Locarno."[46] To a historian writing with the benefit of hindsight "[i]t seems incongruous that a largely disarmed Britain became the primary instrument for the enforcement of peace."[47] But the British did not feel the incongruity because they did not really feel the obligation.

Chamberlain, among other British leaders, regarded the Locarno agreements as a great triumph and a significant turning point, "the real dividing line between war and peace."[48] He basked in the warmth of the widespread praise that poured in. World approval became official with the award in 1926 of the Nobel Peace Prize, which Chamberlain shared with Stresemann and Briand. What he valued most was no specific guarantee, but the "Spirit of Locarno." In November of 1925 he said, "It was the spirit of Locarno to which I attached so much value and which I hoped would inform and guide the policy of the whole world. . . . Our policy was one of appeasement. The world was too narrow to admit of any of us remaining indifferent to the possibilities of a new struggle breaking out anywhere. . . ."[49] That same spirit, once the pact was in effect, would produce a "*détente* which should inevitably follow. . . ."[50] Events had seemed to justify the proud claim Chamberlain had made to the House of Commons in March 1925:

> The British Empire, detached from Europe by its Dominions, linked to Europe by these islands, can do what no other nation on the face of the earth can do, and from east and west alike there come to me the cry that, after all, it is in the hands of the British Empire and if they will that there shall be no war there will be no war.[51]

France had repeatedly appealed to Britain for a guarantee of peace, and in January 1925 Germany had made its appeal. At Locarno, so it seemed, Britain had willed peace, and now there would be peace.

In fact, the British government stumbled into the Locarno treaties to avoid looming disasters caused by its continuing unwillingness to take the lead in shaping a viable peace, without intending to and very much against the original wishes of many, probably the majority, in the Cabinet. A remarkable document, written in the Foreign Office to justify and celebrate the achievements of Locarno and to persuade the dominions to take part, helps to make that clear.[52] The Versailles Treaty, it says, did not bring real peace but only a "precarious armistice" and the problem since has been to turn it into a true peace. Locarno provided the solution and the beginning of its execution.

Had the British considered their situation in realistic strategic terms after Locarno they would not have had cause for such hopeful rejoicing. Both the treaties agreed to at Locarno, however, and the spirit of Locarno were a sham. The basic problem of French, European, and, therefore, British security was not truly addressed and, in fact, made worse. The German advantage over France in population and industrial power would continue to grow, less and less hampered by reparations payments and more than ever assisted by American loans and investments. By 1929, per capita production was higher than it had been in 1913; between 1924 and 1929, German exports doubled. Germany's improvement in organization and investment in industry swiftly outpaced the other European powers.[53] Should the Germans violate the treaties, especially in regard to the Rhineland, Britain's commitment to aid the French was, in reality, less certain than ever.

But in spite of its prosperity and industrial growth and in spite of Locarno, the Germans were neither conciliated nor satisfied. Even such a "good European" as Stresemann worked for the unraveling of Versailles, the restoration of German economic supremacy in Europe, rearmament, and revision of the border with Belgium and, far more grandly, of the entire eastern settlement. He had written to the former Crown Prince that his first goal was to remove foreign troops from German soil. After that he meant to get free of reparations, "protect the ten or twelve million Germans living under the foreign yoke, recover Danzig and the Corridor and revise the frontier in Upper Silesia."[54] Stresemann also wrote of a union with German Austria, and he did not entirely rule out the recovery of Alsace-Lorraine in the future. He told the German Cabinet that the Locarno accords were not meant "'to stabilize the status quo,' but 'to assure peace'; and they did not include any 'relinquishment of former German territory.'"[55]

Stresemann, moreover, was a moderate in the German political spectrum. When he returned from Locarno he and his agreements were savagely assaulted by more radical nationalists. Hitler's Nazi Party urged Stresemann's assassination, and the more respectable German Nationalist Party (DNVP) was angry at the concession of Alsace-Lorraine and of the rest of the agreements. The DNVP withdrew its minister from the Cabinet and caused a government crisis. Army officials told President Hindenburg that Stresemann was handing their country over to the Western Powers. For the rest of Stresemann's life and after he died, criticism continued.

Whatever his own intentions might have been, there were Germans who were entirely unreconciled and ready to use force to restore Germany to dominance whenever the chance should arise. Stresemann's acceptance of the Dawes Plan and the work of the London Conference in 1924 had been denounced in the Reichstag as a "policy of enslavement," and Ludendorff declared, "This is a disgrace to Germany! Ten years ago I won the battle of Tannenberg. Today you have made a Jewish Tannenberg!"[56] Should such people come to power, the agreements made at Locarno provided few realistic means for preventing Germany's rearmament and the forcible revision of the situation in Europe. Such men, General Seeckt among them, were "unaware [of] or unwilling to admit the obvious military advantages of the Locarno Pact. Besides relieving Allied-German tension, a factor which by itself was to prove most advantageous to the Reichswehr's undercover activities, it also enabled Germany to concentrate most of her military planning against the East, where the threat of a clash with Poland was seen as a constant possibility."[57]

Locarno, moreover, went far toward completing the dismantling of the system France had created to protect itself. As a practical matter, France's security after 1925 relied on its own arms, on its alliances with the Little Entente, i.e., Poland, Czechoslovakia, Rumania, and Yugoslavia, especially the first two states, which bordered Germany, and on the British military guarantee of its frontier with Germany. Unless France could protect its eastern allies they would be a great liability instead of an asset, but the only effective way to do so was to attack Germany from the west. Locarno, however, "added one more obstacle against unilateral French acts of force against Germany. . . . So long as the demilitarisation of the Rhineland was guaranteed by Britain any further incursion into the Ruhr or any French attempt to bring military assistance to her eastern allies from the west was not merely illegal but tantamount to war with Britain."[58] A sound defensive strategy, therefore, required a strong offensive component that was mobile and swift and always ready to attack. Such a force and such a strategy could have had a strong deterrent effect on Germany and served as a protection for France's allies, and it was something the French could do for themselves. The Ruhr debacle, however, and the rift it had caused with Britain and the United States, and then the realities of the Locarno settlement, had pushed the French totally onto the defensive, psychologically as well as strategically. Their military planners designed only a mass army that could fight only after a long delay, one entirely unsuited for the most important task. "The French system of alliances rested on strategic nonsense."[59]

Britain's security, however, as its civilian and military leaders recognized from time to time, depended on France. The British, however, suspicious of France and her unwelcome demands, chose to rehabilitate Germany and expect the best from her, cherishing "the illusion that France and Germany were equals as between whom Britain had to hold the scales. . . . While this illusion held British opinion in its grip Germany need not fear an Anglo-French combination against her, save in the most blatant case of German aggression, which no sensible German Government would attempt unless it were strong enough to despise such a combination even if it were formed."[60] The Locarno agreements represented a victory for irresponsibility and wishful thinking at the expense of security and peace. Chamberlain's boast to Parliament was right that in the first decade after the war Britain could "do what no other nation on the face of the earth can do" and that the British were in such a position that "if they will that there shall be no war there will be no war." But that decision would require a cold and clear look at reality, a recognition that for the foreseeable future peace would depend on Britain's willingness and ability to defend France and the new nations of Central Europe against a restored and vengeful Germany, for all the reasons spelled out by the experts in the Foreign Office. In a broader sense, British and European security required the British to accept their role as the leading power, the only one capable of a forward policy to shape the international scene in such a way as to preserve the peace. Such a policy must be backed by a larger, stronger military force planning and working in concert with the French to keep Germany militarily inferior until such time as it could be trusted. The British, however, had fled from such a recognition and such a policy ever since 1919, and they did so decisively in 1925. No more than before were they ready for a turn from the comfortable way of life such an approach would require. "The British desire for 'business as usual' in 1925 had a commonsense flavour about it. But politics are not everywhere run by men whose footrule is the profit and loss account."[61] Locarno was not "the real dividing line between war and peace," but the end of any serious thought of seeking peace through strength and deterrence and the beginning of a policy of appeasement.

9

The Spirit of Locarno

The signing of the Locarno treaties unleashed an outburst of optimism and pacific sentiment. Briand and Stresemann repeatedly announced the friendship of their two countries and competed in expressions of pan-European solidarity. Germany joined the League of Nations. Briand and American Secretary of State Frank B. Kellogg drew up a proposal meant to abolish war. In August 1928, fifteen nations met to sign the "Pact of Paris," in which they condemned recourse to war to solve international disputes, renounced it as an instrument of national policy, and agreed that any future disputes between them would be solved only by peaceful means. They were soon joined by almost every country in the world.

The British Government gazed with complacency on a world they had created.

> Having virtually reassumed the leadership of Europe, she [Britain] can afford the luxury of individual restraint, where others, less reflective and less interested, are not afraid to tread. She can, in fact, hear the privilege of independence without the odium of isolation.[1]

In that spirit, Britain's Chancellor of the Exchequer, Winston Churchill, told the Committee of Imperial Defence that "there was every reason to secure a reduction in the total amount of the Service Estimates."[2]

In 1926, in the early days of the "Locarno Era," the British Foreign Office

prepared a memorandum for its chief cataloguing the government's commitments and policies around the world.[3] It began with a statement of general
goals: to seek peace, to preserve the status quo and the balance of power, and
to protect and pursue British interests abroad. In this Britain was very different
from other countries, such as Germany, Hungary, Russia, Italy, and Japan, all
of whom hoped to regain lost territories or acquire new ones. "We, on the other
hand, have no territorial ambitions nor desire for aggrandisement. We have got
all that we want—perhaps more. Our sole object is to keep what we have and
live in peace." This made the conduct of British policy unique.

> Many foreign countries are playing for a definite stake and their policy is
> shaped accordingly. It is not so in our case. To the casual observer our
> foreign policy may appear to lack consistency and continuity, but both
> are there. We keep our hands free in order to throw our weight into the
> scale on behalf of peace. The maintenance of the balance of power and
> the preservation of the status quo have been our guiding lights for many
> decades and will so continue.

Britain did not pursue such policies for altruistic motives but in its own vital interest. War, quarrels, friction anywhere in the world "spell loss and harm
to British commercial and financial interests." That was why Britain involved
itself in conflicts and tried to help solve them peacefully. "So manifold and
ubiquitous are British trade and British finance that, whatever else may be the
outcome of a disturbance of the peace, we shall be the losers." Britain's far-
flung economic interests complicated its foreign policy. High tariffs and other
discriminatory economic and financial policies in other countries compelled
Britain to complain and put pressure on those countries in defense of British interests, and these actions "do not facilitate good relation or render easier the
conduct of purely foreign policy." That was

> the explanation and the reason of our intervention in almost every dis-
> pute that arises, and one justification of the armed forces which enable us
> to intervene prominently and with authority. Without our trade and our
> finance we sink to the level of a third-class Power. Locarno and the un-
> employed have an intimate connexion.[4]

However hopeful the British mood might be after Locarno, the Foreign Office memorandum recognized future dangers. The fear of a conflict with France
could safely be dismissed, but the need to protect it from "a German revival"
and "Italian ambitions" could not. "It is to our interest to see a strong and
prosperous France . . . [for] the two countries are bound to stand together for
many years to come." The independence of the Low Countries also "will in the

future as in the past remain of vital importance to this country." Even without the Locarno treaties "we should be obliged as in 1914 to fight in order to prevent the absorption or conquest of the Low Countries by any Great Power."[5]

The obvious source of such a threat must be Germany. To be sure, the situation since Locarno was more hopeful. "The policy of appeasement continued and grew . . . culminating in the Locarno Conference. . . . The Locarno Treaty may be regarded as the triumph of the British idea of compromise and conciliation over the continental idea of compulsion." The great question was "what will Germany make of her new position?" Such difficulties as involved the Rhineland and the Saar had become ephemeral, but the problems raised by Danzig, Upper Silesia, Austria, and disarmament would remain serious. In regard to the first two, in spite of its arbitration treaty with Poland, "Germany will never rest until her present wrongs, as she considers them, have been righted." At Locarno Britain refused to make any commitment in Eastern Europe, but "as members of the League we are bound to do our part in resisting any forcible solution of these questions." What action, if any, British interests would require in such a case could not be predicted, but "this country has never in the past taken up arms to resist the dismemberment of Poland. . . ." A German union with Austria was forbidden by the Treaty of Trianon without the permission of the League Council, which was most unlikely. Yet, "sooner or later the union of Germany and Austria will become a live issue." At present the problem was remote, but should the Germans in the future violate the agreement, Britain "would be affected as signatory of the Treaty of Saint-Germain, and of the Covenant of the League of Nations."

It was further evident that the question of general disarmament would arise quite soon. "No German Government will ever be satisfied until the general disarmament foreshadowed in the peace treaties has become a reality." At the Locarno Conference, in fact, the Germans had asked that the amount of armaments permitted to all nations should not only be "as small as possible but also proportional." But Sir Austen Chamberlain rejected that request, saying that "German disarmament remained a thing apart. The other Powers could not agree to disarm in a measure proportionate to Germany's disarmament." Here was a difficulty ominous for future peaceful relations:

> If and when a definite attempt to bring about a general disarmament has been made and failed, the German grievance will become still more acute, and she may be tempted to repudiate or evade her obligations under the Treaty of Versailles to remain disarmed. Any attempt to recreate a navy would presumably be treated as a direct threat to Great Britain, nor would His Majesty's Government acquiesce in a violent repudiation by Germany of her obligations in respect to land armaments, especially if her policy was clearly that of recovering her prewar military strength.[6]

The memorandum accurately stated Britain's goals, past and present, and acutely predicted the sources of future troubles. Where it went badly wrong was in predicting Britain's responses to them. In the next decade the British government would claim to have no responsibility when Germany absorbed Austria, would acquiesce to a major buildup of the German navy, and would look on as the Germans began to build a new military power greater than that of 1914. Most contrary to expectations, the British went to war in 1939 because of a German attack on Poland.

The memorandum made one unstated and inaccurate assumption that was critical: that Britain currently had and would in the future retain decisive military force. It cited with approval the words of Headlam-Morley, the Foreign Office's Historical Adviser: "[I]f in presenting the estimates for naval and military defence, the importance of providing for liabilities under this treaty is shown; then I believe that in the long run the treaty will become effective." The meaning of that, according to the memorandum, was that "the more the nations of Europe become convinced of our readiness to fulfill our guarantee, the less likelihood will there be that we shall be called upon to do so."[7] The flaw in this otherwise admirable reasoning was that the British armed forces were already insufficient to meet the country's responsibilities undertaken of Locarno, as the author had reason to know. In the same year that he wrote, the Chiefs of Staff spoke of the forces available to fulfill Britain's continental guarantees in the first of their annual reviews of imperial defense policy:

> The size of the forces of the Crown maintained by Great Britain is governed by various conditions peculiar to each service, and is not arrived at by any calculation of the requirements of foreign policy, nor is it possible that they should ever be so calculated. Thus, though the Expeditionary Force, together with a limited number of Air Force Squadrons, constitute the only military instrument available for immediate use in Europe or elsewhere outside Imperial territory in support of foreign policy, they are available only when requirements of Imperial Defence permit.
>
> It follows that, so far as commitments on the Continent are concerned, the Services can only take note of them.[8]

The expeditionary force mentioned was "two skeletal divisions made up of units temporarily without other employment." In the next few years the military situation grew worse, and the Chiefs repeated their warnings. In 1928 they wrote that "we cannot, in the early stages of a war, do much, except by naval means, to carry out our obligations under the Locarno Treaties." In 1930 they said, "We have received no instructions to work out plans in fulfillment of that guarantee, and in fact detailed plans have not been worked out. This country is in a less favourable position to fulfill the Locarno guarantees than it was, without any guarantee, to come to the assistance of France and Belgium in 1914." In 1925 and the years to follow, Britain was "impotent to bring serious influence to bear on those developments in Europe on which her security ultimately depended."[9]

Britain's military weakness made a mockery of the sage words of the memorandum connecting Britain's readiness with deterrence. It also undermined whatever advantages might have come from Britain's favored policy of keeping its "hands free." Such a posture might work if the British held such a preponderance of military power that its joining one side or the other would inescapably mean victory. The absence of such preponderance, however, makes deterrence difficult or impossible. Throwing one's "weight into the scale" requires having a weight adequate to tip it in the desired direction. Britain's military capacity after Locarno was at odds with a policy of deterrence.

In the words of the biographers of Stanley Baldwin, the Prime Minister who presided over Locarno and returned to live with its consequences:

> Britain herself retired behind the veil of security, into a form of isolation which persisted into the early thirties; and disarmament, on which the whole imposing structure rested, never came. When the Pact was tested in 1936 it broke, and though the worst was then hidden, the reasons for its failure could not be disguised: no agreement, however binding, can last ten years without constant and careful thought. The mechanism of the Pact rested on military strength; and three out of five of the partners [Britain, France and Belgium] abandoned their strength. Baldwin was to find the fruit mere Dead Sea ashes when he came back to power.[10]

For the moment, however, the "spirit of Locarno" appeared to work. In September 1926, Germany entered the League of Nations as a permanent member and member of the League Council, a symbol of the end of its disgrace and isolation. Briand proclaimed the end of Franco-German antagonism and declared: "Away with rifles, machine guns, and cannon! Make way for conciliation, arbitration, and peace!"[11] For Germany the new approach brought quick dividends. The Cologne zone of the Rhineland was evacuated on December 1, 1925, and the number of troops in the other zones were reduced in the following year. The committee inspecting German disarmament was deprived of any serious function and withdrew entirely in January 1927, leaving the Germans free to continue their violations of the treaty without fear of complaint.

After Locarno, German foreign policy became "a carefully calibrated series of diplomatic steps calculated to achieve detailed and related goals which in their sum would gradually dismantle the Treaty of Versailles." Germany's ultimate goal was to "reconstruct and even to expand the prewar Great Power position of the German Reich."[12] Entry into the League of Nations was not merely a symbol of Germany's return to the status of a great power but part of the revisionist plan.[13] One card that strengthened Germany's revisionist hand was its relationship with the Soviet Union. At Locarno, Stresemann had obtained exemption from Article 16 of the League Covenant, which required Germany to permit transit of League troops to apply sanctions to another country, and from Germany's participation in the sanctions. This weakened the League's capacity to pursue collective security through the application of sanctions. In any quarrel between Poland and Russia, moreover, the Poles would be isolated, since no Western troops could cross Germany without consent. This was a further step toward "weakening the Franco-Polish alliance and the eventual demotion of French continental hegemony."[14]

To reassure the Soviets, alarmed at Germany's entry into the League, Stresemann in April 1926 signed the Treaty of Berlin, which essentially confirmed the Treaty of Rapallo. The first Western reaction was shock and anger, but in May 1927, Chamberlain told Briand: "We are battling with Soviet Russia for the soul of Germany. . . . the more difficult our relations with Russia became, the more important was it that we should attach Germany solidly to the Western Powers."[15]

This remained British policy despite the disturbing news that had come out of Germany the previous December. An article in the *Manchester Guardian* revealed for the first time the secret collaboration between the Soviet and German armies. Two weeks later the Socialist politician Philipp Scheidemann made a speech in the Reichstag revealing in detail the broad range of German disarmament violations. Great sums of money from private sources were going into military spending. Paramilitary patriotic associations were being used by the army to increase its numbers. Scheidemann also revealed the relations between the army and the Russians and "the production of airplanes, poison gas, and ammunition by German firms in the Soviet Union."[16] In response to his questions, the German Minister of Defense replied, "Nothing had been done of which the Foreign Office [under Stresemann] did not have knowledge. The necessary passports issued in the Foreign Office." The revelations caused a sensation in Germany, where Scheidemann was denounced for endangering his country, but the feared reactions from other countries were absent.

Much of the information was dismissed as old hat. Allied experts had been talking about such violations for years. To be sure, the role of the Soviet Union in German rearmament was news, but it had nothing to do with the question at hand, the removal of Allied inspection and military control that was such an important part of the "spirit of Locarno."

> The Allies faced the alternative of either returning to the strict enforcement of each and every provision of Versailles, which would have meant the end of Locarno and all it had come to signify; or else they had to close their eyes to many things that went on in Germany, putting their trust in the good will of Stresemann, who would see to it that his coun-

try lived up to obligations voluntarily undertaken. By the end of 1927, the western powers had gone too far along the second path to turn back.[17]

In 1926, about the time of the *Manchester Guardian* story, rumors were rife that the Germans were preparing a future attack on the Polish Corridor. The Stahlhelm, a paramilitary organization of extreme nationalists hostile to a settlement with the West and to the Weimer Republic, grew to the point that in 1927–1928 its leaders claimed a membership of a million men. A nervous member of the German left warned "that for every French soldier who left the Rhineland ten Stahlhelm troopers would spring up,"[18] yet Stresemann was able to obtain from the Western Powers the troop withdrawals and the end to arms inspections already mentioned. The Germans continued to press for further revision. There were still occupation forces in the Rhineland, and Germany abandoned a conciliatory tone and demanded their prompt evacuation, calling the occupation an "iron curtain."[19] The first of heavier reparations payments under the Dawes Plan would soon come due, moreover, and Stresemann sought reductions, insisting, however, that the Germans would accept no new payment schedule without an end to the occupation.

In August 1929 the powers involved met at The Hague to discuss both problems in what they called "the Conference on the Final Liquidation of the War." Britain was represented by Philip Snowden, Chancellor of the Exchequer in the new Labour government that had recently replaced the Conservatives. The Labour Party, led by Ramsay MacDonald, whose Foreign Secretary was Arthur Henderson, pursued the "spirit of Locarno" with conviction. The new government "was determined to complete the appeasement of Europe by removing yet more of the disabilities under the peace treaty which so upset Germany. . . . Make Germany a contented and fully equal member of the human brotherhood, the Labour Government believed, and the task of achieving lasting peace in Europe would be completed."[20]

Snowden, giving primacy to economic goals, demanded an increase in Britain's share of the reparations payments and the end of the expense of supporting British troops occupying the Rhineland. With ruthless arguments in which "he conceded neither a farthing nor a polite word,"[21] he gained a greater share of reparations for Britain in the new Young Plan, which replaced the Dawes Plan and once again scaled down Germany's payments. Briand pressed for continued inspection of German disarmament and for continuation of the Rhineland occupation until the 1935 date, but the British would have none of it, threatening to remove their own troops from the northern zone unilaterally. Under their pressure the French yielded and agreed to evacuation by June 30, 1930.

The Germans showed no gratitude for the early withdrawal from the Rhineland, although they regarded it as the most valuable result of the settlement of 1929. It gave them the freedom to press harder for a new order in Europe. British diplomats reported a statement from the German Minister of the Interior that "'the Rhineland was not really free owing to its being subject to certain servitudes'—meaning the permanent demilitarization provisions in the Versailles Treaty." The new German Foreign Minister, Ernst Curtius, seemed to be more concerned with German rearmament than with a general disarmament.[22] "Freedom from occupation could be an important step toward revision of Versailles and independence from France rather than a step toward cooperation." In the words of President Hindenburg, the Hague settlement could serve as "a staging area [for the] next assault on the Treaty of Versailles."[23]

Acclaim from all political parties, nonetheless, greeted Snowden on his return from The Hague. Even two years later the editor of the *Observer* said of Snowden's work at The Hague that "insisting on the speedy evacuation of the foreign garrisons, [he] accomplished the best single stroke for peace that any Foreign Minister has achieved since the armistice."[24] Such a reception revealed how widespread was the British endorsement of the Locarno approach. A discontented Germany was the problem. Locarno was seen as the crucial step in turning the Germans from dangerous dissatisfaction that brought confrontation and threatened war to acceptance of the world order and the willingness to seek satisfaction through peaceful means. Germany must be conciliated and engaged, not confronted and isolated. The new approach was to ignore unpleasant facts about German behavior and desires and to assume the best about Germany's intentions and development. Conciliation would bring peace and confidence, which would improve trade and prosperity, which would improve the German mood and strengthen the forces that favored democracy and cooperation.

All this depended on the conviction that there was no real danger of a war against Germany, which made strategic questions irrelevant. In September 1929, for instance, MacDonald told the Tenth Assembly of the League of Nations at Geneva to consider the question of disarmament "on the assumption that the risk of war breaking out is far less than the hope of peace being permanently observed."[25] Should that assumption prove false, however, the results of the Hague Conference would take on a different significance. Even in retrospect it is too much to claim that the evacuation of the Rhineland was "the decisive *military* step" in the breakdown of the peace,[26] but there is evident merit to the argument that if the Rhineland had been occupied until 1935, as required at Versailles, that "would have deterred or prevented even a National Socialist Government from embarking upon a rearmament programme of dangerous proportions."[27] It has been argued that such thinking could not be expected from British leaders in 1929, when in respectable circles conciliation was thought to be the only enlightened policy. "German revanchism" had not yet reached "unmanageable proportions," and it was too soon to give up hope of bringing the Germans back "into the comity of nations." At such a time,

Labour's "policy of appeasing Berlin, while no doubt risky, had much to commend it. . . ."[28]

Another view is less forgiving of the Labour government of 1929: "[T]he gravamen of the charge against them—as against British policy between the world wars as a whole—is not that they failed to foresee the future, but that they deliberately rejected the lessons offered by the past."[29] Behind that entire policy was the belief that the past was irrelevant in a world that was made different by modern conditions. The conventional wisdom of the past must be rejected; strategy, alliances, armaments, military forces had been the causes of wars in the past. The rejection of these things and the way of thinking that went with them is what would bring peace. There was no reason to worry or even think about the strategic consequences of the early withdrawal from the Rhineland, which removed France's capacity easily to prevent the emergence of a dangerous Germany. "The European balance of power, heavily tilted at Locarno, had taken a great lurch away from France and England towards Germany,"[30] but nobody seemed to know or care.

The second vital assumption underlying the British policy of conciliation toward Germany was that economic prosperity would continue and grow, smoothing the edges of German resentment and ambition. That hope was rudely undermined by the Wall Street stock market crash in October 1929. For Germany, even more than other countries, the year 1929, the midpoint in the two decades between the wars, was an important watershed. In October of that year, Gustav Stresemann died, and with him the politically careful, if determined, program for the revision of the Versailles settlement in Germany's favor. In the same month the Wall Street stock market crash gave impetus to a great depression that swept across the industrialized world, causing political shock waves of great significance in Europe, especially Germany.

Germany had been suffering from an economic depression well before the crash. In October 1929 there were already 1.76 million unemployed. By December the number was 3 million and growing fast.[31] The financial panic led the Americans to set up high tariff walls against foreign imports and to recall their loans. The new barriers to exports and the flight of American capital devastated the Germans. Business suffered, unemployment grew, and the results were felt in the political arena. The fortunes of the parties who had always supported the Weimar Republic sank, as the extremist, antirepublican, anticapitalist parties, the Communists and Nazis, gained new strength. Each of them, and others as well, fielded paramilitary organizations that fought one another in the streets.

Leaders of the army were alarmed that the country might disintegrate and fall into civil war, but they were unwilling to take direct responsibility for governing, preferring to work through political intermediaries they hoped to control. It was a delicate task that proved to be beyond their capabilities. In March 1930 the broad government led by the Socialist Hermann Müller fell. General

Groener, Minister of War, and his associate, General Kurt von Schleicher, head of the ministry's political bureau, took leading roles in shaping the new government. Their aim was to select a Cabinet amenable to their views that was above parties, independent of the Reichstag and dependent for its authority on President Hindenburg, who could be trusted to pursue the army's policies.[32] They chose as the new Chancellor Heinrich Brüning of the Catholic Center Party.

Brüning's plan as Chancellor is sometimes interpreted as one seeking to solve domestic problems by achieving success in foreign policy, specifically, to reduce or put an end to the reparations payments and arms limitations imposed by the Versailles Treaty.[33] There is good evidence, however, that foreign policy, in the sense of restoring Germany to political independence and the status of a great power, was his chief concern and that he was prepared to run great risks and cause terrible suffering on the domestic side in order to achieve his goals in the other sphere.

The Chancellor launched a program of the strictest fiscal rigidity with deliberate deflationary consequences, raising taxes and reducing government expenditures, including unemployment insurance, but not reducing the military budget. When this proposal was turned down by the Reichstag, Brüning resorted to the infamous Article 48 of the Weimar constitution, which permitted him to promulgate the law by presidential decree. It was a sharp departure from the principles of republican government, and it would not be the last. Some have regarded it as the death knell for the Weimar Republic. Brüning then called for new elections, hoping to achieve a Reichstag more friendly to his policies, but his political judgment was faulty. The elections of September 14, 1930, produced a great victory for the extremist parties: the Communists won seventy-seven seats, but the greatest winners were Hitler's Nazis. In the elections of 1928 they had received 809,000 votes and twelve seats in the Reichstag. In 1930 they polled 6,400,000, "which meant that 107 brown-shirts were going to march into the new Reichstag."[34]

Political leaders in Britain and America thought of Brüning as an exponent of financial responsibility and political moderation, but his memoirs and other evidence suggest that he had something else in mind. He told the army, the Nationalists, and Hitler that he welcomed their public opposition "so that he could exploit this in diplomacy, . . . by making himself appear as the moderate German to whom concessions had best be made."[35] In October 1930 he explained his plans to the newly influential Adolf Hitler. In the first stage, economic policy would be completely in the service of foreign policy. Deflationary measures of every kind would be used to harden Germany "so that she could resist any external pressure and be in a position to exploit the world economic crisis in order to bring pressure to bear on the remaining Powers."[36] Economic hardship would show the Western nations that Germany could not afford to pay reparations. Germany would become as independent of imports as possible; together with fiscal soundness created by domestic austerity, autaurky would allow Germany to shake free of the Young Plan, reparations, and arms limitations.

Meanwhile, the German economy was in terrible decline. Unemployment grew from 3,000,000 in March when Brüning took office to 4,380,000 in December 1930 and to 5,615,000 a year later, close to 10 percent of the population and a much higher percentage of the workforce.[37] While cutting government expenditures for unemployment benefits and reducing wages and salaries and jobs, however, he refused to make equivalent reductions in the military budget, reflection the political power of the military in the late Weimar Republic and also Brüning's determination to strengthen Germany's position as a great power. At the same time he continued to provide economic support for the inefficient grain-growing Junkers east of the Elbe. This made the price of bread artificially high at a time when wages and other prices were low and placed a burden on industry, on the poor, and on the small mixed and dairy farmers. All of this increased the flight to the extreme parties on the right and left, especially to the Nazis, but Brüning was prepared to run the risk and also to use it to achieve his goals in foreign policy. The very growth of Nazi power and the threat it posed helped to convince the Western Powers to make concessions.

In spite of these developments, and ignoring the evidence of the Germans' rearmament and their determination to continue pressing for the undoing of the European order, even after Locarno, the British government clung to Brüning. As the Foreign Secretary put it in February 1931:

> The fall of the Brüning Government in the present period of political and economic strain might easily have far-reaching detrimental effects on international relationships. . . . It ought, I consider, to be the policy of His Majesty's Government to give it such support and encouragement as they properly can, in order to fortify its position.[38]

Rather than depart from his policy of tight money and retrenchment meant to "discipline" the Germans and demonstrate Germany's incapacity to continue paying reparations, therefore, Brüning would take no measure to lighten the suffering. It seems to have been Brüning's plan to have Germany be the first European nation to emerge from the depression.[39] The result would have been to give Germany an economic and then political domination over states of Eastern Europe, which would entirely undermine France's plan for security through eastern alliances, already badly weakened by the evacuation of the Rhineland.

Brüning's chancellorship was a period of intensified pressure against the Versailles settlement. When France agreed to withdraw from the Rhineland in September 1929, its Foreign Minister, Briand, proposed a new plan for a European federation that somewhat resembled the plan for a united Europe of our own time. He hoped, by involving Germany in a politically and economically integrated Europe, to preserve the states of Eastern and Southeastern Europe and so to defend French security in a new way. The Germans saw it as an attempt to defend Versailles and French domination. Their response was to take a bold and aggressive line. German diplomats pressed for an end to demilitarization in the Rhineland. Brüning went forward with building four armored cruisers, or "pocket battleships," between 1931 and 1934 even as he complained of Germany's poverty and its inability to pay reparations.[40] Sir George Milne, Chief of the Imperial General Staff, wrote a memorandum showing the several ways that Germany was evading the military limitations imposed at Versailles.[41] "Although he knew of these developments, Henderson chose, for a time, to turn a blind eye in the interest of general European conciliation."[42]

Most striking of all was Germany's announcement on March 21, 1931, of the intention to form a customs union with Austria. It was done without the prior notice and discussion characteristic of the Stresemann era, but resembled "a forcing manoeuvre in the Wilhelmine manner;"[43] it was also a precursor of the unpleasant surprises that Hitler would so often present to the world. This action was intended as a step in the direction of gaining new influence in Eastern Europe and, as the French, Poles, Czechs, and Yugoslavs quickly saw, the first step in the Anchluss, the union of Germany and Austria forbidden by the treaties of Versailles and St. Germain. It was also a way of undermining Briand's plan for a federated Europe, although, as the German diplomat Bernhard von Bülow said, "we will dress the matter up with a pan-European cloak."[44] The French responded by using their financial power to break the Creditanstalt bank in Vienna, wreaking economic havoc in Austria, and by bringing the case to the International Court at The Hague, where the union was declared a violation of the treaties. German behavior in this affair was too much for the British Foreign Secretary, Arthur Henderson. For him, "this move decisively demonstrated that the German Government was determined to take selfish and irresponsible actions whatever the consequences."[45] He changed his attitude in the face of clear evidence that he had been mistaken about Germany. In this respect he was all but alone among British leaders.

Germany's behavior aroused suspicions among the other nations and delayed the concessions Brüning sought. Economic effects of the depression and increased public violence between the paramilitary forces of the Nazis and Communists further reduced his political strength. What brought Brüning down, however, was the loss of support from president Hindenburg and from the army, represented by its most political general, Kurt von Schleicher. Hindenburg was unhappy that the Chancellor could not get the Nazis to support an extension of his term as President without a contest. He blames this humiliation on Brüning. The military officers were determined to break through the limitations placed on the German army, and this led them to seek a new and more pliant leader.

Throughout the history of the Weimar Republic the German military leaders worked, often secretly, to build the most effective military force possible with the intention, "under favorable circumstances, to use war as an instrument of policy."[46] Their greatest concern was to achieve a capacity for large-scale mobilization, which required the accumulation of a trained reserve, difficult to achieve so long as conscription was banned. By 1931, Germany's reserves from the last war were becoming too old to fight, and a crisis in reserve manpower loomed. The long-range solution would be to gain freedom from the limiting clauses of the Versailles Treaty, and the army looked to a new Chancellor to achieve that at the forthcoming disarmament conference. Meanwhile, the army encouraged and worked with right-wing paramilitary organizations, especially the Nazi SA. The German government, pressed by the Prussian government, under Socialist control, banned the SA, but by 1932 the army's plans for military expansion contained a role for the SA, so a Chancellor must be found who would protect it.

Schleicher used Brüning's efforts to stop the violence of Hitler's paramilitary SA and SS organizations as the means of bringing him down. He persuaded Hindenburg that Brüning was too responsive to the Socialists and prevailed upon the President to withdrew his support. Since Brüning had been ruling by presidential decree, without the support of Parliament, he was forced to go on May 30, 1932.

Even before the regime of Hitler, however, Brüning's successors had the good fortune to benefit from the work he had done. While he was still in power the Hoover Moratorium suspended reparations payments for a year. At Lausanne in July 1932 the reparations conference revised the Young Plan: Germany would have to make only a token payment in three years, and that would be the end of reparations. Disarmament was also discussed at Lausanne, but the French and British were unwilling to grant the Germans the equality in armaments they insisted upon. At the Geneva Disarmament Conference in September, therefore, the Germans walked out. In response, Britain and the United States put pressure not on the Germans but on the French. In December the conference agreed to the principle of equality of rights for Germany in the field of armaments, and the German military leadership already had firm plans for the restoration of their country's military might.[47] Well before Hitler came to power, therefore, Germany had thrown off some of the most crucial restraints imposed by the Versailles Treaty: occupation of the Rhineland, reparations, and disarmament. When rearmament had been achieved it would be far more difficult to prevent the rejection of what remained.

Even before Hitler's ascension to power and Germany's full remilitarization its leading diplomats favored an aggressive foreign policy that foresaw the complete destruction of the settlement in Eastern Europe, including a fourth partition of Poland.[48] These men, such as Foreign Minister Konstantin von Neurath and State Secretary Bernhard von Bülow, remained in their positions quite comfortably for years after Hitler took over. Hitler had some different goals that went far beyond theirs, but for quite a long way their aims were the same. Sharing common ground with most officials in the foreign office, conservative politicians, and the army, they set forth their views early in March 1933.[49] They sought to tear up what remained of the Versailles Treaty: the Rhineland must be remilitarized and the Saar recovered, along with all the lost territories. These should include, apart from the destruction of Poland, Danzig, Memel, parts of Czechoslovakia, some of Schleswig in Denmark, Malmédy in Belgium, the return of Alsace-Lorraine and Germany's lost colonies. Further plans to be pursued later foresaw union with Austria and the seizure and exploitation of markets and the domination of the economies of the states of Eastern Europe. Bülow's thinking not only encompassed the war aims discussions of 1917–1918, which had conceived of a Polish client state subordinate to Prussia, but also embraced territorial expansion to the east as in 1918, when it had been sanctioned by the Treaty of Brest-Litovsk.[50]

These were the goals not of the frightening leader of the Nazis, but of the comforting, traditional diplomats who negotiated with the Western Powers in 1932 and who contributed to the impression, widespread in Britain and America,

> that Germany had learned from its defeat in 1918, that the country had a moderate, responsible government, and that in military affairs, the Germans now wanted only the disarmament of others, for the sake of their own security. Germans did not want war, and they had no significant military power; thus there was no need to think of trying to balance German military power. If anything, it was French power that needed to be reduced.

The German people's disinclination toward another war was "the only element of truth in this general impression."[51] In the last years of the Weimar Republic, many of Germany's civilian and military leaders continued to aim at the extreme goals formulated during the last war. If even some of them were achieved the result would be to give Germany the same domination of Europe that the Allies had entered the war to prevent. It was only a matter of time until rearmament would permit a determined leader to act to achieve Germany's unacceptable goals.

It is a common opinion that Germany came to be a menace to the peace of Europe only after the Great Depression had shattered its prosperity, discredited the Weimar Republic, and opened the way for the dark forces symbolized by Adolf Hitler and his National Socialist Party. There is, of course, some truth in a view so widely held, for the depression and the rise of Hitler were critically important events without which the course of history would have been very different. The Weimar Republic was neither Nazi Germany nor William II's empire. For the most part, it was a democratic republic with many of the checks on militant aggressive foreign policies that modern democracies have. It is possible that, given time, prosperity, and a strengthening of confidence in and by the unfamiliar democratic regime, interest in the more adventurous and dangerous of its goals would have faded, as the desire to recover Alsace-Lorraine, even by war, had faded in France.

It was possible, but by no means certain. Perhaps, given the lack of a democratic tradition in Germany, the failure of defeat in the war to destroy or even disable the elites of the previous regime, and the extreme improbability of permanent or even long-range economic recovery and prosperity, the success of the Weimar Republic and a consequent forgetting of grievances and ambitions were unlikely. Should the Republic fail, it is important to observe that by the end of the decade of the 1920s, Germany was essentially free of the checks imposed on it by the Versailles Treaty, was rearming with modern weapons and training officers and their men in modern tactics, and was already restored to leadership in industrial power. Almost all Germans were still resentful over the territorial settlement, especially in the east, and its legitimacy and permanence had been undermined by the silence of the Locarno agreements. The nations threatened by Germany's return to independence and power could not effectively resist Germany without the threat of a French attack in the west, yet the chances of such an attack were all but eliminated by the evacuation of the Rhineland, Britain's commitment to disarmament and appeasement, and the purely defensive strategy and cast of mind adopted by France. In these circumstances it is not certain that a European war would have been averted even if Hitler had never come to power. Germany would certainly have pressed an isolated Poland for territorial adjustments that the Poles would surely have resisted. A German attack carried out by a conservative, nationalist regime on Poland would have been less alarming than the one Hitler launched in 1939, but it would have been serious. The German problem was once again at the center of question of European peace, but there was no one either in Germany or elsewhere who was willing and able to take the steps needed to preserve it. That situation had been created by a policy of military weakness, neglect, and appeasement by Great Britain.

In 1950, Winston Churchill distinguished in the House of Commons between two kinds of appeasement: "Appeasement in itself may be good or bad according to the circumstances. Appeasement from weakness and fear is alike futile and fatal. Appeasement from strength is magnanimous and noble, and might be the surest and perhaps the only path to world peace."[52] In the years from 1919 to 1935, it has been said, "the principal tenet of [British] appeasement was concession through strength." Its practitioners did not act from fear; they were not "misguided men who mistook weakness for charity." For them "appeasement was a policy of optimism and hope, even at times of strength."[53] The British statesmen of these years were certainly full of optimism and hope, but it is hard to credit the view that they acted from strength. They swiftly dissipated British military strength and established a policy to make sure it could not quickly be restored. Then they worked to restrain and discourage France's military strength, which was their only tangible defense against the possibility of a revived and revanchist Germany. Finally, they powerfully assisted Germany's restoration as the mightiest industrial power in Europe and put an end to serious checks on its clandestine rearmament, even as they hampered France's industrial recovery and deprived it of tangible means of resisting Germany's growing power. In order to protect its interests and preserve the peaceful world in which alone those interests could flourish, Britain needed to take the lead in Europe, employing its strength to guide international affairs in a healthy direction. Whatever strength Britain may have had after the war, its true weight and effectiveness rapidly diminished and was soon only theoretical. Had the British retained a considerable military establishment, had they made a defensive treaty with France and backed it with concrete military plans and then supported them with the appropriate forces, had they then undertaken such revisions in the Versailles settlement as seemed appropriate and possible and assisted German recovery after French security was guaranteed, such a policy would deserve to be called appeasement from strength. By making a German program of militant defiance obviously suicidal, it would also have strengthened the hand of more moderate politicians like Stresemann. Leaders like Stresemann were nationalists and sought revision of the treaties, but they were rational, practical men who could be deterred in a way that Hitler could not. True appeasement from strength was a policy worth trying, but that is not the policy the British pursued.

British policy, in fact, *was* weak and misguided. It "did not merely display a characteristic escapism and self-deception but, the realities of power and strategy having been left so far behind, now veered positively into fantasy, like an unsound financier who, devoid of cash resources, deludes himself and his creditors with grandiose paper transactions."[54] It is worth considering why the British acted so. Instead of relieving Britain of burdens, victory in the war had vastly increased British imperial responsibilities all over the globe. At the same time, British finances were far more difficult. The national debt had grown from £650 million to £7,500 million, and taxes had quadrupled.[55] Britain's capacity to compete in the modern industrial world was diminishing in comparison with more up-to-date competitors such as the United States and Germany. When, in October 1922, Bonar Law declared, "We cannot act alone as the policeman of the world," he explained that "the financial and social condition of the country makes that impossible."[56] The political parties from Conservative to Labour looked to economic prosperity as the national goal and also as the solution to the problem of war. "The interests of the British Empire in foreign countries," said Stanley Baldwin, "are first of all economic and commercial. When we speak of peace being the greatest British interest, we mean that British trade and commerce, which are essential to the life of our people, flourish best in conditions of peace." Ramsay MacDonald said he repeatedly sought agreements at Geneva in order to attain "international confidence upon which we can base a fabric of peace . . . [because] we want security and stability for the working class and for the economic interest of this country."[57] Such men believed that the restoration of economic well-being would mollify resentments and bring peace. This pointed to assistance for the German economy, to recognizing German economic predominance in Mitteleuropa, to providing credit to help Germany obtain raw materials, and to bringing it back into the international trading system. Their actions rested on "a hope, perhaps a belief, that there could be an economic breakthrough which would avoid war. There was a pervasive 'economism' which believed that states did go to war for economic reasons."[58] To a historian writing soon after the outbreak of World War II it seemed "amazing that the British, even when dealing with Hitler, so frequently put faith in the ability of some purely economic arrangement or settlement to satisfy nations or to divert their attention from political or territorial aspirations unwelcome to Great Britain."[59]

Missing from all this was an understanding that peoples and nations go to war for deeper and less "rational" motives than economics and a recognition of the need to adopt a sound strategy and to provide the military capacity to carry it out. The Germans were openly resentful about issues of territory and nationality and honor that had little to do with economics. They bridled at what they thought were the injustices of the settlement. Yet if Germany was accorded "justice" by the rectification of its frontiers, would this not once again result in its domination of the continent, unless its neighbors once more joined forces against it? "And if she did again dominate the Continent, what security could there be for a Britain who now for the first time in her history really *was* vulnerable? . . ."[60]

The sense of vulnerability emerged not only from these bitter memories of loss in the last war but from intensified fears of even greater dangers in the next. The new terror that threatened was aerial bombardment, and it was generally depicted as irresistible and unbearable. As early as 1922 a subcommittee of the Committee of Imperial Defence reported its estimate of the probable results of an enemy air attack: "Railway traffic would be disorganized, food supplies would be interrupted, and it is probably that after being subjected for several weeks to the strain of such an attack the population would be so demoralized that they would insist upon an armistice."[61] Although it recommended work on ground defenses, it assumed that they would have only a marginal effect. The dominant theory was that bombers could not be stopped. In 1932, Baldwin told the House of Commons: "I think it well . . . for the man in the street to realise that there is no power on earth that can protect him from being bombed. Whatever people may tell him, the bomber will always get through." The only hope was through deterrence provided by an equal threat: "The only defence is offence, which means that you will have to kill women and children more quickly than the enemy if you want to save yourselves."[62]

As early as 1923, Arthur Balfour, serving on another committee that helped set British policy, had reached the same conclusion: the only ultimate guarantee of peace was "the certainty of every civilized man, woman and child that everybody will be destroyed if there is a war: everybody and everything." Here we see the birth of the policy later adopted by the United States in the nuclear age, and still in place today, after the end of the Cold War: Mutually Assured Destruction (MAD), which deliberately eschews serious efforts at defense against attack from the air and relies completely on the terror of retaliation to prevent a future war, leaving no means of defense in case deterrence fails. Had the British kept to it faithfully they would have been devastated and defeated in World War II. There can be no doubt that such memories of losses in the war and fears of such future terrors played a powerful part in shaping policy between the wars. "Some time during these celebrations [of victory] there was formulated that simple phrase which the people not only of Great Britain but of the Dominions resolved should be the epitaph of their million-odd war dead: Never Again. Unfortunately, it was to be more than an epitaph; it was to be a policy—and one which would have disastrous results."[63]

British appeasement in the 1920s was not the work of a narrow group of ideologues isolated from the mood of the rest of the country. Prime Ministers and Cabinets representing the Liberals, Conservatives, and Labour pursued the same course. Some started on that course even before the peace treaties were complete; most of the governing class quickly joined in. Winston Churchill, the doughty nationalist and imperialist, the very symbol of Britain's bulldog tenacity and courage, said in 1921: "The aim is to get an appeasement of the fearful hatreds and antagonisms which exist in Europe and to enable the world to settle down. I have no other object in view."[64] Lesser men held doggedly to that policy even after conditions changed and called for a new assessment, but "appeasement was the corner-stone of inter-war foreign policy."[65] The men who shaped and executed British policy in the 1930s have much to answer for, but it would be a mistake to ignore how bad was the hand dealt them by their predecessors. After 1930, appeasement from strength was no longer an option. The only choice was to continue the well-established policy and continue to yield to German pressure, even as it grew increasingly risky to do so, or to undertake a sharp reversal of course, a policy sure to be unpopular, difficult to bring about, and full of immediate costs and dangers.

10

The Bill Comes Due

The Ethiopian Crisis

The Great Depression that began in 1929, unforeseen and unimagined in the prosperous and hopeful years following Locarno, helped give birth to a suddenly dangerous international situation. In September 1931, Japan invaded Manchuria, the second and more important challenge to the League of Nations and the whole concept of collective security. Like all the other nations, Britain had no intention of taking military action. Sir John Simon, Foreign Secretary of the new National Government, insisted that "he had never for one moment favoured the adoption of the League of any kind of sanctions, not even of an economic character." What concerned him was that even a declaration complaining of Japan's behavior might "provoke a situation that precipitated Japan's resentment." His fear was justified, for the British achieved the neat trick of failing to stop the Japanese while gaining their hostility.[1]

The Manchurian affair compelled the British armed forces and the government to face a few realities. The British took note of their inability even to defend Singapore and Hong Kong, much less to fight the Japanese. In February 1932, Sir Robert Vansittart, Permanent Under-Secretary at the Foreign Office, recognized the danger from Japan, which "may well spread to the Middle East"; Britain alone could do nothing to check it and would be "done for in the Far East" and "must eventually swallow any and every humiliation" there unless the United States was prepared to use force.[2] But during the Manchurian affair the Americans had shown that there was no prospect of that.

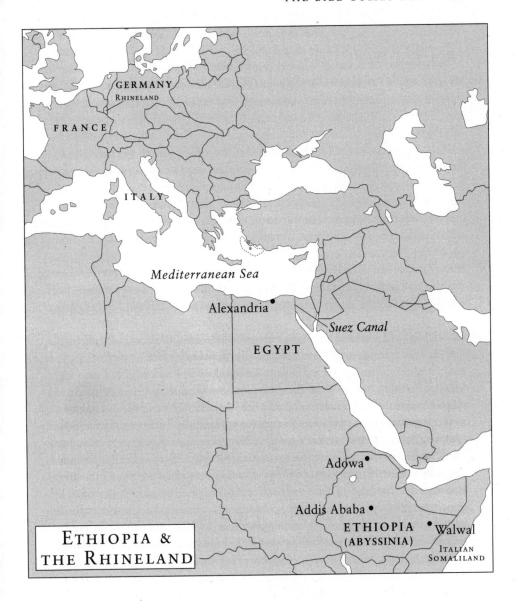

GERMANY
RHINELAND

FRANCE

ITALY

Mediterranean Sea

Alexandria•

Suez Canal

EGYPT

Adowa•

Addis Ababa •

ETHIOPIA
(ABYSSINIA)   •Walwal

ITALIAN
SOMALILAND

ETHIOPIA &
THE RHINELAND

By 1933 an apparently liberal Japan that took part in arms control agreements had turned into an aggressor state increasingly influenced and controlled
by fanatically nationalistic militarists. In January of the same year, Germany
abandoned the liberal and democratic Weimar Republic and turned to a National Socialist regime under a dictator, Adolf Hitler, committed to the destruction of the European order and to conquest by military force.

In the 1920s, Great Britain had rejected the traditional means of meeting
such challenges to its interests and security. The British governments had disarmed swiftly and deeply. In Europe they had refused to maintain their wartime

alliance with France by guaranteeing French security against attack by Germany, preferring to stand aloof and maintain a free hand. They chose not to accept the responsibility of active leadership in maintaining the peace and shaping the situation to make it more secure. All this left them terribly vulnerable to the dangerous new threats that now erupted. The calamities that struck Britain in the 1930s were the product of the self-deluding and irresponsible policies pursued in the 1920s.

In March 1935, even as Britain and France were proposing new disarmament plans to Germany, Hitler declared that, in violation of the Versailles Treaty, Germany had an air force. A week later he rejected the remaining military limitations imposed by Versailles and announced the return of military conscription, proclaiming his intention to replace the army of 100,000 long-term volunteers prescribed at Versailles with a force of thirty-six divisions, about 550,000 short-term conscripts who would provide a deep corps of trained reserves. The new German army would be larger than the French, and such a force would fundamentally change the European balance of power to the disadvantage of the nations that had imposed the peace.

Britain's continued refusal to guarantee French security and its increased withdrawal from continental affairs forced the French to turn elsewhere for protection against a newly formidable Germany. In 1934 the new French Foreign Minister, Louis Barthou, proposed a regional pact to preserve the peace in Eastern Europe, "an eastern Locarno," that would have involved Germany, Russia, the Baltic states, Finland, and Czechoslovakia, and, alongside that, a Franco-Russian pact that would protect each against Germany. This was not, of course, acceptable to Germany, nor to the Poles, who feared Stalin more than Hitler and responded by making an agreement with Germany that further undermined French security. Barthou then sought an agreement with the Soviet Union alone. The growth of power and ambition on the part of Japan and Germany made Stalin more open to cooperation with the Western Powers. With French prodding and support the Soviet Union entered the League of Nations in September 1934 and negotiated a very limited agreement with France. In October an assassin's bullet removed Barthou from the scene, and a month later a new French government put Pierre Laval in his place as Foreign Minister.

The situation he faced was grim. French and British reaction to Hitler's blatant and menacing breach of the peace treaty's disarmament clauses was a weak and useless verbal complaint. The American ambassador in Paris reported that the French response to Britain's unwillingness to do more was "despair and smouldering resentment." Barthou's efforts had failed to produce an eastern Locarno and had brought an agreement with the Soviets that was of little value. Laval was hostile toward the Soviet Union and friendly toward Italy. Without making a clear and open break from Barthou's policies, he made an accommodation with Italy his first important goal.

In July 1934 the Austrian Nazi Party had murdered Prime Minister Engelbert Dollfuss. Britain and France protested, and Mussolini sent two Italian divisions to the Brenner Pass as a threat against a German invasion of Austria. The common fear of the new Germany drew France and Italy closer together. France, especially, felt the need to gain Italian friendship. In 1935 the effects of the generation France had lost in the war made itself felt in the most alarming way. In that year there were 20,000 more French deaths than births. The number of troops from metropolitan France came to only 265,000. For some years the annual recruitment of soldiers fell from the usual 235,000 to an average of 118,000. Although the new conscription law doubled the term of service to two years, the troop estimate for 1936 was only 405,000, compared to the 600,000 Germans who would be in uniform.[4] It would be an enormous advantage if the Italian army could be added to French forces against the German danger, but even if the Italians lent no active support a treaty with Italy would have great strategic advantages. It would free the French from a threat on their southeastern frontier, allowing them to move troops from there to the German front, and it would remove a threat in the Mediterranean. The French were soon able to move ten infantry divisions and two cavalry brigades from the Italian front, and further talks produced military and air force agreements. Italy now became a crucial part of French security policy.[5] In light of Britain's refusal to make a continental commitment backed by adequate military forces, French eagerness for an Italian agreement was natural and inevitable. Since the end of the Great War, British officials, military and civilian, had repeatedly declared that Britain's frontier was on the Rhine, but their policies, military and diplomatic, had driven their allies on the Rhine into the arms of a dictator who was also a reckless adventurer and a threat to the peace.

Several long-standing disagreements, chiefly about African colonies, stood in the way of a Franco-Italian accord, but by the end of 1934, Mussolini had reason to seek a rapprochement. In 1896 the Italian army had been humiliated by the Ethiopians at the Battle of Adowa, one of the rare defeats suffered by a European power at the hands of a non-European nation. Mussolini was determined to avenge the defeat, to begin the restoration of Roman imperial glory, and, perhaps, to turn the thoughts of Italians from his corrupt and nasty Fascist regime and their economic problems.[6] Mussolini appears to have expected French support for his aggression, while Laval claimed to have been surprised by the Italian desire for a complete conquest of Ethiopia.[7] In fact, there is no doubt that he gave Mussolini a free hand in Ethiopia. He knew that Mussolini was planning an attack, that it would violate the League of Nations Covenant and create an international crisis, but he judged it all of less importance than bolstering a crumbling and newly threatened French security. "By a shrug of the shoulders, or a wink," as one French diplomat put it, "Laval was able to convey to Mussolini that he would not be too critical if the latter attempted a military expedition."[8]

The one possible stumbling block in Mussolini's path could be opposition by

Britain. In spite of disagreements and Britain's increased isolationism, France, if forced to make a choice, must, however reluctantly, side with Britain. As the head of the army, General Gamelin, said, "for us Italy is important; England is essential."[9] In January 1935, however, Britain did not seem to be a problem. The British had always maintained friendly relations with Italy since that nation's founding in the nineteenth century, and Mussolini's seizure of power and his establishment of a Fascist dictatorship had not changed that tradition.

On December 5, 1934 Italian and Ethiopian troops clashed at Walwal on the unclear frontier between Ethiopia and Italian Somaliland, providing a pretext for Mussolini's long-planned conquest of the African kingdom. The British government's instinct was to try to work out a compromise of the traditional sort whereby Italy would make some colonial gains at the expense of a non-European victim, but without disturbing the European equilibrium.

Three serious problems stood in the way of such a solution: the character of the Italian regime, the European international situation that had evolved since 1919, and the expectations by the British public that had been shaped in that time. At the heat of Mussolini's Fascist regime was an expansive nationalism that promised the achievement of Italy's status as a true great power and spoke of a restoration of the Roman Empire in the Mediterranean. Mussolini gloried in the proposed strength of his armed forces and the victories and conquests they would achieve. For these purposes Mussolini wanted not concessions but war against a foe so inferior as to guarantee victory. The British government had no deep objection to Mussolini's goal and no desire to annoy him. On the contrary, the emergence of Hitler and the alarming speed of his rearmament made them, like the French, eager to maintain friendship with Italy as a support for European stability and a check on the restoration of German power. Before the Great War it would have been extremely unlikely that an Italian assault on a weak African nation of no particular value or interest to any of the other European powers would have provoked any meaningful reaction from any of them.

The creation of the League of Nations, however, and the accompanying commitments to collective security and to the resistance against aggression changed the situation. Britain's failure to maintain a true alliance with France or an adequate military force was justified to the public under the shield of a commitment to collective security and the League of Nations. English popular opinion had seized upon the idea, and any government that openly played by the old rules and neglected the new commitments would be in serious trouble.

In the winter of 1934–1935, however, this was not yet obvious. Mussolini had considerable contempt for the British, regarding them as soft and dominated by pacifism. The Duce surely remembered their weak, halfhearted performance in the Corfu affair in 1923. If they had cared little and done nothing in defense of the League and collective security then, in the Mediterranean that was so vital to them, why should they do more to stop him now in an African land of no consequence to them? British behavior since the war had under-

mined the respect and awe created by British determination and military performance in the late war and diminished the power to deter unwelcome actions
that had succeeded at Chanak.

Mussolini did not undertake serious discussions with the British, as he had
with the French, because he knew that there would be "strong opposition" to
his plans for Ethiopia. Instead he preferred to allow events to take their course.
The message delivered by Leonardo Vitetti, counselor to the Italian Embassy in
London, on January 29, 1935, however, offered the British a chance to respond
before things got out of hand. Vitetti said that "the Italian Government would
like to exchange views with His Majesty's Government on the respective interests of both governments in Ethiopia." The Foreign Office rightly thought that
Italy's dispute with Ethiopia and its military preparations indicated that the aim
of the Italians "is not merely economic predominance in Ethiopia only, but
the virtual absorption of as much territory as can be achieved without jeopardy. . . ." Mussolini, in fact, had decided on a war of conquest against Ethiopia as early as 1932 and given orders for it in December 1934.[11] The Foreign
Office's only recommendation, however, was to appoint a committee to exam-
ine the nature of British interests in the region, which "should report without
any avoidable delay."[12]

The interministerial commission on Britain's Ethiopian interests was appointed on March 6 under the chairmanship of Sir John Maffey; in spite of the
call for urgency, it did not sign the report until June 18 and did not circulate it
until August.[13] The letter from the Foreign Office that created the commission
invited its members to consider the question broadly, to consider how the Italian action would affect international treaties and the "general political relations" between Italy and Britain. Instead, they examined the matter "from the
narrow standpoint of the British material interests in and near Ethiopia." From
that perspective the commission concluded that Italy would undoubtedly gain
control of Ethiopia "in the next few years," but "no . . . vital British interest is
concerned in and round Ethiopia as would make it essential for His Majesty's
Government to resist an Italian conquest of Ethiopia."[14]

The commissioners were fully aware that larger questions might be involved, the "general situation in Europe . . . the question of how far His
Majesty's Government are prepared to support the League of Nations at the
risk of losing Italian friendship," but left those problems of "high policy" to
others. They recognized that there were more "fundamental" matters, such as
whether the government should agree to an Italian action that would be "a
clear breach of obligations undertaken in at least three international agreements" including the Covenant of the League of Nations and the Kellogg Pact.
They took note of "the moral aspect and the question of how far the wider interests of Great Britain . . . will be served by opposing designs contrary to international obligations." They "took no account" of such issues but "set [them]
aside."[15] These limitations allowed them to decide that no "vital" British inter-

ests would be damaged by an Italian conquest of Ethiopia. That decision, calling only material interests vital, made it easier for the government to ignore Britain's more "fundamental" and truly vital interests, like upholding the principle of collective action against aggressors, on which British security rested.

Meanwhile, the British government made no reply to Mussolini's overture, because no clear and pleasant solution offered itself. Britain's Foreign Secretary, Sir John Simon, had no doubt that "the Italians intended to take Abyssinia,"[16] but he was determined not to get in Mussolini's way to prevent it. Simon was much inclined to pacifism, and he feared that a British war against Mussolini would lead to the Duce's replacement by a Bolshevik regime. Robert Vansittart, Permanent Under-Secretary in the Foreign Office, was no pacifist, but the menace presented by Hitler's Germany was his chief concern. He thought it essential not to alienate Mussolini and drive him into the hands of Hitler.

Some argued that a strong British reaction might have deterred Mussolini. As early as February 1935, Britain's ambassador in Addis Ababa, Sir Sidney Barton, recommended a firm response: "Personally I can think of only one course likely to prevent perpetration of what may be widely regarded as an international crime and that would be for England and France to tell Italy that she cannot have Ethiopia."[17] In the Foreign Office, R. I. Campbell warned, "The Italians begin to think they can go so far as they like. . . . I fear that we may defeat the object in view if we refrain from making our position quite clear." Anthony Eden also wanted a "pretty strong hint" to deter the Italians by telling them that Britain would not sit quietly while Ethiopia was dismembered.[18] That was decidedly not the dominant view at the Foreign Office, which made no formal reply to the Italian overtures as the Maffey Committee went leisurely about its work.

Mussolini was given little reason to believe that the British would get in his way any more than the French. The Italian dictator, who later asserted that he had been willing at this time "to table his case," took Britain's failure to respond as a quiet consent to his ambitions. "In the face of that silence," he said in an interview in September 1935, "there was only one road which remained open to me and I took it."[19] As he moved forward with his preparations "he did not fear the British, and English silence seemed as good as the French wink."[20]

On March 16, Hitler announced his intention to violate the disarmament clauses of the peace treaty. France, Italy, and Britain were alarmed, and their Foreign Ministers met at the Italian town of Stresa on April 11 for consultation. What came out of the conference was a common denunciation of Hitler's announcement and a suggestion that they would stand together against future violations of the treaty. It is not cynical to say that "the 'Stresa front' was a front in the sense of a 'bold front' to conceal inner quaverings, . . . as Hitler correctly assumed."[21] It also encouraged Mussolini's plans to conquer Ethiopia. Mussolini vainly waited throughout the conference for the British to say something about Ethiopia. As a final test he added to the communiqué in which the three powers agreed to oppose "any unilateral repudiation of treaties which may endanger the peace" the words "in Europe"; no one objected. "The French and Italians drew an identical and instantaneous conclusion: the silence was a tacit consent given by the British" to Mussolini's plans for Ethiopia.[22] "The Duce concluded that the path to conquest in Ethiopia was open."[23]

The British soon revealed the emptiness of their commitment to defend what was left of the Versailles Treaty's limitations on German armaments in the newly dangerous international situation. The chiefs of the navy were deeply alarmed by the inadequacy of the resources available to meet their responsibilities in home waters, the Mediterranean, and the Far East. The truculence of Japan and the new threat posed by Germany made the folly of years of retrenchment and neglect of the armed forces, combined with the denial of growing dangers, inescapably clear. The consequences of the errors of the past fifteen years produced a panicky response and serious new errors.

Baldwin, who had become Prime Minister in 1935, was pressed by the Admiralty to accept Hitler's offer to negotiate naval limitations, chiefly because of the threat posed by Japan. In the face of a forthcoming election, convinced that the British people opposed rearmament and connected the Conservatives with it, "Baldwin was inclined to accept any agreement that might provide a counter-argument."[24] The result was a naval treaty that granted Germany the right to build a fleet up to 35 percent of the British, and a ratio of 45 percent in submarines, which could go to parity when the Germans wished.

The treaty gained nothing for Britain. Even if Britain did not build another ship it would take many years for the Germans, who had a fleet of only 86,000 tons, to reach the 425,000 tons that amounted to the 35 percent of British tonnage, and they would need to do so at the expense of their army. The ratio, moreover, might be comforting so long as the entire British navy was kept in the North Sea, but if detachments were needed in the Mediterranean or the Far East it would surely be inadequate. Churchill, out of office and now deeply alarmed by the new threats from Japan and Germany, exclaimed in the Commons: "What a windfall this has been to Japan! . . . The British Fleet . . . will be largely anchored in the North Sea . . . and . . . when this German fleet is built we shall not be able to keep any appreciable portion of the British Fleet so far from home [as the Far East.]"[25]

The diplomatic consequences were no less serious. The Anglo-German agreement was a breach of the Versailles Treaty undertaken without the approval of the other powers. It destroyed the Stresa front and further shook the confidence of the French, which led them to seek help elsewhere, from the USSR, and it widened their rift with Britain. Admiral Raeder, chief of the Germany navy, was right to call the naval agreement "a political success for Germany," because Britain thereby "sanctioned Germany's right thereafter to rearm."[26] Mussolini took courage from Britain's appeasement of Hitler, and the break the Anglo-German naval agreement had caused with France could only have increased his confidence that Britain would not interfere with his plans. The weakness of their armed forces had led the British to do great damage to their diplomatic position and, in a second way, to their capacity to resist aggression and preserve the peace.

The further estrangement of Great Britain from France caused by the naval agreement would be a serious problem during the crisis with Italy. Within a few weeks, Italian forces and equipment were moving through the Suez Canal to get into position for an attack on Ethiopia, and by June the British could no longer ignore the likelihood of a war. Faced with the continuing threat of Japan in the Far East, the growing danger presented by Germany, the evidence of French rapprochement with Italy, and the terrible inadequacy of their own military preparations, the Baldwin government tried to avoid the Hobson's choice that awaited them. They sent Anthony Eden, Minister for League of Nations Affairs, to Rome carrying a proposal that would give Italy part of Ethiopia and, in return, would provide compensation by giving part of British Somaliland to the Ethiopians, but Mussolini rejected it.[27]

The new British Foreign Secretary, Sir Samuel Hoare, was not unaware of the high cost of allowing Italy a free hand to make war against Ethiopia:

> The effect of war upon the influence of the League of Nations will be wholly bad. . . . It would by all ordinary persons be held to be a plain war of aggression for the purpose of annexation by a strong member of the League upon a weaker member. . . . If the League acquiesced in such a purpose it would fall into universal and lasting contempt. . . . [I]f it were formally but ineffectually to condemn the action of the Italian Government . . . Italy would join the growing number of scoffing dissenters. In any event, another and inglorious chapter would have been closed in the history of attempts to substitute a regime of law for international anarchy; and there would have been destroyed one of those factors . . . which join the United Kingdom with France in the political and moral leadership of Europe. In such circumstances the countries of Central and South Eastern Europe, filled already with apprehensions at the growing might of Germany, might well be excused for feeling that a term had been set to whatever stability this leadership had secured to them, and for looking elsewhere than to the League and to the two great conservative democracies for support and guidance.[28]

These turned out to be accurate predictions of some of the costs on the international scene of a successful Italian war of aggression, but Hoare also recognized the threat it would pose to Britain's political condition at home:

> The present crisis is widely regarded in this country as a test not only of the ability of the members of the League to make their own Covenant re-

spected, but as a test of whether the words "collective action" which are often, and rightly, on our lips, really mean collective action in defence of law and order against aggression from any quarter, or whether the security which is being sought is security against Germany, alone. The popular movement in this country in support of the principle of security by collective action might well be arrested unless the principles of the League were steadfastly upheld even at the cost of the apostasy of one or more of the principal members.[29]

This led him to advocate a policy not to "keep Italy step by step within the bounds of the Covenant, so that war if it eventually breaks out may be legitimate war, but rather to prevent war altogether."[30]

But Hoare, like most of his colleagues, remained reluctant to antagonize the Italians, chiefly because of a keen sense of Britain's military weakness. The Defence Policy and Requirements Committee, whose chairman was Prime Minister Baldwin himself, issued a report at the beginning of July 1935, warning that "it is of the utmost importance that this country should not become involved in a war within the next few years. . . . No opportunity should be lost to avoid the risk of war . . . as long as possible." Baldwin personally told Hoare, "Keep us out of war, we are not ready for it."[31]

That opinion rested firmly on the advice of the Royal Navy. Low levels of support over fifteen years found it in a poor state of preparation. The First Sea Lord, Admiral Ernle Chatfield, asked for delay in imposing sanctions on Italy for as long as possible. The Mediterranean fleet lacked sufficient cruisers and destroyers equipped to fight submarines. In August he wrote Vansittart that he was "surprised to find how very unready the other two services were and how long it would take them before they could give effective resistance to Italian action by land or air."[32] Vansittart passed the admiral's views, already acquired in earlier conversations, on to Hoare:

> We must never forget surely that we now have no naval margin at all, and the loss of one or two ships even would be a very serious matter for us. . . . [T]he Mediterranean fleet is probably at present too weak to look after itself vis-à-vis Italy, and if any serious trouble were possible it would undoubtedly have to be reinforced. . . . [T]here must be always the risk of a mad dog coup by Mussolini, and since we cannot in our present weakness afford the consequences of such a coup, we must obviously take every precaution to avoid it.[33]

In passing on Chatfield's letter, Vansittart summarized his own conclusions:

> What it really comes to is this. This country has been so weakened of recent years that we are in no position to take a strong line in the Mediter-

ranean—anyhow not for some time. We are in fact experiencing . . . something of the impotence . . . which we experienced without present hope of remedy in the Far East. I have of course for many years past been stressing our weakness to successive Governments and dwelling on its inevitable political consequences, . . . so Chatfield and the other two Chiefs of Staff will scarcely need the assurance . . . that we shall of course exercise due caution in our conduct and language in Paris.[34]

Hoare took these warnings to heart: "This country has been so weakened of recent years that we are in no position to take a strong line in the Mediterranean . . . we should be very cautious as to how far and in what manner we force the pace in Paris, with an unstable France and an unready England."[35] Throughout the crisis the British government was consistently discouraged from taking stronger action to deter Mussolini from his planned aggression by its sense of military inadequacy.

France's attitude was another deterrent to strong action. The French could not understand Britain's enthusiasm for collective security to defend a backward African nation that still practiced slavery, at the cost of alienating Italy, an ally in the last war and a potential ally against Nazi Germany, when it had been so unwilling to employ it in defense of France's security against German rearmament and revenge. In September at Geneva, Laval, now French Foreign Minister, asked if Britain would be equally willing to apply sanctions in Europe against Germany. Eden could not give a direct and satisfactory answer. Instead he made the case for the League, sanctions, and collective security: to hold the line at Ethiopia would give strength to the league, "and our moral obligation to assist in supporting and enforcing the Covenant correspondingly increased. If, however, the Covenant were now violated with impunity, the authority of the League would be so impaired that its future influence must be negligible in Europe or anywhere else." Laval pointed out that this did not answer the question, and, writing years later, Eden conceded, "This may have been true, but the British Government's wariness *and the state of our defences* [emphasis added] made it impossible for me to promise unconditional support of the Covenant in the future. . . ."[36]

Eden, though unwilling to make war, wanted to impose economic sanctions against Italy. The navy warned that doing so might lead Mussolini to a "mad dog act," to a military action that would bring war. Such a war, however, would require French cooperation, and besides, it would risk a simultaneous attack by Japan and/or Germany for which Britain's naval and military forces were in no way adequate. Britain's military and diplomatic policies undertaken in the previous decade had left it seemingly powerless to take the actions those policies had led the British public to expect.

In these circumstances Hoare met with Laval on September 9 and 10 in Geneva, where they agreed that war was too dangerous to risk, so any military action was ruled out lest it provoke Mussolini. Faced with the need to reconcile contradictory goals, to curb Mussolini, and to avoid the threat of war, Hoare pursued what he called "a double policy . . . of negotiation with Italy and respect for our collective obligations under the Covenant, based on Anglo-French cooperation."[37] The difficulty was that Mussolini was not interested in an acceptable deal and France did not wish to oppose him, so that negotiating with Mussolini was inconsistent with collective security and opposing him was at odds with Anglo-French cooperation.

In spite of that, on September 12, Hoare delivered a speech to the Assembly of the League astonishing in the boldness of what it seemed to say. He promised that Britain's government would be "second to none to fulfill, within the measure of their capacity, the obligations which the Covenant lays upon them. . . . The League stands, and my country stands with it, for the collective maintenance of the Covenant in its entirety, and particularly for steady and collective resistance to all acts of unprovoked aggression."[38] This was no sudden burst of enthusiasm by a single minister but had been crafted with the collaboration of Baldwin and Chamberlain. Hoare later described his intentions: it was to be a "revivalist appeal" meant to put "new life" into the League. "At best, it might start a new chapter of League recovery, at worst, it might deter Mussolini by a display of League fervor. If there was any element of bluff in it, it was a moment when bluff was not only legitimate but inescapable."[39]

For internationalists it was "the very speech which they had always hoped to hear from an English foreign minister in such a crisis," but it was empty bombast, as Hoare was quick to communicate to Mussolini. Through his ambassador in Rome he told the Italian dictator that Britain was eager for a settlement, had no wish to humiliate Italy, and would neither employ military sanctions nor close the Suez Canal.[40] Reassured by such communications, Mussolini rejected further proposals for compromise and invaded Abyssinia on October 3, 1935.

The League condemned Italy's action as a violation of the Covenant, which called for sanctions of some kind. The ones imposed, and these did not go into effect until November 18, were economic only and did not include an embargo on oil, which, apart from military action, was the only sanction that might have caused Mussolini serious trouble. France continued to hold back; indeed, according to Hoare, Laval was secretly intriguing with Mussolini. The debate in Britain revealed the contradiction and confusion that underlay the government's policies and public opinion. The military chiefs, especially the navy, continued to advise against any action that might provoke Mussolini, and leading civil servants such as Vansittart in the Foreign Office and Sir Warren Fisher in the Treasury, their eyes focused on the German menace, were strongly of the same opinion.[41] The ministers shared all these misgivings, but were unwilling to abandon the League and collective security, especially in light of public opinion. That opinion, however, was ill-informed about the realities and unclear about the strategic issues and their implications. The British government had never made clear, if it understood it itself, the necessary relationship between collective security and British military power. The journalist Kingsley Martin reported the arguments presented at a combined Popular Front meeting he attended in Birmingham:

> The first speaker urged that we must carry out economic sanctions, but in no circumstances must the Labour Party support a war. I followed next and said that, though there was good ground for hoping that economic sanctions would be enough, there was a risk that war would follow, that we should be committed to it if there was war and that we ought run the risk. The next speaker thanked me for my frankness and said that since sanctions might lead to war, he was altogether opposed to them. The fourth speaker demanded that Britain should at once take drastic steps, including blocking the Suez Canal, but that there must in no circumstances be a war. . . . [T]he meeting ended with an eloquent expression of the Christian pacifist case by Canon Stuart Morris, who was later to be chairman of the Peace Pledge Union.[42]

The same divisions existed within the Labour Party itself. The leadership supported the League and sanctions; Stafford Cripps denounced the League as "an International Burglars' Union," insisting that "every war entered upon by a capitalist government is and must be an imperialist and capitalist war"; Lansbury continued to oppose anything but passive resistance. The final vote was overwhelming in support of the leadership, but its meaning remained ambiguous: "Nearly all Labour supporters of collective security continued to say: collective security will stop the aggressor, therefore rearmament is unnecessary."[43]

The government won a huge majority in the elections of October 1935 with a platform containing planks supporting sanctions and the League, but the sanctions did not prevent Italian success in Ethiopia. Voices were raised in favor of an embargo on oil for Italy, but the British Cabinet was reluctant. Hoare and his colleagues were afraid that imposing the petroleum sanction would provoke Mussolini into the much-feared "mad dog" act, an attack on the British fleet and a war. The navy warned again of its unpreparedness, and Hoare complained about the "serious gap in our system of Imperial Defences, which were in a weak state as compared with an Italy mobilised for war."[44] Throughout the crisis he and most other British leaders greatly overestimated Italy's military power and readiness, frightened by the knowledge of Britain's long neglect of its own forces.

By December, however, the Cabinet was on the point of approving an oil embargo, when Hoare went off to Paris and produced the Hoare-Laval agreement meant to provide a peaceful settlement without risking such a provocation. It would have given some 60,000 square miles of Ethiopia to Italy. In return Ethiopia would get a narrow corridor to the sea. The British Cabinet approved it and Mussolini was ready to accept it; if the Emperor of Ethiopia would not, so much the worse for him. News of the deal, however, was greeted in Britain by an outburst of angry disapproval. It was widely seen as a reward for aggression, a blow to the idea of the League and collective security and an act of cowardice. Howard was forced to resign and was replaced by Eden, and yet it was not until the end of February that the Cabinet agreed to support oil sanctions, which, in fact, were never imposed. By May, Haile Selassie fled to London and Addis Ababa fell; the war was over. In July 1936 the League ended its sanctions.

In the end, Britain's attempt at a double policy was a disaster that brought about results worse than following either one consistently. Mussolini had achieved his goals, the League and collective security were finished, Britain's prestige was badly damaged, and Italy was alienated, shortly to join forces with Hitler. The democracies seemed weak, indecisive, and cowardly, and their failure and inaction gave courage to their enemies. Lloyd George personified the disgust felt by the British people toward their own government's behavior when he told the House of Commons: "I have never before heard a British Minister . . . come down to the House of Commons and say Britain was beaten . . . and that we must abandon an enterprise we had taken in hand." Pointing to the members of the government on the front bench, he said: "Tonight we have had the cowardly surrender, and *there* are the cowards."[45]

Then and later on, critics blamed the government for not pursuing one of the alternative policies or the other. A few, like Vansittart and Fisher, the navy chiefs, and some Conservative politicians, argued at the time for what they saw as a prudent, realistic policy that recognized British military weakness and the need to hold Mussolini as an ally against Hitler and so was prepared to sacrifice Ethiopia, as Britain would almost surely have done in previous centuries. Such a policy, of course, would have underscored Britain's weakness of will and military power and encouraged further aggression. Whatever its merits, however, a policy purely of *Realpolitik* was all but impossible in the Britain of 1935, as it has remained in Western democratic countries ever since. It is, in fact, a requirement of true realism in the modern world to recognize the inescapable role of what has come to be called ideology but is not very different from what once was called honor. By 1935 the British public would not ignore the commitment to resist aggression, especially on the part of a dictator against a weak country, even without regard to their country's capacity to resist effectively. A government trying to ignore that would be rejected not only as mistaken but, as the reaction of many Conservatives and of Lloyd George made clear, as dishonorable.

What of the alternative, a decision to take strong measures against Mussolini, e.g., an oil embargo, a naval barrier in front of the Suez Canal, even a war? There is reason to think that an oil embargo might have been effective. In 1938, Mussolini told Hitler at Munich that its imposition might have brought him down.[46] In the mood of the day such actions would have gained public support and acclaim. Why did the British government shy away from them? We have seen that they were, in general, eager to avoid a war of any kind. They were especially reluctant to lose the friendship of Italy, probably to the advantage of Hitler. They knew that France did not support such a policy and were reluctant to carry the full burden of a possible war almost alone. Above all, they believed that their military and naval forces were inadequate and unready to fight, a belief that was repeatedly and forcefully presented to them by the service chiefs and officials. The leaders of the navy had a legitimate sense of the inadequacy of their resources caused by fifteen years of disarmament. After the Ethiopian fiasco, Cabinet members awoke to the importance of these shortcomings in British defense capabilities and pressed for improvement. The military assistant secretary of the Committee of Imperial Defence responded in exasperation:

> Deficiencies and financial starvation over 15 years cannot be put right in three months. . . . Goodness knows enough warnings have been given by the Chiefs of Staff—and now the "Frocks" turn round and ask, "Why aren't you ready—we told you in September." To which the reply is, "We told you in 1925 and every year afterwards and you paid no attention."[47]

The result of this combination of attitudes and concerns was an excessive caution, a defensive mentality, an emphasis on risks over opportunities, a willingness to present political opinions in the guise of military estimates, and, most seriously, a loss of strategic imagination. To the government the navy leaders spoke of the threat of Italian airpower but did not take it seriously themselves. Admiral of the Fleet Lord Cunningham confirmed many years later essentially what Chatfield said at the time of the Italian air force.: "[W]e were not disposed to attach too much weight to its ability to affect the issue. As the war was to prove we were right."[48] They emphasized the dangers of fighting alone against Italy, without French help. At one point the Chiefs of Staff sent a report that Cunningham described as "a very pessimistic, not to say defeatist, view of the Mediterranean Fleet's capacity to deal with the Italians."[49] But neither the attitude of the French nor the fear of Italian airpower "seriously affected the supreme confidence of the Admiralty in the ability of its fleet to handle the Italians in the Mediterranean, even in a singlehanded war."[50] What they seemed to fear was that in the course of winning they would suffer such losses as would make them vulnerable and encourage other enemies, Germany, but particularly Japan, to strike and cause Britain to lose the next war. These fears were entirely understandable and natural to any officers with responsibilities far greater than their military resources. They were keenly aware of the danger of an attack in a second theater of war while they were engaged in the Mediterranean, and this led them to overestimate the threat from the Italians alone. One price of having military forces inadequate to sustain a nation's policy and responsibilities is to make its commanders unduly cautious and less capable of using those forces they have to full effect.

In retrospect it is clear that the fears were not justified. Germany was in no condition to take any military action, and Japan was fully occupied in Manchuria and China. As for significant losses caused by Italy, it is hard to take such fears seriously in light of the justified contempt the British officers expressed for the Italian navy, whose performance in the war to come would be far from impressive. Nor did the nervous military leaders give adequate thought to the larger strategic consequences of giving way to a breach of the international order. They failed to see the important advantages for keeping the peace of demonstrating Britain's will and capacity, and they ignored the dangers of inaction and perceived weakness. They thereby failed in their responsibility to keep the peace and succeeded in encouraging those who would break it at Britain's expense.

The lessons learned by the military leaders from the outcome of the Ethiopian crisis, however, were different. They breathed a sigh of relief at the demise of the Covenant and collective security. Now they would be "freed from the vague, wholesale and largely unpredictable military commitments which we at present incur under the League Covenant."[51] But Britain's situation required international alliances and associations to protect its interests and security, and these inevitably must involve "unpredictable military commitments" to interests that seem marginal to one's own if these associations are to function. The military leaders sought to pare down the conditions in which Britain might fight to those which could not provide the needed protection, and the politicians accepted their advice without complaint.

But what if the British had taken a bolder course and taken a clear position in opposition to Mussolini's aggression? It seems more than likely that France and other states would have provided assistance. It is a paradoxical truth that for a nation to lead a coalition into risky actions it needs to show its willingness to act alone, while an unwillingness to act without prior agreement encourages hesitation. Even acting alone, moreover, the British had no good reason to fear the outcome. "To us in the Mediterranean Fleet," wrote Admiral Cunningham,

> it seemed a very simple task to stop [Mussolini]. The mere closing of the Suez Canal to his transports which were then streaming through with troops and stores would effectively have cut off his armies concentrating in Eritrea and elsewhere. It is true that such a drastic measure might have led to war with Italy; but the Mediterranean Fleet was in a state of high morale and efficiency, and had no fear whatever of the result of an encounter with the Italian navy.[52]

Adolf Hitler, it seems, expected Britain to do exactly what Admiral Cunningham described. When the Italians asked him for a loan of ships for their expedition, he told the minister carrying the message:

> Let the Italians have a hundred ships! We'll go back, undamaged. They will go through the Suez Canal, but they will never go further. The British navy's battleship *Repulse* will be waiting there and signalling: "Which way are you going?" "South," the Italians will reply "Oh no you're not," the *Repulse* will reply. "You're going north!" and north they will go.

To his personal adjutant he said:

> If I had a choice between the Italians and the English, then I would take the English. Mussolini is closer to me, but I know the English from the last war. I know they are hard fellows. If Mussolini thinks he can chase away the English fleet from the Mediterranean with his own, he is very much mistaken.[53]

But the English stood aside of their own accord, and Mussolini took Ethiopia. Eden defended his government's policy in the House of Commons by saying that "you cannot close the Suez Canal with paper boats."[54] but Hitler and Mussolini knew that the British ships were of steel and fully capable of stopping the Italian fleet. Admiral Cunningham believed, "Had we stopped the passage of Italian transports through the Suez Canal, and the import of fuel oil into Italy, the whole subsequent history of the world might have been altered."[55] Instead, in the midst of the crisis in which the British were demonstrating their weakness of will, on March 7, 1936, the Germans marched an army into the demilitarized Rhineland, violating the Versailles Treaty, which they had been compelled to sign, and the Locarno Pact, to which they had agreed voluntarily.

The Remilitarization of the Rhineland

The demilitarized Rhineland was the most important element in the security structure for France created by the Versailles Treaty. It made a German invasion of France or the Low Countries all but impossible, and it opened Germany to an attack from the west that would be difficult to resist. This served as a guarantee for the small countries of Central and Eastern Europe, for any aggression in that direction would open Germany to a French invasion and a two-front war. France's security relied on the credibility of the threat that it could attack Germany successfully, and the demilitarized Rhineland was essential to that credibility.

For Hitler the demilitarization was especially damaging. It interfered with his plans for rearmament and for the expansion to the east to achieve *Lebensraum* for the German people. Hitler was in a great hurry. He had huge plans, and he rightly believed that his own participation was necessary for undertaking and achieving them, yet he feared that he might suffer an early death. He must, therefore, force the pace and create opportunities where none seemed to exist. As late as February 1936 he appears to have thought that remilitarization might have to wait until 1937,[56] but the Ethiopian affair, the divisions it caused among the Stresa front powers, and the hesitation and inefficacy of the British and French reaction encouraged him to speed up the timetable.

By November 1935 the French and British began to receive warnings from their ambassadors and others that Hitler would soon move troops into the Rhineland. One of those making the prediction was General Maurice Gamelin, commander in chief of the French army, who warned that Germany would take the Rhineland in order to "neutralize the French Army by constructing on its western frontiers a fortified barrier comparable to our own. . . . Hence, free from any fear of an offense from us, Germany would be completely at liberty to settle the fate of the Little Entente powers."[57]

In spite of their clear understanding of the dire consequences that would follow remilitarization, the French "not only lacked a previously prepared plan for a military countermove to remilitarization but did not even begin to prepare one while all . . . intelligence and diplomatic sources were telling them that such a step was impending."[58] The logic of France's situation from 1919 on required a not very large mobile force always at the ready to perform just such a task as presented itself in March 1936, but that would have meant thinking offensively on a tactical level as part of a larger defensive strategy. Such thinking was rejected not only by the soldiers but also by their civilian masters: one government after another had held to the position that there was no need for the army to be prepared for "spontaneous offensive action." The only plan of action called for a general mobilization of all the forces that would take weeks. What was wanted was "a kind of military flyswatter, supple and relatively unmenacing; instead military doctrine prescribed a sledge hammer."[59]

When Hitler sent his small force into the Rhineland on March 7 his formal excuse was that the Franco-Soviet Pact, clearly directed against Germany, was a violation of the Locarno Treaty that nullified Germany's demilitarization of the Rhineland. Hitler claimed to be ready to negotiate with France and Belgium for new demilitarized zones on either side of their borders, to sign nonagression pacts with them guaranteed by Britain and Italy, to make such agreements also with the eastern states, to work out the guarantees against air attacks so eagerly sought by the British, and to return to the League of Nations when it was properly reformed.[60] Speaking in the Reichstag for foreign consumption that same night, he concluded his speech with the pledge that "now, more than ever, we shall strive for an understanding between the European peoples. . . . We have no territorial demands to make in Europe. . . . Germany will never break the peace." The French ambassador in Berlin characterized all this as follows: "Hitler struck his adversary in the face, and as he did so declared: 'I bring you proposals for peace!'"[61]

Neither the French ministers nor soldiers had any thought of a military response. On the day after the German action the French formally sent a protest to the League. Thereafter, in spite of arguments within the French government and tough talk from French Foreign Minister Flandin to the British about sanctions, even military ones, to be taken, there was no chance that France would move.

The British, too, had been well warned about the likelihood of a German move in the Rhineland, and the new Foreign Minister, Anthony Eden, was aware of its significance. In February he told his colleagues that the disappearance of the demilitarized zone would "not merely change local military values but is likely to lead to far-reaching political repercussions of a kind which will further weaken France's influence in Eastern and Central Europe. . . ."[62] Nonetheless, he was unwilling to fight to protect the zone, preferring to negotiate, using remilitarization as a bargaining chip. Before there was time for negotiation, Hitler moved into the Rhineland. Eden immediately urged the French "not to make the situation more difficult." Over the weekend he wrote a memorandum for the Cabinet arguing against military action or even demands that Germany withdraw its troops. The thing to do was to "conclude with [Germany] as far-reaching and enduring a settlement as is possible whilst Herr Hitler is in the mood to do so."[63]

The government perfectly reflected the feelings of most of the people of Britain. The Conservative member Harold Nicolson did not distinguish between parties when he described the mood in Parliament and looked beneath the surface to explain its source: "The country will not stand for anything that makes for war. On all sides one hears sympathy for Germany. It is all very tragic and sad." In his diary he wrote: "General mood of the House is fear. Anything to keep us out of war."[64]

Ordinary people also took the occupation of the Rhineland calmly. Eden reported the comment of a taxi driver: "I suppose Jerry can do what he likes with his own back garden, can't he?" It was a phrase that reflected the understandable ignorance of most people about the strategic significance of what had happened and of the character of the regime that had carried out the coup, as well as eighteen years in which educated opinion had minimized the threat from Germany, sympathized with its grievances, and complained of the aggressive unreasonableness and selfishness of France. The public found it especially hard to understand what was wrong with the Germans' gaining full sovereignty over a part of their own country, even if that required the violation of international treaties. In the midst of the crisis the British Secretary of State for War told the German ambassador that the British people would not fight on account of the coup in the Rhineland: "The people did not know much about the demilitarization provisions and most of them probably took the view that they did not care 'two hoots' about the Germans reoccupying their own territory."[65] Their leaders had given them no help in understanding that Germany's action acutely changed the balance of power and threatened the peace of Europe and British security. They had said little or nothing of such things over the years, nor did they say anything in 1936. It is not clear that many of them, themselves, understood them.

British policy was to avoid war at all costs, to seek negotiations with Hitler, and to speed the pace of rearmament. The government's unwillingness to fight was strongly supported by the military leadership. The Chiefs of Staff reported that Britain was "perilously exposed in the air and completely open to attack by sea."[66] The army would be able to send no more than two divisions to the continent, and only after three weeks. They would not be mechanized but horse-drawn. They would lack antiaircraft personnel, tanks, antitank guns, and mortars and have a limited amount of artillery ammunition.[67] They insisted that in the event of any conflict with Germany all war materials be withdrawn from the Mediterranean, but even then there would be no swift improvement, because "'the excessive strain' of seven months of 'instant readiness . . . had exhausted practically the whole of our meagre forces.'" Another problem was the slow pace of rearmament after the shrinkage of war industries in the 1920s. "Although manufacturers were working to capacity, the fact was, as Baldwin admitted, 'we have hardly got any armament firms left.'"[68] The Chiefs saw war with Germany as "a disaster for which the Services with their existing commitments in the Mediterranean are totally unprepared."[69]

Soldiers facing broad responsibilities and threats around the globe with resources far too thin to meet more than one can be expected to hesitate to act vigorously to meet even a single challenge lest they endanger their position and their forces elsewhere. That is one of the heavy prices of inadequate military preparation. So it was with the military leaders of Britain in March 1936. Only months before, the Committee on Defence Requirements had begged the ministers to "avoid the simultaneous and 'suicidal' hostility of Japan, Germany, and any power on the main line of communication between the two." Military leaders had worried that a conflict with Italy over Ethiopia might bring on an attack by Japan. Now they feared that a clash with Hitler might cause Mussolini to attack Egypt and also bring about an attack on Britain's Asian interests north of Singapore, which were "at the mercy of the Japanese."[70]

To be sure, these estimates were too despairing, but the excessive caution of British military leaders in the circumstances of the time was entirely to be expected, the natural consequence of the government's foreign and defense policies since the war. The military and naval professionals were keenly aware of how badly their forces fell short of what might be required of them in all eventualities. In such conditions soldiers typically overestimate the strength of potential opponents as they dwell on their own inadequacies.

It is not surprising, therefore, that the generals grossly overestimated the capacity of the Germans. In the Rhineland itself, although General Gamelin claimed that Hitler had placed 265,000 troops there, the actual number was

22,000 men and 14,000 local police.[71] In overall military strength there were seventy-six French army divisions plus twenty-one Belgian against thirty-two German. At sea the Western Powers had an overwhelming superiority. In the air the Germans had an advantage in bombers but not in fighters; besides, the Luftwaffe was hardly out of its infancy. The German Air Staff reported that in the spring of 1936 its strength would not be enough to fight a war against France and *Czechoslovakia* "with the slightest chance of success."[72] In addition, the Czechs and Rumanians had offered France their support. On March 9, thinking France would move, Poland offered to activate its military alliance.[73] If France had moved and all the promises had been kept, well over a hundred divisions would have moved into Germany from several directions at a time when "German rearmament was only beginning and the first conscripts had only been taken into the army a few months before."[74] A.J.P. Taylor was only exaggerating to a degree when he said: "The actual move on 7 March was a staggering example of Hitler's strong nerve. Germany had literally no forces available for war. The trained men of the old Reichswehr were now dispersed as instructors among the new mass army; and this new army was not yet ready. Hitler assured his protesting generals that he would withdraw his token force at the first sight of French action: but he was unshakably confident."[75] In his testimony at Nuremberg, General Alfred Jodl, high in the ranks of the Wehrmacht, said: "Considering the situation we were in, the French covering army could have blown us to pieces." Hitler himself later said: "A retreat on our part would have spelled collapse. . . . The forty-eight hours after the march into the Rhineland were the most nerve-wracking in my life. If the French had then marched into the Rhineland we would have had to withdraw with our tails between our legs, for the military resources at our disposal would have been wholly inadequate for even a moderate resistance."[76]

Frightened by their knowledge of Britain's military weakness in the context of the many responsibilities and menaces it faced around the world, the Chiefs strenuously advised against any use or threat of force. Their civilian masters were in no mood to argue. They accepted the advice that no military option was available. In the Ethiopian affair they retreated from their commitment to the League of Nations and collective security, and in the Rhineland they retreated from their pledges at Locarno, not to mention Versailles. Deprived of the use of military force to uphold treaties and the international order, they had no alternative but to yield to military force, to pursue a policy of appeasement and further retreat. One Foreign Office official found in the diplomats "a feeling of profound relief . . . that there could be no question of endorsing any foreign policy at all since arms were palpably lacking."[77]

The consequences of the remilitarization of the Rhineland were enormous. Hitler emerged much strengthened internally, and Germany's power and influence were greatly increased. His evident success raised the dictator's popularity with the German people to new heights. The American ambassador to London wrote that "an overwhelming majority of Germans' would support any venture which Hitler might undertake. . . ."[78] Hitler's stature with Germany's diplomats and military leaders, mostly carry-overs from the old regime, was much increased, and their willingness to challenge him and his plans was undermined. Success also increased his own self-confidence. As he sped home from a triumphant tour of the Rhineland, Hitler "turned to his cronies in the special train and once again expressed his relief at the limpness of the Western powers: 'Am I glad! Good Lord, am I glad it's gone so smoothly. Sure enough, the world belongs to the brave man. He's the one God helps.'"[79] The inaction of the French and British emboldened him to proceed with his aggressive plans. He was now convinced that France would not attack without British support and that Britain would not fight to prevent Germany from taking Austria or Czechoslovakia.[80]

The most important results were strategic. The presence of a German army in the Rhineland, however small and unprepared, confirmed the French army in its commitment to a purely defensive strategy. The Germans were free to continue building fortifications on their western front that could be held with relatively few troops. Even more important, they could now use all of Germany's industrial capacity to prepare for war. Eighty percent of Germany's coal lay in the Rhineland and the Ruhr, and while these regions were open to French invasion they could not be safely developed and counted on. "The action of 7 March enabled Hitler to launch his four-year programme, which was designed to mobilize the German economy for a large-scale war by the autumn of 1940."[81] France's inaction, moreover, encouraged Belgium to break off its alliance made in the 1920s with France and to move to neutrality, which left a critical gap at the end of the Maginot Line, further increasing France's defensive mentality and putting even the defensive strategy in greater doubt. It helped persuade Mussolini to conclude the "Rome-Berlin Axis" in October 1936, an agreement between the dictators that further complicated France's strategic problems. It also entailed withdrawal of Italian protection from Austria, a prerequisite for Hitler's annexation of Austria. After March 1936, "there could be no doubt that, with the disappearance of the demilitarized Rhineland, Europe had lost her last guarantee against German aggression."[82] That, in turn, meant that the French would not take offensive action in the west if Germany attacked their allies in Eastern and Central Europe. "The Rhineland *coup* sounded the death knell of the eastern pacts. . . ."[83] Prime Minister Sarraut said in April 1936 that "the essential point is that France cannot allow Germany to build fortifications in the formerly demilitarized zone. We would find it impossible to intervene effectively in order to assist our eastern allies."[84] Having permitted the coup, however, the French could not prevent the fortification nor defend their allies.

For many years it was common for historians to look upon the remilitarization of the Rhineland as a critical moment. A typical statement by a distinguished scholar reads: "It was one of the great turning points in history, of
higher significance than what occurred in Munich two years later."[85] That view
was sharply challenged by A. J. P. Taylor:

> It was said at the time, and has often been said since, that 7 March 1936
> was "the last chance," the last occasion when Germany could have been
> stopped without all the sacrifice and suffering of a great war. Technically,
> on paper, this was true: the French had a great army and the Germans
> had none. Psychologically it was the reverse of the truth. The Western
> peoples remained helpless before the question: what could they do? The
> French army could march into Germany; it could exact promises of good
> behaviour from the Germans; and then it could go away. The situation
> would remain the same as before, or, if anything worse—the Germans
> more resentful and restless than ever.[86]

There is no trouble in answering that challenge. A decisive military action by
the French might have humiliated and discredited Hitler, putting an end to his
especially dangerous regime. As Hitler himself told the British ambassador,
"with dictators, nothing succeeds like success."[87] By the same token, nothing
fails like failure. It is also important to ask what might not have happened. Belgium would surely not have sought safety in neutrality. There would be no effective fortifications of Germany's western frontier to deter a French invasion,
the threat of which, in turn, could deter a German attack on France's eastern allies. Finally, the Rhineland would not be available "for its traditional purpose
of providing the assembly area for great armies intended for the invasion of
France and the Low Countries."[88]

A different challenge to the traditional view has more merit. Its advocates
point out that the die had been cast well before 1936. To point to the real superiority of the French army ignores "all those factors of opinion, nerve and determination which made it a foregone conclusion that the superior French
power would not be used in the event." The remilitarization was only "the cul-
mination . . . of all that had already passed between Germany on the one hand
and France and England on the other in the three years since Hitler had come
to power in Germany. . . ."[89] It is possible to go further and say that it was the
result of almost two decades of the refusal to face unpleasant realities, to think
strategically, and to maintain a system of defense and the will to use it that
would be adequate to deter aggression and preserve the peace.

11

The Price of
Self–Deception

Britain paid a horrible price for the follies of the 1920s in the following decade. Her armed forces, too small to meet even the minor challenges of that relatively peaceful era, were completely overwhelmed by the new dangers that appeared. Years of putting off needed maintenance and improvement of those forces meant that the prospect of making good the deficiencies in military capabilities were appalling. Perhaps worst of all, the dramatic contraction of military procurement greatly reduced the military industrial base so that even when the money became available to rearm, it was impossible to spend it. Throughout an increasingly dangerous decade, therefore, Britain's military forces were consistently unprepared to deter aggression, and their weakness helped to undermine further an already timorous foreign policy. At the end of the decade, but for a miracle, the price for England's folly might have cost her freedom.

The Great Depression of 1929 marked a turning point in world history and in England's security. Before that economic calamity, relatively peaceful, relatively democratic regimes governed Japan and Germany, but the depression swept those regimes away. Their replacements, bent on external aggression, set out at once to rearm dramatically, in Germany's case, and to secure regional interests by force in Japan's. The Japanese invaded Manchuria in 1931, while the Weimar Republic perished in 1933. England was confronted at once with the problem of contemplating two wars widely separated—her "2-MRC," or two major regional contingencies, conundrum.

To be sure, the wars in 1933 would have been quite small. Japan was still no match for the Royal Navy (although England could have done little to stop Japan's forces in Manchuria), while Germany was still almost completely defenseless. The preparations for rearmament carefully shepherded through the dangers of the Inter-Allied Control Commission period were still only preparations in 1933 and for some time thereafter. There was every military possibility for England to nip both potential wars in the bud.

The British did not act, chiefly because they lacked the political will to do so. What Japan did to Manchuria, in itself, was relatively unimportant to England, and the claim in England's military power stemming for its obligations to resist aggression under the League Covenant had never seemed strong enough to England's leaders to warrant going to war. We have seen how Germany's overt violations of the disarmament terms of the Versailles Treaty had long since fallen into the same category—unfortunate, but not worth fighting for.

Economic problems also deterred any thought of intervention. The same depression that overturned the Weimar Republic and incited the "war party" in Japan to take control also had devastating effects on England. The relatively sound economy of the late 1920s vanished almost overnight, and the Cabinet once again became, in effect, an Economic War Cabinet to manage the new crisis. In the context of such an internal crisis, the prospect of any war was appalling and to be avoided at almost any costs. Certainly there was no stomach at Whitehall for an "adventure" to the continent or to East Asia, as an operation against Germany or Japan would certainly be called. The very crisis that brought the most serious dangers into being, therefore, also helped to undermine the leading power's will and ability to respond to those dangers.

Apart from these political and economic considerations, however, it is inescapable that England's military ability to respond to those two crises was inadequate. The adoption of the ten-year rule and its establishment on a rolling basis in 1928 specifically meant that the army was not to prepare an expeditionary force for use in a continental war. Since the army was overstrained simply in trying to perform its normal missions of policing and defending the empire, there was no surplus available from which to maintain such a force. There were enough regiments in the British army, to be sure, to have thrown together a force for use on the continent, but thrown-together it would have been, and it would have been weeks or months before British forces could have made their presence felt in any strength.

The Royal Navy's condition was both better and worse. The navy had been maintained at a higher level of readiness across the board and was able, at least, to perform its primary mission of defending England and policing the empire. It was worse, however, because although war against Japan was recognized as a real possibility and it was agreed that a strongly fortified base at Singapore was essential if England was to have any hope of prosecuting such a war, the base at Singapore was unfinished. Efforts to complete it had been underway practically since the end of the World War, but they were repeatedly under-mined both by the government's parsimony and by interservice rivalries. Tren-chard's success in taking missions away from the army in the Middle East emboldened him to attack both the army's and the navy's missions in the Far East. He claimed that aircraft could defend the port better than any guns and that no ship could survive concerted air attack in any case. The navy and the army argued otherwise, but the result was to provide a Cabinet eager not to spend money with an excuse to delay the completion of the Singapore base while a series of committees "studied the matter." The absence of a prepared base at Singapore meant that the prospect of a war with Japan was dangerous in the extreme.[1]

These problems did not escape the attention of the Chiefs of Staff, who brought them dramatically to the attention of the Cabinet in their annual re-view for 1932. The Chiefs surveyed in great detail the effects the ten-year rule had wrought on Britain's military capabilities.

> The position is about as bad as it could be. . . . In a word, we possess only light naval forces in the Far East; the fuel supplies required for the passage of the Main Fleet to the East and for its mobility after arrival are in jeopardy; and the bases at Singapore and Hong Kong, essential to the maintenance of a fleet of capital ships on arrival in the Far East, are not in a defensible condition. The whole of our territory in the Far East, as well as the coastline of India and the Dominions and our vast trade and shipping, lies open to attack.[2]

They wrote that the British battle fleet would require thirty-eight days to sail from its home ports to Singapore, but warned that "in their present weak state, these ports would be liable to capture or, at lest to the destruction of their fa-cilities, before the arrival of the Fleet." Unless these ports were strengthened considerably and quickly, "we should have to assume either that they would be captured or that their facilities would be destroyed in the first month of a war. The position would then become one of the utmost gravity. Improvisations would be required on a vast scale before the Fleet could sail to the East. . . ."[3] If England had to wage war against Japan, therefore, it faced the prospect of significant initial setbacks. The Chiefs did not bother to point out that En-gland's mobilized power was greater than that of Japan and that there was lit-tle doubt who would ultimately win such a contest. They knew perfectly well that the prospect of suffering initial losses of the magnitude they portrayed would deter almost any conceivable British government from taking such a risk.

The Chiefs declared that they had gone into detail in the case of a putative war with Japan because "in those regions we are conceivably within measura-ble distance of a catastrophe." They warned most ominously, however, "As a matter of fact . . . we are equally unprepared for every major commitment that confronts the Services."[4] British naval strength was not great enough, they wrote, to secure England's sea lines of communications. The number of ships available was inadequate, and many were obsolete. Worse still, "even vessels in full commission are not now fully manned, and some 16,000 Reservists would be needed to put the whole Fleet in commission." Whereas in 1918 hundreds of British airplanes and zeppelins patrolled the surrounding oceans on antisubmarine duty, in 1932 there were only fifteen such aircraft available! "The deficiencies in our means for protecting our overseas communications are the more disturbing when it is remembered that we are probably more dependent upon overseas supplies than at any previous time in our history."

Regarding air defense, the situation was very poor. Of fifty-two squadrons that were supposed to be available for the defense of England's skies, only forty-two existed in 1932, and of those thirteen were second-line squadrons. London's antiaircraft defenses were totally inadequate, and those of England's critical ports did not exist at all. The Chiefs reminded the Cabinet of Balfour's words in 1905: "We cannot sleep secure with only a bare margin of probability in our favour." They warned that "there is nothing approaching a bare margin today in the matter of defence against air attack."[5]

The possibility of a continental war was equally appalling:

> For major military liabilities, such as might arise under the Covenant of the League of Nations or the Treaty of Locarno, we are but ill-prepared. In 1914 we intervened on the Continent with six well-equipped and well-trained Divisions within the first month of the War. If to-day we committed our Expeditionary Force to a Continental campaign in response to our liabilities under the Pact of Locarno, its contribution during the first month would be limited to one Division, and during the first four months to three Divisions, arriving piecemeal; and except for the moral effect of its presence on the Continent it could have little effect on the fortunes of the campaign. Even for a War for the defence of India or our other Eastern Possessions, this rate of mobilisation, which cannot be exceeded, would place us in a very difficult position.[6]

The standard against which British military planning in the early 1920s had been judged had been the ability to field a force equivalent to that sent to Europe in 1914. The parsimony of the 1920s had seen to it that Britain could not make even that commitment to any future war, inadequate though it had proved in 1914.

The Chiefs were quick to defend themselves from the charge of having presided over the demise of England's military power:

> Once more we have to repeat that the above situation is due mainly to the assumption that there will be no major war for ten years. It is true

that considerations of finance would very probably have been operative in any event, but they would not have had behind them the same unanswerable argument against even really urgent proposals. Amid the colossal expenditure on development and unemployment . . . we find it difficult to believe that the relatively modest sums required to correct the more glaring defects in Imperial Defence could not have been found.

In 1932 two of the Chiefs, Admiral Field and Air Marshal Salmond, were relatively new, having taken office only in 1930, but the CIGS, General Milne, had been in that position since 1926. The Chiefs noted that there was nothing new in their report and that "the records of the Committee of Imperial Defence show that every year since 1919 the weakness of our position in the Far East has been brought to the attention of successive governments. . . ."[7]

That is true. The rivalry among the Chiefs, however, particularly while Trenchard commanded the Air Staff, militated against the sort of unified demand for more resources that alone might have convinced their political masters. Nor were the Chiefs inclined to make such a demand. On the contrary, as we have seen, apart from the navy's annual stubbornness, which, however, always dissolved, the services accepted their plight. Most of their leaders did not feel it was their place to tell their political masters how much they should spend on armed forces, and they feared to demand too much lest they seem to be out of touch with reality. It is certainly true that the ten-year rule had a horrible impact on the state of England's defenses, and that even without that rule, England's political leaders in the 1920s were unwilling to spend the money necessary to maintain adequate military capabilities. The fact is, however, that England's military leadership accepted an unacceptable situation far too tamely and hid behind the pretext of maintaining proper civil-military relations to avoid stating their case in any way that might have been effective. The armed forces themselves were, in part, to blame, for their weakness in 1932.

The Chiefs described the serious damage the policies of the 1920s had done to England's armaments industries. Using the example of naval construction facilities, they pointed out that whereas 111 ships, including nineteen capital ships, were building in English shipyards in 1914, only thirty-five were building or on order in 1932, of which none was a capital ship. They warned, "If confronted with a sudden emergency we should in many respects be in a worse position than in 1914 in the matter of armament production. . . ."[8] The weakness of Britain's armaments industries would prove to have grave consequences for her efforts to rearm rapidly and stands in astonishing contrast to the detailed preparations the Germans had made, practically under the noses of the IACC, to be able to rearm quickly.

Lastly, the Chiefs called the Cabinet's attention to the effect the ten-year rule had had on public opinion. They wrote, "it seems extraordinary that we alone among the great Powers should have neglected our defences to the point of taking serious risks." In England, they continued, this resulted in part from the fact that other countries trained their citizens in the need to make the necessary sacrifices to defend their countries. "In recent years," however, "particularly since the adoption of the ten years' assumption, not much lead has been given to the British people in this direction, although military security is not inconsistent with a policy of peace." Recruiting, particularly for the army, they reported, was difficult, despite "unprecedented unemployment." The people resented taxation to support defense. Perhaps worst of all was the ignorance and optimism that seemed to pervade people's thinking about the armed forces. The Chiefs noted that the League of Nations Union, an organization "that has contributed so much to national unpreparedness" through its regular opposition to defense expenditure, had called upon England to bring the issue of Manchuria to the League's attention and to demand the application of sanctions. The Chiefs noted that "it must be apparent to any well-informed person that such action might result in a resort to force by Japan, and that the brunt of a war must fall on the British Empire," but the League of Nations Union seemed oblivious to the danger it had helped to create.[9]

The Chiefs found this situation "a not unexpected paradox," and indeed, there was nothing surprising about it. The people who most wish for permanent peace generally place their hopes for such a peace in international organizations. In the heyday of those organizations, when everything seems to be going well, those people are usually the first to demand reductions in defense expenditures on the ground that armed forces are increasingly unnecessary in the peaceful era. When serious aggression begins to undermine the credibility of the international organizations, however, the more intelligent and responsible advocates of those organizations thereupon demand the use of force to maintain them. That is not an unreasonable position—indeed, in this case, it was the only rational position. But it was too late—armed forces once demobilized cannot be called instantly back to life. There was nothing at all unnatural in the successive position of the League of Nations Union and other similar organizations, just something very irresponsible.

The Chiefs summed up their warning, asserting that Britain's weakness constituted a "state of ineffectiveness unequalled in the defensive arrangements of any foreign military power" and "a complete bar to the execution of any policy in Imperial Defence however urgent." But still they did not call for a revolution in defense spending. A disarmament conference was underway in Geneva, and although it was clearly doomed from the start, the government, frightened by the changed situation, put great stock in it. They steadfastly refused to spend money on "offensive" operation at a time when such spending, they felt, would torpedo the conference to which they pinned all their hopes. The Chiefs settled for a lame plea, therefore, to undertake some purely defensive rearmament programs and not to delay that decision to await the results of the disarmament conference. They requested that the ten-year rule be abolished as a matter of course.

When the Cabinet had seen the report, the arguments of which it could not well dispute, it accepted the plea that the ten-year rule be abandoned. Even then, however, it could not face the ramifications of the situation thus presented to it. The danger to England still seemed, in 1932, to be far in the future, while the economic crisis was real and present. The Cabinet decided, therefore, that "acceptance of the Chiefs of Staff report must not be taken to justify increased expenditure on defence without regard to the very serious financial and economic situation that still prevailed."[10] They also rejected the Chief's request not to postpone defense increases until the resolution of the disarmament talks: "[T]he whole subject was closely connected with the question of disarmament and 'required further exploration.'"

The powerful appeal of the disarmament conference was largely emotional and irrational. The appeal of the primacy of economic concerns was more logical. The Treasury argued that "even had Hong Kong and Singapore been ready to withstand a Japanese attack in the recent Far Eastern crisis, no such localised defence would have been worth-while unless Britain had been prepared to sustain major operations in Far Eastern waters." It argued that, "'in present circumstances we are not more in a position financially and economically to engage in a major war in the Far East than we are militarily. It would seem, therefore, that as regards the Far East we must for the time being be content with applying such deterrents as may be available.'" Eighteen months went by and the Cabinet took no action on the Chief's complaints. Pressed by the Chiefs, the Chancellor of the Exchequer responded that "the Cabinet had earlier taken his advice, balanced the risks, and decided that the financial situation had then been the most threatening."[11]

The economic crisis that produced the threats against Britain simultaneously prevented the British from preparing to respond to them. Since Britain had failed to keep up adequate military forces all along, it needed a large influx of cash to make good deficiencies, and that cash was not available. In such a case the leadership is likely to delay, and "study" the proposals of the armed forces in an attempt to dither its way out of the economic crisis. By that point, of course, the foreign situation may worsen, other states with other priorities may devote more of their dwindling resources to defense or to offensive preparations, and the leading power's position may slip even more.

The economic situation, moreover, may help to blind the national leadership to the real peril of its position:

It was in some ways unfortunate that Britain's inability even to contemplate an active Far Eastern strategy in the crisis of 1931–32 should have been so easily explicable in economic terms. Had the acute financial restrictions of the immediate post-depression period not provided so obvious an explanation of military weakness, then it is just possible that the crisis in Manchuria might have induced that far-reaching analysis of the feasibility of an active strategy against Japan in a world war which was, in fact, postponed until 1939.[12]

Had Britain's military been adequate to its missions in 1932, and had willful blindness not prevented the consideration of the possibility of conflict with Japan and its consequences, the economic blinkers the depression offered would not have been so dangerous. When military weakness and inadequacy was added to the picture, however, they became potentially lethal.

The situation had not materially improved by the time of the Chiefs' next review in 1933. The RAF budget introduced in March 1933 was smaller than it had been the year before, and although the army budget was somewhat larger, it was still £2 million lower than the budget of 1931 had been. Worse still, "the increased expenditure, such as it was, was not for any augmentation in the size of the army, in the scale of munitions or in preparation for war. It was merely to replace cuts made a year before 'in face of the danger of national bankruptcy which as then thought—and rightly thought—to be even a greater danger than that of having inefficient fighting services,'" in the words of the Secretary of State for War, Mr. Duff Cooper.[13]

As the Cabinet dawdled in finding the necessary funds to fix their broken armed forces, the world situation continued to deteriorate at a faster rate. In 1933 the Chiefs reported: "In 1930, when our last comprehensive review was submitted, the prestige of the League was believed to be higher than at any time since its foundation. At the present moment that prestige has sunk to a low ebb." The Foreign Office reported in a memorandum written to support the Chiefs' review that "the world seems indeed to have gone steadily downhill. The most flagrant case is that of Germany, which is once more manifestly becoming a public menace; the spirit of that country is worse than at any time before 1914."[14]

The Chiefs then outlined the major dangers to Britain's security: the Soviet threat to Afghanistan (and therefore India), internal instability in China, including the crisis with Japan over Manchuria, Japan's withdrawal from the League of Nations, and "the militarist revival in Germany." Those threats, the Chiefs wrote, entailed three major commitments: "(i) The defence of our possessions and interests in the Far East; (ii) European commitments; and (iii) the defence of India against Soviet aggression."[15] If England's forces could meet those three contingencies, "no difficulties should arise with the remainder."

This strategy was thoroughly sound. England needed to be able to deal with what, in 1933 and for a few years thereafter, would be a relatively minor "continental commitment" against Germany, the threat to her interests and possessions in Asia, which was not so minor, and the "Bolshevik menace" against

India, which was the smallest of the three. She needed, in other words, a "2-MRC" capability plus a little more. This strategy was only stated clearly after the threats emerged, yet it should have been clear from 1925 that such were England's military requirements. By that year the alliance with Japan had been allowed to lapse, and whatever friendly sentiments toward the Japanese the Chiefs then might have harbored, it was utterly irresponsible to fail to provide adequate military force to replace the alliance in protecting England's interests in Asia. If England's de facto obligation to defend France were not enough to argue for the ability to conduct a small continental campaign against a reviving Germany, moreover, the Locarno Treaty imposed a binding treaty obligation to maintain such a capability. The Chief's insistence at that time and since that England's military commitments were not increased by Locarno was false and disingenuous. And it had been clear since the previous century that England needed to maintain a relatively small force to oppose Russian—or Bolshevik—advances in Asia.

All of those requirements should have argued for the maintenance of a 2-MRC-plus capability, at least after 1925. But in 1925 there were no threats. Japan was peaceful. Germany had just entered the League of Nations and signed the Locarno Treaty. Britain's interests were clear and the need to defend them was obvious, but, in the absence of any active danger to those interests, the Chiefs chose not to point out that British military capabilities were not up to task. It was only when threats began to materialize that the services began to speak loudly enough to be heard—and by then it was too late.

The Chiefs of 1933 attempted to make up the lost ground as best they could. They noted that "steps have already been authorised whereby our defensive position in the Far East will tend progressively to improve during the next three years, but we feel that with the general instability of the world conditions, we should be failing in our duty if we did not point out that, in say three to five years' time, when the anticipated military revival in Germany may have been realised, we shall be in a worse position than to-day to implement the Treaty of Locarno, unless the unsatisfactory and inadequate means at our disposal are increased and the general position is rectified." Three to five years from 1933 would have been 1936 to 1938. It would have been extremely valuable to England had her armed forces been in condition to meet her commitments in those years.

The nonsense spouted in the 1920s about what was and was not possible rapidly evaporated in the face of real dangers in the next decade. In those earlier years, we should recall, the Chiefs argued that the Locarno Treaty did not increase England's responsibilities because England would have to defend France and the Low Countries anyway. War with France was, in principle, not considered by the services in preparing their estimates—except for the RAF, which succeeded in using Anglo-French war scares to support its program. In 1933 the Chiefs reported, "By the signing of the Treaty of Locarno . . . we undertook definite commitments, and to that extent made our participation in a European war more likely without in any way reducing our responsibilities in the Far East." It would have been well if that had been admitted—and its consequences considered—when the treaty was signed. The report of 1933, of course, explicitly rejected the notion of any preparations for a war with France. Reality had finally intruded upon England's considerations of her security.

The lack of reality in the 1920s, however, meant that the price of fixing the deficiencies in the armed forces in the 1930s would be astronomical. Thus the admiralty judged that it needed twenty new cruisers in case of a war with Japan and warned that stocks of fuel, ammunition, and equipment were far below what was necessary. In the case of nearly simultaneous war with Germany, in alliance with France, the Royal Navy was sure it could protect England's trade by allowing the French navy to defend England itself, "provided that the European situation remains quiet for a sufficient time to enable us, after sending the Main Fleet to the Far East, to bring forward for service two of the capital ships undergoing large repairs, and assuming additional cruisers as suggested . . . above."[16] Considering the weakness of the German navy in 1933, it is unnerving that the Royal Navy felt it necessary to add so many caveats to its assurance.

The army's situation was appalling. By establishing a system we might now call "tiered readiness," the "Government has, in fact, deliberately accepted the risk of spreading the mobilization of the regular divisions over a period of six months. Our present resources do not permit us even to aim at anything better than to place in the field single divisions in each of the first two months of the war, a third at the end of the fourth month, and the remaining two divisions at the end of the sixth month." Worse still, "the demands for economy have prevented us from providing the modern equipment and the extremely important and expensive item of sufficient reserves of ammunition which would be necessary for war on the continent of Europe, and even for a major contingency on the Frontiers of India." Fixing these problems would require a great deal of money annually over a number of years, and would also require finding the manpower necessary to make good deficiencies in the army. "The most we could do at present if called upon to intervene in Europe, and it is probably well known to both our friends and enemies, would be to provide a small contingent of, say, one or at most two divisions at the outbreak of war, equipping them to a certain extent at the expense of later divisions preparing to go overseas."[17]

Even with such dire warnings, the Chiefs pulled their punch. They did not name a sum that would suffice to cure the armed forces' ills, and they did not outline any procedure that would make it possible to fix such a sum. The establishment of such a procedure was left to the Cabinet, which produced its usual solution: create a committee. Thus was the Defence Requirements Sub-Committee of the Committee of Imperial Defence, formed with instructions to consider Britain's military deficiencies in regard to the three cases the Chiefs had outlined—war in Europe, in Asia, and against the Soviets in India. It was also ordered not to consider possible conflict against the United States, France, or Italy, although the Chiefs had reported that England's position in the Mediterranean was weak and many of her facilities there obsolete. But, of course, Italy was an ally in 1933.

The Defence Requirements Committee consisted of the Chiefs of Staff; Sir Maurice Hankey, secretary of the Committee of Imperial Defence; Sir Warren Fischer from the Treasury; and Robert Vansittart, from the Foreign Office. It reported at the end of February 1934. Fischer recommended at the outset that the Chiefs outline everything they might need without reference to political realities, but the Chiefs cautiously demurred. They felt that it would be imprudent to offer a program obviously beyond what their civilian masters were likely to find acceptable, and they feared that anything they suggested would be cut by 30 or 50 percent in any event. Both Fischer and Vansittart "vainly urged the COS to be less self-denying, and pointed out that increased expenditure was of little value if it did not satisfy definite strategic priorities such as insuring Britain against air attack or providing a territorial Army trained and equipped to reinforce the Expeditionary Force." But the Chiefs were not moved—years of designing budgets aimed at pleasing their masters rather than securing England's security, and years of finding necessary programs rejected for political and financial reasons, had weakened their will to state their case. The Chiefs had become political creatures and could not suddenly go back to being general officers.[18]

The DRC, therefore, proposed only to repair the deficiencies that fifteen years of ten-year rules had allowed to creep into Britain's defenses. It did not consider what would be needed to meet a German or Japanese threat five years thence, unless those threats could be met by the forces already programmed. Even so, just to repair those deficiencies, the bill was staggering. The DRC called for an additional £71 million over five years, with an additional £11 million thereafter.[19] Since the armed services budgets for 1933 had totaled £108 million, that was a daunting sum—an increase of more than 13 percent annually![20] Yet it was not remotely enough. The army was to receive some £40 million of the proposed total, but Sir Henry Pownall, one of the secretaries of the DRC, estimated that it would actually have cost £145 million to produce an adequate expeditionary force and to create the territorial reserve necessary to reinforce it.[21] It would have cost more than England spent on defense for a year just to make good the deficiencies in one service, to say nothing of actually preparing for the war that was to come! That was the legacy of the 1920s.

For all the moderation the Chiefs showed, the Cabinet trembled at the magnitude of their requests, delayed, and reduced them. The Cabinet received the report in early March, but farmed it out to the Ministerial Committee on Disarmament before considering it, finally, in July. By far its least welcome part was the prominence of the army and its expeditionary force, which clearly implied that Britain intended to fight another continental war. The Cabinet as a whole believed that the country would not stand for such a plan, since revulsion against the last war was so strong. Cabinet members argued that what "the people" feared most was the possibility of enemy air attacks on England, and that their "semi-panic," in the words of Chancellor of the Exchequer, Neville Chamberlain, had to be dealt with first and foremost.

At the same time, Chamberlain claimed that the economic condition of the country was still so weak that expenditures on the scale proposed by the DRC were simply impossible. Choices would therefore have to be made among the service programs. Because of the importance of "public opinion" and his belief that the chief menace posed by Germany was in the air, Chamberlain recommended increasing the RAF program and cutting the army program in half to £20 million, of which £6.5 million was to be spent on antiaircraft defenses.[22] Here, for the first time, he openly advocated the policy of "limited liability" in which England would provide air and naval support to France, but no ground contingent. In 1934 he was not strong enough to carry this point—later on his views would be more damaging.

The Cabinet's retreat behind "public opinion's" opposition to ground forces was solidly in the tradition of successive Cabinets since the end of World War I, which had done nothing but encourage such a view on the part of their people. For many years, Prime Ministers assured the English people that they were safe, particularly in the aftermath of Locarno. But many others, military and ex-military, professionals and amateurs, had been raising the specter of indiscriminate bombing, death, and destruction raining from the skies. It was clear in 1934 that England's air defenses were inadequate. The government, which desperately did not want to fight another continental war, did nothing to explain the need for ground forces to the people. Before long, however, members of the government would join the people in calling attention to the menace from the air. The public opinion the Cabinet cited as the need for the reduction in the army's deficiency estimates in favor of the RAF's was, largely, a creature of its own creation.

One historian of this first episode in the weary effort to restore Britain's emaciated armed forces to health concludes his account as follows:

> It is not unfair to end this story of the first deficiency programme on a note of bleak frustration. A balanced programme of £75 million had been amended to one only two-thirds that size, and so altered in distribution that the air gained at the expense of the other two arms for reasons far from convincing on military grounds alone however much they appealed to the general public. In his announcement to the House of Commons on 30th July, the Government spokesman, Mr. Baldwin mentioned only the measures designed to strengthen the Royal Air Force. And even this modest announcement was greeted by the Leader of the

Opposition with the words "We deny the need for increased air armaments."[23]

These events are of fundamental importance in understanding the pernicious effect of ten-year rules and similar acts of willing into the distant future all possible significant threats. The invasion of Manchuria and the fall of the Weimar Republic combined with the clear beginnings of German rearmament came "out of the blue sky"—no one expected them, no one foresaw them. To the military eye, these events were clear evidence that the time to turn around had come—England was in danger, not immediately, but in the near future. In a sense, these practiced eyes were right. If England had started rearming vigorously in 1933–34, it might have been in position to meet the German attacks of 1940 on reasonably solid ground, although, even then, it would have been a near-run thing.

But events that tell the strategist that the time has come for rapid preparation need not suffice to persuade politicians to open the public coffers quickly and wide, especially when those events are triggered by a global economic crisis that has hit hard at home. Still less do those events, the subject of much confusion, ignorance, and controversy, suffice to galvanize public opinion behind such expenditures. The man-on-the-street is apt to wonder what Manchuria is to him and why Germany should not, after all, be allowed to have an army like any other state. The government should have provided answers to those questions. It should have provided the explanations, guidance, and leadership its people needed to understand the danger and the response that was needed. But the government was itself unclear about these very things and had been claiming for years that all was serene and that England's defenses were in excellent shape. In modern democracies events that reveal the need to abandon ten-year rules and to begin rearming swiftly rarely trigger the needed responses in time to produce effective deterrence or smaller military actions that can prevent a great war.

Rearmament takes time. It creates a window of opportunity in which aggressors may seek to gain maximum advantages before the democratic states that would oppose them have the strength to do so. The delay between the moment when rearmament begins and when their forces are fit to fight constitutes a period in which deterrence becomes extremely difficult. Armed services, feeling inadequate in their strength, often just after writing piercing exposés of all that is wrong with them are likely to counsel politicians against undertaking "dangerous" policies in the world. They often insist that the politicians "buy time" with appeasing policies of friendly "engagement" lest the war come too soon, before they are ready. They are apt, in other words, to undermine what sentiments exist for strong deterrence and to ensure, thereby, that whether or not they are ready, the war will come.

The British tried to rearm. Service estimates increased from £109 million in

1933 to £384 million in 1938—an increase of 350 percent in five years.[24] But it was still not enough. The army had resisted mechanizing its forces fully in the 1920s and early 1930s (although where it would have found the money to do so is unclear), but by 1935 it was evident that they must be mechanized. Plans for good tanks were not ready; factories were not tooled to produce them. The RAF would have had an easy time mass-producing obsolete fighters and bombers, but their new designs were not complete and the factories unready. The long period of tiny military expenditures, in fact, had serious eroded the armaments industries, so that for much of the rearmament period factories were overwhelmed with orders they could not fill. The situation was exacerbated by the government's unwillingness to disrupt the peacetime economy in any serious way by preempting civilian factories and facilities, requiring multiple shifts, or altering union regulations. At times the problem was not lack of money but lack of factory capacity.

The results were devastating. The expense of fixing what was broken, let alone preparing forces to fight the threatening war, supported Chamberlain's natural inclination against ground forces. When he became Prime Minister in 1937, therefore, "limited liability" became England's policy, and the army's rearmament program aimed only at extra-European threats, in addition to being scaled back. Priority went to the RAF. Thus in October 1938, Sir Thomas Inskip, the Minister for the Coordination of Defense, reported:

> By 1 August 1939 the re-equipment of the Regular Army should be virtually complete except for armoured fighting vehicles, anti-aircraft guns, and chemical warfare companies. But its scale of equipment and reserves would still be calculated on the basis of an Eastern theatre, a basis inadequate for the Continent. The present scale of equipment for the Territorial divisions would not even allow them to train effectively on embodiment. No fully equipped Territorial formation could take the field until at least eight months after the war began.[25]

This dangerous state continued, despite increasingly frantic efforts to reequip the army before the storm broke.

In July 1939, the field force that would sail to the continent in defense of France, was still woefully inadequate to its task:

> [T]here were available only 72 out of 240 heavy anti-aircraft guns and only 30 percent of the approved scale of ammunition; only 108 out of 226 light anti-aircraft guns and 144 out of 240 anti-tank guns. . . . In August a War Office spokesman admitted that only 60 infantry tanks were available, against a total requirement of 1,646. As for training, there had been no large-scale Army manoeuvres for several years and Ironside had been counting on the September exercises to get I Corps

into good order. As he gloomily noted in his diary, the units he had observed lacked even rudimentary tactical skills, Thus in September the
first four divisions of the Field Force sailed to France inadequately
trained and short of every type of equipment, especially guns and tanks.
The remainder of the growing citizen army at home was reduced to "a
token force of semi-trained troops" lacking the equipment for realistic
training.[26]

The Royal Air Force, which had received the most attention during the rearmament, was in better shape, but was still far smaller than the German air force
and, on the whole, less well trained. The Royal Navy was not prepared for the
task of coping with simultaneous wars in Asia, the Mediterranean, and the Atlantic.

It is easy to point to the catastrophes that resulted from these policies. Singapore was never finished and British forces were swept out of it in days by a
surprise Japanese attack. The fleet, far too weak to oppose the Japanese in any
event, never had a chance to try to rescue its critical base. When the Japanese
struck in 1941, Britain lost its predominance and most of its influence in Asia
forever. The British Expeditionary Force, as expected, turned out to be far too
small to turn the tide. The moral factor of its mere presence was not enough to
cheer the French as the panzers ripped through their ranks. The miracle of the
escape of Britain's army at Dunkirk was the only bright light in a dismal campaign. Nor did England's armored forces perform well at first on their own.
Failures in doctrine and organization, equipment, and training led to embarrassing defeats in Africa before material superiority and the Americans finally
began to overwhelm the Axis Power in 1943.

Bad as that showing was, it should have been worse. The British army expected that it would have to deploy rapidly to the European theater to reinforce
the French as the Germans attacked. It was known that the Germans would
seek a rapid decision in such a war and that time would be of the essence. But
the BEF, as we have seen, was totally unprepared for that sort of war. Had the
Germans struck France rather than Poland in 1939, the BEF would almost certainly have been embarrassed and annihilated—even if it had arrived on the
continent before the campaign had passed it by. Untrained, ill-equipped, and
confused, it was not a combat force in 1939. Only Hitler's decision to go east
before going west gave the BEF the vital nine months in which to deploy, train,
and make good its material losses. At that, it was too small to affect the campaign in any material way.

The worst story of all was in the air. Although the danger of air attack on
England had been apparent since 1916, and although successive governments
had proclaimed it the single most important danger, and although numerous
schemes and programs were developed and partially implemented, England
was not up to the task of defending its people against air attack. Two decades

of complacency and inadequate programs opened England's skies to the Luft-waffe's bombers. But for a fortuitous set of circumstances, the RAF might well have lost the Battle of Britain. It was, at any rate, on its last legs when the Germans turned from their goal of destroying it to the more satisfying but enormously less militarily effective aim of killing English people. Many of those who died in England's cities died unnecessarily. Many deaths could have been averted if the expansion of the RAF and England's air defense system had started (when rearmament began in the early 1930s), even from the base of programs announced in the 1920s. Instead they first had to strain to carry out those unfulfilled programs—leaving not enough time to meet the growing danger.

That is the story of all England's armed services. The decade of the 1920s, a time of complacency and peaceful hopes, had created such deficiencies, had hollowed out England's forces to such an extent, that the hole they found themselves in when the crisis came was too deep to climb out of. Politicians, forced, at last, to face the costs of making good those deficiencies, blanched and turned away, hoping that "limited liability" and airpower—which England did not have in sufficient strength—would be a magic bullet. But there are no magic bullets in war. Only responsible planning and the maintenance of adequate military forces at all times could have avoided this horrible crisis and guarded against the terrible price England paid in 1940 and 1941.

Britain's policy in the 1920s and the early 1930s suffered from a fatal flaw—the flaw of groundless optimism and willful blindness. Having failed truly to conquer Germany and to resolve the basic problem a powerful unified Germany posed to Europe, the Allies imposed a harsh but unenforceable peace on their partially defeated foe. They created an international organization they hoped would maintain stability thereafter, relying on their dictated peace to keep the only real enemy they could see suppressed and unable to rise again.

But the League of Nations was nothing without the armed might of the democratic states of the world behind it. The others looked to England for leadership. England looked away. At Corfu it allowed the international organization so important to its thinking to be undermined and humiliated—and declared the outcome a triumph. As the inspectors revealed a large and sophisticated effort in Germany to subvert the terms of the peace, England's leaders condemned the French for trying to enforce it. Having alienated Germany with insulting and oppressive peace terms, they sought to smooth over the crisis with a meaningless treaty, made the more meaningless by England's manifest inability to execute it militarily. They then declared that peace had dawned and that no further danger was visible—no war, they assured soldiers and civilians alike, need be feared before ten years had elapsed from any given date. All efforts could be turned to reaping the fruits of England's efforts in the late war, to making England "a land fit for heroes."

Heroes would be needed, indeed, to set right what was allowed to go wrong in that time. England's failure in test after test to maintain the order it had helped to create in 1919 undermined international stability and allowed the international situation to whirl rapidly out of its control. So decisive was England's lead in power and influence in 1919 that it took more than a decade, and an unforeseen economic crisis, finally to bring into being the obvious threats to international peace that had been lurking in the wings all along. Every year that went by, England became relatively weaker and more withdrawn from the international scene. Thrust into the position of leadership in 1919, England abdicated. The vacuum was filled by her enemies. By June 1940, England was alone. Its allies had been crushed. Its own forces had been hammered into the ground. Its own cities would soon be pounded from the sky and its citizens killed in their homes. With its life on the line, it had no more of its own resources to fall back on, nothing else to bring to bear. All might have been lost—but for a miracle. When Japan bombed Pearl Harbor, Churchill knew that England would win the war. He can be excused for not reflecting at that moment on how little even he, not to mention England's other leaders, had done in the years of peace to deserve that victory.

PART II

The United States
After the Cold War

12

The New World Order

The Cold War

In 1989 the wall separating East from West Berlin, the best-known symbol of the Cold War and the "Iron Curtain" dividing Europe, came down. Within two years the Warsaw Pact that subordinated the nations of Eastern Europe to the Soviet Union dissolved, its members newly free and independent. A reunited Germany joined the Western nations in NATO. On Christmas Day, 1991, the Soviet Union disappeared, to be replaced by a Commonwealth of Independent States. Russia lost control over Byelorus, Ukraine, and the Baltic states, driving its borders far to the east. The Communist Party was out of power and discredited. Boris Yeltsin, the new Russian President, was committed to a broad program of reform in the direction of democratic government and a free market economy. Without the firing of a shot the Cold War was over.

After a half-century of intense and dangerous competition that sometimes involved war with and against proxies, and at least once seemed to threaten direct and nuclear war, the United States found itself without a serious opponent or a "peer competitor," the only remaining "superpower." Few who examined the scene in the years following World War II could have predicted such a remarkable outcome. Within a decade, Europe was informally but firmly divided in the context of an informal and uncertain peace. No sooner was the old war over than a new one between victorious allies seemed to threaten the world. Out of such unpromising beginnings grew a peace that lasted for a half-century without a major war, concluding with the peaceful collapse of one of the com-

COLLAPSE OF
YUGOSLAVIA

petitors in the Cold War and excellent prospects for peace in the future if the
relevant nations would learn the proper lessons from this great and surprising
success.

The end of World War II found Europe in a shambles, potentially a prey to
poverty, misery, and the political and military power of the Soviet Union. Only
the United States had the economic and military power to restore a balance in

Europe, but the Americans began their traditional practice of rapid demobilization, disarmament, and withdrawal from commitments overseas. The threat from the Soviet Union and the onset of the Cold War, however, imposed a recognition and acceptance of reality, changing American attitudes and policies. The imposition of Communist regimes in Eastern Europe, the menace to the independence of Greece and Turkey, the coup in Czechoslovakia, the blockade of Berlin presented immediate dangers that enabled America's leaders to persuade their people to undertake the responsibility of continuous engagement to create and preserve an international order compatible with their ideals and interests.

The long-range strategy pursued by the United States and its allies was the policy of containment gradually adopted in the early years of the Cold War, set forth in its first form by George F. Kennan. America's policy should be guided by traditional, realistic considerations of power: to restore the balance of power in Europe, to frustrate Soviet efforts to expand its power and influence and in that way persuade Soviet leaders to change their behavior.[1] This could be accomplished chiefly by economic, political, and psychological means, by surrounding the Soviets with strong, confident nations and societies that were able to defend themselves against intimidation of one sort or another. Kennan, however, understood the importance of military forces in achieving these ends. "You have no idea," he said, "how much it contributes to the general politeness and pleasantness of diplomacy when you have a little quiet armed force in the background . . . [Its existence] is probably the most important instrumentality of U.S. foreign policy."[2] He also hoped that a successful policy of containment would subject the Soviet empire to internal strains that might dismantle it. He even thought that a frustrated Soviet regime might one day crumble internally and suffer an overthrow of the dictatorship.[3]

Early in 1950, Paul Nitze replaced Kennan as the head of the State Department's Policy Planning Staff. He and his staff were charged with producing a comprehensive statement of national security policy, the general foundation of strategy Kennan had never written, the document known as NSC-68. It sought to frustrate the Soviet Union's goals of expanding its power by undermining and overawing other nations. Confronted by steady, determined resistance, its leaders might change their ways and live in peace, behaving in tolerable ways. The goal was to get the Soviets to accept the "specific and limited conditions requisite to an international environment in which free institutions can flourish, and in which the Russian peoples will have a new chance to work out their destiny."[4] NSC-68 sought to provide a plan to provide these conditions.

Nitze called for a vast increase in America's military capacity and expenditure to permit resistance by conventional forces, not merely by the menace of the atomic bomb, whose credibility had been undermined by its acquisition by the Soviets. There was considerable opposition to the high cost of the program by those who feared the American economy would be ruined by so great an expense, but the outbreak of the Korean War in June seemed to have confirmed the evaluation of the situation presented by NSC-68, which became the foundation stone of American foreign policy.

The policy laid out in these years was a rare example of a state making a rational evaluation of the problems it faced, the nature of its opponent, and the character of the threat it posed to stability and peace, then deciding on a reasoned course of action and the sacrifices and commitments needed for success. It was a realistic and nuanced approach that gave full weight to the importance of ideas, economics, institutions, culture, and to the need to adapt to change at the same time as it rested on the understanding of the need for military power and the manifest willingness to use it when necessary.

The adoption of the fully shaped policy of a long-range commitment to a policy of international engagement backed by powerful military forces required a sharp break from America's past. Contrary to its traditions, the United States joined in a continuing alliance with nations in Europe and later in other parts of the world. It consciously undertook the chief burden of preserving the peace under conditions tolerable to itself and its allies, gearing its economy for the purpose and even adopting military conscription in peacetime. These taxing and extraordinary measures were taken to meet what American leaders took to be serious and imminent threat, but their policy was also shaped by their understanding of the origins of World War II. These they took to be the failure of the Western democracies to meet their responsibilities after World War I, their withdrawal into isolation, their unwillingness to bear the costs of keeping the peace, which required the capacity and will to resist detrimental changes in the balance of power caused by dissatisfied states using subversion, threats, and military force to achieve their purpose.

For a time, however, weakened and divided by the war in Vietnam and by domestic travails, American leaders wavered, reverting to an earlier model. They seemed to be in retreat, seeking to win peace through unilateral reduction of their military power and attempts at appeasement, but during the period of what was called détente, culminating during the Carter administration, expansion of Soviet power and influence around the globe grew in extent, boldness, and intensity to an unprecedented level. It was only the Soviet invasion of Afghanistan in 1979 that produced a turn away from détente and toward a return to a policy of containment resting on increased military strength and political will.

Carter was succeeded by Ronald Reagan, a well-known critic of détente identified with the older policy of containment through strength who ran on a platform calling for rejection of the SALT II arms limitation agreement and a swift increase in defense spending to gain military preponderance over the Soviet Union.

The Reagan administration moved quickly to keep its promises to increase America's military strength. There is reason to believe that the pressure applied by the growth of America's military strength, particularly the exploitation of its lead in technology to produce advanced weapons, helped to move the Soviets toward change. Alexander Bessmertnykh, Deputy Foreign Minister under Gorbachev, had made the connection between the Americans' firmness and the progress of arms control clear.[5] "As for the Soviet Union, we were already feeling the pressure of the arms race. Gorbachev wanted to go on with the reforms and the continued arms race, and especially the nuclear area, was a tremendous hindrance to the future of those reforms."[6]

The Reagan administration's approach of seeking to keep the peace from a position of strength fit the circumstances well. The President appears to have sought to achieve security through negotiation after a position had been achieved that was so strong as to discourage dangerous ambitions. He was prepared to negotiate arms agreements that truly reduced the threat of nuclear war so long as they did not give the Soviets an advantage. Confident that the Western way of life would triumph in a competition free of intimidation, he was prepared to seek accommodation. His insistence on doing so from a position of strength and the confidence the American people had in him and his approach made such arrangements possible. As one scholar, by no means uncritical of Reagan, has put it:

> Others may have seen in the doctrine of "negotiations from strength" a way of avoiding negotiations altogether, but it now seems clear that the President saw in that approach the means of constructing a domestic political base without which agreements with the Russians would almost certainly have foundered, as indeed many of them did in the 1970s. For unless one can sustain domestic support—and one does not do that by appearing weak—then it is hardly likely that whatever one has arranged with any adversary will actually come to anything.
>
> It fell to Ronald Reagan to preside over the belated but decisive success of the strategy of containment George F. Kennan had first proposed more than four decades earlier. For what were Gorbachev's reforms if not the long-delayed "mellowing" of Soviet society that Kennan had said would take place with the passage of time?[7]

The collapse first of the Soviet empire, then of the Communist Party, then of the Soviet Union itself was, of course, chiefly an internal phenomenon. Its main cause was certainly the perverse unsuitability of the Soviet economic, social, and political system that might well have brought it down someday, in any case. The role of Gorbachev was also very important. His attempt to reform a system incapable of reform inadvertently but surely hastened the collapse. The peaceful resolution of the Cold War, however, was not inevitable. It would be a mistake to minimize the role played by the United States and its allies in bringing it to a peaceful end. It is not only that the leaders of the Soviet Union might have been less cautious and brought on a war through recklessness. In the 1970s the leaders of the United States came very close to abandoning the strategy that succeeded, thereby encouraging the very adventures that might have touched off a war in response. From the Kennedy administration after the Cuban Missile Crisis through the Soviet invasion of Afghanistan, American administrations began a process of unilateral disarmament and appeasement under the title of détente, an apparent failure of will that reduced America's power and prestige, encouraging the Soviet leaders to undertake adventures that might have sparked a conflict. The return to the original policy of containment and deterrence through superior power after Afghanistan permitted the decay of Soviet power to take place in a context of resigned inferiority rather than dangerous adventure.

The collapse of the Soviet Union and the end of the Cold War demonstrated the soundness of the policy and strategy adopted by the United States after World War II. Its leaders resisted the powerful historical, geographic, and political tendencies that had led their predecessors to isolation and irresponsibility after World War I. Instead, they chose to accept the burden of preserving the peace by constructing an international order that would require the United States to expend money and effort, to make sacrifices and run risks, and to make these commitments indefinitely. Rarely has a nation's grand strategy achieved so brilliant a result. Contrasted with the disaster produced by the very different policy pursued by the Western democracies between the world wars it would seem to have provided clear guidance for the future efforts to protect American interests, foremost among them the preservation of general peace.

In 1989, when the Berlin Wall came down, George Bush was President of the United States. He was a veteran of World War II and of the Cold War that followed. In theory, at least, he had learned their lessons. In the summer of 1990 he began to formulate the idea of a "new world order" in which the United States "henceforth would be obligated to lead the world community to an unprecedented degree. . . ."[8] Later, he would spell out his idea more fully: the United States, "as the leading democracy and beacon of liberty," with its economic, political, and geographical advantages, has "a disproportionate responsibility to use that power in pursuit of a common good. We also have an obligation to lead." Because it is generally perceived "as benign, without territorial ambitions, uncomfortable with exercising our considerable power," the United States has a special opportunity.

> Among our most valuable contributions will be to engender predictability and stability in international relations, and we are the only power with the resources and reputation to act and be broadly accepted in this role. We need not . . . become embroiled in every upheaval, . . . but we must act—whenever possible in concert with partners equally committed—when major aggression cannot be deterred. . . .
>
> The present international scene, turbulent though it is, is about as much of a blank slate as history ever provides, and the importance of American engagement has never been higher. If the United States does

not lead, there will be no leadership. It is our greatest challenge to learn from this bloodiest century in history. If we fail to live up to our responsibilities, if we shirk the role which only we can assume, if we retreat from our obligation to the world into indifference, we will, one day, pay the highest price once again for our neglect and shortsightedness.[9]

President Bush's understanding of the situation and its requirements is accurate. For all the differences in its resources and position and in the condition of the world in 1919, Britain might have been spared great travail had its leaders understood their opportunities and responsibilities with equal clarity and followed the advice of Headlam-Morley, the Historical Adviser at the Foreign Office. He had written:

> It is on Great Britain and if necessary on the British Empire, that in the time of emergency the world must depend for the necessary force. In this matter we have a very peculiar position. The whole arrangement is . . . of vital necessity to ourselves; on the other hand, we alone of all the nations concerned have, and can have in the future, no direct territorial interests. It is therefore essential that the world should be made to understand that our accession to any such agreement will be the symbol of a firm resolution at all costs to enforce its observance. There must be no hedging, no justification for the suspicion that we might on some finesse of interpretation attempt to avoid our engagements. . . . The world must understand that in the future, as in 1914, those in this country who are in principle most opposed to war, will actively and vigorously support a war undertaken in defence of law and justice against aggressive violence.[10]

Even with so perceptive an understanding, however, George Bush found it difficult to convert this broad vision into a practical plan of action, to hold to it in the face of real challenges, and the great pressures, foreign and domestic, that always work against the pursuit of such a policy.

President Bush understood, in the American system of government, how greatly the formation and execution of policies and strategies in defense of peace and the nation's security and interests depend upon the President.

> The president must take seriously his constitutional role as the chief foreign policy maker, developing objectives and setting priorities, doing what is right for all even if it is unpopular, and then rallying for the country. The challenge of presidential leadership in foreign affairs is not to listen to consensus, but to forge it at home and abroad. Nowhere is this leadership more critical than in creating a new domestic consensus for the American role in the world.[11]

The Gulf War

The first great test of President Bush and the people he led, even before the end of the Cold War, came from a most unexpected direction, from Iraq—by coincidence the first test of British resolve after the Great War. On August 2, 1990, Iraqi forces, by order of the country's leader, Saddam Hussein, invaded Kuwait. In spite of abundant advance indications, Saddam's invasion of Kuwait came as a great surprise. Since 1984 the United States had befriended Iraq as a counterweight against its larger, potentially more powerful, and virulently anti-American neighbor Iran. It had favored and assisted Iraq in its war against Iran and continued that policy afterward. The Americans understood that Iraq's leader was ambitious and something of a rogue. One student of his career has described his image of himself as "a reincarnation" of such ancient Mesopotamian heroes as Gilgamesh, Sargon of Akkad, Nebuchadnezzar, Saladin, and even the god Dumuzi-Tammuz. The war with Iran had made him the head of the leading regional power. And now he wanted a new victory to pave the way for his greater ambitions: "He intended to become the Gulf's greatest power . . . the pace-setter for the whole Arab world. Finally . . . his ambition was to become the most influential leader of the Third World. Beyond the immediate rewards of money and an excellent harbor, then, the long-term stakes were global power and glory.[12] If he lacked the potential power of the Hitler with whom Bush compared him, his ambitions earn him a place at least alongside Benito Mussolini.

He was a military dictator who repressed his own people, especially the Kurdish minority, against whom he had used chemical weapons. He was attempting to build his own nuclear weapon, and he had amassed the largest army in the region, reckoned by some to be the fourth-largest in the world. He had used it to launch and win the war against Iran. He had been on good terms with the Soviet Union, acquiring most of his military equipment from that source. He was bitterly hostile to America's ally in the region, threatening that "we will make fire eat half of Israel if it tries to do anything against Iraq."[13]

American policy, nontheless, was to avoid confrontation with Saddam, to maintain good relations with him and continue to supply him with credits, grain, and even the high technology that he might use for sophisticated weapons. It was based on the assumptions that Iraq was still needed to balance Iranian power and that, as National Security Adviser Brent Scowcroft said, it was possible "to make this guy a reasonable responsible member of the international community."[14] But Saddam was not inclined to be reasonable. He was badly short of money and deeply in debt, a considerable part of it owed to Kuwait, which insisted on repayment. To meet his needs he wanted the OPEC states to reduce the production of oil in order to raise its price. The leaders of Kuwait, however, preferred to allow market forces to work. Apart from these considerations, there was a quarrel between Iraq and Kuwait over the control of some islands in the Gulf.

In July 1990, Saddam launched a diplomatic assault on Kuwait, outlining a variety of "grievances," and began to mass large numbers of troops and tanks along its border. He demanded "the raising of oil prices to over $25 a barrel; the cessation of Kuwaiti 'theft' of oil from the Iraqi Rumailia oilfield and the return of the $2.4 billion 'stolen' from Iraq; a complete moratorium on Iraq's wartime loans; the formation of 'an Arab plan similar to the Marshall Plan to compensate Iraq for some of the losses during the war [against Iran].'"[15]

The United States responded by stating that it would support "the sovereignty and integrity of the Gulf states" and by insisting "that disputes be settled peacefully and not by threats and intimidations,"[16] but it regarded Iraq's efforts as aimed at intimidation rather than war. When Ambassador April Glaspie was called to see Hussein, she continued the conciliatory policy her government had not ceased to pursue. Saddam treated her to some tough talk: " 'If you use pressure we will deploy pressure and force. We cannot come all the way to you in the United States but individual Arabs may reach you.' To emphasize his point, he observed that the Americans lacked Iraq's readiness to lose 10,000 men in a day's combat."[17] She remained conciliatory, assuring Saddam that she had direct instructions from the President to try to improve relations with Iraq. Congress had tried to impose economic sanctions but the administration had blocked them. The administration understood Saddam's need for funds; many Americans also wanted higher oil prices. The setting of oil production quotas was strictly a matter for the Arabs, and Saddam's insistence that Kuwait should not exceed them deserved Arab support. Although she repeated the American view that disputes must be settled peacefully, she also stated that the United States had no opinion on the border dispute between Iraq and Kuwait. "The natural interpretation for Saddam to put on this, especially in the light of his opening harangue, was that the United States was still offering him a hand of friendship while urging him to be good."[18]

There seems little doubt that the weakness of American policy encouraged Saddam to move against Kuwait. It has been characterized as an "ambiguous policy combining threats with appeasement."[19] The threats came chiefly from Congress and the appeasement from the administration. Asked by a congressman what would happen if the Iraqis crossed into Kuwait, a State Department official replied that the United States would be very much concerned but that it had no treaty obligations to use force. Congress, in any case, would not have supported anything but economic sanctions. Saddam had good reason to believe that the United States would not get in his way. From his ambassador in Washington he heard there were "few risks of an American reaction in case of an intervention in Kuwait."[20]

The failure of the United States effectively to deter Saddam resulted, in part, from the Bush administration's refusal to face the fact that it had not succeeded in moderating Iraq's behavior but also on the highly influential role of General Colin Powell, Chairman of the Joint Chiefs of Staff and a powerful force in shaping American strategy, diplomatic as well as military. Powell has been called one of a "new breed of American commander," skillful in dealing with Congress and the media, "wise in the ways of Washington." Legislation passed in 1986 gave the chairman new powers that Powell exploited fully, "wielding power and influence beyond that exercised by any previous chairman." In the Gulf War he was the overwhelmingly dominant military figure, and once the war started his influence over the civilians who were ostensibly making policy decisions was formidable. The chief influence on Powell's thinking was the Vietnam War, which had an effect on American military leaders similar to the impact the fighting in World War I had on British generals after that war. Memories of Vietnam and the Tet offensive had paralyzed American soldiers just as recollections of Flanders and Passchendaele had paralyzed British generals who remembered not only the bitter experience of casualties expended in ground offensives that produced little or no military gain but also the terrible criticism of the generals who ordered them. General H. Norman Schwarzkopf, who would lead American forces in the Gulf War, told a reporter: "I *hate* what Vietnam has done to our country! I *hate* what Vietnam has done to our army! The government sends you off to fight its war. It's not *your* war, it's the government's war. . . . And suddenly a decision is made, 'Well, look, you guys were all wrong.' "[21] Never again would they expose their armies to conditions in which they could not be certain of having a decisive advantage and a prospect of victory without heavy casualties and of being immune themselves to charges of stupidity, incompetence, or callous bloody-mindedness.

Powell's thinking was similar:

> If force was to be used, it should be overwhelming, and its application should be decisive and preferably short. Military intervention should not be undertaken unless the outcome was all but guaranteed. The aims in using force needed to be precisely defined beforehand, and as soon as they were achieved American forces should be quickly extracted, lest the Pentagon slide into a quagmire. American casualties had to be held to a minimum.

The political experience of Vietnam led him to fear that the American public would turn against the military in any other kind of war. These ideas formed the conventional wisdom of most of the army's leadership, but the chairman held them so strongly that in the Pentagon they were called the "Powell Doctrine." General Powell exercised vital influence in the preliminaries to the war, in its conduct, and in its conclusion.

On the very eve of the war the administration, in the face of clear evidence of the massing of Iraqi forces, refused to believe that Saddam would attack

Kuwait, to issue a tough and unmistakable warning to Saddam, or to move new military forces to the region for purposes of deterrence.

On August 2 the Iraqi army invaded Kuwait with a force much greater than was needed for its easy conquest. The invasion was a textbook case of aggression. "Few disputed the need for Iraq to withdraw: even Iraq's friends did not attempt to make a case for Kuwait's annexation."[22] American interests were also very much involved. A key to the crisis was oil. With Kuwait in his control, Saddam Hussein controlled 20 percent of the world's known oil reserves. If he took Saudi Arabia that percentage would double. Even if he only overawed the Saudis, as his control of Kuwait would surely do, he could count on a dominant voice in the councils of OPEC and the policies it pursued.

Those opposed to the use of force during the debate over how to respond to the crisis frequently trivialized the issue of oil, casting it simply as a desire to keep the price of oil low for the United States and its allies. Its true importance was as a part of grand strategy. Any state that controlled so large a percentage of the world's petroleum could wield a powerful economic weapon for political purposes. Under a ruthless and ambitious leader such as Saddam Hussein, with the wealth he would acquire from petroleum sales, Iraq could build a large and powerful army equipped with modern weapons. Unchallenged, it would overnight change the political balance in the Middle East, compelling the moderate Arab states loosely aligned with the United States to join the side of Iraq and turmoil. The prospects would then grow for a serious war in the region with the United States at a disadvantage, without friends or bases. William Hyland, editor of the journal *Foreign Affairs,* a former Deputy National Security Adviser, painted a persuasive and alarming picture: "The Saudis would be looking down a gun barrel. And we would be asking for an Arab-Israeli war in five years in which nuclear weapons would probably be used by both sides. . . . The issue is this: Can we tolerate the continued existence of Saddam Hussein with his military machine intact?[23] A few also understood that it was an important test for the character of international relations in the new era. Deputy Secretary of State Lawrence Eagleburger pointed out that the Iraqi aggression would set "all the wrong standards" for the post–Cold War world—telling local dictators that "now the rules of the game might have changed to make it possible to get away with aggression."[24] It was plain that aggression in the Middle East was bound to entangle the United States. Beyond that, "Coming at a defining moment in the emergence of a post–Cold War order, the invasion was a critical test of collective security in the new context."[25]

Richard Cheney, Secretary of Defense, quickly saw the danger. The United States could not permit "a man like Saddam Hussein, with his military force and his willingness to use it, to in effect have a chokehold on the lifeline of the world's economy."[26] America's military leaders, however, did not seem to grasp the strategic importance of Saddam's control of Kuwait. After the invasion, Powell was reluctant to use military force to drive the Iraqis out. At the first meeting of the National Security Council after the invasion he asked, "'Don't we want just to draw a firm line with Saudi Arabia?' That country was the real U.S. interest."[27] It was not an inquiry but a proposal. "Powell said he saw the issue as deterrence—stopping Saddam from coming into Saudi Arabia." From that moment until he was forced to abandon it, "containment" of Saddam within Kuwait was the policy he favored.[28]

The choice of such a policy revealed an extraordinary failure to understand the larger strategic situation. We now know that Saddam already had stocks of chemical and biological weapons and was making rapid progress toward the acquisition of nuclear ones. Drawing the line at Saudi Arabia would have left Saddam with his ill-gotten gains earned by flagrant aggression, with his large military force intact, and with his prestige in the Middle East enormously enhanced for having faced down the United States, the West, and the world. As a failure to stand against Kemal's Turkish army at Chanak would have done to the British in 1922, a failure by the Americans to drive the Iraqis from Kuwait would have badly damaged their prestige in the volatile Middle East and around the world and their ability to influence the course of events toward peace and good order. It would have been a success for Saddam at least as significant as the remilitarization of the Rhineland had been for Hitler.

In his reluctance to use force, Powell received strong support from most American military leaders. Like Generals Wilson and Milne when Kemal challenged the British at Chanak, but with infinitely less justification, they warned against taking military action. Before Congress, Powell's two immediate prede- cessors as JCS Chairman, Admiral William Crowe and General David C. Jones, both called for the continuation of economic sanctions against Saddam instead of launching a war. Crowe said: "If, in fact, the sanctions will work in 12 to 18 months instead of six months, the trade-off of avoiding war with its attendant sacrifices and uncertainties, would, in my estimation, be worth it."[29] Crowe could claim no expertise in the effects of economic sanctions, nor did he take note of the effect of a long delay on the American forces in the field or on the insecure inter- national coalition President Bush had cobbled together against Iraq. America's CIA and the British Joint Intelligence Committee, however, who could claim some such expertise, concluded that economic sanctions would not work.[30] The judg- ment of the best scholarly study of the Gulf War is that "the economic weapon by itself seemed unlikely to bring Saddam to heel, at least during the time-frame in which it would also be possible to sustain the complementary political and mili- tary pressures, without which the sanctions could not be maintained."[31]

Before the onset of hostilities, nonetheless, one military leader after another indicated reluctance to fight. General Merrill McPeak, Air Force Chief of Staff, later told a reporter, "None of the Chiefs was itching for a fight. They did not want an offensive operation if there was any other honorable way out for the United States."[32] The army's General Thomas Kelly received the news of Sad- dam's invasion with pessimism: " 'There's nothing we can do,' he said. With no heavy grounds—tank divisions—in the area, there was no effective way to meet Saddam's thrust. Kelly said that the military didn't want to get involved in a land war in Southwest Asia, thank you anyway." He was firm and clear in his rejection: "We hope you political types aren't dreaming. . . . If we're thinking of taking on the Iraqis in any way, I want to voice a note of caution. . . . We can't have a land war."[33] General Schwarzkopf agreed with his colleagues. He told Powell that "he was not sold on offensive operation as the solution. Pushing Saddam out of Kuwait at this point would be dirty and bloody. 'Did they know that back in Washington?'"[34] In 1923 the British Treasury had resisted the imposition of economic sanctions against Mussolini for his invasion of Corfu with this argument: "We do not believe banking or trading community will accept bureaucratic control and dislocation of trade unless essential to prosecuting a war in which national feelings are intensely aroused."[35] In the words of a Washington reporter regarding Saddam's invasion of Kuwait: "The Vietnam Syndrome was alive and well—the military didn't want to use force unless everyone else approved. . . . Waging war was impossible without a galvanizing event such as Pearl Harbor, or a moral and emotional crusade."[36]

But not everyone did approve. Retired military officers and civilian political and defense experts across the political spectrum expressed similar views and made dire predictions about the doubtful outcome of a war against Saddam and its high cost in American casualties. The same views were strong in Congress. As the embargo against Iraq failed to work and the prospect of war came closer, antiwar congressmen insisted that congressional approval was necessary. The most powerful leaders of the Democratic majority in both Houses were opposed, and they were joined by some Republicans. Senator William Cohen, later Secretary of Defense in the Clinton administration, told the President: "I hope you will resist the calls that are being made for an offensive action." He warned that the President's current popularity and support would quickly erode once the casualties began: "When there comes a point that there is blood in the sand the Congress—which is following its constituents now—will again do so, and follow them in the opposite direction."[37]

As more time passed with no result, opponents argued for more time to allow the sanctions to work. Always the most powerful theme was the dread of casualties, which made any policy other than war more attractive. Senator Edward M. Kennedy of Massachusetts made a speech typical of the arguments of the opposition:

Let there be no mistake about the cost of war. We have arrayed an impressive international coalition against Iraq, but when the bullets start flying 90 percent of the casualties will be Americans. It is hardly a surprise that so many other nations are willing to fight to the last American to achieve the goals of the United Nations. It is not their sons and daughters who will do the dying. Most military experts tell us that war with

Iraq will not be not be quick and decisive, as President Bush suggests: it'll be brutal and costly. It'll take weeks, even months, and will quickly turn from an air war to a ground war with thousands, perhaps even tens of thousands of American casualties. . . . [W]e're talking about the likelihood of at least 3,000 American casualties a week with 700 dead, for as long as the war goes on.[38]

As British political opposition, war-weariness, and reluctance to accept international responsibilities, fostered by bitter memories of casualties in the Great War, had hampered Lloyd George's government while encouraging Kemal and the Turkish nationalists in 1922, so did similar tendencies impede President Bush's policy of resistance by weakening the adherence of allies and encouraging Saddam. That America had not escaped the "Vietnam syndrome" was well known to its friends and foes, and it presented serious problems to Bush and his administration as they tried to respond to the threat posed by Saddam. There was

> a lingering anxiety that the United States, despite its great power, was fundamentally strategically incompetent. The members of the coalition dependent upon American strength, as well as the Iraqis gearing themselves to oppose it, could all look to the Vietnam experience and wonder about the ability of the United States to sustain a commitment when the going gets tough. The most important "lesson" drawn from this experience was that support for a war would wobble once the losses mounted. It was suggested that the United States became unable to prosecute the war in Vietnam because public opinion could not stomach nightly scenes of war on television and the mounting lists of casualties.[39]

The decision to go to war in the Gulf after the Iraqi invasion of Kuwait, first to protect the other states in the region, then to force the aggressor to withdraw, seems to have been the work chiefly of one man, George Bush,[40] as the decision to defy the Turks at Chanak had been chiefly due to the determination of Lloyd George. As the British Prime Minister had the support of only a small group in his Cabinet, Bush was strongly backed only by his National Security Adviser, General Brent Scowcroft, and his Secretary of Defense, Richard Cheney. Most of his military advisers, however, although they performed well once the decision for war was taken, were reluctant to undertake it, and so were some of his leading civilian advisers. In his goal he was not supported by the military chiefs or the Secretary of State.

The first challenge the administration faced after the invasion was to persuade the Saudis to permit the placement of large numbers of American forces in Saudi Arabia. With Saddam's tanks pointed like a dagger at their heart it might seem they would welcome American protection without hesitation, but they greeted the American offer cautiously. They did not trust the Americans' commitment, fearing "that they might send over some aircraft as a gesture but then not follow it through, thereby leaving the Saudis to face the consequences alone."[41] President Bush was concerned that the Saudis might select "the appeasement option." The Saudi ambassador in Washington, Prince Bandar Ibn Sultan, reminded Scowcroft of the time in 1979 after the fall of the Shah of Iran when President Carter had sent squadrons of F-15s to Arabia as a gesture of support, only to announce when the planes were halfway there that they were unarmed. Bandar said that "the consequences had been devastating to the Saudis and lived on. Frankly, he said, we're worried. Do you guys have the guts or don't you? 'We don't want you to put out a hand and then pull it back and leave us with this guy on our border twice as mad as he is now.' "[42] Bush had great difficulty persuading the Saudis, paying the price for previous American hesitation and timidity. He succeeded by telling Bandar, "I give you my word of honor, I will see this through with you."[43] Only by giving his personal pledge could the President of the United State convince the Saudis of American seriousness and commitment and persuade them to accept American forces.

In spite of the administration's assurances, the Saudis' doubts and hesitation were well justified. As the decision on war drew closer, congressional opposition remained firm. Late in November, Speaker of the House Tom Foley told the President that he needed to consult the new Congress in January before taking any action. He thought they would support economic sanctions for another year. When the President rejected the suggestion, Foley told him; "If after January 15th you decide to go to war, you'll have to come to Congress," and Senate Majority Leader Mitchell agreed. Secretary of State James Baker asked if Congress would agree at least to an offensive limited to airpower, but Mitchell said no. Senator Richard Lugar, Republican of Indiana, pointed out that seven times in the meeting the congressman had refused the President's appeals for support. "It just seems inconceivable that we are going to leave it at this," he said. But there was no promise of support. Two weeks earlier, Secretary Cheney, himself a former congressman, had met with a group of congressmen who provided no consensus for support. "He found himself thinking of August 1941, just four months before Pearl Harbor, when the House was able to muster only a one-vote margin for continuing the Selective Service System."[44]

It was chiefly to deal with congressional opposition that Bush agreed on November 30 to go "an extra mile for peace" by offering direct talks with Iraq to achieve a peaceful resolution of the Gulf crisis. He would send Baker to Baghdad and would himself meet with Iraqi Foreign Minister Tariq Aziz in Washington. The well-informed Bandar regarded Powell and Baker as "the members of the Bush inner circle least inclined to go to war against Saddam,"[45] but it was the pressure from the domestic political situation that made Baker's suggestion attractive. The United Nations had authorized the use of force, intensifying public apprehension and Congressional opposition. As the chances of war grew, public support was weakening. Sam Nunn, chairman of the Senate Armed Services Committee and a most powerful figure on defense and military questions, was vigorously opposed, and two former chairmen of the JCS were testifying against fighting a war. Baker's most effective argument was that the President "had to stop the political bleeding."[46]

The "last mile for peace" alarmed America's allies, who feared it might be the first mile to retreat. Prince Bandar thought that "Americans would never understand Arabs. A peace offering 24 hours after the United Nations victory would send precisely the wrong message to Saddam: a message of weakness." He told Scowcroft, "To you sending Baker is goodwill; to Saddam it suggests you're chicken." His own conclusion was that "Bush and Baker had given Saddam great comfort at what should have been the Iraqi leader's moment of greatest distress."[47]

Bandar was right about Saddam's reaction: "He was ecstatic." From the first he had sought direct negotiations with the United States, to no avail. Just when the UN resolution had put the greatest pressure on Saddam to retreat, however, the American offer gave him new courage. He interpreted it "in the context of his evident troubles at home, as the start of a climb-down. Perhaps he had been right, after all, in telling ambassador Glaspie . . . that the United States did not have 'the stomach' for a costly war." The Iraqi press exulted, "The enemy of God, the arrogant President of the United States, George Bush, had consistently opposed dialogue . . . his initiative is [therefore] a submission to Iraq's demand . . . namely, the need to open a serious dialogue on the region's issues." From Baghdad the BBC reported, "There's no mistaking the feeling here that President Saddam Hussein has got the Americans on the run."[48] Whatever chance there may have been to convince Saddam to draw back without a war, deterred by the credible threat of force, was entirely undermined by opposition at home that encouraged the administration to act as though it lacked the will to fight.

At last, amid great nervousness on the part of America's allies, Baker met Aziz at Geneva on January 9, 1991. No agreement resulted, but the negotiations served their political purpose in the United States. The vote on a motion authorizing the use of force against Iraq took place in Congress on January 12. In the House it passed 250 to 183, but in the Senate, even after all that had occurred, it passed only by the close vote of 52 to 47. If three senators had gone the other way the motion would have lost.

Many wondered why Saddam was willing to risk a war he was bound to lose against so powerful an opponent. Dennis Ross, head of Policy Planning in the State Department, offered an explanation to a reporter in October 1991:

What I underestimated was his [Saddam Hussein's] perception of our resolve. He just didn't believe us. He had watched CNN . . . and his concept of the [congressional] debate was that it was a sign of weakness.

Debate and dissent meant that we would fall victim the same way we fell victim in Lebanon and the same way we did in Vietnam. . . . He thought we were hamstrung domestically.[49]

In the same way, dissenting public statements by the Liberal politician Asquith and the Conservative Bonar Law had encouraged Kemal further to challenge the courage and determination of the British leaders in defense of Chanak.

The leading scholars on the Gulf War come to conclusions similar to those of Ross:

> [T]he problem was not only Saddam's misguided confidence, based on his defensive success against Iran, but also the mixed signals from Washington including the "mile for peace" initiative, which came over as reflecting American weakness, in the sense of deteriorating popular support.
>
> Consequently, the Administration failed to convince Saddam of the seriousness of its intention . . . the Iraqi leader remained confident that through a combination of bluster and inducements he might strengthen the peace camp in the West to such an extent that war would be averted.[50]

Saddam, however, as Thucydides said of the Spartans, was a convenient enemy. He was given countless opportunities to withdraw, with his army, weapons, and country intact. He might fear domestic repercussions, but events have shown his remarkable powers of survival, even after a terrible defeat. Had he pulled out of Kuwait the United States would have withdrawn its forces, and, in a while, his military power would have begun to impose its influence upon the region again. The Americans would be far away and would find it very hard to rally themselves and their allies for another effort. The real danger posed by Iraq was less its occupation of Kuwait than the combination of Saddam's vast ambitions and his powerful military force. The stated American policy, limited to the restoration of Kuwaiti independence, would have left both of these in place had not Saddam's stubborn miscalculation forced the hand of the United States.

He was equally convenient in his conduct of the war. Thirty-eight days of devastating bombing changed neither his stubbornness nor his military deployments. The bulk of his forces remained dug in facing Saudi Arabia while his enemies went around his right flank and through his debilitated and demoralized front line. In four days his army was smashed and routed, suffering heavy casualties. For weeks before the offensive, American television and newspapers had been filled with dire predictions, often by experienced military officers and experts not previously associated with pacifism or the antiwar movement. The war would be long and hard and the casualties great. There was much talk of body bags and disastrous losses. This was fantastically unrealistic. Prince Bandar had a far more accurate understanding of the true military situation:

Everything will be over in a matter of hours. Do you know what happens to tanks in the desert? They are absolutely unprotected targets for the air force, in which we have an overwhelming superiority. They will burn like matches. Don't overestimate the fighting ability of the Iraqi army. . . . Don't exaggerate the number of [allied] casualties, either. This operation will be backed up by the most up-to-date electronics. It will be a surgical attack.[51]

In fact, casualties in battle amounted to 148 Americans dead and 458 wounded and 92 dead and 318 wounded from the other members of the coalition.[52]

In just over 100 hours, coalition forces captured over 73,700 square kilometres of territory. Fifteen percent of Iraq was under coalition control. The Iraqi army which had been in occupation had been effectively cut to pieces. No more than seven of the original forty-three Iraqi divisions were capable of operations. . . . [A]fter all the gloomy predictions of thousands of casualties, the total was remarkably small.[53]

Bush had repeatedly compared Saddam Hussein with Hitler and indicated that his removal from power was one aim of the war. The Republican Guard comprised Saddam's best and most loyal troops, and its destruction had been a main goal of the operation, but at the war's end a considerable part of that force, with its tanks, had escaped to safety, in condition to preserve its leader's power and to crush the resistance of the Shiites, Kurds, and his other opponents. The decision to end the fighting was taken in Washington, before the American ground forces had cut off the escape route of the fleeing Iraqi forces; "the commanders who knew the most about the battlefield were not asked for their views. . . . Powell and the White House decided to end the war based on initial, fragmentary intelligence reports instead of waiting for a fuller accounting." They hastened to end the war less for military or diplomatic reasons or the dictates of international policy than out of considerations of public relations and domestic policies. Powell "was determined that the military would erase the stain of Vietnam and come out of the Gulf War victorious with its honor intact." That meant avoiding casualties, the appearance of unnecessary killing of Iraqis, and an involvement in the postwar settlement of Iraq. The Secretary of Defense attempted to justify the decision by portraying Saddam as a bastion of stability and order:

If we'd gone to Baghdad and got rid of Saddam . . . then you've got to put a new government in his place and then you're faced with the question of what kind of government are you going to establish in Iraq? Is it going to be a Kurdish government or a Shia government or a Sunni government? How many forces are you going to have to leave there to keep it propped up?[54]

He did not ask the question of how many forces would be needed to contain Saddam if he was permitted to stay in power. The evidence is clear, moreover, that the fear of Saddam's fall and the political chaos of a consequent collapse of the state of Iraq was not behind the American decision to leave him in place. Bush's repeated denunciations of Saddam surely encouraged the rising against him by the Shiites in the south and the Kurds in the north that broke out in February 1991. In March, Bush said: "It seems unlikely that he can survive. . . . People are fed up with him. They see him as the brutal dictator he is."[55] But he did survive and took terrible revenge on his internal enemies. On a mountain full of Kurdish refugees Secretary of State Baker saw some of the results for himself. He was handed a letter expressing the Kurdish view of the American decision to end the war: "All Iraqis were waiting for freedom and democratic regime in Iraq. But the mistakes and wrong decisions that allowed the Iraqi regime to use tanks and helicopters caused this tragedy." Baker was deeply moved by the terrible plight of the men, women, and children who were starving and freezing all around him. He set in motion a major effort to provide the Kurdish refugees with humanitarian aid that certainly saved many lives, but he realized that the problem remained: they "eventually had to be able to return home free from future threat of the persecution and harassment that had sent them fleeing for their lives." But the most he was willing to do was to press for a plan of setting up "safe havens" and refugee camps in northern Iraq, which did not solve the Kurds' problems.

Baker reports the widespread criticism of his administration's policies that followed:

> Our detractors accused us of inciting the Kurdish and Shiite rebellions against Saddam in the days immediately following the end of the war, then dooming them by refusing to come to their aid, either through U.S. military action or covert assistance. These are many of the same voices who also allege that Desert Storm was halted prematurely for political reasons, and that United States forces should have gone on to Baghdad and occupied large portions of Iraq.

The only defense he offers against these charges is "We never embraced as a war aim or a political aim the replacement of the Iraqi regime." But the next sentence gives the game away: "We did, however, hope and believe that Saddam Hussein would not survive in power after such a crushing defeat."[56] Yet the removal of Saddam by internal rebellion by Shiites, Kurds, and others would have produced just the same "chaos" the policy of aborting the fighting was meant to avoid. It is hard to escape the conclusion that the American government wanted the result without paying the price. For all Bush's brave statements to the contrary, his actions in Iraq showed that the "Vietnam syndrome" was still in place and that the understanding of what was needed to establish a "new world order" and the willingness to do it were lacking. The day after the war ended, President Bush drew a hopeful lesson from it: "I think because of what happened we won't have to use U.S. forces around the world. . . . I think out of all this will be a newfound—put it this way, a reestablished credibility for the United States of America."[57] Only a few days after the smashing victory, however, a reporter asked him why he seemed so somber—"aren't these great days?" The President replied:

> You know, to be very honest with you, I haven't felt this wonderfully euphoric feeling that many of the American people feel. . . . But I think it's that I want to see an end. You mentioned World War II—there was a definitive end to that conflict. And now we have Saddam Hussein still there—the man that wreaked this havoc upon his neighbors.[58]

This latter statement proved to be the more foresighted. The premature end of the war left Saddam in power, with much of his military force intact and with the capacity to continue work on weapons of mass destruction, nuclear, chemical, and biological, that would allow him to threaten and destabilize the region. Like the Versailles Treaty in 1919, it destroyed the defeated state's power for the moment without ending its threat over time. Saddam continued to harbor a potent combination of resentment and ambition that required constant vigilance and control by the victors if he was not to threaten the peace and safety of the region. He defeated hopes of his imminent demise by brutal actions aimed at crushing internal dissension on the part of Shiite and Kurdish opponents and cowing all others.

The victory of Desert Storm, therefore, did not become the first step in a clear, vigorous, and steady policy of active peacekeeping in the world after the Cold War. The hasty, confused, and unsatisfactory conclusion of the Gulf War became instead the pattern for a hesitant, confused, and unsatisfactory foreign policy carried on first for the rest of the Bush administration and then by its successor. "The uncanny decision to end the Gulf War without overthrowing Saddam Hussein and leaving his apparatus of terror still largely intact . . . marked the stillbirth of the 'New World Order.'"[59]

Yugoslavia

No sooner had the Gulf War ended than a new challenge tested the Bush administration's commitment to shaping the international scene in the pursuit of stability, peace, and American interests. Within months the state of Yugoslavia began to collapse. As early as 1989, Slobodan Milosevic, leader of the Serbian Communist Party, brought about the suspension of autonomy in the provinces of Vojvodina and Kosovo as part of a drive to gain power as the leader of a renewed wave of Serbian nationalism.[60] Fearful of the drive for a "Greater Serbia," the other nationalities broke with the Yugoslav Communist League and held multiparty elections in the spring of 1990. These produced noncommunist nationalist governments in Croatia and Slovenia and, in Bosnia, a noncommunist regime divided proportionately among the three major ethnic groups, Muslims, Croats, and Serbs. In Serbia the Communists won, and Milosevic was elected President.

Yugoslavia's federal constitution provided for a rotating presidency, and a Croat was due to take his turn on May 15, 1991. The incumbent Serb, however, refused to be replaced. "This was in effect a Serbian coup d'état."[61] This act and the reactions to it, clear indications that Slovenia and Croatia would seek independence, made it plain that the disintegration of Yugoslavia was imminent. The American desire was for a combination of unity and democracy, but these were at odds. A democratic solution would certainly lead to the independence of those two republics, at least, destroying the unity of the Yugoslavian state. Unity could be preserved only by force. A CIA estimate made in the fall of 1990 predicted that Yugoslavia would probably dissolve within two years. It forecast that Serbia would not permit Slovenia and Croatia to convert Yugoslavia into a loose confederation in which their independence would be protected, that the Albanians in Kosovo would rise up in arms against the Serbs, that Serbia would instigate armed uprisings by the Serbs in Croatia and Bosnia, and that violent ethnic conflict might become a true civil war. The CIA's opinion was that neither Europe nor the United States could preserve the Yugoslav state. With the exception of Kosovo, where the predicted events were delayed by some years, the forecast "proved dead accurate."[62]

The prospect of a serious civil war in Europe would be a grave problem, not only for the prospects of a "new world order" of peaceful settlement of disputes, but also for NATO and, therefore, for the United States. The President, his Secretary of State, and other officials were uncomfortable with the changes that were taking place in Europe, even those that to many might seem to be welcome. As the Soviet Union was dissolving, Bush urged caution on Lithuania and the other Baltic states seeking independence. His advice, given in their capital to the Ukrainian people, urging them to be cautious in separating from the Soviet Union, earned from critics the title "the chicken Kiev speech." He feared that a Yugoslavia disintegrating into violent chaos might encourage a similar development in the Soviet Union. In spite of the CIA estimate, therefore, the Bush administration fixed on a policy of supporting Yugoslav unity and discouraging independence for the constituent states.

On June 21, Secretary Baker came to Belgrade in what the American ambassador, Warren Zimmerman, describes as "a last-ditch effort to head off the violence that we all expected as an aftermath to the destruction of Yugoslavia."[63] In nine meetings with representatives of the several Yugoslav regions, Baker made clear Europe's and America's views and desires. He asked the leaders "to reaffirm their adherence to the principles of the Helsinki Conference, notably the principle that all disputes must be resolved peacefully, borders must not be changed except by consent, and human rights must be protected, particularly minority rights."[64] These were the essential principles that underlay the "new world order," and the American government was expressing its support of them before the outbreak of war. Firmly, Baker emphasized the most important of the principles: "Our critical interest in the Yugoslavia question is its peaceful settlement. We will continue to oppose the use of force or intimidation in resolving political differences."[65]

Baker warned the Slovenes and the Croats against unilateral secession, but he had no doubt that the Serbs were the chief threat to peace, especially their leader, Milosovic, whom he describes as "a man whose whole life has been built on using the past to inflame the present . . . a tough and a liar." He told him that "we regard your policies as the main cause of Yugoslavia's present crisis. . . . You are propelling your people, your republic, and Yugoslavia into disintegration." Coming from the representative of the world's only superpower, which had just demonstrated its devastating military might and the will to use it in the Gulf War, such unusually clear and tough talk ought to have had a decisively deterrent effect, but Baker reports that as a result of all his conversations, "I convinced no one. . . . These people were headed right into a civil war, and yet nothing seemed capable of changing their minds."[66]

Baker should not have been surprised. While making clear what the United States did and did not want he also revealed the limits of what it was prepared to do to achieve a desired result. He warned of nonrecognition and international isolation, but never mentioned sanctions or the use of force. Zimmerman, the former ambassador, denies that Baker's talks gave Milosevic a "green light" for his future aggressions, but admits that neither was there a "red light," because "the U.S. government had given no consideration to using force to stop a Serbian-JNA [Yugoslavian army] attack on Slovenia or Croatia." In spite of its tone and the overwhelming power that could stand behind it, Milosevic and his generals accurately understood the American message. They

> had lived by force, and they understood it. What they read between the lines of the Baker visit was that the United States had no intention of stopping them by force. It might isolate them and make them pariahs, but that, they concluded, was an acceptable risk."[67]

On June 25, only a few days after Baker's conversations, Croatia and Slovenia declared their independence from Yugoslavia. The next day the Yugoslav army invaded Slovenia, where there were few ethnic minorities and still fewer Serbs, but was beaten back and quickly forced to accept its secession and independence. The picture was different in Croatia, where there was a considerable Serb minority. The invading Yugoslav army was some seventy percent Serbian and soon began supporting Serbs in Croatia as the fighting turned into a deadly and intensifying war.[68]

Until then, the European countries had given little notice to events in the Balkans, but the outbreak of war caught their attention. Yugoslavia shared frontiers with Italy and Greece; for those countries, at least, the conflict could not be ignored, and the others were shaken by the first serious and extended fighting on the continent since World War II. The moment, moreover, seemed ripe for the burgeoning and increasingly confident European nations to assert themselves in the international arena. The year 1992 was scheduled to be a landmark in the formation of the European Community, the Soviet Union was in decline, and everywhere there was talk of the coming European superpower. Jacques Poos, Luxembourg's Foreign Minister, proclaimed, "This is the hour of Europe, not the hour of the Americans." Jacques Delors, chairman of the European Community Commission, said, "We do not interfere in American affairs. We hope they will have enough respect not to interfere in ours."[69] Europe appeared confident and eager to accept its post–Cold War responsibilities for preserving peace and order in its own region, and the Americans were only too happy to leave the matter to them. James Baker reported the general opinion in Washington that "it was time to make the Europeans step up to the plate and show that they could act as a unified power. Yugoslavia was as good a test as any."[70] David Owen put the situation neatly:

> There was a feeling that Europe could do it all on its own. . . . Europe wanted to stand on its own feet—Yugoslavia was the virility symbol of the Euro-federalists. This was going to be the time when Europe emerged with a single foreign policy and therefore it unwisely shut out an America only too happy to be shut out.[71]

The resulting disaster demonstrated the incapacity of the Europeans to act effectively without American leadership and the impossibility of the United States' escaping its responsibilities for long.

In Croatia the Yugoslav army occupied itself with taking territory for the Serbs and cutting the main part of the country off from the Dalmatian coast. Soon they shifted their focus to attacks on civilians. They shelled and bombed Dubrovnik, destroying its resort hotels, but their assaults on the eastern cities of Vukovar and Osijek were even more fierce. In that region the fighting between Serbs and Croats

> was reminiscent of World War II's fratricidal killing. Civilians bore horrors of the conflict. . . . In Vukovar, under siege for eighty-seven days, only a fourth of its traumatized inhabitants who had not fled or been driven out survived, mostly by living in cellars. There were 2,300 dead; the town itself was totally leveled.[72]

By the time a UN-sponsored truce went into effect in November the Serbs controlled one-third of Croatia, 10,000 people had been killed, 30,000 soldiers and civilians had been wounded, and 730,000 Croats and Serbs had become refugees, living in other Yugoslav republics or elsewhere in Europe.[73]

In spite of these events the Europeans rejected any use of force to stop the fighting. Zimmerman points out that no one, for instance, considered using military action to stop the shelling of Dubrovnik, even though "the JNA's artillery on the hills surrounding Dubrovnik and the small craft on the water would have been easy targets." Military action then, he says, would have saved the city and

> [t]he Serbs would have been taught a lesson about Western resolve that might have deterred at least some of their aggression against Bosnia. As it was, the Serbs learned a different lesson—that there was no Western resolve, and that they could push about as far as their power could take them.[74]

Instead, the Europeans limited their actions to sending in unarmed volunteer monitors in white uniforms that made them look like ice cream vendors; they met weekly at The Hague to discuss events and vainly tried to arrange lasting truces. The EC appointed Britain's Lord Carrington as mediator, and he was soon joined in that role by Cyrus Vance acting for the UN. They negotiated a truce in November, but violence continued.

European actions were hampered, among other reasons, by divisions based on old attachments. The British and French had sympathies with the Serbs based on alliance in the two world wars, but the Germans felt close to the Croats and Slovenes. Germany pressed for the recognition of the breakaway republics while the French and British resisted. At last, on December 23, the Germans, on their own, recognized the independence of Slovenia and Croatia. The EC followed suit three weeks later. In February a referendum, boycotted by the Bosnian Serbs, produced a vote for independence for the republic of Bosnia-Hercegovina. On April 6 the Europeans granted recognition, and the next day the United States recognized all three new republics, leaving only a rump Yugoslav federation. At once, the JNA launched rocket attacks on the Bosnian capital of Sarajevo, the beginning of terrible new violence to come.

By the summer of 1992, ethnic warfare in Bosnia was rampant. Bosnian Serbs were declaring autonomous regions, and gangs of masked men were blocking roads into Sarajevo. Serbs fought against the Muslims and Croats in cities and villages. The air force of the Yugoslav Federation attacked Bosnian towns. Soon the Serbs controlled two-thirds of Bosnia, and their military power was far greater than the Bosnians'. Events were making it impossible for the world to ignore what was happening. Vast numbers of refugees fled their homes, and television screens were soon full of testimony and pictures revealing Serbian concentration camps and mass rapes, which were part of a conscious policy of "ethnic cleansing" meant to drive the victims from the land claimed by the Serbs. Although atrocities were committed on all sides, the Western countries had no doubt that the Serbs were the aggressors and the chief perpetrators of a deliberate program of terror for political ends.

Western inaction had a high price:

> As it became clear that the West was going to do nothing, the Croats and the Bosnian Croats were increasingly encouraged to join in the dismemberment of Bosnia. Like the Serbs, the Croats were accurately reading the signals sent by the West, and adjusting their policies accordingly. . . . Many critics of the U.S. policy worried about the effects of the Serbian example of being rewarded for military aggression, on extreme nationalists and tyrants in other countries. But the real effect was on the Croats in Bosnia. As 1992 ended, and especially after the spring of 1993, it was clear that the Croats had already absorbed the lesson provided by the appeasement of the Serbs and were starting their own war of aggrandizement in Bosnia.[75]

The European nations could not agree on an effective policy, and it soon became clear that the main priority of the West was not to stop aggression or to solve the problem: "It was to dampen the violence enough so that an intervention would not be necessary, and public unease over the violence and atrocities would be limited."[76]

Try as it might, the American government could not ignore the failure of its European allies to stop the fighting. Secretary Baker reports being moved to action as early as April 1992 by a visit from the Bosnian Foreign Minister, who told him, "As we speak, sir, people are dying. They are killing civilians as if they were animals. These are real people who are dying. We are not talking politics anymore." The meeting reminded Baker of the one with the Kurdish refugees on the mountain less than a week before. He called it "one of the most emotional meetings I had as Secretary of State."[77] The resulting action consisted of seeking to gain public support for Bosnia in the news media and seeking support for "ostracizing" Milosevic and Serbia. Since the American policy was to stand aside and let the Europeans handle the situation, Baker tried to press them toward more effective measures and quickly discovered European impotence. The EC would not act except with a unanimity that was almost impossible to achieve in light of the contrary prejudices of its members. "This," says Baker, "further undermined the negotiations, as the parties in the region quickly learned to play the Europeans off against one another, effectively neutralizing the EC."[78]

By the end of May, Baker had concluded that the Europeans could not be relied upon to stop the war and preserve order, even in their own neighborhood, and so informed President Bush:

The Europeans want to be active but need a push from us to do so—even when it's on an issue where they want to be in the lead and should be in the lead. Collective engagement works and multilateral responses can be real but tend not to get energized unless we serve as the catalyst.[79]

In light of this understanding and the administration's continued concern with the growing disaster in Bosnia, why didn't the United States act? The government clearly stated why the events in Bosnia were important. American officials said that "the determination of President Milosovic to create a 'Greater Serbia' posed an enormous challenge to the international community." Bush denounced the "vile policy" of ethnic cleansing and the deliberate murder of innocent civilians, calling them a "humanitarian nightmare." Secretary of State Lawrence Eagleburger, who succeeded Baker in August 1992, explained:

The civilized world simply cannot afford to allow this cancer in the heart of Europe to flourish, much less spread. We must wrest control of the future from those who would drag us back into the past, and demonstrate to the world—especially to the world's one billion Muslims—that the Western democracies will oppose aggression under all circumstances, not oppose it in one region and appease it in another.[80]

Nor did the Americans have any doubt about who was at fault. Bush and Baker consistently held Serbia and Milosovic to blame, denounced him repeatedly, and pressed for diplomatic and economic measures to punish them. The United States pressed its allies not to recognize the rump Yugoslav Federation, suspended it from the Commission on Security and Cooperation in Europe (CSCE), withdrew its own ambassador from Belgrade, considered an oil embargo on Serbia, and finally persuaded the UN to impose a complete economic embargo.

None of this had the desired effect, as the atrocities in Bosnia continued. Why didn't the United States, at last, use military force, "the one instrument," Baker admitted, "that might change the course of the war"? In June, in fact, Baker went to Scowcroft to discuss such an action, but "we both knew the President didn't want to, and shouldn't, get involved in an open-ended military commitment in the former Yugoslavia. We both knew as well that the Pentagon was deeply opposed to any military involvement in Bosnia, for reasons we both appreciated."[81] This is the same rhetoric that has been and is still used by any American leader who wishes to avoid the use of military force for any reason: to state the choices as though the only two available are inaction or an "open-ended" involvement with great numbers of ground forces who would take heavy casualties, without any guarantee of achieving the desired results. Suggestions for the employment of intermediate means are rejected as impractical or not considered at all. In a television interview, Lawrence Eagleburger testily responded to critics of the administration's formulation of policy options:

I'm not prepared to accept arguments that there must be something between the kind of involvement of Vietnam and doing nothing, that the *New York Times* and the *Washington Post* keep blabbing about, that there must be some form in the middle. That's, again, what got us into Vietnam—do a little bit, and it doesn't work. What do you do next?[82]

Even after the Gulf War the Vietnam syndrome dominated.

Once again, General Powell, Chairman of the Joint Chiefs, was against even the most limited forms of military intervention. "As soon as they tell me it's limited, it means they do not care whether you achieve a result or not. As soon as they tell me 'surgical,' I head for the bunker."[83] The general, however, did not recommend unlimited military force instead. He doubted the value of an air exclusion zone in Bosnia and thought limited bombing would be of no use. Powell's views were widespread among his military colleagues, "who recalled the Vietnam 'quagmire.'"[84]

But as the horrors mounted and the victims were increasingly visible on the television news programs, the pressure against inaction mounted. Anthony Lewis, a columnist of the *New York Times,* repeatedly attacked the weakness of the government's policy. He asserted that the President should have rallied public opinion, as he had against Saddam. Bush, he argued,

had been a veritable Neville Chamberlain in refusing to face the challenge of Yugoslavia, refusing to provide international leadership and to call for the military action that everyone knows is needed to stop Serb aggression. If Bush had had the courage to act, the horror in Yugoslavia would have ended long ago. When the Serbs began lobbing shells into Dubrovnik a year ago, a few air strikes would have stopped them and headed off the tragedy that followed.[85]

Baker decided to propose the use of force only to assure the delivery of humanitarian aid that the Serbs were preventing. The plan was to move an aircraft carrier into the Adriatic, to impose a naval blockade to enforce economic sanctions, to cut the oil pipeline that ran into Rumania, and "to demonstrate willingness to conduct multilateral air strikes . . . as necessary. . . ." The last three actions would be taken under UN authority, with explicit congressional support and without U.S. ground forces. Knowing that the military and the Defense Department would oppose these measures as the first step on a "slippery slope," Baker ignored them and went straight to the President, whose "initial inclination to stay completely away from the Yugoslav imbroglio militarily had been altered by the continuing horrors in Bosnia and by his disappointment with the Europeans' inability to get their act together,"[86] and, one might add, by the pressure of media and political criticism.

Bush stood with Baker against Cheney and Powell, the UN issued an ultimatum to the Serbs, and Bush and Baker got widespread approval from the European countries. The UN flag flew over Sarajevo's airport, and American relief flights flew safely into the city. "The Serbs for the moment had backed down."[87]

All this suggests that a similar stand taken earlier might well have avoided bloodshed and warfare. Until the war spread to Kosovo in 1999, anytime the United States made clear its intention to use military force to achieve its demands, the Serbs and the other participants understood its significance and either gave way at once or yielded soon after its application. There is good reason to believe that a resolute decision in the summer of 1992 would have put an end to the fighting and forced a truce, providing for negotiations toward a lasting peaceful settlement, however difficult to achieve. But that is not the lesson the Bush administration learned. It would use force only to permit humanitarian relief, but not "to resolve the underlying conflict."[88] It would apply a Band-Aid to the symptoms but refuse to cope with the causes of the disease.

Baker left the State Department soon after these events to take charge of Bush's faltering reelection campaign. Afterward he defended the administration's policy against its critics:

> And now as this is written [1995], almost three years later, the "humanitarian nightmare" in the heart of Europe continues. I do not believe it could have been prevented by any combination of political, diplomatic, and economic measures. In my opinion, the only way that it might have been prevented or reversed would have been through the application of substantial military force early on, with all the costs, particularly in lives, that would have entailed—and by everyone's reckoning, in that environment the casualties would have been staggering. President Bush's decision that our national interests did not require the United States of America to fight its fourth war in Europe this century, with the loss of America's sons and daughters that would have ensued, was absolutely the right one. We cannot be, and should not be expected to be, the world's policeman, and the necessary support by the American people for the degree of force that would have been required in Bosnia could never have been built or maintained.[89]

Here is the familiar litany: America had no "vital interest" in the issues; the only effective solution would require vast military forces and frightening casualties; the American people would never support such a policy. The same arguments were marshaled by opponents of the Gulf War, and similar ones were at work in 1922 when Bonar Law wrote of the British during the Chanak crisis: "We cannot act alone as the policeman of the world."

President Bush soon found himself in a campaign for reelection in which the war in Iraq played a different role than expected. The feeling grew, as a consequence of its ambiguous ending but without justification, that the war had been in vain. The caution that permitted the survival of Saddam and the rape of Bosnia did not have its intended political effect.

> The public euphoria and patriotic fervor that swept across an America exultant in the wake of the Gulf War faded even more swiftly than the yellow ribbons that adorned the trees, bushes, and fences of Desert Shield and Desert Storm. The streets had hardly been swept clean of the debris from the last ticker-tape parades when America awoke with a gigantic hangover. Persistent recession and growing unemployment gnawed at the country's vitals. The president who could do no wrong suddenly could do nothing right: George Bush, bewildered, watched his approval ratings in the polls plunge from just over 90 percent during the war to only 35 percent as he began seeking re-election.[90]

During the election of 1992 the incumbent candidate, whose will and diplomatic skill were the key elements in the great and important victory in the Gulf, was advised to stay away from the subjects of foreign affairs and defense. The managers of his opponent created a widely popular campaign button bearing the admonition "It's the Economy, Stupid." The opportunity to achieve a more complete victory in Iraq, to use the resulting credibility to lead a coalition of allies to impose a peaceful solution to the problems of Yugoslavia, and to produce a reasoned and persuasive argument for an active role in preserving peace and order in the world had slipped by.

Even so, President Bush and his equally reluctant successor, for all their twisting and turning, have found it impossible to escape the threat posed even by a defeated and damaged Saddam Hussein or to abandon the unwelcome responsibilities arising from the troubles in Yugoslavia, suggesting that America's interests there, too, are real and significant, as members of the Bush administration sometimes admitted. American actions then and later showed that when the United States was ready to lead, others would follow. The effects of the ultimatum on the shelling of Sarajevo in the summer of 1992, moreover, showed, as later events would demonstrate, that determined and serious use of limited force could have great success.

The Bush administration refused to recognize the evidence before them and left office unrepentant, stubbornly defending their mistakes in Iraq and Yugoslavia. One student of the Yugoslav policy rejects that defense:

The lesson that should have been learned, and explained to the public, is that the costs paid to pursue foreign-policy objectives should be proportional to the objectives being sought. . . . The rationale of the Bush administration leads to complete inaction. . . . If the U.S. subscribes to the now-obsolete doctrine that wars can only be fought all-out with objectives, costs, and end-points clearly defined and visible, then the U.S. will play a far too limited role in shaping a world that needs a U.S. military involvement. The Bush administration, seeking the certainty of victory, but with limited cost, was reduced to a sterile rhetoric that was helpless before a Serbian leadership that had taken its measure, and acted accordingly.

The former ambassador to Yugoslavia is also critical:

A doctrine precluding any military engagement except an absolutely sure thing would keep American power on the sidelines of almost every imaginable future crisis. . . . The refusal of the Bush administration to commit American power early in the Bosnian war . . . was our greatest mistake of the entire Yugoslav crisis. It made an unjust outcome inevitable and wasted the opportunity to prevent over a hundred thousand deaths.[92]

The Bush administration left to its successor a nasty situation in Yugoslavia that was growing nastier by the day, a problem that would not solve itself and could not be ignored. Six years later, thousands of American troops were on the ground in Bosnia and more prepared to enter Kosovo, a region newly plunged into ethnic strife and warfare, threatening to grow even more menacing. Another legacy was an Iraq still under Saddam Hussein, who would soon make it clear that his ambitions and capacity to upset the stability of the entire region, though reduced, was still significant and dangerous, requiring repeated American military attention. The vision of establishing a "new world order" in which the United States led a broad alliance in defense of international stability and human rights had become cloudy and uncertain. American actions were ambiguous, halfhearted, and contradictory, and the government had failed to establish a clear policy for the future, much less to provide the well-reasoned basis needed to gain support for a new world order at home and abroad.

13

The Peace Dividend

T he end of the Cold War marked a change in the international system fully as fundamental as those brought about by the end of the Napoleonic Wars, World War I, and World War II, and American grand strategy necessarily required a complete overhaul. For more than forty years, America's strategy had been designed to face the Soviet threat, and our armed forces had been shaped for that purpose. A strategic nuclear triad of land-based bombers, ICBMs, and nuclear missile submarines had been created with the sole purpose of deterring Soviet aggression. The U.S. Navy existed primarily to protect the critical sea lines of communication to Europe and, under water, to hunt and kill Soviet missile submarines. The U.S. Army and the tactical components of the U.S. Air Force were built to defend Western Europe from Soviet conventional attack. The rationale for the size, structure, budget, doctrine, and posture of all the services generally and of each service in particular died with the death of the Soviet Union.

It was not easy to replace the Soviet threat as the underpinning of American strategy and force structure. The need to deter a nuclear attack on Europe or the United States, or a conventional invasion of Western Europe, greatly simplified American strategy, reducing it to more easily resolved questions of ways and means. Just as the British in World War I might debate whether to focus on ground forces and commit large numbers of conscripts to the Western Front or to focus on naval forces and "peripheral operations" against Germany's allies, so Americans could debate the relative merits of fighting the Soviets in the third world, relying on nuclear deterrence, or seeking to redress the conventional balance in Europe. But in both cases, the objective was clear, the need for a large commitment of resources was widely recognized, and the most important debates were over tactical and operational questions. The end of the Cold War rendered those tactical debates irrelevant and replaced strategic certainty with strategic confusion.

With the passing of the Cold War, Americans had, for the first time in decades, to ask themselves what role they wanted to have in the world. What were their interests in the absence of a Soviet threat? What should their objectives be? Only then could they ask how the armed forces could help to achieve those objectives and defend those interests, and the answer to those questions would allow consideration of the size, structure, and nature of the armed forces necessary for the new era.

Surprisingly, there was little significant debate among the leadership either in Congress or the administration over what America's role and interests in the new world should be. The debate that drove the development of America's armed forces instead pitted those, primarily in the administration, who sought to craft a strategy and a force structure tailored to a relatively long view of the new era and those, primarily in Congress, who continued to think only in the old threat-based paradigm of the Cold War. The confusion in the debate has contributed to the disjunction between America's stated national security strategy and the force structure it has been maintaining to support it.

A Confusing Ending

The philosophical basis for the doctrine of containment had addressed more than the danger posed by communism, but it did not seem that way to the policy makers and the American people who fought and won the Cold War. To most of them, America's active engagement in the world was the direct result of the danger posed by communism in the shape of the Soviet Union. When that specter was removed, most Americans were at a loss to understand what their role in the world should be and, therefore, what the military strategy and structure of America's armed forces should be.

This confusion was increased by the nature of the Cold War's conclusion. The Napoleonic Wars ended spectacularly with allied generals leaving the conference table in Vienna to defeat Napoleon's forces for the last time at Waterloo. World War II ended in Europe with the complete occupation of Germany and the death of Adolf Hitler, and in Asia with the unconditional surrender of Japan in response to the second atomic bomb. The end of World War I was considerably less clear, as we have seen. The end of hostilities came in November 1918, but the Versailles Treaty was not signed until June 1919 and the problem of enforcing the terms of that treaty remained for several years after that. Britain, however, began to demobilize almost immediately after the signing of the armistice and found itself uncomfortably weak in the face of the apparent determination, for the moment, of the Germans to refuse to sign the treaty seven months later. The drawn-out ending of the war led to confusion in England's leadership, which, in turn, created unforeseen dangers for Britain's security and hampered efforts to develop a new strategy and force structure appropriate for the new era.

In similar fashion, the Cold War ended gradually, in several stages, and so equivocally that no treaty between the formerly warring states has been or will be signed, and no formal readjustment of their mutual relationship has been undertaken. The consequences of this ambiguity for national strategy have been dramatic and form part of the reason for America's failure to develop a coherent and appropriate strategy for the new international system and its failure to consider carefully what will be the requirements of the armed forces now and in the future to execute such a strategy.

The dissolution of the Soviet Union took place unexpectedly in 1991. In August a group of senior leaders opposed to perestroika and the collapse of the Soviet empire captured Gorbachev in his Crimean retreat, seized power in Moscow, and attempted to reverse the reforms. The August coup collapsed ignominiously, however, and the leaders were arrested. A wave of declarations of independence throughout the Soviet Union followed, which the formation of the Commonwealth of Independent States did little to mask. Gorbachev had resigned all his posts by the end of the year, and the Union of Soviet Socialist Republics formally ceased to exist on December 31.

The Soviet Union's retreat and decline had been under way for several years, and the gradual nature of its collapse had an important effect on the debate over America's future strategy and force structure. Although President Bush began speaking of a "new world order" in which the United States would be more dominant, he and almost all of his senior military and civilian advisers, as well as congressmen, the media, and the public, continued to regard the Soviet Union as the most critical threat to American security. The debate over changing America's national security strategy before late 1991, therefore, revolved around adjusting that strategy vis-à-vis the Soviet Union. The debate over adjusting the size of America's armed forces likewise focused on the impact of the changing Soviet threat. The slow death of the Soviet Union thus encouraged America to focus on its own increasing safety and security and to ignore its increasing responsibilities in a world that was about to become much more complicated than it had been for the previous half-century.

For all the real danger the Soviet Union had presented to the established order in the world, it had also, paradoxically, been a force for stability. It imposed an unwelcome control over relations between and within old enemies in the countries of Central and Eastern Europe and the Middle East. Cold War rivalries limited the independence of peoples in Africa, Central Asia, the Indian subcontinent, and Southeast and East Asia to engage in military conflict. As the victor in the Cold War, as the nation with the greatest stake in international trade and, therefore, international peace, and as the only remaining super-power, the leader of the only forces capable of resisting challenges to that peace, the United States found itself in a more fluid new world.

America's vital interests in maintaining peace and stability in the Middle East, in Europe, and in East Asia did not pass with the passing of the Soviet Union. The waning of Soviet power, however, unleashed former Soviet client states in the Middle East such as Iraq, led to the collapse of the communist states of Europe, including Yugoslavia, and on the one hand freed China from concern for its northern frontier while on the other it deprived North Korea of the last support that had kept it from desperation. During the Cold War, all of these regions had been, to a considerable extent, self-balancing. Both the United States and the Soviet Union had contrived to damp down the Arab-Israeli wars and to contain the Korean War and keep it from escalating. Fear of the superpower to its north had kept China at once relatively passive and rela-tively well inclined toward the United States. If in the future the United States wished to pursue its critical interests of peace and stability in these regions, a much more active foreign policy, backed by adequate military means, would be required.

America's situation in 1991 strongly resembled Britain's in 1919. Instead of finding a sharp diminution of its responsibilities and threats to its interests, of which the general peace was the greatest, the United States would face the emergence of a host of lesser, but often serious, threats in place of the one great menace recently overcome. The general expectation that the demise of the So-viet Union would permit a broad relaxation, a turning away from foreign af-fairs and obligations, ignored the new realities.

The size and power of America's armed forces at the time of victory in the Cold War, enhanced and maintained even though there had been no serious fighting for a decade and a half, was impressive. That power should not con-ceal, however, the powerful opposition to defense spending that it always needed to overcome. The Reagan military buildup, although ultimately suc-cessful in its goal, faced strong hostility in Congress. As Gorbachev's reforms began to take hold, that hostility turned to demands for reductions in defense spending. Beginning with the 1986 budget, defense appropriations were lower every year and had fallen 10 percent by 1990.

The debate over the desirability of reducing America's armed forces and de-fense budget intensified in 1990, partly in response to the voluntary and invol-untary reductions in Soviet capabilities. Some argued that reducing America's defenses would speed the Soviets' reforms, while others argued that unilateral reductions would delay further reforms by removing the pressure that had driven them. The key point is that the debate centered on the Soviet Union and its present and future capabilities. In 1990 almost all policy makers assumed that whatever the shape of the future world, it would contain a Soviet Union in some form, and that the Soviet Union, however peaceful its future intentions, would continue to constitute the most significant threat to America.

The desire to cut the defense budget became more urgent because of the economic situation. After the sharp expansion of the economy in the 1980s, the slowdown of the early 1990s appeared dramatic. Many people blamed the increasing budget deficit on the Reagan military buildup. Fear of the ever-growing budget deficit and national debt, moreover, helped to exaggerate the significance of the economic downturn. These fears would cost President Bush his job in 1992, but they also greatly strengthened the demand for a "peace dividend"—the reprogramming of defense money to domestic programs.

By 1990, political considerations made it clear to all that reductions, and therefore changes in the national security strategy and in the national military strategy and the armed forces, were inevitable. The diminishing Soviet threat solidified the happy assumption that those changes would result in dramatically smaller and cheaper armed forces. Although no one said it in those words, all understood, as Prime Minister Lloyd George had, that if defense spending did not go down sharply, everyone would wonder what we had fought the war for. It was in this context that America's armed forces would be shaped for the new era.

The Peace Dividend

The recognition that military budget cuts were inevitable was not slow to dawn on the military leadership, nor were they slow to recognize the objective changes that seemed to make such cuts appropriate. Since the late 1970s the size of American armed forces had been based on the assumption that they would have to confront a Soviet attack with little or no warning. The Soviet peacetime army in Europe and in the Soviet Union itself was so large and so apparently ready to fight at a moment's notice that it was not considered safe to assume that the United States would have the chance to prepare before the outbreak of hostilities. This assumption, among other things,[1] led the army to maintain most of its combat power in the active component, while relegating much of its combat support and combat service support (CS/CSS—logistics, communications, transportation, etc.) to the reserves. The United States would not have time, it was thought, to call up combat units from the reserves right away, but there would be time, if the active component was strong enough to halt the initial Soviet blow, to call up CS/CSS units and, over time, the combat forces in the National Guard.

Congress was sensitive to the warning-time question, and most congressmen apparently accepted the assumption that the Soviet threat was the most significant over the long term. Thus in January 1990, Congressman Ike Skelton recommended the following procedure for defense budget programming:

The JCS Chairman would be given a planning top line and a set of planning assumptions. For example, the top line might be a defense budget of $275 billion in fiscal year 1996—in 89 dollars—and $250 billion in fiscal year 2000. The assumptions for this top line might include a greatly reduced Soviet threat as a result of stringent strategic and conventional arms control agreements and at least 6 months warning time of a Soviet buildup that might lead to hostilities.[2]

The appearance of budget toplines in this discussion is extremely significant. We should recall that the establishment of budget toplines in England reflected a willingness to accept armed forces that were not necessarily capable of fulfilling the national strategy. Thus in 1920, the Cabinet had a budget topline of £75 million for the army and the RAF combined and then focused efforts on reducing the "extraordinary expenditures" associated with Britain's troubles in Iraq, Ireland, Palestine, and elsewhere.[3] The correct procedure for evaluating the forces needed for those contingencies, Churchill had argued, was "first, to fix the amount that may be spent. Secondly, to give the administering department the power of choosing the policy within those limits. And thirdly, having chosen its policy, to indent upon the War Office or the Air Ministry for the military force required." In the 1920s this policy led to the maintenance of armed forces that fit within preset budgetary constraints, but were wholly inadequate to support the national military strategy and provided continual support for arguments against involvement in crises around the world on the grounds that such involvement might force service estimates above the agreed-upon topline. For Britain in the 1920s, the adoption of budget toplines represented a willingness *not* to meet strategic requirements. In the 1990s, that same willingness began to appear combined with a similar confusion about what armed forces the national strategy required and, even, what the national strategy should be.

The most telling comments in the congressional debate were the calls to reorient our national priorities fundamentally. In February 1990, Representative Byron Dorgan offered the following comments on the "Harvest of Peace Resolution":

The remarkable political developments in Europe . . . have made it even clearer that we must reorder our budgetary priorities.

Over 40 years ago we faced and met one of the major challenges of our 200 years of experience. That challenge was feeding the hungry in war-ravaged regions, rebuilding a devastated Europe, promoting and nurturing democracy in Germany, Japan, and Italy, and protecting the West from the threat of Soviet aggression. The successes we are now enjoying are the fruits of sacrifices we made. It would be pleasant, if in the afterglow of the good news from Europe and in view of the dramatic improvement in United States-Soviet relations, we could relax, take it easy, and forget our domestic and global responsibilities. However, the decline in our schools, the decay of our highways and bridges, and the increase in poverty and homelessness in our communities will not be reversed unless we reorder our priorities. If we fail to invest in programs to reverse this decline, our productivity and our economic competitiveness will be eroded as well.

Our Nation's strength depends not only on a sturdy defense, but in meeting the needs of our people so that they can contribute to the growth of a healthy society and a robust economy.[4]

He did not, like Lloyd George in 1919, call explicitly for the creation of a "land fit for heroes," but the implication is clear. No one disputed the belief that the weakening of the Soviet Union would allow us to reduce our armed forces significantly, while many argued that America should turn inward and address domestic problems they felt had been neglected during the Cold War and, particularly, the Reagan years. Demands for a "peace dividend" abounded.

The Bush administration did not follow the path of Lloyd George. Secretary of Defense Dick Cheney long remained skeptical of the changes in the Soviet Union and believed that only America's continued strength could force the Soviets to adopt the necessary further reforms. He greatly feared that if American military power was reduced too quickly, the Soviets might halt or even reverse their own reductions as their desire to maintain and recover what they could of their empire overcame their fear of America's power and commitment to oppose them. Cheney had to be dragged repeatedly into supporting arms control initiatives and defense reductions.[5] The defense budget he and President Bush sent to Congress in February 1990 contained only a 10 percent reduction. Since Cheney did not believe that a fundamental reorientation of America's strategy and force structure was necessary, no such revised strategic vision was offered with that budget proposal. The results were politically costly—the Democratic Congress charged the administration with "old-thinking" and mindless conservatism, and a number of congressmen and senators tried to take the initiative in setting defense policy away from the administration altogether. The most prominent of these was the chairman of the Senate Armed Services Committee, Sam Nunn.

In March and April 1990, Nunn attempted to outline a new military strategy for America in the new era.[6] His proposals focused on the Soviet Union as the only significant threat for the future. Although he attacked the administration's failure to develop a strategy and an assessment of the threat appropriate to the new international system, Nunn fell into precisely the same trap.

In the new international environment, Nunn said,

the threat of a large-scale Warsaw Pact attack against Western Europe has virtually been eliminated, and the chances of any Soviet "go-it-alone" attack across Eastern Europe are very remote. . . . Because more than half of our defense budget has traditionally been spent on European security—deployment of forces in Europe, the early reinforcement of Europe, or later-arriving reinforcement—these developments have enormous consequences for the size of defense budgets and our conventional force structure.

He suggested that the collapse of the Soviet Union would render about half of America's force structure superfluous.[7] He also pointed to Defense Department estimates that America would have increased warning of a possible Soviet attack, using that argument directly to support defense reductions:

Even if one deems it necessary to hedge against the possibility, however remote, of a reestablishment of a Soviet invasion threat against Western Europe, it does not necessarily follow that the appropriate precaution is to maintain huge American standing armies on guard in Europe.

Test pilots talk of "turning inside your opponent" when they speak of one aircraft's capability to outmaneuver another. I believe a similar standard should now serve as NATO's measure for judging the adequacy of its defense posture. We cannot determine as an absolute matter if the greatly diminished Soviet threat is reversible. This is a highly subjective judgment of intentions.

NATO's criterion should be whether the alliance is capable of maintaining deterrence at lower levels and mobilizing and rebuilding to higher levels in time if a Soviet buildup begins.

In short, this question of the West's ability to mobilize faster than the enemy can get ready for war has to be the future measure of the adequacy of our conventional forces and our conventional deterrent. This view requires a different concept of "warning time"—that is, warning that the Russian bear is no longer hibernating but is emerging from its den.[8]

This line of reasoning errs in its exclusive focus on the Soviet threat, but this argument contains a more subtle flaw as well. The notion that America and NATO can rely on their capability to "turn inside their opponent" is misleading and dangerous. In the first part of the present work, we showed precisely how Britain failed to respond rapidly and forcefully enough to the first indications of German rearmament and, furthermore, why that failure was likely, if not inevitable. Nunn's assumption, like Britain's ten-year rule, relied on the belief that America would see the earliest signs of danger and would immediately respond with sufficient force not merely to be ready to defeat its opponent, but to be strong enough again to deter him. The story of Britain in the interwar years suggests the dangers of such a complacent belief.

Nunn repeatedly minimized the dangers of regional threats and their significance for the size of the armed forces needed and for the direction they must give to American strategy. He admitted, for instance, that U.S. reliance on Persian Gulf oil was steadily increasing and that the "root causes" of instability in that region "have not yet begun to be resolved." He pointed out, however, that the contingency plans of the early 1980s for the Rapid Deployment Force called for "up to 200,000 troops and several carrier battle groups moving to the region to attempt to halt any Soviet invasion of Iran at the Zagros Mountains." Such plans were clearly outdated. He conceded, to be sure, "The United States has never acquired capabilities sufficient to implement this strategy," concluding lamely, "but we have aimed in that direction." He made no recommendations whatever about how to meet the dangers to America's interests resulting from the potential instability in the Middle East, or about what sort of armed forces would be required to do so. Having identified a serious potential threat and admitted America's incapacity to meet it, he blithely proceeded as though it did not exist.

The Soviets' withdrawal from Afghanistan led Nunn to ignore the continuing strategic importance of the Middle East and to argue for defense cuts. "I agree," he said, "that our strategy for southwest Asia should now be focused on scenarios requiring fewer forces and matériel than that particular scenario [a Soviet invasion]."[9] Ten months later, 650,000 American troops were in the Persian Gulf fighting a non-Soviet invader.

The increase in warning time that Nunn relied upon to argue for cuts in force size also prompted him to propose increased roles for the National Guard and the service reserves. He argued that America should greatly reduce its forward presence in Europe and turn forward-deployed forces away from combat missions toward "reception" missions. They should remain prepared to receive and train reserves sent from the United States in response to the "many months" of warning time we would have before a Soviet attack.

Whatever its merits in regard to the Soviet threat, it was not appropriate to the broader range of threats facing the United States in the new era. In the same speech he spoke of America's reliance on Middle Eastern oil and warned that "the Persian Gulf region is also one of the most heavily armed regions in the world. Tanks abound, many countries have modern, high-performance tactical aircraft, and ballistic missiles are widely proliferated, including both surface-to-surface and antiship missiles. Any U.S. intervention in support of a friendly government must expect to encounter a high-threat environment." He did not, however, say how his proposed new plans would affect such problems, concluding merely, "Our ability to provide this assistance will require an improved logistics infrastructure in the region, including pre-positioned supplies and matériel."[10]

Senator Nunn complained of the Bush administration's failure to offer a new strategic vision, but this most experienced and best-informed congressional speaker on defense matters offered little more than a version of the same armed forces, scaled down even further, with modernization and procurement of most systems delayed or halted altogether. He did not identify specific new threats, propound a new strategy, or address a significant alteration of the force structure to meet the new realities. In March–April 1990 the only question was how much should be cut now that the Soviet Union was dying.

The Base Force

Unlike the Congress, the Defense Department was largely successful in trying to free itself from the Cold War paradigm. In separate but converging efforts, Chairman of the Joint Chiefs of Staff General Colin Powell and Undersecretary of Defense for Policy Paul Wolfowitz developed a new basis for American strategy and a new concept for shaping its military resources called the Base Force. The Base Force explicitly rejected the Soviet threat as the principal yardstick against which to judge America's military capabilities, taking as its basis instead America's new role as the sole surviving superpower. It also came to be known as a regional defense strategy because of its decision to determine the size of forces required by their need to respond to major regional threats. It was the right strategy for the short term, and also more farsighted than anything being discussed in Congress, although it, too, suffered from important problems.

Virtually from the moment he took office as Chairman of the JCS, Colin Powell sought to redesign America's armed forces to deal with the emerging strategic realities.[11] From the outset, he saw the development of a new strategy to support selected, managed defense cuts as essential to protect the armed forces from the irrational and uncontrolled cutting he feared a hostile and unconvinced Congress might force upon them:

> Congress, independent national security think tanks, and self-styled freelance military experts were blanketing the town with proposals. We had to get in front of them if we were to control our own destiny. Paul Wolfowitz . . . and his new team began to work. I was determined to have the Joint Chiefs drive the military strategy train, so I had scoped out certain ideas, even if they represented hunches more than analysis. I wanted to offer something our allies could rally around and give our critics something to shoot at rather than having military reorganization schemes shoved down our throat.[12]

Powell portrays the new regional strategy he would propose as his own, but it is clear that it had deeper roots than that. A Joint Strategic Capabilities Plan produced in 1988 "considered the possibility of a U.S.–Soviet confrontation that could erupt into global war as the most serious threat to U.S. interests . . . [but] argued that calculated Soviet aggression in Central Europe was unlikely. The more likely threats were indigenously caused conventional regional conflicts with little likelihood of direct Soviet intervention."[13]

General Lee Butler, who became the director of the Strategic Plans and Policy Directorate of the Joint Staff (J-5) in August 1989, had already set forth a farsighted view of the new strategic era:

> On the basis of his assessment of developments in the Soviet Union, General Butler concluded that the Cold War was over, communism had failed, and the world was witnessing a second Russian Revolution. He examined the implications for U.S. strategy of the success of the policy of containment. In his view, the world was entering a multipolar era, in which superpowers would find it increasingly difficult to influence events militarily. In addition to the decline of the Soviet Union and the further evolution of West European alliance relationships, the coming era would see the rise of new hegemonic powers, increasingly intractable regional problems, and the global impact of disastrous Third World conditions.
>
> General Butler maintained that the United States was the only power with the capacity to manage the major forces at work in the world. Implementing this new use of U.S. power in order to shape the emerging world in accordance with U.S. interests would require a coherent strategy that defined U.S. vital interests, decided the role of the military, and then set the necessary forces in place.

With political realism General Butler also "anticipated that budgetary retrenchment would lead to a major restructuring of the armed forces. If they did not undertake this task themselves, they would find reductions forced upon them."[14]

Powell sketched out his own predictions in November 1989:

> I wrote down what I foresaw in the Soviet Union: "Rise of opposition parties, Western investment, market pricing, and Gorbachev still supreme authority" . . . Soviet military budget cuts of 40 percent, manpower cuts of 50 percent, a cap on naval shipbuilding—in short, a Soviet force intended strictly for a "defensive posture" . . . by 1994, "No Soviet forces in Eastern Europe"; "Warsaw Pact replaced"; "East Germany gone"; all Eastern-bloc countries "neutral states with multiparty systems" . . . Germany, "reunified," and Berlin, "undivided" . . . Of course, trouble spots would persist, and I identified them as "Korea, Lebanon, the Persian Gulf, Philippines." I made another heading, "Potential U.S. involvement," and under it listed two places, "Korea, Persian Gulf."

As a consequence,

> I began matching these projections to a commensurate strength and structure for the U.S. military. And here, going almost entirely on gut feelings, I wrote, "From a 550-ship to a 450-ship Navy, reduce our troop strength in Europe from 300,000 to between 75,000 and 100,000, and cut back the active duty Army from 760,000 to 525,000." The Marines, the Air Force, and the reserves would be cut as well.[15]

Powell and the Joint Staff refined the concept over time, and by February advocated a Base Force composed of four major packages. An Atlantic Force, the largest, would be prepared to deal with contingencies in Europe and Southwest Asia. It would contain heavy forces based in the United States and the transportation assets needed to move and supply them. The Pacific Force would maintain a forward presence in Japan and Korea with smaller reinforcements in the United States. The Strategic Force would control America's nuclear arsenal and strategic systems, while a Contingency Force composed primarily of light, rapidly deployable forces would be available for short-notice operations like Just Cause, the U.S. invasion of Panama to remove Noriega. The force would have the following composition: "12 active and 8 reserve Army divisions, 16 active and 12 reserve Air Force tactical fighter wings; 150,000 personnel in the 3 active Marine Corps division/wing teams and 38,000 in the reserve division/wing team; and 450 ships, including 12 carriers."[16] It would represent a reduction of 24 percent in the active component and 42 percent in the reserve component and would be completed by 1994. Powell argued that this force would "not only meet U.S. defense needs in the new era but provide an expandable base upon which a larger force could be reconstituted should the need arise."

Powell won adoption for the Base Force concept in the late summer of 1990, and his victory was signaled by President Bush's address to the Aspen Institute in which he outlined the regional defense policy on August 2, 1990. The evening before the address, Iraq invaded Kuwait, but the speech was given largely as prepared. Bush boldly presented the new strategy and force structure:

> In a world less driven by an immediate threat to Europe and the danger of global war—in a world where the size of our forces will increasingly be shaped by the needs of regional contingencies and peacetime presence—we know that our forces can be smaller. . . . [W]e calculate that by 1995 our security needs can be met by an active force 25 percent smaller than today's. America's armed forces will be at their lowest level since 1950.[17]

The formal reorientation of America's military policy toward regional threats rather than the Soviet Union was the most important change enunciated in this speech; not far behind it in importance was the section headed "come-as-you-are conflicts."

Nunn and many others had used the increased-warning-time argument to justify placing greater reliance on the reserves. Bush's Aspen speech implicitly rejected that argument:

> Such threats [as the Iraqi invasion of Kuwait] can arise suddenly, unpredictably, and from unexpected quarters. U.S. interests can be protected only with capability which is in existence and which is ready to act without delay. . . . As we saw most recently in Panama, the U.S. may be called on to respond to a variety of challenges from various points on the compass. In an era when threats may emerge with little or no warning, our ability to defend our interests will depend on our speed and agility. We will need forces that give us global reach. No amount of political change will alter the geostrategic fact that we are separated from many of our most important allies and interests by thousands of miles of water.
>
> In many of the conflicts we could face, we may not have the luxury of matching manpower with pre-positioned material. We will have to have air- and sea-lift capacities to get our forces where they are needed, when they are needed. A new emphasis on flexibility and versatility must guide our efforts.[18]

The President also called for continued investment in research and development, because "the U.S. has always relied upon its technological edge to offset the need to match potential adversaries' strength in numbers," and in readiness.

The new strategy was also embodied in the Annual Report of the Secretary of Defense of January 1991, which described the Atlantic, Pacific, and Contingency Forces of Powell's conception (the Strategic Force was dealt with in a separate section) and explicitly laid out the requirement for the armed forces to be able to handle two major regional contingencies simultaneously:

> In addition to providing air, naval, and ground combat forces needed to deter, and if necessary to respond to possible conflict, this approach provides the capability to deal with more than one concurrent major regional contingency. In addition, this approach would use reserve forces to augment and support forces deployed in prolonged and/or concurrent contingencies, and provide a sustaining base for other forward-deployed forces.[19]

With these principles publicly explained, the report established the basis for the post–Cold War American strategy and force structure, and all changes since have been relatively minor modifications.

The Base Force After the Gulf War

The timing of the enunciation of the Bush administration's strategy for the post–Cold War era was unfortunate. Powell and Cheney had intended to hold a news conference following Bush's Aspen address to flesh out the details of the Base Force plan. Then they had planned a campaign to explain the new strategy and force structure to the Congress and the American people and to seek national support for it. Those plans were upstaged by the Iraqi crisis and had to be canceled or scaled down.[20] This very important change in American policies never thereafter received the attention and discussion it needed and deserved.

After the end of the ground campaign in Iraq, however, the defense budget became a primary concern to Congress once again, and the administration began pressing its policies more aggressively. In testimony before the House Armed Services Committee in March 1991, the Principal Deputy Under Secretary of Defense for Policy and Resources, I. Lewis Libby, used the Gulf crisis to illustrate the administration's strategy:

> [T]he Gulf crisis reminds us of the sobering truth that local sources of instability will continue to foster conflicts, small and large, across the globe. Regional crises are likely to arise or to escalate unpredictably and on very short notice.
>
> There is often no substitute for U.S. leadership in areas of concern to us. Such crises will require, if necessary to respond, that we be able to do so rapidly, often very far from home, and against hostile forces that are increasingly well armed with conventional and unconventional capabilities.[21]

Most of the congressmen on the committee, however, were not much interested in the strategic background to the Base Force or the arguments advanced by Libby for maintaining the capabilities necessary for that strategy. Instead, the chairman of the committee, Representative Les Aspin, attacked the plan, as he would consistently thereafter, for failing to take into consideration the changes in circumstances that had occurred since the Base Force plan had been crafted.

Aspin asked Admiral David Jeremiah, the Vice Chairman of the Joint Chiefs of Staff, who spoke after Libby's testimony, "In what way has this [plan] changed in the light of Desert Storm, and if it hasn't changed, how come it hasn't changed?" Admiral Jeremiah answered that as there had not yet been time to analyze the lessons of the Gulf War (which had ended two weeks before), the plan obviously did not take them into account. One lesson he thought should be learned was that "many of the things that we were able to do here a future adversary would work very hard to try to minimize, particularly the access to host nation support, the port facilities, and things that were available to us and the time lines that we were able to drive." Aspin replied only, "So let me just see if I can understand. What you're saying is that this plan is essentially the way it was worked out before Desert Storm."

One member of the committee, Representative Dellums, however, argued that he could already see the lessons of the Gulf War:

> I believe that, against the backdrop of Desert Storm, what we have learned is that our extraordinary technological capability has so thoroughly altered the battlefield that it has enormous impact on the issue of force structure. . . . In a yesterday war, maybe it took 150 men to assault a bunker. In the context of Desert Storm, you now realize that, with smart bombs', cruise missiles' standoff capability, you could hit the same bunker with enormous capacity to kill—in fact, beyond most of our comprehension. So one doesn't have to be too bright a mathematician to realize that that has implications for force structure. You don't need the 150 persons.
>
> Second example, by virtue of our technological advancements, we have, with respect to our tanks on the one hand, improved dramatically our survivability and, on the other hand, increased our lethality. So that it would seem to me that one can draw from that that you don't need the same number of tanks in a modern force, because, on the one hand, more tanks survive, fewer tanks have the same capacity to destroy that a larger number of tanks did in the past. One doesn't have to be a brilliant mathematician to know that, if that is, indeed, the case, and I make that assertion, that if you need fewer tanks, you need fewer personnel, which would again have enormous impact upon personnel.

Dellums argued that in the Gulf War, "the ground forces were really not a major factor, or certainly mobilization of significant thousands of massive forces was an irrelevant, unnecessary, antiquated idea, given our major spending in research and development, which gave us this great technological capability."

Aspin pursued the same theme, asking if there was "an argument that . . . if you have a more capable technological force, that you can, therefore, do with less forces." Libby pointed out that we really needed to evaluate Desert Storm before drawing conclusions, but this had no effect on Dellums and Aspin. Admiral Jeremiah made the very important point—but to little avail—that we cannot count on having the same freedom to use our precision weapons systems unopposed in the future: "We will have a much more hotly contested engagement potentially in the future. And the freedom to exercise some of that capability in delivering air-to-ground munitions may or may not be available to us."

Later, Aspin asked a fundamental question: "Under this base force concept, could we repeat the Desert Storm?" Admiral Jeremiah answered:

> I think the answer to that, as you have heard from a variety of witnesses so far, has been "yes, but/no, but." Yes, in the sense that ultimately I think we could accomplish the objective. No, in the sense that we would do it in precisely the same way. And I think . . . the circumstances would change. This force has the capability of doing it, but with greater risk. . . . As you draw down the numbers of forces here, you're going to have fewer forces available in Europe, for instance . . . and you would have a greater risk in our ability to reinforce in areas around the world such as Korea or some other hot spot where we would have a requirement to do so.

Representative Skelton pressed his point: "Had we not had a strong military capability worldwide, including Europe which was there for the Soviet threat, we would not have been able to have pulled this off as we did." Admiral Jeremiah responded, "[E]xact replication of what we did we could not do. We would have to—we would do it with difficulty, and we would do it with increased risk." Although the January 1991 DoD Annual Report to the President and Congress stated that the Base Force was intended to be able to conduct two simultaneous major regional contingencies (MRCs), Admiral Jeremiah's testimony revealed that from the first it did not have that capability.

Aspin did not pursue that issue, asking instead, "How were the forces in this base force concept sized?" Admiral Jeremiah responded, "This is the base force. We don't perceive that we can go below this force structure and carry out missions that have been assigned. . . . [W]e feel that these packages that we have described give us the ability to carry out our force strategic objectives." Not satisfied, Aspin asked:

> What is the scenario, though, that you anticipate. I mean, do you anticipate one contingency, two contingencies? . . . What kind of a strategy have you got built into this base force concept? Are you looking at being able to handle one contingency like the Persian Gulf and being able to, at the same time then, have enough force that would—in the rest of the world that would discourage people from trying to take advantage of it? Are you looking at a two-contingency force? Are you looking at being able to do a Persian Gulf plus a Libya—the Liberia rescue operation at the same time? Are you thinking in terms of doing a—handling a Korea and a Persian Gulf at the same time? What are the kinds of things you're looking at here?

Admiral Jeremiah responded:

All of the above, as you point out and as I tried to point out in our testimony. And when we're looking at scenarios, we're looking at threat, we look at all of those things. We're not trying to size it to a specific 2½, 1½, 1.3 here and 1.4 there. What we're trying to have is a force that allows this country to respond to requirements. . . . I mean, there is a continuum of risk and of likelihood of occurrence in which we tried to posture a force that we felt would cover the most likely kinds of scenarios that we might see against the most likely kinds of threats we have, without going so large in the force structure that we would not have the ability to sustain it at the levels of readiness or the modernization that is necessary to support it. So . . . the direct answer to your question is that we did not size it on "x plus y" scenarios. We sized it on the continuum of scenarios that we expect and the size of the force you want to try to have to address all of that.

Admiral Jeremiah's answer was self-defeating. The Base Force plan seems not to have been designed against any particular threats or individual scenarios, although a number of scenarios were considered during its formulation. It was designed just as Admiral Jeremiah said—as a force that was as small as it could be and still, in the judgment of the Defense Department, carry out the missions the Defense Department believed it would be called upon to accomplish. There was nothing inherently wrong in such an approach to force-sizing—on the contrary, it was in many ways superior to the scenario-driven force-sizing programs later adopted. The absence of a specific set of scenarios publicly acknowledged and described, however, made it a much harder plan to sell to Congress.

General Powell, the plan's author, repeated the presentation of the Base Force strategy with little variation in his testimony before the House Appropriations Committee in September 1991.[22] Two issues received special prominence at that hearing, however, that had been largely ignored at the previous one: reserves and reconstitution.

Powell made it clear that he regarded the reduction of the reserve and national guard forces as essential:

With the decade of the '80s the Army kept its active end strength constant. The Reserves grew from roughly 575,000 up to roughly 767,000, a significant increase in the size of the Reserves during the Reagan years. Why?

The reason was because we had not taken care of our European needs. We needed to fix our force structure. What for? To fight a European war. Where? On the central plains of Europe. And we built up the Reserves for that reason.

The Army now is coming down to 535,000. Why? Because we're

bringing half of its force structure if not more out of Europe. Why? Because that situation has fundamentally changed. We want to bring the Reserves down for the same reason. . . .

If I am not permitted—we are not permitted to bring the structure down in a sensible way, we are going to have to find outlay dollars to pay for it, one-one. You either get that by reducing additional active force below what I believe is a prudent level, or you have to try to find enough procurement programs at a three-to-one outlay authorization rate that you won't find, and the final answer is we go where we always go, we take it out of [operations and maintenance accounts], you affect training, readiness, quality of life, and you're on your way to a hollow force.

Powell's argument reflected the fact that the administration had sought to cut the reserves for the previous two years and failed in the face of congressional resistance. The same argument would repeatedly run into trouble in the post–Cold War era.

One assumption underlying cutting the reserves remained unstated: they are unsuited to low- or no-warning conflicts of the sort the administration's strategy believed America would be involved in. Reserves take time to locate, mobilize, train, and deploy. When the administration contemplated responding swiftly to Desert Shield–like operations, it could not find a meaningful role for the reserves. Only in the case of a large-scale war against a revived Soviet Union or a similar threat, they thought, would the reserves be relevant.

For the case of the more serious danger of a revived Soviet threat, however, Powell had little to offer. He proposed a plan whereby two National Guard divisions would be maintained in cadre, in addition to the six reserve divisions he meant to keep in the force structure, although they would not be manned. He explained:

When we were faced with a situation of conflict breaking out in Europe in 10 days or two weeks, then you had to try to get everything ready to go there quickly. But we're now faced with a situation where warning time is almost kind of irrelevant. It would take months, if not years and years, for the Soviets to try to reconstitute, even if they had the will to do so. Therefore we can now start to lower our reinforcement and reconstitution requirements.

Powell thereby proposed to create a hollow reserve army while avoiding a "hollow army"; the notion of maintaining two divisions in cadre was completely inadequate to the scenario Powell envisaged of confronting a reviving Soviet-style global threat. Although he always highlighted the issue of reconstitution, it was plain that his force had no real capability for it. Like many others, he wished the revival of a major threat so far away into the future as to be irrelevant for current planning concerns.

The Aspin Plan

The Base Force was hard to sell politically, ironically, because it was well thought out. Realizing that it was impossible to predict who America's enemies would be, even in the short term, let alone the longer period for which the Base Force was designed, the Bush administration made little effort to describe in any detail how it arrived at the force size it advocated. This approach was intelligent in an uncertain era, but it was a major political vulnerability, since it lent an air of vagueness and confusion to the testimony of administration officials who sought to defend the plan before a skeptical Congress. Aspin seized on that apparent vagueness and sought to preempt the administration by offering a defense "strategy" and force structure of his own.

In a series of addresses and House Armed Services Committee papers in January and February 1992, Aspin sought to attack the Base Force and to propound his own vision of an even smaller and cheaper defense establishment. He asked, "If the base force concept was the answer to the first Russian Revolution, which took the Warsaw Pact out of play, what is the right answer to the second revolution, which has now taken the Soviet Union out of play?"[23] He wondered, "[I]f a force structure of a 25 percent cut was right when the Warsaw Pact disappeared, which sounds roughly right to me, what is the right answer if the Soviet Union now disappears?"

Aspin first attacked the Bush administration's attempt to craft a strategy and force structure without first identifying the enemies at whom they were aiming:

> General Powell told the *Washington Post* on May 31st, 1991, that, quote, "We are the major player on the world stage, with responsibilities and interests around the world," end quote, and we need to retain that superpower capability.[24] Former Defense Secretary Jim Schlesinger wrote recently in *Foreign Policy* that the basis for future U.S. forces should, quote, "not simply be the response to individual threats but rather that which is needed to maintain the overall aura of American power." End quote.

Aspin responded to proposals of Powell and others as follows:

> If the Soviet threat is gone, how do you design the forces? Three different notions: one is the minimum requirements for a superpower, another

is a capabilities-based force structure, and a third is the minimum requirements to maintain the organizational health. The trouble with all of
them, of course, is that it doesn't tell you how much is enough. And the
trouble is going to be, I think, with anything other than a threat-based
force structure, it's going to be awfully hard to get the taxpayers to pay
for it.

He added, "None of these . . . is very helpful in terms of deciding how much is
enough," and

I don't think the taxpayers are likely to warm to the notion of capabilities, base forces, or that this is what you need to have as a superpower,
or this is what you need to maintain the health of the organizations. It
isn't that maintaining the health of the organization, or becoming the superpower, or maintaining capabilities isn't important, it's just that it's a
difficult sell politically.

Just as the British had throughout the 1920s, Aspin prejudged the political environment and helped bring about the self-fulfilling prophecy. It is hard to
know, in advance, what "the people" will support if given policies are strenuously proposed and vigorously defended. It is impossible to say what can or
cannot be accomplished through the use of presidential and congressional leadership before that leadership is applied. But the argument that "the people won't
support it" is a comforting one for politicians who desperately do not want to
pursue a particular policy. Throughout the interwar period, such an argument
was used to prevent the maintenance of an expeditionary force for the continent—the people won't support plans for a continental war. It was used to keep
defense expenditures down—the people won't support higher taxation for armaments. In both cases successive governments did everything in their power to
persuade the people *not* to support such policies, which they themselves did not
favor. It was not surprising, therefore, that the people, indeed, did not support
them. Aspin operated in the same way. Desperate to move away from the apparent vagueness and "excessiveness" of the administration's proposed structure, he used the argument that "the people would not support it" to defend his
own pet approach to the problem. He concluded, "So I think that basically
you're back to the notion of the threats. I don't think you can put together a defense budget which is totally divorced from the threats."

Aspin then outlined his own proposal for determining the structure and size
of America's armed forces in the post–Cold War world:

Essentially the concept that we're playing with is trying to do this in
terms of Iraq equivalents or Panama equivalents. Without the Soviet

Union, the long pole in the tent is probably Saddam Hussein and Desert
Storm—Iraq of Saddam Hussein and Desert Storm.

So you start with a basic force concept that looks at what we needed
to deal with that threat. Then we look at other parts of the world in
terms of Iraq equivalence. What is North Korea? Is that a three-quarters
of an Iraq? Or is that an Iraq and a half? What is Syria? What is Libya?
What is Iraq post–Desert Storm? Is it one-quarter of an Iraq? Or is it half
of an Iraq? Or is it an eighth of an Iraq? . . .

And you figure how many forces we needed to fight Iraq before Desert
Storm, look at those kind of notions around the world, and then decide
the old question how many do you want to deal with simultaneously,
and try and get to a U.S. force structure by that kind of a means.

Aspin recognized that the Desert Storm force would have to be modified in a
number of ways to respond to crises in various theaters. He noted that its size
and composition, as well as the size and composition of the armed forces as a
whole, depended upon how many major conflicts one thought America should
be prepared to handle right away, how rapidly America's armed forces needed
to be in theater, and how long they would have to remain after the end of hostilities. At the same time, he assigned numerical values to likely contingencies
(post–Desert Storm Iraq received a rating of 0.3 "Iraq equivalents") around the
world.[25]

He also began to apply a name to his methodology: a "Bottom-Up Review."
He argued that the Bush administration's defense budgets had been top-down
efforts: "What we have seen and what people are talking about so far is kind of
force structure by subtraction" whereby the Cold War force structure is simply
reduced to meet budgetary guidelines. His "bottom-up" method, he argued, assumed no starting force structure, but simply looked at the likely missions the
armed forces would have to carry out, determined what forces would be needed
for those missions, and calculated the overall force structure on that basis. He
came to conclusions very different from those offered by the Bush administration.

In three House Armed Services Committee papers published in January,
February, and March 1992, Aspin delineated four alternative future force pos-
tures.[26] He described the alternatives in terms of the capabilities they provided
to meet likely scenarios, and he based the requirements for forces for each scenario on force packages used in recent crises he regarded as similar. Thus option A would allow the armed forces to conduct a Gulf War equivalent, a
"Kurdistan-style relief crisis," and to purchase additional sealift; option B
added an "air power defense of South Korea" (Aspin never believed that
ground forces would be necessary in that theater); option C added a "Panama-
style invasion," while option D added an additional "Kurdistan-style relief cri-

sis."[27] Option C, which was Aspin's preferred option, would cut $48 billion more than the Base Force proposal (which cut $43 billion) over the five-year program for defense spending, and 300,000 more troops. It would reduce the number of air force tactical fighter wings to ten (from fifteen in the Base Force), of active army divisions to nine (from twelve), and of marine divisions to two (from two and a third).[28] It was the classic "1-MRC" force structure.

The Base Force Counterattacks

The normal annual preparation and submission of the defense budget provided Cheney the opportunity to respond. In a budget briefing in January 1992, he said:

> [The] new regional defense strategy was announced by President Bush in Aspen, August 1990, the same day that Saddam Hussein invaded Kuwait. And that strategy was designed not simply to react to reductions in the Soviet threat, but also to shape the future security environment. We built our regional defense strategy and the base force that implements it not by merely cutting down from Cold War levels, but by judging what would be needed to further democracy and our national security interests in the post Cold War world.[29]

Directly challenging Aspin's criticisms that the national strategy and force structure could be determined only by preparing to respond to discrete threats, Cheney emphasized instead the uncertainties of the new era:

> Shaping our future security environment means more than simply accounting for changes in anticipated threats, as some have suggested. World events have repeatedly defied even near-term predictions. In early 1989 no one predicted Eastern Europe would escape Soviet domination by Thanksgiving. In early 1990 few predicted that America would be headed for war by Labor Day, or that more than half a million men and women would be in Saudi Arabia by New Year's 1991. In early '91 few predicted the Soviet Union would be gone by Christmas. In earlier times we have failed to predict the Soviet development of atomic weapons, Sputnik, the North Korean invasion of South Korea or the Japanese attack on Pearl Harbor. These are significant failures of prediction of major events in very short time frames. And as time lengthens, as we have to deal with longer time horizons our capacities to predict grow even less precise.
>
> The history of the Twentieth Century is replete with instances of major, unanticipated strategic shifts over five, ten or twenty year time

frames. Sophisticated, modern military forces take many years to build and develop. And a proper appreciation for uncertainty is therefore a critical part of any realistic defense strategy that builds forces that are going to allow us to deal with crises five, ten, or twenty years hence.

We cannot base our future security on a shaky record of trying to predict threats or a prudent recognition of uncertainty. Sound defense planning seeks to help shape the future, to actually alter the future. And that's what the President's regional defense strategy seeks to do.

Restating the last point more concretely, Cheney argued, "It's important for us to remember that future peace and stability in the world will continue to depend in large measure upon the willingness of the United States to deploy forces overseas in Europe, the Pacific and the Middle East, and to retain high quality forces here at home."

Cheney also addressed the problem of deterrence in a regional strategy:

The future may also come to depend upon others' perception of our will and our capability to reconstitute forces and to deter or defend against strategic attack should that prove necessary. Maintaining that posture, maintaining U.S. presence around the world and maintaining the capacity to respond in a crisis will be absolutely crucial in heading off future crises and dissuading future aggressors from challenging our vital interests. . . . We can help shape our future environment and hedge against both anticipated threats and uncertainty.

This strategy was entirely different from Aspin's. Whereas Aspin saw the United States in a purely reactive role, maintaining armed forces ready to repel aggressors after they had attacked, conducting the odd humanitarian mission here or there (but not in two places at once), Cheney saw the armed forces playing an active role in shaping the future development of the international environment. By remaining large enough and positioned well forward, he argued, America's armed forces could make America's involvement in the world and commitment to repel aggression clear, even as they made the task of actually repelling aggression easier for themselves. This was a critical and irreducible difference between the two conceptions.

Another critical difference was the time frame of focus of the plans. Aspin's concept did not look beyond the immediately foreseeable future. He did not address the question of what he would do should the international situation change, but he probably would have argued that we would change our force structure in a timely way to match. Cheney and the other members of the administration, however, clearly focused on the future and, within that focus, emphasized the impossibility of knowing with any certainty what would happen even in the nearest term, let alone in the long term. Whereas "Aspin assumes that current threats are representative of future threats [and] his arguments are necessarily couched in terms of current capabilities . . . the keys to the Cheney argument are the central role of uncertainty in planning (and implicitly the penalty for guessing wrong) and the need to shape, not just respond to, future environments."[30] Cheney's emphasis on uncertainty led to an emphasis on the need to "protect difficult-to-replace capabilities in an uncertain world. . . ."[31]

In fundamental ways, Aspin's program represented a return to the sort of thinking that had characterized British planning in the 1920s, while Cheney's was an effort to break away from that trap. Aspin largely divorced force structure and strategy, imagining that crises would pop up and American armed forces would deal with them. He did not consider the role the armed forces played in supporting U.S. foreign policy, nor did he consider the effects of military weakness on the formation and execution of that policy. In this he paralleled the British Chiefs of Staff of the 1920s. They gave little or no thought to the relationship between strategy and force structure except to call for changes in strategy to reflect their military weakness. Their focus was continually on present threats and problems and attempting to bring "strategy in line with our capabilities." In that way, they consistently failed to make a strong case for any strategy that might deter the appearance of new threats or for the forces needed to pursue such a strategy. Cheney, on the other hand, broke from that tradition. His focus was not on near-term threats, which were mostly within the capacity of projected American forces to handle, but on the longer-term problem of deterring larger threats and being able to defeat them if deterrence failed.

But the long-term focus and emphasis on uncertainties in the Bush administration's arguments still proved a political liability, as they appeared to many to cover vagueness and attempts to preserve larger armed forces than were really necessary. Thus Cheney was asked "why the force structure [he proposed] has remained essentially unchanged in the process of the changes we've seen just in the last six months." He responded:

> We think that plan's a good one, it moves us in the direction of dramatic change in the overall size of the U.S. military, and we don't think we ought to change that plan every six months or 12 months based upon developments either on Capitol Hill or overseas.
>
> We also think . . . that base force is built upon a structure of the national strategic assumptions that underlie it. . . . But if you believe, as we do, in the fundamental proposition that we want to retain our strategic deterrence and deploy strategic defenses; that we want to remain forward deployed overseas in Europe and the Pacific; . . . deploy a crisis response force here at home; and have the capacity to reconstitute forces—those are sort of the four basic elements of that new regional strategy—then we need a base force that . . . we've recommended to the Congress. We think we need 12 active Army divisions. . . .

We got to that point . . . based upon starting with scrapping the old strategic assumption of the all-out global war that would begin with a land attack by the Soviets into Western Europe, to focusing on regional contingencies and we think we need that size force in order to be able to implement that strategy.

In response to Aspin's most serious challenge, that the Base Force did not account for the complete collapse of the Soviet Union, which occurred almost eighteen months after the Aspen speech, Cheney said:

Now, nothing has changed with respect to that fundamental set of assumptions. What has happened, of course, is that in the Soviet Union it's disintegrated fairly rapidly, but we had assumed continued positive developments in our new strategy anyway. What has happened in the Soviet Union that most dramatically affects our plans is—that hadn't already been taken into account, is the pace at which we think they will modernize their forces in the future, as I mentioned, the extent to which their economic collapse will make it more difficult for them to field increasingly sophisticated types of weapons systems. And therefore, what we've gone after in our own budget in response to those changes is to change our own modernization plan in significant ways and change our whole acquisition strategy. That's a pretty fundamental change. It does not go to force structure. But you don't always respond to some change in the world with a change necessarily in our force structure.

This argument came closest to meeting the challenge directly, but Cheney still failed to make the most essential and telling point. Of Aspin's two "Russian revolutions," the first, the collapse of the Warsaw Pact, affected the force structure of only the conventional forces, while the second, the collapse of the Soviet Union itself, affected that of only the strategic forces. Only through the medium of the Warsaw Pact could Soviet conventional forces pose any real threat to the West, let alone to America. If the Base Force truly took account of the disappearance of the Soviet conventional threat, as the Bush administration claimed it did, then clearly no further reductions in that force were required in light of the disappearance of the Soviet Union, which did not affect the conventional balance in any meaningful way.

From a strategic standpoint, however, the disappearance of the Warsaw Pact had little effect on the Soviets' ability to attack the United States with nuclear weapons, thus justifying very few changes in America's strategic posture, while the disappearance of the Soviet Union was a critical change in that equation. The Bush administration, however, rarely made this distinction clear and so continually appeared to be defensive and evasive in answering Aspin's charges.

Even the Bush administration, moreover, accepted the argument that because the Soviet Union was collapsing or had collapsed, it was appropriate to retard the modernization of the armed forces, canceling many programs and dramatically slowing down the research, development, and procurement of new systems. Cheney pointed out that any new acquisition program

> was always based upon our assessment of what the Soviets were doing, how soon they'd field a new capability and then you would begin from that point forward to develop our own capabilities and a timeframe by which you expected you had to have them in the force. Clearly that basic fundamental first set of assumptions about what the threat is going to be is what's changed so dramatically and what allows us now to back off the process, not pursue it in as aggressive a fashion as we have in the past in terms of getting new equipment fielded with the force and being able to take more time to do it right. . . .

Although Cheney recognized the importance of technology for America's success, he believed that "if you're going to change our strategy and our force structure based upon the changes that have occurred in the world, then you go after modernization."

The same congressmen who pointed so emphatically to the importance of technology in our victory in the Gulf raised no questions when presented with a budget that dramatically slowed the modernization of the armed forces. As the debate over whether and how to cut the armed forces beyond the Base Force raged, therefore, the Bush administration's cuts in modernization went largely unchallenged.

The annual budget cycle soon provided the principal antagonists with the opportunity for direct conflict, when Cheney and Powell testified before the House Armed Services Committee, of which Les Aspin was the chairman.[32] In this testimony, Cheney and Powell stated their strategy and view of the future clearly, and once again, Aspin failed to understand it or simply ignored it, focusing, instead, on the problems or possibilities of the moment.

He restated his "two revolutions" thesis:

> I think that historians looking back on this period will say that in a very short time we have had two revolutions in the threat posed by the Soviet Union and the Warsaw Pact. What concerns me about the budget being presented today is that the base force concept which is at the heart of this budget being presented today was drawn up after the first revolution and I think does not fully incorporate the second. . . . The base force budget you have submitted looks to me very much like a one-revolution budget in a two-revolution world.

Cheney, too, restated his position, but this time he gave a clearer and more co-gent description of the strategic view underlying the Base Force:

> These reductions are developed not based upon the somewhat sobering prospects that we faced a year ago, the war in the Gulf and the Soviet re-formers under siege, but rather were based upon the promise that the collapse of the Berlin Wall represented some 15 months before that pres-entation was made and upon the new regional defense strategy that Pres-ident Bush first outlined at Aspen August 2nd, 1990, the same day that Saddam Hussein invaded Kuwait.
>
> That strategy was not designed simply to react to expected reductions in Soviet forces and the Soviet threat, but to do something else, and this is a key point: to shape the future security environment. Strategy is no good if all it is designed to do is to allow us to respond militarily to the next crisis. It serves an even more important purpose, and that's to allow us to shape the future, to determine the outcome of history, to have an im-pact on whether or not threats even arise and whether or not we ultimately have to use those forces that we have built and deployed over the years.

The focus on the future he recommended reflected the enormous improvement in America's security situation with the end of the Cold War:

> Today we have no global challenger except with respect to strategic nu-clear forces. No country is our match in conventional military power or the ability to apply it. There are no significant alliances hostile to our in-terests. To the contrary, the strongest and most capable countries in the world are our friends. No region of the world critical to our interest is under hostile, non-democratic domination. With the defeat of Saddam Hussein, near-term threats in that region are small relative to our capa-bilities and those of our allies. We have, in fact, won great depth for our strategic position.
>
> The threats to our security have become more distant, not only phys-ically, but in time as well. A challenger to our security would have to overcome our formidable alliances and the qualitative advantages that we displayed so successfully in Desert Storm. The events of the last four years have provided America with strategic depth in which to defend our national interest, the kind of depth that we've lacked for decades.

He ended this positive vision with a note of caution: "I want to remind the com-mittee that never—never—in this century have we ever gone through one of these periods of downsizing the force and done it right."

He warned:

We've gained so much strategic depth that the threats to our security, now relatively distant, are harder to define, but it's important for us to take advantage of the position that we have to preserve those capabilities that we need in order to keep those threats small. If we fail to maintain the necessary level of military power, we are likely to find that a hostile power will try to fill the vacuum and present us with a regional challenge once again. And this will, in turn, as it has previously, force us to higher levels of defense expenditure at a higher level of threat and a greater risk of war.

He offered the committee a stark choice:

We can make the investments required to maintain the strategic depth that we've won, which is much less than the investments required when we had none. Or we can fail to secure those advantages, and eventually, the threats will not be remote, they will not be vague or difficult to discern, and we will not have the alliances and capabilities required to deal with them. We will wish then that we had made the much smaller investment that we ask today to preserve the depth of our strategic position.

He concluded his presentation with an important admonition: "[T]he decisions we're making in the period immediately ahead have one and only one purpose. They constitute preparation for the next time we go to war. And there will be a next time; there always is." This was as explicit a statement of the lessons of Britain's experience between the two world wars as could be hoped for. It went beyond the complacent "we have got all we want, perhaps more" of English strategic thought to an understanding of the need to look far into the future and to be prepared to pay the price of maintaining America's advantages. It is tragic that so clear an exposition of the true lessons of the past at such a critical time should have fallen on truly deaf ears.

In his testimony, Powell explained why America should shoulder the burden of maintaining international stability:

One of the most striking features of this new world we face is that America is the sole remaining superpower. We are also the preeminent force for stability in the world. So we have to be very, very wise in the way we adjust our military posture to the changes that are taking place. Our friends know that we seek no territory, we do not aspire to a position of hegemony in any region, but we cannot ignore our responsibility as the leader of the free world to lead the entire world community along the path of peace and prosperity and democracy. . . .

In a very real sense, the primary threat to our security and the security of our friends is instability and being unprepared to handle a crisis or war that no one expected or predicted.

He attacked, once again, the notion that defense planning in the post–Cold War era should be based upon visible threats, arguing that it must, instead, be based on ensuring that America has the capabilities to intervene decisively in every critical region, whether or not a visible threat exists there. He noted that the National Military Strategy concluded with a quotation of Winston Churchill's: "The conventional wisdom is that war is too foolish, too fantastic to be thought of in the 20th century. Civilization has climbed above such perils. The interdependence of nations, the sense of public law, have rendered such nightmares impossible. . . . Are you quite sure? Pity to be wrong."

Powell's and Cheney's presentations clearly laid out the strategic principles underlying the Base Force concept, but Aspin remained fixated on the "two revolutions" theme. In the first question of the hearing, he asked, "[I]f you can make new changes . . . in the strategic system, based upon Boris Yeltsin and the new world, why can't we do some other things in terms of the conventional forces? It seems to me that what we really need is something that allows for the second revolution, particularly in the conventional forces."

Cheney responded directly: "I think there's an assumption underlying your question that I don't accept, and that is that the only justification for our force structure is the size of Soviet forces or conditions inside the Soviet Union." He argued that the Soviet Union had been abandoned as an important element in sizing the conventional forces in 1990 and that the Base Force did address the reduction of the Soviet conventional threat. The nuclear balance, he argued, was all that was affected by the "second revolution," and Bush's arms control initiatives were addressing that issue. He concluded, "I don't think . . . that the changes that have occurred in Russia since August lead me in the direction of concluding we need less force structure except in the strategic area, and we have, in fact, made all those adjustments. I don't see it taking down divisions or aircraft carriers because the hardliners failed in their coup attempt in Moscow in August."

Aspin, unyielding, replied that "in planning the base force concept . . . a Soviet threat was still a long pole in the tent. It was one of the regional threats, and I would say a major regional threat." With that "regional" threat gone, he asked, what were the implications for America's force structure? Instead of answering, Cheney changed the subject. He had already made clear that the Base Force was not meant to be able to fight a conventional war with the Soviet Union, since the Defense Department believed that the Soviets would not be able to fight a conventional war for many years. Cheney and Powell, moreover, consistently made it clear that America would need to reconstitute forces to face the Soviets in a conventional war, and that they believed they would have years in which to do so. In the manner of congressional hearings, however, the matter was not resolved.

In a final exchange, Representative Ike Skelton asked Powell if America's armed forces could conduct a successful Desert Storm operation at that moment. Powell said, "Today, yes, sir." Skelton asked if America could repel a massive North Korean conventional attack on South Korea at that moment. Powell replied, "In my judgment, yes, without question, if there was no other major contingency taking place. If there was a Desert Storm taking place at the same time, a little more difficult proposition for us, but probably yes." Powell then added, "[W]hen we go down to the base force, what we are losing is flexibility to handle two scenarios at the same time. We're tying to structure the base force to handle two at the same time, hoping that two at the same time will not occur."

Skelton pressed further, asking if, in 1997 with the Base Force as Powell described it, American forces could still conduct a Desert Storm. Powell replied, "Yes." Skelton asked the same question about a North Korean invasion in 1997. Powell replied, "Yes, with great difficulty and no longer any reserves available to us to handle anything else that came along." Skelton asked, finally, about a Korean contingency and a Desert Storm contingency simultaneous in 1997. Powell answered:

Yes, but at the breaking point.
Skelton: Would you be kind enough to explain the breaking point?
Powell: What I mean is if we were doing another Desert Storm and, at the same time, we were required to respond to Korea, and these were both emergencies that did not give us the opportunity to fully mobilize, for example, all of our Reserve components, to send 7⅔ divisions to Desert Shield/Desert Storm, to provide a large air component to Korea and ground forces to Korea and Marine forces to Korea would strip us of all active forces and would place an immediate demand on the total reserve component to get mobilized as quickly as possible. And, at that point, we would no longer have the capability to deal with anything else that might happen elsewhere in the world.
Skelton: Thank you, General.

And with that, the hearing ended.

Conclusion

The Bush administration won the debate, for the moment. The Base Force became the blueprint for the post–Cold War defense reductions and remained so, with minor changes, while Bush was in office. It was, however, a very limited victory. The Base Force resulted from impressive strategic thinking at an unusually high level. It reflected the Bush administration's understanding that

America should actively engage in shaping the international environment, and that substantial military forces were needed to do so. But the Base Force they designed for that purpose, from the first, did not provide military forces adequate for the period it considered. Although strategically sound and far superior to any competition, the Base Force plan did not provide the means with which to meet the ends at which it aimed.

The Base Force strategy called for armed forces capable of responding to at least two low-warning major regional contingencies at the same time. This was a sensible policy, although it has come under heavy attack virtually since it was propounded on the grounds that it is unlikely that two MRCs would occur at any one time, and it has historically been extremely unusual for America to fight two major conflicts at once. One commentator however, responded as follows:

> Although the United States has rarely been engaged in simultaneous separate combat operations in the past (short of global war), it has had to underwrite deterrence simultaneously in separate theaters—often against independent potential adversaries. Engagement in combat operations in any one theater should not degrade the quality of deterrence in another. A key element of deterrence is the relative ease with which a future U.S. president is seen as able to bring superior force to bear (without having to pay the domestic political price of mobilization to meet a threat that can be quickly withdrawn).[33]

A more recent study of the 2-MRC requirement came to a similar conclusion:

> The United States should obviously be prepared to fight and win one war quickly and decisively. However, if the United States had only that level of capability, its freedom in crisis might be constrained because of "self-deterrence." That is, because of a lack of reserves, the government might be dangerously overcautious about reacting to aggression. Further, if it did react to aggression at the MRC level, it would be virtually inviting aggression elsewhere. In a world with a variety of potential aggressors, that is not a minor issue.[34]

We have seen that the British were "self-deterred" in just that way during the Ethiopian crisis of 1935, shrinking from their preferred policy of stopping Mussolini, quite unnecessarily, because of their forces' inadequacy to respond to a Japanese attack should it come at the same time.

The same study considered the likelihood of such a scenario arising: "Does anyone doubt that if a Korean war broke out, Saddam Hussein would consider new adventures?" It concluded, "Even if the name of the game is deterrence, two—not one—is the right number."[35]

The argument over the need to meet two simultaneous MRCs or only one played a great part in the debate over the armed forces' size and posture for the rest of the decade, and remains so until today. An important element shaping that debate is that the Base Force is considered a 2-MRC force because the Bush administration said it ought to be and treated it as if it were. But it was not. The testimony of Powell, Jeremiah, and others made clear that the Base Force could not handle two simultaneous MRCs similar in scale to the Gulf War. Their statements that it should be able to do so, even when they knew it could not, have powerfully influenced the subsequent debate.

The Bush administration also spoke often of the need to respond rapidly and decisively to aggression, a capability demanded by its commitment to deterrence. But the Base Force was to be no more capable of rapid response than the Gulf War force had been—and everyone knew that force had moved far too slowly. Powell described a contingency force composed primarily of light forces; he frequently said that as many as three heavy divisions belonged to that force, but he never addressed the problem of how those heavy divisions could be moved anywhere rapidly. Nor did the Bush defense budgets contain resources adequate to purchase additional airlift and sealift assets. Even Aspin recommended increasing those categories of funding, about the only increases he ever advocated.

The Base Force plan also went wrong in its decision to retard or cancel a great many modernization programs, both in the research and development phase and in the procurement phase. Few opponents challenged the administration on that issue at the time, but it would become critical as the argument for a "revolution in military affairs" based on the Gulf War grew louder. In the discussions on increasing modernization funding in the years after the Bush administration almost all proposed increases would bring the modernization budget only up to where it had been before the Base Force cut it.

Another serious problem with the Base Force is that it claimed to preserve the capability to reconstitute larger forces to face a revived Soviet threat or a new threat on a similar scale, but the reality was quite different. No adequate reconstitution capability was built into the Base Force, either to reform disbanded units or to maintain the military industry that would be critical to such reconstitution. Even the administration's opponents in Congress took an interest in this issue, since it related directly to jobs in congressional districts at a time of economic crisis. Nevertheless, when the administration decided to cut the armed forces dramatically and to reduce and delay modernization substantially, the resources with which to maintain a healthy military industry simply were not there. For all of the strategic soundness of the administration's vision, it still could do little more than wave the idea of a revived major threat off into the irrelevant future.

The largest failing of the Base Force, finally, was that it failed to convince its opponents of any of its fundamental assumptions. For all of the efforts of

Cheney, Powell, Wolfowitz, Libby, and others, it remained the partisan defense program of the Bush administration, foisted on Congress through a budget deal. Its opponents were neither mollified nor enlisted—Aspin, having listened patiently while Cheney explained that his assumptions were flawed and his understanding of the Base Force strategy was wrong, continued to deliver addresses misrepresenting the Base Force, accusing the Bush administration of lacking a strategy, and demanding a "two revolution" defense budget.

The very complexity and subtlety of the strategic rationale for the Base Force remained a political weakness. Nunn's and Aspin's focus on immediately visible threats was dangerously wrong. Nunn's argument that America could "turn inside" a reviving opponent was specious—America has never done so, nor is it in the nature of liberal democracies to begin to rearm at the first sign of danger. On the contrary, even when a potential enemy begins arming heavily, the first inclination of liberal democracies is frequently to refuse to rearm dramatically, hoping thereby to quell tensions and avoid an "arms race" that is regarded as the likely precursor to a war no democracy wishes to fight. That, at any rate, was the experience of Britain confronted with a rearming Germany in the 1930s, and neither Nunn nor Aspin ever offered any reason to suggest that America would do better.

Their determination to focus on visible threats, in fact, fell precisely into the most dangerous trap that faces a nation such as the United States in its moment of triumph and security. In truth, there were no credible threats in 1991 or 1992 that would have justified forces much larger than Aspin was proposing. Judging only by the yardstick of reality at the time, it could be argued that Aspin's force structure, based as it was on the need to defeat an Iraq that had already been defeated, was itself excessive. The threat-based focus of the congressional proposals, moreover, obscured the critical role the United States could play in shaping the international environment and deterring wars, rather than fighting them, as Cheney repeatedly argued. But the threat-based program had one decisive advantage—it was easy to understand and easy to explain, and it lent itself to colorful charts and diagrams. It just happened to be wrong.

The failure of the Bush administration to convince its opponents or move the debate in its desired direction, no doubt, seemed small in light of Bush's enormous popularity in 1990 and his success in pushing the Base Force through a hostile Congress. In 1992, however, this deficiency emerged as the most important of all, for Bush lost the election and the unconvinced opponents of the already inadequate Base Force took power, determined to focus on tangible threats and, thereby, to distribute yet another peace dividend.

14

Increased Commitments, Reduced Forces

T he Bush administration made a serious effort to establish a strategy appropriate to the postwar world, although the resources it allocated to defense were inadequate to support it. Clinton did not attack that strategy in the campaign, nor did he repudiate it as President. On the contrary, his public pronouncements and strategy documents largely accepted and even expanded upon the activism and engagement the Bush administration advocated. Whereas Bush had fought to maintain defense resources at the minimum level necessary to support his strategy, however, Clinton showed little interest in the growing mismatch between his proclaimed strategy, U.S. military involvement in the world, and the resources available to support that strategy and involvement. The consistent failure to address that mismatch has had disastrous consequences both for the military and for American foreign policy.

"It's the Economy, Stupid"

Since the 1950s the Soviet Union's possession of the military capability to destroy significant portions of the United States in minutes had ensured that defense policy and national strategy were important components of every presidential election. The two parties changed sides on the issue over time—Kennedy ran on the "missile gap" platform; Reagan profited from Carter's foreign policy failures—but most campaigns saw efforts by each candidate to spell out a vision of defense and foreign policy distinct from his opponent's. The

1992 campaign saw the exact opposite—Bush and Clinton described strategies and defense budgets that seemed little different one from the other. Clinton boasted, in fact, that defense cuts he proposed constituted only 5 percent of the Bush defense budget.

This apparent sameness on defense reflected the fact that both candidates regarded defense and foreign policy as largely irrelevant to an electorate that was flushed with victories in the Persian Gulf and the Cold War, but deeply concerned about an economic downturn. In debates and speeches the candidates rarely spoke about defense and then only in platitudes. A Clinton campaign button summed it up: "It's the economy, stupid."

The sameness of the Bush and Clinton defense programs during the campaign was only apparent, however. Bush regarded defense and foreign policy as his strong suit and had fought with a Democrat-controlled Congress to defend defense, even sacrificing other initiatives to do so. He believed in the strategy developed by Colin Powell, Dick Cheney, and Paul Wolfowitz and regarded it as a priority to maintain the resources he believed necessary to support that strategy. His advocacy of defense was balanced by a congressional desire to cut more and faster, which led to damaging compromises in the size and funding of the armed forces. The election of Bill Clinton destroyed the balance completely.

During the campaign, Clinton enthusiastically adopted the phraseology of Les Aspin's alternative defense plans, specifically Aspin's "Option C," which proposed significant defense cuts beyond the Base Force. He promised to cut defense spending by $60 billion over the five-year Future Years Defense Plan (FYDP) beyond the cuts already contained in the Bush budget. He made it plain that domestic policy would be the dominant concern of his administration and foreign and defense policies would be entirely subordinate to it. Promising to "focus like a laser beam" on the economy, he made it clear that he expected the defense budget to pay the bill for domestic initiatives.

Clinton did not advocate a return to isolationism, however. Wary of being perceived as another Democratic presidential candidate who was "soft on defense," he adopted the phraseology of the regional defense plan, spoke of engagement in the world, and frequently advocated more aggressive foreign and military policies than Bush pursued. Clinton pressed for the use of force in Somalia and Bosnia and criticized the Bush administration for hanging back. He swore that he would maintain armed forces that were trained, ready, well armed, and not "hollow." Even during the campaign it was evident that the disconnection between strategy and force structure, already becoming visible in the Bush administration, would expand dramatically under the Clinton administration. Clinton's foreign policy was certain to write checks that his armed forces would not be able to cash.

Clinton's election gave Aspin the chance to implement the changes he had proposed. In his Senate confirmation hearings, however, Aspin made it very clear that he did not regard himself as a free agent but felt bound by the campaign promises Clinton had made. He promised, therefore, that as Secretary of Defense he would cut another $60 billion from the defense budget and reduce the size of the armed forces' personnel from 1.6 million to 1.4 million, both Clinton campaign pledges.

Aspin's testimony before the House Armed Services Committee emphasized the degree to which campaign promises aimed at solving domestic problems determined the shape of the defense budget even before the new administration had been able to review the situation and formulate a policy. A troubled Representative Floyd Spence said that "we haven't completed the new assessment, bottoms-up kind of review. But we've already decided on the end figure, you see? Is that clear. I just want you to understand, you see." Aspin responded, "We're dealing with the world as we have to deal with it. We came into office. We needed to put together a defense budget, a '94 defense budget. We hadn't done the bottom-up review." He assured Spence that if the Bottom-Up Review (BUR) showed that less money was needed, then the defense budget would be adjusted downward, and if it showed that more money was needed, "we go back to Bill Clinton. As part of this bottom-up review, we're going to engage, not just the Pentagon here, but the whole administration."[1] The notion of going back for more if the BUR indicated that more was necessary would prove to be overly optimistic. In the meantime, the Department of Defense budget for 1994 was some $16 billion or 6 percent lower than that for 1993.[2]

The Bottom–Up Review

Even before conducting the thorough review of America's post–Cold War strategy and defense posture that he claimed the Bush administration had failed to perform, therefore, Aspin and the new President had established a firm budget topline determined not by military necessity but by domestic politics. The Bottom-Up Review, therefore, had the task not of determining the size, structure, and organization of the armed forces necessary to support a given strategy, but of matching resources of a predetermined size against a desired strategy. There was no particular reason for this process to result in armed forces that were adequate to support the strategy, and, like the process of making British defense policy in the early 1920s, it did not do so.

The BUR abandoned the Base Force's emphasis on shaping the international environment, preserving the "strategic depth" America had won in the Cold War and the Gulf War and maintaining stability in critical regions. Like Aspin's work as chairman of the House Armed Services Committee, the BUR focused entirely upon currently visible threats, evaluating the resources necessary to meet them solely in terms of recent military operations.

To the extent that the BUR had an underlying strategic concept, it was

"Base Force lite." Like the Base Force, the BUR argued that the most important danger facing the United States in the post–Cold War world was regional challenges, and that the most important task the armed forces had to be prepared to execute was that of fighting two nearly simultaneous major regional contingencies (MRCs).[3] The BUR diverged from the Base Force strategy, however, in its focus on responding to regional threats rather than heading them off.

Solemnly warning that America must remain engaged in the world lest a "precipitous U.S. withdrawal from security commitments" trigger "global instability and imbalance," the BUR nevertheless failed to outline a military component for that engagement:

> This strategy of engagement will be defined by two characteristics: prevention and partnership. It advocates preventing threats to our interests by promoting democracy, economic growth and free markets, human dignity, and the peaceful resolution of conflict, giving first priority to regions critical to our interests. Our new strategy will also pursue an international partnership for freedom, prosperity, and peace. To succeed, this partnership will require the contributions of our allies and will depend on our ability to establish fair and equitable political, economic, and military relationships with them.[4]

It concluded:

> Our primary task, then, as a nation is to strengthen our society and economy for the demanding competitive environment of the 21st century, while at the same time avoiding the risks of precipitous reductions in defense capabilities and the overseas commitments they support.[5]

The unstated assumptions underlying this "strategic" vision were that the world was moving toward broad acceptance of American values, that this movement could best be achieved by nonmilitary means, and that the greatest challenge America faced in the future was economic and social, not military.

The BUR continually emphasized the "opportunities" that went along with the dangers of the new era. Security partnerships offered the opportunity to get more security for less money by relying on allies. The collapse of America's enemies greatly expanded the number of nations that could become our allies in regional conflicts:

> During the Cold War, repressive regimes that were direct adversaries of the United States dominated vast regions of the globe. Today, the countries that pose direct dangers to us are far fewer, and the countries that may join us in thwarting the remaining regional dangers are far more numerous.[6]

By implication, the BUR argued that the Base Force had seen only the dangers of the new situation and did not reap the advantages, in the form of a further peace dividend, that the end of the Cold War offered. In doing so, it ignored the reverse side of its own arguments—that the superpower confrontation had restrained many regional conflicts that were now free to explode.

By focusing on threats, moreover, instead of the more nebulous but more sophisticated arguments of the Base Force strategy, the BUR provided many arguments for failing to use military power to influence the developing international situation, but few arguments in favor of the use of power in that way. This failing was particularly evident in its treatment of smaller-scale conflicts (SSCs):

> Through overseas presence and power projection, our armed forces can help deter or contain violence in volatile regions where our interests are threatened. In some circumstances, U.S. forces can serve a peacekeeping role, monitoring and facilitating the implementation of cease-fire and peace agreements with the consent of the belligerent parties as part of a UN or other coalition presence. In more hostile situations, the United States might be called upon, along with other nations, to provide forces to compel compliance with international resolutions or to restore order in peace enforcement operations. In some cases, such as Operation Just Cause in Panama, we may intervene unilaterally to protect our interests. Finally, our armed forces will continue to play an important role in the national effort to halt the importation of illegal drugs to the United States.[7]

It is the qualifiers that are illuminating in this description of the possible uses of U.S. military power to preserve global stability. Overseas presence and power projection can help contain violence *where American interests are threatened. In some circumstances* American forces can perform peacekeeping or peacemaking missions. At other times the United States might be called upon to engage in more serious efforts to preserve international stability, which it might do along with other nations. Larger-scale operations, like Just Cause, are justified *if they protect America's interests.*

Nowhere did the BUR link major military missions with the preservation of international order or stability in critical regions. On the contrary, it offered instead a list of prescriptive conditions that must be met before U.S. forces should be introduced:

- Does participation advance U.S. national interests?
- Are the objectives clear and attainable?
- How will the intervention affect our other defense obligations?

- Can the United States contribute capabilities and assets necessary for the success of the mission?

Each question is, in itself, valid. Put together and decoded, however, these conditions are a recipe for avoiding engagement. Since the definition of "U.S. national interests" is necessarily vague, it offers no assistance in arguing for or against any particular operation. The requirement that objectives be clear and attainable, however, will almost always militate against involvement in peacemaking and peacekeeping operations. Such operations by their nature are murky, end states are difficult or impossible to define, and forces may be required for a long time—longer than the term of office of any given President or Secretary of Defense, which is to say forever. If the clarity and attainability of the mission was the yardstick by which interventions were to be judged, few situations could measure up.

The point is not that the Clinton administration sought to avoid becoming involved in peacekeeping or other stability operations. On the contrary, such operations proliferated in the Clinton years. The BUR, however, offered no strategic rationale for American military involvement in such operations and, giving little thought to the strategy, gave less thought to the implications for resources of such operations:

> Fortunately, the military capabilities needed for these operations are largely those maintained for other purposes—major regional conflicts and overseas presence. Thus, although specialized training and equipment may often be needed, the forces required will, for the most part, be selected elements of those general purpose forces maintained for other, larger military operations.

The BUR applied the same principle to SSCs that the Base Force had, assuming that forces large enough to conduct MRCs could conduct smaller missions as well. That was true as far as it went, but it did nothing to evaluate what size armed forces would be required to conduct the multiple SSCs likely to be occurring at any given time while at the same time remaining ready to accomplish the more challenging and critical mission of deterring or responding to MRCs. That lacuna was unfortunate in a strategic concept developed in 1990; it was far less acceptable in a concept developed as U.S. forces were engaged in Somalia, as the situations in Haiti and Bosnia deteriorated, and as tensions with Iraq and North Korea increased. Looking only for threats (which SSCs clearly were not), the BUR ignored the ways in which day-to-day military reality would interfere with the armed forces' ability to carry out the fundamental strategy it advocated.

Reviewing Major Regional Conflicts
from the Bottom Up

Aspin had always disliked the apparent vagueness of the Base Force, its failure to identify an enemy, to describe the scenarios against which it determined how large the armed forces should be, to define exactly what an MRC was, and so forth. The BUR wasted no time in clarifying these matters. The composition of an enemy force that would make a conflict an MRC was defined precisely:

400,000–750,000 total personnel under arms
2,000–4,000 tanks
3,000–5,000 armored fighting vehicles
2,000–3,000 artillery pieces
500–1,000 combat aircraft
100–200 naval vessels, primarily patrol craft armed with surface-to-surface missiles, and up to 50 submarines
100–1,000 Scud-class ballistic missiles, some possibly with nuclear, chemical, or biological warheads.[8]

These criteria described a force considerably smaller than the one Suddam Hussein fielded in 1990, which included a million men under arms, 5,000 tanks, 5,000 armored fighting vehicles (AFVs), 3,000 artillery pieces, and numerous mobile Scud launchers.[9] It came much closer to describing the Iraq of 1992, which had an estimated 400,000 men under arms, 2,300 tanks, 3,000+ armored fighting vehicles, and so forth.[10] It also described North Korea's armed forces reasonably well.[11]

That the description of an MRC opponent matched postwar Iraq and North Korea was no accident, for the BUR remedied another supposed defect of the Base Force by explicitly identifying the threats that determined the size of America's armed forces as Iraq and North Korea:

For planning and assessment purposes, we have selected two illustrative scenarios that are both plausible and posit demands characteristic of those that could be posed by conflicts with other potential adversaries. . . . While a number of scenarios were examined, the two that we focused on most closely in the Bottom-Up Review envisioned aggression by a remilitarized Iraq against Kuwait and Saudi Arabia, and by North Korea against the Republic of Korea.[12]

There was to be no uncertainty here. Although warnings that these two cases were only illustrative abounded, the BUR made clear that the threat posed by nearly simultaneous conflicts in Iraq and Korea was the basis for the force structure it proposed. Threat-based planning had superseded planning based on the need to shape the international environment.

It is interesting to note, in addition, that the two threats Aspin selected were only the most visible and obvious. At that time, five other countries (not considering American allies) had capabilities similar to, or in excess of, the MRC-enemy posited by the BUR: Syria, Egypt, India, Pakistan, and Vietnam.[13] Omitting India and Pakistan, which may or may not form a self-balancing regional tension, Egypt was an ally, although not entirely stable, while Vietnam remained hostile and Syria an implacable foe. Syria and Vietnam, what is more, were not suffering from the effects of a catastrophic military loss, like Iraq, or of an impending economic collapse, like North Korea.

They were credible as military threats, but they had the fatal disadvantage of not then being on the national radar screen. For all their latent or open hostility, neither was actively opposing U.S. policy or thwarting U.S. desires at that time. The potential MRC opponents Aspin chose, therefore, were not the most challenging enemies at that time, nor the most dangerous in the long term, but the ones that had already been nationally identified as threats. This choice would have important consequences for the future of the debate over the size of the armed forces.

The BUR also ignored the forces of the state with the largest armed forces in the world, China, as well as a state, even in decay, with conventional armed forces considerably in excess of the BUR-defined MRC foe: Russia. To be sure, war with China would not be a "regional contingency," while Russia's armed forces were assumed to be so decrepit that they would be unable to pose a serious threat to Western Europe for ten years.[14] Yet the decision to exclude these states from the BUR calculus is significant.

If North Korea was a threat in 1993, so was China. Both states adhered to the communist ideology that was antithetical to American interests during the Cold War. Both blithely ignored international norms regarding the treatment of their citizens, periodically behaving so brutally as to force America into an openly hostile position. Both maintained enormous armed forces far beyond what the defense of their territory and interests required. Both had as open objectives the conquest or absorption of another state with which the United States was allied. Why was war with North Korea included as a planning factor in the BUR while war with China was not? The likeliest motive cannot be ignored: war with China was unthinkable because no American armed forces posture that was remotely within the realm of the politically conceivable could support such a conflict. Whatever the motivation, the result is clear. The single most powerful and dangerous potential foe was excluded from the evaluation of America's defense needs. Whatever foreign policy might require, whatever American interests might be threatened, the BUR took no steps to ensure that America's armed forces could oppose those of China in 1993, 1997, or at any time in the future.

The exclusion of Russia's conventional forces was even harder to justify (something the BUR did not attempt to do). Although it might be eight to ten years before Russia could pose a conventional threat to American interests on anything like the scale it had during the most recent conflict, exactly the same could be said of Iraq. Russia, after all, was suffering only from political confusion and economic dislocation, both of which had seriously degraded her armed forces. Iraq, however, suffered from both of those factors but, in addition, it was subject to a rigorous regime of economic and military sanctions, substantial portions of its infrastructure, military and civilian, had been physically destroyed, and it was cut off from the sources that had armed it in the past. Although the Russian conventional threat to drive through Germany and France was a long way off, Russia's threat to its neighbors was considerably nearer than any immediate threat Iraq might pose.

It may be that Aspin equated any conflict with Russia with nuclear war and felt that the nuclear balance would continue to paralyze any Russian efforts to reclaim its "lost" territories or otherwise endanger its neighbors. The evidence, however, suggests that this was not the reason. The "ten-year rule" was alive and well. The BUR did not address the potential threat from Russia because Aspin waved it off into the comfortably distant future:

> [A]bout the [Russian] conventional forces . . . we cannot imagine that they would be in a position to threaten Western Europe the way we did back in the old days under the Cold War, et cetera, before 1989. But a military that is still improbably the most effective organization or force in the Soviet Union under a different leadership could be a threat to its neighbors—Ukraine, the Baltics, things like that. . . . [I]f you're sizing and shaping your forces based upon regional threats, that suddenly probably becomes the biggest regional threat out there. And let's suppose we were designing our forces based upon regional threats, and we went on the assumption that the biggest threat out there could probably be handled with a Desert Storm kind of force, and I think that's true, without the Soviet Union. If . . . Russia suddenly reconstitutes itself as a threat to its neighbors, that would be, all of a sudden, a regional threat out of there of some consideration, and that would be part of our planning forces for the future. We'd have to figure that as a possible contingency and that would affect our defense budgets.[15]

Aspin here confused several important concepts. The Russian armed forces in 1993 were in disarray, but so were those of Ukraine, the Baltic States, Belarus, the states of the Caucasus, and most of the former Warsaw Pact states. Some time would have to pass before the Russian military was capable of offensive operations on a large scale, and a major political turnabout would be required, but it would not necessarily be many years before such a situation could arise as Aspin seemed to imply.

That the "warning time" for a Russian invasion of Western Europe had increased to a decade or more was not a new concept in 1993—it had served as the basis for the approach to the Base Force in 1990. A contemporary student of the Base Force noted:

> U.S. planners now assume that the old theater-strategic operation, or a surge operational-strategic-level attack across the old inter-German border with the Pyrenees as goal, could not be mounted without the U.S. intelligence community obtaining and understanding indicators eight to ten years in advance.
>
> For program planning, we also assume that during this eight-to-ten-year period, the United States can reconstitute forces for defense of Europe while the Russians are doing the same for their offensive capability. During that time, we assume that we can rebuild forces and materials instead of having maintained them on active duty, in the Ready Reserves, or prepositioned in Europe. U.S. forces reconstituted for a major war in Europe need be adequate only to deter or defend against a Russian attack—not launch a theater-strategic offensive operation.
>
> In short, the need for the old, massive, short-term (14-day) mobilization has diminished. The threat planning assumption that once drove NATO toward a two-week mobilization requirement has been replaced with a threat assumption, for programming purposes, that now gives the alliance eight to ten years to respond.[16]

But that eight-to-ten-year period, which is as comfortably far into the future as Aspin implies, is the period before the Russians might be in a position to plan, as the Soviet Union did, to conquer all of Western Europe in thirty days. The threat of serious Russian operations aimed at more moderate goals that, nevertheless, would pose major dangers to U.S. national security could arise in a much shorter time:

> An eight-to-ten-year warning does not mean that the Russians cannot launch . . . an attack at the tactical, or perhaps, even the operational level in Europe in less time. There is probably some period of time associated with still realistic, but lesser, threats from Russia that is less than two years and more than two weeks. A major regional contingency involving the USSR in Europe should be, and is, in our program-planning contingencies.

Aspin had vigorously attacked the Base Force for using an MRC against the Soviet Union as "the long pole in the tent" for determining the size of the armed forces—a charge Colin Powell had hotly denied. Aspin had even gone so far as to assert in 1992 that "the residual Soviet conventional forces will be incapable of external aggression for years to come."[17] He came into office believing that he need not even plan for an MRC against Russia, and the BUR reflected that assumption. According to the BUR, America's armed forces were not to consider possible conflict, even regional conflict, with Russia or with China, and it was assumed that America would have ample warning time in which to prepare ("reconstitute") her forces for any such struggles.

This situation was in many ways parallel with the complacency with which interwar British governments contemplated the potential threats from Germany and Japan. Having deluded themselves into believing that Germany was disarmed when it had, in fact, made extensive preparations for a rapid rearmament, successive British governments forbade their military to consider the problem of sending an expeditionary force to the continent, just as Aspin excluded even the possibility of an MRC against Russia on no firmer basis. Worse still on both cases was the ignoring of another potential threat that could pose a significant danger in a much shorter time frame: Japan in the 1920s or China today. Japan had recently been Britain's ally, but the abandonment of the Anglo-Japanese alliance had alienated England's old partner. The calm that reigned in Tokyo and seemed to bode well for democratic, peaceful progress would prove ephemeral, and when it did, it would emerge that the military strength to underwrite a large-scale Japanese offensive in East Asia was already in existence.

China, recently America's uncomfortable partner in the struggle against Soviet hegemony, has been antagonized by a wide variety of American positions since the end of the Cold War, of which Bush's denunciation of the Tiananmen massacre, weak though it was, was the foremost. Since then a state of more or less continual tension has reigned in Sino-American relations, and the obvious potential *casus belli,* China's desire to regain control of Taiwan, remains. At the same time, Chinese military power is large and growing ever more dangerous, whatever nuclear secrets China may or may not have stolen. There was no reason in 1993 whatsoever to exclude a war with China from contingencies for which America's armed forces must be prepared except that, like a British war with Japan in the 1920s, it was too horrible to contemplate. Since the publication of the BUR, however, the prospect of war with either Russia or China has been almost completely excluded from the discussions about the proper size of America's conventional armed forces. The ten-year rule and willful blindness once again have won out over more rational and responsible strategic thinking.

Having simplified the problem by excluding the two most dangerous potential cases, the BUR described the course of the generic MRC and outlined the American forces required to win one. The BUR assumed that American forces would need to respond to an MRC that arose from an unexpected attack by a regional aggressor against an American ally. American forces, therefore, could not be in the theater of operations at the outset of hostilities. The conflict that ensued could be broken into four distinct phases. During the "halt phase," American and allied forces would seek to stop the advance of enemy armored forces.[18] During the buildup phase, reinforcements would hasten to the theater, stiffen the defense, and prepare for the counteroffensive phase to follow. In that phase American and allied forces would "decisively defeat the enemy." When that had been accomplished, the last phase would consist of ensuring postwar stability.[19] This phasing was simply the description of what had happened during the Korean War and the Gulf War. Like the rest of the BUR, it looked at past conflicts to provide the context within which a force could be designed to meet clearly visible current threats.

The BUR then described the forces that would be required in each phase. Phase one, the "halt phase," would be conducted, on the American side, almost entirely by airpower. Such ground troops as participated would belong to America's ally, because "[P]rimary responsibility for the initial defense of their territory rests, of course, with our allies." What, exactly, such a stricture might mean in the case of such vastly outnumbered states as Kuwait and Saudi Arabia was unclear. Because of the dramatic reductions in America's overseas presence since the end of the Cold War, moreover, there were not likely to be significant American forces of any service in the theater of operations when hostilities broke out. The reliance on airpower reflected a strategic reality that had already been created—with the pious note that sovereign states have the "primary responsibility" to defend their own territory, the BUR simply sought to lend legitimacy to a predetermined policy.

Airpower had not halted the North Korean invasion in 1950, nor could airpower alone have halted an Iraqi attack into Saudi Arabia in August 1990. What made us think it would do so in the future? Magic!

> As coalition operations in the Gulf War demonstrated, advanced precision-guided munitions can dramatically increase the effectiveness of a fighting force. Precision-guided munitions already in the U.S. inventory (for example, laser-guided bombs) as well as new types of munitions still under development are needed to ensure that U.S. forces can operate successfully in future MRCs and other types of conflicts. New "smart" and "brilliant" munitions under development hold promise of dramatically improving the ability of U.S. air, ground, and maritime forces to destroy enemy armored vehicles and halt invading ground forces, as well as destroy fixed targets at longer ranges, thus reducing exposure to enemy air defenses.[20]

The notion of victory through airpower, first trumpeted by Trenchard, was alive and well. At the end of World War I, the RAF argued and the Cabinet largely accepted that "mechanization," by which was meant the development of aircraft and tanks, could be used to offset Britain's inferiority in ground forces. This argument was used to maintain the institutional identity of the RAF, to defend RAF budgets, and to seize for the RAF missions that would otherwise have gone to the army or the navy. The suppression of the rebellion in Iraq and the subsequent maintenance of peace in that country was, like the Gulf War, used to show that airpower could replace ground forces more economically both in lives and in money. As in the Gulf War, there were limitations to the success of airpower, and sharp limitations to the degree to which airpower *alone* had "succeeded." But credulous Cabinets and congressmen were more pleased with the prospect of replacing "manpower," and, therefore, reducing expenditures, by substituting new machines than they were interested in exploring reality. In both cases, airpower became a panacea that cured the host of ills caused by military weakness—right up to the time the nation faced a serious test of strength.[21]

The BUR's emphasis on a "halt phase" conducted primarily by long-range, stand-off weapons systems marked a fundamental change in America's strategic planning. The Base Force had emphasized the importance of maintaining America's lead in high-technology systems, and that emphasis increased between May 1990 and the end of Bush's term in office. But the Base Force never proposed to rely on technology alone to solve strategic problems. Above all, it did not propose to rely on systems that had not yet been designed or fielded to do so, but that is precisely what the BUR did. In an address to the graduating class of the National Defense University, one of several addresses announcing and pushing the BUR, Aspin elaborated on the BUR's reliance on yet-to-be developed technologies.[22] He argued that stopping the enemy assault quickly was probably the most important and most daunting task facing the American forces responding to an MRC. "The requirement to halt regional invasions early," he said, "looked very much like an insoluble problem until very recently," but he added that "two high-tech responses operating synergistically have combined to give us a much better chance." The two were "smart anti-tank munitions" and "electronic battlefield surveillance."

> For the first time it appears possible that air and missile forces will be able to kill large numbers of armored vehicles quickly from the air, land and sea—and that's the key. For the first time, highly deployable early arriving forces will be able to kill armor quickly and in large numbers. This would be a real revolution, and it looks like we can do it while minimizing U.S. losses.

The keys to that capability Aspin identified as "sensor-fused weapons that seek their own targets" and "smart mines." Both types of weapon would be dispersed by the B-2 bomber, which "can deploy from the United States and attack armored columns on the first day of the war." In the theater of operations, "F-15E and F/A-18 aircraft could kill as many as five to ten armored vehicles per sortie rather than engaging one vehicle at a time." He concluded, "These weapons and platforms present new possibilities never before available. If we could just realize their potential, we will have a solution to the problem of quickly blunting an invasion."

He conceded that this "revolution" relied upon developments in battlefield surveillance that had not yet been quite realized. In order to take advantage of the new weapons, "[W]e must be able to detect the main concentrations of the enemy force, process and analyze the information, and then pass it to the shooters before it becomes obsolete." He noted, however, that despite some successes in this area, "there's much to be done." For instance,

> most of these systems for dissemination of intelligence imagery can't talk to each other. Many of our strategic reconnaissance assets were prepared primarily to monitor the former Soviet Union and were often overtaxed in support of tactical missions. And most important of all, we have much to learn about orchestrating the operation of hundreds of sophisticated systems into one coherent operation.

One of the virtues of these systems, Aspin noted, was that "they do not require radical changes in force structure." On the other hand, "we have not yet acquired some of these systems and of course they have not yet been tested in combat."

This argument was also similar to one of the fundamental flaws of the airpower argument in the 1920s—much of the technology Trenchard's plans relied upon was not in existence when his strategies were adopted. Many of the capabilities essential to carry out the RAF's schemes did not exist until during or after the next war! Long-range accurate bombing, for instance, proved to be an extremely difficult technological nut to crack—in a certain sense, it was only the development of the "smart weapons" of which Aspin was so fond that cracked it. Worse still, British bombers that could hit Berlin from bases in England did not exist throughout the interwar period, despite the fact that Trenchard's strategy relied upon having such a capability. What is perhaps more interesting is that a number of technological developments unforeseen by the RAF in the 1920s would profoundly change the nature of air warfare—radar, for instance. Basing current strategy and force structure on yet-to-be fielded or perfected systems is an extremely dangerous course of action, as the British experience shows, but it remains extremely attractive because of the opportunities it offers for *current* rather than future savings, even if they are not warranted.

The BUR was not the first sign of Aspin's love affair with airpower. Before the BUR had been announced, Aspin had already advocated relying upon airpower to handle any Korean contingency when he was the chairman of the House Armed Services Committee. That assumption had been critical to Aspin's "Option C," the force structure he proposed as congressman that Clinton adopted when running for office, most similar to the force structure ultimately adopted by the BUR. The commitment to using airpower to "halt" the enemy in the second MRC while ground forces dealt with the first, it appears, remained firm in the process of conducting the BUR.

Aspin tried to state that "one-MRC" strategy boldly, in the form of a "win-hold-win" strategy he floated briefly as a "trial balloon" in June 1993,[23] but his frankness was politically maladroit. He tried to argue that airpower would blunt one enemy offensive while ground forces finished off another, and then switched theaters to "clean up" whatever the air force had not killed. Senior military officers, however, immediately dubbed the plan "win-lose-lose" and the "win-hold-oops strategy." The armed forces supporting the "win-hold-win" strategy were reported to consist of ten active army divisions, ten aircraft carriers, and twenty air force tactical wings.[24] Aspin explicitly linked the "win-hold-win" strategy with the advances he saw in technology:

> In what aides described as a trial balloon, Aspin suggested yesterday that a two-war strategy is not needed because breakthroughs in weapons and sensor technology will permit the United States to hold off a second adversary with only a small commitment of forces. After the main weight of American military power defeats the first adversary, it would be shifted to attack the second.

The story continued:

> But officers from all services note that Aspin is acknowledging the risk of simultaneous conflicts while proposing answers that do not yet exist in the U.S. inventory. . . . Even under the Bush administration's plan, the U.S. military could not have fought two major wars quite simultaneously, according to documents obtained and reported by the *Washington Post* last year. If faced, for instance, with imminent aggression by North Korea while already fighting in the Persian Gulf, U.S. commanders under the Bush administration's scenario would divert "a small portion" of their cargo-carrying ships and planes in an "attempt to delay outbreak of a conflict in Korea for as long as possible." They would then seek to win decisively in the gulf before sending most of their forces to Korea.
>
> During the buildup to the 1991 Persian Gulf War, one officer said, the Joint Staff staged a concurrent war game against North Korea. Although the United States eventually won that imaginary conflict, one officer involved said "we had a few breathless moments."

There were eighteen divisions in the American army at the time of the Gulf War, twelve in the Base Force plan, and ten in Aspin's proposed plans. The "two-MRC" capability of the armed forces proposed by the BUR was nonsensical except under the assumption that airpower would deal almost entirely with one crisis. Colin Powell, defending the Base Force in 1992, admitted that even the larger Base Force would face high risk and tough times in trying to fight both in Korea and in Iraq in 1997. Aspin's BUR force structure could not possibly be billed as a 2-MRC force.

And yet it was. The unpleasant reaction to the "win-hold-win" concept convinced Aspin to withdraw it. Within a week he announced his commitment to the 2-MRC capability: "After much discussion and analysis in this bottom up review, we've come to the conclusion that our forces must be able to fight and win two major regional conflicts and do it nearly simultaneously."[25] But the BUR force structure did not change. Accused of simply changing the name of the strategy from "win-hold" to "win-win," a senior Defense Department official denied that the force structures were the same. Between the "win-hold" structure Aspin had proposed and the "win-win" structure the BUR adopted, "[t]he major differences are the additional aircraft carrier and several 'force enhancements' that will compensate for the weaker 'win-hold' structure. . . . 'We think that in light of those enhancements we have largely gotten over that. . . .' "[26] The new structure, however, contained the same number of army and marine divisions and air force wings as the "win-hold" structure had. By contrast, the *Washington Times* reported that a Defense Department study set the force necessary "to win two major regional conflicts at nearly the same time" at "20 combat divisions, both active and reserve, 12 aircraft carriers, five Marine Expeditionary Brigades and 24 air wings." The BUR provided a force structure of about one-half that size. What was absolutely clear was that the BUR force could not fight two MRCs at once: "We never claimed any of the options were for fighting two wars simultaneously. . . . The key issue though is not the force structure, it is mobility. We cannot move forces in two directions at the same time."

Although Aspin explained the need for a 2-MRC capability eloquently on a number of occasions, his Bottom-Up Review did not provide that capability. Accepting its own claims, it provided the capability to conduct two "nearly simultaneous" MRCs. The truth was that it could do so only under the most optimistic circumstances. A 1995 study of the BUR conducted by the General Accounting Office argued that many of the assumptions underlying the BUR's strategy were overly optimistic. The GAO identified five specific assumptions that it regarded as "questionable":

- Forces would be redeployed from other operations, such as peace-keeping, to regional conflicts, and forces would be redeployed between regional conflicts. However, critical support and combat forces needed in the early stages of a regional conflict may not be able to quickly redeploy from peace operations because (1) certain Army support forces would be needed to facilitate the redeployment of other forces and (2) logistics and maintenance support needed for specialized Air Force aircraft would have to wait for available airlift.

- Certain specialized units or unique assets would be shifted from one conflict to another. However, two war-fighting commands, in an ongoing study of the two-conflict strategy, have raised questions about shifting assets between conflicts.
- Sufficient strategic lift assets, prepositioned equipment, and support forces would be available. However, the Army lacks sufficient numbers of certain types of support units to meet current requirements for a single conflict.
- Army National Guard enhanced combat brigades could be deployed within 90 days of being called to active duty to supplement active combat units. However, National Guard combat brigades are currently experiencing difficulty meeting peacetime training requirements critical to ensuring their ability to deploy quickly in wartime.
- A series of enhancements, such as improvements to strategic mobility and U.S. firepower, are critical to implementing the two-conflict strategy and would be available by about 2000. However, some enhancements, such as additional airlift aircraft, may not be available as planned.[27]

The BUR recognized that handling two MRCs at the same time would require the withdrawal of U.S. forces from any other military activities, the call-up and deployment of all National Guard combat brigades, and the deployment of almost every military asset in the armed forces. The GAO report argued that although the BUR assumed that the Department of Defense would be able to shift all these forces around at will, there was reason to think that it would not be able to do so.

Aspin had repeatedly stressed the inadequacy of the airlift and sealift capacity of the armed forces both in criticizing the Bush administration's defense plans and in promoting his own. The strategy the BUR adopted for coping with the 2-MRC scenario, however, put the greatest possible stress on that lift capacity. The withdrawal of most American forces from forward positions in Europe and the Pacific meant that almost all of the forces for any MRC would have to be deployed from the continental United States. In addition to that massive deployment, for which Aspin admitted the United States did not have the lift necessary in the event of two simultaneous MRCs, the BUR would also require that forces deployed overseas in peacekeeping or other smaller-scale contingencies disengage from those operations and redeploy to one or the other of the MRCs almost instantaneously.

The GAO report pointed out many flaws in that assumption. Assuming that units involved in smaller-scale contingencies could withdraw from them at once, they would have to take some time to reacquire the necessary level of warfighting readiness before engaging in combat. Even if they could do so almost instantaneously, however, they would not be able to move quickly, because the aircraft and ships they needed would be busy racing U.S. forces and supplies to the forces engaged in dangerous combat operations in the MRCs. That problem aside, the response to the MRCs was likely to be extremely jumbled, because forces would have to be deployed as they became available, rather than as they were needed. If the commander of one MRC required a B-2 bomber force or an F-15E wing or a heavy division, he might be able to get it when he needed it, or he might not, depending on the readiness of those units and on whether or not lift was available to move them. The conduct of both MRCs would be far from the carefully planned and executed precision operation that the finely balanced plans required it to be. It would be a desperate scramble.

The GAO report pointed out still another problem with the BUR's faith that airpower could save the day by noting that although the high-tech aircraft and their crews required for that mission could, themselves, fly to the theater of operations, their supplies, ground crews, and spare parts could not. The fuel to keep the B-2s and F-15s flying, the high-tech ammunition they would need to fire at the enemy, the ground crews needed to keep them operating, and the spare parts essential to keep them functional all would have to be moved by some of the precious airlift capacity, which, it was already clear, would be badly overstrained. The image Aspin offered of B-2s crushing an enemy armored attack by flying from the United States on the first day of the campaign was simply a mirage.

The BUR force saved $91 billion over the course of the Future Years Defense Plan. Of that savings, reductions in modernization programs accounted for $53 billion, planned closure of military bases $19 billion, and reductions in the size of the armed forces $24 billion.[28] Despite the critical importance of leading-edge technology and of the development of technological systems that had not yet been designed and fielded to the strategy that underlay the BUR, modernization programs accounted for almost 60 percent of this most recent edition of the peace dividend. Many critics of the Clinton administration were not pleased by the BUR because they felt it cut defense too deeply, but despite these reductions, the BUR cost too much.

The federal deficit promised to be much larger than Clinton had bargained for when he took office, and his pledge to cut $60 billion from the defense budget grew to a determination to cut $104 billion. The BUR found all but $13 billion of those reductions. The BUR suggested that further savings might be possible by increasing the Defense Department's efficiency, further reducing strategic forces, or closing more bases, but all of those notions depended upon factors not under the Defense Department's control. Aspin had assured a skeptical Congress that if the BUR revealed the need for additional funds beyond what the President's cuts permitted, he would "engage the whole administration" and not just the Pentagon in the discussion. It was now clear that the Defense Department would need to absorb that cut, and more.

By the time Clinton had taken office it was already obvious that even the Bush administration's defense budgets were too small to support the Base Force by more than $10 billion, which Clinton permitted to be added back to the defense budget. Despite the magnitude of Aspin's cuts, however, evidence immediately began to pile up that once again, the budgets for defense would not support even the reduced armed forces the administration proposed. Estimates of the shortfall varied from a few billion dollars to hundreds of billions.[29] Higher-than-expected inflation rates, Congress' refusal to allow the administration to freeze military pay, and many other factors exacerbated the situation, so that in November Aspin informed Clinton, in a memorandum that was subsequently leaked, that the Defense Department urgently needed an additional $50 billion over the course of the FYDP.[30]

White House Budget Director Leon Panetta responded, "I think the president has pretty much made a commitment that he wants to stick to those numbers. . . . I think the basic path has been set. . . . The president has made very clear . . . he does not feel that there is any room there for changes." Within a week, the $50 billion defense budget gap had been "revised" to $31 billion, mostly by revising future assumptions about inflation. Regarding the remaining gap, one news story noted, "Senior Pentagon and White House officials asserted yesterday that they can close a widely publicized gap between Pentagon spending plans and available funding without compromising military readiness, but they declined to say how."[31] Aspin then resigned as Secretary of Defense.

The reasons for Aspin's resignation remain uncertain. In addition to the feud over the defense budget, Aspin had come under heavy criticism for the disaster in Mogadishu earlier in the year, and for his role in attempting to implement Clinton's policies banning discrimination against homosexuals in the military. The legacy of his tenure as Secretary of Defense was clearer. He had reformulated the military policy of the United States to suit the threat environment of the early post–Cold War years, "rationalizing" the Base Force and eliminating its annoying vagueness.

In the process he had reduced the post–Cold War armed forces to their final form: ten active army divisions, fifteen National Guard enhanced readiness brigades, three marine active divisions, twenty air force tactical wings, eleven active and one reserve navy carrier. The armed forces were smaller, both in terms of the number of units and the percentage of gross national product represented by the defense budget, than at any time since before World War II. In the end, demobilization for America after the Cold War meant what it had for England after World War I—the demobilization could only be finished if the final product was less than any force that had been maintained after the outbreak of hostilities.

Another legacy of Aspin's tenure was the death of strategic vision. In order to provide firmness and reality to his proposals, Aspin had turned to the threats that were immediately available and universally recognizable. In doing so, he destroyed the philosophical basis for American defense strategy. The Base Force strategy had begun with an argument about what America's role in the world should be, elaborated that argument into a strategy for handling the most serious challenges likely to face that role—regional aggression on a large scale—and concluded by offering a force structure that was inadequate, to be sure, but developed within an overall strategic concept. The BUR offered no vision of America's role in the world, relying instead on treaty commitments and preexisting deployments to justify intervention in two specific regions. It offered no guidance for dealing with aggression elsewhere in the world.

If the two threats for which it purported to maintain forces seemed to fade in intensity, as they soon did, it left its already inadequate budget and force structure dangerously exposed to still further reductions. To make matters even more dire, the strategy relied upon possible developments in weapons technology to offset the excessive cuts in force structure, even as it reduced the modernization funding necessary to bring about those changes. But the Clinton administration defense budgets were inadequate to support even the BUR force.

The divergence of military policy from foreign policy had been one of the most important factors crippling Britain's ability to influence world events in the 1920s or even to react to them in the 1930s. The need to support France, the League of Nations, and the Versailles Treaty imposed a series of requirements on the military forces of Great Britain. Other requirements flowed from the need to defend the empire and to police it. Still other requirements involved maintaining stability in the Far East and the Mediterranean. Rational defense policy should have examined all of those requirements and designed armed forces to match them. Only then should the necessary balancing of what the armed forces needed and what they could have, given the current economic and political climate, have been considered.

But neither the Chiefs of Staff nor any government approached the matter in that way. The problems of Western Europe entailed contemplating the possibility of another war on the continent, even if only to consider how to prevent it, and that was anathema. The problems of East Asia were relatively new—Japan was viewed traditionally as a friend, and the prospect of fighting a war in that area was disturbing. It was so clearly beyond the capacities of the armed forces of the time, moreover, that it, too, became a prohibited line of thought. The League of Nations, it turned out, was to have run the world by itself—

when the League began presenting checks to Britain's armed forces to cash, as it did at Corfu and later on Abyssinia, it emerged that British governments refused to honor their notes.

The Base Force had attempted, at least, to consider what requirements America's role in the world imposed upon its armed forces. It developed a military strategy that was the perfect counterpoint to a foreign policy designed to support that role. It failed, even so, to provide armed forces adequate to support the policy it advocated. The BUR did much worse. It explicitly rejected any serious strategic thinking, as the British had, and turned away from obvious threats for no other reason than that to consider them would reveal how inadequate was the force structure it proposed. The American military was no more eager to "police the world" in Somalia, Haiti, or Bosnia than Britain's military had been to do so in the Middle East, the Mediterranean, or East Asia. In both cases, militaries that knew they were overstretched by their primary missions attempted to fight off missions they saw as secondary. In the process, they undermined their own credibility with administrations that occasionally sought to do the right thing, but worse still, they failed to call attention to the mismatch between the resources they had been given and the resources they needed to fulfill both primary and secondary missions.

Throughout the 1920s and 1930s successive Chiefs of Staff regularly failed to dissuade governments that sought to take military action from doing so. Their opposition to that action invariably marginalized them and prevented them from developing military structures of adequate size and organization to support the actual foreign policy being pursued. The American military has largely failed to learn this lesson. Its opposition to operations in the Balkans continues to this day, and opposition to Haiti and Somalia never abated. As a result, part of the fight over American military strategy, as over British military strategy, has been badly misplaced. It should not be a question of whether or not the armed forces can intervene in such smaller conflicts, but of what they need to be able to intervene in them without compromising their ability to fulfill their major missions.

The most dangerous parallel between the two situations has been that in both cases, the resources given to defense were fixed before the resources needed to support the stated foreign policy had been determined. No governmental process in either state worked to ensure that the armed forces would be able to support the foreign policy that was being pursued. Instead, it became increasingly necessary for successive military leaders to oppose particular elements of the foreign policy, or to demand further resources, or to conceal the fact that the armed forces were not capable of carrying out their missions, generally all three. With the adoption of the BUR, the Clinton administration locked America into this pattern so similar to the one that had eviscerated Britain's armed forces in the interwar era, and America has shown, so far, no sign of breaking out of it.

15

Kicking the Can
Down the Road

When William Jefferson Clinton entered the White House in January 1993 he led a nation that had no match in economic, political, and military power. In spite of the incompleteness of the triumph over Iraq, the credibility of American power, earned in the lightning military victory over Saddam Hussein's army, was greater than ever. Contrary to the rhetoric of the 1992 campaign, America's economy, by far the largest in the world, was on the rise, on its way to the greatest prosperity in the history of the world, increasing its relative advantage over competitors and making a mockery of the assessments and predictions of the "declinists" of the previous decade. In the political realm, America's role as leader of the world's nations supporting peace and stability had been greatly enhanced. The opportunity to abandon the hesitation and timidity that hampered the Bush administration, to set forth a clear policy of leading an international effort to discourage the use of force, and to shape the international environment to preserve peace, the greatest American interest, had never been so great or the cost so easily bearable.

As a candidate, however, Clinton did not seem a promising figure to lead such an effort. The governor of a small southern state, he had no experience in foreign affairs and apparently little interest in them. His problem was increased by the Democrats' image as weak in defense and foreign policy and by his own personal history. Unlike all his predecessors for three decades he had never performed military service and was accused of improperly evading it during the Vietnam War and of denouncing American policy in a foreign country as a student at Oxford. He chose, therefore to attack Bush's record in foreign affairs

SOMALIA

from the right. He assailed Bush for appeasing Saddam Hussein before the Gulf War and for abandoning the Iraqi people to his untender mercies after it; he blamed Bush for "coddling the old communist guard in China" and asserted that China's violation of human rights should be punished by economic sanctions, promising to "link China's trading privileges to its human rights record and its conduct on trade and weapons sales."[1] Clinton demanded intervention in Somalia to feed the starving people and the reversal of Bush's policy of turning back boats of refugees from Haiti. He called for a more active and aggressive American role in Bosnia, including the use of American military forces to assure the delivery of supplies to the civilians in Sarajevo. "President Bush's policy toward the former Yugoslavia," he said, "mirrors his indifference to the massacre at Tiananmen Square and his coddling of Saddam Hussein. . . . Once again, the administration is turning its back on violations of basic human rights and our own democratic values."[2] After the election, even before taking office, he reversed his policy on Haitian refugees. As President he abandoned Somalia at the first loss of American life; he steered clear of Bosnia as long as possible; he reversed the policy of tying American economic relations with China to that nation's behavior, engaging in a policy that many called appeasement; his tentative policies toward Iraq have led to the end of all inspection of its production of weapons of mass destruction.

A clue to the inconstancy he would bring to American foreign policy as President was provided by candidate Clinton's response to the Gulf War. On the eve of the congressional vote to give President Bush authority to wage war against Saddam Hussein, Clinton was asked by hawkish Democrats to sign a newspaper ad in favor; he promised to consider the matter, but never responded. After the war he was asked how he would have voted had he been in Congress. He answered, "I guess I would have voted with the majority if it was a close vote. But I agree with the argument the minority made."[3]

Observers have tried to characterize the administration's hesitant, confusing, and often contradictory policies in some coherent way. One scholar describes them as "some combination of retrenched internationalism, economism and Wilsonianism, with a dash of new, liberal internationalism."[4] Any attempt at systematic description is bound to produce a pastiche, for since 1993 America has not pursued a coherent plan for foreign and defense policy but relied on a reluctant, reactive series of actions and avoidance of actions whose one continuing, underlying aim has been to put important decisions and their consequences off far into the future, with luck until the next administration has taken office. In June 1995 the President, in irritation, described the Bosnian policy pursued to that point by his administration: "We need to get the policy straight or we're going to be kicking the can down the road again. Right now we've got a situation, we've got no clear mission, no one's in control of events."[5] The President's words are a just description of the Bosnian policy and of American foreign and defense policy in the Clinton years.

In the campaign of 1992, Clinton had promised to "focus like a laser beam" on the economy.[6] After the election, Secretary of State designate Warren Christopher asserted that the voters had "embraced governor Clinton's concept that the strength of the economy is the foundation of foreign policy."[7] Clinton had run against an opponent whose chief strength was foreign policy and beaten him by minimizing its importance compared with domestic issues. The new Secretary of State said, "I make no apologies for putting economics at the top of our foreign policy agenda."[8] The President himself compared the United States to "a big corporation competing in the global marketplace."[9]

Catching the general American mood after the end of the Cold War, Clinton pictured himself and the American people as "homeward bound," concerned chiefly with domestic questions, with restoring and increasing American prosperity, reducing defense expenditures, and improving economic competitiveness and the quality of American life, with foreign policy serving an ancillary role. In support of that priority, administration officials argued that America's position abroad rested on the strength of its economy at home and painted a dark picture of its current state. In September 1993 the President's National Security Adviser, Anthony Lake, said that "above all, [the United States is] threatened by sluggish economic growth." In May, Peter Tarnoff, Under Secretary of State for Political Affairs, presented no less gloomy a description of American incapacity in foreign affairs caused by its economic weakness: "Economic interests are paramount. We simply don't have the leverage, we don't have the inclination to use military force, we certainly don't have the money . . . to bring to bear the kind of pressure that will produce positive results."[10] Although other officials rushed to diminish the force of these off-the-record background remarks, there is every reason to believe they accurately represented the views of Clinton and his administration.[11] They seemed to accept the views of the "declinists" who spoke of America's diminished capacity to compete economically and to exercise effective leadership in the world. As a British scholar has put it, "the Administration appeared to accept Henry Kissinger's assertion that 'America now finds herself in a world which she cannot dominate, but from which she cannot simply withdraw.'"[12] In May 1994, Clinton put it this way: while the United States "cannot turn our backs on the rest of the world," it "cannot solve every problem and must not become the world's policeman."[13] Like James Baker in the Bush administration he unconsciously echoed the words of Bonar Law, alarmed by the British stand at Chanak in 1922. The comparison reveals how ludicrous were the assertions of the American leaders in the 1990s. Bonar Law's Britain faced real and serious economic problems, although timidity and retreat still did not serve its interests and security. The United States of Bush and Clinton, on the other hand, was in the midst of probably the greatest economic boom in the twentieth century. There was plenty available both for guns and butter; what was lacking was the will to undertake the task at hand, the responsibility of shaping a peaceful and secure world environment.

To be sure, there were arguments to support a policy of retrenchment. The budget deficit and national debt had grown significantly in the previous decade, even as the economy boomed. For years Republicans had been calling for their reduction without new taxes. A significant portion of congressional members, especially the younger ones, pointed to the end of the Cold War as a reason to reduce foreign entanglements and defense expenditures. The old, isolationist tradition of the Republican Party began to reappear in the new circumstances. These political considerations made it easier for the new administration to move in the direction it wanted to go.

The President himself, however, was truly unhappy in the realm of foreign affairs:

> The real problem was that Clinton had trouble defining policy, even in a given case, and seemed not very interested in foreign policy. He seemed uncomfortable talking about it. Unlike every President since Truman, Clinton had no regularly scheduled meetings with his foreign policy team.[14]

Dick Morris, a close political adviser of long standing, wrote that Clinton "had no special vision of his foreign policy. He reacted, more or less reluctantly, to global concerns when they intruded so deeply into American politics that he had to do something."[15] Though foreign policy is always influenced by domestic politics, under Clinton domestic considerations seem always to predominate.

The two most prominent members of the foreign policy team, Secretary of State Warren Christopher and National Security Adviser Anthony Lake, had been members of the Carter administration, and they and their President were widely seen as "soft" in foreign affairs and reluctant to use force when needed. One journalist wrote that the arrival of Clinton and his friends represented "the maturing and . . . the vengeance of the anti-Vietnam generation."[16] It was no surprise that such men should take a cautious, minimal view of America's role in the world.

One way to try to cope with the unwelcome intrusion of foreign affairs was to try to leave the responsibility to others. As the British in the 1920s had put their hopes in the League of Nations, so the Clinton administration championed the idea of "multilateralism," by which they chiefly meant the United Nations. This approach is made clear in a document published in 1994 called *The National Security Strategy of Engagement and Enlargement,* "which articulates most extensively" the Clinton foreign policy strategy.[17] It lists three main objectives: security, bolstering the economy, and spreading democracy around the world. "Enlarging the community of market democracies earned a place in the document's title, but fell behind promoting [American] economic prosperity in the hierarchy of strategic goals." It speaks of the need for American leadership, "but a selective leadership that implies selective engagement." It mentions the need for a strong defense but asserts, "No matter how powerful we are as a nation, we cannot secure those goals unilaterally. . . . The threats and challenges we face demand cooperative, multinational solutions."[18] The document contains

> a watered-down version of the controversial Presidential Review Directive (PRD) 13, drafted in August 1993, which identified the United Nations as the primary peacekeeping vehicle and laid out a framework for committing U.S. forces to a permanent UN army under foreign com-

mand. In PRD 13, multilateral operations were viewed as a way to save money and spread political and military risk.[19]

Although so novel a scheme could not be implemented, the Clinton administration approached its first challenges in that spirit, "with high hopes that many of the new crises could be dealt with through the peacekeeping machinery of the United Nations—as a way of sharing resources and responsibilities."[20] America's Ambassador to the United Nations, Madeline Albright, put a bright face on the policy with the phrase "assertive multilateralism," but she emphasized the noun by using the administration's favorite cliché, "the United States is not the world's policeman."[21]

Events soon put the new administration's policies to the test. Continued attention was required in dealing with the delicate problems of the former Soviet Union and Eastern Europe, the relationship with China, the troubled and troubling North Korea, Haiti, and the lingering the unclear commitments in Somalia, Bosnia, and Iraq.

Somalia

The United States became significantly involved in Somalia late in the Bush administration. War against Ethiopia and internal insurrection in 1978 had brought about both an economic and humanitarian and a political crisis. Five hundred thousand refugees from the disputed Ogaden region fled into Somalia, putting unbearable pressure on its food supply, exacerbated by the conflict between regional clan chieftains. "The first of these developments helped to create an economy of dependence on humanitarian aid; the second locked the country into the pattern of regional and global rivalries that persisted until the end of the Cold War."[22]

The crisis became more acute with the overthrow of the dictator Siyad Barre in January 1991. He had been a corrupt and brutal ruler, but his overthrow by a collection of ill-assorted clan leaders propelled Somalia swiftly toward anarchy and starvation in a situation intensified by traditional Somali culture. The nineteenth-century English explorer Richard Burton "had described the Somalis accurately as a 'fierce and turbulent race of republicans' who lacked both chiefs and experience of centralised government." In the chaos that followed the removal of the dictator Barre, the situation had deteriorated, and "the Somalis lived in what amounted to a state of chronic political schizophrenia, verging on anarchy."[23]

To the old problems of excessive population, civil war and the deliberate destruction of farmland and livestock were added. Soon, the UN estimated, some 300,000 people had died of starvation and 700,000 had fled the country. Fighting and looting by the various factions greatly interfered with efforts to deliver humanitarian aid. Security had become a vital issue in dealing with the terrible famine, whose consequences were dramatically reported and shown in newspapers and on television screens around the world. "The question was how it was to be alleviated in a country where central government had lapsed."[24]

By August 1992 a third of the population of southern Somalia, between 1.5 and 2 million people, was in immediate danger of death by starvation and the number of those suffering from malnutrition approached 80 percent of the total. The Red Cross was spending some 35 percent of its world budget in Somalia.[25] The problem remained how to deliver the needed supplies safely, and this presented a special difficulty for the UN, for "there was no precedent for deploying UN forces on a humanitarian rather than a peacekeeping mission when there was no government with which to negotiate. . . ."[26] Although Secretary-General Boutros-Ghali obtained a resolution authorizing 3,500 men to provide armed protection for deliveries, the number was far too small to be effective and the first 500 of them did not go into action until September, when circumstances had changed significantly. It soon became obvious that without strong support and involvement by the United States, "the UN lacked the organizational resources and its members the political interest or will to fashion a coherent strategy for Somalia."[27]

The Bush administration adamantly refused to be drawn into Somalia in any way. It resisted the UN's desire to send in five hundred armed troops to protect the food shipments. The UN sent only fifty unarmed observers instead and then asked for a larger armed force, and the administration objected again, asserting that the Congress would refuse to pay for any additional forces. The *New York Times* reported, "This token force was all the Bush Administration felt it could prudently support."[28] The election campaign was on, and the administration wanted to protect the President from any potentially embarrassing entanglement in foreign affairs. On August 14, however, came a sharp reversal in policy. The United States undertook "Operation Provide Relief," flying food and medical supplies in U.S. Air Force planes, using a small number of military personnel, to places in the Somali interior cut off by bandit clans.[29] The action won the endorsement of Democratic candidate Bill Clinton. So sharp a reversal has been explained as "an irresistible sip of painless Third World heroism, with no backwash,"[30] but, almost on the eve of the Republican convention, it must have been a political response to criticism. Boutros-Ghali had chided the United States and its allies for their lack of concern for Somalia compared with the fighting in the former Yugoslavia, calling the latter "a rich man's war."[31] A *New York Times* editorial was even more pointed:

> What's amazing is not resistance in Congress, but the silent acquiescence of George Bush. The Administration is in the peculiar position of agreeing to thousands of peacekeepers in chaotic Yugoslavia while balking at

a battalion in Somalia. What does Mr. Bush say to African protests that race accounts for the difference?[32]

By August, criticism of inaction had grown to the point where the Senate passed a resolution calling for sending UN armed guards "with or without the consent of Somali factions."[33] In spite of the greatest determination to stay aloof and even to limit UN involvement, publicity in the media and political pressure forced the Bush administration to take the first reluctant step toward involvement in a purely humanitarian venture with military consequences.

The food deliveries met with little trouble from the Somalis, but the White House, the State Department, and the Pentagon "remained adamantly opposed to any escalation in American involvement."[34] The American mission, though helpful, was only a drop in a very large bucket. The looting, killing, and starvation continued and appeared in the communications media in all its horror. On November 25, Boutros-Ghali wrote "that 'the situation is not improving' and that conditions were so bad that it would be 'exceedingly difficult' for the United Nations' existing operation in Somalia to achieve its objectives."[35] Defeated in the presidential election, liberated from internal political considerations, Bush took the lead in changing American policy toward Somalia. "As the architect of the 'new world order' he evidently felt it incumbent on him 'to do something.' "[36]

The United States devised a plan that would send some 30,000 troops, most of them American, to permit the effective distribution of humanitarian aid. It would gain control of airports, ports, roads, and distribution centers and was prepared to use force for the purpose. As General Colin Powell, chairman of the Joint Chiefs, put it: "It's sort of like the cavalry coming to the rescue, straightening things out for a while and then letting the marshals come back to keep things under control."[37] Even now, the Bush administration was very careful to make clear that this was a "circumscribed mission intended to stabilize the military situation only to the extent needed to avoid mass starvation, and the United States expected to hand the matter back to the United Nations in three or four months."[38]

President-elect Clinton greeted the action warmly: "I have felt for a long time that we should do more in Somalia," he said. "The thing I think is so heartening is that the United States is now taking the initiative. . . . I think it is high time. I'm encouraged, and I applaud the initiative of President Bush and his administration."[39] On December 3 the Security Council unanimously adopted Resolution 794 authorizing the participating nations to use "all necessary means to establish . . . a secure environment for humanitarian relief operations in Somalia."[40] In a letter to the Secretary-General, Bush was careful to spell out the limits of America's commitment: "I want to emphasize that the mission of the coalition is limited and specific: to create security conditions which will permit the feeding of the starving Somali people and allow the transfer of this security function to the UN peacekeeping force." He made it clear that he expected that to happen soon and that the American and coalition forces would leave at that time.[41]

On December 9, American troops landed in Somalia. Almost at once, tension arose between Boutros-Ghali and the Americans. The Secretary-General always wanted to enlarge the mission to include general disarmament of the Somali warlords, widespread pacification, and what was called "nation building." The Americans, on the other hand, "were apt to stress the limited and short-term character of their intervention."[42] Within a few weeks, however, they were successful in opening supply routes and delivering relief. By the end of the Bush administration, "humanitarian assistance was regularly flowing to critical areas. Mediation efforts were progressing, with all major factions agreeing to a conference on national reconciliation in mid-March."[43]

Even before the change of administration, events were beginning to change the character of the mission. The original calm that followed the intervention began to collapse, as fighting resumed in several places. To deal with that, the Americans, in spite of worries about "mission creep," were compelled to patrol more aggressively and to disarm people carrying weapons. Still, just before Clinton's inauguration, the Americans "staged a symbolic withdrawal of several hundred Marines as a prelude to eventual UN control of the mission," and "many other U.S. units left during the following months."[44]

The departing administration, no doubt, thought it would be allowed to "tiptoe away" from its humanitarian effort, but "American prestige was now invested in the United Nations operation whether they liked it or not,"[45] as the Clinton administration soon discovered. Although the Democrats had campaigned on the slogan of "assertive multilateralism," which the Somalia intervention seemed to exemplify, at first the administration pressed for American withdrawal as planned. As fighting became more serious late in February, however, it began to seem that even greater forces would be needed to prevent disaster, and the idea of swift withdrawal began to fade. "The real shift, however, came on March 26," when the Americans successfully pressed the Security Council to adopt Resolution 814. It asked the special representative of the Secretary-General (the recently appointed retired American admiral Jonathan Howe) "to assume responsibility for the consolidation, expansion, and maintenance of a secure environment throughout Somalia" and asked for money for "the rehabilitation of the political institutions and economy of Somalia."[46] The new American representative to the United Nations, Madeline K. Albright, greeted the resolution with enthusiasm: "With this resolution we will embark on an unprecedented enterprise aimed at nothing less than the restoration of an entire country as a proud, functioning and viable member of the community of nations."[47] The UN force prescribed by Resolution 814 included 20,000 troops, 8,000 American logistical support staff, and about 3,000 civilians. The Americans also undertook to provide a special "quick reaction" tactical force of 1,000 troops when needed.[48]

On May 4 the United States military formally turned over command of the international force to the UN, some five months later than had originally been planned. They left behind, however, about 5,000 American troops of a total of 27,000 UN soldiers. A month later, Secretary of State Christopher proudly announced that "we have phased out the American-led mission to Somalia, and taken the lead in passing responsibility to a United Nations peacekeeping force. . . ."[49] Even before his announcement, UN forces were facing increasing trouble from Somali warlords, chief among them Mohammed Farrah Aideed. On June 5 he led an attack on UN forces from Pakistan, killing twenty-three and wounding perhaps fifty others.[50] The next day the Security Council unanimously passed a resolution calling for the arrest of Aideed, Admiral Howe placed a bounty on his head, and American forces went on the attack with helicopters and assault teams to defeat and capture the warlord. It was on June 7 that Christopher sent a cable to his ambassadors announcing that "for the first time there will be a sturdy American role to help the United Nations rebuild a viable nation-state [in Somalia]."[51] The character of American involvement had changed from a humanitarian effort to deliver food and supplies, using military force to protect it, to offensive actions meant to defeat Somali opponents and pacify the country. "In the early summer of 1993 the official view was that, having broken new ground with resolution 794, the United States could not afford to have the Somali operation fail."[52]

As fighting continued during the summer the U.S. Congress grew restless. Senator Robert Byrd called for the withdrawal of American forces. In hearings before a House subcommittee, UN Ambassador Albright defended the American role in Somalia as an example of the "assertive multilateralism" she favored. Somalia was one of that category of states she called "failed societies . . . where effective government has collapsed, or anarchy reigns, or the economy is hopeless, or humanitarian calamity overwhelms the country and the people are sliding into an abyss." America's success in dealing with these and other foreign policy challenges, its credibility as a superpower, required "multilateral engagement," which itself required the exercise of "leadership within collective bodies like the UN." The goal in Somalia was to promote "a durable and political settlement . . . [and] rebuilding Somali society and promoting democracy. . . ."

> After the enormous effort made by the U.S. and other nations . . . to reverse famine in Somalia, I believe it would be folly now to permit conditions to deteriorate again. Had there not been a UN response to the June 5th killings, the UN's credibility in Somalia would have been fatally undermined.[53]

In spite of criticism the administration held to its policy through the summer. On August 27, Secretary of Defense Les Aspin declared: "We are staying there now to help those people rebuild their nation. . . . President Clinton has given us clear direction to stay the course with other nations to help Somalia."[54] In spite of such language, Aspin and the other relevant officials in Washington were reluctant to increase the number and visibility of American forces in Somalia. When Admiral Howe requested additional forces to pursue Aideed, and particularly for Rangers and the specially trained Delta Force, Aspin and General Powell held back. On August 8, however, four American soldiers in Mogadishu had been blown up by a remote-controlled mine. Powell and others in the administration now pressed Aspin, and the special forces requested were sent.[55]

These casualties made the administration nervous about pursuing a military track alone, since, as one well-informed reporter has observed, "Congress was beginning to squawk, and there was the possibility of having to send twenty-five thousand troops to Bosnia."[56] Clinton and his advisers now tried to move along a two-track approach, seeking a diplomatic solution even as they were committed to a vigorous military policy of seeking out and trying to capture Aideed, without telling the soldiers in the field to hold back their efforts or strengthening their capacity to achieve their goal. In September a rift was growing between the military men in Mogadishu and "the military brass in the United States" who were more in tune with the views of their political masters and "felt that the UN had to scale back its objectives" to avoid "mission creep."[57]

It was in these confused circumstances that the officers in charge in Mogadishu asked for reinforcements in the form of Bradley armored vehicles, M-1 tanks, artillery pieces, and assault helicopters. The response came on September 23 from Secretary Aspin, who "was uncomfortable accelerating the disparity between the two tracks and turned down [General Thomas] Montgomery's [Montgomery was in charge of U.S. forces in Somalia] requests for tanks and artillery and [General William F.] Garrison's [Garrison was commander of special operations] requests for AC-130 Specter gunships."[58]

On October 3, without this equipment, a team of Rangers and troops from the Delta Force undertook an airborne assault from Blackhawk helicopters on a suspected hideout of Aideed. The result was disaster. Eighteen Americans were killed and seventy-seven wounded. One soldier was taken hostage, and the picture of another, dead and unclothed, being dragged through the streets was shown all over the world. A later study by the Joint Chiefs concluded that "even if the tanks [requested by Montgomery] had arrived in time, they would have been of little use in the Mogadishu firefight,"[59] but that conclusion is unconvincing as a general exculpation. There is excellent reason to believe that if the helicopters delivering the troops had been accompanied by additional air forces with greater firepower, such as the requested AC-130 gunships or Apache helicopters, the fire from the Somalis could have been suppressed and the disaster averted. If the force sent to extract the soldiers after the mission had been made up of the armored Bradley vehicles and M-1 tanks, their firepower could have been brought to bear for the same purpose. More important, the protection offered by these armored vehicles would have obviated the need for the defeated and wounded Rangers to *walk* out of the center of Mogadishu through enemy-held areas back to their bases. It seems fair to conclude that the hesitation, confusion, and halfheartedness of the administration, which proceeded on a double-track policy without providing the military with the forces needed to pursue its track safely and effectively, bore considerable responsibility for the disaster at Mogadishu.[60]

Afterward the question was asked why, "given the fact that the administration was shifting its emphasis—or thought it was—to the political track, it had taken place at all. Why weren't the commanders in the field given new instructions?"[61] In a heartrending appearance before the Senate Armed Services Committee in May 1994, Larry E. Joyce, a retired army officer who had served two tours in Vietnam and whose son was killed at Mogadishu, asked a similar question: "If the President had already decided, in September, to seek a diplomatic solution with Aideed, why were the Rangers ordered on October 3 to conduct a raid that, by its very nature, would be the most dangerous mission yet?"[62] The Clinton administration, according to one commentator, "had come to this pass via a series of casually made decisions," and the answer to Larry Joyce's question "was shrouded in ambiguity, if not outright confusion." They asserted that

> putting more emphasis on a political settlement didn't mean the hunt for Aideed would be called off. The theory, according to [Anthony] Lake, was that the military and diplomatic pressures were complementary. "The policy was never to stop trying to get Aideed," Lake said. Aspin said afterward, "The Pentagon's understanding of the policy was to move to more diplomatic efforts but snatch Aideed on the side, if you can."[63]

News of the firefight in Mogadishu produced furious criticism in the country and the Congress. On October 7, Clinton, fearful that Congress might insist on an earlier date, announced that all American forces would leave Somalia by March 31, 1994. This effectively put an end to the UN operation in Somalia, because the other participating governments soon announced their decision to withdraw. By September 1994 the UN mission was at an end. When its last troops, protected by U.S. Marines, pulled out in March 1995, Secretary Christopher claimed, "We leave the country in a lot better shape than [when] we went in."[64] To be sure, the successful delivery of food saved at least 100,000 lives and perhaps many more, but the country was left in sorry condition. The warlords were never disarmed or tamed, and the prospect remained of recurring famine in the future. Four years after the withdrawal of the last UN forces the newspapers reported that "Somalia is in the middle of a food crisis, with up to one million people facing shortages and 300,000 at risk of serious nutritional problems. Reaching those people in a country with no government, where disputes between clans are settled at the point of a rifle is a logistical nightmare."[65] A reporter observed, "With most agencies gone and clan warfare continuing in the only nation in the world with no central government, Somalia has been largely left on its own, for good and bad."[66] It is hard to think of such an outcome as much of a success. A reporter observed one important lesson of Somalia: "Broader public pressure to keep combat casualties low—always a goal but now a condition for a military mission's success—may restrict the kinds of relief and peacekeeping tasks America joins."[67] To the world it appeared that the Americans had "cut and run" at the first sign of casualties and raised doubts of its willingness to run even the smallest risks or pay the smallest price in defense of the "new world order."

Many Americans saw it as a caution against any repetition of humanitarian interventions, attempts at "nation building," or what one commentator called international "social work." A congressman made the inevitable comment "The American public is fed up that Uncle Sam is called on to be the world's policeman."[68] The United States' experience in Somalia has had consequences much greater even than the immediate loss of life and the blow to American prestige. "Mogadishu has had a profound cautionary influence on U.S. military policy ever since. . . . So, for better or worse . . . the U.S. government (and the UN) looked on as genocidal spasms killed a million people in Rwanda and Zaire, and as atrocity was piled on atrocity in Bosnia."[69]

The American experience in Somalia, nevertheless, revealed how difficult it is in the new era for the United States to ignore great humanitarian disasters that appear to have military solutions and how difficult it is to resolve them. It would be hard to think of a place less important in itself. It had no strategic, economic, or political significance for the United States. It would also be hard to think of two presidents with a stronger instinct to avoid involvement than Bush and Clinton, yet each found himself unable to stay out. The first attempted a superficial intervention and a quick withdrawal but would have found it hard to withdraw had he remained in office. The second undertook a deeper solution but provided neither the commitment nor the means to achieve it and fled the scene when the first reverse and the first casualties caused a storm of protest at home. The fiasco in Somalia would have a significant deterrent effect on future interventions, effectively ruling out even the thought of putting troops on the ground almost anywhere, but, even so, it could not overcome the powerful forces that continued to press for intervention in trouble spots when the occasion arose.

Haiti

On October 17, 1993, just two weeks after the firefight at Mogadishu, some forty "armed vagabonds" prevented the American warship *Harlan County* from landing in the harbor at Port-au-Prince, Haiti. "The mob was shooting in the air and threatening to block the disembarkation of the American soldiers who had gone to Haiti at the behest of the UN." There were also pictures of Haitian thugs kicking the car carrying the top U.S. diplomat there, thus forcing it, too, to speed away to safety. These pictures appeared not long after photographs and film clips had shown jubilant Somalians dragging the bodies of dead Americans through the streets of Mogadishu and dancing on the burned-out hulks of armored personnel carriers.[70]

In the months that followed, cablegrams from the American Embassy in Haiti repeatedly reported that "from the moment the *Harlan County* turned around, the United States lost all credibility."[71]

The United States' latest involvement with Haiti began in September 1991, when a military coup overthrew President Jean-Bertrand Aristide. In his eight months in office he had made anti-American speeches, advocated radical programs of redistribution of Haitian wealth, and ruled in an authoritarian manner, and he was accused of sanctioning "necklacing," putting a gasoline-filled tire about a victim's neck and setting it afire. A CIA report suggested he was insane, but the Bush administration denounced the coup, insisted on the return of Aristide to office, and gave him asylum. The brutality and misery caused by the ruling junta sent thousands of Haitians fleeing their island on flimsy boats heading for the United States, chiefly Florida; the Bush administration's policy was to turn them back.

During the presidential campaign of 1992, Clinton accused his opponent if "racial politics" in turning the refugees back, promising that he "wouldn't be shipping those poor people back," if elected.[72] After he took office, however, he reversed his position. The numbers of refugees and the opposition in America, especially from Florida, were so great that the President restricted admission of Haitians even more than before and set up a blockade of the Haitian coast to stop the migration.[73] Aristide was not a comfortable protégé for American policy, but he was the first popularly elected president in Haitian history. He had strong political support in the Congress, especially in the Black Caucus, and also generally in liberal circles, members of the Kennedy family among them, so Clinton "took a strong personal interest" in restoring him to office.[74]

In June 1993 the United States backed a UN resolution in favor of an embargo on oil and military supplies and froze the assets of Haiti's new military leaders in an attempt to put pressure on them, with no success. In July, however, the United States and the UN were able to mediate an agreement between Aristide and the military junta to end sanctions in return for a promise to restore the President by the end of October. It was in connection with this agreement that the *Harlan County* incident occurred. The mission was meant to carry out the provisions of the accord to train the Haitian army and police force and to help rebuild the country's infrastructure. Although the mission involved only a couple of hundred American Seabees and Canadian troops, the Pentagon opposed it, in part because of the military's opposition to "yet another nation-building exercise."[75] The ship waited in the harbor for two days while the administration tried to decide whether it would look worse to be turned away or be kept impotently waiting in the harbor and at last decided to have the ship depart. "So on Tuesday, October 12, the world was treated to a picture of the mighty United States sailing away from a clutch of rioters." It could not fail to appear ludicrous when Clinton, "trying to look forceful in the face of this second humiliation in little over a week," said, "I want the Haitians to know that I am dead serious about seeing them honor the agreement they made."[76]

The United States persuaded the UN to reimpose economic sanctions and sent its own ships to enforce the embargo. Ordinary Haitians suffered terribly from its effects, but General Raoul Cedras and the junta refused to go. Refugee flights increased, some of the refugees, in flight on inadequate boats, dying at sea. Those who made shore were located at the Guantanamo Bay naval base in eastern Cuba or in Panama. Clinton then threatened further sanctions if the generals did not retire by January 15, 1994, to no effect. The date passed with no action. A new plan proposed that Cedras resign his military post and Aristide name a new Prime Minister, but both sides rejected it. "Neither believed that Washington had the resolve to carry out a coherent policy. The administration's credibility plummeted."[77]

Soon Clinton faced heavy political criticism at home. From one direction came dire warnings against using military force against the junta, with the ritual invocations of Vietnam and quagmires and body bags. From the other, the Black Caucus in Congress demanded that he stop turning away refugees, act more forcefully to restore Aristide, and stop forcing compromises on him. Aristide himself attacked the administration's refugee policy as "racist" and "criminal."[78] In the spring of 1994, Randall Robinson, head of the TransAfrica Forum, went on a hunger strike to protest administration policy toward Haiti. "In an extraordinary statement for an American President, Mr. Clinton not only admitted that his policy had failed, but also left the impression that he was somehow powerless to change course." Clinton said: "I understand and respect what he is doing. . . . And we ought to change our policy. It hasn't worked. . . . He ought to stay out there. We need to change our policy." Clinton was apparently distressed, repeatedly telling his aides of the atrocities committed by the junta, "They're chopping people's faces off." But Robinson was not impressed by the President's comments, complaining:

> To have the President suggest that the policy should change and I should stay out there on a hunger strike while he abdicates his responsibility is deeply disturbing. . . . The President can make the policy effective and humane with the stroke of a pen, but he hasn't changed a thing. It's sad to say, but he appears to be without a moral compass.[79]

By this time Congressman David R. Obey, chairman of the House Appropriations Committee, publicly called for an American invasion of Haiti to remove the military junta and hold new elections, and he was soon joined by others. The Pentagon, however, made it clear "that it has no appetite for putting American troops in Haiti, even as military trainers and civil engineers. . . ." The team of reporters covering Haiti for the *New York Times* concluded that "the United States may have a long way to go before it can convince the military leadership and the people of Haiti of the seriousness of its intentions."

The embargo was tightened, but the only effect was to increase the misery of the Haitian people, so that the number of refugees also multiplied. The administration cut off travel visas and commercial air flights to Haiti and froze the assets of individual Haitians in the regime, all to no avail. As political pressures mounted, the administration moved reluctantly toward military action, obtaining a resolution from the Security Council authorizing an invasion to restore "democracy and the prompt return of the legitimately elected president." Unlike the resolutions authorizing the assault on Iraq in 1991, this one carried no deadline, and American officials said that they had not decided to invade but that a decision to use force was "still weeks away."[80]

By September, however, an invasion was generally expected. On the 15th the President appeared on television to prepare the American people, "amid mounting criticism from Congress that he had waited too long and done too little to steel the public for the prospect that American lives could soon be at risk."[81] Beginning with the usual disclaimer, he said: "I know that the United States cannot, indeed should not, be the world's policeman," but concluded that "when brutality occurs close to our shores it affects our national interests."[82] Clinton announced that he was prepared to send ground forces to remove Haiti's military junta, saying, "The message of the United States to the Haitian dictators is clear. Your time is up. Leave now or we will force you from power."[83] He presented four reasons for armed intervention: to protect the Haitians' human rights, to restore democracy, to prevent masses of refugees fleeing to the United States, and to preserve American credibility.

This was the first speech the President had ever made about Haiti. The administration's previous timidity, the shifting nature and ambiguity of its policy, and the resulting failure previously to make the case to the American people made the new apparent firmness hard to sell. The public, the press, and the politicians questioned that Haiti involved American interests or was an American responsibility. Democratic congressmen who heard the speech said that "the case is not strong enough to require an invasion," and complained, "There was no rationale before the speech, and there was no rationale after the speech." The Republicans were more pointed. Republican Senator McCain spoke of the lessons of Vietnam: "[W]e cannot involve ourselves militarily without the support of the American people." Republican Senator Lugar pointed out that Clinton had ignored similar atrocities in Bosnia and said that "the President's argument that Haiti's proximity to the United States was critical seemed to be an attempt to absolve himself of a weak foreign policy." Former members of the Bush administration pointed to the lessons of Somalia, "when televised pictures of a dead American soldier being dragged through the streets of Mogadishu at the end of a rope brought a national outcry." A statement by an organization headed by Brent Scowcroft, Bush's National Security Adviser, warned that in considering "an invasion followed by nation-building, we should all keep Somalia in mind."

The price of pursuing a foreign policy without a clear direction and without an effective and continuing effort to educate the public was reflected in polls showing that two-thirds of the American people "oppose any military solution."[84] Congressman David Skaggs reflected a widespread opinion when he said, "There's just a gut-level sense in this country that the interests of the United States in this matter are not serious enough to justify the use of the military."[85]

The one argument that won at least the grudging respect of commentators concerned American credibility. Previous American statements, actions, and inactions raised serious questions in that regard. A Republican congressman opposed to invasion conceded that hesitation by Clinton now would make him " 'a laughingstock' both at home and abroad." As if to prove the point, France's Foreign Minister, Alain Juppé, told reporters, "with a hint of exasperation, that he could not quite understand why the United States has waited so long. 'The signals from the Administration have been a little bit contradictory.' "

Members of the Clinton administration were keenly aware of its credibility problem. A Washington reporter described their thinking:

> Clinton Aides privately acknowledge that they believe it especially important to establish U.S. reliability in Haiti because the Administration has failed notably to maintain its credibility in earlier tests.
>
> In Somalia, Clinton hastily announced a withdrawal of U.S. troops after a gun battle last October in Mogadishu killed 18 U.S. troops.
>
> In Haiti, the U.S. Navy attempted to land police trainers last fall but turned away when they encountered a band of the regime's gunmen on the dock.
>
> "We have some impressions to live down," one official said. "Some of the impressions are unfair, but there they are."

For these reasons Clinton's National Security Adviser put American credibility at the top of the list of reasons for the invasion: "[W]e must make it clear that we mean what we say. Our actions in Haiti will send a message far beyond our region—to all who seriously threaten our interests."[86] The incremental deterioration in America's reputation for reliability and resolve was the main concern that seemed to be driving Clinton's administration to the use of armed force and to another difficult experiment in nation-building.

Even then the President was visibly reluctant to use military force. "Clinton's unhappiness at the prospect of a military clash has been palpable: One visitor who saw the President . . . said that he spoke of the prospect of war . . . as if he still had not made up his mind." At the last moment, former President Jimmy Carter conveyed an ambiguous message to the President from General Cedras inviting discussions, and Clinton seized on it. A week earlier he had rejected a proposal from Carter for such a mission, but now he sent Carter, General Colin Powell, and Senator Sam Nunn on a visit to Haiti that "offered Clinton one final hope for escape from a war he does not relish."[87] A reporter wondered why the President was so eager to get the junta out without armed force, "especially when Defense Secretary William J. Perry said only this afternoon that invasion troops could dispatch the junta in a matter of hours, . . . even though it again made him look indecisive and inconsistent in foreign policy—the very things for which he has been criticized throughout his Presidency."[88] Some speculated that the delay for talks was meant to appease critics and that even the failure of talks would provide a stronger basis for the final assault, "but in the end, officials agreed, Clinton's main motive was simpler: He just doesn't want to go to war."[89]

With 20,000 U.S. troops prepared to invade, the Haitian generals agreed to leave, and the troops landed peacefully and unopposed on September 19. A few weeks later, Aristide returned to the presidency, but "Operation Restore Democracy was almost anticlimactic after months of Hamletlike indecision in the White House. Clinton's irresolution, in fact, detracted from what might otherwise have been a display of presidential power and decisiveness."[90]

In March 1995 the United States turned over the overseeing of Haiti to the UN, although some 2,500 American troops remained as part of the UN force. On the last day of the month, President Clinton came to Haiti to celebrate the success of the mission. To the American soldiers he said:

> Thank you for bringing back the promise of liberty to this long-troubled land. . . . Seven months ago, the world wondered whether the United States could summon the will to protect democracy in this hemisphere, . . . now the world knows once again the United States will honor its commitment and stand up for freedom.[91]

To be sure, the flight of refugees ceased, General Cedras and his associates were gone, and the elected President was restored, but the possibility of democracy and liberty, not to mention economic improvement and reasonable political stability, remained more than dubious. Political murder and lesser violence resumed at once. Parliamentary and presidential elections were marked by extremes of fraud and intimidation. In 1996 one scholar described the situation in Haiti as follows:

> The rulers are the main threat to life, limb and private property. Reforms are in abeyance and privatization of government assets is still a mere

promise. Near anarchy lurks in the vast shanty towns of Port-au-Prince as factions occasionally battle each other in the streets. Pro-Aristide vigilantes settle old scores against opponents and intimidate current opposition figures. Aristide, although titularly not the president, exerts power from behind the scenes.[92]

By March 1999 the situation had deteriorated still more. Haiti has been without an effective government since June 1997, when the Premier resigned and accused President René Préval, a protégé of Aristide's, of corrupting the recent election in favor of Aristide's party. Préval dissolved Parliament and appointed a new Premier by decree. The dismissed legislators successfully called on the nations of the world not to recognize the new government, which stopped vitally needed foreign aid from coming to Haiti. On March 26, 1999, he appointed still another new government by decree, promising new elections, in hopes of ending the crisis, but the opposition gave no sign of confidence in the fairness of new elections and seemed likely to continue to boycott the political process. A member of the majority party in the previous Parliament predicted that " 'this government . . . will peruse Preval's antidemocratic project' to concentrate power in the president's hands. . . ."[93] Even more chilling was the resumption of refugee flights. On March 25, 1999, the report of the loss of a forty-foot wooden sailboat carrying some three hundred Haitian refugees in a storm off the Bahamas produced the information that such attempts had been increasing for two years, that the U.S. Coast Guard had stopped 258 Haitians trying to reach Florida in the three months of 1999, and that the Bahamian coast guard had intercepted about 560 in the previous week alone.[94] It seemed clear that the United States had not solved the Haitian problem, but merely "kicked it down the road."

Conclusion

The Clinton administration had set out to pursue a policy of "aggressive multilateralism," relying upon the United Nations. Implicit in its stated foreign policy objectives of American engagement in the world and support for democracy and stability around the world were the bases for U.S. involvement in Somalia and Haiti. In the end, it was the need to defend America's credibility and prestige in the world that primarily drove that involvement. The similarities with the earliest crises that faced Britain in the 1920s are clear. Then the need was to support the League of Nations and the Peace Settlements in crises at Chanak and Corfu, and those goals were publicly much discussed by the British governments of the time. In each case, however, British prestige and the need to preserve England's credibility in places where it was already committed drove involvement.

But in the 1990s as in the 1920s, the involvement was always reluctant and minimal, and pursued unclear objectives. The British and the Americans both had turned inward, and they saw foreign policy as a distraction from the really important issues of the day, which were all domestic. Then and now, military involvement, however small, was seen as dangerous, because it might lead to unwanted and expensive escalation. It is astonishing that Clinton should have feared a war against the pitiful dictators of Haiti, but less astonishing in the light of the collapse of America's policy in Somalia. The adage "Once burned, twice shy" applies to politicians almost more than to any other group of people. Somalia had taught the Clinton administration that *any* American casualties might be regarded as unacceptable, and they sought, therefore, to avoid any commitment of American forces to dangerous situations. Similarly, the Baldwin government had learned from Lloyd George's mistake—the British people did not want to fight a war, even against rebellious Turks. As a result, Baldwin was determined from the outset to avoid a war against the Italians, despite the fact that it was quite clear the Italians had absolutely no hope of winning.

But the most telling similarity is the most baleful. In each case, the British and American leaderships enunciated the general principles that compelled them to intervene: the need to protect their credibility, and to support the international organizations to which they looked to maintain the peace and stability of the world. In each case, things went, or seemed as though they might go, badly wrong. Unforeseen dangers arose, fears mounted. At Chanak, for all the courage with which Lloyd George contemplated war with Attaturk, he ended up forsaking the objectives that had engendered the conflict in the first place and attempting to declare a victory, having achieved only a few of his aims. So it was in Haiti: the real objective of restoring stability and democracy in that land was not achieved, despite the Clinton administration's apparent, but reluctant, willingness to use force. In the end it was necessary to declare that the simple restoration of Aristide was victory in itself and that all was now well—when it was patently quite ill.

In Somalia the situation was much worse. Having identified the crisis as the critical test of the new multilateralism, just as Corfu was identified as the critical test of the viability of the League of Nations, Clinton failed the test. At Corfu, Baldwin, fearful of any war with Italy, however certain the outcome, permitted the crisis to be taken out of the League's hands and settled unjustly at the expense of the victimized power, Greece. The blow to the League was devastating and the encouragement to international predators was strong. In Somalia, the Clinton administration visibly cut and ran at the smallest loss of American life, abandoning the UN, Somalia, and the policy of internationalism. The declaration of victory following the crisis, like that following Mussolini's retirement from Corfu, was worse than hollow, it was absurd. The legacy of both crises, however, proved to be serious and far-reaching.

16

Proliferation and Blackmail

The Bottom-Up Review confidently asserted that of the two nearly simultaneous conflicts for which America's armed forces had to be prepared, the one in North Korea could be largely dealt with through the use of airpower. Although defense documents never said so, it was clearly implied that that one would be fairly easy. The enormous lethality of American airpower in the Gulf War could be used to similar effect in the tightly constrained passes through which the North Korean forces had to come. It should have been quite shocking to policy makers, therefore, when during a conflict with North Korea over its nascent nuclear weapons programs, the costs of fighting that lesser major regional conflict were deemed by the Clinton administration to be too great to face. The problems with America's defense posture, evident during the Gulf War and exacerbated since that time by further defense cuts, in time undermined America's strategy and diplomacy. As a result of that military weakness, America would turn away from the important objective of fighting the proliferation of nuclear weapons and backing the newly reenergized international organization charged with that task.

The Nonproliferation Problem

The end of the nuclear tensions of the Cold War brought a new nuclear danger into sharper focus: the danger of the proliferation of weapons of mass destruction (WMD), including nuclear, biological, and chemical weapons and the sys-

tems for delivering them. The increased attention to proliferation reflected, in part, the fear that out-of-work Soviet nuclear, biological, and chemical weapons experts would sell their services to the highest bidders, or that the bankrupt and hungry Russian armed forces would do so. The collapse of the bipolar world order, moreover, meant that the Soviets could no longer be relied upon to control the behavior of their clients. It was not in the Soviets' interest for Iraq or North Korea to develop indigenous WMD capabilities that would have made them independent of the USSR and dangerous in their own right, and the Soviets discouraged such developments. The collapse of the Soviet

Union, however, left Iraq, North Korea, and other former clients desperate for cheap military might even as it removed the pressure from Moscow to refrain from developing nuclear capabilities. Nonproliferation became a critical issue in the post–Cold War world.

The Bush administration recognized the importance of nonproliferation in its official statements but did not give it priority. The last defense policy paper produced by the Cheney Pentagon included "limits on the spread of militarily significant technology, particularly the proliferation of weapons of mass destruction along with the means to deliver them" among the last goals of American strategy after the provision of humanitarian assistance.[1] Aspin's Defense Department, however, promoted to first place

> [d]angers posed by nuclear weapons and other weapons of mass destruction (WMD), including dangers associated with the proliferation of nuclear, biological, and chemical weapons and their delivery systems, as well as those associated with the large stocks of these weapons that remain in the [former Soviet Union].[2]

Regional dangers, dangers to democracy in the former Soviet Union, and economic dangers to national security came after the WMD threat.

The Clinton administration inherited complicated proliferation problems in both Iraq and North Korea. In this area, as in others, the end of the Gulf War had not resolved the problem in Iraq, while the Bush administration had avoided taking decisive action in the face of indications of problems in North Korea. Despite the increased focus in defense policy documents on the proliferation problem, however, the Clinton administration has signally failed to take adequate steps to resolve dangerous situations in both Iraq and North Korea. There is reason to believe that the relative weakness of America's military position and Clinton's unwillingness to engage in significant military operations are major factors in that failure.

The North Korean Nuclear Threat

The origins of the North Korean nuclear program date back to the 1970s, but indications that the Democratic People's Republic of Korea (DPRK) might actually be able to build nuclear weapons soon did not appear until the 1980s. In 1982, American satellites identified a nuclear reactor vessel under construction at Yongbyon, sixty miles north of Pyongyang, the capital. In 1986, satellites detected indications that the North Koreans had conducted explosion testing, essential to preparing to build a bomb, near that site. The next year, satellites noted that a building under construction near the Yongbyon reactor seemed to have the pattern characteristic of the spent fuel processing plants that produce plutonium, the critical ingredient for nuclear weapons. A year later, they saw a second, larger reactor under construction at Yongbyon.[3]

Shortly after taking power in 1985, Mikhail Gorbachev came to an agreement with the DPRK under which the Soviets would provide light water reactors (LWRs) if the DPRK joined the Nonproliferation Treaty (NPT), which Pyongyang did two weeks later. Gorbachev wanted to head off the Korean nuclear weapons program by providing reactors not suitable for producing weapons-grade plutonium, but more than adequate for supplying the DPRK's power needs. The steady decline of Soviet power, however, placed this deal in abeyance; North Korea became impatient, and the nuclear program moved ahead, despite its new commitments under the NPT.

When the Bush administration took office in 1989 it had ample evidence that a serious effort was under way in North Korea to develop nuclear weapons, but took action only reluctantly and cautiously. One official noted, "The real problem was the policymakers' reluctance to face the issue, an avoidance of reality that probably flowed from the realization of the scope and difficulty of the problem."[4] Rather than confront the DPRK directly, the Bush administration sought instead to bring international pressure to bear on Pyongyang through North Korea's friends by briefing the Soviets and the Chinese about the DPRK's nuclear program. When that failed, a similar brief was provided to South Korea and Japan, sparking a short flurry.

The flurry was brief, in part, because at the turn of the decade prospects for a thaw on the Korean peninsula appeared good. Kim Il Sung, the aged dictator who had ruled Korea for more than forty years, had objected to inspections by the International Atomic Energy Agency (IAEA) required by the NPT on the grounds that his country was threatened by the presence of American weapons in South Korea. The Bush administration undertook to meet that objection by removing all U.S. nuclear weapons from Korean soil, a fact announced by South Korean President Roh Tae Woo in December 1991. The American olive branch, coupled with pressure from China and the collapse of the Soviet Union, persuaded Pyongyang to seek to normalize relations with the South. Negotiations begun in October 1991 led to an "Agreement on Reconciliation, Nonaggression and Exchanges and Cooperation between the South and the North" signed in December 1991. This agreement went further than any previous attempt to bring peace to the divided peninsula. Although the DPRK refused to deal with its nuclear program in the agreement itself, moreover, it promised to work out a separate accord with the South addressing that issue.

Surprisingly, even that effort bore fruit. Negotiations on the nuclear issue began on December 26 at Panmunjom and concluded with an agreement on the last day of the year. Both sides promised not to "test, manufacture, produce, receive, possess, store, deploy or use nuclear weapons" or to "possess nuclear reprocessing and uranium enrichment facilities." They agreed to reciprocal inspections of each other's nuclear sites by a Joint Nuclear Control Commission. North Korea's reasonableness came at a price, however. The South agreed to cancel the 1992 Team Spirit exercises, an annual activity in which U.S. and South Korean forces practiced reinforcing southern defenses against a northern attack. The North had long objected to these exercises, seeing in the movement of U.S. troops, ships, and warplanes to South Korea a provocation. The United States went even further, however, arranging a direct meeting between State Department representatives and DPRK officials in New York in January 1992.[5]

A direct meeting between American and DPRK officials with no outsiders was unprecedented. Throughout the Cold War, American policy had been to eschew direct contacts with North Korea and to avoid even indirect contacts in which the South did not participate. The North Koreans, for their part, desperately wanted to develop direct relations with the United States and grasped at this break in precedent eagerly. The meeting helped seal agreement on what was apparently the last major sticking point.

Although North Korea had signed the NPT in 1985, it had still not executed an agreement with the IAEA providing for inspections of its nuclear sites at the end of 1991. A succession of IAEA errors and North Korean excuses had permitted this foot-dragging, but the issue came to be the central problem in North-South relations that threatened to delay or stop the promised improvement in relations. The cancellation of Team Spirit and the promise of direct U.S.–DPRK talks seems to have convinced Kim Il Sung that the time had come. The DPRK signed an agreement with the IAEA on January 30, ratifying it in April.[6]

The IAEA with which North Korea signed an inspections agreement in 1992, however, was not the same agency it had been in 1985 when the DPRK joined the Nonproliferation Treaty. Throughout the Cold War, the IAEA's inspection procedures had been relatively lax—so much so that the agency had given Iraq a clean bill of health before the Gulf War. The revelation at the end of that conflict that Iraq had a multibillion-dollar nuclear weapons research program spread out at sites dispersed throughout the country that the IAEA had totally missed was a humiliation for the agency. The IAEA responded: "In the face of withering criticism for ineffectiveness and timidity, the IAEA under Director General Hans Blix underwent an upheaval in personnel and a sea change in attitudes, from complacency to alertness about suspicious nuclear activities."[7] In 1991, Blix asserted the agency's right to conduct "special inspections" of suspect sites as well as to receive and act upon intelligence provided by member nations.

The Bush administration, eager to ensure that North Korea's deeds matched its words, began providing such intelligence in September 1991. U.S. satellite imagery, nuclear laboratories, and even "virtual reality" tours developed from aerial photographs were provided to Blix and his team prior to their first pre-inspection visit to the DPRK in May 1992. "Armed for the first time with extensive independent information about the nuclear programs that they were checking, the IAEA's leaders and its corps of international inspectors were determined not to be hoodwinked or embarrassed again. North Korea became the first test case of their new capabilities and attitudes."[8]

The sophistication and determination of the IAEA inspection teams caught the North Koreans quite by surprise. The DPRK had entered into its new relationship with the IAEA apparently honestly, reporting a nuclear program that in size and location closely matched what Western intelligence agencies suspected.[9] The North Koreans even reversed their previous claims that they were not interested in processing spent fuel by presenting Blix and his team with a vial containing ninety grams of plutonium. No doubt believing that they could fool the IAEA as Iraq had done, Pyongyang clearly sought to trade its seeming openness for Western benevolence, trade, and diplomatic relations.

The pre-inspection of Blix's team in May produced some evidence that all was not well. Blix noted that much of the nuclear program was housed in very deep underground bunkers that served to protect or hide it (or both) from Western eyes and weapons.[10] The first two sets of normal inspections, in June and July, produced increasing disquiet, but little concrete evidence of wrongdoing. As late as September 17, Blix reported that the IAEA's work in North Korea was "proceeding well" and according to schedule.[11]

Despite the apparent success of the IAEA's inspections, however, tensions had again begun to rise on the peninsula. Talks aimed at hammering out the details of the North-South nuclear agreement to permit short-notice inspections in both countries stalled. The DPRK officials began to complain that they were receiving no recompense for allowing the IAEA inspections to continue and to demand that they be allowed to inspect American military bases in the South. At the same time, North Korea strenuously objected to provisions proposed by the South that would have permitted inspections of suspect sites by the Joint Nuclear Control Commission at eight hours' notice.

It is tempting to argue that South Korea and the United States did not do enough to compensate North Korea for the loss of its secrecy, to argue that progress in North-South relations "came to a halt in the second half of 1992, in part because the United States and South Korea slowed the implementation of their highly successful diplomacy of the previous two years."[12] Furthermore,

A disturbing pattern had begun to emerge. North Korea appeared intent on delaying the North-South inspection regime and its threat of challenge inspections. And South Korea and the United States made this strategy possible, by refusing to rob North Korea of its excuses by allowing inspections of U.S. facilities in the South and taking other steps. In retrospect it is difficult to understand why Washington and Seoul did not move more energetically to defuse North Korean arguments about U.S. bases by simply opening them to outside inspection, as many U.S.

military officers had long agreed that this would pose no threat to security. But no such initiative was forthcoming.[13]

There were, in fact, two excellent reasons for not meeting North Korea's demands. The first, and most important, was that the DPRK should not have been insisting on compensation for inspections it was bound by treaty to permit. All signatories to the NPT avow that they will not pursue nuclear weapons programs and that they will permit inspections by the IAEA. This avowal is not contingent upon compensation by the international community but results from the good-faith assertion that the signatory is not pursuing nuclear weapons. From the first, however, the DPRK made it clear that it regarded its adherence to the terms of the NPT as contingent on the good behavior of the international community, specifically South Korea and the United States, and not something it was legally obligated to observe. Offering to compensate the DPRK for fulfilling its own obligations threatened to establish its unique position with regard to the NPT, something that the Bush administration was wisely unwilling to do.

The second reason for not paying Pyongyang off was that the demands made by the DPRK reflected efforts to delay and minimize inspections rather than rational objections that could be met. North Korea sought to delay the inspections and minimize their impact because, from the first, Pyongyang never intended to give up its nuclear weapons program. It was prepared to accept whatever compensation the West would offer, but it seems likely that new roadblocks and new demands would have followed each capitulation. For the IAEA quickly discovered that for all the apparent openness Pyongyang manifested in May and June 1992, the DPRK continued to lie about and conceal the extent of its nuclear program.

North Korea had not anticipated that the United States would place its highly sophisticated nuclear weapons laboratories at the disposal of the IAEA and was shocked when the third round of IAEA inspections in September uncovered its concealment. Using highly sophisticated procedures, the IAEA revealed that the plutonium sample the North Koreans had presented to Blix could not have been produced from the waste the inspectors saw, and that instead of the one instance of plutonium separation reported by Pyongyang, at least three separate instances could have occurred. This evidence was enough to convince the IAEA that "there must be some more plutonium . . . whether it is grams or kilograms, we don't know." The North Koreans rapidly became concerned:

North Korea grossly underestimated the agency's measurement capability. . . . They never expected us to be able to perform isotopic analyses. They could not understand this or explain the [test result] differences. The more they learned, the more they provided manufactured responses.

We had to approach them harder and harder as they realized we were going to discover their wrongdoings.[14]

The crisis was coming to a head. For the IAEA the issue was critical: "After its
disastrous performance in Iraq, the agency (and its leading members) was anx-
ious to show that it had teeth. As the primary international proliferation
watchdog group, the IAEA could not afford another major gaffe and still retain
any semblance of credibility."[15] The issue was no less critical for North Korea,
however, which faced either the collapse of any hope of international opening
and foreign aid or the loss of its nuclear program, which it seems to have held
very dear. The confrontation came quickly.

Alarmed by the North's delaying tactics and the ominous reports of the
IAEA, the United States and the Republic of Korea (ROK) announced in October that plans were proceeding for the 1993 Team Spirit exercise "in the absence of meaningful improvements in South-North relations, especially on
bilateral nuclear inspections."[16] At almost the same time, the South Korean intelligence agency reported that it had uncovered a vast North Korean spy
ring—the largest since 1948.[17] North Korea called the resumption of the Team
Spirit exercise a "criminal act" and the spy-ring charges a "preposterous fal-
sity." The DPRK promptly broke off all talks with South Korea, including the
negotiations over nuclear inspections, asserting that the Team Spirit announcement constituted "an act of provocation breaking the U.S. promise not to make
nuclear threats."[18] In November, IAEA officials in North Korea offered to allow
the DPRK to revise its original report on the status and location of its nuclear
programs so that it might save face. Pyongyang instead denounced the IAEA official as an "agent of the CIA" and refused to cooperate with the IAEA at all.

By the end of 1992 two "suspect sites" had come to figure prominently in
the IAEA's concerns about North Korea's nuclear weapons programs. U.S.
satellites had revealed not only an outdoor site located near the Yongbyon com-
pound and patterned after solid and liquid nuclear waste sites used near Soviet
and Iraqi facilities, but also that North Korean workers had been hard at work
covering that site with earth and landscaping it to conceal it from further observation. Another nearby site contained a large building that early satellite
passes had shown to consist of two floors. Later passes, however, revealed that
the North Koreans had covered the lower floor with earth and landscaping, and
inspectors who explored the building were unable to find any evidence of the
lower floor, which the North Koreans denied existed.[19]

Concerned by the discrepancies over the dates and amounts of plutonium
separated by the DPRK, Blix wasted no time in calling for "special inspections"
of these two "suspect sites"—the first such inspections ever demanded by the
IAEA—in December 1992. Recognizing the seriousness of the issue, the UN Security Council backed up the request by declaring itself "able to take punitive
action if IAEA inspection requests were ignored, saying that nuclear prolifera-

tion constitutes a threat to international peace and security. Thus North Korea was set to become the first test of the more vigorous international consensus against nuclear proliferation that had arisen in the wake of the discoveries about Iraq's nuclear program."[20]

The DPRK adamantly refused to allow the special inspections, claiming that the sites were "conventional military" facilities and the IAEA demand was "an unpardonable provocation aimed at infringing on and violating its sovereignty and dignity."[21] The Clinton administration, which had inherited this dangerous situation, initially kept up its predecessor's tough line. In February, the actual satellite photos that revealed the extent of North Korea's cheating were shown in closed session to the IAEA board. The board was deeply impressed. It resolved on February 25 that inspections of the suspect sites were "essential and urgent," and directed Director General Blix to report back on DPRK compliance within one month. The board offered this one-month grace period to palliate Chinese concerns, but noted that if the DPRK refused to cooperate, "it would take the issue to the Security Council for international sanctions or other actions."[22] The DPRK, naturally, refused utterly to cooperate.

It is easy to come to different conclusions about the causes of the crisis. Some argue:

> Apparently, the lessons of the previous year—that specific offers and incentives combined with a generally favorable negotiating climate had produced results—had faded from the memories of some South Korean and U.S. officials. Admittedly, evidence did emerge that the North was cheating, and North Korean officials showed little inclination to make major concessions in the North-South talks on denuclearization. At the same time, however, there may have been an opportunity to meet these setbacks with intensified diplomatic efforts and a slightly deepened embrace of the North, which would have represented a continuation of the previous year's successful diplomacy. As it was, U.S. and South Korean officials—particularly leaders in Seoul, feeling somewhat betrayed by the lack of progress in the JNCC talks—decided to reverse the diplomatic approach and revert to the old pattern of conveying messages through hard-line signals and threats.[23]

This view overlooks how high the stakes in this conflict were becoming. North Korea was increasingly trapped by the unexpected ramifications of its adherence to the NPT and its increasing isolation in the Post–Cold War world. For the international community, however, the test was even more important:

> By this time, the credibility and international standing of both the IAEA and North Korea were at risk, with the stakes very high for both sides. If the IAEA could not secure international backing for inspections when

there was evidence of cheating, its newly asserted authority could be defied with impunity, and the post-Iraq drive against nuclear weapons proliferation would be set back decisively. For Pyongyang, the danger was that this would be only the first of increasingly intrusive inspections it regarded as masterminded by hostile U.S. intelligence.[24]

Nonproliferation inspections will never be pleasant for the countries that are seeking to develop nuclear weapons (and even for those that have no such desires). Such states will always seek every opportunity to delay, lie, and fend off attempts at serious inspections of suspected sites. The crisis of 1993 was a critical test of the "teeth" of the inspection regime that would certainly be watched by all states interested in their own nuclear programs. Accommodating the North Koreans would establish the principle that a developing nuclear weapons program could be traded for international benefits. Failing to implement the inspection regime would establish the fact that nuclear weapons programs could be developed with impunity. The room for concessions by the West was extremely small.

Team Spirit 1993 was scheduled to begin on March 9. On March 8, Kim Jong Il, DPRK supreme military commander and heir apparent, placed North Korea on a war footing because of the exercise he described as a "nuclear war test aimed at a surprise, preemptive strike at the northern half of the country."

> Senior military officials, told that an attack might be imminent, were ordered to evacuate to underground fortifications. All military leaves were canceled, the heads of all soldiers were shaved, steel helmets were worn, and the troops were issued rifle ammunition. In Pyongyang armored cars were drawn up in rows near security headquarters and armed police checked military passes, while in the countryside the civilian population was mobilized to dig trenches near their homes as protection against air attack.[25]

The DPRK sought to use the war scare it thus created to justify its refusal to comply with IAEA demands, but Blix rejected all excuses. Facing this continuing demand for inspections it felt it could not allow, North Korea renounced its adherence to the NPT on March 12.

The renunciation of the NPT stunned the world—North Korea was the first state in the treaty's history to do so. The precedent thus set was alarming. Any NPT adherent that felt its nuclear secrets were about to be discovered could, first, stall and delay hoping for compensations and then, failing that, withdraw from the treaty without yielding its secrets. The treaty and the cause of nuclear nonproliferation could be upheld only by rigidly adhering to its requirements and strongly supporting the efforts of the IAEA to investigate suspicious activities. This policy has seemed to some to be "a narrow, legalistic interpretation of nonproliferation policy" that led directly to "stalemate, confrontation, and perpetual crisis on the peninsula."[26] In fact, it was the only meaningful conception of nonproliferation policy possible, and the stalemate, confrontation, and crisis resulted from North Korea's determination either to maintain its nuclear weapons program or to use it to blackmail the West into significant concessions. Any attempts to "see the situation from the DPRK's perspective" would lead inevitably to the demise of any effective nonproliferation regime. Considering the direct U.S. involvement in supporting that regime, moreover, both in Korea and in Iraq, backing off would result in considerable damage to America's prestige and credibility.

It should have been obvious in 1992 that a North Korean withdrawal from the NPT, or similar aggressive step, was conceivable and, at the same time, unacceptable. Long-range contingencies for dealing with such eventualities should have been developed and, perhaps, been implemented in their initial phases. The U.S. elections, however, prevented the development of long-term policy by the outgoing administration, while the incoming administration had no opportunity to consider its long-term goals before being thrust willy-nilly into the heart of the conflict. The DPRK's withdrawal from the NPT, therefore, caught the administration unaware and unprepared, and a scramble to develop reasonable options ensued.

Some in Seoul proposed a carrot-and-stick approach, threatening sanctions, severance of diplomatic relations, or even military action, on the one hand, while promising cancellation of Team Spirit exercises, increases in trade, security arrangements, and so forth on the other. The Joint Chiefs of Staff opposed such an approach:

> "Under no circumstances should you engage [the North Koreans] in negotiations. You should not reward them. You should punish them," recalled a State Department official. But the official added, "As soon as you said, 'How do you mean, punish them?' of course the JCS would back away from any military options."[27]

In Seoul even the Defense Ministry opposed the use of military action at that stage, warning that a "surgical strike" against the reactors at Yongbyon would produce full-scale war on the peninsula. "Negotiations quickly emerged as the consensus solution in Washington, not because they appeared to be promising, but because nobody could come up with another feasible plan to head off a crisis in Northeast Asia."

The American effort to avoid conflict followed two tracks. To deal with the IAEA's pressure for a stronger, more confrontational stance, the Clinton administration proposed insisting upon the maintenance of "continuity of safeguards"—allowing IAEA officials to change films and batteries in monitors at North Korean sites—rather than insisting on the inspections Blix demanded.

The administration also chose to reopen a direct dialogue with Pyongyang, accepting de facto Pyongyang's assertion that the crisis "was not a matter to be discussed in the UN arena but a problem that should be resolved through negotiation between the DPRK and the U.S."[28]

It appears that the decision to separate American policy from the IAEA was taken deliberately. William Perry, who was Deputy Secretary of Defense in 1993 and Secretary of Defense in 1994, writes, "Initially the U.S. government supported the IAEA position. But beginning in 1993 some in the Pentagon . . . began to have their doubts." The IAEA's position, they felt, "might be consistent with the NPT and IAEA procedures, but from the point of view of security for our troops in Korea and our allies in the region, it demanded both too little and too much of North Korea." Mere inspections were not enough, after all, to guarantee America's security—the North Korean nuclear program should be eliminated. On the other hand, "the special inspections only reinforced the North Koreans' belief that they were being singled out by the IAEA for discriminatory treatment, while offering little security benefit." Les Aspin and Perry then began to argue that the United States "should switch from the IAEA position to a new position emphasizing a demand that North Korea freeze all of its future nuclear operations but deferring 'special' inspections of past operations." Since it seemed clear that North Korea was determined to turn its conflict with the IAEA into one with the United States, "it was important, we argued, that the United States have its own policy, supportive of but independent of the IAEA."[29]

This decision, which led to meetings between North Korean and American officials in June, marked the first serious split between Washington and the IAEA. It is eerily reminiscent of England's decision to accept Mussolini's arguments that the Corfu crisis was not suitable for discussion in the League of Nations, where his supporters would have had a hard time controlling the debate, but must be addressed by the Conference of Ambassadors, where the crisis could be more conveniently shelved. In the process, England had severely damaged the credibility of the League of Nations, upon which it sought to rely to guarantee international peace and security. The abandonment of the IAEA, upon which the United States sought to rely to guarantee its security from the widespread proliferation of weapons of mass destruction, ran similar risks.

Unlike the League of Nations, which accepted its defeat gracefully, the IAEA continued to fight. It recognized that its credibility relied upon the strict enforcement of the NPT, especially in places like North Korea that sought to hedge and fudge. The IAEA, moreover, held the upper hand. At any moment it could declare that "continuity of safeguards" had been lost, thereby triggering the international crisis the Clinton administration now increasingly sought to avoid. But the IAEA, in the end, was no stronger than Washington's will to oppose Pyongyang. Nonproliferation was hostage to America's desire to avoid war at almost all costs.

Under the terms of the Nonproliferation Treaty, member states could withdraw but only after a ninety-day waiting period, which was up on June 12. As the IAEA continued to press Pyongyang to allow inspections and the North Koreans continued to insist that their announced withdrawal placed them in a "special status" immune to such inspections, Washington prepared to negotiate. On June 2, ten days before the ninety-day waiting period was up, Robert Gallucci, Assistant Secretary of State for Politico-Military Affairs, met with the North Korean Deputy Foreign Minister, Kang Sok Ju, in New York. By June 11, the day before North Korea's withdrawal from the NPT would take effect, they had worked out a joint statement. In return for a North Korean announcement that it would suspend its withdrawal from the NPT "for as long as it considers necessary," Washington gave the DPRK assurances that it would not "'use armed forces, including nuclear weapons, nor threaten' such use against the North" and agreed to continue a bilateral dialogue with Pyongyang.[30] The announcement appeared to defuse the crisis, although the underlying conflict arising from Pyongyang's unwillingness to abide by the terms of the NPT and its agreements with the IAEA remained. Like the decision to remove the Corfu issue from the purview of the League of Nations, however, the joint statement had a significance beyond its content:

> For the North Koreans, a joint statement with the United States was an achievement of immense importance. A year earlier, at the end of the Kanter–Kim Yong Sun talk, the Bush administration had refused to issue such a document. Even though vague in many respects, the joint statement this time was of great symbolic value to the Foreign Ministry and to others in Pyongyang who were arguing for making a serious effort to bargain with the Americans on the nuclear program. Even if it had only described the weather in New York, the statement would have been tangible evidence that the United States had recognized the legitimacy of North Korea and was willing to negotiate. By raising the stakes with its nuclear program, North Korea suddenly had become important to the United States. . . . If North Korea's objective had been to seize the attention of Washington and force it to negotiate seriously on a bilateral basis, its strategy had succeeded brilliantly.[31]

It was becoming clear that North Korea held a winning hand. In exchange for a return to the unacceptable situation before the announcement of North Korea's intention to withdraw from the NPT, the Clinton administration had made important concessions. In the continuing DPRK–U.S. discussions, therefore, Pyongyang was encouraged to raise the bidding even higher.

In a July meeting, Kang proposed to Gallucci that if the West provided light water reactors, not suitable for building nuclear weapons, to North Korea, then North Korea would abandon its graphite reactors (and, by implication, its nuclear program). In a formal statement, Gallucci responded that "the United States would 'support the introduction of LWRs and . . . explore with the DPRK ways in which LWRs could be obtained,' but only as part of a 'final resolution' of nuclear issues."[32] October saw an even more aggressive move by Pyongyang. North Korea offered a package deal to resolve the whole situation, and included in that deal not only the nuclear issue, but the whole Korean security problem. In exchange for remaining in the NPT, submitting to regular IAEA inspections, and "discussing" the special inspections, Pyongyang demanded a permanent end to the Team Spirit exercises, the lifting of American economic sanctions, and the convening of yet another round of direct talks.[33] This proposal was too obvious and too bold. The IAEA, moreover, was not yet willing to throw in its hand.

It had never accepted the minimalist notion of "continuity of safeguards," and, with Pyongyang's withdrawal from the NPT in abeyance, it insisted on implementing the full range of verification measures, including the special inspections. One observer argues, "To have worked so painfully throughout the spring of 1993 to avoid a North Korean rejection of the NPT only to have the IAEA return to the very demand that had sparked the crisis in the first place seemed hardly logical."[34] The reverse, however, is true. In order to avoid implementing the inspections it was bound to allow as a signatory to the NPT, North Korea had manufactured a series of crises, relying on the unwillingness of the West to impose its desires by force. With the last crisis apparently settled by Western concessions in other areas, it was only natural that the IAEA should seek to get on with its job of ensuring that nuclear weapons did not proliferate. Since nothing had been done to alleviate Blix's suspicions about the two "suspect sites," moreover, it made sense for him to continue to insist on special inspections. And since, finally, North Korea either had secrets to hide or wished to appear that it had secrets to hide in order to enhance its bargaining position, the demand for special inspections continued to be an insuperable obstacle to ending the crisis.

Director General Blix presented a report to the UN General Assembly on November 1. He could not have been unaware of Washington's desire to avoid confrontation: "While no U.S. official had directly discouraged Blix from declaring the continuity of inspections broken, Assistant Secretary Gallucci and others did make clear the difficulty of the U.S. position and the potential consequences of an unambiguous statement in that direction."[35] Blix, therefore, made a strong report to the General Assembly, stopping short of declaring the loss of "continuity of safeguards." The result was a vote of 140 to 1 urging the DPRK "to cooperate immediately" with the IAEA. Only Pyongyang dissented; China abstained.[36]

An air of crisis lingered in Washington, Seoul, and Pyongyang. Les Aspin made a series of unguarded and probably unwise remarks indicating that war on the Korean peninsula was dangerously near. Columns and editorials argued that the time for talking had passed and the time for action was near. Clinton himself added to the crisis environment by declaring that "North Korea cannot be allowed to develop a nuclear bomb" despite the fact that his administration estimated that Pyongyang could already possess a bomb. Some weeks later Aspin "corrected" the President's statement, asserting that North Korea could not be allowed to become a nuclear power, implying that its possession of a nuclear bomb or two might be acceptable.[37]

In response to Pyongyang's "package deal," Washington put its own package on the table. On November 15, the Clinton administration proposed a two-phased agreement. In phase one, North Korea would allow regular IAEA inspections and would renew its dialogue with the South. In return, the 1994 Team Spirit exercise would be canceled and another round of direct U.S.–DPRK talks convened. In phase two, IAEA inspections of the two disputed sites would be permitted while the United States would offer diplomatic recognition, trade, and investment concessions to Pyongyang. The rewards for Kim Il Sung's continued intransigence grew dramatically.[38] But Clinton could not control either his allies or his own media sufficiently to maintain such a deal.

On January 26, 1994, the *New York Times* reported that the United States was sending reinforcements to South Korea, including Patriot antimissile batteries.

> Deploying the Patriots had been under consideration since December, when they had been requested by the United States military commander in Korea, General Gary Luck, as a precautionary measure in case war broke out and North Korean Rodong missiles were fired against American military targets. Luck's December request had been temporarily shelved because of State Department objections that the deployments could upset the negotiations with North Korea over resuming the international inspections. But when Michael Gordon, the *Times* Pentagon correspondent, made a reporting trip to the South and returned with information about the potential Patriot deployment, "The White House went into a panic," Gordon recalled later. Fearful that the administration would be charged with withholding vital military equipment from American troops—as had been the case when a U.S. peacekeeping unit had been overwhelmed in Somalia the previous October—the White House immediately began briefing members of Congress on the Patriot request, and National Security Adviser Anthony Lake telephoned Gordon to tell him that Luck's request was in the process of being approved—giving rise to an exclusive story in the *Times*.[39]

Even as word of the Patriot deployments hit Pyongyang, however, the South Korean Defense Ministry announced plans to hold the 1994 Team Spirit exercise. The South Koreans had been becoming increasingly alarmed by the solidifying direct U.S.–DPRK relationship. Some in South Korea felt that America was cutting them out and would strike a deal with the North that would not adequately protect South Korea's interests. Others were angered that South Korea had renounced its nuclear reprocessing capabilities in order to gain concessions from the North that did not appear to be forthcoming. In attempting to give ground to Pyongyang, Washington had not reckoned on the chips its allies had to play.

Nor had the IAEA abandoned its efforts. As the North threatened to respond to the "new war maneuvers the United States has been pursuing behind the screen of the DPRK–USA talks," the IAEA declared that February 21 was its deadline for inspecting the Yongbyon sites. "Unless an agreement could be reached by then, the international agency said, it would turn the stalemate over to the UN Security Council for action."[40] The United States had no alternative but to begin informal discussions with the other permanent members of the Security Council about sanctions, while the Pentagon prepared to send a thousand additional troops to the South as part of Team Spirit. North Korea, warning that it would consider sanctions of any sort an act of war, continued to drag its feet, agreeing to accept the IAEA inspectors, but refusing to grant them visas.

The deadline came and went amid bickering, but more DPRK–U.S. negotiations in New York on February 25 seemed to produce the necessary breakthrough. On March 1, the IAEA was to be allowed to return to Yongbyon to ensure "continuity of safeguards," the North-South dialogue was to be resumed, the 1994 Team Spirit exercise was to be canceled, and the United States and North Korea were to announce the third round of high-level talks to begin on March 21.[41]

The agreement broke down almost immediately. The North-South talks went nowhere, and North Korea began to denounce America's insistence on them as a precursor to direct U.S.–DPRK talks. Worse still, the North Koreans continued to impede the IAEA inspectors, preventing them from doing anything more than change batteries and film in monitoring equipment. Despite the fact that Pyongyang had agreed to allow the inspectors to carry out radiation sweeps throughout the Yongbyon facility and to enter the reprocessing plant, the DPRK barred them from doing so. Even as the inspectors were being hindered in their tasks, moreover, Pyongyang attempted to negotiate with the United States, offering to allow full inspections in exchange for South Korean concessions during the talks. America and South Korea refused, the inspectors were not allowed to inspect, and North Korea stormed out of the North-South negotiations.[42]

American officials, diplomatic and military, felt that war was near at hand:

> For Robert Gallucci, the spring of 1994 had an eerie and disturbing resemblance to historian Barbara Tuchman's account of "the guns of Au-

gust," when in summer 1914, World War I began in cross-purposes, mis-understanding, and inadvertence. As he and other policy makers moved inexorably toward a confrontation with North Korea, Gallucci was conscious that "this had an escalatory quality, that could deteriorate not only into a war but into a big war." Secretary of Defense William Perry, looking back on the events, concluded that the course he was on "had a real risk of war associated with it." Commanders in the field were even more convinced. Lieutenant General Howell Estes, the senior U.S. Air Force officer in Korea, recalled later that although neither he nor other commanders said so out loud, not even in private conversations with one another, "inside we all thought we were going to war."[43]

War appeared likely after March 15, when the IAEA, frustrated beyond bearing, ordered its inspectors home and announced that it "could not verify that there had been no diversion of nuclear materials to bomb production." The IAEA board voted to turn the issue over to the UN Security Council for action. The United States began consulting Seoul about planning for the Team Spirit exercise, began negotiating with other Security Council permanent members regarding sanctions, and canceled the third round of U.S.–DPRK talks.[44] The crisis was at hand—it would only get worse.

The North Koreans made it clear to the inspectors that they intended to "refuel" the reactor very shortly. During the refueling process, the spent fuel rods in the reactor would be removed and fresh rods inserted. The spent fuel rods, however, contained plutonium as a natural by-product of their reactions, perhaps enough plutonium for five or six nuclear bombs, according to Perry.[45] The IAEA insisted that it was critical not only that it be allowed to supervise the defueling, or removal of the rods, from the reactor, but that it be allowed to segregate those rods and test them to determine the history of the reactor. In this way, the IAEA could determine whether plutonium had already been diverted from the core, in addition to preventing further such diversions. Needless to say, the DPRK refused to allow such sampling, although it offered to allow IAEA inspectors to watch the refueling process.

The United States had made it clear to North Korea that a failure to comply with IAEA demands regarding refueling the reactor would terminate U.S.–DPRK talks, but "a U.S. official familiar with the contents of the meetings said, 'We didn't lay down with great force and clarity that this was a drop-dead issue.' " Worse still, "most of the U.S.–North Korean discussion before the spring of 1994 had been about the refueling of the reactor, not about defueling, or unloading the current stock of irradiated fuel rods. 'If North Korea understood, they chose to ignore it.' "[46]

The IAEA, for its part, refused to send inspectors at all if North Korea would not meet its demands. Washington supported the IAEA, but only extremely reluctantly. Gallucci described the IAEA's workings as "medieval or perhaps Talmudic, depending on what religious metaphor you use." A Department of Defense official referred to Blix as a " 'fanatic' who was single-mindedly protecting his agency with little thought for the overall consequences." A former ambassador to Korea called the inspectors "a bunch of eager proctologists, making painful inquiries without holding out any benefits to North Korea."[47]

It was not the IAEA that could not see the big picture, however, but, increasingly, the Clinton administration. Fixated by the danger of war in Korea, many U.S. officials seem to have seen the IAEA's demands as bargaining positions to be traded, bringing North Korean concessions that would end the crisis. The IAEA, however, saw its demands as the minimum necessary to do its job of preventing North Korea and other states from acquiring any nuclear weapons. By abandoning the IAEA's determination to hold special inspections, the Clinton administration was tacitly agreeing to allow Pyongyang to keep whatever weapons-grade plutonium it might already have hidden away. It was agreeing, therefore, to allow Pyongyang to maintain a very small stockpile of nuclear weapons, if Pyongyang could complete their development. How many such weapons could the North Koreans have hidden? Three, four, or five? In the next iteration of such a crisis, either with Pyongyang or with some other rogue state, how many weapons could be hidden before the crisis came? Ten or twenty? If the United States was serious about preventing the proliferation of nuclear weapons, then it should have supported the IAEA's positions without argument. As time went on, however, the United States became increasingly less serious about nonproliferation as it had to face ever more seriously the real danger of war and its consequences.

On May 18, 1994, Secretary of Defense Perry asked Chairman of the Joint Chiefs of Staff General Shalikashvili and the commander of U.S. forces in Korea, General Luck, to describe for him a contingency plan to destroy the Yongbyon facilities. He writes:

> The plan for an attack on the reactor site had been presented to a small, grim group seated around the conference table in my office. The plan was impressive; it could be executed with only a few days' alert, and it would entail little or no risk of U.S. casualties during the attack. Additionally, it had been designed so that it entailed a low risk of North Korean casualties and a very low risk of radiation release into the atmosphere. The North Koreans, of course, could have rebuilt the facilities destroyed by the attack, but without question it would have achieved its objective of setting back their nuclear program many years.

The United States did not attack the Yongbyon nuclear facility, however, because

General Shalikashvili and I had concluded that such an attack was very likely to incite the North Koreans to launch a military attack on South Korea. Even though the North Koreans would surely lose this second Korean War, they could cause hundreds of thousands, perhaps millions of casualties before being defeated. Therefore, I decided against recommending this option to the president at that time.[48]

Perry does not report that he, Shalikashvili, and Luck presented the results of their meeting to President Clinton at the White House the next day. There, they warned that war in Korea would cost 52,000 U.S. casualties and 490,000 South Korean casualties in the first ninety days, as well as $61 billion, of which the United States would receive very little back from its allies.[49] "To the surprise of most journalists and experts who had been following the crisis—but who did not know about the nature or conclusions of the military meetings—the administration suddenly veered back toward diplomatic efforts, offering to convene its long-postponed third round of high-level negotiations with Pyongyang despite the unloading of the nuclear reactor."

Despite the continuing refusal of Pyongyang to allow the IAEA to supervise the defueling of the reactor, in fact, Washington was quick to seize on the one positive aspect of the crisis—the IAEA inspectors, allowed to return in May to Yongbyon, announced that they could ensure that continuity of safeguards had been maintained. Despite the fact that "for some time U.S. officials had made very clear that one North Korean action in particular would automatically trigger a drive for sanctions: the unsupervised refueling of the main Yongbyon reactor," the Clinton administration offered to resume the U.S.–DPRK high-level negotiations on May 20, the day after Luck, Perry, and Shalikashvili had briefed the President on the costs of a new Korean war.

Despite Washington's desire for agreement, however, the situation soon threatened to spiral out of control once again. The North Koreans managed to defuel their reactor much faster than anyone had anticipated, and conducted the process in such a way, furthermore, as to ensure that it would be impossible to reconstruct the past history of the reactor. On June 2, therefore, the IAEA issued a statement that "its ability to verify the reactor's past history had been 'lost.'" Blix said, "'All important parts of the core' had been unloaded. . . . The situation, he declared, is 'irreversible.'"[50] Fear of triggering a North Korean attack by taking out the Yongbyon reactor stayed Clinton's hand militarily. It was left to seek UN sanctions against North Korea, which he did, even though that option, too, ran the risk of goading North Korea into war. But what would war mean?

On June 14, Perry once again called a meeting with General Luck, the Joint Chiefs, and the commanders of U.S. forces in the Pacific and the Persian Gulf to develop a series of options for addressing not only war in Korea but how to meet America's security requirements in the Persian Gulf at the same time. General Luck's estimates at that meeting were even more pessimistic: that there would be a million people dead, of whom 80,000 to 100,000 would be Americans, that the operation would cost more than $100 billion, and that property destruction would amount to $1 trillion. "The extent of the death and destruction, in the American calculus, would depend to a great degree on the speed with which a counterattack could be mounted by U.S. reinforcements called for in the war plan."[51]

The meeting drew up three options for dealing with the immediate crisis. Option one would send an additional 2,000 troops to Korea that could support the introduction of larger reinforcements. Option two would increase the amount of combat airpower in Korea, add another carrier battle group, and send 10,000 troops to the South to augment the 37,000 already there. Option three added an even more significant reinforcement of the ground forces available in South Korea. "Even this option did not provide enough U.S. forces to fight a general war on the peninsula—Operation Plan 5027 [for war in Korea] reportedly called for more than 400,000 reinforcements to do that."[52] Perry and the Joint Chiefs favored option two: "Perry hoped that such a dramatic increase in American forces would combine more serious preparations for war with an element of additional deterrence, highly visible to the North Koreans."

Perry describes the war plan discussions with great confidence, in retrospect:

> Our review of General Luck's plans took two long days and resulted in some modifications. In particular, we wanted the plan to fully reflect that nuclear weapons were not the only weapons of mass destruction that North Korea had been working on. They clearly had chemical weapons, and their interest in biological weapons and ballistic missiles was also evident. . . . As for the one or two nuclear weapons that North Korea might conceivably have built with the plutonium from the first few fuel rods, Luck concluded that although North Korea could use them to add to the carnage of the war, they would not change the eventual result, namely, the defeat of North Korea.

This happy conclusion ignores the fact that it was the threat of that carnage, rather than a fear of failing to defeat North Korea, that consistently stayed the President's hand. Perry continues:

> With these modifications, we concluded that we could deal with any contingency that the North Koreans could present us and still not be vulnerable to an opportunistic "second front" started by Iraq. In short, in a few

days we had updated the plans for fighting two major regional contingencies. . . . I decided to submit the modified contingency plans immediately to the president for his review and approval, along with my
recommendation in support of General Shalikashvili's request for a large,
immediate increase in our forces deployed in Korea.[53]

It is amazing how focusing on the minute details of military operations can divert the attention of strategic planners away from reality. No one doubted that
the United States and the ROK would defeat North Korea, nor that America
would prevent Iraq from attacking Kuwait or Saudi Arabia at the same time.
American victory, in 1994, was never in doubt. The question at all times was
"How much would it cost?" The answer to that question was always "Far too
much." And so the Clinton administration regularly sought to avoid military
confrontation, even when diplomacy was clearly failing.

It is hard to see how the plan adopted in mid-June could be regarded as an
adequate 2-MRC plan. Discussions surrounding the 2-MRC concept during
Aspin's tenure had made it clear that even if the forces for dealing with both
contingencies were available, which seemed unlikely, there was barely enough
airlift and sealift necessary for moving them all to one contingency, let alone
two nearly simultaneously. No details, furthermore, are available about the
composition of the 400,000 reinforcements required to win a Korean war, but
we should note that as of January 1994 there were 540,000 soldiers in the U.S.
Army, total.[54] It is not at all clear how much force a full-scale Korean war
would have left for a simultaneous Iraqi attack.

Perry's confidence appears to be misplaced for yet another reason: there is
evidence that the North Koreans would not have waited tamely for America to
build up its massive forces. Perry himself admitted:

We saw the development on the one hand as being provocative. That was
the downside. On the other side, we saw it as demonstrating a seriousness of purpose. . . . We didn't know enough about the Korean mentality
to know how to gauge the negative aspects versus the positive aspects of
the signal we were sending. Therefore, I chose in my own thinking to set
that signal aside, not knowing how to assess it, and recognizing we could
have either of these two possibilities.[55]

Other American military officials felt that they did know enough about the Korean mentality to fear the worst:

"I always got this feeling that the North Koreans studied [the Gulf War]
more than we did almost," said a general with access to all available in-

telligence. "And they learned one thing: you don't let the United States build up its forces and then let them go to war against you. . . . So I always felt that the North Koreans were never going to let us do a large buildup. They would see their window of opportunity closing, and they would come." Adding to this officer's apprehension was a chilling fact not well known outside the U.S. Command: at Panmunjom in May, a North Korean colonel told a U.S. officer: "We are not going to let you do a buildup."[56]

It does not appear that the contingency plans accepted in June were prepared for a full-scale North Korean preemptive attack, something that seemed quite likely to officers on the scene. Perhaps an American defeat on the peninsula was not entirely out of the question.

The issue never came to the test. Former President Jimmy Carter, who had become increasingly concerned as the crisis appeared to move to war, sought and received permission from the Clinton administration to travel to Pyongyang for a direct meeting with Kim Il Sung. He was briefed by Gallucci and others on the situation and was determined, even at that late hour, to bring peace to the peninsula. And so he did. Even as Perry, Shalikashvili, and the other military leaders were briefing the President about the three options available to him, Carter called the White House to inform Clinton that Kim Il Sung had agreed to freeze North Korea's nuclear program and to allow the last of the remaining IAEA inspectors to stay at Yongbyon. In return, he had assured Kim that he would press Clinton to convene the third round of high-level U.S.–DPRK talks. He also informed Gallucci that he intended to announce his "breakthrough" to the world in a few minutes through an interview with CNN.[57]

Carter announced dramatically that in "fairly definitive and important discussions with President Kim Il Sung," Kim "committed himself to maintain the [IAEA] inspectors on site in the disputed nuclear reactor position and also to guarantee that surveillance equipment would stay in good operating order . . . [s]o long as good faith efforts are being made jointly between the United States and North Korea to resolve the entire nuclear problem." Asked whether there was any agreement about permitting inspections of the two disputed sites, Carter responded, "Well, the commitment that I have received is that all aspects of North Korea's nuclear program would be resolved through good faith talks, but not just unilaterally or letting them look back at these old sites that were created before North Korea joined the non-proliferation treaty. . . . But that particularly sensitive item would have to come as a result of very careful and very mutually trustworthy discussions between the United States and North Korea." Carter misspoke—the Yongbyon facilities under dispute were constructed in the late 1980s, after Pyongyang had joined the NPT. Carter also represented

Pyongyang's willingness to "discuss" the special inspections as a new break-through, which it was not. It became clear, in fact, that Carter's "deal" amounted to this: in return for Western help in obtaining light water reactors, Pyongyang would agree to negotiate directly with Washington, but not with the IAEA, about the outstanding issues, including the special inspections that had sparked the crisis. It was not much of a deal at all.[58]

The White House was not overjoyed. Feeling that it had been upstaged by Carter and that there was little new in the deal he offered, the administration insisted on raising the ante. In addition to what Pyongyang had offered, the White House insisted that a freeze on the North Korean nuclear program remain in effect for the duration of the talks, specifically forbidding North Korea to refuel and restart the Yongbyon reactor or to reprocess the fuel rods that had been removed. Carter was aghast, fearing that these demands would break his "deal," but he had underestimated how much Pyongyang wanted to end the conflict on such satisfactory terms. Kim Il Sung accepted Washington's terms in short order.[59]

The Carter deal and the White House's response formed the basis of the Agreed Framework between the United States and the DPRK signed on October 21, 1994. In the Agreed Framework, North Korea pledged to remain a member of the Nonproliferation Treaty (although not of the IAEA), to freeze its nuclear program and, "eventually," dismantle it, to forgo reprocessing of its spent fuel, and to allow implementation of its IAEA safeguards agreement. The construction of the two larger graphite reactors near Yongbyon would be halted; the reprocessing facility would be sealed. In return, it would receive two light water reactors from the West. With regard to the IAEA's inspections of the suspect sites and attempts to determine whether or not North Korea had hidden away any plutonium, those issues were put off into the future: the DPRK was obliged by the Agreed Framework to satisfy the IAEA on those points only before the delivery of "significant nuclear components of the first LWR to be constructed in North Korea." "If the LWR project is to proceed beyond that point, special inspections must be conducted if requested by the IAEA."

In addition to the two LWR reactors, to be furnished by South Korea and Japan through a Korean Energy Development Organization directed by the United States, North Korea was also to receive "500,000 tons of heavy fuel annually for use in a specific power plant" in order "to compensate the DPRK for loss of energy production" from abandoning its graphite reactors. In addition, the liaison offices would be established in Pyongyang and Washington that would "open a channel to deal with other issues that concern us." "There is also a commitment on the part of the U.S. and DPRK to move to full diplomatic relations at the ambassadorial level as other issues of concern are resolved. . . . We plan to reduce economic and financial restrictions selectively on U.S. citizens' dealings with the DPRK, in close consultation with the congress." The

United States also restated its pledge not to use nuclear weapons against the DPRK as long as it remained a member of the NPT regime.[60]

Just taken on its own merits, this deal was a breathtaking accomplishment for North Korea. From being a pariah state with which the United States scorned to have any relations at all, North Korea had become the focus of attention in Washington for months, and had received the promise of expensive nuclear technology, fuel deliveries, trade benefits, and even the long-coveted diplomatic relations with the United States. The hateful IAEA had been cut out of the deal almost completely, since the United States had agreed, in the end, that Korea's nuclear program was not a matter fit to be discussed in the international arena but one that should be dealt with on a bilateral basis. North Korea's threat to develop a nuclear weapons program, the reality of which remains, to this day, unclear, proved an extremely powerful bargaining chip with which to break out of the isolation and irrelevance into which the end of the Cold War had plunged this most recalcitrant of communist dictatorships. The Clinton administration had demonstrated to all who might be watching that a powerful armed force, a willingness to use it, and the threat of a developing WMD program, whether or not it was real, could buy a trapped and disintegrating nation a very great deal.

But that is just taking the agreement on its own merits, something, it appears, the North Koreans had no intention of doing. Since the 1994 agreement the IAEA has been allowed to monitor the Yongbyon sites, on the whole, with minimal interference from the North Koreans. Any efforts, however, to verify North Korea's original declarations regarding the extent of its nuclear program and the amount of plutonium it might have separated have been brushed aside. In August 1998, moreover, North Korea launched a multistage ballistic missile over the main island of Japan. It appears logical to many that such an aggressively pursued ballistic missile program must be accompanied by a renewed nuclear weapons program. As of this writing, reports circulate freely that there is, indeed, a renewed nuclear weapons program in the works, deep in newly dug underground bunkers. In recent exchanges the North Koreans have shown every indication that they are up to their old games—in early 1999 they offered to allow the United States to inspect one site, if the United States paid for the privilege in hard currency and food aid. Whatever the truth of the current rumors, one thing is clear. The Agreed Framework froze the nuclear program that the United States could see then, although it effectively put off indefinitely the important question of determining exactly how much plutonium the North Koreans might have separated. The IAEA inspectors, however, are highly constrained in their activities, and the North Koreans seem determined to continue to insist on compensation for any openness regarding their program. Considering the tight, centralized control the Kim Jong Il regime exercises over the country and the miles of underground facilities already dug for conventional military purposes, to say nothing of new construction, for which there is some current evidence, it is impossible to say that the Agreed Framework has ended the North Korean nuclear threat. At best, it has delayed or postponed it for some years.

It seems clear that North Korea continues to have a nuclear program today and that the cause of international nonproliferation has been dealt a serious blow in large part because of American military weakness in 1994. The forces deployed in South Korea itself were quite clearly inadequate by themselves to halt a Northern attack. The happy picture painted first by Aspin and then by Perry that a DPRK attack would be crushed by overwhelming U.S. airpower also appears to have been mythical. Since the notion that Korea can be easily handled by forces, particularly air forces, available under the notional 2-MRC policy remains a key assumption of U.S. strategy, this assertion requires some justification. One cannot, of course, prove that a given force is or is not adequate to a military task without putting it to the test. But the facts are quite clear. In 1994 the Clinton administration contemplated actions that might lead to a North Korean attack several times. Each time senior military advisers, including the commander on the spot, outlined what the costs and risks of those options would be. Each time the administration was driven by that analysis to accept less than its policy called for. Whether or not the forces available to the commander of U.S. forces in Korea were adequate to achieve ultimate victory on the peninsula, they were very clearly inadequate to avoid the self-deterrence that results from a perception of danger.

The experience of the Korean crisis made clear, as General Luck realized explicitly, that in the face of an armed and ready enemy the United States cannot expect to be able to reinforce its positions in the leisurely fashion that suited the circumstances of the Gulf War. That fact leaves open only two options: be strong enough on the ground before hostilities are contemplated to deter action, or be able to reinforce to overwhelming strength so rapidly that the enemy's defeat at an acceptable cost to the United States and its allies is ensured. It was clear from the experience of 1994 that the American armed forces then in being were inadequate for this purpose, and it should have been clear that that inadequacy had led to a major foreign policy setback, the full effects of which have yet to be felt. But those armed forces were still in the process of cutting down. The North Korean crisis did not delay that drawdown. The first lesson of 1994 went unheeded, and, five years later, it remained unlearned.

American reactions to North Korean threats resembled those of the British to the menace posed by Mussolini's Italy, first at Corfu in 1923 and then in regard to Ethiopia in 1936. In each case a smaller power violated the rules on international order to achieve its ends and avoided punishment by the world-class power. The great power, stretched to the limit by its refusal to provide military forces strong enough to meet its world responsibilities, flinched for fear that the lesser power might launch a "mad dog act" and turned to appeasement rather than risk a confrontation. In the earlier instances, British hesitation undermined Britain's international reputation and that of the world order that was meant to preserve peace. Soon, it encouraged even more dangerous threateners of the peace and order of the world who, in turn, soon brought on a great war. In the later instance, the story is yet to be told.

17

Another Versailles

The Clinton administration inherited yet another dangerous legacy from its predecessor. With the 1920s in mind, the peace the victorious coalition imposed on Iraq in 1991 bears a troubling similarity to the peace imposed on the Germans in 1919. Its terms were harsh enough to engender resentment, hatred, and the desire for revenge in the hearts of Iraqis without providing a satisfactory long-term defense against a revived Iraq. The complicated and detailed terms of that peace, spelled out in numerous UN Security Council resolutions, virtually ensured years of conflict during which Iraq would repeatedly violate provisions—violations small enough in themselves not to merit serious military action but significant enough, taken together, to undermine the security of the peace. The fatal flaw of the peace of 1991, like that of 1919, was less that it was too harsh or too soft, but that it was too difficult to enforce and did not address the fundamental problems of the region. Since imposing that peace on Iraq and the world, the United States has been more willing than England was to use force to enforce its terms (although less willing than France), but no more successful in maintaining either the credibility of the peace or the integrity of the coalition essential for its long-term survival.

The Peace Terms Compared

Both in 1919 and 1991, the victorious forces had not overrun the defeated country, had not seized the defeated capital, and had not destroyed the entire enemy army. In both cases, the key decision makers feared the "chaos" that would follow such a total victory far more than the more remote danger of a revived threat emanating from the old enemy. The absence of a complete military occupation of Germany and Iraq and of the complete destruction of their armies meant that there were limits to the strategic effectiveness of the peace. Attempts to impose terms harsher than the defeated people found tolerable or to enforce the terms agreed to were met by resistance and threats of renewed conflict. The determination to maintain the territorial integrity of the defeated states rendered the victors captive to the instability of the vanquished—military operations by the Germans and the Iraqis conducted to suppress minority uprisings in violation of the peace terms were, in the end, permitted in both cases, and they had to be, in light of the victors' unwillingness to allow the breakup of the German and Iraqi states. That unwillingness, however, ensured that both Germany and Iraq would retain their considerable capacity for regional domination over the long term and that they would be major players in the regional balance far into the future, regardless of the character of their regimes and the dangers they posed.

In both cases the victors tried to use the terms they imposed to eliminate the threats posed by the defeated powers in the near future, while seeking ways to change the nature of the defeated regimes so as to bring them back into the community of nations, thereby eliminating the long-term threat. The terms were harsh in demanding unilateral disarmament, especially in weapons thought to be particularly lethal and useful for regional aggression, and in economic sanctions and financial punishments designed to keep the defeated powers economically, and therefore militarily, weakened for a considerable time. The long-term hope rested on peace conditions requiring the defeated powers to adopt democratic political systems, for the belief was widespread, then as now, that democratic regimes are much less likely to undertake aggression.

The Peace of 1991

Saddam Hussein was a very convenient enemy, but not as convenient as he might have been. He completely misjudged the resolve of the West, particularly the United States, to oppose his invasion of Kuwait, and then he conducted his foreign policy, as well as the war itself, in a manner seemingly calculated to keep the coalition together and Iraq isolated. But Saddam was shrewd enough to accept the coalition's terms and to surrender before his military might had been entirely destroyed and before Iraq itself was occupied. In that way he averted the destruction of his regime that further intransigence might have provoked.

The Bush administration has offered many justifications for not continuing the war and occupying Iraq. President Bush lamented that "the lack of a 'battleship *Missouri*' surrender unfortunately left unresolved problems, and new ones arose."[1] He was "disappointed that Saddam's defeat did not break his hold on power, as many of our Arab allies had predicted and we had come to expect. The abortive uprising of the Shi'ites in the south and the Kurds in the north did not spread to the Sunni population of central Iraq, and the Iraqi military remained loyal." The most basic explanation offered was and remains this: "Breaking up the Iraqi state would pose its own destabilizing problems. . . . Trying to eliminate Saddam, extending the ground war into an occupation of Iraq, would have violated our guideline about not changing objectives in midstream, engaging in 'mission creep,' and would have incurred incalculable human and political costs."[2] This combination of the ever-present Vietnam syndrome and the desire to halt a superbly successful war before it was tarnished in any way proved to have its own "incalculable human and political costs." Bush's lament that there was no "battleship *Missouri*" surrender was quite apt—the end of the Gulf War proved to be similar not to the successful end of World War II, which resolved the German problem fully, but to the catastrophic end of World War I, which only exacerbated it.

No formal peace treaty has been signed between Iraq and any of the coalition powers, but the United Nations Security Council resolutions passed during and after the war have laid out the general conditions for the peace. On August 2, 1990, the day Iraq invaded Kuwait, the Security Council passed Resolution 660, which condemned the invasion and required Iraq to move its forces back to the positions they had occupied prior to the invasion. Resolution 661, adopted on August 6, imposed a nearly complete blockade upon Iraq—only medical supplies and foodstuffs sent "in humanitarian circumstances" could be exported to Iraq, while nothing could be imported from Iraq. These two resolutions formed the basis of the coalition demands and punishments before the beginning of Operation Desert Storm.

The nearly complete destruction of Iraq's armed force in the Kuwaiti Theater of Operations (KTO) did not lead to the unconditional surrender of Iraq or to the destruction of all of Iraq's military assets. The victors, accordingly, issued a series of demands in the form of Security Council resolutions that Iraq had to accept in order for peace to be restored in the region. The incentives for Iraq to agree were the continued presence of coalition forces in Iraq and the continuation of the complete economic embargo until the Security Council decided that Iraq had complied with its demands. The scale of the victory made the demands of April 1991 much greater than those of August 1990.

On April 8, the Security Council adopted Resolution 687, which laid out in detail the peace terms the coalition sought to dictate to Iraq. It must abandon its claims on Kuwaiti territory, abandon its chemical, biological, and nuclear weapons programs, which were prohibited by treaties to which Iraq was already a party, as well as its ballistic missile program, which is not prohibited by any treaty. The appropriate international agencies were to inspect all the elements of these four programs and then destroy them. Iraq must also cease all "flights of combat aircraft," even within its own territory, and renounce the use of international terrorism.

Security Council Resolution 688 of April 5, 1991, explicitly confirmed the territorial integrity of Iraq, but the Iraq-Kuwait border required readjustment because of the vagueness of the prewar demarcation line. A Security Council commission would be established to determine the permanent demarcation line, and, because the current border resulted, in part, from Iraqi encroachments on Kuwaiti territory, the border commission was likely to give territory back to Kuwait.

The Security Council also imposed a series of economic conditions upon Iraq. One cause of the Gulf War had been Saddam Hussein's refusal to repay the vast sums he owed Kuwait as a result of war loans Kuwait had made during the Iran-Iraq war. Resolution 687 required Iraq to honor all of its prewar debts and to pay reparations to compensate Kuwait and other coalition powers for their suffering during the war. Iraq would be allowed to sell a certain amount of oil, determined by the Security Council, and was required to use a percentage of the proceeds to service its debt and reparations and another percentage to feed its people. In all other respects the economic embargo was to be kept in place pending Iraq's acceptance of all of the Security Council's conditions and the Security Council's determination that Iraq had fully complied.

These basic demands contained important similarities with the peace terms imposed on Germany in 1919. Although the size, strength, and organization of the Iraqi army was not regulated, the elimination of Iraq's ballistic missile program constituted enforced unilateral disarmament beyond what was required of any other state, and the "no-fly" zones that arose from the U.S. interpretation of Resolution 687 restricted the use of Iraq's air force even in Iraqi airspace for so long as that resolution remained in force. The provisions enforcing various international bans on chemical, biological, and nuclear weapons were, technically, simply compelling Iraq to accept conditions it had already agreed to accept by signing the relevant treaties. In fact, by linking highly intrusive inspections with the lifting of economic sanctions, the Security Council was compelling Iraq to accept a higher level of enforcement of those agreements than any other state.

These requirements were neither unjust nor inappropriate; on the contrary, they seem in retrospect to have been inadequate in light of Saddam's continued determination to violate international norms and to pursue aggressive policies. Taken together, however, they constituted the imposition of unilateral partial disarmament on a state that had been beaten badly, but neither crushed nor occupied. Above all, they were requirements that were every bit as unacceptable to Saddam as the restrictions placed on the German army would be to German leaders even before Hitler. Like the disarmament clauses of the Versailles Treaty, they had the prospect of engaging the coalition in a series of relatively small conflicts over inspections, combat aircraft flights, and other violations, no single instance of which was likely to merit the use of significant force. The continuation of complete economic sanctions, however, like the establishment of crippling war reparations in 1919, meant that the coalition, like the Allies, had no threat *except* the use of force. Both the Germans and the Iraqis would spend the several years following the cessation of hostilities continually testing the bounds to see how far they could push before their opponents were willing to fight. And in both cases the pattern was the same—the pariah regime would push ever harder and farther, generally, but not always, avoiding actual conflict, but gradually eroding the will of coalition powers to enforce the unwieldy treaty and, thereby, eroding the integrity of the coalition and the treaty itself.

The situations of 1919 and 1991, however, differed in two crucial ways. In 1919 the alliance facing Germany depended on two major powers, England and France, following the retreat of America from the world scene. France, dreading the long-term might of a rearmed Germany, feared moving more aggressively than England could accept lest it find itself forced to confront Germany alone. England, for its part, rapidly came to regret the harshness of the Versailles Treaty and to resent the obligations it placed upon it to be ready to use force to maintain it. Thus England, the power that must largely determine the coalition's policy toward Germany, was extremely reluctant to use force to support the treaty, while France was reluctant to act alone. These factors prevented the disputes over Germany's violations of the disarmament clauses from becoming serious. Since 1991, however, America has been both the leading power militarily in the Gulf and the power with the most at stake in supporting the peace imposed in 1991.

For that reason, the disputes over Iraqi disarmament have been more extended and violent as the Americans have behaved somewhat more responsibly than Britain did in seeing to it that violations of the peace conditions did not go unpunished. The other major difference, however, has had an extremely baleful effect. The hideous sufferings of the German people during the war had eroded the legitimacy of the Kaiser's government to a dangerous extent. Popular belief in October 1918 that the government might refuse to make peace, therefore, led to the abdication of the Kaiser and the collapse of the German Empire into revolution. The Weimar Republic that emerged from the ashes of that revolution was a wholly different creature from the imperial government that had started the war. Both the Allies and the Germans had the chance, in 1919, to start over. In 1991, although Bush and others claim that they hoped that Saddam would fall to an internal coup, they did nothing to compel Iraq to change either its ruler or its form of government. The revolutions that challenged Saddam in the immediate aftermath of the Gulf War proved abortive. As a result, eight years after the war, America is forced to continue to deal with the man whose aggressive designs fomented the conflict in the first place. Whereas in Germany after 1919 a new regime was created that, in many respects, had different needs, goals, and ambitions from the one that had gone before, in Iraq after 1991 the same regime still bided its time, changed its ambitions not at all, and determined to exact personal vengeance for its humiliation. Although the peace dictated in 1991 was considerably less harsh than that of 1919, the challenge of actually imposing it on so recalcitrant and tyrannical a regime would prove to be considerably greater.

The First Kurdish Rebellion

The ignominious collapse of the German army in 1918 touched off a string of revolutions and disturbances that transformed the German system of government. The even more humiliating collapse of the Iraqi military in 1991 also touched off rebellions and disturbances throughout the country, but the state structure and leadership weathered the storm. The main reasons for this difference were that where the Kaiser's government had vacillated and delayed coming to terms, Saddam surrendered promptly and while much of his armed force was still alive. The Allies of 1918 were, moreover, willing, if necessary, to invade Germany, utterly destroy her army, and occupy her territory; the coalition of 1991 desperately sought to avoid such an outcome.

When the Kurds revolted in their northern homeland as the Gulf War drew to a close, therefore, Saddam was able to find loyal troops to suppress the uprising. The Bush administration was criticized then and since for failing to support this uprising, but it was held captive by its determination to maintain the territorial integrity of Iraq. Brent Scowcroft reported years later, "I frankly wished [the uprising] hadn't happened. I envisioned a postwar government being a military government. . . . It's the colonel with the brigade patrolling his palace that's going to get him [Saddam] if someone gets him."[3] Another official noted at the time of the uprising. "Our policy is to get rid of Saddam Hussein, not his regime."

The United States, accordingly, waffled in response to the suppression of the Kurds. Bush decided to enforce the no-fly zone he had declared in the northern portion of Iraq, and U.S. warplanes shot down Iraqi aircraft in that zone in March.[4] At the same time, the United States decided that helicopters did not fall under the no-fly zone ban and allowed Saddam to use his attack helicopters to butcher the lightly armed Kurds. This was a minor point, for the Iraqi army even after the Gulf War was more than strong enough to deal with the disorganized and ill-equipped Kurds. Without foreign intervention, the rebellion in the north never had a chance.[5]

The Kurdish uprising posed a complicated and painful problem for the victorious coalition. As Saddam's forces crushed the rebels, hundreds of thousands of Kurds fled toward Turkey and Iran, creating a massive refugee crisis. Apart from the humanitarian nightmare, Turkey's difficulties with its own Kurdish population ensured that the coalition could not ignore the crisis entirely. As a result, an agreement between the UN and Iraq in April 1991 created a demilitarized security zone in much of Iraqi Kurdistan and put the northern no-fly zone on a sounder legal footing. In accord with this agreement, the UN stationed 500 monitors in the area to oversee and protect humanitarian relief operations.[6]

These measures, although they generated continual crisis and conflict between the coalition and Saddam, were not enough to solve the problem. Saddam stationed more than 150,000 troops along the border of the developing Kurdish autonomous region and instituted a strict economic blockade on the area that exacerbated the humanitarian crisis.[7] Direct conflict with U.S. and UN forces alternated with desultory negotiations with the Kurds that went nowhere.

The Bush administration did not welcome the Kurdish uprising and the subsequent need to establish the northern no-fly zone. Since the United States was committed to maintaining the territorial integrity of Iraq, the most obvious solution—the establishment of an autonomous Kurdish state—was impossible. But Saddam was determined to crush the Kurdish rebellion with great brutality to demonstrate his continued control. That brutality, however, was a blow to the prestige of the United States and the coalition, while the humanitarian horror Saddam was determined to create in Iraqi Kurdistan evoked powerful indignation in the world community. The United States was forced, then, to keep the Kurds in Iraq, despite the Kurds' continuing efforts to achieve independence or at least autonomy, even as it tried to prevent Saddam from butchering them. During the same period the rebellious Shiites in southern Iraq received similar treatment. Immediately after the Gulf War, American prestige and credibility, as well as the credibility of the "peace" following that war, became intimately entangled with the enforcement of the northern and southern no-fly zones and the treatment by Saddam Hussein of his own citizens.

The Kurdish problem continued to expand as the success of the Iraqi Kurds encouraged their Turkish cousins to step up their attacks on the Turkish regime. To counter that threat, the Turks, claiming that the Kurdish "safe haven" in northern Iraq was a staging ground for terrorists aimed at Ankara, began to launch attacks into Iraqi territory against their own Kurdish rebels. The Iraqi Kurds, for their part, had immediately broken into two major camps that almost immediately came to blows. The post–Gulf War years saw continuing efforts by Turkey and Iraq to make use of the intra-Kurdish conflict to suppress Kurdish terrorism in Turkey and the Kurdish independence movement in Iraq, as the United States and its allies stood by.

UNSCOM

In the meantime, major problems had developed in the enforcement of the other peace conditions, especially those concerning Iraq's disarmament. UN Security Council Resolution 687 created a UN Special Commission (UNSCOM) that would receive Iraq's declarations defining its nuclear, chemical, biological, and ballistic missile programs, would conduct on-site inspections to verify those declarations, and would oversee the destruction of weapons and equipment that were part of those programs. In its mandate and functions, UNSCOM was very similar to the Inter-Allied Control Commission that had enforced the disarmament provisions of the Versailles Treaty. It was similar in another important respect as well: just as Brigadier General Morgan had been forced to resign from the IACC for taking a stronger stance against German violations of the treaty than some in his government could accept, so a major figure of UNSCOM, Scott Ritter, felt compelled to resign from that commission when he became convinced that his government was not willing to back the commission in spite of Iraq's clear violations of its disarmament commitments. And, like Morgan, Ritter wrote a book to warn the world of the dangers he saw that also catalogued his commission's efforts to disarm the beaten foe.[8]

The Iraqis, like the Germans, greeted the commission that was to disarm them with hostility and even violence. The coalition did not make the same mistake that the Allies had made in 1919 of asking their enemy to create a parallel liaison organ, but it appears that the Iraqis took the initiative and created such an organ on their own:

> Even as the Security Council was putting the finishing touches on the creation of UNSCOM, Saddam Hussein was summoning his inner leadership for the purpose of creating a special committee to decide which weapons capabilities would be turned over and which would be kept. This committee had an additional task. It would have to devise a mechanism to conceal the weaponry retained along with related information and material from the inspectors.[9]

The Germans began their disarmament process by delaying for months the declarations of proscribed equipment they were obliged to render to the IACC; the Iraqis did not delay those declarations, they simply lied in them:

> Of nineteen ballistic missile launchers held by Iraq at the end of the Gulf War, only ten were declared. The other nine went into hiding, part of an operational ballistic missile force that Saddam wanted desperately to keep intact;

Of approximately 140 long-range ballistic missiles, known as the Al-Hussein or its variant, the Al-Hijara, only forty-five were declared and submitted to UNSCOM for disposition;

While declaring its program for modifying standard, short-range Soviet-supplied Scud missiles to the 650-kilometer range Al-Hussein, it kept secret its indigenous ballistic missile production of operational Al-Hussein missiles;

Similarly, it declared aspects of its massive chemical weapons inventory and production capabilities, but thousands of bombs and artillery shells filled with deadly substances were hidden, including munitions and production equipment associated with the highly lethal VX—a nerve agent that Iraq never acknowledged possessing;

Iraq did not declare any aspect of its biological weapons program in the initial declaration to UNSCOM, nor did it declare any aspects of its nuclear weapons program.[10]

The inspectors tried to find what the Iraqis were hiding, and Iraq undertook to stop them from doing that.

The first conflict came in June 1991 when an inspection team attempted to intercept an Iraqi convoy loaded with equipment supporting Iraq's nuclear weapons program. The convoy's guards fired warning shots over the heads of the inspectors and drove off, although the equipment was subsequently destroyed under UNSCOM's supervision.[11] The incident resulted in the passage of another Security Council resolution affirming UNSCOM's authority to conduct such inspections. The most important Iraqi attempt to defeat the inspections was a massive effort to destroy a great deal (although by no means all) of Iraq's nuclear, biological, chemical, and missile manufacturing systems and weapons, and to conceal the most critical components. Thus on the eve of what was to be a dramatic UNSCOM inspection backed with intelligence information derived from sophisticated Western sources, the Iraqis announced that they had already destroyed the material to be inspected and "invited" the inspectors to "verify" that destruction. The idea of verifying from piles of charred and melted metal that particular weapons had been destroyed was surely daunting, but the inspectors undertook it nevertheless, and found that the material they were allowed to see could not account in mass for the weapons and systems Iraq had claimed to have destroyed. The Iraqis responded by asserting that some of the material had been, for some unknowable reason, melted into metal ingots—they now invited the inspectors to look at clean bars of metal and "verify" that they once had been components of WMD systems! When the inspectors declined and asked, instead, to see the documentation describing these systems, the Iraqis demurred: "Unfortunately, according to Baghdad, the entire affair had been top secret and carried out precipitously; there was no documentation."[12]

But this deception plan was inadequate, for the Iraqis were still determined to maintain the critical components of their WMD programs and the UNSCOM inspectors were forever threatening to find those components. The Iraqis refused to allow the UNSCOM teams to use helicopters, barred inspectors from sites, or tore documents from their hands. Repeated demands by the Security Council, coupled occasionally with threats if Iraq did not comply, won most of the individual points—inspectors ultimately were allowed to visit each site, usually got the documents, ultimately were able to use helicopters, and so forth. What Iraq was gaining by these tactics was time.

Like the Germans before them, the Iraqis knew that the inspections would not continue indefinitely. The coalition was so fragile that only Saddam's belligerence had kept it together through the Gulf War, and it started to break up almost immediately afterward. If Saddam could walk the fine line of mollifying the international community by yielding, in time, to the inspectors while keeping them from finding his most critical secrets by delaying their inspections long enough to play a shell game with those secrets, in the long run he would win. The inspections would stop and his secrets would be preserved. So do defeated states behave when they are determined to undermine disarmament restrictions, and that is a fundamental flaw in the notion of coercive disarmament.

Saddam played this game extremely well. In July an inspection team was prevented from searching for records in the Ministry of Agriculture. Five team members began a round-the-clock surveillance of the ministry to ensure that the Iraqis did not remove critical materials or documents. The Security Council moved swiftly to declare Iraq's actions a "material and unacceptable breach by Iraq" of the terms of the cease-fire.[13] The crisis quickly escalated into a full-blown test of the viability of the inspections regime. The White House let it be known that it was consulting with Britain and France on military actions that the coalition allies might take if Iraq failed to comply, while the Iraqis took the opportunity to denounce the entire inspections arrangement and to call for the annulment of the punitive terms of the cease-fire.[14]

Iraq also refused to issue visas to UN relief workers and stalled in negotiations to continue the work of UN guards and humanitarian groups in Iraq, particularly Kurdistan. A UN guard in Kurdistan was killed while he slept, and grenades were thrown at a UN guard residence. Just like the German press during periods of tension with the IACC, the Iraqi press began a violent campaign, denouncing the inspectors and threatening them. Mass demonstrations in the streets of Baghdad became daily occurrences, with people slashing the tires of UN vehicles and defacing them.[15]

As the crisis heated up, the Iraqis interjected elements of subtlety into their violence, offering to allow the UNSCOM team to inspect the Agriculture Ministry, but only if no Americans participated. Ritter, a member of that UNSCOM team, reports:

For over three weeks that July Iraq had refused us access, defying UNSCOM and the Security Council and threatening the safety of the inspectors. Mass demonstrations of thousands of civilians, who had been handed eggs and vegetables by the egg-and-vegetable quartermasters of the regime, had pelted us as we sat in our cars. This onslaught had failed to pry us loose from the perimeter of the ministry, and now the Iraqis tried a more direct tactic. They assaulted us with skewers and knives. Unarmed and with no mandate for self-defense, the team had no choice but to withdraw and await the outcome of the Security Council discussion of the issue.[16]

The White House warned in what came to be the classic phrase, "We are not ruling out any option, including the use of military force."[17]

But the near-unanimous support for military action that had existed before and during the Gulf War had evaporated. The Bush administration sought Security Council support for a new resolution authorizing military intervention to force Baghdad to allow the inspections, "possibly with a series of air strikes. . . . But several days of preliminary consultations here have convinced some diplomats the three big powers are unlikely to muster the backing they are seeking from more than a handful of the 15-member Security Council." The Bush administration and its two remaining loyal allies, France and Britain, argued that Iraq's violation of the terms of the cease-fire agreement gave them all the authority needed to conduct further attacks,[18] but only five months after the war, Bush's carefully constructed international consensus, essential for the difficult task of maintaining coercive disarmament against Iraq, was evaporating.

With the withdrawal of the UN team from its stakeout around the Agriculture Ministry, every hour that went by heightened the likelihood that the Iraqis would first remove all sensitive material and then "cave in" to the UN. In fact, it was the UN that caved in to Iraq: the day after the withdrawal of the inspection team, the UN offered a "compromise plan" in which only small teams of inspectors would enter the Agriculture Ministry.[19]

Rolf Ekeus, the head of UNSCOM, insisted: "We are not negotiating and even less compromising. . . . We have no authority to compromise. . . . We are talking about modalities for the inspection to be carried out." At the same time, he "emphasized the urgent need for a solution, both to ensure the continued safety of his inspection teams in Baghdad and to reduce the opportunity for Iraqi officials to remove any relevant documents that might be in the Agriculture Ministry."[20]

The "non-negotiations" soon stalled over Iraq's demand that no American, British, or French inspectors enter the site; the Iraqis wanted the inspectors to be Chinese or Indian. Ekeus suggested that they could perhaps be Finns, Swedes, and Germans,[21] and his "non-compromise" resolved the crisis. Iraq agreed to allow a UN team to inspect the building six days after the stakeout had ended. He acknowledged that "most probably, this building has been quite effectively cleaned out," but insisted "there may be some material of significance for us, covering all aspects."[22] Although the Bush administration described the exclusion of U.S. members from the inspection team as "unacceptable" and a "deal-breaker," the deal went through.[23] The inspection team was to consist of two Germans, a Finn, a Russian, a Swede, and a Swiss. Two American inspectors were nominally part of the team, but would not be allowed to enter the building.[24]

Everyone declared victory. Ekeus said that the "threat of military action" had added "an element of reality" into his discussions with the Iraqis. The Iraqis were publicly delighted that no Americans were to enter the building. Privately, they can only have been even more pleased that they had been able to gain six critical days in which to remove any incriminating material from the building. Bush claimed that Iraq had "caved in," while Iraq claimed that Baghdad "had established a precedent and that international inspectors could no longer enter buildings on their own terms"[25] Some in the administration appeared to agree with Iraq: " 'The Defense Department is puzzled by the compromise because it appears to give Iraq the ability to decide the composition of the inspection team, which it clearly has no right to do,' a senior Defense Department official said." The rest of the administration tried to put a good face on it: "It was not that critical that the inspector that goes inside carry an American passport." Indeed it did not matter at all, in one sense, for the building had been cleaned out quite thoroughly and the team found nothing.

The crisis highlighted the enormous difficulties facing the Americans in their attempt to enforce the disarmament imposed on Iraq after the Gulf War. Saddam Hussein could instigate a crisis whenever he chose. In any crisis, he needed only to delay the inspections long enough to remove the incriminating material. America, constrained by the need to maintain national and international support for military action, could not strike while "negotiations" were going on. As the crisis went on, however, it became apparent that the Bush administration wanted to conduct a military strike. They moved the military pieces necessary into the theater, tested international support, developed domestic support—and the Saddam "caved in" in time to avert the strike, but only after he had sanitized the site to be inspected. The United States had certainly allowed this crisis to go on far too long, creating the conditions for a compromise that would render the whole inspection meaningless. Enforcement of inspections was a no-win proposition.

The Southern No–Fly Zone

The "resolution" of the July crisis set the stage for further incidents. Shortly after the Gulf War, Iraqi Shiites in the south began a rebellion as widespread, if not as effective, as the one the Kurds started in the north. It collapsed even more quickly than the Kurdish resistance, and by mid-March 1991, Saddam declared the Shiite rebellion over.[26] The rebels did not all perish or surrender but retreated into the marches of southern Iraq. By August 1992 reports indicated that five or six divisions, including Republican Guard units, supported by artillery, helicopters, and fixed-wing aircraft, were attacking the marshy refuge of the Shiite rebels. The coalition declared a no-fly zone in the south, which grounded Iraq's aircraft in the region but did nothing to stop the ground offensive.[27] The southern no-fly zone became the scene of the next conflict between Iraq and the United States over the enforcement of the peace.

On December 27 a U.S. aircraft patrolling the zone shot down an Iraqi MiG-25. The outgoing Bush administration recognized the flight as "the latest of several attempts by Saddam to test whether the United States, during the final days of the Bush administration, will enforce fully the United Nations restrictions upon Iraq after its defeat last year in the Persian Gulf War." Bush ordered the aircraft carrier *Kitty Hawk* into the Gulf as a "signal of U.S. determination" to oppose Iraq's moves.[28]

The United States did not fear Iraqi fighters, already proved to be no match for U.S. planes flown by U.S. pilots, but word that Iraq was deploying surface-to-air missiles into the southern no-fly zone was much more worrying. No UN resolution barred Iraq from deploying SAMs wherever it would, nor did the declaration of the no-fly zone explicitly ban such deployments into that area. The deployment of the missiles, coincident with incursions into the no-fly zone, however, might be part of a plan to "lure the Americans into range of the surface to air missiles so that Baghdad can avenge the downing of the Iraqi MiG."[29] On January 6 the United States presented Iraq with an ultimatum signed by France, Britain, and Russia, giving Saddam forty-eight hours to remove the missiles.

The Iraqis declared that they had every right to move their civilian and military material within their borders without external interference but began to remove some of the missiles from the southern zone. Cloud cover over the southern zone prevented U.S. satellites from seeing exactly what was going on[30] and complicated Bush's policy options: "There were a lot of missiles moving around. . . . There were missiles going north. What we don't know for certain is whether they are staying north."[31] The deadline passed without any action.

Saddam then created a new crisis by declaring that UNSCOM teams would not be allowed to fly their own aircraft into and out of Iraq, but must charter Iraqi aircraft or travel overland. At the same time, hundreds of Iraqi troops crossed into the demilitarized zone between Iraq and Kuwait, seizing weapons and equipment they had been forced to leave behind at the end of the Gulf War. The Security Council declared the ban on flights a "material breach" of the cease-fire; the situation continued to be extremely tense.[32]

The conflict Saddam was courting arrived. On January 10, Iraq barred an

UNSCOM plane from entering Iraqi airspace and then began reactivating surface-to-air missiles that had been deployed to the northern no-fly zone. On January 13, 110 allied aircraft struck eight sites in Iraq, all related to the air defense systems Iraq had reemplaced in or near the southern no-fly zone. At the same time, Bush ordered a 1,000-man battalion task force to Kuwait. He had originally approved a much broader air strike that would have hit command and control facilities, airfields, and suspected WMD sites throughout Iraq, but had chosen the reduced strike at the last minute. The administration said the reason for that decision was that Bush wanted to "make a political point. The point is that this was so fast, efficient, low-key and limited that we can do it again one day from now or two or three. Clinton can do it without much stress."[33] Asked directly if he thought the strike would "work," Bush answered, "Well, I don't know what 'work' means, but I am confident that I will continue to insist that [Saddam] abide by these resolutions, and we will—we've taken action and I hope we'll convince him that he must do that."[34] It seems likely that Saddam received a different message from the one Bush sent.

The attacks aimed at "military airfields, missile sites, radar installations, bunkers, facilities to which UN inspectors have been denied access and possibly even the headquarters of Iraq's air force in Baghdad."[35] Repeatedly Bush and administration officials declared that the cause of the strikes was not just the most recent crisis, but a broad pattern of Iraqi violations of the peace terms and that the aim of the strikes was to force the Iraqis into compliance. But in the wake of the strikes, the definition of success changed dramatically. The strike was smaller and considerably less accurate than many expected, missing half of its intended targets and leaving three of four SAM launchers intact, yet

> despite the limited goals and lesser returns, President Bush declared that the attack had achieved its chief goal. "The skies are safer" for allied planes and Hussein has been sent a clear warning, he said. "They [the coalition aircraft] went in there with a wide array of defensive equipment threatening them, and that threat has been severely reduced. That's the bottom line, that's the important point," said Bush.[36]

With three or four launchers left intact, the reduction in Iraq's defenses in the area were hardly "severe." Nor did Saddam get the message Bush was trying to convey, for two days after the strike, Iraq again threatened to shoot down UNSCOM aircraft flying in Iraqi airspace.

Saddam continued to stall while "negotiating." He offered to allow UNSCOM inspectors to fly in their own aircraft, but only if they avoided the no-fly zones. The Bush administration rejected the offer and struck a facility near Baghdad suspected of being part of Iraq's nuclear weapons program. The facility had already been inspected by UNSCOM and found to be "mothballed," but the White House declared that the strike "also helps in the process of eliminating nuclear weapons."[37] This was the first time America had attacked Iraq without the participation of other coalition members, and it was the first time that a strike was limited to cruise missiles. The administration said openly that the absence of any aircraft was designed to ensure that there would be no U.S. casualties.

On the day Clinton took office, Iraq backed down, announcing it would permit UNSCOM inspectors to fly wherever they pleased in their own planes and announcing a "cease-fire" over the no-fly zones. Within a few days, however, the situation was back to normal—UNSCOM inspections continued, with constant harassment by the Iraqis, although not enough to attract international attention, and other low-key tests of the no-fly zones persisted.

By attacking on multiple fronts, challenging the prospective territorial adjustments, the inspections, and the no-fly zones, Saddam succeeded in confusing the issues and gaining a point. Although he had to back down on the question of UNSCOM, the most public and dramatic of the issues, he escaped chastisement for the cross-border raids. At the same time he was able to test the continuing strength of the coalition and find it weakening: British and French participation in the first raid was desultory; the second raid was conducted only by American forces. He also succeeded in displaying his unpredictability. In all previous crises he had pushed to the edge of conflict and backed away. This time he made it clear that the United States could not count on such a retreat. In the future, it would be the United States, not Iraq, that faced the danger of falling into a predictable pattern. Lastly, he continued to delay the inspections with impunity—punishment came for interfering with UNSCOM, not for delaying it. Both the outgoing Bush administration and the incoming Clinton administration made it clear that however long Saddam took to allow the resolution of a crisis, there would be no punishment after he surrendered. That precedent was very dangerous.

Clinton Takes Charge

The first test of the Clinton administration's determination to enforce the peace terms was not auspicious. On June 6, 1993, UNSCOM inspectors notified Iraq of their intention to install monitoring cameras in a plant suspected of continuing Iraq's ballistic missile program. Iraq demurred, claiming that monitoring operations could come into operation only after the Security Council had declared Iraq to be in compliance with its obligations under Resolution 687 and had lifted the economic embargo. This was a ploy designed to end the inspections at once and proceed to "monitoring" and the end of economic sanctions,[38] and it was an obvious misreading of the resolutions, which commanded Iraq to comply with UNSCOM's monitoring efforts even as it complied with continued inspections.

The UNSCOM report left no doubt of the importance the commission attached to compelling Iraq to adhere to the terms of the resolutions:

> Iraq has, through its conduct since the last report, consistently demonstrated its desire to limit the Commission's inspection rights and operational capabilities through seeking to place restrictions on inspectors in the course of their work. . . . the Commission has no doubt that [these actions] form part of a long-term campaign to establish a practice for the conduct of inspections that would severely restrict the rights provided in the plans for ongoing monitoring and verification and relevant Security Council resolutions. Iraq is thus clearly seeking to assert for itself the right to interpret how the resolutions should be implemented. Included in this campaign have been attempts by Iraq to dispute the Commission's instructions on the destruction of equipment intended for the production of banned weapons; to restrict the scope of inspections and information gathering; to restrict access and impose delays on inspections; to restrict the exercise of the Commission's aerial rights; to impose limits on the duration, size and composition of inspections; to require advance notice of inspection activities; and to limit the right to take photography. . . . [W]hen taken together, these incidents add up to a major impediment that would effectively impede credible long-term monitoring and verification. This again underlines the need to obtain from Iraq as soon as possible its formal acknowledgment of its obligations under resolution 715 (1991), so that the Council's requirements laid down in that resolution can be met.[39]

The commission stated the problem clearly. Each incident of Iraqi opposition might be insignificant in itself, but the effect of all of the incidents together was to undermine the inspections and the enforcement of the terms of the peace.

The Clinton administration's first reaction to this report was to warn that "quite serious" consequences would result from Iraq's refusal to comply with UNSCOM's demands. At the same time, however, the White House said that the United States "was not contemplating any immediate resort to military force."[40] Then, on June 26, twenty-three Tomahawk cruise missiles struck an intelligence complex in downtown Baghdad. The justification for the strike was the discovery of evidence that Iraq had attempted to assassinate former President Bush during his visit to Kuwait in April. Clinton's explanation contained no reference to the standoff with the arms inspectors. He declared, instead, that his objective was "to send a message to those who engage in state-sponsored terrorism, to deter further violence against our people and to affirm the expectation of civilized behavior among nations. . . . Our intent was to target Iraq's capacity to support violence against the United States and other nations and to deter Saddam Hussein from supporting such outlawed behavior in the future."[41] The strike, once again, was a unilateral U.S. action with no coalition partners taking part. The French, who had been described as eager to participate in earlier chastisements of Saddam, declared that although they "understood" the strike, they did not "seek either the destabilization or the dismemberment of the Iraqi state."

Like Bush's attack in January, this strike consisted solely of sea-launched cruise missiles so as to avoid putting any American lives in danger, and its effects immediately came into question. Military reports pointed out that Iraq had other facilities and means for collecting and processing intelligence and claimed only that Iraq's intelligence capabilities had "suffered a major setback."[42] Clinton's national security team, however, made more dramatic claims that "we did in fact cripple the Iraqi intelligence capacity, which was the intent of the action." In the press, experts quickly exposed the exaggeration in the claim of having "crippled" Iraq's intelligence capabilities with one strike of twenty-three missiles on a single target.[43] The Clinton administration had succeeded in sending a signal to Saddam Hussein via cruise missile that it was "tough" and was willing to use force against him. From the standpoint of fundamental U.S. interests and long-term policy, however, the raid was a disaster that played into Saddam's hands.

Bush had always been careful to act within the confines of multilateralism, however tight they might have been. His unwillingness to risk the collapse of widespread international support for his policy toward Iraq sometimes seemed an unwillingness to take the lead internationally and to push unwilling partners to take necessary actions. It helped lead to his refusal to defeat Saddam completely in war and to the terribly complicated situation in which he was forced to rely on international sanctions to achieve what he had chosen not to achieve by force.

By 1993, the United States was firmly committed to a policy of sanctions and equally firmly committed not to settle the Iraqi issue by force. Clinton was not willing to revisit that fundamental question—for all the application of force during his administration, his policy, at its root, always relied exclusively on the functioning of sanctions. But sanctions require solid and broad international support. Saddam was well aware of that, and had obviously tried in the last days of the Bush administration to find ways of breaking up that support. Nothing could serve Saddam's turn better in that regard than transforming the conflict between Iraq and the world community into a conflict between Iraq and the United States. The unilateral military strike helped in that transformation.

The attack was unfortunate in its timing as well, coming a day after Washington had denounced Iraq's failure to comply yet again with UNSCOM's inspectors and shortly after the release of a damning UNSCOM report. The Clinton administration was careful to dissociate the two events—too careful, in fact. The unilateral strike on Iraq and the subsequent need to justify the attack with the evidence of Iraq's complicity in the plot to assassinate Bush pushed the inspections issue off the table and, in fact, shelved it completely. Clinton had served Saddam's goals again by helping to distract attention from an important challenge to the enforcement of the peace terms and by forcing the United States onto the diplomatic defensive in its need to justify this unilateral attack. This timing, so unfortunate from the standpoint of long-term U.S. policy, was particularly inexplicable considering that a trial of the assassination-plot suspects was under way in Kuwait at the time, and had not been completed when the missiles struck. The strike was evidence that the new administration was confused about its policy with regard to Iraq and was in danger of confusing action with policy.

For some time after the missile attack, Iraq's presence on the world scene diminished. Although sparring with UNSCOM continued on a low level, no new crises erupted, and UNSCOM reported progress in its work. The cameras that Iraq had opposed in June were installed and operational in September.[44] It was little remarked upon that Iraq's intransigence and Clinton's ill-timed attack gave Iraq an additional four months of delay during which there was no monitoring of the site, for UNSCOM was finally moving in the general direction of declaring Iraq in compliance with the arms control provisions of the cease-fire. For bizarre reasons of his own, however, Saddam interrupted the placid pace of events, provoking a dramatic new crisis in October 1994.

The October Scare

The UN Border Commission, established in 1991 to review the disputed Iraq-Kuwaiti border, issued its final report in May 1993, defining a new border that gave Kuwait greater control over valuable oilfields. At the same time, it reduced Iraq's access to the port facilities at Umm Qasr. The UN moved speedily to accept the commission's report and to declare the new border "inviolable." Iraq moved equally quickly to denounce the new border and to engineer a series of incidents along it.[45] Iraq began moving elements of three Republican guard divisions from their permanent encampments around Baghdad toward the Kuwaiti border on October 7, 1994.

The Clinton administration immediately ordered the deployment of an additional aircraft carrier, a marine amphibious group with about 2,000 marines, and a number of maritime prepositioning ships to the Persian Gulf, and alerted 20,000 ground troops for possible deployment to the Gulf region. The administration estimated that Iraq would soon have a force of 60,000 men equipped with 700 tanks and 900 armored personnel carriers along the Kuwaiti border.[46]

Iraq raised the stakes on October 8, declaring that it would end all cooperation with the United Nations unless the embargo on its oil exports was lifted immediately.[47] When the threat was made, American forces were down to

12,000 troops, twenty-four combat aircraft, and two cruise missile ships in the Gulf region.

> Because the American ability to defend Kuwait is so limited, the Pentagon did not promise today that it could stop an Iraqi attack if one were launched right away. Rather, Pentagon officials spoke in terms of "punishing" the Iraqis if they crossed the Kuwaiti border. The officials today issued a pointed warning that an Iraqi attack on Kuwait would prompt an American cruise missile attack against Baghdad.[48]

Had Iraq been serious in its intention to invade Kuwait again, the threat of a mere cruise missile attack on Baghdad coupled with the admission that the coalition could not stop the attack would have been a green light. That Iraq had no such intention should not have made the manifest weakness of U.S. forces in the region less alarming.

In spite of their belief that Iraq would not attack, the administration announced that more than 36,000 ground troops were on their way to the Gulf, although they would now confront more than 80,000 Iraqis.[49] American forces would take some time to arrive in the theater of operations, even with the benefit of prepositioned equipment in Kuwait and aboard ships in the Gulf. One analyst noted, "Even with American airpower, the troops there would be in peril if Iraq attacked soon," although "by attacking the American unit, Iraq would be committing itself to war with the United States." He continued, "Recognizing the vulnerability of the initial American deployments, top Administration officials went out of their way today to publicize new air deployments and to threaten punishing missile and air attacks against Baghdad if Iraqi forces attacked Kuwait."[50]

America's deterrent in the Gulf rested, as it had in 1990, on America's ability to bring overwhelming force to bear over time, rather than on capabilities available immediately in the region. The differences were that forces were now deploying into Kuwait, not Saudi Arabia, that Iraq was much weaker than it had been in 1990, and the credibility of Clinton's threats was much greater while their tone was much stronger. At the same time, America's response to the crisis of October 1994 demonstrated once again that even in an area of known tension and high priority to the United States, any significant American military response would be delayed by days or even weeks. And Iraq had shown that it could present a tangible threat, even weakened as it was, long before overwhelming American forces could appear on the scene.

The crisis was short-lived. By October 10 the Iraqis announced that their forces were withdrawing to the north and east, away from the Kuwaiti frontier. The U.S. administration was not slow to realize, however, that Iraq held a winning hand if it had only to drive its tanks in the direction of Kuwait to trigger a massive deployment of American forces: "'We cannot have this situation where he can create an international crisis' simply by moving his forces south, one official said." On the other hand, Secretary of Defense William Perry noted, "We do not want to have large numbers of U.S. forces pinned down in Kuwait and Saudi Arabia."[51]

But what to do instead? The Gulf War coalition was splintering ever faster with word that UNSCOM was moving toward monitoring and away from the inspection and destruction of Iraqi proscribed materials. That decision would pave the way for the elimination of sanctions, which France favored for economic and Russia for political reasons. Both countries pressed for diplomatic rather than military solutions to the current crisis. Even Turkey appeared to signal that it might not be willing to allow the United States to use its bases for strikes against Iraq. Britain continued to stand firm, and less expectedly, so did Egypt, but the coalition was clearly fraying.

The cracks in the coalition began to show clearly as Washington outlined a plan to prevent Saddam from repeatedly moving forces toward Kuwait to provoke painful and expensive American responses. The concept was to establish a demilitarized zone extending some distance to the north of the Iraq-Kuwaiti border.[52] The French torpedoed the plan, first announcing that they felt the American buildup had been generated more by domestic American politics than by the situation in the Gulf, and then refusing to consider the buffer plan at all. Even Britain's reception of the idea was lukewarm at best.[53] At the same time, it emerged that the Defense Department had alerted a total of 155,000 ground troops for deployment to the Gulf despite the fact that Iraq claimed it was already withdrawing its forces.[54] That alert brought the total number of U.S. forces in theater, in transit, or alerted for deployment to 210,000, of which 194,000 were ground troops.[55]

The United States quickly backed off the demand for a "no-drive" zone to accompany the southern no-fly zone, some officials claiming that no such zone had ever even been proposed! One analyst noted that although coalition resistance to the plan and Arab concerns about the collapse of the Iraqi state were important restraints, "[s]ome of the limits on the United States are self-imposed: The Clinton administration is unwilling to go to war to bring down Saddam. In recent days, President Clinton cautioned advisers against overreaching in their current aims on Iraq. The goal right now, he argued, was simply the protection of Kuwait. . . ."[56] Once again the definition of victory changed in midcourse so that it would prove to be achievable at an acceptable cost.

By the end of the month that definition of victory was achieved. Saddam's forces withdrew, and Kuwait was safe. The UN Security Council condemned the Iraqi action and demanded that Iraq desist from threatening its neighbors, but the resolution did not authorize force to oppose deployment of forces within Iraq, nor did it create a "no-drive" zone. Iraq was free to test America's resolve again by deployments to the south—as it did again in August 1995 and January 1996.[57]

This crisis was a clear defeat for American policy. It showed that the Gulf War coalition was dead and could not be revived even in the face of Iraqi threats against Kuwait. The British military contribution to the buildup in October 1994 was desultory, while the French put one frigate to sea in the general direction of Iraq from the French port of Djibouti. France and Russia indicated that they would not support the U.S. plan to solve the problem in the long term. Both states declared themselves in sympathy with Iraq's demand for the lifting of economic sanctions, even during the crisis, thereby putting themselves directly at odds with the cornerstone of the Clinton administration's policy toward Iraq.

Saddam must have emerged from this crisis greatly encouraged by the collapse of the coalition against him. A relatively minor deployment (80,000 troops of an army of more than 400,000 moved from the central part of the country to the southern portion) required preparations for an American deployment of more than 200,000. That deployment was much faster than it had been in 1990, but it was still slow enough that Saddam probably could have taken Kuwait, although, once again, he could not have held it against an American counterattack. The deployment also sent the Secretary of Defense scurrying to the Gulf states to demand monetary contributions to offset U.S. expenses. Not only was America unwilling to fight, it was unwilling to pay the bill for deterrence. If Saddam chose to repeat this sort of provocation, the time would certainly come when the American response would lag sufficiently to offer him an opportunity for success. During similar crises in 1995 and 1996, in fact, the United States did not deploy significant numbers of ground troops, sending prepositioning ships, cruise missile platforms, and aircraft instead. Saddam underlined his contempt for the U.S. actions in 1994 by having one Republican Guard division stop its retreat well south of its permanent base for more than a day for no apparent reason. The real reason was obviously to send a "signal" of his own.

The crisis of October 1994 revealed yet another, more general, problem in American policy. When the United States capitulated to North Korea earlier in 1994, buying Pyongyang off with the promise of light water reactors. Saddam was watching. In a conversation with Rolf Ekeus, head of UNSCOM, after the crisis had passed, Iraqi foreign minister Saeed Sahhaf

> raised the issue of Washington's willingness to strike a deal with North Korea, which has been refusing an international inspection of two suspected nuclear storage sites, while U.S. officials were rejecting any reward to Iraq for its tolerance of similar inspections. "What does North Korea get for its refusal," Ekeus quoted Sahhaf as saying. "They get a $4

billion light-water reactor, get a couple billion dollars in addition, plus unlimited oil deliveries. What do we get? We get nothing."[58]

The Iraqis had learned the right lesson, but had applied it at the wrong time. The Clinton administration was willing to appease states with WMD capabilities tied to powerful conventional threats to U.S. allies. They were not so craven, however, as to do so twice within the space of six months, nor to appease a defeated state already compelled to accept international inspections and sanctions. The bad timing reflected Saddam's customary incompetence and impatience. A different opponent, or the same one in the future, may not be so conveniently inert.

Lifting the Curtain

The October crisis did not fundamentally divert the direction and pace of UNSCOM's work. By December 1994, UNSCOM was all but ready to declare Iraq in compliance with the disarmament terms of the peace. The commission noted in its December report that Iraq had been generally cooperative and helpful, and the few instances of Iraqi obstruction were "minor"—apart from the October crisis. It had progressed from inspection and destruction of proscribed programs to "ongoing monitoring and verification," and a system for such monitoring was up and running. The report concluded:

> While the preceding paragraphs inevitably dwell on outstanding issues where further work remains, much progress has been made during the period under review towards the fulfillment of the Commission's mandate. All items verified as being proscribed have now been destroyed. The ongoing monitoring and verification system is provisionally operational. The major elements for chemical and missile monitoring are in place. Interim monitoring in the biological area is about to commence. Testing of the system had begun, and a mechanism for monitoring Iraq's trade in dual-purpose items (the export/import mechanism) has been elaborated and appears to meet with approval.[59]

Ritter notes that "UNSCOM by 1995 had moved toward accepting most of the Iraqi declarations concerning past proscribed programs, and in a report to the Security Council in June of that year, Ekeus stated that once Iraq's biological weapons program declaration was verified, UNSCOM would be ready to issue its clean bill of health."[60] At the beginning of 1995, Iraq had fooled the world, successfully concealing its weapons programs and the means for their resurrection.

The evidence for such an assertion materialized quite suddenly in August

1995. In July, Saddam began, once again, to insist upon a fixed timetable for the elimination of sanctions. In early August he declared that unless such a timetable was established by the end of the month, Iraq would cease cooperating with the inspectors. But on August 8, 1995, the situation was transformed. General Hussein Kamel Hassan, Minister of Industry and Minerals and formerly chief of the Military Industrialization Corporation (MIC), which had overseen the development of Iraq's nuclear, biological, chemical, and missile programs, defected to Jordan along with his wife, one of Saddam's daughters, and his brother, Saddam Kamel, who was married to another of Saddam's daughters.

Hussein Kamel's defection completely undercut the Iraqi position, and the Iraqis were not slow to realize their predicament. In a letter to Ekeus sent even before Ekeus had interviewed Kamel, the Minister of Oil invited him to Baghdad, where he was informed that Kamel had hidden important documentation concerning Iraq's proscribed programs without the knowledge of the senior Iraqi leadership. Ekeus was taken to a farm belonging to Hussein Kamel, where he found, locked in a chicken coop, boxes containing half a million pages in print, disk, and microfilm, documenting Iraq's illegal programs.[61]

The documents and the discussions both with the Iraqis, who, for a time, sought damage control by conciliating the commission, and with Hussein Kamel were devastating to Saddam Hussein. They revealed that Iraq possessed highly advanced programs to develop nuclear, biological, and chemical weapons, that it had indigenous capabilities to produce Al-Hussein missiles, that it had "weaponized" its biological agents contrary to its repeated declarations, and that it maintained an extensive and sophisticated mechanism for concealing all its illegal activities. The documents themselves were among those that Ritter had tried in vain to retrieve from the Agriculture Ministry in 1992, and they revealed a massive effort to locate and conceal or destroy documentation relating to these programs that Iraq had repeatedly declared did not even exist.

The Iraqis tries to mollify the commission with a new and sometimes preemptive openness. It soon became clear to them, however, that, armed with this evidence of their perfidy, the Clinton administration would not permit the elimination of the sanctions. The administration, unlike the British in the 1920s, refused to be hoodwinked again, once having had the curtain raised on its enemy's deception. The UN Special Commission, what is more, was a far more independent agency than the IACC had been; it would have been much harder to muzzle that body even had the administration wanted to do so. The result was that a situation that had been moving toward accommodation and resolution (albeit on totally false premises) now lurched rapidly back to one of continual confrontation. Following Hussein Kamel's revelations, the Clinton administration declared that its objective was not merely to enforce the disarmament clauses of the cease-fire, but to remove Saddam Hussein. As long as he was in power, they said, sanctions would remain in place and efforts to unseat him from within would continue.[62]

Saddam's ouster had been the true aim of America's policy since the end of the Gulf War, but allies' objections had prevented its adoption as the explicit purpose of the sanctions imposed by the cease-fire. The fear that the Americans would not be satisfied even by full Iraqi compliance with the disarmament provisions had probably driven Saddam's defiance in October 1994 and July–August 1995, and had certainly driven France to distance herself from the coalition and even, in October 1994, to denounce America's actions in defense of Kuwait. Now this coalition-splitting objective became the open aim of the U.S. government, and sanctions became the tool whereby Clinton expected to achieve it.

The Battle of Irbil

The coalition's fragmentation only increased over time. On August 31, 1996, Saddam Hussein sent some 30,000 men and over 100 tanks into the "safe haven" of Kurdistan to seize its capital, Irbil. Clinton took advantage of this incursion to launch forty-four cruise missiles against air defense targets in *southern* Iraq and to extend the *southern* no-fly zone. No action whatsoever was taken against the Iraqi forces engaged in reconquering Kurdistan, although the incursion into that region was the only justification publicly given for the U.S. attacks.[63] The Clinton administration claimed success, in that the cruise missiles mostly hit their targets and the southern no-fly zone was extended by fiat. What is more, Saddam's forces withdrew from Kurdistan within a few days. Yet the incursion and the American response were further victories for Saddam in the complicated calculus of Versailles-style peaces.

There were probably two main causes for the Iraqi incursion. Despite continued American efforts to bring the two rival Kurdish factions struggling for control of their war-torn region together in opposition to Iraq, civil war continued to rage within the "safe haven." The instability caused by this civil war deeply worried both Turkey and Iran, each of which has large Kurdish minorities and feels continually threatened both by any manifestations of Kurdish nationalism and by the prospect of large-scale refugee problems that had been created by the Kurdish uprising of 1991 and might be created by continued conflict in that region. Since the suppression of the 1991 Kurdish rebellion, Turkish troops had repeatedly violated Iraqi territory in pursuit of their own Kurdish guerrillas, who used the war-torn region as a staging and recruiting base. In the months preceding the August 1996 crisis, Iranian forces had started to make similar incursions, even forming an alliance with one of the Kurdish factions during one such incursion in March 1996. These violations of Iraqi territory were unacceptable to Saddam, as they would be to any sovereign state, and he had probably become legitimately concerned that Kurdistan could either be taken from him, precipitating the breakup of Iraq, or become the staging base for Iranian attacks or demands upon him.

At the same time, the humanitarian determination of the United Nations to allow Iraq to sell oil to procure food for its starving people probably provided the proximate cause for the invasion. In an agreement signed shortly before the Iraqi attack, the UN pledged to allow Iraq to sell $2 billion worth of oil over a period of six months, the proceeds from which could be used only to procure essential supplies for Iraq's needy—most of the population. The oil was to go via Iraq's pipeline that ran through Turkey; the UN's decision, therefore, promised to be lucrative not only for Iraq, but for Turkey as well, since the latter would be able to collect its ordinary transit fees on oil sent through its pipeline.

The oil-for-food deal posed two immediate problems for Saddam in Kurdistan, the region through which the Turkish pipeline ran. It meant that UN monitors would soon be entering that ravaged land to oversee the distribution of humanitarian aid under the agreement. The presence of such a group would pose an obstacle to the political games Saddam was playing in that region in order to secure its reconquest and repacification. Also, with civil war raging and order disrupted, it would be quite easy for any of the Kurdish groups to sabotage the pipeline to spite either Baghdad or Ankara or both together. Only by securing the pipeline could Saddam ensure the necessary income the deal would provide him, and only by securing Kurdistan could he secure the oil.[64]

On traditional grounds of power politics, the United States had no interest in stopping Saddam from securing Kurdistan. Instability in the Gulf region resulting from the breakup of the Iraqi state was the main reason given in 1991, and throughout the years since, for failing to invade Iraq and topple Saddam by force. Yet the continued strife in Kurdistan was one of the most inflammatory sources of instability in the state of Iraq, and had, in fact, brought the armed forces of Iraq, Iran, and Turkey into conflict with various Kurdish factions and, almost, with each other. From the standpoint of regional security, which the U.S. administrations esteemed so highly, the settlement of the Kurdish "problem" was a good thing. From the international standpoint, it was even better, since it would secure the oil pipeline that made the oil-for-food deal possible. Turkey was likely to be particularly pleased with such an attack, for although it feared and distrusted Iraq, it hated and distrusted the Kurds more and had previously pressed Saddam to intervene and put an end to the strife. A cold calculation of America's interests called for Saddam to crush the Kurds, and any aggressive response to such an operation was certain to receive little support in the international community.

And so it was: Turkey refused to allow the United States to use forces based at Incirlik to participate in the attack; Saudi Arabia similarly refused to allow U.S. forces on its territory to assist in the strike. France once again distanced itself from the action, stating again that the action was designed to assist President Clinton in his reelection campaign and had nothing to do with the UN or the international community—Saddam Hussein's actions in his own territory, the French proclaimed, were his own business and should not be subject to punishment. Russia and China openly denounced the attack. No UN resolution formally authorized the attack—the Clinton administration made the extremely tenuous claim that previous resolutions had already done so—because any such resolution would have been vetoed had it been proposed. Great Britain supported the strike, but took almost no part in it. Nor was the strike spectacularly successful even in attaining its extremely modest objectives: Iraq's air defense capabilities in the southern no-fly zone were hurt, but hardly crippled. Nothing, of course, prevented Saddam from installing the Kurdish faction loyal to him in Irbil, destroying his enemies, and reasserting his control over the entire region—which he did.

Even so, the Clinton administration had little choice but to respond to Saddam's attack on Irbil. The creation of the Kurdish safe haven and the northern no-fly zone in 1991 had invested American prestige and the credibility of the peace settlement in that dangerous land. In 1991 and later the United States had repeatedly warned Iraq that it would not tolerate Iraqi operations in the safe haven. By claiming that the 1991 Security Council resolutions authorized the United States to use force to oppose the incursion, moreover, the Clinton administration ensured that the Iraqi attack, if allowed to succeed, would undermine the peace itself. But Kurdistan is not on the sea, and America's regional allies opposed military action against Iraq on that issue. Even if the Clinton administration had not been determined to avoid large-scale war in the Gulf at all costs, it is doubtful what could have been done in 1996 to keep Saddam out of Kurdistan. The very nature of the peace created in 1991 virtually ensured that such an attack would come, that it would be effectively unopposable, and that it would be a blow to the peace itself.

The U.S. strike on Iraq in September 1996 was similar in many respects to the French occupation of Frankfurt and Darmstadt in 1920 in response to Germany's suppression of the Ruhr uprising of that year.[65] In both cases, the attacking power found itself in the extremely uncomfortable position of having to take action to maintain the peace, knowing that such action would be merely a gesture, incapable of changing the course of events in the region, and would also inflame unwilling allies and greatly complicate the politics of the alliance.

Similar confusion about objectives was also apparent in both cases. The French coveted the Ruhr and hoped to keep it or, at least, to keep it out of the hands of the Germans, yet coalition politics prevented them from making such a condition part of the peace, or even from publicly declaring it as an objective. In the same way, the United States hoped to maintain indefinitely the untenable situation wherein Kurdistan was nominally under Iraqi suzerainty, which would not alienate the Turks and the Iranians who opposed an independent Kurdistan, but was also not really part of Iraq. In 1991, as in 1919, however, coalition politics made even the public declaration of such an objective impossible. The invasion of the Ruhr and the strike of September 1996, therefore, pursued objectives that could not be publicly proclaimed and would not have been internationally supported. The most that could be said for either was that it made France, on the one hand, or the United States, on the other, "feel good" that at least "something had been done" to uphold the peace and punish the unrepentant aggressor. In truth all that either did was to deepen the hatred of Germany or Iraq and further divide an already crumbling alliance. Such an outcome was an almost inevitable result of the nature of the peaces of 1919 and 1991.

The End of Inspections

The Kurdish incursion served another purpose for Saddam as well by distracting attention from yet another conflict over inspections that had been brewing since March. The defection of Hussein Kamel and his revelations placed UNSCOM in an excellent position to attack the wall of secrecy Saddam Hussein had erected behind which to hide his continuing WMD programs. Hussein Kamel had revealed that the concealment was a consciously orchestrated program directed by Saddam's closest and most trusted agents. Acting under Saddam's orders, they had microfilmed and digitized key documents so that they could be more readily hidden, had decided which hardware components must be preserved, and had destroyed a great number of superfluous documents and unnecessary hardware to reduce the amount of damaging material UNSCOM might find. The concealment operations involved delaying inspectors, sometimes only for a few hours, so that critical materials could be moved or, if the delays were longer, could be destroyed.[66] Intelligence provided by Western sources confirmed in 1998 that Saddam's security organizations were issuing orders to local units to conceal documents even as the inspectors inspected other areas. At one point, Ritter reports, the UNSCOM team was held up by Iraqi minders who feigned confusion while boxes of material were removed in trucks in sight of the UNSCOM team.[67]

These tactics were almost always effective; it was in the nature of such an inspection regime that they be so. Each time the Iraqis delayed or refused entry to an UNSCOM team, an international incident of some variety ensued. But it was always impossible for the United States to move unilaterally, let alone with any allied support, instantly, as soon as the inspection was blocked. The Iraqis always had a reason for refusing that had to be demonstrated to be false to an increasingly credulous international community, and American forces in the Gulf theater were always reduced in the relaxation of tensions following every crisis, both to save money and to have those precious forces available for operations elsewhere. American military power in the Gulf region, therefore, always had to be built back up again to launch or threaten another attack. Even in these trivial exercises of American military might, America's military weakness proved hampering. In the inevitable days and weeks that the military diplomatic deployments required, the Iraqis could almost always defeat any given inspection.

It was clear by mid-1996 that Iraq was continuing a program designed to protect its future capabilities to produce chemical and biological warheads and the missiles to deploy them.[68] It was also clear that this program entailed the deliberate deception of UNSCOM and obstruction of its work. It was clear above all that such a program of deception and obstruction would work, at least to preserve the knowledge base Iraq needed to restart its WMD programs the minute the inspectors finally left. And Saddam Hussein had made it brutally obvious that he intended to do precisely that.

The coalition powers should have discontinued the inspections on their own and come to terms with the situation. Either it was acceptable to the United States and the other powers for Iraq to maintain the ability and the determination to develop large WMD stockpiles and the mechanisms for delivering them, or else they must take serious action, not to enforce the failing inspections, but to change the situation in Iraq. Repeated missile strikes made clear that only an invasion could do that, but invading was the one thing the United States was absolutely unwilling to consider—so much so that as the crises continued, it became normal neither to deploy nor even to alert U.S. ground forces, as if to reassure Saddam that nothing worse than pinprick missile strikes would ever threaten him.

But Washington was unwilling to accept or admit that the inspections had become a fig leaf for Saddam rather than a threat to him. It was less frightening to believe that they might be made to work than to face the alternatives that really existed: a rearmed, revitalized Iraq, or an invasion. As time went on, the Clinton administration increasingly placed its hopes on the long-term effects of sanctions, but evidence soon mounted that sanctions were a bent reed. If nothing else, the humanitarian nightmare in Iraq, engineered largely by Saddam, had caused such a furor in the international community as to compel the United States to accept the oil-for-food deal. But that deal inevitably undercut the sanctions, whatever conditions were placed upon the money actually sent to Iraq, for any money used to alleviate the starvation of Iraq's citizens could be retrieved by Baghdad dollar-for-dollar. For all Saddam's brutality, Iraq had been spending money to keep its people from starving. As time went on, the amount of oil Iraq was allowed to sell for food was steadily increased, sometimes at the very same time Saddam defied UNSCOM and the United States. If the harsh sanctions in place before 1996 when Saddam was weakest had not toppled him, there was little hope that the increasingly weaker sanctions after that time would bring down his increasingly strong regime.

These contradictions reached a crescendo in November–December 1998, when Saddam finally declared that he would not cooperate with UNSCOM any longer and stuck to that declaration. In response, the United States launched Operation Desert Fox, a four-day extensive strike by bombers and cruise missiles against a wide variety of targets in Iraq. The strike was worse than a forlorn hope—it was an admission of defeat. The ostensible objective, apart from "punishing" Saddam, was to "degrade" his WMD program. The much more massive airstrikes of 1991 had failed to do that; UNSCOM inspections had done a much better job, but had been foiled throughout 1998 in their attempts to locate critical documents and materials. The very fact of Saddam's obstruction of the UNSCOM inspections meant that the United States could not have had the targeting information needed for its high-tech weapons with their pinpoint accuracy. It is certain that Desert Fox did not destroy Saddam's WMD capabilities, and it is highly unlikely that it degraded them seriously.[69] What is certain, however, is that it brought the inspections to an end. Since the United States was unwilling to invade, and since Desert Fox clearly indicated the maximum level of effort the United States was willing to use, Saddam had absolutely no incentive to yield any more, since even his obstructions of December 1998 had not shaken the determination of his international allies to undermine the sanctions regime. With Desert Fox the inspections farce came to an end and a critical component of the peace of 1991 had perished.[70]

Conclusion: The Flawed Peace, Versailles 1991

Iraq is no threat now to its neighbors, except Kuwait, and no threat to that state as long as the United States is committed to defend it. The UNSCOM inspections have been effective at eliminating any current threat Iraqi WMD programs might pose, despite the significant questions that remain regarding Iraq's biological weapons capabilities. Iraq's army was significantly damaged during the Gulf War and has not been rebuilt. Despite the successful operations of 1994 in the deployment toward Kuwait or 1996 in the pacification of Kurdistan, it is clear that the Iraqi armed forces are not capable of large-scale sustained aggression at this time. To that extent the peace of 1991 has been effective.

But, like the peace of 1919, that of 1991 was fundamentally and fatally flawed. In both cases the victorious powers failed to address the basic issues, the Americans after 1991 more so than England and France. Bush repeatedly proclaimed the wrong objective for Desert Storm, declaring that the liberation of Kuwait was his only goal. Since then, both American administrations have repeatedly declared that the elimination of Saddam's weapons of mass destruction is the only obstacle in the way of permanent peace. It is as though France and Britain went to war in 1914 in order to liberate Belgium and continued sanctions against Germany after 1918 to prevent her from acquiring tanks and aircraft.

The Allies after 1918, especially England, were not that ill-advised, but they, too, failed to reckon with the extent of their problem. The imposition of the disarmament clauses of the Treaty of Versailles implied that it was "German militarism" that had been the difficulty and that the forcible elimination of German military power would permanently secure the peace. But German militarism was not at the root. The true problem was that before 1914, Germany had acquired the ability to field military forces capable of vying for regional hegemony and, more important, had developed the burning desire to use them for that purpose. The disarmament provisions did not really strike at that ability, which is latent in any populous, industrialized state—they merely put off the evil day until some period after the end of inspections, unless the Germans decided of their own accord not to continue to pursue aggressive policies.

The imposition of sanctions in the Versailles Treaty, both economic and military, unintentionally ensured that the Germans would not choose such a peaceful course. The harsh terms of the treaty were an affront to all Germans and a grievance nurtured for twenty years. The sufferings imposed on the Germans by the Allied embargo, which persisted until 1920, and then Allied reparations, which persisted for much longer, were all laid at the feet of the Allies despite the fact that the German government greatly increased that suffering by its intransigence. The terms of the peace treaty, indeed, sowed the seeds for the next war by creating resentment and the determination to undo the peace even as they failed to destroy the German capability to do so in the long run.

The peace of 1991 has had a similar effect. It is clear that Saddam's own intransigence (and sometimes his deliberate policy) has vastly increased the suffering of his own people—if he had adhered to the peace terms he signed in 1991, the sanctions would have been lifted long ago. If he had accepted the oil-for-food program when it was first offered to him, thousands of Iraqis would be alive and healthy who are now sick or dead. But the resentments for those actions are not likely to fall on Saddam. He controls the media in Iraq, he controls the system of education and propaganda. He has used all these tools to teach his people that the United States is to blame for their suffering—and the international facts are not altogether at odds with that reading. The embargo has come to be seen by many, not only Iraqis, as a U.S. weapon, and the forces of the United States have repeatedly attacked Iraq. The Iraqis may come to hate or despise their current leader enough to remove him, unlikely though that seems now, but it is extremely unlikely that their resentment of the United States will dissipate with that action. It is highly likely, on the contrary, that any successor government in Iraq, even a nominal democracy in that state, will be determined to reverse the verdict of the Gulf War and avenge a decade of horrible suffering.

The peace of 1991 may have generated, if anything, stronger resentment than that of 1919.

Has it been as successful in curbing Iraq's military power as the Allies had been after World War I? Far from it. On the contrary, Iraq is now relatively far stronger militarily than Germany was in 1927, an equivalent number of years after the peace. Iraq's army numbers in the hundreds of thousands, its infrastructure has not been destroyed, its command and control arrangements have not been disturbed. Any lessons it learned in the Gulf Wars and in the years following have been preserved. The Iraqis do not face the daunting prospect of rebuilding their army from cadre, as the Germans did. They have merely to rearm, reequip, and retrain a functioning organization. That is a far easier task.

From the standpoint of proscribed weapons, the Iraqis are probably in about the same position the Germans had been in. Neither state had, eight years after the conflict, any militarily useful proscribed weapons. But the Germans had an extensive theoretical program aimed at determining the optimum design, production methods, doctrine tactics, and organizations required to produce, field, and use tanks and aircraft. Their military industry, although nominally converted to peacetime uses, was specifically designed to be ready for a rapid transition to the production of those weapons. A corps of specialists in both aircraft and armored warfare was carefully preserved within the *Reichswehr*'s ranks. The most dangerous activities were carried on outside Germany's borders by states not within the purview of the IACC and not vulnerable to Allied retributions. These factors allowed the German state to rearm with such rapidity following the decision to do so in 1932, even before Hitler had come to power. When Hitler's determination was added to these latent capabilities, Germany's rearmament proceeded at an astronomical pace.

That pace was made possible by the apparently minor violations of the disarmament treaty Germany had conducted throughout the 1920s. The IACC knew about those violations; its members reported them to their governments. But what were Britain and France to do? Should they invade Germany because proscribed documents were found at a Krupps plant? Should they assault because inspectors were blocked from visiting a regimental barracks? It is in the nature of such treaties that each violation is so minor in itself that it could not possibly be used to justify war. And although the pattern of violations begins to provide such a justification a few years after the peace, the will to fight a war to rearrange the flawed international system fundamentally, which had been too weak when the peace was signed, had vanished altogether. The small violations had to be tolerated; the pattern of obstruction had to be accepted, even though it was clear to those who could see that the basis was laid thereby for a rapid reversal of the disarmament.

If the sanctions are finally lifted, as they surely will be before too long, Saddam will not lack for funds. He has shown that his first priority is taking care of his armed forces, particularly his WMD programs. It is likely that those programs will see a massive infusion of cash as soon as the cash become available. Before or after that time, he will have succeeded in bringing an end to the no-fly zones. Those zones now serve no purpose—the Shiite rebellion has been crushed, and Saddam never needed aircraft to suppress the Kurds. But the United States has invested a considerable amount of national prestige in them, and their abandonment, like the remilitarization of the Rhineland in 1935, will be a serious blow to United States credibility. The rapid rebirth of Iraq's armed forces is likely to follow. What will happen then can only be guessed.

The course of events makes it clear that the Bush administration was wrong in failing to invade Iraq and to accept the burden of maintaining regional stability in the aftermath of that invasion, just as it is clear in historical retrospect that the Allies' failure to invade Germany in 1918 sowed the seeds for future conflict. For the Allies, of course, such an option was not available—Wilson's offer of a peace based on the Fourteen Points and the Germans' acceptance of that offer precluded any further fighting. Bush and his allies have claimed that they similarly had no choice—the coalition, they say, would have fallen apart had they proceeded into Iraq, but the evidence for that is not convincing. However that may be, the results have been baleful. The victors repeated an error of the past by attempting to compensate with a harsh peace for an incomplete victory.

The fundamental problem the Iraqis present in the Middle East is that they can field an armed force strong enough to vie for regional hegemony and that they have shown the stubborn will to do so. Nothing that has happened in 1991 or since has changed that fact. The unstable peace the United States imposed in 1991, like the one the Allies imposed in 1919, has only delayed the awful day.

But past decisions and events were not inevitable, nor are those of the future. The French invasion of the Ruhr in 1923, like Desert Fox, brought about the end of armaments inspections and dealt the death blow to the disarmament provisions of the treaty. It did so because England refused to support its erstwhile ally, while France was not willing to make the effort on its own to take adequate action. England's refusal and France's unwillingness were not inevitable. They resulted from misreadings in London and Paris of the real situation and of where their interests lay. They resulted from the unwillingness to make a realistic, continuing, and adequately armed commitment to enforce a peace that could not stand on its own. For that commitment they substituted a wishful belief that the problem had already largely been solved and that there was really no need to go to war. Those wishes were unavailing, as events would show all too soon. The absence of a striking historical analogy made it easier to make the mistake.

The United States has no such excuse in pursuing its current policy toward Iraq. The example of the 1920s ought to have provided a warning from the start. The "minor" violations Saddam has been pursuing have not been minor, and the "measured" responses have not measured up to the real threat. The revelations of Hussein Kamel in 1995 should have resulted in direct action to redress the fundamental problem—the persistence in Iraq of an aggressive regime determined to seek regional hegemony. There was nothing inevitable about the failure to respond—that failure resulted from the conscious decision of policy makers to avoid a problem they had reason to know was real. They avoided it because the consequences of dealing with it were too unpleasant, while the consequences of giving in seemed much smaller.

They are not. The Gulf War failed to resolve the fundamental problem, and the peace imposed only delayed its reappearance for as long as the United States ensured the enforcement of the peace's provisions. The costs of continuing to enforce even this inadequate peace are likely to be very great. By the spring of 1999 the United States and its NATO allies were deeply distracted by their war in Yugoslavia, itself, no doubt, encouraged by American timidity toward Iraq. Their air forces were so overstretched as to make it ever more difficult to enforce the no-fly zones. Saddam's development of WMDs had gone on for months, unmonitored and unchecked. The prospect loomed of a negotiated end to the war in Yugoslavia that would leave another brutal leader in power, having survived the halfhearted efforts of the United States and its allies, whose alliance was in the process of disintegration. The nations with the chief responsibility for preserving peace and order in the world might soon find themselves facing the reality of two angry and determined military dictators who had succeeded in defying them and lived to tell the tale, a fact not unnoticed by two dissatisfied outsiders potentially far more powerful.

18

A Legacy of
Half Measures

However unhappy were the legacies from the Bush administration in Somalia and Haiti, the most troubling was the situation in the former Yugoslavia. During the presidential campaign of 1992, Clinton had taken advantage of Bush's inactivity in the face of widely publicized horrors to attack from the right. He called for stronger economic sanctions against "the renegade regime of Slobodan Milosevic," and for the right of Western warships to strike "against those who are attacking the relief effort" to help those under attack by the Serbs. When pictures of Serbian concentration camps filled American television screens, Clinton demanded that the U.S. press NATO to make air attacks to save the Bosnians from "deliberate and systematic extermination based on their ethnic origins." He insisted that the UN, with American support, must do "whatever it takes to stop the slaughter of civilians and we may have to use military force. I would begin with airpower against the Serbs." Soon after the election he announced in words reminiscent of Bush's determined promise to restore the independence of Kuwait that "the legitimacy of ethnic cleansing will not stand,"[1] a statement that suggested a more active role in Yugoslavian affairs by the new regime. "It seemed a clear pledge that President Clinton would bring the great power of the United States to bear on the task of achieving justice in the Balkans."[2] Any such expectations were swiftly dispelled. Prime Minister Baldwin had predicted the American response to Japan's conquest of Manchuria in 1931. "You will get nothing out of Washington but words, big words, but only words."[3] So it was, too, in 1993.

The new President turned his attention to Bosnia almost at once. The fighting in Yugoslavia had temporarily subsided, and some European countries had contributed soldiers who were serving as "peacekeepers" in Bosnia. On February 5, 1993, Clinton told his advisers, "If the United States doesn't act in situations like this nothing will happen. . . . A failure to do so would be to give up American leadership." He decided to use American planes to drop food to Muslims, to ask the UN to authorize a no-fly zone, and to tighten economic sanctions. The United States would become involved in the Vance-Owen discussions; it would repeat Bush's warning to the Serbs not to make trouble in Kosovo, and it would help enforce any agreement that could be made to stop the fighting. In the words of Anthony Lake, "The key to it was our willingness to take part in the implementation of a peace agreement. Otherwise we wouldn't be taken seriously."[4]

On February 10, Secretary of State Christopher announced these decisions publicly at a State Department briefing, the first of a long series of public statements by the Clinton administration that explained the international situation and America's interests in it without producing effective action. Christopher began with a slap at the inaction of his predecessors:

> We inherit at this early in our administration a tragic and dangerous situation. . . . During that period, the West has missed repeated opportunities to engage in early and effective ways that might have prevented the conflict from deepening. . . . [A]n early and forceful signal might well have deterred much of the aggression, bloodshed, and ethnic cleansing.

Although all this took place "far from our shores . . . we cannot afford to ignore it. . . ." The United States had a humanitarian interest—"Our conscience revolts at the idea of passively accepting such brutality"—but it had strategic interests, too. Here Christopher enunciated the concern most basic for a nation whose greatest national interest is the preservation of international peace and stability: the attack on Bosnia, a new member of the UN, "challenges the principle that internationally recognized borders should not be altered by force." But this conflict threatened to spill over borders to Kosovo and Macedonia, producing a general Balkan war, affecting Albania, Greece, and Turkey.

Christopher also pointed to these events as a

> crucial test of how [the world] will address the concerns of religious and ethnic minorities in the post–Cold War period. . . . Bold tyrants and fearful minorities are watching to see whether ethnic cleansing is a policy the world will tolerate. If we hope to promote the spread of freedom, if we hope to encourage the emergence of peaceful ethnic democracies, our answer must be a resounding "no."

The Secretary made clear that the United States did not intend to impose a so-lution and made the usual disclaimer: "The United States is not the world's po-liceman. We cannot interpose our forces to stop every armed conflict in the world." He concluded, however, with a statement of commitment to a respon-sible American policy in the new era:

> Yet we are the United States of America. We have singular powers and influence. We are committed to Europe's stability. Our values and inter-ests give us reason to help create an international standard for fair treat-ment of minorities; therefore we have reason to participate actively, urgently in this effort. This is an important moment for our nation's postwar—post–Cold War role in Europe and the world. It tests our abil-ity to adopt new approaches to foreign policy in a world that is funda-mentally changed. It tests our commitment to nurturing of democracy and the support of environments in which democracy can grow and take root. It tests our willingness and that of our allies to help our institutions of collective security, such as NATO, evolve in ways that can meet the demands of a new age. And it tests what wisdom we have gathered from this bloody century, and it measures our resolve to take early concerted action against systematic ethnic persecution.[5]

This fine statement, however, also turned out to be largely only "words, big words, but only words." As one scholar describes the Clinton administration's actions: "The new White House had a tendency to pronounce on principle, pre-varicate in practice and preempt the policies and plans of others." Whatever its statement of principles, "it was never commensurate either with circumstances or its own degree of commitment, given its absolute domestic priorities." In practice, American policy "graduated from virtually no action to little action—the sum of which was to distract international diplomacy and divert any pres-sure for serious engagement by the U.S."[6]

Discussions within the administration in February quickly revealed little taste for action. John Fox, a State Department official who took part, described their character. Practical proposals that avoided the extremes of a major and disastrous commitment like that in Vietnam or complete inaction were ruled out: "[T]he people who wanted to do something got the rhetoric, but the people who didn't want to do anything got the policy." Before long it became clear that "there would be little if anything done to follow through on the campaign pledges."[7]

From the first, without formally opposing it, the Clinton administration had scorned the Vance-Owen plan on the grounds that, behind a verbal screen of multiethnicity, it ratified ethnic cleansing, but the administration was not prepared to use American force to support a different solution. Bosnian Serb at-tacks in mid-February on Srebinica and other eastern Bosnian towns, however, soon showed vividly on television the horrible consequences of ethnic cleansing. The only American response was the institution of a drop of food and medicine into Bosnia by air as a purely humanitarian gesture. Clinton was rapidly backing away from his earlier political demands and talk of military action. He swiftly decided not to commit American ground troops in any circumstances. He began to distance the United States from involvement and to contradict statements he and his associates had made. Only weeks after Christopher's briefing, with its refusal to ignore events "far from our shores" or to allow ethnic cleansing to stand, its commitment to new American initiatives, Clinton suggested that the problems were too hard to solve and that the United States was already doing what it could: "The hatred between all three groups . . . is almost unbelievable . . . it's centuries old. That really is a problem from hell. And I think the United States is doing all we can to try to deal with the problem." Christopher himself spoke of a war in Bosnia as "a humanitarian crisis a long way from home, in the middle of another continent."[8]

But the atrocious pictures on television and the administration's earlier rhetoric would not allow the problem to go away. In an odd way the Clinton administration contributed to the crisis by encouraging the Bosnians to resist with greater determination, the opposite of what the UN and the Europeans desired. In Bosnia the UN served a purpose similar to that of the League of Nations at Corfu in 1923 and on other occasions. It provided a surrogate for the great powers, performing embarrassing acts of retreat and surrender that would be difficult for the nations themselves. Their "dirty little secret" was that they wanted peace in Bosnia at almost any price. "The terms of the peace were . . . almost irrelevant. It did not have to be a just peace or even a peace that could be maintained."[9] Any peace that avoided further involvement, especially military, would do. Whatever the true meaning or intention of Clinton's words, the Bosnian Muslims took them seriously. When the Americans opened a new embassy in Sarajevo in the spring of 1994, Yasushi Akashi, the UN Secretary-General's representative in Bosnia, was furious. "If anything emboldens the Muslim government to fight on it is things like this," he said. "They can point to that and say, 'See, the Americans are with us.' We can only hope that the failure of NATO to come to their aid will convince them the U.S. cavalry isn't around the corner."[10] There was a feeling among many European "peacekeepers" that the Bosnians were the problem: "[t]he Bosnian side . . . from the UN perspective had . . . the bad taste to be in earnest about the freedom of their country. . . ."[11] As Lord Crewe had blamed the Greeks for not having the decency to trump up false evidence against themselves in the Corfu affair, from the UN perspective "it was unfortunate that the Bosnian government refused to 'come to its senses and surrender.'"[12] It is hard not to think of the remark of an officer of the British Foreign Office a month before Hitler marched into Austria: "Personally, I almost wish that Hitler would swallow Austria and get it over." A month after the Anschluss he wrote to a colleague: "Thank goodness Austria's out of the way."[13]

Clinton's rhetoric, "insofar as he used it as a substitute for meaningful action," was disastrous for the Bosnian resistance.

> [T]he policy of his administration was not only more duplicitous but in many ways more damaging than Bush's had been. . . . [Bush] was too timid and shortsighted . . . ; but Bush had never promised the U.S. cavalry might be on the way. Clinton had promised strong action—had vowed America would help—and when confronted with the need to supply it, he had offered words; those words did more than disappoint— they instilled hope which the Bosnians paid for with blood.[14]

The new attacks on Srebinica drew enormous attention from the media, enough to force Clinton to consider new policies. By now they were so eager to put an end to the embarrassing problem that they were prepared to accept a revised version of the Vance-Owen plan, accepted by the Muslims but not by the Serbs. Clinton said, "We've got to do everything we can to put a full-court press diplomatically to secure the agreement of the Serbs."[15]

But diplomatic pressure alone would not suffice; some military pressure would also be required. The least unattractive choices were to lift the arms embargo in Bosnia or to use air strikes against the Serbs. Both faced problems. The embargo had been in place since 1991, and its effect greatly favored the Serbs, who could draw on the weapons of the old Yugoslav army while the Muslims were without adequate arms. Lifting the embargo could help level the field without cost to the United States. The trouble with that plan was that it would intensify the war, to which the European NATO members, with troops on the ground as "peacekeepers," were opposed. During the time the Muslims were rearming, moreover, the Serbs could be expected to do them terrible harm before the new weapons could arrive.

The Europeans also opposed air strikes while their troops were on the ground. A further barrier came from within the administration itself. American military leaders, led especially by Chairman of the Joint Chiefs Colin Powell, resisted military action. Intelligence estimates were pessimistic about the effectiveness of air strikes alone. The only approach likely to work, they said, was the use of considerable ground forces supported by airplanes. The use of ground troops was quickly ruled out, leaving airpower as the only possibility, but Powell argued against that, as well. "'What is the end point?' He'd say, 'If we bomb Serb military targets in Bosnia and that doesn't bring them to the conference table, then what?'"[16] Powell is well known to have been opposed to any military engagement in Yugoslavia and to be a major victim of the "Vietnam syndrome" in general. He records that an exasperated Madeline Albright asked him, "What's the point of having this superb military that you're always talking about if we can't use it?" Powell wrote, "I thought I would have an aneurysm."[17] Yet his warnings about the need for clear political goals and the need to be prepared for the possible military consequences were well-founded. The President has repeatedly and publicly rejected the use of ground troops, though it should have been obvious that any serious attempt to compel a just and lasting solution might require their use. It was, therefore, infinitely more difficult to deter the Serbs from continued violence or to compel them to come to terms. The American refusal to even think of using ground troops resembled Britain's doctrine of "limited liability" in the 1930s, each severely reducing the chance to deter aggression.

Still the pressure for action built. By mid-April new horrible pictures from Srebinica appeared on television. Republicans in Congress fixed on the superficially attractive plan to lift the arms embargo and criticized Clinton for refusing to do so. Senators from both parties called for air strikes. The Bosnian Serbs rejected the revised Vance-Owens proposal. Clinton responded, once again, with words. He expressed outrage at the Serbian refusal. The United States and Europe must now consider "things which at least previously have been unacceptable." Returning to the tone of the previous February, he reasserted the need to stand up "against the principle of ethnic cleansing. . . . [T]his is not just about Bosnia." The U.S. must "force the consideration of all possible options." Responding to a question, he said, "At this point, I would not rule out any option except the option I have never ruled in, . . . American ground troops." A few days later, he revealed his true hesitation, saying, "The U.S. should always seek an opportunity to stand up against—at least speak out against—inhumanity."[18]

Hesitant or not, Clinton needed to act. "By saying so often that something must be done to stop the ethnic cleansing, he had got himself into a corner. Whatever his misgivings, doing nothing wasn't an option."[19] At last, on May 1, Clinton decided on a plan called "lift and strike," to lift the arms embargo and carry out air strikes if the Serbs attacked in the interim. Immediately he sent Secretary Christopher to Europe to try to bring America's allies along. The British and French indicated their opposition in advance, and an acute reporter observes, "There was no real reason for the President and Christopher to believe that the trip would succeed. They had set themselves up for an embarrassing failure."[20]

If not successful in its stated purpose, however, Christopher's mission to Europe has been called "a brilliant achievement" in a different sense.

> For it provided President Clinton with an effective alibi for his own inaction. If the President had not moved to lift the arms embargo against the Bosnians or to ready air strikes against the Serbs, this was because the Europeans had troops on the ground, and, try as he might, he could not bring them around to accept his proposals.

There is reason to doubt the sincerity of the mission. Belgium's Foreign Minister reported his sense that Christopher "had felt very clearly that there was not a good possibility to convince the Europeans."[21] Nor did he press the case with the necessary force. An American official described Christopher's instructions:

> Chris's mission was to seek support for this approach, but there never was a view that he should say, "This, or else." If we'd bet the ranch, said to the French and English, "This threatens a fundamental breach in our relationships," we could perhaps have got the Europeans—kicking and screaming—involved. But this would have made it an American problem. We would have taken over. We have viewed it as a European problem where we'd helped out."

When Christopher returned to Washington he referred to the policy as a "loser" and said that the only way to get the Europeans to agree was to "pressure them very hard, which carried risks, and that he didn't recommend it."[22] The Europeans were never prepared to take the lead. "They expected the Americans, in matters of true import, to lead, not to ask."[23] Whatever his original intention, Clinton, too, soon backed away from "lift and strike." He discovered that there was little enthusiasm in Congress for the plan, and he read a book that impressed upon him the centuries-old history of the conflict in Yugoslavia. After hearing the President, Secretary of Defense Aspin told some colleagues, "Guys, he's going south on this policy. . . . We have a serious problem here. We're out there pushing a policy that the President's not comfortable with. He's not on board."[24]

The plan was soon abandoned, "and the President of the United States looked feckless."

> He had talked and talked about the moral imperative of doing something about Bosnia, and done nothing. He had said publicly that he would be coming up with a strong policy, one that could well involve military action, and he had failed to do so. He had reacted to what he saw on television, and his mind seemed easily changed. He had also claimed, disingenuously, to be closer to an agreement with the Europeans than he was. Whatever the policy should have been, Clinton's way of making it didn't engender confidence.[25]

These problems resulted chiefly from the Clinton administration's lack of a general understanding of the problems facing the United States after the Cold War and of the will to shape and conduct a policy to meet its difficulties. It was clear that the only way to succeed with the American plan was to take the lead itself and not leave things to the Europeans. "But from the outset the U.S. had wanted to avoid leadership. . . . It was neither prepared to act unilaterally, having clearly committed itself to 'multilateralism,' nor to provide leadership. As there was absolutely no will to shift on this issue, the Administration's policy had run into a dead-end."²⁶ They developed considerable skill in devising the appropriate rhetoric that spoke of America's need to prevent the use of violence between nations or ethnic groups within them, but their actions and inaction regularly failed to match their language.

After the failure of "lift and strike," Christopher "moved methodically to shut down the Bosnia policy."²⁷ To save appearances the United States sent 300 American troops to join the United Nations Protective Forces (UNPROFOR) in Macedonia in a show of helping to contain the crisis. At a congressional hearing, Christopher tried to distance the United States from the Bosnian affair, speaking of ancient hatreds among the contending ethnic groups, all of whom, he said, committed atrocities. "At heart," he said, "this is a European problem." Scrambling for the appearance of some action, the Europeans had invented a scheme for establishing six "safe areas" in Bosnia for the Muslims, and on May 6 the UN passed a resolution calling for the halt of attacks and the withdrawal of the Serbs from those towns. To undermine a meeting proposed by Russian Foreign Minister Alexander Kozyrev to consider real international protection of these areas, Christopher called a meeting of his own, to which he invited Kozyrev and the French, British, and Spanish foreign ministers. In the resulting document the signatory nations agreed to protect the "safe areas" by force, if required. "This 'Joint Action Plan' was a minimalist approach—another form of containment—designed to smooth things over among the Western allies and to co-opt Kozyrev. . . . [It] sanctioned Serb aggression in Bosnia and offered the unpleasant possibility of six permanent Muslim camps." Christopher meant the troops in Macedonia and the Joint Action Plan to serve as "substitutes for 'lift and strike' and as initiatives that could make the Bosnia issue go away—or at least appear to."²⁸

Bosnia was tucked away only briefly, because in July, President Clinton was again deeply troubled by television reports showing the horrors resulting from the Serb siege of Sarajevo. He instructed his advisers to create plans for doing something about Sarajevo; this time he would even consider using ground troops, but criticism by the military chiefs quickly put an end to that idea. Instead it was decided to seek a negotiated settlement, using air strikes in aid of diplomacy, to force the Serbs to the table. This time the United States should be prepared to act alone if its allies would not cooperate. On this occasion it was Lake who sought allied help, and he made a forceful case. If Sarajevo collapsed it would be a terrible blow to NATO and to America's relations with its allies and would harm them in the eyes of all the world's Muslims. At an August 2 meeting of NATO the members agreed to prepare air strikes against the Serbs if "the strangulation of Sarajevo and other areas continues."

The "if" left considerable room for wobbling, and the British and French required the UN's approval before NATO could act. Still, the agreement represented some progress toward the Americans' goal, but "[a]s a result of a combination of Serb guile and lack of will on the part of the United States and its allies, the air strikes never occurred."[29] The Serbs allowed enough supplies to get through to make the question of "strangulation" arguable and then entered peace talks, which provided an escape from the idea of bombing.

The fact of peace negotiations presented an urgent new problem to the Clinton administration. They had promised to commit some 25,000 American troops as peacekeepers if an agreement was reached, as now seemed possible. They do not seem to have considered that problem seriously, but the Congress was already restless about Somalia and was talking of withdrawing troops from there. How could the administration prevent that while asking for more troops to send to Bosnia? In Congress, opposition would arise from those who wanted to send no troops anywhere but also from those who wanted no peace agreement in Bosnia that rewarded Serbian aggression. Misgivings grew within the administration.

Events saved them from the full embarrassment of decision when the Bosnian peace talks collapsed on September 29. The United States and its allies used this as a pretext for abandoning the idea of air strikes and for taking no action. The President's brief determination had "gone south" again because of political fears, foot-dragging by the allies and his own military advisers, and his own timidity.

> For the second time in the year, the President had reacted emotionally to television pictures of what was happening in Bosnia, and had an enthusiasm to do something—and then backed off (not before making strong statements about his intentions). He provided no steady leadership on the subject within the government, to the American people, or internationally. He was passive, and changeable—like a cork bobbing about on the waves. He was torn between his emotional responses and his domestic imperative, which always prevailed.[30]

Late in January 1994, French Foreign Minister Juppé urged Christopher to put pressure on the Muslims to make an agreement, but the Secretary of State declined; a bad deal forced on the Bosnians would be too embarrassing politically at home. At the same time, Clinton showed his renewed timidity by telling the press, "I don't think that the international community has the capacity to stop people . . . from their own civil wars."[31] Bosnia was no longer a matter of Serb aggression but a "civil war," one that the world was helpless to bring to an end. The latest American attempt to put "the problem from hell" aside came to an end, however, with another televised horror. On February 5, 1994, a 120-mm mortar shell landed in a major marketplace in Sarajevo, killing sixty-eight people in "a bloody holocaust whose immediate aftermath television cameras were able to capture."[32] The impression of the scene was strong enough to move the United States and NATO to issue an ultimatum to the Serbs to move their heavy weapons outside an "exclusion zone" around Sarajevo by a stated time and date. If the shelling resumed in the interim or if the weapons were not removed, NATO would launch air strikes.

Although they never fully complied with the ultimatum, the Serbs withdrew and turned over enough weapons to satisfy NATO. For the first time the allies had used the threat of force, and it seemed to work. In fact, the Bosnian Serb leaders Radovan Karadzic and General Ratko Mladic had defied the ultimatum for ten days until British Prime Minister John Major flew to Moscow to enlist the help of the Russians. There President Boris Yeltsin expressed anger at the actions of NATO and the ignoring of Russia. He sent to Karadzic an offer to supply Russian troops to "protect Serb neighborhoods and to watch over Serb weapons." The Serbs in Sarajevo cheered when the Russian forces arrived. "How could NATO pilots drop their bombs while Russian soldiers patrolled Serb neighborhoods?"[33] It was not the last time that the Russians would play a problematic role in the Yugoslav turmoil.

This limited achievement for the threat of force was followed by a diplomatic success by the United States. After months of American mediation, Croats and Muslims in Bosnia accepted in March 1994 the Washington Federation Agreement. It provided for an association, the Federation of Bosnia and Hercegovina, a multiethnic state which might at a future date join with Croatia. The goal was to isolate the Bosnian Serbs and, in the end, bring them into the confederation. In the near term the agreement would end the fighting between Croats and Muslims, make it easier for the non-Serb Bosnians to get weapons, and shift the balance of military power against the Serbs.[34]

The Bosnian Serbs, angered by the new developments, launched a series of defiant acts, including assaults on the UN's "safe areas," especially Gorazde. The American response was divided and weak. The new Secretary of Defense, William Perry, and the new Chairman of the Joint Chiefs, General John Shalikashvili, made public statements indicating that the United States did not intend to become involved, producing somewhat contradictory statements by Christopher and Lake. The double check-off system for air strikes, requiring both NATO and UN approval, made any military response difficult and ultimately produced a "puny" action. "The few bombs dropped were on tents, a tank, and three armored personnel carriers." A NATO ultimatum finally caused the Serbs to stop the attack, leaving the badly damaged city of Gorazde still surrounded by Serbs.[35]

The shelling of the Sarajevo marketplace had produced the formation of the "Contact Group," consisting of the United States, Britain, France, Germany, Italy, and Russia. In July they announced a plan that would have given 51 percent of Bosnia to the Croat-Muslim Federation and 49 percent to the Serbs. This amounted to an acceptance of an ethnically divided Bosnia, a reversal of American policy, "but the fiction was still perpetrated that the state of Bosnia was a united and sovereign state of the three ethnic groups, and this was still unacceptable to the Serbs."[36] The Muslims accepted, but the Serbs, who controlled 70 percent of the land, rejected it. Instead of employing serious air strikes, which the allies and the Russians opposed, the Contact Group adopted a "carrot and stick approach" aimed at Milosevic and the Serbian government in Belgrade. They would impose stricter sanctions on Serbia and would make Gorazde, Sarajevo, and four other Muslim towns "safe areas," threatening air strikes and the lifting of the arms embargo if they were violated. If Milosevic, however, cooperated, cut off supplies to Karadzic, and worked to bring the Bosnian Serbs around to accept the Contact Group's plan, they would ease sanctions. Milosevic put apparent pressure on Karadzic, announced a breach with the Bosnian Serbs, and agreed to monitors watching the border to prevent supplies from reaching them, but violations continued. When the Serbs removed some heavy weapons from the exclusion zone around Sarajevo, "the UN, the U.S., and NATO agreed to retaliation—which consisted of one strike on one gun emplacement in an abandoned area."[37] There was no possibility of ending the arms embargo, which the Europeans and the Russians opposed.

By autumn of 1994 American policy in Bosnia was a shambles.

> There was no policy toward Bosnia, or put differently, there was a different policy for every crisis. Each unexpected development required the ad hoc fashioning of a new response, a response often at odds with previous responses, and often including threats for which there was no follow through.[38]

This chaotic situation resulted from the absence of a general, overall American foreign and security policy and from the continuing influence of the Vietnam syndrome, deterring military action that might be extended in time and produce casualties.

In the spring of 1995, "U.S. policy was in even more disarray than usual. The UN role had come to a dead end. The 'Contact Group' was moribund."[39] The Bosnian Serbs took advantage of the situation to launch powerful attacks on the "safe areas" in eastern Bosnia and on Sarajevo. In the last week in May, "Mladic's soldiers helped themselves to the tanks and cannons and mortars that had been handed over to United Nations troops . . . and began bombarding Sarajevo."[40] This led British General Ruppert Smith of UNPROFOR to undertake retaliation from the air, which, in turn, led the Serbs to take some 370 UN hostages, "many of whom were then chained to NATO target objectives and tauntingly displayed on Serbian television."[41] In the next few days the Serbs shot down an American fighter plane and seized a UN observation post in Srebinica, one of the "safe havens." The "carrot and stick" policy toward Milosevic was a failure and "the UN 'peacekeeping' mission appeared close to collapse, its authority nil."[42]

The Clinton administration was in desperate need of a new policy because developments at home and abroad required a decision that could no longer permit a solution to be deferred. The House of Representatives voted 318 to 99 to lift the arms embargo in Bosnia, and the Senate voted similarly, 60 to 29, allowing UNPROFOR to withdraw before the embargo was lifted. Representative Lee Hamilton said, "[T]he dominant factor was frustration about Bosnia and the administration's handling of it."[43] The taking of hostages had already caused serious talk among the Europeans about withdrawing the troops of UN-PROFOR, and they had always said they would do so if the arms embargo was lifted. This was a terrible prospect, for the withdrawal of the UN "peacekeepers" could well be a dangerous and costly operation, and *the United States was committed to providing some 20,000 American soldiers to the force needed to extricate them.*

During 1994, America and NATO had put together a detailed plan called Operation Determined Effort. It would be a dangerous mission involving American helicopters and 20,000 American troops in a nighttime operation that was certain to produce casualties. The President had publicly promised to provide the American forces, although he had never read or approved or been told the details of the plan. He grasped its import only on June 14, 1995, when Richard Holbrooke told him that the United States had few options in Bosnia. because "NATO has already approved the withdrawal plan. . . . It has a high degree of automaticity built into it, especially since we have committed ourselves publicly to assisting NATO troops if the UN decides to withdraw." The President replied, "What do you mean? I'll decide that when the time comes." To which Holbrooke responded, "Mr. President, it's decided." The President asked Christopher, "Is this true?" To which the Secretary gave his assent.[44]

Without a full grasp of what they were doing, the President and the administration had stumbled into a situation that would require the use of military force in Yugoslavia, whichever route they took.

The suddenly material prospect of French and British troops carrying out a fighting retreat, with thousands of American troops supporting them—images of bodybags sent back to the United States, containing Americans killed for no other reason than to cover a humiliating failure—had begun to concentrate American minds.[45]

Since Clinton's policy, shaped mainly by domestic political concerns, had always given a central place to avoiding the use of ground troops, and inaction would lead to that result, he needed to find a new policy to end the fighting.

The pressure grew as the Serbs continued their assaults on the "safe havens," and Srebinica, besieged for two years, fell on July 11. Once again television showed "harrowing pictures of Muslim women being herded into buses, and draft-aged men being led away to an unknown fate (later determined to have been a massacre, one of several)—'ethnic cleansing' before our very eyes."[46] The same events affected the Europeans, too. The French especially began to take a tough line and suggest various forms of action, although they and the British continued to oppose a major bombing campaign.

New military developments were far more important in changing the situation. On March 4 the Croatian army launched Operation Storm, an attack that swiftly drove the Serbs from Krajina and all the land recently taken from the Croats. More than 150,000 Serbs fled into Bosnia, a greater ethnic cleansing than the Croats had suffered a few years before. The United States had secretly abetted the efforts leading to this offensive, ignoring and even assisting the delivery of weapons to the Croats. They had helped them find a private American military consulting firm that included a former Army Chief of Staff and a former director of the Defense Intelligence Agency, and Operation Storm "seemed to bear striking resemblances to current American military doctrine."[47]

The Croat offensive had a powerful influence, especially on the Western powers.

> Mesmerized by the Serbian juggernaut and the "lessons" of Vietnam, the Western allies had stood by helplessly as the Serbs intimidated their foes, committed atrocities with little but rhetorical resistance from the West, and met only symbolic military opposition. Now the Croatian army cleared the territory of the Serbian military in a matter of days, and the world saw panic-stricken Serb civilians fleeing the territories in which they had lived along with the Bosnian Serb troops that were supposed to be protecting them. . . . With the Serbs shorn of their aura of invincibility. . . . the allies could now summon the courage to conduct their own offensive against them.[48]

Clinton faced the humiliation of renewed Serbian aggression and domestic criticism with the approach of a new presidential election, and he could not ignore the frightening dead end to which his policy was leading: the need to send ground troops to help extract the UN peacekeepers. The President was now forced to choose "between sending American troops to cover an ignominious retreat—'to implement a failure' . . . —or sending them to ensure an end to the war."[49]

This prospect propelled him to more decisive action than ever before. As a well-informed reporter puts it, "Clinton now recognized the danger to his presidency posed by Bosnia."[50] The administration drafted a plan to divide Bosnia between Muslims and Serbs (although formally retaining a unitary state) and offering Milosevic the lifting of sanctions. This would be backed by a threat to lift the arms embargo and to launch serious bombing strikes. There was not much new in this, but the new circumstances might make the threat credible to Milosevic. As to the Muslims, they would have to go along, like it or not. In a discussion in the White House, Lake said, "'If the Bosnians are the bad guys, they don't get the strike or the arms. They get lift and leave.' Everyone knew that would mean they would be overrun."[51] There was some talk of "refusing to ratify ethnic cleansing" or of "rewarding aggression." Among those discussing the plan, "some officials were pained by the charge—and their own knowledge—that the settlement in effect rewarded 'ethnic cleansing,' but they knew no other way to end the war, without making it bloodier."[52] Clinton sent Lake on a mission to seven European countries and presented a plan in a style very different from Christopher's earlier efforts on behalf of "lift and strike." Lake said that President Clinton had already decided this course, urging the Europeans to join. "The thrust was that they had better help get the diplomatic track going in earnest or all hell would break loose and the United States was going to do all those crazy things like bomb the Serbs."[53]

Although the Europeans were pleased at the prospect of new negotiations, they were still reluctant to use force, but they were persuaded to go along. Richard Holbrooke, who had called the reaction to the Bosnia affair "the greatest collective failure since the 1930s," was put in charge of the negotiations with the three ethnic groups, but there was little progress. The Serbs continued to shell the "safe haven" of Gorazde, and NATO failed to retaliate. Then on August 28 the Serbs shelled the Sarajevo marketplace again, killing thirty-seven people. The administration debated whether or not to retaliate. The Bosnian Serbs said they were ready to negotiate, and there was fear that new bombings might interfere. On the other hand, the Muslims refused to join the talks unless there was retaliation. At last, on August 30, a massive bombing attack was launched and continued until September 7, when the Serbs and Muslims accepted an outline of a peace agreement.

The final talks, at Wright-Patterson Air Force Base near Dayton, Ohio, began on November 1 and lasted three weeks. They ratified the sovereignty and independence of Bosnia-Hercegovina, which, in some metaphysical way, was to be both a unitary and a dual state. The central federal government would have a collective presidency and would control foreign policy, customs and immigration, law enforcement, monetary policy, communications, and transportation. There would also be two other governmental entities, the Federation of Bosnia and Hercegovina and the Republika Srpska, each with its own legislative and executive bodies, chosen in internationally supervised free and democratic elections. Human rights were to be respected, and there was to be cooperation with the War Crimes Tribunal. There was to be free movement within the country, and refugees were to have the right to return to their homes or be compensated for losses incurred in ethnic cleansing. Both entities would be permitted "to establish parallel special relationships with 'neighboring' countries," which clearly looked to future associations between the Federation of Bosnia and Croatia and between Republika Srpska and Serbia. "Bosnia would be partitioned, but no one, especially the Americans, would admit it."[54]

Each side was to withdraw its forces behind cease-fire lines, and there were limitations on all arms and especially heavy weapons. The peace would be enforced by 50,000 to 60,000 NATO troops, including 20,000 Americans. The Russians participated under NATO command. The Implementation Force (IFOR) was scheduled to leave after one year, in December 1996. It was obvious to many that the deadline was both unrealistic and an encouragement to disruptive forces. During the year it became evident that Bosnia was strongly divided and that a withdrawal of the NATO troops would lead to renewed warfare. No serious effort was made to arrest the accused war criminals. American officials were still paralyzed by the fear of casualties. Not only Vietnam but also Mogadishu dominated their memories; "the loss of even one soldier might threaten the mission. . . . Certainly they did not intend to risk American troops to capture Karadzic or Mladic or to escort refugees back to their homes."[55] American attempts to intervene in domestic politics to elect more moderate candidates failed. The elections to the Bosnian Parliament in September 1998 produced victories for "hard-line nationalists," including the supporters of Karadzic. "The net result was a further hardening of the Bosnian partition, and, consequently, an increased likelihood of an indefinite occupation by NATO troops."[56] Almost immediately after his reelection in November 1996, Clinton announced that the forces would stay until July 1998. In December 1997 their stay was extended without a deadline. At this writing they are still in Bosnia with no plan for withdrawal.

Ever since the start of the Yugoslav crisis in 1991, skeptics had dismissed the notion that the use of force could produce desired results. They argued that airpower could accomplish nothing important; only the insertion of hundreds of thousands of ground troops would avail. But the success of the powerful air attacks in 1995 showed that such doubt was excessive. Air attacks had brought an end to the fighting in Bosnia and encouraged the hope that the threat of force, combined with diplomacy, would work again in the future, if needed. The peace that had been achieved, however, was far from satisfactory. It had not punished aggression nor undone "ethnic cleansing," but, to a significant degree, ratified both. One ingredient in its success had been the active cooperation of Slobodan Milosevic, whom the United States and NATO regarded as an aggressor and a war criminal. The outcome was far from a convincing deterrent against a new aggression in the future. The American situation resembled Britain's at Lausanne in 1923. Like the British, the Americans, since they were not prepared to commit the necessary forces, were not "in a position to dictate peace" but had to negotiate "on an equal footing, discussing every clause and line in the same way as we discuss Bills in the House."[57] Four years after the settlement the NATO troops were still in place in Bosnia and essential to avoid violence, an outcome that was far from Clinton's goal of achieving a "self-sustaining peace." If NATO's goal was the establishment of stability on its borders, it, too, stood on shaky ground. The skeptics still had reason to doubt the efficacy of military power confined to the sea and air.

In fact, there were special conditions present in Bosnia in 1995 that made possible even the limited and dubious success achieved at Dayton. The victory of Croat armies on the ground and the threat they posed to the Serbs softened the latter's resistance. Milosevic had much to gain from putting the Bosnian Serbs under his control and much to lose from a continuation of the war. He could strengthen his position at home by betraying his ethnic cousins in Bosnia. There was no reason to assume that such favorable conditions would exist in case of a future challenge met by airpower alone.

Even so, the peace achieved at Dayton showed the costliness and timidity of previous hesitation to use force in aid of a solution. An experienced observer of international relations had this opinion:

> Had Clinton made the kind of commitments in spring of 1993 that he did in the late summer of 1995, he could have ended the war and saved thousands of lives—and perhaps staved off the crisis in Kosovo. The difference was that in 1993 Clinton concluded that Bosnia would not determine the fate of his presidency but that a messy foreign entanglement would jeopardize his domestic agenda. Not until two years later, when he saw that Bosnia would indeed jeopardize his presidency, did he act.[58]

A new challenge soon erupted, not in Bosnia but in Kosovo. The Serbs had long regarded Kosovo as a sacred homeland because of its historical importance and its religious shrines. It was the site of a famous defeat by the Turks in 1389 that remains an occasion of great patriotic importance to Serbia. By the 1990s, however, 90 percent of its inhabitants were ethnically Albanians and of the Muslim faith. Only the remaining 10 percent were Serbian Orthodox Christians. Under the Yugoslavia constitution of 1974, Kosovo, with its predominantly Albanian population, enjoyed autonomy, much to the chagrin of many in the Serbian minority. Milosevic was born in Kosovo, and his political career really came alive when he went to his native region in 1987 and told "the resentful Serbs . . . that the Kosovar Albanians 'shall no longer dare to beat you.'"[59] Two years later he revoked Kosovar autonomy, stirring fear and discontent there, but making a name for himself among pan-Serbian nationalists.

Kosovo's troubles, its strategic position, and the dangers it posed of the spread of a major war in the Balkans brought it to American attention as Yugoslavia began to break up.

> There was a growing fear that the fighting would spread to the Yugoslav province of Kosovo. . . . [I]t could draw in Albania. Refugees might flee to neighboring Macedonia, with the Serbs in hot pursuit; fighting be-

tween Serbs and Macedonians would begin. . . . The Greeks and Bulgarians, both claimants to Macedonia, might decide to intervene. Inevitably, the Turks would become involved. The nightmare of a huge Balkan war loomed.[60]

The danger was great enough that, in spite of its hands-off policy, the Bush administration in one of its last acts issued its "Christmas Warning," saying that "in the event of conflict in Kosovo caused by Serbian action, the United States will be prepared to employ military force against the Serbs in Kosovo and in Serbia proper."[61]

The Clinton administration took the same position, regarding it as the "geopolitical limit, the 'red line,'" as one of its officials later called it. In April 1993, Christopher envisioned the most serious consequences arising from trouble in Kosovo. He expressed fear that if Serbia gained influence in Macedonia or Kosovo, "[i]t will bring into the fray other countries in the region—Albania, Greece, Turkey. . . . So the stakes for the United States are to prevent the broadening of that conflict to bring in our NATO, and to bring in vast sections of Europe, and perhaps, as happened before, broadening into a world war."[62]

In spite of such dire forebodings, neither administration took concrete steps to safeguard Kosovo, which was largely forgotten during the Bosnian war. The Dayton agreement ignored Kosovo entirely. "The Americans were in a hurry; they *needed* a Bosnia agreement, only Milosevic could deliver it to them, and he knew it; and he would brook no diplomatic meddling in what was unquestionably 'Serb land.'"[63] There was, however, a price to be paid for this avoidance. The most prominent leader of the Albanian Kosovars was Ibrahim Rugova, a pacifist who urged nonviolent methods in seeking independence for his people. During the collapse of Yugoslavia he had restrained the hotter heads among them with the prospect that a final settlement would take care of their needs, but Dayton decidedly did not do so. By paying no attention to Kosovo it did great harm to the position of Rugova and his policy and strengthened the hand of the militant guerrillas called the Kosovo Liberation Army (KLA), which began attacking Serbian police. The Serbs retaliated, killing KLA members and innocent civilians and burning Kosovar villages. As the Serbs brought in larger and more powerful military forces the KLA began to receive arms through Albania. "Europe's worst nightmare, another Balkan war, seemed likely."[64]

The United States branded the KLA "terrorists," a fair enough description but one that could not fail to encourage Milosevic's assaults against the Kosovars. On February 26, 1998, he unleashed an attack near Drenica, his first serious offensive in Kosovo. He thus challenged the threats made by both the Bush and the Clinton administrations to oppose such an action. Secretary of Defense Cohen put the matter plainly: "The first question we had to ask was whether the Christmas warning was still on the table. And the fact is the Christmas warning was not on the table. We were not prepared for unilateral action."[65]

Nor were they well prepared for joint action. The leadership the Clinton administration had with difficulty mustered to achieve the bombings that produced the Dayton agreement had quickly dissipated. NATO allies, especially France, were reluctant to act in Kosovo at all, and others were hesitant to use force, yet any concerted action required unanimity. Some of the NATO allies had troops on the ground in Bosnia, and this too caused hesitation. One American policy maker told a reporter, "The idea of using force over the objection of allies who have troops on the ground subject to retaliation, is fantasy-land. Allies do not do that to each other." The troops in Bosnia, of course, were not lightly armed blue helmets but heavily armed forces, including Americans, who would not easily suffer retaliation, but the statement reveals the administration's own hesitancy.

Over the next year there was also talk of needing UN approval for various military actions. The Contact Group, moreover, containing the chief NATO countries and Russia, posed a special problem, for it allowed the Russians to cause trouble. Clinton tried to get Yeltsin's help in moderating Milosevic, but, as a British scholar pointed out in June 1998, "the genius who masterminded the Russian war in Chechnya is hardly likely to support a NATO intervention that could be seen as supporting secessionists. . . . [Events] confirm that Russia will collaborate with Milosevic in whatever fudge the latter comes up with to avoid punishment."[66] Resistance from the allies and the Russians increased the administration's own hesitations. There was not yet the kind of gun pointed at the head of American leaders that had produced the Bosnia bombing, and they turned to gentler measures.

The American government in 1995 was of a different stripe from the "small group of resolute men" who led Britain at the time of Chanak, when Churchill and his colleagues, facing remarkably similar problems of risky military operations, political troubles, and reluctant allies, chose to make a stand. Churchill described their prospects and their determination:

> The Government might break up and we might be relieved of our burden. The nation might not support us: they would find others to advise them. The Press might howl, the Allies might bolt. We intended to force the Turk to a negotiated peace before he should set foot in Europe. The aim was modest, but the forces were small.[67]

In 1995 and thereafter, America's forces, though significantly depleted, were far greater than Britain's in 1921, but its leaders lacked the foresight and will to risk their use. As Kosovo heated up, some American NATO planners considered placing a substantial ground force on the Kosovo border in Macedonia as a deterrent to Serbian aggression. Such a move could well have avoided further trouble, but it gained no support, and the crisis deepened.[68]

Serbian violence in Kosovo crossed the "red line" drawn by Bush and Clinton and should have invoked the promise to "employ military force . . . against the Serbs in Kosovo proper," but "[i]t seemed . . . that the red line had begun to fade; Clinton officials now spoke not of war planes and tanks but of 'using every appropriate tool we have at our command,' and making 'the Serb economy . . . head further south.'"[69] France and Russia objected even to severe economic sanctions, and contradiction and confusion reigned within the Clinton administration and within NATO. Secretary of State Madeline Albright had always favored a forceful approach to Yugoslav problems, but was rarely able to prevail within the administration. She decided, according to an aide, "to lead through rhetoric" in shaping opinion on all sides. At a meeting with the Contact Group in Rome on March 7, 1998, she announced: "We are not going to stand by and watch the Serbian authorities do in Kosovo what they can no longer get away with doing in Bosnia."[70]

But that is exactly what the United States and its allies were doing. Milosevic was unable to do such things in Bosnia because there were heavily armed NATO troops on the ground, something he would not permit in Kosovo and something that Clinton would not even contemplate imposing upon him. Clinton's special envoy repeated the warning, previously made by Bush and Christopher in February. In March the Contact Group insisted on the removal of Serb security forces from Kosovo and the participation of an international mediator in future talks between Rugova and Milosevic. "Nevertheless, in May, after Richard Holbrooke interceded on behalf of his old Dayton sparring partner, the United States unilaterally lifted sanctions and bullied Rugova into bilateral talks with Milosevic."[71] In compensation, Rugova was invited to the White House on May 27, where the president assured him, "We will not allow another Bosnia to happen in Kosovo."[72] But no plans or promises were made to back up the promise.

This combination of threats and retreats, in fact, was reminiscent of American behavior toward Bosnia, in which rhetoric encouraged the Bosnian Muslims to stand fast, only to allow them to be harried and slaughtered while the Americans looked on. In the spring of 1998, "tough talk by the United States may well have encouraged the KLA, while the weakness of support for sanctions relieved pressure on Milosevic."[73] In June, NATO agreed to draw up military plans and the Contact Group warned Milosevic of their serious intent, but during the spring and summer Serbian forces continued to wreak havoc in Kosovo, driving a quarter of a million from their homes.

At a meeting of NATO defense ministers in Vilamoura, Portugal, in September, NATO's Secretary-General, Javier Solana, bitterly said that the Serbs were "mocking the alliance with a slow-motion offensive aimed at keeping NATO in its torpor." He reported that a Serb official had joked that "a village a day keeps NATO away."[74] Secretary Cohen adopted a new urgency, calling on the alliance to take on a new role. "If NATO could not muster a threat to Milosevic under these circumstances . . . what was the point of the alliance?"[75]

The NATO allies continued to argue over the need for explicit UN approval for military action, but on September 24 the Americans finally convinced them to issue an ultimatum ordering Milosevic to draw back his forces. Then, on October 13, NATO issued the first "activation order" in its history, which authorized a three-phase bombardment of Yugoslavia. Even then, they confined permission only to the first and lightest phase, although this was not publicly announced.

With this threat as his weapon, Richard Holbrooke again went to Milosevic and in October gained agreement to a cease-fire in Kosovo and the withdrawal of police and troops who had not been there prior to 1998. The Serb leader also accepted the presence of unarmed international inspectors and overflights by NATO planes to monitor compliance. Clinton wasted no time in claiming victory, a triumph of diplomacy backed by force, the basis of a lasting peace. He represented Milosevich as having "agreed to internationally supervised democratic elections in Kosovo, substantial self-government and a local police—in short, rights the Kosovars have been demanding since Mr. Milosevic stripped their autonomy a decade ago."[76]

That did not accurately represent the full situation. In exchange for the agreement, Milosevic demanded the cancellation of the NATO order authorizing air strikes. NATO went so far as to suspend the order, but not to cancel it, and this enraged him. According to an American present, he called it "a declaration of war." At a meeting to discuss implementation of the October agreement, NATO commander General Wesley Clark asked why he had not withdrawn some of his forces. Milosevic denied the forces were there or that he had agreed to remove them. "We have no extra forces," he told Clark. "NATO must do what it must do."[77] It was not long before the October agreement was a shambles.

What led Milosevic so readily to defy the mighty NATO alliance, armed with an order to unleash an air campaign against his country, when a previous air attack had led him to yield? First, Kosovo was not Bosnia. It was the ancestral homeland of the Serbs and much less lightly to be yielded. It was the place Milosevic had made his name, where he had promised Serbian domination. The memories of Somalia and Haiti and many previous American and NATO hesitations, reversals, and retreats in Yugoslavia also encouraged a further test of their will. Clinton's behavior in Iraq, moreover, provided further evidence that the United States might be thwarted by determined defiance. Saddam Hussein repeatedly defied the United States, which replied with rhetoric, threats, and an occasional use of missile and air attacks that were dismissed as "pinpricks." The result after several years of the game was an increase in Saddam's power at home, a splintering of the coalition Bush had put together against Iraq, and the gradual removal of the restraints fettering America's enemy. Over the fall and winter of 1998–1999, Saddam was winning the battle of wills, and Milosevic could not fail to take heed. Finally, Clinton's repeated declaration in advance that the United States would not use ground forces, America's equivalent of "limited liability," undermined the seriousness of American intentions.

As Serb forces withdrew from Kosovo, civilian refugees came down from the mountains and KLA troops came with them. On January 15, 1999, Serb forces assaulted the village of Racak, murdering forty-five Kosovar victims. This was a provocation that could not be ignored. Four days later the Clinton administration decided on the elements of a plan that would be presented as an ultimatum: "One was to make a credible threat of military force. The other was to demand the attendance of the parties at a meeting at which the principal demands would be decided in advance by the Contact Group, including Russia. The basic principles were nonnegotiable, including a NATO implementing force."[78] Even confronted by such a provocation the administration was prepared to allow the Russians a hand in decisions. The military force still would be limited to air strikes. The "implementing force," to be sure, must be ground troops, but these would be "peacekeepers," used only with the permission of Milosevic, and Secretary Cohen and Chairman of the Joint Chiefs General Henry H. Shelton resisted even that mission.

By January 30 the NATO allies decided to support the ultimatum backed by the threat of air strikes, but, according to Secretary Albright, "they wanted a conference that would be their equivalent of Dayton."[79] Between February 6 and 17 a conference met at the castle of Rambouillet, near Paris. This was to be no Dayton, however. There was no defeat by the Croatian army to sober Milosevic, who chose not to attend in person. Nor did any high-ranking NATO general take part. NATO presented its demands: the Serbs were to withdraw most of their troops from Kosovo, accept 28,000 armed peacekeepers, and accept a transition to autonomy for Kosovo in three years. If they rejected these terms by the end of the talks the allies would commence bombing.[80] The Serbs objected especially vigorously to the presence of armed troops, without which there could be no guarantee of Kosovar security and therefore no agreement. The Albanian Kosovars were also unwilling to accept a promise of autonomy within Yugoslavia without a firm date for a referendum on full independence. Secretary Albright tried to persuade the Kosovars to sign the agreement, which would force the Serbs to sign or have the bombing begin, but to no avail. The meeting ended in failure. At last, in Paris on March 18, the Albanians were persuaded to sign, but the Serbs refused. Holbrooke was sent on a last vain effort to persuade Milosevic, who was unshaken by the threat of bombardment, and two days later the bombing began.

It later became clear that Milosevic had for months been preparing a military attack on Kosovo called Operation Horseshoe, meant to sweep the Albanians from Kosovo in a matter of weeks. After a month of bombing, the Serbs had driven hundreds of thousands of Albanian Kosovars from their homes and across the borders of neighboring countries such as Macedonia, Montenegro, and Albania, at the cost of enormous human suffering and the spread of instability in the Balkans. The allies continued to insist on the success of their bombing missions even as Kosovo was being "cleansed" of its Albanian citizens and the Serbian people rallied loyally about Milosevic. Russia rattled its saber, making threats against the allies, even as the Americans desperately sought its help with Milosevic. On April 5, 1999, while the Serbs were clearing Kosovo of most of the Albanian Kosovars, Clinton announced, "The ethnic cleansing of Kosovo cannot stand as a permanent event," but he still stated firmly that he would not employ American ground troops.[81] Pressure on the Clinton administration grew, both within the United States from Democratic and Republican senators and then even from such NATO allies as Britain and France, to use fighting ground forces to defeat the Serbs and restore the Albanian Kosovars.

The President's indecisive leadership could not produce the unity, determination, and clear strategy that could swiftly end the war that its indecision had produced. In an odd and ominous way, Clinton's performance seems to have deserved the description that Lloyd George posthumously gave to Sir Edward Grey, the British Foreign Secretary whose indecision and lack of clarity had helped bring on World War I. Like Grey he wanted "to pursue a European policy without keeping up a great army,"[82] and like Grey

> [h]e lacked the knowledge . . . vision, imagination, breadth of mind and that high courage, bordering on audacity, which his immense task demanded. . . . [He was] a pilot whose hand trembled in the palsy of apprehension, unable to grip the levers and manipulate them with a firm and clear purpose . . . waiting for public opinion to decide the direction for him.[83]

Late in the spring, powerful new voices began to demand preparations for the use of ground troops to end the fighting, at least to put pressure on Milosevic to yield. In the United States, Republican Senator John McCain gained wide attention and made himself into a serious contender for the presidential nomination by championing that cause. In Britain, Prime Minister Tony Blair expressed himself with increasing force in the same direction. Grudgingly, the Americans made statements and took preliminary steps that made such an action seem possible. The Russians, who were deeply afraid of a NATO ground action in Yugoslavia, began to serve as a more useful intermediary in negotiations between NATO and Milosevic. At last, after more than ten weeks of bombing, the Serbs accepted an agreement to withdraw their forces from Kosovo and allow UN forces, with NATO at their core, to enter and protect the returning Kosovars and allow autonomy to them. The protecting forces would need to remain for a long time, the destruction of Kosovo would cost vast sums to repair, and how many of roughly a million Kosovars driven from their homeland would choose to return remained to be seen.

At this writing, NATO and the United States appear to have avoided a humiliation for the United States and NATO that would have decisively damaged their prestige and their ability to preserve peace and order even in Europe, without needing to launch a full-scale war on land, on sea, and in the air, and accepting the cost in money and blood. This result came at the cost of many lives, vast losses in property, and great expense to the NATO countries.

Some observers took these developments as evidence of the folly of becoming involved in the affairs of "faraway peoples" in places of no vital importance to the United States. But such an inadequate and shortsighted understanding of American interests is far less common than it once was. Even after so unsatisfactory a performance by its leaders, such timidity and inconsistency, such an absence of a clear and powerful message of what was involved, even while the military effort was disappointing and inconclusive, an increasing majority of Americans supported the air war and even the use of ground troops. The memory of two world wars and of the half-century of the Cold War could not lightly be obliterated, and those who explained the importance of the events in Yugoslavia to the future of peace and order in the world gained a grateful audience.

To such important considerations were added the extraordinary power of modern communications technology. Isolationism in the old style was impossible. The power of satellite television delivering vivid pictures of the suffering caused by aggression could not be ignored. The American people had come to regard such horrors as unacceptable and expected their government to do something about them. A truly realistic foreign policy would need to take into account a greater public awareness and insistence on a foreign policy that accorded with the public's values.

The century, and now the last decade, had shown, instead, the deep folly of trying to ignore breaches of the public order in the hope that they would not affect us. Once again, two American Presidents, both cautious and determined to avoid entanglements in difficult and complicated foreign quarrels, had been unable to avoid such entanglement. By trying to ignore the problem, to leave it to others, whether the UN or NATO, by declaring it to be of no vital interest to the United States, by refusing to use any force once involved and then to use adequate force once committed, they found themselves making the very mistakes that brought defeat and disaster in Vietnam, the fear of which had played so great a role, first in their failure to act and then in their inadequate response. As the Holocaust survivor and Nobel Peace Prize winner Elie Wiesel made a tour of Kosovar refugee camps in June of 1999 he said that if the West had taken action a decade earlier the horrors of ethnic cleansing in Kosovo might have been averted. "We could have foreseen Kosovo. Why," he asked, "didn't we?"[84] A strong and firm reaction by the Bush administration in 1991 to the collapse of Yugoslavia might have averted almost any violence and produced stability without war. By 1993 it would have taken more effort and greater cost by the Clinton administration to avert the disaster that ravaged Bosnia, but a firm ac-

tion backed by convincing military power could have done the job and prevented the calamity of Kosovo. By the spring of 1999 a major military effort
would be needed to restore peace and order and to avoid the collapse of NATO,
but the United States and its allies could only be brought to it late and with the
greatest difficulty.

At this writing the cost of the hesitant and timid policy in Yugoslavia was
becoming manifest. Milosevic continued his dictatorial rule in Belgrade, perse-
cuting and suppressing opposition. Montenegro remained uneasily within the
state of Yugoslavia, eager to escape the isolation from the West that union with
Serbia imposed on it, afraid to risk an attack by Milosevic should it secede, a
source of instability in the future. Bosnia was ethnically divided but relatively
quiet thanks to the continued occupation by NATO forces, years after their
withdrawal had been promised.

The greatest troubles were in Kosovo, where Albanians and Serbs remained
at each others' throats, especially in its northern region bordering on Serbia and
most fiercely in the divided city of Mitrovica. In Kosovo it was clear that ethnic
warfare would break out in the absence of adequate NATO military forces, but
the European countries were failing to supply the troops they had promised and
the United States refused to make up the difference. Serbs were emboldened to
resist NATO efforts to search for arms and to attack NATO troops with stones
and other weapons. The Clinton administration and NATO officials found reason to accuse Milosevic of "fomenting violence" in Mitrovica "to keep Kosovo
unsettled" and to keep the northern region for Serbs only.[85] An anonymous
French official's opinion was that "Kosovo has become a quagmire. Nobody
has a solution."[86] Clinton may have succeeded in kicking the problem beyond
his own administration, but his successor would inherit the danger that would
not go away of itself.

Conclusion

T he United States at the end of the millennium is not England between the wars. The challenges and opportunities of the 1990s were not precisely the same as those of the 1920s, nor will the first decade of the new millennium precisely repeat the pattern of the 1930s. It has not been the purpose of this work to draw precise parallels between particular events of the last interwar years and those of the present years. The analogy is much broader and more fundamental than that. It lies in the similarities between the strategic positions of England and the United States with respect to the rest of the world and, above all, in the general pattern of self-deluding pseudoengagement that both countries pursued. The main purpose of drawing that parallel is to ask the question: Is America today in danger of suffering a fate similar to that which befell Britain in the 1930s? The answer, we believe, is yes.

Pseudoengagement

America today is not isolationist, nor was England then. Both governments' stated policies were those of engagement—with France and Germany and the League of Nations in England's case, with NATO, Russia, China, and the United Nations Organization in America's. In both the postwar years saw the frequent deployment of American or British armed forces, including the less frequent deployment of ground forces. In both cases powerful national interests around the globe, economic, political, and emotional, prevented domestically oriented political leaderships from simply turning inward and forsaking the outer world.

Yet neither America nor England was seriously committed to shaping the international environment, a task that only they, as the leading global powers of their time, could perform. Their leaders proclaimed a determination to shape the environment, a powerful commitment to "engagement"; they declared that America's or England's interests required participation in the world and even the use of force to shape it. But almost invariably, when crises demanded decisive action, leaders hesitated to commit military forces, sought "peaceful" resolutions to crises, preferred "economic leverage" and "negotiated settlements" to the effective and necessary use of armed might.

In both cases, the deployment of ground forces was particularly anathema. The memory of the First World War burned strongly in England in the 1920s and 1930s. English leaders sought to avoid policies that might drag England into a major ground campaign anywhere, lest it turn into another World War I even in miniature. The circumstances that had created the trench stalemate that dominated British military thought were unusual, due not only to the technology of the time, but also to the size, shape, and nature of the Western Front—the same technologies produced radically different results in almost every other theater of war. War with Turkey in the early 1920s, or with Italy, or with Japan, would not have produced a trench-warfare bloodfest like the battles of the Somme and Passchendael. But the memory of those awful conflicts horrified the postwar generation of leaders, and paralyzed their willingness to do what was needed to preserve the general peace.

America's fear of using ground forces results from a more complicated history. The "Vietnam syndrome" continues to paralyze American leaders as the memory of the trenches did the British. The notion of "mission creep," rooted in the belief that the gradual expansion of America's role in Vietnam caused that loss, defeats any solid understanding of the relationship of politics and war. The notion that a state can enter a war with a clearly defined mission and "endstate" and pursue the war without changing either, whatever circumstances arise, and arrive, thereby, at the desired outcome, is absurd and impossible in the real world. Things change and missions will creep—or shrink—and sometimes they must be allowed to do so. There is no escape from the responsibility of judgment and no reason to believe that inaction is safer than action.

But the "mission creep" syndrome, too, is here to stay, and it is as enervating as the memory of the Great War was to the British. The introduction of ground forces anywhere in the world, be it Bosnia, Somalia, Haiti, or Iraq, brings cries of "Vietnam" and "mission creep." Opponents of such deployments always argue that things will get out of hand, that the United States cannot be the world's policeman, that the war will bog down, drag out, and expand, and American forces will have to "be there" for forty years or forever.

Ironically, the successful Gulf War has contributed to the same end. The false notion that "air power won the Gulf War" has been exposed and refuted by the evidence, but it continues to be asserted and believed, and it serves to strengthen the argument against the use of ground forces. America's ground forces in the Gulf War suffered virtually no casualties, nevertheless, ground forces today continue to be associated with casualties, as with mission creep. The Gulf War, moreover, has changed America's definition of success in war— it is not enough to win; the victory must come at almost no cost. There is no reason to believe that the American people would not, in fact, accept casualties, even large casualties, in a war they understood and supported, but America's political leaders refuse to take the risk, even when the cause requires some risk of losses. Both a recent victory and a recent defeat have brought America to nearly the same strategic limitations that Britain imposed on itself in the 1920s—engagement must not be prolonged, must entail no casualties, and, must, almost always, avoid the use of ground forces. (This is the sort of pseudo-engagement that has been America's real policy in the 1990s, as it was England's in the 1920s. Its consequences were disastrous for England and threaten to be the same for the United States.)

In the crises they faced in the 1920s, the British appeared to "win" each one. After the conclusion of each Britain's leaders could always claim that they had "defused" the crisis, "stood firm," and "insisted" on the acceptance of their terms. The British put down an Iraqi rebellion, Mustafa Kemal came to terms in Turkey, the Italians gave Corfu back to the Greeks, and the Germans came back into the community of nations. What was overlooked was that the Iraqi rebellion was partly put down, but partly bought off, that Kemal came to terms more favorable than what Britain had declared to be the minimum acceptance conditions, that Mussolini returned Corfu to Greece, but that Greece was humiliated and the League of Nations badly undermined. The Germany that joined the League of Nations, moreover, was unrepentant, was secretly violating the disarmament agreements, determined to reverse the whole basis of the peace, having preserved the industrial and military basic capability to do so. In each case, the superficial "victory" was a more fundamental defeat.

The main cause for each defeat was the unwillingness and inability to use adequate military force. Iraq was bought off because the prospect of defending the area over the long term was judged to be too expensive. The British yielded to most of Kemal's terms because they could not bear the thought of a ground war with Turkey, although Kemal's forces would have been no match for England's mobilized strength. In the same way Italy stood no chance in a war against the British Navy over Corfu, but the prospect of war was unacceptable to Britain's leaders. And the Treaty of Locarno in 1925, which undermined any practical commitment to defend France against an attack by Germany, resulted directly from the fact that Britain was unwilling to support France diplomatically and unable, because of its unilateral disarmament, to support France militarily; it was a fig leaf to cover Britain's weakness. In this way military weakness, which resulted from the unwillingness seriously to contemplate war, made a mockery of the "engagement" openly proclaimed.

The sum of these defeats, though portrayed as victories, had a devastating effect on England's position at the turn of the decade, undermining alliances and causing estrangements. More and more, the British had to face the world alone and unaided where but a few years earlier they had held the chance to forge a powerful alliance—the most formidable in the world. Nor were the true winners in each crisis, or the rest of the world, deluded by the declarations of victory by England's leaders. Turkey's Kemal, Italy's Mussolini, and Germany's Stresemann knew that they had faced down the British. They and others who saw their success and Britain's hesitation were emboldened by those successes.

Only the British were deceived by their leaders' declarations—everyone else noted that Britain's bark was far worse than her bite. Such "victories" and the repeated assurances by their leaders that all was well, backed by military assumptions that removed all possible danger into the distant future, undermined any will among the English people to maintain adequate defenses or to preserve the peace by firm action. Successive prime ministers proclaimed that "the people" would not support greater defense expenditure or stronger foreign policies. They never tested that hypothesis, but their words and inaction helped to make it true.

Since 1991 America has pursued the same program of pseudoengagement and the repeated declaration of false victories. Of the foreign crises tackled by the Bush and Clinton administrations since the Gulf War, almost all against their will, not one has been truly successful. Somalia was a catastrophe; there the declaration of victory rings hollowest of all. The intervention in Haiti was timid, halfhearted, and inadequate to fix the situation there, which seems to be descending rapidly toward the sort of chaos and horror that led to the intervention in the first place. Intervention in Bosnia seems superficially to have been most successful; it changed the situation in that region decisively, but, in contradiction to the language of the Dayton accords that ostensibly preserves Bosnia as a unified multiethnic state and reverses the process of ethnic cleansing, the United States has been forced to accept its permanent division and to ratify, de facto, the detestable process of ethnic cleansing. At that, the chief reason for the turn of the tide there was a military victory by the Croatians over the Bosnian Serbs. What is not at all clear, however, is that the situation would remain stable if United States forces withdraw. Unless the United States is prepared to remain deployed in Bosnia indefinitely, the situation may well rapidly revert to brutal civil war.

The belated and limited commitment to Bosnia did not achieve America's most important goals in the Balkans, which included preventing the spread of the war to Kosovo. During a period of limited warfare that excluded ground forces, hundreds of thousands of Albanian Kosovars were driven from their homes to neighboring countries and refuges around the world. The withdrawal

428   WHILE AMERICA SLEEPS

of the Serb armies permitted the return of most of them, and this has been declared a victory, but the perpetrator of the horrors attendant upon the war, the Serbian leader Slobodan Milosevic, remains in power. Ethnic hatred between Serb and Albanian in Kosovo is more intense than ever. It is clear that a new war would break out in the absence of adequate NATO military forces, which the NATO countries are reluctant to supply. Yet American and European troops are committed, with no end in sight.

The situation in Iraq and North Korea may be the most alarming of all. In Iraq the United States has repeatedly "punished" Saddam Hussein, both with air strikes and with an economic embargo. But the inspections are over. Saddam has already had months to develop his WMD programs further, and conceal them better. The Gulf War coalition has collapsed utterly and the Kosovo operation has driven a wedge between the United States and its NATO allies and emboldened China and Russia to impede their efforts. Sanctions, already deeply undermined by the oil-for-food program, are quickly disappearing. Before long, Saddam, or his successor, will begin rearming his conventional forces and perfecting his missile and weapons of mass destruction. A new crisis in the Gulf is highly likely.

The situation is similar in North Korea. In 1994 the threat posed by North Korean development of dangerous nuclear weapons led not to a confrontation with the United States, but to a bribe to Pyongyang whose continuation resembles the tribute a weak young American nation paid to the Barbary pirates at the beginning of the nineteenth century. Repeatedly the North Koreans have demanded and received further bribes simply to keep their part of the bargain. Evidence continues to mount that they are not keeping their bargain. North Korean engineers keep perfecting the arts of digging deeply and concealing from above—what we do not know about their WMD programs is almost certainly much greater than what we know. The United States has given the North Koreans every incentive to consider some sort of "mad dog" act by the weakness of its military forces in the south and its patent inability to reinforce them before the North has struck. The declaration of victory in 1994 may have deceived many Americans; it surely did not fool Pyongyang.

What have other states learned from America's policies since the Gulf War? They have not learned that America is willing to summon the force needed to defeat aggression, that the development of weapons of mass destruction and the means to deliver them will not be tolerated, that ethnic cleansing and politically driven mass starvation will be prevented or severely punished. They have not seen an America that is truly engaged in the world, willing to risk the lives of its sons and daughters when needed to preserve the global stability on which peace and prosperity rest. On the contrary. The message America has sent to the aggressors and oppressors of the world has been that their depredations run only a limited risk. The most likely American response will be neglect, at first, followed by some attempt at negotiation. If, at last, driven to action, the Americans attack, it will be from the air, employing limited rules of engagement, and it will not destroy the aggressor. Ground forces will almost certainly not be used until the aggressor himself invites them in as part of a negotiation that gives him most of what he wants. Above all, he should be sure to develop weapons of mass destruction. Even the hint of such a program in a threatening country will bring high-level American officials on top-secret missions to bribe its leaders to abandon the program. They will probably be able to keep the bribe and to pursue the programs they like, as well. These are the lessons America has given the world in the past eight years in Somalia, Haiti, Rwanda, Bosnia, Kosovo, Iraq, North Korea, China, and elsewhere. Americans should not imagine that the would-be dictators of the world have not learned them.

But psuedoengagement has had the same effect in America as it had in England—it has gravely complicated the efforts of those who favor real engagement to make their case. A succession of declared victories and the repeated assurances that the United States is in a "strategic pause" have helped undermine whatever support there might have been for maintaining adequate military forces or for pursuing an adequate foreign policy. America even has its own versions of the ten-year rule. In 1991 it was announced that America would have at least ten years' warning before a resurgent Soviet threat took the stage. Since then, the armed services have announced programs for modernization that assume there will be no serious enemy even into the more distant future. The basic modernization document from the Joint Chiefs of Staff is Joint Vision 2010. The Army After Next series of war games posit scenarios more than twenty years out. The air force conducted a valuable and insightful study called Air Force 2025.

The armed services are right to look so far into the future to see what sort of wars they should be prepared to fight—the formalized, forward-looking theoretical consideration of future war is an important positive element differentiating the current era from that of the 1920s, when such prospects were considered only by individual thinkers. What is more, there are excellent budgetary, political, and technological reasons why the services should focus their future-thinking so far into the distance. The problem is that the twenty- or twenty-five-year period has dominated the strategic realm.

Two major defense reviews followed the Bottom-Up Review of 1993: the report of the Commission on Roles and Missions in 1995, and the report of the Quadrennial Defense Review in 1997. Both came, fundamentally, to the same conclusions: the U.S. should be prepared to fight two nearly simultaneous major regional contingencies, should pursue an aggressive policy of modernization, should look to improvements in administrative and functional efficiency to save money, and should accomplish its tasks with the BUR force structure. Following the QDR, however, the report of the National Defense Panel, established to review the review, came to different conclusions. The NDP argued, "The United States needs a transformation strategy that enables us to meet a range of security challenges in 2010–2020 without taking undue risk in the interim."[1] It is possible to do that, the NDP argues, because the United States is "in a relatively secure interlude following an era of intense international confrontation." The NDP advocated abandoning the 2-MRC capability in order to make it easier to find funds for the technological transformation it proposed.

The concept of a "strategic pause" and the notion that the United States will face no major threats before 2010, probably before 2020, is a dangerous parallel to the ten-year rule. It has made it easy to stretch out acquisition and research and development on the grounds that the United States is still "way ahead" of any potential aggressor. Worse still, it has supported the increasingly widespread belief that the current force structure is, if anything, extravagant for dealing with this "relatively secure" period. But the most dangerous part of the argument urges the United States to be prepared to fight only the next world cataclysm—not to be ready to head it off through deterrence or by a swift, devastating response to nip a growing threat in the bud.

The ten-year rule led England to pursue a similar strategy. The rule was canceled at just about the right time—1932 was ten years before the Germans imagined they could be ready for war. Nor would England have been unprepared for war in 1942, judging by the advances made in the late 1930s. By 1942, the RAF would have been in condition to turn back the Luftwaffe in the Battle of Britain. It is even possible things would not have come to such a pass, for by 1942, the British Expeditionary Force could have been a force to reckon with—fully mechanized with modern equipment and, most important of all, having had considerable time to train. Naval deficiencies are harder to correct quickly, but it is quite possible that a better English showing in Western Europe (assuming that the Germans were not deterred by England's growing power) would have deflected the Japanese attack in the Pacific.

These are all might-have-beens, because the war did not start in 1942. It started in 1939 when neither Hitler nor the British expected it. It started in considerable part because of Britain's inability to deter it. We have seen how military weakness encouraged already timorous national leaders to avoid stopping German aggression in 1936 or 1938. Britain's weakness in those crises, and the knowledge that its rearmament would not be complete until 1942, encouraged Hitler to believe that he would not be opposed in 1939. He did not reckon on the fact that, ready for war or not, Chamberlain could not afford to back down again.

The problem with a ten-year rule is that it creates a window for aggression. Any state that can prepare for conflict faster than the state that imposes a ten-year rule on itself will be encouraged to do so, because delay might prove fatal. But the enemies of democracies can usually transform their militaries much faster than the democracies can. They do not need to worry about a parliament or congress voting funds or about the competing demands of civilian industries and workforces for resources that weaken the military program. They do not need to fear that elections will turn them out of office if they call upon their civilians to make too many sacrifices.

Ten-year rules undermine a nation's ability to influence international affairs in the intervening period. They become excuses to underfund the military—on the grounds that the gaps will be made good when the crisis is visible—and thereby create an enormous deficit that must be redressed when the crisis has come. In the 1930s, the deficit in military capabilities created by the ten-year-rule policies of the 1920s was so great that successive British governments alternately underfunded the rearmament and tried to ignore the problem altogether, hoping it would go away. Not until 1938 did they face the problem squarely—and allowed the army, for instance, to plan on sending an expeditionary force to France!

We have shown how military weakness, combined with the desire to ignore unpleasant international realities, has led America to abandon control of the international scene, shirk its responsibilities, and place global stability and its own security in jeopardy. The last question we must ask is: has America allowed its military might to run down so far that the cost of restoring it might drive future administrations faced with real warning signs to ignore the dangers or seek unrealistic solutions? The answer, again, we fear, is yes.

America's Military Weakness

The British experience between the wars reveals how the inadequacy of military forces to cope with worldwide responsibilities can cripple a nation's will to combat even a single challenge for which its power is more than enough. It has long been questionable whether America's post–Gulf War commitment to a 2-MRC capability was real, whether the forces the United States retained after the defense drawdowns were adequate to fight two real, nearly simultaneous major regional conflicts. The question arose at the very first, when Defense Secretary Aspin originally described the BUR plan as a win-hold-win force structure, but later decided virtually the same force structure to be capable of fighting two MRCs. By 1994, informed critics were openly questioning America's capability to prosecute this strategy, one defense expert asserting, "Logistically, you just can't do it."[2] But the Clinton administration would not be moved. Challenged by such critics, then Secretary of Defense William Perry declared, "It's an entirely implausible scenario that we'd fight two wars at once."

It may be implausible that the United States would fight two MRCs nearly simultaneously, but it is not at all unlikely that it might face two simultaneous major regional aggressors who should be opposed. It nearly faced precisely such a situation in 1994 when, for reasons of his own, Saddam once again threatened to invade Kuwait and, a few months later, Pyongyang threatened to invade South Korea. Almost 200,000 ground forces were put on alert for deployment to Kuwait. The Korean war plan reportedly called for some 400,000 troops to meet that contingency. During the Iraqi crisis, more than 20,000 U.S. soldiers were in Haiti. The total stated requirements for a war on the Korean peninsula, the defense of Kuwait (but not an invasion of Iraq, which was not considered), and a minor contingency in Haiti, then, were more than 620,000 troops. In 1994 there were 541,300 soldiers in the U.S. Army and 174,200 in the U.S. Marine Corps, for a total of 715,500 potential ground troops in all, assuming that all were available to deploy, ready to fight, and suitable for the missions at hand.[3] None of those assumptions, of course, were valid. Both Korea and Iraq are theaters that favor the use of heavy forces, armed with tanks and Bradley armored personnel carriers—light units and marines could not have done all that was necessary. By 1998 the fit was even tighter: the U.S. Army and U.S. Marine Corps active force structure had been reduced to only 661,000.[4]

Apart from the extremely serious question of whether the United States had enough airlift and sealift capacity to manage one, let alone two MRCs, this fit was much too tight for comfort. Military planners cannot strive, like efficient businessmen, to have precisely the right number of products, parts, or people and not one more. In business when stocking policies have aimed at such perfection but things go wrong, money is lost. In war when things go wrong and the margins of error are so small, people die unnecessarily, ground is lost, time is lost, and the situation changes, usually for the worse. The United States does not fight wars within margins so tight. Faced with the prospect of such a dangerous conflict, American leaders are far more likely to flinch, give in, declare victory, and withdraw than to risk sending inadequate forces to war. This military weakness helped deter the United States from taking more serious action in 1994 against Korea, and surely helped shape the decision to launch the counterproductive Operation Desert Fox against Iraq in 1998. It is certain to be a continuing factor in the calculation America's leaders must continually make as America's potential foes grow in power and determination during this era of "relative security."

As in Britain during the interwar years, the generally pacific mood of the populace has caused serious problems in recruiting for the armed forces. Even for those already serving, the situation is relatively bleak. Beginning in 1994, reports began to surface that the readiness of the armed forces to fight a war on short notice was eroding—training could not be paid for, equipment was breaking down, overworked people were burning out and leaving the services. The House and Senate armed services committees began taking testimony and uncovered many problems. By 1998 it was widely recognized that the readiness of the armed forces had eroded seriously. The Marine Corps Commandant, General Charles Krulak, and other senior military officers warned that the services could not support the 2-MRC strategy with their current resources; neither the training nor the personnel were there to make it possible. By the end of that year, all four service chiefs had told Congress that the defense budget was too small by at least $17 billion per year. Since then, the debate has focused on how much should be added to the budget, with "realistic" numbers floating between $10 and $20 billion annually.

The threat has not yet emerged; no "Japan" has yet invaded "Manchuria" to warn us that we must now prepare in earnest. No "Hitler" has yet come to power in any "Germany" to threaten destabilization and aggression on a massive scale. Even so, it is clear that such dollar amounts are in the same category as the £40 million voted to the British armed services in 1933, less than half of the £90-odd million the services identified as the "minimum" to meet the programs already in existence and clearly inadequate to meet the real needs of the situation. For the United States today, $20 billion a year will not fix the problem.

The military deficit is probably already too great for any "reasonable" politician to contemplate, and it will only get worse. Not only have readiness and "quality-of-life" issues (which affect recruiting and retention of qualified people) suffered badly, but the experiences even of the past few years show that the armed forces are too small. Worse than that, since at least 1995, the Department of Defense has been forced to reprogram money earmarked for modernization toward readiness and current operations. The systems that America will need to fight the major war of 2010 or 2020 are not now in place and are being developed too slowly or not at all. America is not ready now to face a major challenge, and current plans, even in light of current proposals to increase the defense budget, will not make it ready to face a major challenger in the future.

Nor will it be able to correct the situation quickly. Just as Britain's military industry contracted sharply with the reduction of defense budgets in the 1920s, so America's military industry has "converted" to civilian production and gone through its own process of reduction and reorganization. The capacity to mass-produce weapons is largely gone—it will not be quickly restored. To make matters worse, it is not clear that the high-technology weapons our forces now use can be mass-produced quickly. Smart munitions are highly delicate, sensitive pieces of equipment—gone are the days of acres of factory floor covered with hundreds of B-24 bombers in simultaneous construction. We may well find ourselves in the position the British experienced during the early 1930s—money for rearmament may appear, but it may be impossible to find any factory able to fill the orders.

America, Wake Up!

The story of America's military weaknesses is widely known and less and less disputed. Some defense experts advocate cutting the armed forces still further in order to fund modernization programs that are desperately important. They point to the "opportunity cost" of maintaining readiness now (supposing that it were being maintained) at the price of unpreparedness for the high-tech battlefield of the future. But weakness now has a much higher opportunity cost that has attracted virtually no attention to date—it may cost us the opportunity to avoid war in the future.

The rhetoric of the Clinton administration, if not its actions, has been generally sound. The United States is the "indispensable nation"; it must remain engaged in the world. Where the rhetoric has been wrongheaded is in the old phrase, used by Bonar Law in 1922 and again and again by British and Americans ever since, that "we are not the world's policeman." But it is the experience of the past century and the one before it that to preserve the peace of the world requires a "police force." If the United States is not to take a leading part in such a constabulary, who will? If the United States will not take the lead, spend its treasure, and risk its sons and daughters to maintain stability and peace in the world, who will? The most significant differences between England in the 1920s and America today point up the dangerous foolishness and needlessness of our hesitation. England suffered from serious economic, social, and political dislocations for much of the interwar period. Compared to potential friends and foes alike, her ground forces were insignificant unless maintained at a level unknown in England except for the Great War. Her defense capabilities could only barely be made adequate to her global requirements, and that process would have entailed a great deal of fiscal and emotional pain.

America faces none of those problems. The American economy enjoys a greater prosperity than any it has ever known—if this is an "era of constrained resources," then resources are and always will be constrained. Economically, conditions will never be better than this. America can maintain ground forces adequate to her global needs, as well as air and naval forces that, unlike England's, brook no challenge from any existing foe. Above all, America has suffered no such recent calamity as World War I. The continued wounds received from the "Vietnam syndrome" are self-inflicted and unnecessary. There is no reason whatsoever why America should not accept the burden fate laid upon her in 1991 and pay the price for doing so. The price of failure to accept it will be very much higher.

This warning, in many respects, is already too late. The cost of repairing our military deficiencies will already be staggering. The international situation has already begun to slip from our control. The Gulf coalition has shattered; NATO and the United States risk drifting apart. Challengers to the status quo proliferate, along with weapons of mass destruction and the means to deliver them. The English had this dubious advantage over today's America, that England was bombed in World War I—there was no need to argue on behalf of the need for air defense (although the solutions proposed and adopted were inadequate all the same). Americans today, at least judging by the actions of their leaders, do not understand their risk in this regard. In the war of 2020, certainly, of 2010, possibly, perhaps even earlier, America will not be immune to direct attack anymore. And it has done, so far, much less than the British at an equivalent point to address that danger.

America's course now is much harder than it would have been had it followed a prudent path after the Gulf War. Its Iraq policy is in ruins; it will not be resurrected. The threat from North Korea has only been delayed. In the wings, Russia, which was friendly in 1991, is increasingly restive. China grows ever stronger and more technologically capable—sources of conflict with her are obvious. If ever there was a "strategic pause" it is gone. Now the United States must begin to gird itself for the next round of conflict.

Comparisons of this or that present policy to Munich are premature—we have not yet entered our 1930s, our period of crisis. But our 1920s are drawing rapidly to a close. It is likely that the turning point for us now, as it was then, will be an unforeseen change in the international environment, probably economic. A major downturn often drives more moderate leaders from power and replaces them with aggressive regimes. Their leaders often seek to recoup economic loss with material, political gain. A major recession or depression, moreover, is certain to turn the United States even more inward just as the international situation most demands its attention. It will take away the resources needed to rearm its denuded armed forces even as it most needs to do so.

Although professional historians have written this study, this is not merely an academic discussion. A situation very like ours faced another great democracy this century. Warnings that England was sleeping came too late to do any good. We hope that this one comes in time. America must wake up, look realistically to its position in the world and to its defenses. It must strengthen its alliances by demonstrating the willingness to bear its inescapable responsibilities. It must make the necessary commitments and be ready materially and morally to meet them. Should it falter and delay, as the British did, the price of failure will be higher, nor will there be a powerful ally, safely across the ocean, to snatch safety and victory from the jaws of defeat.

Notes

Introduction

1. Winston S. Churchill, *Marlborough, His Life and Times* (London, 1947), vol. 1, pp. 427–28. The original publication was in 1933.

1: The Brave New World

1. Brian Bond, *British Military Policy Between the Two World Wars* (New York, 1980), p. 3.
2. David Lloyd George, *Memoirs of the Peace Conference* (New Haven, Conn., 1939), vol. 1, pp. 11–12.
3. Keith Jeffery, *The British Army and the Crisis of Empire, 1918–1922* (Dover, N.H., 1984).
4. Lloyd George, p. 98.
5. Ibid., emphasis in original.
6. These positions were separated on February 13, 1921, with the creation of the Air Ministry.
7. "Memorandum by the Chief of the Air Staff on Air Power Requirements of the Empire," Great Britain, Cabinet Papers, CAB 24/71, 9 December 1918.
8. Both "strategic bombing" and "blitzkrieg" are terms so controversial and so much abused as to have lost practically all meaning. Strategic bombing includes concepts ranging from "any use of airpower beyond the battlefield," to "city-busting," the deliberate annihilation of enemy cities or civilians, to nuclear war. Sykes's definition is rather all-inclusive—the RAF had not yet begun to argue for a particular view of what "strategic bombing" would be, but saw it simply as the argument for an "independent," war-winning mission for an *independent* Royal Air Force. "Blitzkrieg" is the term used after the fact by the Western press to describe the method of attack of the German armored forces in their attacks on Poland and France in 1939 and 1940. It was never a German doctrinal term and, in fact, relates more to operational techniques than to any body of thought or doctrine. For these purposes, it is used as it has commonly been used in the West to denote the combination of armored thrusts and ground-attack aircraft.
9. Major General Sir C. E. Callwell, *Field Marshal Sir Henry Wilson: His Life and Diaries* (New York, 1927), vol. 2, p. 151. Hereafter referred to as Wilson Diaries.
10. Wilson to Admiral Cowan, April 1919, ibid., p. 182.
11. Wilson Diaries, p. 183.
12. "The Military Situation Throughout the British Empire with Special Reference to the Inadequacy of the Numbers of Troops Available," forwarded by the Secretary of State for War, Winston Churchill, May 3, 1919, CAB 24/78, pp. 349–50. Hereafter cited as Military Situation.

13. Ibid., p. 1.
14. Charles Townshend, *The British Campaign in Ireland, 1919–1921: The Development of Political and Military Policies* (New York, 1975), pp. 17–19.
15. Cited in John Darwin, *Britain, Egypt, and the Middle East: Imperial Policy in the Aftermath of War, 1918–1922* (London, 1981), p. 72.
16. Military Situation, p. 2.
17. Ibid.
18. Viceroy's telegraph of 18 April, cited in Jeffery, *British Army*, p. 100.
19. Wilson Diaries, pp. 182–83.
20. Military Situation, p. 3.
21. Wilson Diaries, entry for January 26, 1919, p. 166.
22. Military Situation, p. 3, emphasis in original.
23. Ibid., pp. 3–4.
24. Wilson Diaries, entry for May 6, 1919, p. 190.
25. Ibid., entry for June 18, 1919, p. 199.
26. Ibid.
27. "Navy Estimates 1919–1920: Further Admiralty Memorandum for the War Cabinet," 5 July 1919, CAB 24/93, pp. 197–98.
28. "Navy Votes, Memorandum by the Chancellor of the Exchequer," 8 July 1919, G.T. 7646, CAB 24/83, p. 203.
29. "The Financial Situation, Memorandum by Dr. Addison," 28 July 1919, G.T. 7830, CAB 24/85, p. 281.
30. "Navy Votes, Memorandum by the Chancellor of the Exchequer," 8 July 1919, p. 203.
31. Ibid.
32. "Post-War Naval Policy, Admiralty Memorandum for the War Cabinet," G.T. 7975, 12 August 1919, CAB 24/86, p. 511.
33. Ibid., p. 512.
34. War Cabinet 606A, Draft Minutes of a Meeting held at 10 Downing Street, SW, on Tuesday, August 5, 1919, at 11:30 A.M., CAB 23/15, p. 156. Partially reproduced in John Robert Ferris, *The Evolution of British Strategic Policy, 1919–1926* (London, 1989), p. 20.
35. War Cabinet 606A, p. 164, emphasis added.
36. Ibid., p. 165.
37. See below.
38. War Cabinet 616A, Draft conclusions of a Meeting held at 10 Downing Street, SW, on Friday, August 15, 1919 at 11:30 A.M., CAB 23/15, pp. 270–71.
39. Ferris devotes considerable effort to showing that the "ten-year rule" is not all it is made out to be, and certainly should not be regarded as the shackle that kept the services from doing what they ought. This view is correct, as far as it goes, but misses the forest for the trees, as we argue below. Ferris, *Evolution,* chap. 2, *passim.*
40. We will present our interpretation of the meaning of the ten-year rule for the interwar period as a whole below.
41. See below.
42. Although Churchill had suggested something like it at the August 5 Cabinet meeting in which he advocated giving the services a lump sum of money and letting them figure out what to do with it. By that he meant to keep the politicians from involving themselves from all the petty details of the running of the service, but he certainly opened the armed forces up to the imposition of a ceiling on expenditures with this tactic.
43. Wilson Diaries, p. 208. We can find no evidence that any such detailed evaluation of the army's needs was presented to the Cabinet in 1919.
44. G. T. 7846, CAB 24/85, p. 308.
45. Ibid., p. 309, emphasis added.
46. Ibid., p. 310.
47. "Armies and Economics, Memorandum by the Secretary of State for War," 4 August 1919, G.T. 7882, CAB 24/84, p. 406.

2: Britain's Defense Dilemma

1. Raleigh, Sir W. A., *The War in the Air,* Oxford, 1937, p. 11.
2. Keith Jeffery, *The British Army and the Crisis of Empire, 1918–1922* (Dover, N.H., 1984), p. 150.
3. Ibid., p. 84.

4. "Summary of Army Estimates, 1920–21," Great Britain, Cabinet Papers, CAB 24/91, pp. 603–4, February 7, 1920.
5. Winston Churchill, "Memorandum covering Army Estimates, 1920–21," February 7, 1920, CAB 24/97, p. 608.
6. "Army Estimates, 1920–21, Conclusions of a meeting of the Cabinet Finance Committee held on February 9, 1920," CAB 24/98, p. 215.
7. Ibid.
8. Ibid., p. 216.
9. Ibid., p. 218.
10. Sir Henry Wilson, "Possibility of Reducing the Garrison of Iraq," February 20, 1920, CAB 24/99, p. 44.
11. "Note by the Secretary of State for War Covering four Memoranda," May 20, 1920, CAB 24/106, p. 65.
12. Hugh Trenchard, "Preliminary Scheme for the Military Control of Iraq by the Royal Air Force," CAB 24/106, p. 69.
13. "Note on the Causes of the Outbreak in Iraq, CP 1790," CAB 24/110, p. 428.
14. Aylmer Haldane, "The Situation in Iraq," CP 2217, December 2, 1920, CAB 24/116, p. 59, emphasis added.
15. Eliezer Tauber, *The Formation of Modern Syria and Iraq* (Portland, Ore., 1985), p. 300.
16. "Telegrams relating to Iraqi Situation," CP 1796, CAB 24/110, p. 454.
17. Sir Henry Wilson, "Palestine and Iraq," CP 1320, CAB 24/106, p. 74, May 6, 1920.
18. Sir Henry Wilson, "Policy Regarding Garrisons of Egypt and Palestine, and Iraq and Persia," CP 1320, CAB 24/106, p. 75, May 5, 1920.
19. Winston Churchill, "British Military Liabilities," CP 1467, CAB 24/107, p. 250, June 15, 1920.
20. Ibid., p. 253.
21. Emphasis in the original.
22. Hugh Trenchard, "British Military Liabilities," CAB 24/107, p. 262, June 14, 1920.
23. "Army, Navy, and Air Force Supplementary Estimates, Memorandum by the Chancellor of the Exchequer," July 20, 1920, CP 1656, CAB 24/109, p. 296.
24. "Telegram from Viceroy, Army Department, to Secretary of State for India, dated 3rd September 1920," CP 1844, CAB 24/111, p. 424.
25. "Reinforcements for Iraq," CP 1843, CAB 24/111, p. 423, September 9, 1920.
26. Jeffery, p. 60.
27. "The Work of the Royal Air Force in Iraq," CP 2652, CAB 24/120, February 19, 1921, pp. 289ff. This report was circulated to the Cabinet with marginal notes by the Air Staff, a note by the Deputy Chief of the Imperial General Staff, and a reply to that note by the Chief of the Air Staff, in February 1921.

3: The First Challenge to Peace

1. Harold Nicolson, *Curzon: The Last Phase 1919–1925* (Boston and New York, 1934), p. 62.
2. Ibid., p. 99.
3. Martin Gilbert, *Winston S. Churchill,* vol. 4, *1916–1922, The Stricken World* (Boston, 1975), p. 482.
4. Nicolson, *Curzon,* pp. 76–77.
5. John Darwin, *Britain, Egypt, and the Middle East: Imperial Policy in the Aftermath of War, 1918–1922* (London, 1981), p. 173.
6. Gilbert, *Winston Churchill,* p. 472; F. S. Northedge, *The Troubled Giant, Britain Among the Great Powers, 1916–1939* (London, 1966), p. 135.
7. Gilbert, *Winston Churchill,* pp. 472–73; G. H. Bennett, *British Foreign Policy During the Curzon Period, 1919–24* (London, 1995), p. 81.
8. Gilbert, *Winston Churchill,* p. 473.
9. Nicolson, *Curzon,* p. 247.
10. Northedge, *Troubled Giant,* p. 141.
11. Nicolson, *Curzon,* p. 249.
12. June 17, 1920, Appendix II to CAB 23/22.
13. June 18, 1920, Appendix I to CAB 23/21.
14. June 17, 1920, Appendix II to CAB 23/22.
15. Ibid.
16. June 18, 1920, Appendix III to CAB 23/22.

17. E.g., Darwin, *Britain, Egypt, and the Middle East*, p. 14: "By contrast with the pragmatism of his approach to German and Russian questions, Lloyd George's burning commitment to the destruction of Turkey as a European power, or as an expansive force in Asia, has often appeared curiously irrational."
18. *Ibid.*, p. 15.
19. Gilbert, *Winston Churchill*, pp. 478–79.
20. *Ibid.*, p. 480.
21. Nicolson, *Curzon*, p. 250.
22. Gilbert, *Winston Churchill*, p. 488.
23. Northedge, *Troubled Giant*, p. 143.
24. *Ibid.*, p. 146.
25. Nicolson, *Curzon*, p. 251.
26. Northedge, *Troubled Giant*, p. 145.
27. Gilbert, *Winston Churchill*, p. 498.
28. In a letter to Churchill on December 23, 1920, Lord Derby wrote, "I am practically certain the French, and absolutely certain the Italians have made advances to him [Kemal] behind our backs." Cited in Gilbert, *Winston Churchill*, pp. 501–2. He was right on both counts.
29. Bennett, p. 82: "That the Entente Powers no longer spoke to Turkey with a united voice was brought home to the British Cabinet in January 1921 by reports that propaganda, indicating that the French and Italians favoured revision of Sèvres, was being spread in Asia as far as Afghanistan."
30. Darwin, *Britain, Egypt, and the Middle East*, p. 209.
31. Northedge, *Troubled Giant*, p. 147.
32. David Walder, *The Chanak Affair* (London, 1969), pp. 149–51.
33. Darwin, *Britain, Egypt, and the Middle East*, p. 226.
34. 157 H.C. Deb. 5s. Cols. 2001–2002 (August 4, 1922).
35. See Nicolson's account of Churchill's critique, *Curzon*, pp. 265–67.
36. *Ibid.*, p. 265.
37. *Ibid.*, p. 270.
38. Darwin, *Britain, Egypt, and the Middle East*, p. 233.

4: The Paper Lion Roars

1. F. S. Northedge, *The Troubled Giant: Britain Among the Great Powers, 1916–1939* (London, 1966), p. 150.
2. Conclusion of Cabinet 48(22), September 7, 1922, CAB 23/31, and Conclusions of Cabinet 49(22), September 15, 1922, CAB 23/31.
3. Martin Gilbert, *Winston S. Churchill*, vol. 4 (London, 1975), p. 820.
4. Ibid.
5. Ibid., p. 821.
6. "Memorandum by Mr. H. G. Nicolson respecting the Freedom of the Straits," DBFP, vol. xviii, Appendix I, pp. 974–83.
7. Ibid., p. 976.
8. Darwin, *Britain*, p. 227.
9. Gilbert, *Winston S. Churchill*, vol. 4, p. 827.
10. John Darwin, *Britain, Egypt, and the Middle East: Imperial Policy in the Aftermath of War, 1918–1922* (London, 1981), p. 270.
11. Ibid., p. 271.
12. John Robert Ferris, *The Evolution of British Strategic Policy, 1919–1926* (London, 1989), p. 119.
13. Darwin, *Britain, Egypt, and the Middle East*, p. 234.
14. Gilbert, *Churchill*, vol. 4, pp. 824, 829.
15. Rumbold to Curzon, September 13, 1922, DBFP, vol. xviii, no. 24, p. 22.
16. Gilbert, *Churchill*, vol. 4, pp. 829–30.
17. Winston S. Churchill, *The Aftermath* (New York, 1929), pp. 423–24.
18. Gilbert, *Churchill*, vol. 4, p. 826.
19. Ferris, *Evolution of British Strategic Policy*, p. 119.
20. Nicolson, *Curzon*, p. 272, n. 1.
21. Ibid., p. 272.
22. Gilbert, *Churchill*, vol. 4, p. 829.
23. Nicolson, *Curzon*, p. 272; Gilbert, *Churchill*, p. 829.

24. Nicolson, *Curzon*, p. 273.
25. The interview was reported in a telegram received by Curzon on September 15. See DBFP, vol. xviii, pp. 79–80, n. 28.
26. Ibid., p. 45.
27. Ibid., p. 6.
28. Ibid., no. 27, pp. 25–26.
29. Curzon to Rumbold, September 16, ibid., no. 32, p. 29.
30. Gilbert, *Churchill*, vol. 4, p. 833.
31. Ibid., p. 834.
32. Cited in Ferris, *Evolution of British Strategic Policy*, p. 120.
33. Cited in Northedge, *Troubled Giant*, p. 151.
34. DBFP, vol. xviii, no. 48, Annex, "Draft of Invitation to Angora Government," pp. 84–85.
35. Gilbert, *Churchill Companion*, vol. 3 (London, 1977), pp. 2029–30.
36. Ibid., p. 2049.
37. Gilbert, *Churchill*, vol. 4, p. 843.
38. DBFP, vol. xviii, no. 78, pp. 117–18.
39. Gilbert, *Companion*, vol. 4, p. 2053.
40. Ibid., no. 68, pp. 109–10.
41. Gilbert, *Churchill*, vol. 4, p. 830.
42. DBFP, vol. xviii, no. 78, pp. 117–18, n. 1.
43. The judgment is made in Gilbert, *Churchill*, vol. 4, p. 845.
44. DBFP, vol. xviii, no. 79, p. 118, n. 1.
45. Gilbert, *Churchill Companion*, vol. 4, p. 2059, Harington's telegram to the War Office, September 30, 1922.
46. Gilbert, *Churchill*, vol. 4, p. 836.
47. DBFP, vol. xviii, no. 79, p. 118, n. 1.
48. Gilbert, *Churchill Companion*, vol. 4, p. 2058.
49. Gilbert, *Churchill*, vol. 4, p. 851.
50. DBFP, vol. xviii, October 6, 1922, no. 102, pp. 156–57; Gilbert, *Churchill*, vol. 4, p. 856.
51. DBFP, vol. xviii, no. 91, p. 140.
52. Rumbold to Curzon, October 6, 1922, DBFP, vol. xviii, no. 96, pp. 144–45.
53. Rumbold to Curzon, October 4, 1922, DBFP, vol. xviii, no. 91, p. 140, n. 2.
54. Gilbert, *Churchill*, p. 858.
55. Rumbold to Curzon, October 6, 1922, DBFP, vol. xviii, no. 97, p. 146.
56. Curzon to Rumbold, October 6, 1922, DBFP, vol. xviii, no. 95, p. 144.
57. "British Secretary's Notes of a Meeting between the French President of the Council, the British Secretary for Foreign Affairs, and the Italian Chargé d'Affaires," October 6, 1922, DBFP, vol. xviii, no. 106, p. 161.
58. Bennett, *British Foreign Policy*, p. 88.
59. Ibid., p. 167.
60. Crowe to Rumbold, October 7, 1922, DBFP, vol. xviii, no. 111, p. 178.
61. Rumbold to Curzon, October 10, 1922, DBFP, no. 117, p. 183, n. 2.
62. Rumbold to Curzon, October 8 and 9, 1922, DBFP, vol. xviii, nos. 112 and 115, pp. 178–79, 181–82. In the latter message Rumbold wrote that the British admiral on the scene had been instructed to prepare to clear all Turkish ships from the Bosphorus, and "I assume that these orders have been given . . . because you anticipate that conference in Mudania will break down today or because of continued advance of Kemalist detachments from Ismid to Constantinople" (p. 182).
63. DBFP, no. 112.
64. DBFP, no. 117, p. 184.
65. Ibid., p. 183.
66. Gilbert, *Churchill*, vol. 4, p. 860.
67. DBFP, no. 119, pp. 186–87, n. 4.
68. Nicolson, *Curzon*, p. 283.
69. Cited in Bennett, *Curzon*, p. 90.
70. Nicolson, *Curzon*, p. 282, says that Curzon has "one essential objective in view, namely the restoration of British diplomatic credit."
71. Ibid., pp. 324–25.
72. Curzon to his wife, January 1, 1923, cited in David Gilmour, *Curzon* (London, 1994), p. 563.
73. Northedge, *Troubled Giant*, p. 154.
74. Ibid., p. 331.

75. Ibid.
76. Ibid., pp. 312–13.
77. Ibid., pp. 339–40.
78. Ibid.
79. Northedge, *Troubled Giant*, pp. 154–55.
80. Nicolson, *Curzon*, pp. 347–48.
81. Ibid., p. 350, n. 1.
82. Nicolson, *Curzon*, p. 349.
83. Northedge, *Troubled Giant*, p. 157.
84. DBFP, vol. xviii, p. x.
85. Northedge, *Troubled Giant*, p. 157.
86. Ibid., pp. 153, 155.
87. Gilmour, *Curzon*, p. 566.
88. Bennett, *Curzon*, pp. 92–94.
89. Gilmour, *Curzon*, p. 565.
90. Nicolson, *Curzon*, pp. 275, 285.
91. Northedge, *Troubled Giant*, p. 152.
92. Ferris, *Evolution*, p. 119.
93. Northedge, *Troubled Giant*, p. 152.
94. Ferris, *Evolution*, pp. 120–21.
95. Conference of Ministers, September 27, 1922, CAB 23/39.
96. Bennett, *Curzon*, p. 93.
97. Letter to J. C. Robertson, October 7, 1922, in Gilbert, *Companion*, p. 2080.
98. Ferris, *Evolution*, p. 121.
99. Darwin, *Britain*, p. 45.
100. R. Boothby, *I Fight to Live*, p. 28, cited in A. J. P. Taylor, *English History, 1914–1945* (Oxford, 1965), p. 191.

5: Retreat from Responsibility

1. In May 1923 Stanley Baldwin succeeded Bonar Law as Prime Minister. Lord Curzon remained Foreign Secretary.
2. DBFP, vol. xxiv, no. 612, p. 936. The fullest account of the affair is James Barros, *The Corfu Incident of 1923, Mussolini and the League of Nations* (Princeton, N.J., 1965). The description of the murder is on pp. 22–24.
3. Arnold Toynbee, *Survey of International Affairs, 1920–1923* (London, 1925), pp. 348–49.
4. Barros, *Corfu*, p. 32.
5. DBFP, vol. xxiv, no. 617, p. 944.
6. Toynbee, *Survey*, p. 349; DBFP, vol. 24, 618, pp. 944–55.
7. Barros, *Corfu*, pp. 68–69.
8. Alan Cassels, *Mussolini's Early Diplomacy* (Princeton, N.J., 1970), p. 99.
9. Ibid. Raffaele Guariglia, *Ricordi 1922–1946* (Naples, 1949), p. 29, says that Mussolini, at first, "undoubtedly nourished the mad hope of being able to gain possession of the island. . . ." Cassels, *Mussolini's Early Diplomacy*, p. 99, says, "The Fascist leader's conduct throughout the Corfu crisis bore out this conviction."
10. Dennis Mack Smith, *Mussolini's Roman Empire* (London, 1976), p. 5.
11. DBFP, vol. xxiv, no. 634, pp. 963–68; Toynbee, *Survey*, p. 349.
12. Barros, *Corfu*, p. 73.
13. Nicolson, *Curzon*, pp. 368–69.
14. DBFP, vol. xxiv, no. 624, p. 950.
15. Ibid., p. 652.
16. Ibid., no. 626, p. 953.
17. Ibid., no. 627, p. 954.
18. K. Middlemas and J. Barnes, *Baldwin* (London, 1969), p. 195.
19. Nicolson, *Curzon*, p. 370.
20. DBFP, vol. xxiv, no. 639, p. 971.
21. Ibid., p. 972, n. 9.
22. Ibid., no. 628, p. 956.
23. Ibid., no. 629, p. 957, n. 1.
24. Nicolson, *Curzon*, p. 371.

25. Barros, *Corfu,* p. 36 and n. 9.
26. Ibid., p. 111.
27. Barros, *Corfu,* p. 112.
28. Nicolson, *Curzon,* p. 371.
29. DBFP, vol. xxiv, no. 655, p. 986.
30. Nicolson, *Curzon,* p. 371.
31. Gordon A. Craig, "The British Foreign Office from Grey to Austen Chamberlain," in Craig and Felix Gilbert, *The Diplomats* (Princeton, N.J., 1953), p. 37.
32. H. Stuart Hughes, "The Early Diplomacy of Italian Fascism, 1922–1932," in ibid., p. 220.
33. Guariglia, *Ricordi,* p. 30.
34. Alan Cassels, *Mussolini's Early Diplomacy* (Princeton, N.J., 1970), p. 110.
35. Barros, *Corfu,* 109. See also Arnold Wolfers, *Britain and France Between Two Wars* (New York, 1940), pp. 321–64.
36. DBFP, vol. xxiv, no. 629, pp. 957–58.
37. Ibid., no. 664, pp. 995–96.
38. Ibid., p. 996.
39. Ibid., no. 655, pp. 986–87.
40. The purpose of the message was clearly to squelch any idea of serious resistance to Italy. It was sent to Cecil in Geneva at the suggestion of Tyrrell, to restrain the ardent champion of collective security, "if only to bring it home how little the authors of the Covenant thought of practical difficulties." Lest the message be lost on Curzon, he added: "It all means that putting Art[icle] 16 into action means creating a state of war." Tyrrell's minute to ibid., p. 986, n. 1.
41. Henry de Jouvenel, "France and Italy," *Foreign Affairs,* vol. 5 (1927), no. 4, p. 538, says that "the English delegates showed that they were giving the matter [of a naval action] the most serious consideration."
42. Antonio Salandra, *Memorie Politiche, 1916–1925* (Milan, 1951), p. 104, cited in Barros, *Corfu,* p. 178.
43. DBFP, vol. xxiv, no. 677, p. 1012 and n. 1.
44. Barros, *Corfu,* p. 179.
45. Ibid., p. 180.
46. Kenneth Edwards, *The Grey Diplomatists* (London, 1938), pp. 86–87, cited in Barros, *Corfu,* p. 180, n. 65.
47. Barros, *Corfu,* p. 181.
48. Ibid., p. 183.
49. Ibid., p. 305.
50. Cassels, *Mussolini,* p. 110, says: "By September 3, Poincaré agreed to bail Italy out."
51. Ibid., p. 111.
52. DBFP, vol. xxiv, no. 657, p. 988.
53. Cassels, *Mussolini,* p. 112.
54. Ibid., pp. 112–13.
55. DBFP, vol. xxiv, no. 682, p. 1016.
56. Ibid., p. 1016.
57. Barros, *Corfu,* p. 231. Greek town officials had been replaced by Italian military personnel, trenches were dug, mines were laid in the channel, and public buildings, including the customs house, had been taken over. See nn. 4 and 5.
58. Cassels, *Mussolini,* p. 117.
59. Barros, *Corfu,* p. 241; Cassels, *Mussolini,* p. 118.
60. Barros, *Corfu,* p. 239. Cassels, p. 118, calls Crewes statement "an unmistakable ultimatum."
61. Barros, *Corfu,* pp. 241–42.
62. Cassels, *Mussolini,* pp. 118–19.
63. DBFP, vol. xxiv, no. 735, p. 1074.
64. Cassels, *Mussolini,* p. 120.
65. Barros, *Corfu,* p. 246.
66. DBFP, vol. xxiv, no. 735, p. 1076, n. 9.
67. Ibid., no. 735, pp. 1073–76.
68. The quotation is from a message from Curzon to Crewe on September 26, cited in Barros, *Corfu,* pp. 281–82, n. 24. Essentially the same language is to be found in a telegram from Curzon to Crewe on the same date in DBFP, vol. xxiv, no. 725, p. 1066.
69. DBFP, vol. xxiv, no. 725, pp. 1066–67.
70. Sheldon Whitehouse, American chargé d'affaires in Paris, quoted in Barros, *Corfu,* p. 249.

71. Stanley Baldwin to Lord Curzon, September 14, 1923, cited from the Curzon Papers in Barros, *Corfu*, pp. 252–253.
72. DBFP, vol. xxiv, p. xv. See also Appendix, pp. 1106–15, which contains Harenc's discussion of the commission's final report.
73. Barros, *Corfu*, p. 281.
74. Ibid., p. 283.
75. Ibid.
76. DBFP, vol. xxiv, no. 744, p. 1088.
77. Denis Mack Smith, *Mussolini's Roman Empire* (New York, 1976), p. 6.
78. Guariglia, *Ricordi*, p. 31.
79. Gaetano Salvemimi, *Mussolini Diplomatico (1922–1932)* (Bari, Italy, 1952), p. 70.
80. Smith, *Mussolini*, p. 6.
81. Guariglia, *Ricordi*, p. 14.
82. H. Stuart Hughes, "The Early Diplomacy of Italian Fascism, 1922–1932," in Craig and Gilbert, *Diplomats*, p. 221. See also Cassels, *Mussolini*, pp. 127–45.
83. Smith, *Mussolini*, p. 6.
84. Barros, *Corfu*, Appendix C, "Memorandum by Sir Eric Drummond of the Corfu Incident," pp. 317–20.
85. Martin Gilbert, *A History of the Twentieth Century*, vol. 1, *1900–1933* (New York, 1997), p. 660.
86. Gilmour, *Curzon*, p. 590.
87. Nicolson, *Curzon*, p. 372.
88. Barros, *Corfu*, p. 313.
89. Salvemini, *Mussolini Diplomatico*, p. 69. Barros, *Corfu*, p. 303, compares it with both Manchuria and Italy's conquest of Ethiopia in 1935.
90. Cassels, *Mussolini*, p. 126.
91. Barros, *Corfu*, p. 123.

6: The Search for Security

1. For an interesting discussion of the question see Gerhard L. Weinberg, "The Defeat of Germany in 1918 and the European Balance of Power," *Central European History*, vol. 2 (1969), pp. 248–260.
2. Cited in F. S. Northedge, *The Troubled Giant: Britain Among the Great Powers, 1916–1939* (London, 1966), p. 103.
3. Ibid., p. 104.
4. Later, there was a dispute in the House as to whether or not there was a single dissent. See 150 H.C. Deb. 5s, Cols. 53–55.
5. Northedge, *Troubled Giant*, p. 105.
6. Ibid., p. 102.
7. Comte A. F. B. de St-Aulaire, *Confession d'un vieux diplomate* (Paris, 1953), p. 566.
8. 150 H.C. Deb. 5s, Col. 42.
9. Ibid., Col. 55.
10. Correlli Barnett, *The Collapse of British Power* (London, 1972), p. 321.
11. Memorandum by Sir E. Crowe, February 12, 1921, in DBFP, vol. 17, no. 38, p. 56.
12. Anne Orde, *Great Britain and International Security 1920–1926* (London, 1978), p. 11.
13. Martin Gilbert, *Winston S. Churchill*, vols. 4–5 (London, 1975–77), *Companion*, vol. 4, parts 1–3, (1976–1977), pp. 1545–46.
14. Northedge, *Troubled Giant*, p. 225.
15. DBFP, vol. xvi, no. 110, p. 787.
16. Memorandum by Marquess Curzon of Kedleston on the question of an Anglo-French Alliance, December 28, 1921. In DBFP, vol. 16, pp. 862–70.
17. DBFP, vol. xv, no. 1, pp. 6–7.
18. Orde, *Great Britain*, p. 16.
19. DBFP, vol. xvi, p. 789.
20. Orde, *Great Britain*, p. 17.
21. Ibid., p. 18.
22. Ibid., pp. 24–25.
23. Ibid., p. 26.
24. Northedge, *Troubled Giant*, p. 229.

25. Orde, *Great Britain,* p. 35.
26. Ibid., p. 36.
27. Cited in ibid., p. 66.
28. Ibid.
29. DBFP, vol. xxvii, no. 180, p. 256.
30. Sir James Headlam-Morley, "The Guarantee Treaties, 1814–5—1919: A Comparison," in *Studies in Diplomatic History* (New York, 1930), pp. 146–56. His relevant memoranda were collected and edited by Kenneth and Agnes Headlam-Morley.
31. Ibid., p. 156.
32. "England and the Low Countries," in ibid., pp. 156–57.
33. Ibid., p. 164.
34. Ibid., pp. 170–71.
35. Ibid., pp. 178–79.
36. Ibid., pp. 183–84.
37. Ibid., pp. 186–87.
38. Ibid., pp. 188–89.
39. Ibid., pp. 189–90.
40. Ibid., pp. 190–91.
41. 150 H.C. Deb. 5s, Col. 42, February 7, 1922.
42. Ibid., Col. 186, February 8, 1922.
43. Ibid., Col. 1920, February 7, 1922.

7: The Unraveling of Versailles

1. One of the senior British members of that commission, Brigadier General J. H. Morgan, has left an account of its activities: *Assize of Arms: The Disarmament of Germany and Her Rearmament (1919–1939),* vol. 1 (New York, 1946). Morgan conceived an almost racial hatred for the Germans, and his account is a tendentious effort to persuade the leaders of the world in 1946 not to repeat the mistakes of 1919. Perhaps the shrillness of its tone has convinced later historians to avoid reliance upon it, but it is quite easy, in fact, to distinguish Morgan's relation of events of which he was directly aware or in which he participated from the exaggerated conclusions he drew from them.
2. Ibid., pp. 23–24.
3. Ibid., pp. 31–32.
4. Ibid., pp. 65–67.
5. "Note by the Chief of the Imperial General Staff on His Visit to the Rhine, March 7th to 17th, 1920," CP 919, Great Britain, Cabinet Papers, CAB 24/101, pp. 107–8.
6. "Violations of the Peace Treaty by Germany: Memorandum by the General Staff," CP 1030, 7 April 1920, CAB 24/103, pp. 116–17.
7. F. S. Northedge, *The Troubled Giant: Britain Among the Great Powers, 1916–1939* (London, 1966), pp. 162–63.
8. Hajo Holborn, *A History of Modern Germany, 1840–1945* (Princeton, N.J., 1982), p. 583.
9. Morgan, *Assize of Arms,* pp. 183ff.
10. "Memorandum of the German Minister of Defence on the Maintenance of an Army of 200,000 men," 20 April 1920, CAB 24/104, pp. 383ff.
11. "Destruction of German War Material," CP 1132, 22 April 1920, CAB 24/104.
12. "German Request to Maintain an Army of 200,000. Allied Declaration in Answer to German Note," CP 1184, 26 April 1920, CAB 24/104, pp. 381ff.
13. Northedge, *Troubled Giant,* p. 167.
14. Ibid., p. 168.
15. Ibid., p. 169.
16. Ibid., p. 171.
17. "Execution of the Treaty of Peace with Germany," Cabinet Paper 1381, 4 June 1920, CAB 24/106, pp. 261ff.
18. The Great General Staff, which had formerly run the Imperial German Army, was abolished by the Treaty of Versailles. To replace it the Germans created the *Truppenamt,* or "troops administration," which became an underground general staff. Seeckt was the head of this organization.
19. In F. L. Carsten, *The Reichswehr and Politics, 1918–1933* (New York, 1966), p. 113.
20. "The German Situation from a Military Aspect. Memorandum by the General Staff," CP 1782, 16 August 1920, CAB 24/110, pp. 412ff.

21. Emphasis added.
22. "Note Presented by the British, French, Italian, Japanese and Belgian Ambassadors at Berlin," 4 June 1925, Cmd. 2429. For a summary of that report, see "Summary of the Final Report of the Inter-Allied Military Comission of Control into the General Inspection of German Armaments, February 15, 1925," in *Documents on British Foreign Policy,* First Series, vol. XXVII, 1925, No. 592.
23. Ibid., No. 592, p. 959.
24. Ibid., pp. 960–61.
25. See, for instance, ibid., No. 650, pp. 1060ff.
26. Morgan, *Assize of Arms,* pp. xvi–xvii.
27. Ibid., p. xiii.
28. Barton Whaley, *Covert German Rearmament, 1919–1939: Deception and Misperception* (Frederick, Md., 1984).
29. Ibid., p. 11.
30. Ibid., p. 13.
31. Ibid., p. 14.
32. For a discussion of the complicity of the German government and the relations between the *Reichswehr* and its civilian masters, see Hans W. Gatzke, *Stresemann and the Rearmament of Germany* (Baltimore, 1969). There can be no doubt that successive German governments were aware of what the *Reichswehr* was up to and that they were, in fact, deeply complicit—even Stresemann, the architect of the Locarno Treaty.
33. Whaley, *Covert German Rearmament,* p. 25.
34. Ibid., p. 26.
35. Ibid., p. 29.
36. Ibid., p. 31.
37. Ibid., p. 32.

8: The Locarno Treaty

1. Sally Marks, "1918 and After: The Postwar Era," in Gordon Martel, ed., *The Origins of the Second World War Reconsidered* (Boston, 1986), p. 29.
2. K. Middlemas and J. Barnes, *Baldwin* (London, 1969), p. 180.
3. Sally Marks, "The Myth of Reparations," *Central European History,* vol. 2 (1978), p. 236.
4. Maurice Baumont, *The Origins of the Second World War,* translated by Simon de Couvreur Ferguson (New Haven, Conn., and London, 1978), p. 16.
5. W. A. McDougall, "Political Economy versus National Sovereignty: French Structures for German Integration after Versailles," *Journal of Modern History,* vol. 51 (1979), pp. 18–19.
6. Correlli Barnett, *The Collapse of British Power* (London, 1972), p. 327.
7. A. J. P. Taylor, *The Origins of the Second World War,* 2nd ed. (New York, 1985), p. 52.
8. Sally Marks, *Illusion of Peace* (New York, 1976), p. 61. Since there was no majority for the Protocol in the Labour Cabinet, it would have been defeated even if the Conservatives had not won the election. See F. S. Northedge, *The Troubled Giant: Britain Among the Great Powers, 1916–1939* (London, 1966), p. 247.
9. Jon Jacobson, *Locarno Diplomacy, Germany and the West 1925–1929* (Princeton, N.J. 1972), p. 16.
10. Anne Orde, *Great Britain and International Security 1920–1926* (London, 1978), p. 82.
11. DBFP, vol. xxvii, no. 180, p. 255.
12. Orde, *Great Britain,* p. 56; Northedge, *Troubled Giant,* p. 253.
13. DBFP, vol. xxvii, no. 181 (January 7, 1925), p. 260. Chamberlain was unpersuaded. He minuted: "I do not understand Lord D'Abernon's reason for thinking union between the Imperialist leaders in Germany [and] the Communists in Russia 'unthinkable.' After all, who started the Russian revolutionaries on their task [and] why not again." Lt. Col. T. Heywood, of the general staff, wrote a response to D'Abernon's memorandum that challenged and undermined it thoroughly. Heywood concluded that the strategic realities would have found France alone in a war with Germany (without British support): "at the present moment she would undoubtedly be equal to the task, but her superiority is bound to decrease steadily in the course of the next few years." Ibid., no. 203, p. 309.
14. DBFP, vol. xxvii, no. 191, p. 286.
15. Ibid., pp. 286–89.
16. Ibid., vol. xxvii, no. 186, p. 269.

17. Ibid., pp. 270–71.
18. Ibid., pp. 271–73.
19. Ibid., no. 205, p. 312.
20. Ibid., pp. 311–18.
21. Ibid., p. 311, n. 1.
22 John Robert Ferris, *The Evolution of British Strategic Policy, 1919–1926* (London, 1989), p. 152.
23. Ibid., p. 153. The evidence for Chamberlain's actions and intentions is ambiguous. Lord D'Abernon, on the basis of informal information, wrote in his diary: "The main argument adduced by opponents of the scheme was that the unilateral pact with France against Germany would throw that country into the arms of Russia. It was further desired to proceed with the negotiations for the conclusion of a wider Mutual Pact of Guarantee on the basis of the German effort of January. Chamberlain bowed to the majority." *An Ambassador of Peace: Lord D'Abernon's Diary* (London, 1930), vol. 3, p. 155. That pictures a two-step process in which Chamberlain's first proposal is defeated before he adopts a second. In a letter to D'Abernon, Chamberlain said that from the first he had pressed for a French alliance first in order later to bring in Germany and that he could not have achieved the quadruple alliance without pressing for the one with France alone. Orde (*Britain*, p. 91, n. 1) questions the accuracy of his memory. Ferris (*Evolution*, p. 211, n. 28), citing a communication from Chamberlain to Crowe, says that "by mid February 1925 Chamberlain began to favour a quadruple pact rather than an Anglo-French alliance."
24. Orde, *Britain*, p. 84. For a similar evaluation see C. Baechler, *Gustave Stresemann (1878–1929), De l'impérialisme à la sécurité collective* (Strasbourg, 1996), p. 584.
25. Northedge, *Troubled Giant*, p. 255.
26. Orde, *Britain*, p. 90.
27. Ferris, *Evolution*, p. 153.
28. H.C. Deb. 181, Cols. 714–15.
29. McDougall, "Political Economy," p. 19.
30. Orde, Britain, p. 86.
31. Jacobson, *Locarno*, p. 3.
32. Ibid.
33. Even these arbitration agreements were nonbinding, therefore not enforceable, which understandably worried the Czechs and Poles.
34. H.C. Deb. 5th Ser., vol. 188, Col. 419.
35. Piotr S. Wandycz, *The Twilight of French Eastern Alliances, 1926–1936* (Princeton, N.J., 1988), p. 20.
36. Marks, *Illusion*, p. 71.
37. At the time of Locarno, however, evacuation of the Rhineland was not scheduled until 1935.
38. Marks, *Illusion*, p. 70.
39. Ferris, *Evolution*, p. 154.
40. Jacobson, *Locarno*, p. 38.
41. Ferris, *Evolution*, p. 154.
42. Barnett, *Collapse*, p. 332.
43. Ibid., p. 333. The comment was made by Lord D'Abernon, British ambassador to Berlin, perhaps "the true father" of Locarno. Marks, *Illusion*, p. 65.
44. Taylor, *Origins*, p. 54.
45. Northedge, *Troubled Giant*, p. 266.
46. Jacobson, *Locarno*, p. 36.
47. Marks, *Illusion*, p. 72.
48. Northedge, *Troubled Giant*, p. 267.
49. DBFP, Series 1A, vol. 1, no. 83, p. 122.
50. Ibid., no. 2, p. 18.
51. H.C. Deb. 5s, Col. 318 (March 24, 1925).
52. DBFP, Series 1A, vol. 1, no. 1, pp. 1–17. It is entitled "Foreign Office Memorandum respecting the Locarno Treaties" and dated January 10, 1926. The author is J. C. Sterndale Bennett of the Central Department of the Foreign Office.
53. Ibid., p. 334.
54. Northedge, *Troubled Giant*, p. 253.
55. Hans W. Gatzke, *Stresemann and the Rearmament of Germany* (Baltimore, 1969), p. 114.
56. Craig, *Germany*, p. 514.
57. Gatzke, *Stresemann*, p. 38.
58. Northedge, *Troubled Giant*, p. 270.

59. Barnett, *Collapse,* p. 328.
60. Northedge, *Troubled Giant,* pp. 271–72.
61. Northedge, *Troubled Giant,* p. 272.

9: The Spirit of Locarno

1. From a Foreign Office memorandum cited in C. J. Bartlett, *British Foreign Policy in the Twentieth Century* (London, 1989), p. 35.
2. Correlli Barnett, *The Collapse of British Power* (London, 1972), p. 333.
3. DBFP, Series 1A, vol. i, Appendix, pp. 846–81.
4. Ibid., pp. 846–47.
5. Ibid., pp. 850, 854.
6. Ibid., pp. 855–58.
7. Ibid., p. 849.
8. Chiefs of Staff Sub-Committee Review of Imperial Defence, June 22, 1926, COS 41, CAB 53/12.
9. Michael Howard, *The Continental Commitment* (London, 1989), p. 95 and n. 180.
10. K. Middlemas and J. Barnes, *Baldwin* (London, 1969), p. 359.
11. Sally Marks, *Illusion of Peace* (New York, 1976), p. 80.
12. Marshall M. Lee and Wolfgang Michalka, *German Foreign Policy 1917–1933: Continuity or Break?* (Leamington Spa, Hamburg, and New York, 1987), p. 98.
13. Ibid., p. 86.
14. Lee and Michalka, *German Foreign Policy,* pp. 86–87.
15. Jon Jacobson, *Locarno Diplomacy: Germany and the West 1925–1929* (Princeton, N.J., 1972), p. 123.
16. Hans W. Gatzke, *Stresemann and the Rearmament of Germany* (New York, 1969), p. 74.
17. Ibid., p. 13.
18. Gordon A. Craig, *Germany 1866–1945* (New York, 1978), p. 522.
19. Marks, *Illusion,* p. 99.
20. Barnett, *Collapse,* p. 335.
21. Ibid., p. 104.
22. David Carlton, *MacDonald versus Henderson* (London, 1970), p. 67.
23. Jacobson, *Locarno,* p. 365.
24. Carlton, *MacDonald versus Henderson,* p. 55.
25. Ibid., p. 75, n. 1.
26. The argument is made in Quintin Hogg, *The Left Was Never Right* (London, 1945), p. 121.
27. Carlton, *MacDonald versus Henderson,* pp. 55–56. Carlton admits the viability of this argument but regards it as persuasive only in hindsight.
28. Ibid., p. 56.
29. Barnett, *Collapse,* p. 336, n. 1.
30. Ibid., p. 336.
31. Carlton, *MacDonald versus Henderson,* p. 57.
32. Gordon A. Craig, *The Politics of the Prussian Army, 1640–1945* (Oxford, 1955), pp. 436–37.
33. Craig, *Germany,* p. 554.
34. Ibid., p. 542.
35. E. W. Bennett, *German Rearmament and the West* (Princeton, 1979), p. 49.
36. Heinrich Brüning, *Memoiren, 1918–1934* (Munich, 1972), p. 203, cited in Lee and Michalka, *German Foreign Policy,* p. 115.
37. Craig, *Germany,* p. 553.
38. DBFP, 2nd Ser., vol. 2/1, no. 348.
39. Ibid., pp. 121–22.
40. Craig, *Germany,* p. 555.
41. DBFP, vol. 2/1, Appendix II.
42. Carlton, *MacDonald versus Henderson,* p. 72.
43. Ibid., p. 556.
44. Marks, *Illusion,* p. 116.
45. Carlton, *MacDonald versus Henderson,* p. 72.
46. Bennett, *German Rearmament,* p. 507.
47. Ibid., pp. 209–72.
48. Lee and Michalka, *German Foreign Policy,* p. 136.

49. Their memorandum is published in G. Wollstein, "Eine Denkschrift des Staatssekretärs Bernhard von Bülow von März 1933. Wilhelminische Konzeption der Aussenpolitik zu Beginn der nationalsozialistischen Herrschaft," *Militärgeschichtliche Mitteilungen,* vol. 1 (1973), pp. 77ff. It is the chief source for the discussion in Lee and Michalka, *German Foreign Policy,* pp. 144–48.
50. Lee and Michalka, *German Foreign Policy,* p. 145.
51. Bennett, *German Rearmament,* p. 506.
52. Martin Gilbert, *The Roots of Appeasement* (London, 1966), p. ix.
53. Ibid., pp. 11–12.
54. Barnett, *Collapse,* p. 332.
55. Ibid., p. 76.
56. Keith Robbins, *Appeasement* (Oxford, 1988), p. 30.
57. Arnold Wolfers, *Britain and France Between Two Wars* (New York, 1940), p. 209. Baldwin spoke in 1923, MacDonald in 1934.
58. Robbins, *Appeasement,* p. 34.
59. Wolfers, *Britain and France,* p. 209.
60. Howard, *Continental Commitment,* p. 80.
61. Ibid., p. 82.
62. Barnett, *Collapse,* p. 436.
63. Howard, *Continental Commitment,* p. 74.
64. Ibid., p. ix.
65. Gilbert, *Roots,* p. 54.

10: The Bill Comes Due

1. Correlli Barnett, *The Collapse of British Power* (London, 1972), pp. 302, 305.
2. Telford Taylor, *Munich, the Price of Peace* (New York, 1979), p. 208.
3. F. S. Northedge, *The Troubled Giant: Britain Among the Great Powers, 1916–1939* (London, 1966), p. 403.
4. G. W. Baer, *The Coming of the Italo-Ethiopian War* (Cambridge, Mass., 1967), p. 70.
5. Ibid., pp. 84–85.
6. On the origins of Mussolini's policy see ibid.
7. For the French side see Franklin D. Laurens, *France and the Ethiopian Crisis, 1935–1936* (The Hague, 1967).
8. Joseph Paul-Boncour, cited in Baer, *Coming,* p. 83.
9. Baer, *Coming,* p. 87.
10. Raffaele Guariglia, *Ricordi 1922–1946* (Naples, 1949), p. 215.
11. DBFP, Second Series, vol. xiv, p. viii.
12. Ibid., no. 192, pp. 180–83. Memorandum from Foreign Office to Colonial Office, March 6, 1935.
13. Ibid., p. ix.
14. Ibid., p. 775.
15. Ibid., p. 744.
16. Cited in Baer, *Coming,* p. 91.
17. DBFP, Second Series, vol. xiv, no. 163, p. 158.
18. DBFP, Second Series, vol. xlv, no. 175, p. 167, n. 4.
19. Baer, *Coming,* p. 93.
20. Ibid., p. 95.
21. Ibid., p. 377.
22. Baer, *Coming,* p. 122.
23. Taylor, *Munich,* p. 225.
24. Gordon A. Craig, *Germany 1866–1945* (New York, 1978), p. 687.
25. Taylor, *Munich,* p. 224.
26. Ibid., p. 222.
27. Barnett, *Collapse,* p. 359.
28. DBFP Second Series, vol. xiv, no. 403, p. 436.
29. Ibid., pp. 437–38.
30. Ibid., p. 437.
31. Taylor, *Munich,* p. 227.
32. DBFP Second Series, vol. xiv, no. 431, p. 470.

33. Ibid., no. 427, p. 465–66.
34. Ibid., no. 434, p. 474.
35. A. Marder, "The Royal Navy and the Ethiopian Crisis of 1935–36," *American Historical Review,* vol. 75 (1970), p. 1328, n. 4; p. 1329.
36. Barnett, *Collapse,* p. 364.
37. Ibid., p. 228.
38. Taylor, *Munich,* p. 229.
39. Ibid.
40. Barnett, *Collapse,* p. 366.
41. Taylor, *Munich,* p. 227.
42. Barnett, *Collapse,* p. 370.
43. A. J. P. Taylor, *English History, 1914–1945* (Oxford, 1965), p. 382.
44. Barnett, *Collapse,* p. 372.
45. Taylor, *Munich,* p. 233.
46. P. O. Schmidt, *Hitler's Interpreter* (London, 1951), p. 112.
47. A. Marder, "The Royal Navy and the Ethiopian Crisis of 1935–36," *American Historical Review,* vol. 75 (1970), pp. 1355–56.
48. Ibid., p. 1344.
49. Ibid., p. 1339.
50. Ibid., p. 1338.
51. Ibid., p. 1356.
52. Ibid., p. 1340.
53. L. Mosley, *On Borrowed Time: How World War II Began* (London, 1969), p. 7. For the sources of the quotations see p. 477.
54. J. T. Emmerson, *The Rhineland Crisis* (London, 1977), p. 246.
55. Marder, "Royal Navy," p. 1341.
56. Gerhard L. Weinberg, *The Foreign Policy of Hitler's Germany: Starting World War Two 1937–1939* (Chicago, 1980), p. 241; Craig, *Germany,* p. 688.
57. R. J. Young, *In Command of France, French Foreign Policy and Military Planning 1933–1940* (Cambridge, Mass., and London, 1978), p. 119.
58. Weinberg, *Foreign Policy,* p. 243.
59. Young, *Command,* p. 120.
60. Craig, *Germany,* p. 690.
61. W. L. Shirer, *The Collapse of the Third Republic* (New York, 1969), pp. 261–62.
62. Taylor, *Munich,* p. 241.
63. Ibid., p. 243.
64. Ibid., p. 244.
65. Weinberg, *Foreign Policy,* p. 259.
66. Emmerson, *Rhineland Crisis,* p. 136.
67. Ibid., p. 137.
68. Ibid.
69. Taylor, *Munich,* p. 245.
70. Emmerson, *Rhineland Crisis,* p. 139.
71. Craig, *Germany,* p. 691.
72. Taylor, *Munich,* p. 248.
73. For a good discussion of Czech and Polish relations with France during the Rhineland crisis see Piotr S. Wandycz, *The Twilight of French Eastern Alliances, 1926–1936* (Princeton, N.J., 1988), pp. 431–47.
74. A. Bullock, *Hitler: A Study in Tyranny* (New York, 1962), pp. 342–43.
75. Taylor, *Origins,* p. 97. Gerhard L. Weinberg, in *The Foreign Policy of Hitler's Germany: Diplomatic Revolution in Europe, 1933–1936* (Chicago, 1970), p. 252, believes that the Germans were to stage "a fighting withdrawal," which implies the willingness to risk a war, but Hitler "clearly did not think the contingency very likely." Weinberg also reports that Hitler had a "last minute attack of nerves" (p. 253) before issuing the final orders.
76. Schmidt, *Hitler's Interpreter,* p. 320.
77. Emmerson, *Rhineland Crisis,* p. 145.
78. Ibid., p. 237.
79. J. C. Fest, *Hitler,* translated by Richard and Clara Winston (New York, 1974), p. 499. Craig, *Germany,* p. 691, translates part of the passage: "The world belongs to the man with guts! God helps him."

80. Emmerson, *Rhineland Crisis,* p. 238.
81. Ibid., p. 239.
82. Ibid., p. 248.
83. A. Adamthwaite, *France and the Coming of the Second World War 1936–1939* (London, 1977), p. 41.
84. Ibid.
85. Hajo Holborn, *A History of Modern Germany, 1840–1945* (Princeton, N.J., 1945), pp. 769–70.
86. Taylor, *Origins,* p. 101.
87. Emmerson, *Rhineland Crisis,* p. 237.
88. Barnett, *Collapse,* p. 385.
89. Ibid., pp. 385–86.

11: The Price of Self-Deception

1. The various proposals, counterproposals, and arguments can be seen throughout Great Britain, Cabinet Papers, Chiefs of Staff Subcommittee of the Committee of Imperial Defense, CAB 53 for this period. See also John Robert Ferris, *The Evolution of British Strategic Policy, 1919–1926* (London, 1989), for a general overview, and James Neidpath, *The Singapore Naval Base and the Defence of Britain's Eastern Empire, 1919–1941* (London, 1981).
2. Committee of Imperial Defense, Chiefs of Staff Sub-Committee, "Imperial Defence Policy: Annual Review for 1932 by the Chiefs of Staff Sub-Committee," C.O.S. 295, CAB 53/22, pp. 273ff, p. 4.
3. Ibid., p. 5.
4. Ibid., p. 6, emphasis added.
5. Ibid., pp. 6–7.
6. Ibid., p. 7.
7. Ibid., p. 4.
8. Ibid., p. 8.
9. Ibid., p. 10.
10. N. H. Gibbs, *History of the Second World War,* United Kingdom Military Series: *Grand Strategy:* vol. 1, *Rearmament Policy* (London, 1976), p. 80.
11. Ibid., p. 81.
12. Ibid., pp. 81–82.
13. Ibid., p. 82.
14. Committee of Imperial Defence, Chiefs of Staff Sub-Committee, "Imperial Defence Policy: Annual Review (1933)," CAB 53/23, pp. 136ff, p. 2.
15. Ibid., p. 4.
16. Ibid., p. 11.
17. Ibid., pp. 11–12.
18. Brian Bond, *British Military Policy Between the Two World Wars* (New York, 1980), pp. 196–97. See Sir Henry Pownall, *Chief of Staff: The Diaries of Lieutenant General Sir Henry Pownall,* ed. Brian Bond, vol. 1, *1933–1940* (London, 1972), pp. 24–25.
19. Gibbs, *Rearmament Policy,* p. 98.
20. Service budgets are given in ibid., p. 532.
21. Bond, *British Military Policy,* p. 199.
22. Ibid., p. 207.
23. Gibbs, *Rearmament Policy,* p. 127.
24. Ibid., p. 532.
25. Bond, *British Military Policy,* p. 288, emphasis added.
26. Ibid., pp. 328–29.

12: The New World Order

1. The discussion of the policy of containment here owes much to the valuable works of J. L. Gaddis: *The United States and the Origins of the Cold War 1941–1947* (New York, 1972); *Strategies of Containment* (New York, 1982); and *The United States and the End of the Cold War* (New York, 1992).
2. Gaddis, *Strategies,* p. 39.
3. M. P. Leffler, *A Preponderance of Power: National Security, the Truman Administration, and the Cold War* (Stanford, 1992), p. 181.

4. Thomas H. Etzold and John Lewis Gaddis, *Containment: Documents on American Politics and Strategy, 1945–1950* (New York, 1978), Document 52, pp. 390–91.

5. Transcript of the second session of the conference, "A Retrospective on the End of the Cold War," sponsored by the Woodrow Wilson School of Public and International Affairs at Princeton University, p. 22. I am grateful to the sponsors for providing me with transcripts of the meetings.

6. Ibid., VI, p. 2.

7. Gaddis, *End,* p. 131.

8. George Bush and Brent Scowcroft, *A World Transformed* (New York, 1998), p. 400.

9. Ibid., pp. 565–66.

10. Ibid., pp. 170–71.

11. Ibid., p. 566.

12. Amatzia Baram, "The Iraqi Invasion of Kuwait: Decision-Making in Baghdad," in Barry Rubin and Amatzia Baram, eds., *Iraq's Road to War* (New York, 1993), p. 26.

13. Lawrence Freedman and Efraim Karsh, *The Gulf Conflict, 1990–1991: Diplomacy and War in the New World Order* (London, 1993), p. 32.

14. A. L. George, *Bridging the Gap* (Washington, D.C., 1993), p. 36.

15. Freedman and Karsh, *Gulf,* p. 48.

16. Ibid., p. 51.

17. Ibid., p. 52.

18. Ibid., p. 53.

19. Ibid., p. 58.

20. Ibid., p. 59.

21. C. D. B. Bryan, "Operation Desert Norm," *New Republic,* March 11, 1991, cited in Barry Rubin, "The United States and Iraq: From Appeasement to War," in Barry Rubin and Amatzia Baram, eds., *Iraq's Road to War* (New York, 1993), p. 266.

22. Ibid., pp. 73, xxxi.

23. *Washington Post,* December 2, 1990, p. H1.

24. Freedman and Karsh, *Gulf,* p. 76.

25. John Dumbrell, *American Foreign Policy: Carter to Clinton* (London, 1997), p. 157.

26. *American Foreign Policy Current Documents: 1990* (Washington, D.C.: Department of State, 1991), pp. 528–29.

27. Bob Woodward, *The Commanders* (New York, 1992), p. 209.

28. Ibid., pp. 232, 283–86.

29. Ibid., p. 318.

30. Freedman and Karsh, *Gulf,* pp. 196–97.

31. Ibid., p. 198.

32. Woodward, *Commanders,* p. 300.

33. Ibid., p. 213.

34. Ibid., p. 293.

35. BDFP, vol. 24, no. 655, pp. 986–87.

36. Woodward, *Commanders,* p. 211.

37. Ibid., p. 273.

38. *New York Times,* January 11, 1991, p. A8.

39. Freedman and Karsh, *Gulf,* p. 283.

40. Some accounts have rightly called attention to the powerful support lent by British Prime Minister Margaret Thatcher, with whom President Bush met at Aspen, Colorado, on the afternoon of August 2, before he had told anyone his views about what should be done. He has since written that "Margaret and I saw the situation in remarkably similar ways." George Bush and Brent Scowcroft, *A World Transformed* (New York, 1998), p. 319. Later in the crisis, frustrated by the American delay in taking action, she is reported to have said to the President's plea for patience: "All right, George, all right, but this is no time to go wobbly." Michael R. Beschloss and Strobe Talbott, *At the Highest Level* (New York, 1993), p. 254. The evidence seems best to support the view that at their meeting in Aspen on August 2nd, "Bush was already inclined to take a tough line. Of all the leaders in the Western alliance, however, Thatcher was the most resolute when it came to the Iraqis, and she reinforced Bush's determination to take a firm stand." Michael R. Gordon and General Bernard E. Trainor, *The Generals' War* (Boston, 1995), p. 36.

41. Woodward, *Commanders,* p. 87.

42. Ibid., p. 221.

43. Ibid., p. 222.

44. Ibid., p. 311.

45. Ibid., pp. 284, 310.
46. Ibid., p. 324.
47. Ibid., pp. 322–23.
48. Freedman and Karsh, *Gulf,* pp. 236–37.
49. George, *Bridging,* p. 84.
50. Freedman and Karsh, *Gulf,* p. 434.
51. Beschloss and Talbott, *At the Highest Level,* pp. 277–78.
52. Ibid., p. 409.
53. Ibid., p. 408.
54. Secretary Richard Cheney, cited in Freedman and Karsh, *Gulf,* p. 413.
55. Cited in Mark Almond, *Europe's Backyard War: The War in the Balkans* (London, 1994), p. 38.
56. James A. Baker, *The Politics of Diplomacy, Revolution, War, and Peace, 1989–1992* (New York, 1995), p. 435.
57. Gordon and Trainor, *Generals' War,* p. 467.
58. Ibid., p. xv.
59. Almond, *Europe's Backyard War,* p. 37.
60. Carol Rogel, *The Breakup of Yugoslavia and the War in Bosnia* (Westport, Conn., 1998), pp. 18–20.
61. Ibid., p. 24.
62. Warren Zimmerman, *Origins of a Catastrophe* (New York, 1996), p. 84.
63. Ibid., p. 133.
64. Baker, *Politics of Diplomacy,* pp. 479–80.
65. Ibid., p. 480.
66. Ibid., pp. 481, 483.
67. Zimmerman, *Origins,* p. 137.
68. Rogel, *Breakup,* p. 25.
69. Wayne Bert, *The Reluctant Superpower: United States Policy on Bosnia 1991–95* (New York, 1997), 139.
70. Baker, *Politics of Diplomacy,* p. 637.
71. Quoted in Bert, *Reluctant Superpower,* p. 138.
72. Rogel, *Breakup,* p. 25.
73. Ibid., p. 26.
74. Zimmerman, *Origins,* p. 158.
75. Bert, *Reluctant Superpower,* p. 155.
76. Ibid., p. 157.
77. Baker, *Politics of Diplomacy,* p. 645.
78. Ibid.
79. Ibid., p. 647.
80. Bert, *Reluctant Superpower,* p. 160.
81. Baker, *Politics of Diplomacy,* p. 648.
82. Cited in Bert, *Reluctant Superpower,* p. 163.
83. Ibid., p. 157.
84. Ibid., p. 158.
85. Paraphrased in ibid., p. 153.
86. Baker, *Politics of Diplomacy,* pp. 648–49.
87. Ibid., p. 650.
88. Ibid., p. 649.
89. Ibid., p. 651.
90. *U.S. News and World Report, Triumph Without Victory: A History of the Gulf War* (New York, 1993), pp. xix–xx.
91. Bert, *Reluctant Superpower,* p. 123.
92. Zimmerman, *Origins,* p. 216.

13: The Peace Dividend

1. It is asserted that Army Chief of Staff General Creighton Abrams deliberately put critical CS/CSS units in the reserves in order to compel any President contemplating significant deployments to call up the reserves and, therefore, obtain the support of the nation for his activities. In this way, it is said, Abrams hoped to avoid the sort of war on the sly waged by Lyndon Johnson in Vietnam. On the other hand it is clear that speed of deployability of guard and reserve combat forces

also played a role. See Stephen M. Duncan, *Citizen Warriors: America's National Guard and Reserve Forces and the Politics of National Security* (Novato, Calif., 1997), p. 144 and n. 37.

2. "Call for a New National Security Strategy," House of Representatives, January 24, 1990, p. H79.

3. See Chapter 2.

4. House Concurrent Resolution 259, The Harvest of Peace Resolution, Hon. Byron L. Dorgan, Extension of Remarks, February 20, 1990, p. E279.

5. See, e.g., George Bush and Brent Scowcroft, *A World Transformed: The Collapse of the Soviet Empire, the Unification of Germany, Tiananmen Square, the Gulf War* (New York, 1998), pp. 208–10.

6. These speeches (March 22 and 29, April 19 and 20) were collected into a pamphlet: Center for Strategic and International Affairs, Sam Nunn, *Nunn 1990: A New Military Strategy* (Washington, D.C.), 1990.

7. "The Changed Threat Environment of the 1990s," in ibid., pp. 17–18.

8. Ibid., p. 27, emphasis in the original.

9. Ibid., pp. 34–35.

10. Ibid., p. 53.

11. There has always been considerable tension in the Pentagon between the "civilian" side, the Office of the Secretary of Defense (OSD), and the "military" side, the Joint Staff. This tension, among other things, has led to a partisan discussion about the taking of credit for the Base Force concept—Colin Powell's autobiography and the history of the development of the Base Force produced by his office during his tenure as Chairman of the Joint Chiefs of Staff claim that the idea was his, in the first instance, was perfected by particular individuals on the Joint Staff, and was sold to the civilian leadership over the opposition of Wolfowitz and OSD. Powell claims that OSD held a much more pessimistic view of the Soviet situation and held out against his desire to abandon the Soviet threat as the principal force-sizing factor. Wolfowitz and Cheney have not publicly told their part of the story, but it seems clear from what evidence is available that reality is more complicated than Powell and his supporters make out, although they were certainly much slower than Powell to lose their fear of a Soviet revival. See Lorna S. Jaffe, *The Development of the Base Force, 1989–1992* (Washington, D.C., Office of the Chairman of the Joint Chiefs of Staff, 1993); and Colin L. Powell with Joseph E. Persico, *My American Journey* (New York, 1995).

12. Powell, *My American Journey*, p. 437.

13. Jaffe, *Development of the Base Force*, p. 2.

14. Ibid., p. 8.

15. Powell, *My American Journey*, p. 436. A somewhat different version can be found in Jaffe, *Development of the Base Force*, pp. 14–15, specifying 10–12 divisions for the army, 400 ships including 12 carriers for the navy, and a reduction in the U.S. Marine Corps from 197,000 to 125,000–150,000.

16. Jaffe, *Development of the Base Force*, p. 21.

17. Dick Cheney, *Annual Report to the President and the Congress, January 1991* (Washington, D.C., 1991), p. 131.

18. Ibid., pp. 132–33.

19. Ibid., p. 5.

20. Jaffe, *Development of the Base Force*, p. 37.

21. I. Lewis Libby, testimony before the House Armed Services Committee, 12 March 1991.

22. Colin Powell, testimony before the House Appropriations Committee, 25 September 1991.

23. Les Aspin, "Understanding the New Security Environment," an address to the Atlantic Council of the United States, 6 January 1992.

24. The article Aspin refers to was an editorial by Stephen Rosenfeld entitled "Gulf Giddiness; Gen. Powell needs to get specific on what contingencies lie ahead," that appeared on page A19. It was a hostile editorial that began, "Gen. Colin Powell, the country's celebrated military commander, has uttered one of those indiscreet and illuminating truths that would have put him in the doghouse if he were not Gen. Colin Powell, the country's celebrated military commander."

25. Les Aspin, address to the Washington Land Warfare Forum in Arlington, Va., 24 January 1992.

26. Les Aspin, "An Approach to Sizing American Conventional Forces for the Post-Soviet Era," House Armed Services Committee Paper, 24 January 1992; "An Approach to Sizing American Conventional Forces for the Post-Soviet Era: Four Illustrative Options," House Armed Services Committee Paper, 25 February 1992; and "Defense 1997 Alternatives: Supplemental Materials," House Armed Services Committee Paper, 24 March 1992.

27. Patrick E. Tyler, "Top Congressman Seeks Deeper Cuts in Military Budget," *New York Times,* February 23, 1992, p. 1.
28. Art Pine, "House Leaders Back Call for $114 Billion in Defense Cuts," *Los Angeles Times,* February 26, 1992, p. A13.
29. Defense Department Budget Briefing by Richard B. Cheney, Secretary of Defense, Colin Powell, Chairman of the Joint Chiefs of Staff, and Donald J. Atwood, Jr., Deputy Secretary of Defense, 29 January 1992.
30. James A. Winnefeld, *The Post–Cold War Force-Sizing Debate: Paradigms, Metaphors, and Disconnects* (Santa Monica, Calif., 1992), pp. 4, 7.
31. Ibid., p. 2.
32. Hearing of the House Armed Services Committee, 6 February 1992.
33. Winnefeld, *Post–Cold War Force-Sizing Debate,* p. 19.
34. Paul K. Davis and Richard L. Kugler, "New Principles for Force Sizing," in Zalmay M. Khalilzad and David A. Ochmanek, eds., *Strategy and Defense Planning for the 21st Century* (Santa Monica, Calif., 1997), p. 97.
35. Ibid., p. 98.

14: Increased Commitments, Reduced Forces

1. Les Aspin, Testimony before the House Armed Services Committee, March 30, 1993.
2. Fiscal year Department of Defense outlays, from Department of Defense, *Annual Report to the President and the Congress,* 1998. In constant FY98 dollars, the reduction was $24 billion or 8 percent.
3. Les Aspin, *Report on the Bottom-Up Review* (Washington, D.C., 1993), p. iii (hereafter cited as *BUR*).
4. Ibid., p. 3.
5. Ibid., emphasis in the original.
6. Ibid., p. 7.
7. Ibid., p. 9.
8. Ibid., p. 13.
9. U.S. Department of Defense, *Conduct of the Persian Gulf War: Final Report to Congress* (Washington, D.C., 1992), p. 9.
10. Figures from International Institute for Strategic Studies, *The Military Balance 1991–1992* (London, 1992). Estimates of Iraq's forces remaining after the Gulf War are, of course, uncertain and controversial. For a full treatment of the controversy and more detailed and conflicting strength estimates, see Anthony H. Cordesman and Ahmed S. Hashim, *Iraq: Sanctions and Beyond* (Boulder, Colo., 1997), pp. 233ff.
11. North Korea fielded armed forces of 1.1 million men under arms equipped with more than 4,100 tanks, 4,200 armored fighting vehicles, 6,000 artillery pieces, 732 combat aircraft, 400 ships, and numerous surface-to-surface missiles.
12. *BUR*, p. 14.
13. IISS, *Military Balance.*

Country	Personnel	Tanks	AFVs
Egypt	420,000	3,190	3,000+
Iran	528,000	740	750
Iraq	382,500	2,300	3,000+
Syria	404,000	4,350	4,000+
India	1,265,000	3,100	1,200
N. Korea	1,111,000	4,100+	4,200+
S. Korea	750,000	1,550	2,000+
Pakistan	565,000	2,000+	800
Vietnam	1,041,000	1,800+	3,500+
MRC	400,000	2,000	3,000

14. For this "ten-year rule" see, among others, the conversation between Les Aspin and Congressman Ronald Dellums in a hearing of the House Armed Services Committee, 30 March 1993.
15. Ibid.
16. James John Tritten, *Our New National Security Strategy: America Promises to Come Back* (Westport, Conn., 1992), pp. 140–41.

17. "Aspin says Soviet conventional capability no longer a threat," *Defense Daily*, January 24, 1992, p. 123.
18. Since Korea and Iraq were the two scenarios considered, the only MRC threat contemplated was a large-scale armored assault.
19. *BUR*, pp. 15–16.
20. Ibid., p. 18.
21. See Richard P. Hallion, *Storm over Iraq: Air Power and the Gulf War* (Washington, D.C., 1992), for the airpower triumphalist view; and Eliot A. Cohen, Thomas A. Keaney, et al., *Gulf War Air Power Survey* (Washington, D.C., 1993), for a more balanced view.
22. Les Aspin, Address to the National Defense University's Commencement Ceremony, 16 June 1993.
23. "U.S. May Drop 2-War Capability; Aspin Envisions Smaller, High-Tech Military to 'Win-Hold-Win,'" *Washington Post*, June 17, 1993, p. A1.
24. Ibid.
25. Les Aspin, remarks to the U.S. Air Force Senior Statesman Symposium, Andrews Air Force Base, Maryland, 24 June 1993.
26. Bill Gertz, "Did Aspen switch only the label?; 2-war scheme a lot like 1-war plan," *Washington Times*, September 3, 1993, p. A1.
27. United States General Accounting Office, *Bottom-Up Review: Analysis of Key DoD Assumptions*, GAO/NSIAD-95-56, Washington, D.C., 1995, p. 5.
28. *BUR*, p. 108. Those savings were partially offset by $5 billion added for counterproliferation activities and contacts with the states of the former Soviet Union.
29. United States General Accounting Office, *DoD Budget: Evaluation of Defense Science Board Report on Funding Shortfalls* (Washington, D.C., 1994).
30. "Aspin Says 5-Year Strategy Requires $50 Billion More," *Washington Post*, December 11, 1993, p. A12.
31. "Pentagon Spending Gap Revised to $31 Billion," *Washington Post*, December 18, 1993, p. A8.

15: Kicking the Can Down the Road

1. T. H. Henriksen, *Clinton's Foreign Policy in Somalia, Bosnia, Haiti, and North Korea* (Stanford, Calif., 1996), p. 5.
2. Elizabeth Drew, *On the Edge, The Clinton Presidency* (New York, 1994), p. 138.
3. Thomas L. Friedman in *New York Times*, October 4, 1992, p. A1.
4. John Dumbrell, *American Foreign Policy, Carter to Clinton* (London, 1997), p. 179.
5. Bob Woodward, *The Choice* (New York, 1996), p. 255.
6. W. B. Berman and E. O. Goldman, "Clinton's Foreign Policy at Midterm," *The Clinton Presidency: First Appraisal*, Colin Campbell and Bert A. Rockman, eds. (New York, 1995), p. 291.
7. Dumbrell, *American Foreign Policy*, p. 179.
8. Ibid., p. 181.
9. P. Krugman, "Competitiveness: A Dangerous Obsession," *Foreign Affairs*, vol. 73 (1994), p. 29.
10. Berman and Goldman, "Clinton's Foreign Policy," p. 300.
11. Reporters from the *Washington Post* (May 27, 1993, p. A45) wrote that although Tarnoff had used rather "blunt and rough-edged terms" the remarks of other administration officials "did not differ significantly from what President Clinton and Secretary of State Christopher have said about the U.S. being unable to play the role of 'the world policeman.'" They told of a television interview in which Christopher spoke "in terms that closely parallel" what Tarnoff had said earlier that same day. After Lake's speech in May a syndicated columnist reminded his readers of Tarnoff's statement that "U.S. engagements abroad would be limited by economic and political constraints. Secretary of State Christopher and other senior officials disavowed his comments, but their statements since then—including Lake's speech Tuesday—have largely agreed with Tarnoff." *Chicago Sun-Times*, September 22, 1993, p. 37.
12. Dumbrell, *American Foreign Policy*, p. 179.
13. Berman and Goldman, "Clinton's Foreign Policy," p. 300.
14. Drew, *On the Edge*, p. 112.
15. Dick Morris, *Behind the Oval Office* (New York, 1997), p. 245.
16. Martin Walker, in *Guardian*, February 4, 1994, cited in Dumbrell, *American Foreign Policy*, p. 180.
17. Berman and Goldman, "Clinton's Foreign Policy," p. 302.
18. Cited in ibid.

19. Ibid.
20. Drew, *On the Edge,* p. 112.
21. Dumbrell, *American Foreign Policy,* p. 185.
22. Ioan Lewis and James Mayall, "Somalia," in James Mayall, ed., *The New Interventionism 1991– 1994* (Cambridge, 1996), p. 8.
23. Ibid., p. 101.
24. Ibid., p. 108.
25. Jonathan Stevenson, *Losing Mogadishu* (Annapolis, 1995), p. 11.
26. Lewis and Mayall, "Somalia," p. 109.
27. Ibid.
28. *New York Times,* July 20, 1992, p. A3; July 23, 1992, p. A21.
29. *New York Times,* August 15, 1992, section 1, p. 1.
30. Stevenson, *Losing Mogadishu,* p. 53.
31. Ibid., p. xii.
32. *New York Times,* April 28, 1992, p. A22.
33. *Christian Science Monitor,* August 6, 1992, The U.S., p. 1.
34. Lewis and Mayall, "Somalia," p. 110.
35. John R. Bolton, "Wrong Turn in Somalia," *Foreign Affairs,* January/February 1994, p. 57.
36. Ibid.
37. Stevenson, *Losing Mogadishu,* p. 51.
38. Bolton, "Wrong Turn," p. 57.
39. UPI, "Washington News," November 26, 1992.
40. Lewis and Mayall, "Somalia," p. 112.
41. Bolton, "Wrong Turn," p. 58.
42. Lewis and Mayall, "Somalia," p. 112. See also Bolton, "Wrong Turn," p. 59.
43. Bolton, "Wrong Turn," p. 60.
44. Henriksen, *Clinton's Foreign Policy,* p. 9.
45. Lewis and Mayall, "Somalia," p. 115.
46. Bolton, "Wrong Turn," p. 60.
47. Ibid.
48. Lewis and Mayall, "Somalia," p. 116; Bolton, "Wrong Turn," p. 60.
49. Michael R. Gordon, "Christopher, in Unusual Cable, Defends State Department," *New York Times,* June 16, 1993, p. A13.
50. Bolton, "Wrong Turn," p. 60.
51. Gordon, *New York Times,* June 16, 1993, p. A13.
52. Lewis and Mayall, "Somalia," p. 115.
53. Federal News Service, Hearing of the International Security, International Organizations and Human Rights Subcommittee, "U.S. Participation in UN Peacekeeping Missions," June 24, 1993.
54. Bolton, "Wrong Turn," p. 62.
55. Drew, *On the Edge,* pp. 321–22.
56. Ibid., p. 322.
57. Ibid., p. 331.
58. Stevenson, *Losing Mogadishu,* p. 105; Drew, *On the Edge,* p. 331.
59. Drew, *On the Edge,* p. 331.
60. On May 12, 1994, the Senate Armed Services Committee held hearings on U.S. military operations in Somalia that gave considerable attention to the raid of October 3, 1993. Generals Montgomery and Garrison were present. Although their testimony varied to some degree, neither was willing to claim that the absence of the requested equipment was decisive or even very significant. Montgomery, who had asked for the tanks and armored troop carriers, testified that if they had been available "it would have reduced the time it took to reach Task Force Ranger. The M1A1 tank would have been invulnerable to rocket-propelled grenade fire of the type used by the militia, and the Bradley fighting vehicles would have been less vulnerable than the Malaysian vehicles. This force would have significantly increased fire power and speed." Montgomery here is talking about the relief force after the helicopter was shot down and the great firefight in its defense had already begun. He does not consider the use of such vehicles, instead of mere trucks, in the original ground force sent to pick up the men of the task force even in case of success. Had the M1A1s and Bradleys been there, instead of the trucks, their firepower could have prevented a serious attack on the helicopter and its defenders. General Garrison at first resisted the conclusion that the absence of requested equipment was relevant. Asked by Senator Nunn if the presence of armor during the firefight would have made a difference, he replied: "I do not believe it would have had

any kind of a significant impact upon the casualties that we suffered." Later, Senator Cohen put harder and more specific questions that produced different answers:

SEN. COHEN: Let's come back to this issue of the question of the use of Bradleys or M-1s. . . . You talk about the power and capability, fire power capability of the M-1 tank . . . , or let's say the Bradley in this particular case. High—greater fire power capability—what, 25mm cannons on the Bradley, greater armor, speed, all of which I assume . . . is designed to give greater protection. Right? For your forces.

GEN. GARRISON: That's part of it, yes, sir. Greater protection and it'll give it greater shock power and effectiveness on the battlefield. . . .

SEN. COHEN: Now, . . . when the attack was first carried out and our forces rappelled down and they were on the ground, that when the helicopter first went down, those forces that were on the ground that tried to get to the helicopter came under attack. Is that not correct?

GEN. GARRISON: That is correct.

SEN. COHEN: And at that time the best we had available were some five-ton trucks that had been heavily sandbagged?

SEN. GARRISON: And also some armored HUMVEES.

SEN. COHEN: Right, but they were unable to punch through to get to the crash site?

GEN. GARRISON: Not that they were unable to punch through. They had the detainees on board those vehicles. Also they suffered some casualties in their movement, so the decision was made to bring them back to the airfield.

SEN. COHEN: Is it your judgment now, as opposed to under the pressure of the conflict at that time, that the presence of Bradleys would have saved lives under those circumstances? There were lives lost on the ground by our forces at that time, were there not, trying to get to the crash site?

GEN. GARRISON: There is no question that to use Bradleys, as opposed to using light-skin vehicles, would always be preferential.

SEN. COHEN: And in your judgment, would the probability, . . . is it not more probable you save more lives with greater fire power, speed and protection?

GEN. GARRISON: I am absolutely certain that would have been the case.

General Garrison, the man who had requested them in vain, was asked if the AC-130 gunships would have made a difference. At first he firmly said they would not have, but Senator Nunn returned to the question:

SEN. NUNN: [A]re you saying that an AC-130 gunship would not have made a difference then on October 3rd and 4th, had you had one, or are you saying—what are you saying?

GEN. GARRISON: I am saying that the AC-130, from a psychological standpoint, would have been magnificent. The Somalis were petrified of the AC-130. So from a psychological standpoint, there is no question it would have been beneficial. From the visual or video capabilities, day and night, and from the firepower associated with the AC-130, I believe that I had more than enough capability to offset not having the AC-130 there.

If, however, the AC-130 had been there and had "petrified" the Somalis, presumably there would have been no firefight, no casualties, and no disaster. In saying he had enough firepower without the gunship General Garrison must be thinking of an imaginary situation in which the mission would be successful, no helicopters would be downed, and therefore no troops would be pinned down by hostile fire in protecting it. In the real situation there obviously was inadequate firepower to suppress the Somali attacks, as the outcome and anyone who has seen the films of the battle can attest. The presence of AC-130 gunships would certainly have been helpful and might well have averted the disaster entirely.

61. Drew, *On the Edge*, p. 323.
62. Federal Document Clearing House, Testimony May 12, 1994, Larry E. Joyce, Veteran, Senate Armed Services, U.S. Military Operations in Somalia.
63. Drew, *On the Edge*, pp. 319, 322, 323–24.
64. Eric Schmitt, "Somalia's First Lesson for Military Is Caution," *New York Times*, March 5, 1995, section 1, p. 10.
65. Mark Turner, "Somalia at the Point of a Gun," *Financial Times* (London), March 20, 1999, USA Edition, International, p. 4.
66. Ian Fisher, "Tayeglu Journal: Again, Somalia Is Staring at Starvation," *New York Times*, March 19, 1999, p. A4.

67. Schmitt, "Somalia's First Lesson," p. 10.
68. Democrat James Traficant of Ohio, cited in ibid.
69. Mark Bowden, *Black Hawk Down: A Story of Modern War* (New York, 1999), p. 335.
70. William F. Woo, "Deciding What's Worth Fighting For," *St. Louis Post-Dispatch,* October 17, 1993, p. 1B.
71. Elaine Sciolino, "Haitian Impasse," *New York Times,* April 29, 1994, p. A1.
72. Henriksen, *Clinton's Foreign Policy,* p. 22.
73. Ibid., p. 23.
74. Drew, *On the Edge,* p. 332.
75. Margaret D. Hays and Gary F. Wheateley, *Interagency and Political-Military Dimensions of Peace Operations: Haiti—A Case Study* (Washington, D.C., 1996), pp. 10–11.
76. Drew, *On the Edge,* p. 334.
77. Henriksen, *Clinton's Foreign Policy,* p. 24.
78. Ibid.
79. Sciolino, "Haitian Impasse."
80. Richard D. Lyons, "U.N. Authorizes Invasion of Haiti to Be Led by U.S.," *New York Times,* August 1, 1994, p. A1.
81. Douglas Jehl, "Showdown in Haiti," *New York Times,* September 16, 1994, p. A1.
82. Doyle McManus, "Call to Arms Based on U.S. Credibility," *Los Angeles Times,* September 16, 1994, p. A1.
83. Jehl, "Showdown in Haiti," p. A1.
84. R. W. Apple, "Showdown in Haiti: Perspective," *New York Times,* September 16, 1994, p. A1.
85. Jehl, "Showdown in Haiti," p. A1.
86. R. W. Apple, "Showdown in Haiti: Perspective," p. A1.
87. Doyle McManus, "11th Hour Envoys Open Escape Route for Clinton," *Los Angeles Times,* September 17, 1994, p. A1.
88. R. W. Apple, "Changing Tack on Haiti," *New York Times,* September 17, 1994, section 1, p. 1.
89. Ibid.
90. Henriksen, *Clinton's Foreign Policy,* p. 27.
91. Douglas Jehl, "From Haiti, Images of a Foreign Policy Success," *New York Times,* April 1, 1995, Section 1, p. 4.
92. Henriksen, *Clinton's Foreign Policy,* p. 29.
93. Michael Norton (Associated Press), in *Boston Globe,* March 26, 1999, p. A8.
94. Michael Norton, "Boat Carrying Haitians Sinks Near Bahamas," *Boston Globe,* March 25, 1999, p. A27.

16: Proliferation and Blackmail

1. Dick Cheney, *Defense Strategy for the 1990s: The Regional Defense Strategy* (Washington, D.C., 1993), p. 3.
2. Les Aspin, *Annual Report for 1994* (Washington, D.C., 1995), p. 3.
3. Don Oberdorfer, *The Two Koreas: A Contemporary History* (New York, 1997), pp. 250–54.
4. Cited in ibid., p. 255.
5. Ibid., pp. 263–67.
6. Ibid., p. 267.
7. Ibid.
8. Ibid., p. 268.
9. Michael J. Mazarr, *North Korea and the Bomb: A Case Study in Nonproliferation* (New York, 1996), p. 83.
10. Ibid., p. 84.
11. Ibid., p. 87.
12. Ibid., p. 85.
13. Ibid., p. 88.
14. Oberdorfer, *Two Koreas,* pp. 270–71.
15. Mazarr, *North Korea,* p. 81.
16. Oberdorfer, *Two Koreas,* p. 272.
17. Mazarr, *North Korea,* pp. 88–89.
18. Oberdorfer, *Two Koreas,* p. 274.
19. Mazarr, *North Korea,* pp. 94–95.
20. Oberdorfer, *Two Koreas,* p. 277.

21. Mazarr, *North Korea,* p. 96.
22. Ibid., p. 98; and Oberdorfer, *Two Koreas,* p. 278.
23. Mazarr, *North Korea,* pp. 98–99.
24. Oberdorfer, *Two Koreas,* p. 278.
25. Ibid., p. 279.
26. Mazarr, *North Korea,* p. 102.
27. Oberdorfer, *Two Koreas,* p. 283.
28. Mazarr, *North Korea,* p. 116.
29. Ashton B. Carter and William J. Perry, *Preventive Defense: A New Security Strategy for America* (Washington, D.C., 1999), p. 127.
30. Oberdorfer, *Two Koreas,* p. 286; and Mazarr, *North Korea,* p. 121.
31. Oberdorfer, *Two Koreas,* p. 287.
32. Ibid., pp. 289–91.
33. Ibid., p. 293.
34. Mazarr, *North Korea,* p. 126.
35. Ibid., p. 132.
36. Oberdorfer, *Two Koreas,* p. 294.
37. Mazarr, *North Korea,* p. 134; and Oberdorfer, *Two Koreas,* p. 295.
38. Oberdorfer, *Two Koreas,* p. 295.
39. Ibid., p. 300.
40. Ibid., p. 301.
41. Ibid., pp. 302–3.
42. Mazarr, *North Korea,* pp. 148–49.
43. Oberdorfer, *Two Koreas,* pp. 305–6.
44. Ibid., p. 303.
45. Carter and Perry, *Preventive Defense,* p. 128.
46. Oberdorfer, *Two Koreas,* p. 309.
47. Ibid., p. 310.
48. Carter and Perry, *Preventive Defense,* pp. 128–29.
49. Oberdorfer, *Two Koreas,* p. 315.
50. Ibid., p. 310.
51. Ibid., p. 324.
52. Ibid., pp. 324–25.
53. Carter and Perry, *Preventive Defense,* p. 130.
54. Aspin, *Annual Report for 1994,* p. D-1.
55. Oberdorfer, *Two Koreas,* p. 325.
56. Ibid., pp. 325–26.
57. Ibid., p. 330.
58. CNN, "Carter Says North Korea Won't Expel Nuclear Inspectors," June 16, 1994.
59. Oberdorfer, *Two Koreas,* p. 332.
60. "U.S.–Democratic People's Republic of Korea Agreed Framework," taken from United States Mission to International Organizations in Vienna Web site on April 15, 1999.

17: Another Versailles

1. George Bush and Brent Scowcroft, *A World Transformed: The Collapse of the Soviet Empire, the Unification of Germany, Tiananmen Square, the Gulf War* (New York, 1998), p. 488.
2. Ibid., p. 489.
3. David Wurmser, *Tyranny's Ally: America's Failure to Defeat Saddam Hussein* (Washington, D.C., 1999), p. 11.
4. Anthony H. Cordesman and Ahmed S. Hashim, *Iraq: Sanctions and Beyond* (Boulder, Colo., 1997), p. 77.
5. Ibid.
6. Ibid., p. 78.
7. Ibid., p. 79.
8. Scott Ritter, *Endgame: Solving the Iraq Problem—Once and for All* (New York, 1999).
9. Ibid., p. 32.
10. Ibid., p. 33. See also Cordesman and Hashim, *Iraq,* p. 291.
11. Ritter, *Endgame,* p. 34.
12. Ibid., pp. 34–36.

13. "UN Body Tells Iraq to Yield to Inspectors," *Boston Globe,* July 7, 1992, p. 2.
14. "U.S. Warns Iraqis to End Standoff with U.N. Inspectors; Allies Consulted on Possible Military Action," *Washington Post,* July 16, 1992, p. A14.
15. "Saddam Stiffens Against U.N. Role; Iraq Stalls Inspectors, Refuses to Grant Visas," *Washington Post,* July 18, 1992, p. A15.
16. Ritter, *Endgame,* p. 37.
17. "UN Team Retreats After Iraqi Attack," *USA Today,* July 23, 1992, p. 1A.
18. "U.S. Allies Seek to Rally Support for Strike on Iraq," *Los Angeles Times,* July 23, 1992, p. A1.
19. "UN Offers Inspection Compromise to Baghdad," *Chicago Sun-Times,* July 24, 1992, p. 7.
20. "Bush Trip Canceled in Iraq Crisis," *Washington Post,* July 25, 1992, p. A1.
21. "U.N., Iraq Stalled in Talks," *Washington Post,* July 26, 1992, p. A1.
22. "Iraqi Building Likely 'Cleaned Out'—U.N. Team to Search for 'Traces,'" *USA Today,* July 27, 1992, p. 4A.
23. "U.N., Iraq Stalled in Talks," *Washington Post,* July 26, 1992, p. A1.
24. "Baghdad Agrees to U.N. Inspection: Long Impasse Ends," *New York Times,* July 27, 1992, p. A1.
25. "Iraq Won Its Point on U.N. Inspectors, Top U.S. Aides Say," *New York Times,* July 28, 1992, p. A1.
26. Cordesman and Hashim, *Iraq,* p. 102.
27. Ibid., p. 104.
28. "Iraqis Again Violate 'No-Fly' Zone Ban," *Washington Post,* December 30, 1992, p. A12.
29. "U.S. Urging Allies to Threaten Iraq on Action in South," *New York Times,* January 6, 1993, p. A1.
30. "Iraq Claims Legal Right on Missiles," *Washington Post,* January 8, 1993, p. A1.
31. "U.S. Allies Let Deadline Pass," *Washington Post,* January 9, 1993, p. A1.
32. "U.S. Says Baghdad Removed Missiles," *New York Times,* January 10, 1993, p. 1; "Iraqis Seize Arms Interned in Kuwait," *Washington Post,* January 11, 1993, p. A1.
33. "U.S. Delivers Limited Air Strike on Iraq," *Washington Post,* January 14, 1993, p. A1.
34. "Raid on Iraq: Excerpts from Bush's Remarks: Allies 'Did the Right Thing,'" *New York Times,* January 14, 1993, p. A9.
35. "Bush Decides on Major Iraq Raids If Defiance Goes On," *Los Angeles Times,* January 13, 1993, p. A1.
36. "U.S. Calls Attack a Political Success Despite the Misses," *Los Angeles Times,* January 15, 1993, p. A1.
37. "U.S. Attacks Iraq Nuclear Site," *Los Angeles Times,* January 18, 1993, p. A1.
38. Fifth report of the Executive Chairman of the Special Commission, established by the Secretary-General pursuant to paragraph 9 (b) (i) of Security Council resolution 687 (1991), on the activities of the Special Commission, UN Document S/25977, 21 June 1993, paragraph III. A. 9. (a) (iv).
39. Ibid., paragraph III. A. 9 (e).
40. "Clinton Bluntly Warns Iraq to Yield to Arms Inspectors," *New York Times,* June 26, 1993, p. 4.
41. "Clinton: U.S. Needed 'to Send a Message,'" *Washington Post,* June 27, 1993, p. A20.
42. "U.S. Calls Baghdad Raid a Qualified Success," *Washington Post,* June 28, 1993, p. A1. Dispute also arose because three of the missiles struck homes in a residential area near facility, causing civilian casualties.
43. "Raid on Baghdad; Clinton Overstates Impact of Raid, His Aides Warn," *New York Times,* June 29, 1993, p. A6.
44. Sixth report of the Executive Chairman of the Special Commission, established by the Secretary-General pursuant to paragraph 9 (b) (i) of Security Council resolution 687 (1991) on the activities of the Special Commission, UN Document S/26910, 21 December 1993.
45. Cordesman and Hashim, *Iraq,* p. 186.
46. "U.S. Sends Force as Iraqi Soldiers Threaten Kuwait," *New York Times,* October 8, 1994, p. 1.
47. "Iraq Threatens to End UN Role If Oil Export Ban Is Not Lifted," *New York Times,* October 9, 1994, p. 10.
48. "Pentagon Moving a Force of 4,000 to Guard Kuwait," *New York Times,* October 9, 1994, p. 1.
49. "36,000 U.S. Ground Troops Due in Gulf," *Washington Post,* October 10, 1994, p. A1.
50. "Threats in the Gulf: The Military Buildup," *New York Times,* October 10, 1994, p. A1.
51. "Clinton Doubts Iraq's Word on Retreat," *Washington Post,* October 11, 1994, p. A1.
52. "Threats in the Gulf: Kuwait—Keeping the Iraqis Back," *New York Times,* October 11, 1994, p. A1.

53. "U.S. Allies Block Iraq Buffer Plan," *Los Angeles Times,* October 13, 1994, p. A1.
54. "Threats in the Gulf: The Tactics," *New York Times,* October 12, 1994, p. A1.
55. Anthony H. Cordesman, *U.S. Forces in the Middle East: Resources and Capabilities* (Boulder, Colo., 1997), p. 79.
56. "U.S., in Easing Pressure on Iraq, Feared Coalition Breakup and Shiite State," *Washington Post,* October 14, 1994, p. A34.
57. Cordesman, *U.S. Forces,* pp. 78–79.
58. "UN Aide Links Iraqi Troops Thrust to Frustration on Disclosure," *Washington Post,* October 27, 1994, p. A19.
59. Eighth report of the Executive Chairman of the Special Commission established by the Secretary-General pursuant to paragraph 9 (b) (i) of Security Council resolution 687 (1991), on the activities of the Special Commission, UN Document S/1994/1422, 15 December 1994, IV. 35.
60. Ritter, *Endgame,* pp. 46–47.
61. UNSCOM Report of 11 October 1995, UN Document S/1995/864.
62. "U.S. Intensifies Efforts to Topple Iraqi Regime," *Los Angeles Times,* August 27, 1995, p. A1.
63. Cordesman and Hashim, *Iraq,* pp. 86–95.
64. Ibid.
65. See Chapter 7.
66. See Ritter, *Endgame, passim;* and the semiannual reports of UNSCOM to the Security Council.
67. Ritter, *Endgame,* pp. 187–88.
68. It is not clear if they came to regard the nuclear program as less important or if, because it is much harder to conceal the components for such a program, they recognized that it was impossible to do so. By 1997, UNSCOM semiannual reports increasingly discounted the possibility that a nuclear program of any significance continued to exist.
69. See Cordesman, *U.S. Forces;* Cordesman and Hashim, *Iraq.*
70. Attempts to restart the inspections process continue, of course. Even if they succeed, however, Saddam has already had months in which to identify and conceal any materials they might still find. Nor is there any reason to think that he would agree to inspections that are in any way serious.

18: A Legacy of Half Measures

1. Quoted in Mark Danner, "America and the Bosnia Genocide," *New York Review of Books,* December 4, 1997, pp. 58, 65; and "Clinton, the UN, and the Bosnian Disaster," *New York Review of Books,* December 18, 1997, p. 66. I have learned much from Danner's series of brilliant articles.
2. Danner, "Clinton," p. 67.
3. Quoted in Correlli Barnett, *The Collapse of British Power* (London, 1972), p. 301.
4. Elizabeth Drew, *On the Edge: The Clinton Presidency* (New York, 1994), p. 116.
5. Federal Information Systems Corporation, Federal News Service, State Department Briefing, February 10, 1993.
6. James Gow, *Triumph of the Lack of Will: International Diplomacy and the Yugoslav War* (New York, 1997), p. 208.
7. Danner, "Clinton," p. 68.
8. Ibid., p. 76. Many have drawn the comparison between Neville Chamberlain's description of Czechoslovakia as "a faraway country of which we know nothing."
9. David Rieff, *Slaughterhouse, Bosnia and the Failure of the West* (New York, 1995), p. 174.
10. Danner, "Clinton," p. 75.
11. Rieff, *Slaughterhouse,* p. 179.
12. Wayne Bert, *The Reluctant Superpower: United States Policy in Bosnia 1991–95* (New York, 1997), p. 167.
13. Telford Taylor, *Munich, the Price of Peace* (New York, 1979), p. 617, quoting Sir Alexander Cadogan.
14. Danner, "Clinton," pp. 75–76.
15. Drew, *On the Edge,* p. 148.
16. Ibid., p. 149.
17. Colin L. Powell, *An American Journey* (New York, 1995), p. 576.
18. Drew, *On the Edge,* pp. 151, 153. About the last statement she observes: "There was quite a disparity within that one sentence."
19. Ibid., p. 153.

20. Ibid., p. 155.
21. Danner, "Clinton," p. 78.
22. Drew, *On the Edge*, p. 156.
23. Danner, "Clinton," p. 78.
24. Drew, *On the Edge*, p. 157.
25. Ibid., p. 159.
26. Gow, *Triumph*, p. 218.
27. Drew, *On the Edge*, p. 160.
28. Ibid., pp. 162–63.
29. Ibid., p. 279.
30. Ibid., p. 283.
31. Ibid., p. 410.
32. Mark Danner, "Bosnia: The Turning Point," *New York Review of Books*, February 5, 1998, p. 37.
33. Ibid., p. 39.
34. Bert, *Reluctant Superpower*, p. 213.
35. Drew, *On the Edge*, p. 412.
36. Bert, *Reluctant Superpower*, p. 215.
37. Drew, *On the Edge*, p. 430.
38. Bert, *Reluctant Superpower*, p. 217.
39. Elizabeth Drew, *Showdown* (New York, 1996), p. 243.
40. Mark Danner, "Bosnia: The Great Betrayal," *New York Review of Books*, March 26, 1998, p. 43.
41. Carole Rogel, *The Breakup of Yugoslavia and the War in Bosnia* (Westport, Conn., 1998), p. 38.
42. Drew, *Showdown*, pp. 244–45.
43. Ibid., p. 248.
44. This is the product of two accounts, one reported by Hobrooks and quoted in Mark Danner, "Slouching Toward Dayton," *New York Review of Books*, April 23, 1998, p. 59, and the other in Bob Woodward, *The Choice* (New York, 1996), pp. 256–57.
45. Danner, "Bosnia: The Great Betrayal," p. 43.
46. Drew, *Showdown*, p. 243.
47. Mark Danner, "Operation Storm," *New York Review of Books*, October 22, 1998, p. 74.
48. Bert, *Reluctant Superpower*, pp. 222–23.
49. Danner, "Slouching," p. 61.
50. Drew, *Showdown*, p. 252.
51. Woodward, *Choice*, p. 266.
52. Drew, *Showdown*, p. 252.
53. Woodward, *Choice*, p. 267.
54. William G. Hyland, *Clinton's World: Remaking American Foreign Policy* (Westport, Conn., 1999), p. 41.
55. Mark Danner, "Endgame in Kosovo," *New York Review of Books*, May 6, 1999, p. 10.
56. Ibid., p. 44.
57. See Chapter 4.
58. Hyland, *Clinton's World*, p. 47.
59. Mark Danner, "Endgame," p. 11.
60. Hyland, *Clinton's World*, p. 31.
61. Quoted in Danner, "Endgame," p. 10.
62. Ibid.
63. Ibid., p. 11.
64. Hyland, *Clinton's World*, p. 44.
65. Barton Gellman, "The Path to Crisis: How the United States and Its Allies Went to War," *Washington Post*, April 18, 1999, p. A1.
66. Jane M. O. Sharp, "Not Another Bosnia," *Washington Post*, June 18, 1998, p. A25.
67. Winston S. Churchill, *The Aftermath* (New York, 1929), pp. 423–24.
68. Private communication to authors.
69. Danner, "Endgame," p. 57.
70. Gellman, "Path to Crisis," p. A1.
71. Sharp, "Not Another Bosnia," p. A25.
72. Elaine Sciolino and Ethan Bronner, "Crisis in the Balkans: The Road to War," *New York Times*, April 18, 1999, section 1, p. 1.

73. Hyland, *Clinton's World,* p. 45.
74. Gellman, "Path to Crisis," p. A1.
75. Sciolino and Bronner, "Crisis," p. 1.
76. Ibid.
77. Ibid.
78. Gellman, "Path to Crisis," p. A1.
79. Sciolino and Bronner, "Crisis," p. 25.
80. Danner, "Endgame," p. 11.
81. Steven Lee Myers, "Serb Forces in Kosovo Under Attack as Weather Clears," *New York Times,* April 6, 1999, p. A1.
82. Niall Ferguson, *The Pity of War* (New York, 1999), p. 57.
83. David Lloyd George, *War Memoirs* (London, 1933–36), vol. 1, pp. 56–60, cited in Ferguson, *Pity of War,* p. 57.
84. David Rhode, "Wiesel, a Man of Peace, Cites Need to Act," *New York Times,* June 2, 1999, p. A14.
85. Jane Perlez, "NATO Chief Makes a Plea for More Peacekeepers," *New York Times,* February 24, 2000, A3.
85. Ibid.

Conclusion

1. National Defense Panel, *Transforming Defense: National Security in the 21st Century: Report of the National Defense Panel* (Washington, D.C., 1997), p. 1.
2. "Some Doubt U.S. Ability to Fight Wars on 2 Fronts," *New York Times,* October 17, 1994, p. A9.
3. Department of Defense, *Annual Report,* 1996, Table C-1.
4. Department of Defense, *Annual Report,* 1998, Table C-1.

Bibliography

Britain Between the Wars

Adamthwaite, A. *France and the Coming of the Second World War 1936–1939*. London, 1977.

Baechler, C. *Gustave Stresemann (1878–1929), De l'impérialisme à la sécurité collective*. Strasbourg, 1996.

Baer, G. W. *The Coming of the Italian-Ethiopian War*. Cambridge, Mass., 1967.

Barnett, Correlli. *The Collapse of British Power*. London, 1972.

Barros, James. *The Corfu Incident of 1923: Mussolini and the League of Nations*. Princeton, N.J., 1965.

Bartlett, C. J. *British Foreign Policy in the Twentieth Century*. London, 1989.

Baumont, Maurice. *The Origins of the Second World War*. Translated by Simone de Couvreur Ferguson. New Haven, Conn., and London, 1978.

Bennett, E. W. *German Rearmament and the West*. Princeton, N.J., 1979.

Bennett, G. H. *British Foreign Policy During the Curzon Period, 1919–24*. London, 1995.

Bond, Brian. *British Military Policy Between the Two World Wars*. New York, 1980.

Bullock, A. *Hitler: A Study in Tyranny*. New York, 1962.

Callwell, Major General Sir C. E. *Field Marshal Sir Henry Wilson: His Life and Diaries*. New York, 1927.

Carlton, David. *MacDonald versus Henderson*. London, 1970.

Carsten, F. L. *The Reichswehr and Politics, 1918–1933*. New York, 1966.

Cassels, Alan. *Mussolini's Early Diplomacy*. Princeton, 1970.

Craig, Gordon A. *Germany 1866–1945*. New York, 1978.

———. *The Politics of the Prussian Army, 1640–1945*. Oxford, 1955.

———, and Felix Gilbert. *The Diplomats*. Vol. 1. Princeton, N.J., 1953.

Darwin, John. *Britain, Egypt, and the Middle East: Imperial Policy in the Aftermath of War, 1918–1922*. London, 1981.

Emmerson, J. T. *The Rhineland Crisis*. London, 1977.

Ferris, John Robert. *The Evolution of British Strategic Policy, 1919–1926*. London, 1989.

Fest, J. C. *Hitler*. Translated by Richard and Clara Winston. New York, 1974.

Gatzke, Hans W. *Stresemann and the Rearmament of Germany*. New York, 1969.

Gibbs, N. H. *History of the Second World War*. United Kingdom Military Series. *Grand Strategy*. Vol. 1, *Rearmament Policy*. London, 1976.

Gilbert, Martin. *A History of the Twentieth Century*. Vol. 1, *1900–1933*. New York, 1997.

———. *The Roots of Appeasement*. London, 1966.

————. *Winston S. Churchill*. Vols. 4–5. London, 1975–77. *Companion*. Vol. 4, parts 1–3. 1976–77.

Gilmour, David. *Curzon*. London, 1995.

Great Britain, Government. *Documents on British Foreign Policy*. First Series. 25 vols. Various editors. 1947–1984.

Guariglia, Raffaele. *Ricordi 1922–1946*. Naples, 1949.

Headlam-Morley, Sir James. *Studies in Diplomatic History*. New York, 1930.

Hogg, Quintin. *The Left Was Never Right*. London, 1945.

Holborn, Hajo. *A History of Modern Germany, 1840–1945*. Princeton, N.J., 1982.

Howard, Michael. *The Continental Commitment*. London, 1989.

Hughes, H. Stuart. "The Early Diplomacy of Italian Fascism, 1922–1932." In Craig and Gilbert, *The Diplomats*. Princeton, N.J., 1953.

Jacobson, Jon. *Locarno Diplomacy: Germany and the West 1925–1929*. Princeton, N.J., 1972.

Jeffery, Keith. *The British Army and the Crisis of Empire, 1918–1922*. Dover, N.H., 1984.

Jouvenel, Henry de. "France and Italy." *Foreign Affairs*, vol. 5 (1927).

Laurens, Franklin D. *France and the Ethiopian Crisis, 1935–1936*. The Hague, 1967.

Lee, Marshall M., and Wolfgang Michalka. *German Foreign Policy 1917–1933: Continuity or Break?* Leamington Spa, Hamburg, and New York, 1987.

Lloyd George, David. *Memoirs of the Peace Conference*. New Haven, Conn., 1939.

Marder, A. "The Royal Navy and the Ethiopian Crisis of 1935–36." *American Historical Review*, vol. 75 (1970).

Marks, Sally. "1918 and After: The Postwar Era." In Gordon Martel, ed., *The Origins of the Second World War Reconsidered*. Boston, 1986.

————. "The Myth of Reparations." *Central European History*, vol. 2 (1978).

Martel, Gordon, ed. *The Origins of the Second World War Reconsidered*. Boston, 1986.

McDougall, W. A. "Political Economy versus National Sovereignty: French Structures for German Integration after Versailles." *Journal of Modern History*, vol. 51 (1979).

Middlemas, K., and J. Barnes. *Baldwin*. London, 1969.

Morgan, Brigadier General J. H. *Assize of Arms: The Disarmament of Germany and Her Rearmament (1919–1939)*. Vol. 1. New York, 1946.

Mosley, L. *On Borrowed Time: How World War II Began*. London, 1969.

Neidpath, James. *The Singapore Naval Base and the Defence of Britain's Eastern Empire, 1919–1941*. London, 1981.

Nicholson, Harold. *Curzon: The Last Phase 1919–1925,* Boston and New York, 1934.

Northedge, F. S. *The Troubled Giant: Britain Among the Great Powers, 1916–1939*. London, 1966.

Orde, Anne. *Great Britain and International Security 1920–1926*. London, 1978.

Pownall, Sir Henry. *Chief of Staff: The Diaries of Lieutenant General Sir Henry Pownall*. Ed. Brian Bond. Vol. 1, *1933–1940*. London, 1972.

Raleigh, Sir W. A. *The War in the Air*. Oxford, 1937.

Robbins, Keith. *Appeasement*. Oxford, 1988.

Salvemimi, Gaetano. *Mussolini Diplomatico (1922–1932)*. Bari, Italy, 1952.

Schmidt, P. O. *Hitler's Interpreter*. London, 1951.

Shirer, W. L. *The Collapse of the Third Republic*. New York, 1969.

Smith, Dennis Mack. *Mussolini's Roman Empire*. London, 1976.

St-Aulaire, Comte A. F. B. de. *Confession d'un vieux diplomate*. Paris, 1953.

Tauber, Eliezer. *The Formation of Modern Syria and Iraq*. Portland, Ore., 1985.

Taylor, A. J. P. *English History, 1914–1945*. Oxford, 1965.

Taylor, Telford. *Munich, the Price of Peace*. New York, 1979.

Townshend, Charles. *The British Campaign in Ireland, 1919–1921: The Development of Political and Military Policies*. New York, 1975.

Toynbee, Arnold. *Survey of International Affairs, 1920–1923*. London, 1925.

Walder, David. *The Chanak Affair*. London, 1969.

Wandycz, Piotr S. *The Twilight of French Eastern Alliances, 1926–1936*. Princeton, N.J., 1988.

Weinberg, Gerhard L. "The Defeat of Germany in 1918 and the European Balance of Power." *Central European History*, vol. 2, (1969).

————. *The Foreign Policy of Hitler's Germany: Diplomatic Revolution in Europe 1933–1936*. Chicago, 1970.

————. *The Foreign Policy of Hitler's Germany: Starting World War Two 1937–1939*. Chicago, 1980.

Whaley, Barton. *Covert German Rearmament, 1919–1939: Deception and Misperception*. Frederick, Md., 1984.

Wolfers, Arnold. *Britain and France Between Two Wars*. New York, 1940.
Young, R. J. *In Command of France: French Foreign Policy and Military Planning 1933–1940*. Cambridge, Mass., and London, 1978.

The United States After the Cold War

Almond, Mark. *Europe's Backyard War: The War in the Balkans*. London, 1994.
Aspin, Les. *Annual Report for 1994*. Washington, D.C., 1995.
——. *Report on the Bottom-Up Review*. Washington, D.C., 1993.
Baker, James A. *The Politics of Diplomacy, Revolution, War, and Peace, 1989–1992*. New York, 1995.
Baram, Amatzia. "The Iraqi Invasion of Kuwait: Decision-Making In Baghdad." In Barry Rubin and Amatzia Baram, eds., *Iraq's Road to War*. New York, 1993.
Bert, Wayne. *The Reluctant Superpower: United States Policy in Bosnia 1991–95*. New York, 1997.
Beschloss, Michael R., and Strobe Talbott. *At the Highest Level*. New York, 1993.
Bolton, John R. "Wrong Turn in Somalia." *Foreign Affairs*, January/February 1994.
Bowden, Mark. *Black Hawk Down: A Story of Modern War*. New York, 1999.
Bush, George, and Brent Scowcroft. *A World Transformed: The Collapse of the Soviet Empire, the Unification of Germany, Tiananmen Square, the Gulf War*. New York, 1998.
Carter, Ashton B., and William J. Perry. *Preventive Defense: A New Security Strategy for America*. Washington, D.C., 1999.
Cheney, Dick. *Annual Report to the President and the Congress, January 1991*. Washington, D.C., 1991.
——. *Defense Strategy for the 1990s: The Regional Defense Strategy*. Washington, D.C., 1993.
Cohen, Eliot A., Thomas A. Keaney, et al. *Gulf War Air Power Survey*. Washington, D.C., 1993.
Cordesman, Anthony H. *U.S. Forces in the Middle East: Resources and Capabilities*. Boulder, Colo., 1997.
——, and Ahmed S. Hashim. *Iraq: Sanctions and Beyond*. Boulder, Colo., 1997.
Danner, Mark. "America and the Bosnia Genocide." *New York Review of Books*, December 4, 1997.
——. "Clinton, the UN, and the Bosnian Disaster." *NYRB*, December 18, 1997.
——. "Bosnia: The Turning Point." *NYRB*, February 5, 1998.
——. "Slouching Toward Dayton." *NYRB*, April 23, 1998.
——. "Operation Storm." *NYRB*, October 22, 1998.
——. "Endgame in Kosovo." *NYRB*, May 6, 1999.
Drew, Elizabeth. *On the Edge: The Clinton Presidency*. New York, 1994.
——. *Showdown: The Struggle Between the Gingrich Congress and the Clinton White House*. New York, 1996.
Dumbrell, John. *American Foreign Policy: Carter to Clinton*. London, 1997.
Duncan, Stephen M. *Citizen Warriors: America's National Guard and Reserve Forces and the Politics of National Security*. Novato, Calif., 1997.
Etzold, Thomas H., and John Lewis Gaddis. *Containment: Documents on American Politics and Strategy, 1945–1950*. New York, 1978.
Ferguson, Niall. *The Pity of War*. New York, 1999.
Freedman, Lawrence, and Efraim Karsh. *The Gulf Conflict, 1990–1991: Diplomacy and War in the New World Order*. London, 1993.
Gaddis, J. L. *Strategies of Containment*. New York, 1982.
——. *The United States and the End of the Cold War*. New York, 1992.
——. *The United States and the Origins of the Cold War 1941–1947*. New York, 1972.
George, A. L. *Bridging the Gap*. Washington, D.C., 1993.
Gordon, Michael R., and General Bernard E. Trainor. *The Generals' War*. Boston, 1995.
Gow, James. *Triumph of the Lack of Will: International Diplomacy and the Yugoslav War*. New York, 1997.
Hallion, Richard P. *Storm over Iraq: Air Power and the Gulf War*. Washington, D.C., 1992.
Hays, Margaret D., and Gary F. Wheateley. *Interagency and Political-Military Dimensions of Peace Operations: Haiti—A Case Study*. Washington, D.C., 1996.
Henriksen, T. H. *Clinton's Foreign Policy in Somalia, Bosnia, Haiti, and North Korea*. Stanford, Calif., 1996.
Hyland, William G. *Clinton's World: Remaking American Foreign Policy*. Westport, Conn., 1999.
International Institute for Strategic Studies. *The Military Balance 1991–1992*. London, 1992.
Jaffe, Lorna S. *The Development of the Base Force, 1989–1992*. Washington, D.C., 1993.

Khalilzad, Zalmay M., and David A. Ochmanek, eds. *Strategy and Defense Planning for the 21st Century.* Santa Monica, Calif., 1997.

Krugman, P. "Competitiveness: A Dangerous Obsession." *Foreign Affairs,* vol. 73 (1994).

Leffler, M. P. *A Preponderance of Power: National Security, the Truman Administration, and the Cold War.* Stanford, Calif., 1992.

Lewis, Ioan, and James Mayall. "Somalia." In James Mayall, ed., *The New Interventionism 1991–1994.* Cambridge, 1996.

Mayall, James, ed. *The New Interventionism 1991–1994.* Cambridge, 1996.

Mazarr, Michael J. *North Korea and the Bomb: A Case Study in Nonproliferation.* New York, 1996.

Morris, Dick. *Behind the Oval Office.* New York, 1997.

National Defense Panel. *Transforming Defense: National Security in the 21st Century: Report of the National Defense Panel.* Washington, D.C., 1997.

Nunn, Senator Sam. *Nunn 1990: A New Military Strategy.* Washington, D.C., 1990.

Oberdorfer, Don. *The Two Koreas: A Contemporary History.* New York, 1997.

Powell, Colin L., with Joseph E. Persico. *My American Journey.* New York, 1995.

Rieff, David. *Slaughterhouse: Bosnia and the Failure of the West.* New York, 1995.

Ritter, Scott. *Endgame: Solving the Iraq Problem—Once and for All.* New York, 1999.

Rogel, Carole. *The Breakup of Yugoslavia and the War in Bosnia.* Westport, Conn., 1998.

Rubin, Barry, "The United States and Iraq: From Appeasement to War." In Barry Rubin and Amatzia Baram, eds., *Iraq's Road to War.* New York, 1993.

———, and Amatzia Baram, eds. *Iraq's Road to War.* New York, 1993.

Stevenson, Jonathan. *Losing Mogadishu.* Annapolis, 1995.

Tritten, James John. *Our New National Security Strategy: America Promises to Come Back.* Westport, Conn., 1992.

U.S. Department of Defense. *Conduct of the Persian Gulf War: Final Report to Congress.* Washington, D.C., 1992.

U.S. *News and World Report. Triumph Without Victory: A History of the Gulf War.* New York, 1993.

United Nations Special Commission. Eighth report of the Executive Chairman of the Special Commission established by the Secretary-General pursuant to paragraph 9 (b) (i) of Security Council resolution 687 (1991), on the activities of the Special Commission, UN Document S/1994/1422, 15 December 1994.

———. Fifth report of the Executive Chairman of the Special Commission, established by the Secretary-General pursuant to paragraph 9 (b) (i) of Security Council resolution 687 (1991), on the activities of the Special Commission, UN Document S/25977, 21 June 1993.

———. Sixth report of the Executive Chairman of the Special Commission, established by the Secretary-General pursuant to paragraph 9 (b) (i) of Security Council resolution 687 (1991), on the activities of the Special Commission, UN Document S/26910, 21 December 1993.

United States General Accounting Office. *Bottom-Up Review: Analysis of Key DoD Assumptions.* GAO/NSIAD-95-56. Washington, D.C., 1995.

———. *DoD Budget: Evaluation of Defense Science Board Report on Funding Shortfalls.* Washington, D.C., 1994.

Winnefeld, James A. *The Post–Cold War Force-Sizing Debate: Paradigms, Metaphors, and Disconnects.* Santa Monica, Calif., 1992.

Woodward, Bob. *The Choice.* New York, 1996.

———. *The Commanders.* New York, 1992.

Wurmser, David. *Tyranny's Ally: America's Failure to Defeat Saddam Hussein.* Washington, D.C., 1999.

Zimmerman, Warren. *Origins of a Catastrophe.* New York, 1996.

Index

Abrams, Creighton, 453n1
Abyssinia. *See* Italo-Ethiopian War
Adrianople (Turkey), 73, 87
Afghanistan
  Soviet war in, 64, 240, 242, 275
  after World War I, 23, 27, 28
Africa, Clinton's policy in, 333
Agreed Framework (1994), 363–65
Aideed, Mohammed Farrah, 330–32
air policing, 53–54
airpower, 7, 19–21, 27
  Aspin's love affair with, 313–14, 365
  in Bosnia, 414
  British interwar attitude to, 192–93
  Clinton's reliance on, 311–12
  effectiveness of, 55
  in Gulf War, 55, 426
  in Iraqi 1920 revolt, 61–66
  lack of British technology for, 313
  Trenchard's attitude toward, 53–54
  See also Royal Air Force
Akashi, Yasushi, 403
Albania, 420
  Greek border with, 98
  map of, 99
Albanians in Kosovo, 257, 415, 416, 420–21
Albright, Madeline, 326, 329, 330, 404, 418,
  420
Alexander (King of Greece), 74
Al-Hussein missiles, 375, 389
Allenby, Sir Edmund, 23
Alsace-Lorraine, 119, 120, 141, 169, 173,
  190

Ambassadors Conference. *See* Conference of
  Ambassadors
Amery, Leopold, 113, 168, 169
Amritsar massacre (1919), 23
Anglo-Irish Treaty (1921), 47
Ankara (Angora, Turkey), 71, 73–75
  Trenchard's planned bombing of, 96
appeasement
  Churchill on, 190, 193
  interwar policy of, 8, 105, 152, 172, 175,
    178, 183–84, 190–93
  of Iraq, 245
  by U.S. in Cold War, 240, 242
Arab-Israeli wars, 270
Aristide, Jean-Bertrand, 334, 335, 338, 339
Ark Royal, H.M.S., 106
Armenia, 68, 69, 75
  proposed U.S. mandate over, 74
Army After Next war games, 429
Aspen Institute, Bush's speech to, 278–80, 288,
  291, 293, 452n40
Aspin, Les, 280–82, 285–95, 298, 299, 301–2,
  306–7, 309–10, 312–19, 431
  nonproliferation program of, 343
  North Korea and, 352, 354, 365
  Somalia and, 330–31
Asquith, H. H., 15, 88, 253
asymmetrical response, 21
Australia, Britain's requests for troops from, 61,
  82
Austria, 28
  attempted German customs union with, 187
  Dolfuss murder in, 196–97

Austria (*cont.*)
  union of Germany and, 129, 173, 178, 189, 403–4
  withdrawal of Italian protection from, 215
Avazzini (Italian ambassador), 112
Aziz, Tariq, 251, 252, 418

B-2 bomber, 312, 317
Baghdad (Iraq)
  assaults on UN personnel in, 376–77
  Clinton's missile attack on, 382–84
  after World War I, 50, 52, 54
Baker, James, 251–52, 255, 257–59, 261–64, 324
balance of power, 14
Baldwin, Stanley, 8, 90, 400
  as Prime Minister
    British rearmament, 213, 228
    Corfu crisis, 101, 102, 104, 113
    Ethiopian war and, 203, 205, 340
    European recovery as goal, 160
    German rearmament, 159
    Locarno Treaty, 169, 180
Balfour, Arthur James, 38–40, 42, 80, 193
  Anglo-French alliance opposed by, 169
ballistic missiles
  North Korean launching over Japan of, 364
  prohibited to Iraq, 369, 370
  UNSCOM and, 374–75, 381, 389
Baltic states, 21, 27, 28, 40, 257, 308
Bandar Ibn Sultan, Prince, 251–54
Barre, Siyad, 326
Barthou, Louis, 196
Barton, Sir Sidney, 200
Base Force, 276–99, 454n11
  Aspin's alternative to, 285–88, 302, 306–7, 309–10, 312–19
  Bush administration's defense of, 288–96, 312
  under Clinton administration, 301–3, 319
  after Gulf War, 280–85
Basra (Iraq), 50, 52
Battle of Britain (1940), 55, 232, 430
Belarus, 308
Belgian army, 1936 strength of, 214
Belgium
  Britain's rejection of military staff talks with, 171
  fear of Germany by, 164–65
  France and, 123, 215, 216
  in German occupation, after World War I, 145
  in proposed British guarantee to France, 128, 153, 164–65
  reparations to, 142
  in Ruhr occupation, 161
  in Schlieffen Plan, 135
  See also Malmédy

Berlin (Germany)
  Allied troops in, after World War I, 143
  Kapp putsch in, 146–48
  Koch and Kienzle (E) in, 157
  Treaty of (1926), 181
Berlin Wall, 237, 242
Bessmertnykh, Alexander, 240
biological weapons
  Iraqi, 375, 388, 389, 395
  North Korean, 360
Birkenhead, 1st Earl of, 80
Blair, Tony, 421
Blessing (firm), 156
blitzkrieg, 20, 437n5
Blix, Hans, 345–51, 354, 358
Bofors (firm), 156
Bolshevism
  Germany's threat of, 147–48, 151–53
  See also Soviet Union
Bonar Law, Andrew, 88, 96, 191, 253, 265, 324, 434
  Lausanne Conference and, 91–92, 97
  as Prime Minister, 90, 104
Bosnia-Hercegovina, 257, 260–63, 266, 301, 320, 322, 323, 400–15, 423, 427
  Clinton's "lift and strike" plan for, 406
  Contact Group on, 409–10
  Joint Action Plan in, 407
  "safe areas" in, 407, 409–11, 413
  Washington Federation Agreement for, 409
Bottom-Up Review (BUR), 287, 302–20, 341, 429, 431
  GAO on questionable assumptions of, 315–16
Bouillon, Henri Franklin, 88
Boutros-Ghali, Boutros, 327–29
Branting, Karl H., 102
Breslau (warship), 79
Brest-Litovsk, Treaty of, 189
Briand, Aristide, 176, 182
  "could not be trusted," 126
  Franco-British cooperation and, 124–25, 127–28, 181
  Nobel Peace Prize to, 172
  united Europe plan of, 186–87
Britain
  armaments industries in, 159, 213, 221, 230
  foreign policy of
    "blue water" strategists, 135
    British style of diplomacy, 127
    Chanak crisis, 67, 72, 78–87, 95–97, 116, 248, 250, 253, 265, 324, 339–40, 417
    danger of one power dominating Europe, 134
    no territorial ambitions, 177
    splendid isolation, 166
    after World War I, 18, 21, 25–26, 37, 42–43, 49–50, 58, 73
  former Yugoslavia and, 260, 405, 407, 409, 411, 412

France and
  Britain's security dependent on France,
    174–75
  French need for security, 118–39, 160,
    162, 164–75, 195–96
  and 1935 Anglo-German naval treaty,
    201–2
Germany and
  Britain's need for trade with Germany, 160,
    192
  British 1920s policy, 177–78, 183–84
  German forces overestimated, 213–14
  Germany excluded from British war plan-
    ning, 310
  Imperial General Staff memo (1920),
    151–53
  Lloyd George's policy, 137–38, 142, 147,
    149–50, 153, 160
  1935 naval treaty, 201
  reconciliation after World War I, 41–42,
    122, 152, 183–84
  Versailles Treaty as too severe, 140, 142,
    371
Great Depression in, 218, 223–24
Gulf War aftermath and, 386, 387, 392
Italo-Ethiopian War and, 198–210, 213, 297,
    365
Joint Intelligence Committee, 248
military policy of
  Balfour's objections, 38–40, 42
  budget toplines, 272
  economic force seen as substitute for, 41,
    192
  Expeditionary Force, 179, 218, 220, 227,
    230–31, 286, 430
  interwar superficial "victories," 426–27
  interwar weakness, 217, 221–23
  Lloyd George's, 16–28, 33–38, 41–43,
    46–49, 96
  mechanization, 37, 46, 49, 230
  1920–1921 budget, 49–50
  in two major contingencies, 217
  See also ten-year rule
naval policy of, 29–33, 35–36
rearmament of, 213, 227–30, 430
  called unnecessary, 206
Rhine as frontier of, 126, 131, 138, 171, 197
Rhineland remilitarization and, 212–14
in World War I
  1918 military strength, 14
  war aims, 15, 44
as worldwide power after World War I,
    13–15, 191, 233
See also Treasury
British Army
  budgets for
    1920–1921, 49–50
    1934, 228
  Cardwell System, 36
  Chamberlain's inclination against, 228, 230

interwar unpreparedness of, 57–58, 152–53,
    213
in Iraq after World War I, 65–66
1933 report on needs of, 226, 227
pre–World War I, 34–35, 51
after World War I, 16, 21–22, 47, 48
British Empire
  as means to peace, 44, 243
  See also dominions
Brüning, Heinrich, 185–88
Bülow, Bernhard von, 187–89
BUR. See Bottom-Up Review
Burton, Richard, 326
Bush, George
  Clinton's denunciation of, 321–23
  defense policy of, 273, 276, 278–79, 285,
    287–96, 298–99, 301, 312
  foreign policy of
    Haiti, 334
    Korea, 344, 347, 353
    nonproliferation policy, 343
    Yugoslav policy, 257–58, 261–66, 404,
      416–18, 422
  Gulf War and, 244–45, 248, 250–52,
    254–56, 379–81, 383, 395
    enforcement of inspections, 377–78
    Kurdish rebellion, 255, 372, 373
    policy will give rise to future war, 398
    why he ended war, 254, 368–69
  Iraq's attempt to assassinate, 382–84
  new world order of, 242–43, 255–58, 269
  1992 election lost by, 271
  Somalia mission and, 326, 327–29
  Tiananmen massacre denounced by, 310,
    323
Butler, Lee, 277
Byrd, Robert, 330

Cadogan, Alexander, 112
Cambon, Pierre Paul, 112
Campbell, R. I., 200
Canada, Britain's requests for troops from, 61,
    82
Cannes Conference (1922), 125, 127–28,
    168
Carrington, 6th Baron, 260
Carter, Jimmy, 240, 300, 325, 338
  in Iran crisis, 251
  Korean mission of, 362–63
Caucasus, British troops in, 58, 126
Cavan, 10th Earl of, 80, 85
Cecil, Lord Robert
  as "collectivist," 104
  Corfu crisis and, 101–3, 105–8
Cedras, Raoul, 335, 338
Chamberlain, Neville, 91, 263
  appeasement policy of, 8
  and German rearmament, 159
  "limited liability" policy of, 230
  proposed 1934 military budget cut by, 228

Chamberlain, Sir Austen, 29–31, 80, 178, 205
  Nobel Peace Prize to, 172
  and security of France, 133, 163, 167–72,
    174, 181
Chanak crisis, 67, 72, 78–87, 95–97, 116, 248,
    250, 253, 265, 324, 339–40, 417
Chatfield, Ernle, 203, 204, 208
Chechnya, 417
chemical weapons
  Iraqi, 244, 375, 389
  North Korean, 360
Cheney, Richard, 247, 250, 251, 264, 273, 280,
    288–95, 299, 343
China
  Gulf War aftermath and, 392
  military policy of, 8, 310
  North Korea and, 344, 349, 354
  Soviet collapse and, 270
  Tiananmen massacre in, 310, 323
  United States and
    Clinton's policy, 322–23
    excluded from U.S. war planning, 307, 310
    tension and hostility, 2, 310, 435
Christopher, Warren, 323, 325, 330, 332,
    401–3, 405–7, 409, 411, 416
Churchill, Winston
  Anglo-French alliance opposed by, 169, 171
  on appeasement, 190, 193
  on British complacency after Ryswick, 3
  on conventional wisdom about war, 295
  While England Slept, vii, viii
  1930s warnings by, 201
  on Paris Pact, 176
  as Secretary of State for War and Air, 18
    attitude on Turkey, 70, 71, 73, 75, 78,
      80–85, 96–97, 417
    on peacekeeping operations, 52–53
    post–World War I policy, 34–35, 41–43,
      49, 51–52, 57, 58, 272
    repudiated by British people, 91
    on security guarantee to France, 123–24
  in World War II, 233
  World War II predicted by, 124, 132
CIA (Central Intelligence Agency), 248, 257,
    334, 348
Cilicia, 68, 70, 74
Clark, Wesley, 419
Clemenceau, Georges, 38
Clinton, William Jefferson
  Bush's foreign policy attacked by, 321–23
  foreign policy of
    Bosnia, 400–15
    confused and contradictory, 323, 337
    Haiti, 323, 333–40
    his disinterest, 325
    Kosovo, 416–23
    North Korea, 349, 351–66m, 387–88
  Iraq and, 381–95
    Clinton's desire to remove Saddam,
      389–90

  1994 reinforcements sent, 384–85
  Operation Desert Fox, 395, 398
  raid on Iraqi intelligence complex, 382–84
  and Saddam's Kurdistan incursion, 390–93
  military policy of, 300–20
    Somalia mission, 327–33, 337, 340
Cohen, William, 249, 416, 420
Cold War, 237–43
  deterrence in, 5, 267
  end of, 237–38, 267–70, 341–43
  international stability a result of, 269–70,
    342–43
  U.S. demobilization after, 319
  U.S. policy after, 406–7
  See also Soviet Union
collective security, 98, 103, 117, 162, 194, 198,
    200, 202–7, 218
  British military power and, 206
Cologne (Germany), 163, 167, 168, 180
Commission on Roles and Missions, 429
Commission on Security and Cooperation in
    Europe (CSCE), 262
Commonwealth of Independent States, 269
computers, British mechanization compared to
    use of, 46
Conference of Ambassadors, 39, 40
  in Corfu crisis, 98–99, 101–5, 108–14, 352
Conference of Ministers (1921), 84
Congo (Zaire), 333
Constantine I (King of the Hellenes), 74–76
Constantinople (Istanbul)
  Allied occupation of, 70, 71, 75, 79–80, 90
  and British resistance to Kemal, 78–79
  Constantine's attempted seizure of, 76
  in Sèvres treaty, 69, 70
Contact Group (for former Yugoslavia),
    409–10, 417, 418, 420
containment, 239–41, 268
Cooper, Alfred Duff, 224
Corfu crisis (1923), 98–117, 232, 249, 339–40,
    352, 353, 365, 403, 426
counterinsurgency as manpower-intensive, 47
Cox, Sir Percy, 55–56
Creditanstalt bank (Vienna), 187
Crewe, 1st Marquess of, 103, 110–14, 116, 403
criminal organizations, international, 2
Cripps, Sir Stafford, 206
Croatia, 257–61
  Operation Storm of, 412
Crowe, Sir Eyre, 122–23, 132, 167, 168
Crowe, William, 248
CSCE (Commission on Security and Coopera-
    tion in Europe), 262
Cuban Missile Crisis (1962), 242
Cunningham, Sir Andrew, 208–10
Curtius, Ernst, 183
Curzon, 1st Marquess, 58
  Anglo-French alliance opposed by, 169
  Corfu crisis and, 99, 101–10, 112–14, 116
  and guarantee to France, 129, 168

at Lausanne Conference, 90–94, 97
Middle Eastern hopes of, 50
on proposed Franco-British alliance, 125–27
and rehabilitation of Germany, 122
Turkish policy and, 69, 73, 77, 80, 81, 83, 85
   Poincaré interview, 88–89
Czechoslovakia, 28, 39, 40
   France and
      French security, 124, 130, 131, 133, 170, 174
      in Rhineland crisis, 214
   possible disappearance of, 136
   possible German invasion of, 129
   possible redrawing of frontier of, 136
   tanks produced in, 157
   See also Munich crisis (1938)

D'Abernon, 1st Viscount, 163–64
Daily Express, 92
Daily Mail, 81, 94, 95, 103
Danzig, 124, 133, 141, 173, 178, 189
Darmstadt (Germany), 146, 392
Dawes Plan, 161, 173, 182
Dayton (Ohio) agreement, 413, 415–17, 427
Defence Requirements Committee, 226–27
Dellums, Ronald V., 281
Delors, Jacques, 259
democracy
   Clinton's policy of spreading, 325
   foreign policy of, 43
   postwar demobilization of, 3–7
   realpolitik as impossible for, 207
   rearmament in, 229, 299
Derby, 17th Earl of, 91
Desert Storm. See Gulf War
deterrence
   in Bush's regional strategy, 289, 297
   in Cold War, 5, 267
   and Ethiopian crisis, 297
   preparedness and, 4
Deutsche Zeitung, Die, 143
digitization, 46
disarmament
   British support of, 124, 125, 140
   of France, 162
   Geneva 1932 conference on, 188, 222–23
   of Iraq after Gulf War, 374
   proportional, 178
   in Versailles Treaty, 141, 142, 154–55, 158,
      159, 396
   See also naval disarmament
Dodecanese Islands, 69, 100, 101
Dolfuss, Engelbert, 196–97
dominions (British Empire)
   in Chanak crisis, 81, 84
   Corfu crisis and, 103
   Lloyd George's policy on, 61, 81–82
Dorgan, Byron, 272
Doyle, Larry, 332
Drenica (Kosovo), 416
drugs, U.S. armed forces in war against, 304

Drummond, Sir Eric, 115
Dubrovnik (Croatia), 259, 260
Dyer, Reginald, 23

Eagleburger, Lawrence, 247, 262, 263
East Africa, airpower in, 54
Eastern Europe
   British interests in, 136
   Locarno Treaty and, 170, 178
   map of, 119
   after World War I, 40, 42
East Prussia, 141
EC. See European Community
Eden, Anthony, 200, 202, 204, 207, 210, 212
Egypt
   British armed forces in, 22, 26, 28, 34, 35,
      37, 46, 48, 50
      possible withdrawal, 50
   British interwar fear of attack on, 213
   current military forces of, 307
   Gulf War aftermath and, 386
Ekeus, Rolf, 377–78, 387–89
electronic battlefield surveillance, 312–13
England. See Britain
Erenkeui (Turkey), 86
Estes, Howell, 357
Ethiopia
   map of, 195
   See also Italo-Ethiopian War
ethnic cleansing, 261, 262, 400–403, 405,
   412–14, 421, 422
Eupen, 170
Europe, map of, 119
European Community (EC), 259–61
exit strategies, 53

F-15 fighters, 313, 317
F/A-18 aircraft, 313
faraway peoples, becoming involved with, 422
Field, Sir Frederick, 221
Finland, German submarines developed in, 158
Fisher, Sir Warren, 205, 207
Fiume, 25, 115
Flandin, Pierre, 212
Foch, Ferdinand, 24, 26, 145, 146, 148
Fokker aircraft, 156
Foley, Thomas, 251
Foreign Affairs magazine, 247
foreign policy
   in democracy, 43
   force needed as backing of, 4, 239, 290, 319
Foreign Policy magazine, 285
Fourteen Points, 15, 398
Fox, John, 402
France
   Britain and
      British guarantees against Germany,
         118–39, 160, 162, 164–75, 195–96
      proposed alliance, 124–28, 153
      1697 peace, 3

France (*cont.*)
  Corfu crisis and, 101–5, 108–12, 114, 117
  foreign policy of
    French style of diplomacy, 127
    limitations after World War I, 14
    1930s rapprochement with Italy, 196–200
  former Yugoslavia and, 260, 405, 407, 409,
    411, 412, 418
  Germany and
    Herriot predicts war in ten years, 168
    reparations, 130, 142, 161–62, 170
    Versailles Treaty as too soft, 140
  Gulf War aftermath and, 383, 386, 387,
    391–92
  Italo-Ethiopian war and, 204–7
  military policy of
    decrease in number of soldiers, 197
    defensive emphasis, 174
    "spontaneous offensive action" rejected,
      211
  1940 defeat of, as unforeseen, 6
  Rhineland remilitarization and, 211–16
  Ruhr occupied by, 104, 108, 122, 123, 130,
    149, 153–54, 161–62, 170
  in Syria, 69
  Turkey and, after World War I, 70, 74, 75,
    79–82, 85, 88–90
Frankfurt (Germany), 146, 392
Franz Ferdinand (Archduke of Austria), 99
Freikorps, 143, 150
French army
  black troops in, 145
  1936 strength of, 214
  post–World War I demands on, 38–39
French navy, 30, 226
Future Years Defense Plan (FYDP), 301, 317,
  318

Gallipoli Peninsula, British 1921 defense of, 78,
  80–86, 90
Gallucci, Robert, 353–54, 356–58, 362
Gamelin, Maurice, 198, 211, 213
GAO. *See* General Accounting Office
Garrison, William F., 331
Gdansk (Poland). *See* Danzig
Geddes, Sir Eric, 18
General Accounting Office (GAO), 315–17
Geneva Disarmament Conference (1932), 188,
  222–23
Geneva Protocol for the Pacific Settlement
  of Disputes (1924), 162–64, 166, 168
Genoa Conference (1922), 130
genocide, in Africa, 333
German army
  Army Peace Commission, 143–45, 156
  "hasty" demobilization of, 147–48
  rearmament of, 155–59, 164, 174, 179, 181,
    188, 190, 196, 200, 218, 310, 397
  Versailles Treaty regulation of, 141, 142,
    146, 147, 149, 152, 154

German Nationalist Party (DNVP), 173
German navy, 141
  in 1935 Anglo-Germany treaty, 201
  submarines developed in Finland for, 158
Germany
  Britain and
    British occupation, after World War I, 24,
      27–28, 38, 41–42, 49, 59
    pre–World War I British Army policy,
      34–35
    rehabilitation sought by Britain, 122
    Churchill's hope of reconciliation with,
      41–42
  Communists in, 184, 185, 187
  Constitution repudiated by Brüning, 185
  economics and finance of
    Great Depression, 184–86, 189–90, 218
    inflation, 161
    prosperity of late 1920s, 173
  former Yugoslavia and, 260, 409
  in Locarno Treaty, 168–75, 180–81
  map of, 119
  military policy of
    Hitler's, 196
    reserve manpower crisis, 188
    Schlieffen Plan, 135
  naval policy of, Brüning's "pocket battle-
    ships," 187
  Nazis in, 7, 8, 158, 184–86, 188
  proposed dismemberment of, 118–20, 142
  Rhineland remilitarization by, 7
  Soviet Union and, 40, 137, 151, 164
    interwar cooperation in arms, 157–58
    military collaboration revealed, 181
    Treaty of Berlin (1926), 181
  as threat to peace, 224
    even without Nazis, 190
    French viewpoint, 142
    improbable in 1920s, 6, 183, 225
  Versailles Treaty and
    Allied weakness after World War I, 145–46
    German 1924 failure to comply, 163
    German demand for revision, 147–49
    German dissatisfaction, 136, 144–45, 152,
      173, 183, 396
    German exports of war material, 146, 156
    government obstruction, 143–47, 149–51,
      154, 155
    paramilitary groups, 143, 150, 158, 181,
      184, 187, 188
    signing, 27–28
    Stresemann's desire for revision, 167
    withdrawal of Allied supervision, 180
    See also reparations
  in World War II, Allied bombing campaign,
    55
Glaspie, April, 245, 252
Goeben (warship), 79
Gorazde (Bosnia), 409, 410, 413
Gorbachev, Mikhail, 240–41, 269, 270, 344

Gordon, Michael, 355
government, "priming the pump" by, 47
Great Depression, 184–86, 189–90, 194, 217, 218
Greece, 39
  Albanian border with, 98
  map of, 99
  Turkish territory promised to, 68, 69
  Turkish war of, 27, 46, 71, 73–76, 96
  See also Corfu crisis
Grey, 1st Viscount, of Fallodon, 127, 168, 421
Groener, Wilhelm, 184–85
Guariglia, Raffaele, 104
Guderian, Hans, 157
Gulf War, 2, 8, 244–56, 258, 265, 275, 287, 311, 368–99
  airpower in, 55, 426
  Base Force after, 280–85
  casualties in, 254
  Clinton and, 323
  North Korea as student of, 361–62
  if North Korea had attacked at same time, 314
  peace after, compared to Versailles Treaty, 367–71
  size of Iraqi forces in, 306

Hague Conference (1929), 182–83
Haile Selassie (Emperor of Ethiopia), 207
Haiti, 305, 320, 322, 323, 333–40, 432
  Chanak and Corfu compared to crisis in, 339–40
Haldane, Sir J. Aylmer L., 61–64
Hamid Hasancan Bey, 86
Hamilton, Lee, 411
Hankey, Sir Maurice, 164, 170, 227
Harenc, Major, 113
Harington, Sir Charles, 80, 83, 84, 86–91, 95
Harlan County, U.S.S., 333–35
Headlam-Morley, Sir James, 133–38, 179, 243
Heinkel (firm), 156
Helsinski Conference, 258
Henderson, Arthur, 182, 187
Herriot, Édouard, 132, 162
  Locarno Treaty and, 168
  war with Germany in ten years predicted by, 168
Hindenburg, Paul von, 173, 183, 185, 187, 188
Hitler, Adolf, 185, 189, 195
  goals of, and those of traditional diplomats, 189
  on Italian fleet, 209–10
  Mussolini and, 207, 215
  rearmament and, 158, 196, 200, 397
  Rhineland remilitarization by, 7, 210–16
  Saddam Hussein compared to, 244, 254
  Stresemann attacked by, 173
Hoare, Sir Samuel, 202–7
Hoare-Laval agreement (1935), 206–7

Holbrooke, Richard, 411, 413, 418–20
Holland
  German aircraft produced in, 157–58
  Krupp activities in, 156
Hong Kong, 194, 219, 223
Howe, Jonathan, 329–31
humanitarian missions, 333, 401, 403
  defensive forces for, 327
Hungary, 27, 28, 39, 40
Hyland, William, 247

IACC. See Inter-Allied Control Commission
IAEA. See International Atomic Energy Agency
IFOR (Implementation Force), 414
Imbros, 69
Implementation Force (IFOR), 414
India, current military forces of, 307
Indian Army
  Indian objections to Britain's use of, 60–61
  "renting" to Britain of troops from, 60
Indian Empire
  airpower on Northwestern Frontier of, 55
  as original League of Nations member, 61
  Soviet threat to, 224–27
  after World War I, 23–25, 27, 28, 34, 35, 37, 46, 48, 58
information age, war in, 2–3
Inönü, Ismet. See Ismet Pasha
Inskip, Sir Thomas, 230
Inter-Allied Control Commission (IACC, after World War I), 141, 143–46, 150, 154–58, 397
  UNSCOM compared to, 374, 389
  withdrawal of, 155
International Atomic Energy Agency (IAEA), 344–59, 362–64
Iran (Persia)
  after Gulf War, 8
  in U.S. Cold War strategy, 275
  war between Iraq and, 244
  after World War I, 50, 58, 59, 71, 126
Iraq, 34, 37, 54
  as British mandate, 69
  Clinton's policy towards, 305, 323
  after Gulf War, 8, 266
    end of present U.S. policy, 435
    first Kurdish rebellion, 372–73
    military strength, 397, 398
    revenge desired against U.S., 396
    Saddam stays in power, 371
  map of, 45
  no-fly zones in, 370, 372, 378–81, 390, 392, 398
  possible response to a Korean war by, 360–61, 431–32
  Shiite rebellion in, 255, 378–79, 398
  after Soviet Union's collapse, 270
  United Nations sanctions against, 369, 383, 387, 389–90, 394
  war between Iran and, 244

Iraq (*cont.*)
  WMD weapons of, 244, 248, 256, 343, 345,
    369, 374–75, 398, 428
    Kamel's revelations, 389, 399
    UNSCOM and, 374–81, 393–95
  after World War I, 23, 44–45, 47–48, 59,
    127
    Churchill's proposed pullback, 50–52
    1920 revolt, 55–56, 60–66
    Trenchard's proposal for defense, 52,
      53–55
  See also Gulf War; Kurds; Saddam Hussein
Irbil (Kurdistan), battle of, 390–93
Ireland
  British armed forces in, 22–24, 34, 35, 37,
    46–48, 57
  possible U.S. hostile action over, 29
Ironside, Sir Edmund, 230–31
Irvine, Colonel, 145
Ismet Pasha (Ismet Inönü), 87, 89, 93
Ismid Peninsula (Turkey), 71–73, 79, 80,
    82–84, 90
Israel, Iraq and, 244
Italian air force, 208
Italian navy, 1923 weakness of, 107, 110
Italo-Ethiopian War (1935–1936), 7, 197–210,
    213, 297, 365
  Corfu and, 105, 117, 198
  sanctions against Italy in, 205, 207
Italy
  in Corfu crisis, 98–117, 352
  former Yugoslavia and, 409
  France and, 196–200
  Germany and, Rome-Berlin Axis, 215
  Turkey and
    Italian occupation of Turkey, 68, 70, 74,
      79–80
    negotiations with Turks after World War I,
      74, 75, 79, 82, 85, 88–90
  after World War I, 28, 39, 40

Japan
  British unreadiness against, 201, 213, 218–19
  end of British alliance with, 225, 310
  Manchuria occupation of, 117, 194, 209,
    217–18, 222, 223, 229, 400
  North Korea and, 344
  as threat to peace
    ignored by Britain, 319
    improbable in 1920s, 6, 225
  in World War II
    Allied bombing campaign, 55
    Pearl Harbor bombing, 233
Japanese navy, 30, 107
Jeremiah, David, 280–83, 298
Jodl, Alfred, 214
Joint Nuclear Control Commission (JNCC,
    Korea), 345, 346, 349
Joint Strategic Capabilities Plan, 276–77
Jones, David C., 248

Joyce, Larry E., 332
Juppé, Alain, 337, 408

Kamal Hassan, Hussein, 389, 393, 399
Kang Sok Ju, 353
Kapp putsch (1920), 146–48
Karadzic, Radovan, 409, 410, 414
Karagatch (suburb of Adrianople), 87
Kellogg, Frank B., 176
Kellogg-Briand Pact. *See* Paris, Pact of
Kelly, Thomas, 248–49
Kemal Atatürk (Mustapha Kemal), 37, 46,
    70–71, 73–76
  in Chanak crisis, 78, 79, 61, 82, 90, 253, 426
Kennan, George F., 239, 241
Kennard, Sir Howard, 105
Kennedy, Edward M., 249
Kennedy, John F., 242, 300
  Why England Slept, vii, viii
Keyes, Sir Roger, 106–7
Khartoum (Sudan), 50
Kim Il Sung, 344, 345, 362, 363
Kim Jong Il, 350, 364
Kim Yong Sun, 353
Kissinger, Henry, 324
Kitty Hawk, U.S.S., 379
Koch and Kienzle (E), 157
Korea, 277, 282
  map of, 342
  See also North Korea; South Korea
Korean Energy Development Organization, 363
Korean War, 239, 270, 311
Kosovo, 256, 264, 401, 415–23, 428
Kosovo Liberation Army (KLA), 416, 418, 420
Kozyrev, Alexander, 407
Krajina, 412
Krulak, Charles, 432
Krupp (firm), 150, 156, 157
Kun, Béla, 27, 28
Kurds
  in Iran, 390
  in Iraq, 261, 287, 376, 398
    1996 raid by Saddam, 390–93
    rebellion after Gulf War, 255, 369, 372–73
    Saddam's use of chemical weapons against,
      244
  in Turkey, 372, 373, 390
  after World War I, 75
Kuwait
  attempted assassination of Bush in, 382–84
  border between Iraq and, 370, 379, 384,
    386
  invasion of, 244–56, 278–80, 311, 369
  possible 1994 Iraqi attack on, 384–86
  U.S. commitment to defend, 395
  U.S. renewed presence in, 380, 384–86

Lake, Anthony, 324, 325, 332, 355, 407, 409,
    413
Laroche (French ambassador), 111

Lausanne Conference (1922) and Treaty, 90–95, 98, 100, 107, 414
Lausanne Conference (1932), 188
Laval, Pierre, 196–97, 204–6
Law, Andrew Bonar. *See* Bonar Law, Andrew
League of Nations, 16–17, 19, 43, 44, 224, 319–20
  alliances superseded by, 126
  armed might needed by, 232
  British Foreign Office attitudes to, 104–5
  Corfu defeat of, 100–103, 108–9, 111, 113–17, 232, 340, 352, 353, 426
  economic sanctions by, 105–6, 110, 204, 205, 207
  German membership in, 155, 176, 180
  as "International Burglars' Union," 206
  Japanese withdrawal from, 224
  military sanctions by, 106
  Mosul dispute submitted to, 92–93
  proposed supervision of German disarmament by, 167
  Soviet entry into, 196
  Turkey in, 92
  Zone of the Straits to be controlled by, 69
  See also collective security
League of Nations Union, 222
Lebanon, 277
Lee, 1st Viscount, of Fareham (Arthur Lee), 123
Lewis, Anthony, 263
Libby, I. Lewis, 280, 281, 299
Libya, 287
limited intervention, 263
limited liability, British policy of, 230, 232, 405, 420
Lithuania, 40, 257
Little Entente, 166, 174, 211
Lloyd George, David, 15–28, 32–39, 41–43, 46–49, 271
  dominions policy of, 61, 81–82
  fall of Cabinet of, 90
  foreign policy of, 37, 50–52, 58, 73
    Franco-British relations, 121, 124, 127–31, 137–38
    German policy, 137–38, 142, 147, 149–50, 153, 160
  on Italo-Ethiopian War, 207
  on Lausanne Conference, 94
  summary of military policy of, 35–36
  Turkish policy of, 37, 50–52, 58, 67, 72–73, 75–80, 83–85, 95–96, 250
Locarno, Treaty of (1925), 7, 153–55, 168–75, 178, 184, 190, 225–26, 426
  "eastern," proposed, 170, 196
  failure of, 180
  "spirit of Locarno," 169–70, 172, 173, 176, 180–82
  Stresemann as original proponent of, 168, 169
  two main elements of, 169

logic bombs, 3
London Conference (1922), 130
London Conference (1924), 161, 173
losing the first battle, 4
Louis XIV (King of France), 3
Luck, Gary, 355, 358–60, 365
Ludendorff, Erich, 173–74
Luftwaffe, 214
  antecedents of, 156–59
  British fear of, 228
Lugar, Richard, 251, 337

McCain, John, 336, 421
MacDonald, Ramsay, 192
  Geneva Protocol promoted by, 162
  German conciliation as goal of, 162–63, 182
Macedonia, 401, 415–17, 420
  UNPROFOR in, 407, 410, 411
machinery (mechanization). *See* technology
McNeil, Robert, 94
McNeill, Ronald, 164
McPeak, Merrill, 248
MAD (Mutually Assured Destruction), 193
Maffey, Sir John, 199
Maginot Line, 215
Major, John, 409
Malmédy, 170, 189
Manchester Guardian, 181
Manchuria, 117, 194, 209, 217–18, 222, 223, 229, 400
mandates, 44, 61, 69, 74, 107
Marden, Sir Thomas Owen, 86
Marlborough, 1st Duke of, 3
Martin, Kingsley, 206
Mediterranean Sea, Royal Navy's interwar weakness in, 106
Mehmed IV (Sultan of Turkey), 70
Memel, 189
Mesopotamia. *See* Iraq
Middle East
  future U.S. military needs in, 275
  map of, 45
  See also specific countries
military policy
  foreign policy to be backed by, 4, 239, 290, 319
  people's support of, 286
Milne, Sir George, 24, 72, 187, 221
Milosevic, Slobodan, 256–58, 261, 262, 400, 410, 414–16, 418–21, 423, 428
mission creep, 53, 329, 331, 369, 425
Mitchell, George, 251
Mitrovica (Kosovo), 423
Mladic, Ratko, 409, 410, 414
modernization. *See* technology
Mogadishu (Somalia), 318, 331–32, 337, 414, 45760
Montenegro, 420, 423
Montgomery, Thomas, 331
Morgan, J. H., 146–47, 374, 445*n1*

Morris, Richard, 325
Morris, Stuart, 206
Mosul (Iraq), 50, 52, 91–93
MRC (major regional contingencies)
    1-MRC, 288, 298, 314
    2-MRC
        of Britain in interwar period, 217, 225–26
        BUR definition, 306
        U.S. military policy of, 282, 296–98, 303,
            315, 341, 361–62, 429–32
Mudania truce (1921), 78, 86–90
Mudros Armistice (1918), 68
Müller, Hermann, 184
multilateralism, Clinton's policy of, 325–26,
    329, 330, 339, 340
Munich crisis (1938)
    another scenario for, 40
    prediction of, 136
Muslims
    in former Yugoslavia, 260, 403, 407, 409–13
    post–World War I Turkish settlement and, 69,
        88
Mussolini, Benito, 7, 244
    in Corfu crisis, 99–100, 103–6, 109–17,
        352
    Ethiopian war and, 197–210
    as "mad dog," 105, 203, 204, 206

National Defense Panel, 2, 429–30
National Defense University, 312
National Guard and reserves, U.S., 271, 275,
    283–85, 296, 316, 318
National Military Strategy, 295
National Security Strategy of Engagement and
    Enlargement, The, 325–26
nation-building, 329, 330, 334, 337
nation-states, collapse of, 2
NATO (North Atlantic Treaty Organization), 2,
    137, 257, 274, 309, 399, 434
    in former Yugoslavia, 403, 404, 407,
        409–11, 414, 416–23, 428
    recent expansion of, 7
naval disarmament, Washington Conference
    (1923) on, 123
Nederlandische Vliegtuigenfabriek NV, 156
negotiations from strength, 241
Neuilly, Treaty of, 108
Neurath, Konstantin von, 188
Newfoundland, 82
new world order, 242–43, 255–58, 269
New York Times, 169, 263, 327, 328, 336, 355
New Zealand, Britain's requests for troops
    from, 61, 82
Nicolson, Harold, 76, 79, 82, 90, 92, 93, 95,
    100, 101, 103, 165–67, 212
Nitze, Paul, 239
Nobel Peace Prize, 172
nonaggression, in Locarno Treaty, 169
nonproliferation, 341–43
    North Korea and, 342–66, 428

Nonproliferation Treaty (NPT), 344, 345, 347,
    349–53, 362–64
non-state actors, 2
Noriega, Manuel, 278
North Korea, 270, 287, 296, 305
    chemical and biological weapons of, 360
    multistage ballistic missile launched by, 364
    nuclear threat of, 342–66, 428
    reconciliation of South Korea with, 344–46
    size of forces of, 306
    United States and
        Agreed Framework (1994), 363–65,
            387–88
        direct contacts, 345, 352, 353, 355–56,
            362
        economic sanctions, 354
        threat only delayed, 435
    war expected with, 356–57
NSC-68, 239–40
nuclear weapons, 239
    Cheney-Aspin dispute on, 295
    Iraqi, 244, 343, 345, 375, 381–82, 389
        UNSCOM and, 374–81
    North Korean, 342–66, 428
    proliferation of, 341–43
    suitcase, 2
    in U.S. presidential campaigns, 300–301
    U.S.-Soviet negotiations on, 241
Nunn, Sam, 252, 273–76, 279, 299, 338

Obey, David R., 335
oil
    Iraqi
        conflict with Kuwait on, 344–45, 247
        after Gulf War, 370
        Iraq as early source, 50
        oil-for-food deal, 391, 394
        possible Ethiopian war embargo on, 205–7,
            210
        Saddam's control of 20% of, 247
    OPEC states, 244, 247
Operation Desert Fox, 395, 398, 432
Operation Determined Effort, 411
Operation Just Cause, 278, 204
Operation Provide Relief, 327
Operation Restore Democracy, 338
Osijek (Yugoslavia), 259
Ottoman Empire
    possible restoration of, 79
    See also Turkey
Owen, David, 259, 401, 402, 404

Pakistan, 307
    in Somalia, 330
Palestine, 48, 50–52, 71
    as British mandate, 69
    World War I air war in, 54
Panama, U.S. invasion of, 278, 279, 304
Panetta, Leon, 318
Panmunjom (Korea), 344, 362

Paris, Pact of (Kellogg-Briand Pact, 1928), 176, 199
Paris Note (1921), 83–84, 87
Patriot antimissile batteries, 355
Pax Americana, 3
peace
  British people's 1930s wish for, 206
  international organizations for, 222
  See also war
peace dividend, 3, 51, 271–76
peacekeeping operations
  Churchill on, 52–53
  NATO, 420
  by U.S. military, 304, 305
  United Nations, 328–30
peacemaking operations, 304, 305
Peace Pledge Union, 206
peer competitors, 2, 8, 21, 237
Permanent Court of Justice (World Court),
  Corfu crisis and, 108, 111
Perry, William J., 338, 352, 357–60, 365, 386, 409, 431
Persian Gulf, 282, 360
  as trouble spot, 277
Philippines, 277
Poincaré, Raymond
  and British guarantee to France, 128–30
  in Chanak crisis, 88–89
  Ruhr occupation and, 161
Poland, 39, 40, 58
  France and
    French security, 27–28, 130, 131, 133, 166, 170, 174, 181, 196
    in Rhineland crisis, 214
  Germany and, 178
    German military planning, 174
    1934 pact, 196
    possible attack by Germany, 129, 135, 190
  possible new partition of, 136, 137, 188
Polish Corridor, 141, 165, 170, 173, 182
Poos, Jacques, 259
Powell, Colin
  Base Force concept of, 276–80, 283–85, 292, 298, 310, 454n11
  Gulf War and, 246–49, 254
  in Haiti, 338
  Somalia mission and, 328, 331
  on U.S. military needs for security, 294–96
  Yugoslav crises and, 263, 264, 404–5
Pownall, Sir Henry, 227
Préval, René, 339
pseudoengagement, 426–27, 429

Quadrennial Defense Review (QDR), 429

Racak (Kosovo), 420
radar, 313
Raeder, Erich, 201
RAF. See Royal Air Force
Rambouillet conference (1999), 420

Rapallo, Treaty of (1922), 115, 130, 181
Rapid Deployment Force, 275
Reagan, Ronald, 240–41, 270, 271, 300
Red Cross, in Somalia, 327
regional contingencies. See MRC
Reichswehr. See German army
reparations, 130, 141–42
  British army expenses recovered by, 49, 182
  British opposition to, 122
  Brüning's policy on, 185–86
  Dawes Plan and, 161, 173, 182
  Germany's defaulting on, 147, 148, 150, 161, 173, 182
  German avoidance of reparations, 147, 148, 150, 161, 173, 182
  Hoover Moratorium on, 188
  Locarno Treaty and, 170, 173
  Young Plan and, 182, 186, 188
Reparations Commission, 161, 162
Republican Party, U.S., isolationism of, 324
Republika Srpska, 413
Repulse, H.M.S., 210
revolution in military affairs. See RMA
Rhineland
  Allied withdrawal from, 163, 170, 182–84, 186
  demilitarization of, 120, 131, 137, 141, 169, 183, 187
    in Locarno Treaty, 172
  Germany's remilitarization of, 7, 210–16
  maps of, 119, 195
  in proposed Franco-British treaty, 128–31
  proposed independence of, 120, 121, 161, 166
  See also Cologne
Rhineland Pact (Treaty of Mutual Guarantee), 169–72
Ritter, Scott, 374, 376–77, 388, 393
RMA (revolution in military affairs), 48–49, 62–64, 298
Robertson, Sir William, 24, 28
Robinson, Randall, 335
Roh Tae Woo, 344
Romano Avezzano, Baron Camillo, 110
Ross, Dennis, 252–53
Royal Air Force, 16, 27, 29, 30
  in Battle of Britain, 55, 232, 430
  Chanak crisis and, 96
  interwar weakness of, 220, 231
  in 1920 Iraq revolt, 61–66
  in 1920–1921 budget, 49
  in 1934 budget, 228
  post–World War I role of, 19–21
  Trenchard's proposals on role of, 53–54, 58–59, 311–12
Royal Navy, 16, 29–36, 82, 95, 430
  in Ethiopian crisis, 207–10
  interwar unreadiness of, 107, 114, 201, 203–4, 206, 208–9, 218–20, 231

Royal Navy (*cont.*)
  1933 report on needs of, 226
  suggested Corfu crisis use of, 106–7, 110, 114
Rugova, Ibrahim, 416, 418
Ruhr, 215
  French occupation of, 104, 108, 122, 123, 130, 149, 153–54, 161–62, 170
  German uprising in, 146–49, 392–93
  Locarno Treaty and, 174
Rumania, 39, 40, 81
  France and, 124, 166, 174, 214
Rumbold, Sir Horace, 80, 82–83, 85, 86, 88–90
Russia, 2, 8
  excluded from U.S. war planning, 307–10
  fear of sale of WMD by, 342
  former Yugoslavia and, 407, 409, 414, 417, 418, 420, 421
  Gulf War aftermath and, 386, 387, 392
  possible future European attack by, 308–10
  after World War I, 27, 42
  See also Soviet Union
Rwanda, 333
Ryswick, Peace of (1697), 3

Saar, 120, 142, 189
Saddam Hussein, 2, 244–47, 252–56, 263, 265, 266, 287, 293, 297, 374, 376–80, 383–99, 419, 428, 431
  background of, 244
  Bush accused of "coddling," 322–23
  Clinton's desire to remove, 389–90
  not overthrown after Gulf War, 371
  timely surrender of, 368
Saddam Kamel, 389
Sahhaf, Saeed, 387
St-Aulaire (French ambassador), 124, 129, 132
St. Germain, Treaty of, 108, 178
Sakarya River, battle of (1921), 75–76
Salmond, Sir Geoffrey, 221
SALT II agreement, 240
SAMs (surface-to-air missiles), Iraqi, 379–80
San Remo Conference (1920), 69, 73
Sarajevo (Bosnia), 99–100, 260, 264, 265, 322, 403, 407–10, 413
sarin nerve gas, 2
Sarraut, Albert, 215
Saudi Arabia, 69, 247, 248, 250–51, 253
  in Gulf War aftermath, 391
Scheidemann, Philipp, 181
Schleicher, Kurt von, 185, 187, 188
Schlesinger, James, 285
Schlieffen Plan, 135
Schwartzkopf, H. Norman, 246, 249
Scowcroft, Brent, 244, 250, 252, 262, 337, 372
Scud missiles, 375
Sea of Marmora, German warships permitted by Turks in, 79

Seeckt, Hans von, 150, 174, 445n18
Serbia, 81, 256–66, 400, 410
  Kosovo and, 416–23
Sèvres, Treaty of (1920), 69–70, 73, 75, 76, 92, 94
Shalikashvili, John, 358–59, 361, 409
Shelton, Henry H., 420
Sicherheitspolizei, 149
Silesia, 38, 123, 165, 173, 178
Simon, Sir John, 194, 200
Singapore, 194, 218–19, 223, 231
Skaggs, David, 337
Skelton, Ike, 271, 282, 296
Skoda (firm), 157
Slovenia, 257, 258
smaller-scale conflicts. *See* SSCs
smart weapons, 312–13, 433
Smith, Ruppert, 410
Smuts, Jan, 103
Smuts Report (after World War I), 45–46
Smyrna (Turkey), 27, 46, 69, 70, 73–76, 95
Snowden, Philip, 182–83
Solana, Javier, 418
Somalia, 301, 305, 320, 326–33
  Chanak and Corfu compared to crisis in, 339–40
  map of, 322
  Mogadishu disaster in, 318, 331–32, 337, 414, 457n60
South Korea, 287
  inadequate U.S. forces in, 365, 431–32
  nuclear weapons removed from, 344–45
  Patriot missiles sent to, 355
  reconciliation of North Korea with, 344–46, 356
  Team Spirit exercises by U.S. and, 345, 348, 350, 351, 354–57
Soviet Union, 118
  Afghan war of, 64, 240, 242, 275
  containment of, 239–41, 268
  dissolution of, 237, 241–42, 257, 269–71, 274, 277, 291–92, 342–43
  France and, 1935 pact, 211
  Germany and. *See* Germany—Soviet Union and
  Middle Eastern ambitions of, 50
  Turkey and, 84, 91, 92, 95
  Versailles Treaty rejected by, 136
  after World War I, 40, 68
  See also Cold War
Spa Conference (1920), 149, 150–51
Spartans, 253
Spence, Floyd, 302
Srebinica (former Yugoslavia), 404, 405, 411
SSCs (smaller-scale conflicts), 304, 305, 320
Stahlhelm, 158, 182
Stalin, Josef, 196
Straits
  demilitarization of, 94
  See also Chanak; Gallipoli Peninsula

strategic bombing, 20–21, 65, 437*n5*
  by Germany in World War I, 20
strategic pause, 2, 3, 429, 430, 435
Stresa Conference (1935), 200–201
Stresemann, Gustav, 155, 161, 167–70, 176,
    181–82, 184
  fundamental policy of, 173
  Nobel Peace Prize to, 172
Sudan, 50
Suez Canal, 50, 202, 205–7, 209–10
Supreme Council of the Allied Powers, 70, 74,
    96, 145, 146
Sweden
  Krupp activities in, 156
  tank production in, 157
Sykes, Sir Frederick, 18–21, 25, 26
Syria, 69, 287, 307

Taiwan, 310
Tarnoff, Peter, 324
Taylor, A. J. P., 97, 214, 216
technology
  Aspin on new developments in, 312–13
  in British military policy, 37, 46, 49
  Bush's call for investment in, 279
  Bush's policy on, 292, 298, 312
  current lack of money for, 433
  as substitute for U.S. personnel, 281
  in U.S.-Soviet arms race, 292
  See also airpower
Tellini, Enrico, 98
Tenedos, 69
ten-year rule
  basic problem of, 430–31
  in Britain, 36, 41, 42, 97, 158–59, 218, 219,
    221–23, 227, 229, 274
  U.S. analogies to, 308, 310, 429, 430
terrorism, 2, 3
  Iraq's renunciation of, 370
  Kurdish, 373
Thaon di Revel, Paolo, 107
Thatcher, Margaret, 452*n40*
Thrace, 68, 69, 73, 75, 78, 83, 87, 90, 96
Thucydides, 253
Times (London), 169
Townshend, Sir Charles, 138
TransAfrica Forum, 335
Trapani (Sicily), 107
Treasury (Britain)
  economic sanctions opposed by, 105–6, 249
  on military spending, 29–31
  Treaty of Mutual Guarantee (Rhineland
    Pact), 169–72
Trenchard, Sir Hugh, 20, 58–59, 96, 219, 311,
    313
  on defending Iraq on the cheap, 52, 53–55
Trianon, Treaty of, 108, 178
Trotsky, Leon, 136
Tuchman, Barbara, 356
Turkey, 22, 23, 25, 27
  British forces in, after World War I, 24, 46,
    49, 71–72, 81
    RAF weakness, 59
  Chanak crisis and, 67, 72, 78–87, 95–97,
    116, 248, 250, 253, 265, 324, 339–40,
    417
  exclusion from Europe proposed for, 69
  France and, 1921 treaty, 126
  Gulf War aftermath and, 386, 390, 391
  Italy and, secret agreement (1920), 74
  Kemal's success in, 73–77
  Lausanne Conference and, 90–95, 98
  Lloyd George's policy toward, 37, 50–52, 58,
    67, 72–73, 75–80, 83–85, 95–96, 250
  map of, 68
  Sèvres treaty and, 69–70, 73, 75, 76, 92, 94
  territorial losses of, after World War I, 67–68
Tyrrell, Sir William, 104, 110

Ukraine, 257, 308
United Nations
  Bosnian Serbs' hostages from, 410
  Clinton's support of, 325
  Gulf War and, 251–52
    Border Commission, 384
    general conditions for peace, 369–70
    UNSCOM, 374–84, 386, 388, 393–95
  Haiti and, 334, 336, 338
  nonproliferation and, 348–49, 354, 356, 357
  Somalia and, 326–32
  Yugoslav policy of, 260, 263–64, 400, 403
    UNPROFOR in Macedonia, 407, 410, 411
United States
  Dawes Plan and, 161
  direct attack on, in future wars, 434–35
  foreign policy of
    based on U.S. economy, 324
    new world order, 242–43
    President as chief foreign policy maker, 243
    supported by U.S. armed forces, 290
  in German occupation, after World War I,
    145
  military policy of
    airlift and sealift capacities, 316–17, 361,
      432
    budget toplines, 271–72, 302
    Clinton's, 300–20
    in Cold War, 239–43, 267, 271, 275
    after Cold War, 267–68, 270–99
    current weakness of forces, 433–35
    defense budget too small, 432–33
    end of strategic vision, 319
    homosexuals, 318
    National Guard and reserves, 271, 275,
      283–85, 296, 316, 318
    number of divisions, 315, 318
    public support weakened, 429, 432
    rapid response, 298
    Reagan's, 240–41, 270, 271
    recent lessons to other countries, 428–29

United States (*cont.*)
  reconstitution capability, 298
  reinforcement ability, 365, 385
  superficial "victories" since Gulf War,
    427–29
  traditional policy, 240
  See also Base Force
  "national interests" of, 304–5
  1929 crash in, 184
  1990s deficit of, 271, 317–18, 324
  post–World War I withdrawal from Europe
    by, 14, 74, 120–21, 142, 240
  repayment of war loans demanded by, 142
United States Air Force, 267, 429
  after Cold War, 278, 318
United States Army, 267, 429
  after Cold War, 278
  in Somalia, 331–32
  strength of, 432
United States Marine Corps, 278, 318, 432
United States Navy, 29–32, 267
  after Cold War, 278, 318
Upper Silesia. *See* Silesia

Vance, Cyrus, 260
Vance-Owen plan, 401, 402, 404, 405
Vansittart, Sir Robert, 194, 200, 203, 205, 207,
  227
Venizelos, Eleutherios, 27, 72–75
Versailles, Treaty of (1919), 13–14, 16, 40, 44
  as "Carthaginian Peace," 140
  France guaranteed against German attack by,
    120–21
  German opposition to, 136
  as mere armistice, 172–73
  most serious flaw of, 140–41
  1935 Anglo-German naval treaty as breach
    of, 201
  peace after Gulf War compared to that of,
    367–71, 396
  signing of, 27–28
  Stresemann's desire for revision of, 167
  terms of, 141–42
Vickers (firm), 156
Vietnam, current military forces of, 307
Vietnam syndrome, 53, 249, 250, 255, 263,
  369, 404, 410, 414, 425, 434
Vietnam War, 240, 246, 321, 336
  airpower in, 55
  effect on military leaders of, 246
Vilamoura (Portugal), 418
Vitetti, Leonardo, 199
Vojvodina, 256
Vollmer, Joseph, 157
Vukovar (Yugoslavia), 259

war
  British interwar rejection of, 177, 212–13,
    222, 228
  causes of, 4, 138–39

demobilization after, 3–5
future, viii, 1–5, 9
  British 1920s attitude, 192–93
  as certain, 294
  direct attack on U.S., 434–35
  Headlam–Morley on, 134–38
  impossibility of prediction, 288–89
  Sykes's predictions, 19–20
  Locarno Treaty as end to, 169, 172, 175
  Paris Pact condemnation of, 176
  predictions of end of, 5–6
  as too foolish to happen, 295
War Crimes Tribunal (for former Yugoslavia),
  413
Warsaw Pact, 237, 274, 277, 285, 291, 292,
  308
Washington Conference (1923), 123
Washington Federation Agreement (1994),
  409
Washington Post, 263, 285, 314
Washington Times, 315
weapons of mass destruction (WMD)
  fear of proliferation of, 341–43
  See also biological weapons; chemical
    weapons; nuclear weapons
While England Slept (Churchill), vii, viii
Why England Slept (Kennedy), vii, viii
Wiesel, Elie, 422
Wilson, A. T., 55, 56
Wilson, Sir Henry, 16, 21–28, 37, 51, 67,
  145
  on British army in 1920, 57–58
  on British position in Iraq, 52, 56–57
  British urged to leave Germany by, 145–46
  on danger in Middle East, 71–72
  reduction in commitments urged by, 42, 49,
    59–60
Wilson, Woodrow, 15, 25, 74, 121, 398
"win-hold-win" strategy, 314, 315
WMD. *See* weapons of mass destruction
Wolfowitz, Paul, 276, 299
World Court. *See* Permanent Court of Justice
World War I
  British demobilization after, 5–7, 15–18, 30,
    60–61, 70, 97, 153, 195–96, 208
  fearful memories of, 425
  Germany required to take responsibility for,
    141
  gradual end of, 268–69
  Gulf War's end compared to that of,
    256
  later effect of losses in, 246
  number of British troops in, 14
  results of, 13–14
  Sarajevo of, compared to Corfu, 99–100,
    114
  Turkey and German warships in, 79
World War II, end of, 268
Worthington-Evans, Sir Laming, 80
Wright-Patterson Air Force Base, 413

Yeltsin, Boris, 237, 295, 409, 417
Yongbyon (North Korea), 343–44, 348, 351, 356, 358–59, 362–64
Yugoslavia (Jugoslavia), 39, 40
  collapse of, 256–66, 270
  France and, 124, 174
  map of, 238
  peacekeepers in, 327

See also Bosnia-Hercegovina; Fiume; Kosovo; Serbia

Zeitfreiwilligen, 150
Zeppelins, 20
Zimmerman, Warren, 257, 258, 260
Zone of the Straits, 69, 79, 81, 87, 89
  map of, 68